Social Policy and Policymaking
by the Branches of Government
and the Public-at-Large

Social Policy and Policymaking
by the Branches of Government
and the Public-at-Large

THEODORE J. STEIN

Columbia University Press
New York

Columbia University Press
New York   Chichester, West Sussex

Library of Congress Cataloging-in-Publication Data

Stein, Theodore J.
    Social policy and policymaking by the branches of government and the
public-at-large / Theodore J. Stein.
        p. cm.
    Includes bibliographical references and index.
    ISBN 0-231-11682-9 (cloth : alk. paper)
    1. United States—Social policy. 2. Social legislation—United
States. I. Title.
HN59.2 .S74 2001
361.6′1′0973—dc21   00-063865

Contents

List of Tables

List of Figures

To Gary, for all of my books that you've read
and critiqued, and for the ongoing support that
has sustained me over the years

reface

This text is about social policy; about the ways in which social policy is developed and about the policies and programs that exist to benefit people in need.

All nations develop policies through which they express their position on matters such as income support for people who are financially needy, health care, defense, transportation, foreign relations, immigration, and other matters that affect citizens' lives and the security of the nation. All policies that are developed by a nation touch upon the general welfare of its citizenry, although affecting the day-to-day welfare of its citizens is not always the central policy goal.

For example, the goal of a nation's immigration policy is to limit the number of people who are allowed to enter and establish permanent residence in a country. This goal does not express directly any social welfare concern, meaning that it does not have as a purpose to provide income, food or housing, or any other benefit that people need to survive on a daily basis. Nevertheless, a close reading of immigration policy will reveal humanitarian concerns.

Immigration policy is humanitarian in that it provides a means for political dissidents whose lives may be at risk in their homelands to enter and remain in the United States, and it is humanitarian in that it provides rules for people to follow who wish to come to the United States for the sole purpose of attaining a better quality of life. At the same time, immigration policy protects the social welfare of United States citizens by limiting the absolute number of people allowed to immigrate and by limiting the number of work permits granted to people who wish to enter and find employment and thus to compete with and possibly threaten the livelihood of American citizens.

Of the myriad policies that are developed by governments, there is a unique subset whose main purpose is to affect directly the welfare of its citizens by providing benefits such as income support, food, medical care, and social services and by ensuring that individual characteristics such as race and gender do not interfere with an individual's opportunities to find work, receive an education, and have access to health and social services. Social policies such as these concern us in this text, which is divided into five parts.

Part I contains three chapters. In the first chapter, to help you understand why the study of social policy is critical to your ability to be an effective practitioner, I identify the ways in which the practice of social work is connected to and affected by social policy. In chapter 2, we step back in time to look at the different ways in which social workers in the nineteenth and early twentieth centuries viewed social work practice and how some used social policy as a tool to advocate for clients. In the final chapter of part I, the organization of social services and the ways in which social work practice is affected by social policy are reviewed.

In the first of the four chapters that comprise part II, we revisit social work history. Chapter 4 begins with a review of the development of social policy in the early colonies and subsequently in the newly created United States and takes into account the ways in which social policy was used as a tool to support discrimination against minorities as well as to rectify some discriminatory acts.

Chapter 5 addresses the subject of agenda setting, which asks, "Of the myriad issues that concern the public-at-large, such as domestic violence, and lack of health care, how do some capture the attention of policymakers and result in a policy to address the identified problem?" Having reviewed this issue, we turn our attention in chapter 6 to the process that is followed by the legislative, judicial, and executive branches of government, and by the public-at-large, in crafting social policy. In chapter 7, we look at the process used to create the federal budget and to allocate funds to social programs.

There are six chapters in Part III. Poverty is the subject of chapter 8. We consider definitions of poverty, how poverty is measured, and shortcomings in the ways poverty is measured, and the question "Who is poor?" is addressed. In the five chapters that follow, a range of policies that try to alleviate poverty and provide government assistance to poor people are reviewed. This exploration begins in chapters 9 and 10, where we look at programs that provide cash assistance to retired workers (chapter 9) and programs that provide cash assistance to families with dependent children, people with disabilities, and able-bodied adults who are not raising children (chapter 10). A range of social policies provide food benefits and assist some people with housing needs. These are discussed in chapter 11, which is followed by a review, in chapter 12, of policies that provide health benefits. In the final chapter of part III, our attention focuses on civil rights statutes that were enacted to eliminate discrimination in employment, housing, and education and to ensure nondiscriminatory access to services by providing avenues of legal redress for people who are subject to discrimination. Unlike policies that provide, food, housing and medical care, civil rights policies confer "status," because their goal is to place all members of society on an equal footing by eliminating race- or gender-based discrimination and, in some instances, discrimination that is based on sexual orientation.

In part IV, our attention turns to social services. Social services is a broad concept that includes different forms of assistance that range from day care for preschool age children to residential treatment for people who abuse alcohol or drugs. A series of policies that fund social services are reviewed in chapter 14. Some of the reviewed polices affect children, such as day care, but there are a range of policies that address the needs of children who are at-risk of being neglected or abused, and of children who have been abused and neglected, as well as polices that provide for the care of children whose parents cannot or will not provide care for them. We refer to these policies as child welfare policies, and they are the subject of chapter 15. Educational policies that provide for the educational needs of disadvantaged children and that protect the rights of children with disabilities and those who are homeless to an education are covered in chapter 16.

There are two chapters in the last part of the text. In chapter 17, we look at how social policy is implemented and the role that is played by the actors who effect policy implementation. Included here are employees of administrative agencies, such as the United States Department of Health and Human Services, federal and state judges, administrators of social service programs, and social worker staff. In the last chapter, we revisit the subject of professional social work and the relationship of social workers to social policy. This chapter addresses the subject of "policy practice," which is concerned with the various roles that social workers and others, including the public-at-large, play as they endeavor to effect proposed legislation or to modify existing legislation.

The Use of Terms and Data

The noun "policy" is a generic term that has no specific disciplinary meaning. The term refers to an array of rules that may affect our lives, ranging from those that flash across a movie screen admonishing us not to talk or smoke in a theater to rules that govern whether a client is eligible for disability-based income support. A formal definition of policy appears in chapter 1. Throughout this text, I use the term policy to refer to rules that emanate from legislative bodies, judges, presidents, and governors and from the people in states that allow the public to engage directly in policymaking. The concern in this text is with a narrow set of rules that govern the allocation and reallocation of social resources to ensure that some measure of assistance is given to those in need and to ensure that resources are provided on a nondiscriminatory basis. The terms "statute" and "legislation" refer to policies that are made by federal and state legislative bodies, and I limit the use of either term to actions of legislative bodies. Throughout the text, I refer to actions of the Supreme Court. Unless otherwise noted, the reference is to the United States Supreme Court.

The data in this text come mainly from federal sources. Whether data are current or "old" varies considerably, especially when the federal government is reliant on the states to provide information. Some data refer exclusively to federal matters, for example, the federal budget, including allocations to social welfare programs, and the cost of programs where all funds come from the federal government. In the main, such data reflect the fiscal year in which the text was written. However, data that are compiled from state sources are often "old," meaning that the most recent data may be from 1995 or 1997.

Social Policy and Policymaking

by the Branches of Government
and the Public-at-Large

PART

The purpose of part I is to identify the ways in which the practice of social work is inextricably connected to social policy. The goal is to help you understand why the study of social policy is critical to your ability to be an effective practitioner. To achieve this, you will be introduced to the subject of social policy in chapter 1. Chapter 2 addresses the involvement of social workers in the nineteenth and early twentieth centuries as advocates for social policy as a means of assisting clients. Chapter 3 turns to the current organization of social services and the ways in which social work practice is affected by social policy.

Social policy affects the day-to-day practice of social work in numerous ways, for example, when legislation creates new social programs or modifies existing programs or when courts issue orders that restructure social service delivery systems. Some of the effects on practice may be simple, as when eligibility rules change and workers must learn new standards, or the effects may be dramatic, as is the case with implementing the 1996 welfare laws, which require an entirely new approach to assisting dependent children and their caretakers.

The social worker who understands the policymaking process and who has knowledge of the social policies currently in force has an advantage for at least three reasons. First, there are various ways in which practitioners can participate in the policymaking process and influence the reform and creation of policies that affect their clients. Second, to be effective, practitioners need to know which benefits are available to their clients and the rules for obtaining these benefits. Third, practitioners need to know how different social policies are related; for example, eligibility for income assistance from one policy may make a client automatically eligible for health insurance from another policy.

Social Policy

An Introduction

Most of you who are reading this text will be planning your careers as direct service providers to one of the diverse groups served by social workers: children, the elderly, people with mental health problems, or people with disabilities. You may think of your career in terms of assisting people with any of a number of problems, ranging from insufficient income and poor housing to marital difficulties and problems caused by excessive use of alcohol or illegal drugs. Although some of you may plan careers that focus on macro issues such as the development, implementation, and evaluation of public policy, most of you will not. Many of you may view the subject of policy as irrelevant to your career goals and may consider a required course on social policy as something to be endured.

I set three goals for myself when preparing this text: (1) to make the subject of social policy of sufficient interest so that you will continue to be a student of the subject regardless of the direction your career takes; (2) to familiarize you with policies that may benefit your clients; and (3) to further your understanding of the ways in which social policy may affect your practice and of the ways in which you may affect policy.

This chapter provides an introduction to the subject of social policy. The types of policies covered in this text are identified first, after which a definition of social policy is offered. Next, the roles played by the legislative, judicial, and executive branches of government in policy development are discussed, as is the way in which the public-at-large makes or affects policy through the mechanisms of voter initiative and voter referendum.

All policy, whether concerned with social welfare issues, defense, or foreign relations, reflects social values. The subject of values will be reviewed at length because one cannot understand social policy without an understanding of the values that a society holds concerning its members' responsibility for themselves and its responsibility to provide assistance to individuals who are not able to help themselves. An array of social arrangements and societal beliefs, including but not limited to the work ethic, the role of the family, and the status of women, children, and minorities, affect the passage of policies, the substantive provisions contained in policies, and the willingness over time of the public to support certain policies.[1] The limits of social policy as regards unattainable goals, unworkable interventions, and unintended consequences is the last topic reviewed.

The Policies That Concern Us

All social policy confers some type of benefit. The conferred benefit is often concrete and takes the form of cash, food, housing allowances, social services such as counseling or day care, or payment for medical services. In addition, there are policies whose benefits are less tangible but of critical importance to people who are subject to discrimination. For example, the Civil Rights Act of 1964, the Fair Housing Act of 1988, and the Americans with Disabilities Act of 1990 (collectively called civil rights policies) seek to eliminate discrimination in employment, housing, and education and to ensure nondiscriminatory access to services by providing avenues of legal redress for people who are subject to discrimination. Unlike policies that confer concrete benefits, civil rights policies confer "status," because their goal is to place all members of society on an equal footing by eliminating race- or gender-based discrimination and, in some instances, discrimination based on sexual orientation.[2]

Policy Defined

Definitions of policy abound. To some, policy involves any action, including a failure to act, on the part of government as long as those who are governed are affected.[3] Others rely on more formal definitions, defining as policy "collective strategies . . . fashioned by laws, rules, regulations, and budgets of government . . . that affect or bind the actions of citizens, government officials, processionals, and the staff of social service agencies,"[4] or as government actions "having a direct impact on the welfare of the citizens by providing them with services and income,"[5] or as "the principles that govern action directed towards given ends."[6]

Policy can also be defined in simple terms as the rules that describe how one gains access to the benefits provided by an organization or group. Thus, the rules of a social service agency that describe the processes through which clients must pass to be accepted for service are policy statements. Likewise, the rules that are established for membership in a health club or a professional organization are policy statements. In these simple terms, most of us have had some experience with policy.

However, the policies that concern professional social workers are more complex than these examples suggest. First, all policy is value laden. For example, defense policy expresses a nation's value concerning the maintenance of peace, and it may express a commitment to safeguarding the welfare of people in other nations.

Second, once a unit of government or members of the public act to create a new social policy or amend an existing one, debate often takes place in legislative committees and in formal and informal public hearings. Those with an interest in the proposed policy (legislators, representatives of advocacy groups, or members of the general public) may offer their points of view on how the policy objective is to be achieved and propose alternative methods of reducing or eliminating the problems that the policy seeks to address. In addition, governmental and private research groups may generate data and formulate hypotheses concerning the likely effects that the policy will have and how much it will cost. And position papers are often written by policy analysts that express the support or lack of support of the analysts or the organization that they represent. The substance of debate, which is often memorialized in writing, and the research reports and opinion papers that may be generated cast light on policy objectives and bring to the fore differences of opinion about the merits of the procedures to be put in place to realize the policy objective. These data must be taken into account in any definition of social policy.

Third, all social policies provide a framework for the allocation of scarce resources and describe the available benefits, the qualifications an applicant must possess to be eligible for policy benefits, and what, if anything, people must do to receive benefits.

Fourth, some policies address the future, as when a policy goal seeks to change the behavior of the recipient. Fifth, the social policies that concern us have the force of law, which means that violations of a policy (for example, failure by a practitioner to provide eligible clients with the benefits to which they are entitled, failure by an agency to provide services in a nondiscriminatory manner, or failure by a state to follow the rules that are established by the U.S. Congress for the receipt of federal funds) may subject the practitioner, the social service agency, or the state to legal liability.

From this complex set of conditions, a definition of social policy emerges: social policy (1) is an expression of social values, (2) is arrived at through a process of debate and decision making, (3) produces a framework for the allocation of social resources to defined categories of people for the purpose of resolving or eliminating social problems, (4) often seeks to affect the future behavior of members of society, and (5) has the force of law.

Because all social policy results in the allocation of social resources, social policy has an impact on society as a whole. A brief example follows.

In the summer of 1996, Congress passed and President Clinton signed the Personal Responsibility and Work Opportunity Act (PRWOA) (see chapter 10).[7] The PRWOA eliminated or modified several social programs, including the Aid to Families with Dependent Children Program (AFDC) that provided financial support for certain dependent children and their caretakers and the Supplemental Security Income Program (SSI) that provided financial support for children and adults with disabilities.

The decision-making process that preceded passage of the PRWOA began in March 1995 and continued for approximately seventeen months. This process was lengthy because of extensive debate concerning the values that the PRWOA seeks to advance. Many members of Congress viewed the existing welfare programs as creating and maintaining a class of dependent people, thus undermining individual initiative and the value that Americans place on self-sufficiency. However, because children are the main beneficiaries of some of the programs affected by the PRWOA, the debate focused on the fact that regardless of what members of Congress thought of the adult recipients of welfare programs, the burden of the proposed changes would fall most heavily on children.

The PRWOA replaced AFDC with the Temporary Assistance to Needy Families Program (TANF). The AFDC program had provided an entitlement to cash assistance for eligible children and their caretakers for more than sixty years. An entitlement program is one where all who meet the program's eligibility criteria have a legally enforceable claim to the program's benefit. The TANF program, like the AFDC program it replaced, provides income to needy families so that children may be cared for in their own homes or in the home of a relative;[8] however, in passing the PRWOA Congress made clear that henceforth no individual could state a legally enforceable claim to receive a benefit.[9]

The PRWOA seeks to affect both present and future behavior. First, the law seeks to make government support unattractive by requiring the majority of recipients to work within twenty-four months of the time they begin to receive benefits. The goals of the PRWOA expressly seek to affect future behavior by requiring that a family's participation in the program not exceed sixty months and by setting a series of goals that focus on the behavior of recipients. The goals seek to

> promote job preparation, work and marriage; prevent and reduce the incidence of out-of-wedlock pregnancies and [the policy seeks to] establish annual numerical goals for preventing and reducing the incidence of these pregnancies; and [the policy] encourages the formation and maintenance of two-parent families.[10]

The passage of the PRWOA, therefore, expressed values about personal responsibility and society's responsibility to children, arrived at these values through a process of debate, produced a new framework for allocating benefits that sought to eliminate social problems such as welfare dependency, and sought to change present and future behavior so that society as a whole would benefit from greater workforce participation by welfare recipients and from the reduction in the number of people dependent on welfare.

Policymaking: The Role of the Legislative, Judicial, and Executive Branches of Government and the Power of the Public to Make Policy

Most of the social policies covered in this text are enacted as laws or statutes. These terms are used interchangeably. Under the federal constitution and the constitutions of the individual states, the power to enact laws is reserved to the legislative branch of government; the power to enforce laws, to the executive branch; and the power to interpret laws, to the judicial branch. Despite this constitutional division of power, laws are also made by the executive and judicial branches of government and, in some states, by the public-at-large. A brief discussion of the policymaking role of each branch follows. A detailed discussion appears in chapter 6.

Creating Statutes

Lawmaking by the legislative branch of the U.S. Congress follows a typical pattern. A bill is introduced into either chamber, the Senate or the House of Representatives. The bill is discussed and debated. If supported by members of the House, the proposal is then submitted to the Senate or, if the bill that began in the Senate receives support in that chamber, it is forwarded to the House. The chamber receiving the supported bill follows a process that is nearly identical to the process followed when the legislation was first introduced. If legislation is supported by the House and Senate, but there are differences concerning provisions of the legislation, a committee is convened and charged with resolving the differences and producing an acceptable compromise. With any differences resolved, the legislation becomes law if signed by the president or if two-thirds of senators and representatives vote to override a presidential veto.

EXECUTIVE AND JUDICIARY BRANCHES

The executive and judicial branches of government affect policy in two ways. First, both branches have an "interpretive role." The executive branch interprets policy after Congress delegates to an executive-level agency, such as the U.S. Department of Health and Human Services, the authority to make rules and regulations. Rules are intended to clarify vague statutory terms in order to provide the guidance that is necessary to implement federal laws. For example, federal law requires that states provide independent living services to foster care youth before they are discharged from foster care at the age of majority.[11] The administrator who wishes to find out what programs or services would satisfy the statutory requirement for independent-living programs would turn to the Code of Federal Regulations for details that have been set forth by the Department of Health and Human Services.[12] Properly issued regulations become law (see chapter 6).

In the same way that ambiguous statutory language produces rules, ambiguous statutory language may require a court to interpret congressional intent. For example, the Americans with Disabilities Act (ADA) protects qualified individuals from discrimination based on an individual disability. When Congress passed the ADA, it did not create a list of conditions that would qualify a person as disabled and left this task to various executive level agencies. Despite the active role taken by federal agencies in defining disability, federal trial courts could not agree whether persons infected with Human Immunodeficiency Virus (HIV) were disabled as long as they remained asymptomatic. In 1998, the U.S. Supreme Court settled the question on which lower courts were divided by interpreting congressional intent and ruling that asymptomatic HIV is a disability.[13]

People will disagree as to whether interpretation, by either the executive or the judicial branch, is real policymaking, because either body takes a congressional act as its starting point and interprets rather than makes a new law. This matter will be fully discussed in chapter 6, but some examples of how the executive branch and the judicial branch have actually created policy are noted here.

The president or a state governor has the power to create policy by issuing an executive order. Properly issued executive orders become law (see chapter 6), and executive orders are a powerful tool for policymaking. For example, affirmative action policies have had a broad impact on the welfare of Americans and have engaged public opinion as few other policies have done (see chapter 13).[14] Affirmative action policies have affected the admissions process in higher education by allocating "seats" to incoming students, and these policies have affected hiring and promotion in almost all spheres of American life. Yet this important social policy began not with an action of the U.S. Congress or the legislature of any state, but with an executive order issued on March 6, 1961, by President John F. Kennedy. Executive order 10925 required government contracting agencies to take affirmative action to ensure that applicants are employed "without regard to their race, color, religion, sex or national origin."[15]

The issuance of an executive order meets our definition of policy. The values expressed seek to eliminate discrimination based on a characteristic such as race or sex. The discussion and debate that precede issuance of an executive order may be shielded from public view when it occurs behind the closed doors of a White House office, although the debate surrounding some executive orders, such as President Clinton's "Don't Ask, Don't Tell" order concerning lesbians and gays in the military, was exposed to public view (see chapter 5). Affirmative action policies have resulted in the reallocation of society's resources, and the decision has had a dramatic effect on the behavior of university administrators and employers and on the prospects of those seeking university admissions and employment opportunities.

Courts establish social policy in different ways (see chapter 6). One example will serve to illustrate. In the late 1960s, a group of black employees brought a class action suit against their employer, Duke Power Company, alleging that they were denied opportunities for promotion by a company policy that required a high school education and passing of an intelligence test for advancement.

The suit was brought under Title VII of the Civil Rights Act of 1964. Title VII makes it unlawful for an employer to affect adversely an employee's opportunity for advancement because of the employee's race, color, religion, sex, or national origin. However, Title VII permits employers to utilize tests in making employment decisions as long as the test is not "designed, intended or used to discriminate because of race, color, religion, sex or national origin."[16] The power company argued that their use of the intelligence test was permissible under the latter provision.

The U.S. Supreme Court turned its attention to the question of whether use of the test was permissible. The test was neutral, the court found, meaning that women or men of any race could pass. However, the requirement that one pass the test as a condition for promotion had a different impact on black applicants, who were less likely than white applicants to pass and to have a high school diploma. The Supreme Court held that such "neutral" requirements could survive a court challenge only if they were shown to be necessary to job performance. In other words, the power company needed to demonstrate that only those with a high school education or passing scores on an intelligence test were capable of performing the job in a safe and satisfactory manner. The power company failed to demonstrate that its employment criterion were necessary.

The High Court, in reaching its decision, worked within a statutory framework set by Congress in the Civil Rights Act, but the Court did not simply interpret congressional intent. The product of its actions was policymaking, because the conclusion did not follow logically from the language of the statute. The statute could have been interpreted to require not that the employer prove the necessity of the test but that the employees prove that the power company intended use the test to harm their chances for advancement based on their race.

The Court's decision meets the definition of policy given previously. It expresses a set of values that are basic to the act's purpose of eliminating race-based discrimination but does so by going beyond the express language of the statute, which, again, could be interpreted as excluding only those tests intentionally designed to discriminate. The decision was arrived at through a process of debate and decision making unique to the judicial process (see chapter 6). The result of the decision was the reallocation of social resources, in this case employment opportunity, because black people were given a greater chance to advance within the company. The decision created a framework for analysis that prevails to this day; thus, it affected the future behavior of employers and the future opportunities of employees.

THE PUBLIC-AT-LARGE

The public-at-large may affect policy in one of three ways. The first is the voter initiative, which exists in twenty-two states and the District of Columbia. The initiative refers to the "power of the electors to propose statutes and amendments to the [state] constitution." The second is through the voter referendum, found in twenty-five states, which refers to the power of the public to approve or reject statutes already adopted by the legislature."[17] The third is the ability of the public-at-large to affect the civil agenda of the courts by bringing individual and class action suits (see chapter 5).[18]

These can be powerful and effective tools for proposing, approving, rejecting, and interpreting policy. For example, in November 1996, the voters of California passed the California Civil Rights Initiative (popularly referred to as Proposition 209), which amended the state constitution and ended affirmative action programs in the nation's most populous state.

Social Policy and Social Values

At the beginning of this chapter, I stated that the social policies addressed in this text provide for two categories of benefits. The first category includes policies that provide for concrete assistance in the form of income, food, or housing. The second category includes those policies that confer status by seeking to eliminate race- or gender-based barriers to employment, housing, and education.

Whether a policy confers concrete benefits or seeks to eliminate discriminatory barriers, it expresses the value that society places on helping people in need. However, it would be an error to assume that a commitment to helping those in need is inevitable or that the commitment, if made, will be extended to all members of society. Societies balance their willingness to help against a variety of factors. Some are pragmatic—for example, the amount of money that is available to provide assistance—and others have to do with balancing competing values, which may be expressed in questions such as "Does providing financial assistance to those in need rob people of the incentive to become self sufficient?" or "Do civil rights policies that provide domestic partner benefits to unmarried couples undermine the value that some place on marriage and traditional notions of family?"

In the social welfare arena, the values of greatest importance concern the views that people hold regarding individual responsibility: whether and to what extent an individual is able to change her or his circumstances, and what, if anything, society expects in return from people who receive assistance. In order to discuss values and social policy, policies that confer concrete benefits and policies that confer status, such as civil rights policies, must be separately discussed. Although American civil rights policies date back to the latter half of the nineteenth century, the provision of aid to the needy is as old as the nation itself.

SOCIAL VALUES AND BENEFIT-CONFERRING POLICIES

Americans have always provided some form of concrete assistance to groups of people deemed worthy of help, but they have also shown a great deal of ambivalence toward the needy. This ambivalence has been expressed in both conceptual and practical terms and in the universal compared to selective availability of benefits.

CONCEPTUAL   Two concepts or "models" of social welfare reflect the ambivalence that Americans feel toward providing welfare. These are the "residual" and "institutional" models that are rooted in the English Poor Laws of 1601.[19] Both the residual and institutional models assume that society consists of primary and permanent institutions, but the models differ in the role they assign to the welfare institution.

In a residual model, the primary social institutions are the family, the marketplace, the neighborhood, the church, and the ethnic group.[20] According to a residual model, these institutions are permanent fixtures of society with the capacity to provide for the needs of the less fortunate. The welfare institution is not considered a primary institution and is seen as a sign of social dysfunction and the inability, due to a severe economic recession or natural disaster, for example, of the permanent institutions to cope with social need. No one would seriously argue that the institution of social welfare will ever be permanently eliminated; however, diminishing its importance by restoring the vitality of the permanent institutions is, according to those who subscribe to a residual model of welfare, a goal that society should seek to achieve.

The institutional model, on the other hand, takes the existence of the welfare institution as a given, not as a reflection of social dysfunction. Here, social welfare is a permanent facet of society, made necessary by certain realities, for example, that some percentage of the civilian labor force will always be unemployed even when the economy is strong, and that regardless of their strength, social institutions such as the family and the church may not be able to meet all of the needs of certain populations such as the elderly, children, and people with severe disabilities.

PRACTICAL   The ambivalence that Americans have toward the provision of welfare can also be expressed in practical terms. Practical considerations follow from a concern that the availability of welfare benefits might provide an incentive for people to misbehave in order to receive state support. Consider the following examples.

The SSI provides financial support to eligible people with disabilities (see chapter 10). Until 1996, when the PRWOA was passed, one of the ways in which a child's eligibility for SSI benefits was determined was through a procedure called an Individualized Functional Assessment (IFA). An IFA was conducted if the child's disability did not match one of the disabilities on a list that is used by the Social Security Administration (SSA) to determine whether a person is qualified for income assistance. The IFA gave a child whose disability was not listed a second chance to qualify for benefits if the question, "Is the child able to engage in the normal everyday activities of living, such as . . . speaking, walking, washing, dressing and . . . going to school, etc.?"[21] was answered in the negative. If a child's impairment significantly reduced her or his ability to engage in everyday activities, to acquire the skills necessary to assume an adult role, or to "grow, develop, or mature physically, mentally or emotionally and thus to attain developmental milestones,"[22] she or he was deemed eligible to receive benefits. In 1996, Congress eliminated the IFAs because of a concern that children were being coached by their parents to "fake" mental impairments.[23]

Just as some members of Congress believe that parents may coach their children to "act disabled," some believe that the availability of a welfare check is, if not causal to the decision of a teenager to have a child, associated with that decision. In a 1995 report that dealt with welfare reform, Senators Daniel Patrick Moynihan, Bill Bradley, and Carol Moseley-Braun addressed the issue of the availability of financial support in relation to the number of children born to single women. These senators expressed their concern that the welfare reform proposals then under consideration would end the sixty-year-old AFDC program that provided cash benefits to children and their adult caretakers based on the unsubstantiated belief that elimination of financial aid would eliminate an incentive for women to have babies before they married. Directing their attention to research that sought to answer the question of what relationship, if any, does the availability of welfare benefits have to the rate of births to single women, they said that the claim that ending AFDC would reduce the incidence of out-of-wedlock births was no better than guesswork. Neither policymakers nor researchers have found any incentive, benefit, or other intervention that can do much to cut the unwed pregnancy rate.[24] In 1998, the U.S. General Accounting Office reported that most teenage pregnancies are not planned. By racial or ethnic group, 75 percent of births to black teenagers, 67 percent of births to white teenagers, and 46 percent of births to Hispanic teenagers were unintended.[25]

Finally, most teen births occur in states with the lowest welfare benefits. For example, Mississippi, which has a teen birthrate of 58 births per 1,000, pays a combined AFDC/Food Stamp benefit equal to 39 percent of the poverty level, compared to Vermont, which has a teen birthrate of 11 births per 1,000 and a combined AFDC/Food Stamp benefit equal to 79 percent of the poverty line. Tennessee has a teen birthrate of 71 births per 1,000 and pays 45 percent of the poverty level, compared to Minnesota, which has a teen birthrate of 36 births per 1,000 and a welfare benefit equal to 72 percent of the poverty line.[26]

SELECTIVE AND UNIVERSAL PROGRAMS

Because of the American focus on individual responsibility and the concern that too much federal and state aid will rob people of the incentive to be self-supporting, social welfare benefits in the United States are, with few exceptions, provided on a selective rather than a universal basis. Eligibility for the benefit provided by a selective program requires that the applicant be a member of some category defined, for example, by workforce participation, age, disability, or low income.

Selective programs support the values that are expressed in the residual model of social welfare. Because this model assumes that the growth of welfare reflects some measure of social dysfunction, it seeks to reduce reliance on public programs by designing application procedures to delay and discourage efforts to obtain benefits and to make participants feel as though they have failed because they are not able to display the degree of self-sufficiency that is valued in America. Consider the following report by Nina Bernstein in the *New York Times*:

> Cynthia S. was 7 months pregnant when her husband, Jose, was diagnosed with . . . cancer. At the time, they had three jobs between them . . . After Jose's first operation, Cynthia was just another applicant for relief and Medicaid.
>
> Cynthia waited for hours at the welfare center, only to be sent home to call for an appointment. She called 15 times a day to get through. She submitted hospital records, rent receipts, birth certificates and bank statements.
>
> In late April their second daughter was born. Jose underwent more surgery. They still lacked Medicaid . . . although on paper, the family was eligible three times over for Medicaid benefits. They had no rent money.
>
> The . . . hospital . . . referred Cynthia [to] the Resource, Entitlement and Advocacy Program . . . that . . . wages a . . . rear guard action to capture . . . Medicaid payments . . . [and] every government benefit available to those who come to its . . . office. Eligibility specialists spent up to three hours a day over several weeks calling administrators at the welfare center and . . . Medicaid offices on behalf of Cynthia, Jose and their family. The computers kept spitting out rejections.
>
> By June, Jose's hospital was losing patience. He was scheduled for re-admission for chemotherapy and a bone marrow transplant. The hospital financial department ruled that unless his Medicaid enrollment was completed and he had a billing number, his admission would have to be delayed. "June 13th we were at home crying, thinking, 'Oh my God,'" Ms. S. recalled. "If he doesn't get the chemotherapy, the doctor said the cancer would kill him." The Medicaid number was activated later that day. [27]

Universal programs are antithetical to the residual model of welfare because benefits are available to all, regardless of membership in a given category and regardless of income. Universal programs acknowledge the permanency of the welfare institution. In American life, public education is an example of one of the few publicly funded programs that are universally available. Efforts by the federal government to provide universal health insurance illustrate what may happen when making a benefit universally available becomes a subject of debate.

An estimated 43.4 million Americans lack health insurance.[28] Medicaid, the publicly funded health insurance program for children and adults who have not reached the age of retirement, is not available to the uninsured unless they meet restrictive income standards (chapter 11). In 1993, President Clinton introduced his plan for universal health care coverage, the Health Security Act.[29] The centerpiece of Mr. Clinton's proposal was "managed competition" whereby the uninsured would obtain health insurance from a series of regional health networks. Networks would contract for necessary services and, because they would be competitive, it was argued that they would keep down health care costs. Small businesses, which were expected to provide insurance for their employees, would form a "pool" that would give them purchasing power comparable to larger business entities.[30]

President Clinton's plan was unpopular with at least some segments of the public. The president's plan raised four concerns. First, implementation would require the creation of a large government bureaucracy with the attendant costs of maintaining the bureaucracy and with the imposition on providers and recipients of the complicated rules that are associated with government agencies and that seem, at times, to hinder rather than facilitate access to service. Second, the plan called for employers to insure their workers. The employer mandate raised the fear that the costs to businesses might be so prohibitive that they would cause some to close and some workers to lose their jobs. A third concern was the possibility that consumer choice of physician would be limited, and a fourth concern was that some benefit restrictions were likely to control program costs.

To elicit public support against the president's health plan, the Health Insurance Association of America launched a televised campaign.[31] The campaign introduced the American public to "Harry and Louise," a forty-something couple whose concerns about the Clinton health care plan played into the fears held by many people with private insurance, including the barriers to service that would be created by a government bureaucracy. According to Harry and Louise, the Clinton plan would deprive people of the right to choose their care providers, cut people off from their family doctors, and limit the overall range of services available to many with private insurance.

The irony is that as of 1998, despite the demise of the Clinton health care plan and the fact that the number of uninsured Americans has increased from approximately 36 million in the early 1990s to approximately 43 million in 1997,[32] Harry and Louise's worst fears were coming true. To contain health care costs, employers have reduced the options that are available to workers and thrust people into managed care programs. Enrollment in managed care increased from approximately one-half of the workforce in 1994, when the Clinton plan was introduced, to approximately 85 percent in 1998. In the 1998 midterm elections, public anger over managed care induced candidates in a number of states to campaign for greater choice of doctors, greater access to specialists, and procedures that would ensure the right to appeal decisions made by managed care organizations that restrict choice and the right to sue managed care organizations for malpractice.[33]

SOCIAL VALUES AND CIVIL RIGHTS POLICIES

Civil rights refer to personal freedoms that are guaranteed and protected by the U.S. Constitution and by the constitutions of the various states, such as freedom of speech and of religion and the right of all to equal protection under the law. The civil rights acts refer to a series of statutes that Congress passed to give added force to the rights guaranteed under the federal constitution to ensure that barriers that prevent individuals, because of race, religion, gender, or national origin, from participating fully in society are eliminated.

Civil rights acts date back to the 1860s when, following the Civil War, Congress amended the Constitution and passed civil rights legislation to ensure that the states would not abridge the rights of newly freed slaves. The recent history of civil rights began in 1964 with passage of the Civil Rights Act of that year and continued throughout the twentieth century with passage of the statutes to protect the rights of people with disabilities (Vocational Rehabilitation Act, Americans with Disabilities Act, Individuals with Disabilities in Education Act), the right to nondiscriminatory access to housing (Fair Housing Act), the right not to be discharged from one's employment due solely to age (Age Discrimination in Employment Act).

A sense of fair play and the conviction that it is wrong to deny a person an education or a job because of a personal characteristic such as gender or race is the core value that has underpinned public support for civil rights measures as long as the focus of these laws is on providing equal opportunity.[34]

Probably the most controversial aspect of civil rights policies has been affirmative action, yet as long as affirmative action is defined as creating opportunity in the form of outreach and recruitment, it enjoys public support. Public support wanes, however, when the focus of affirmative action programs changes from providing opportunity to ensuring outcome through the use of quotas or preferences.[35]

For the better part of two decades, public opinion has been consistent in its resistance to racial preferences. For example, the results of a 1986 survey revealed that 75 percent of white persons thought it "very likely" or "somewhat likely" that they would be denied a position because of affirmative action,[36] and in 1993, the results of a Gallup pole showed that 21 percent of white persons said that they had already been victims of reverse discrimination, compared to 36 percent of black persons who said that they had been victims of discrimination.[37] In 1995, 69 percent of women and 76 percent of men responding to a survey conducted by the *Washington Post* reported that they oppose affirmative action largely because of concerns about reverse discrimination.[38] As reported earlier in this chapter, public dissatisfaction with affirmative action caused Californians to support a referendum banning preferences in employment and education. A similar measure passed in Washington but failed in Houston, Texas.

Senator Edward Kennedy recognized what lay at the heart of public dissatisfaction with civil rights policies when he introduced the Employment Non-

Discrimination Act (ENDA) that would ban discrimination against lesbians and gay men in employment. He made an appeal to the American sense of fair play and equal opportunity. Senator Kennedy said:

> "This bill . . . requires simple justice for gay men and lesbians who deserve to be judged in their job settings—like all other Americans—by their ability to do the work. Under th[is] act lawsuits could not be brought to increase the number of lesbians or gays in the work force based on under-representation . . . In addition . . . preferential treatment, including quotas, is prohibited."[39]

Because public opinion polls show that a majority of Americans support the goals of ENDA, it would appear that fair play is an enduring and consistent social value.[40]

The Limits of Social Policy

Beginning in the 1960s with the War on Poverty (see chapter 10), a school of thinking developed that held that all social problems could be redressed by social policy.[41] This proposition has proven to be false. At times, policy is limited because it is based on incorrect assumptions about human behavior, and at times policy assumes that interventions will be effective when there are no data to support that expectation. At other times, policy produces unexpected consequences that exacerbate rather than relieve the problem that the policy was intended to resolve. The remainder of this chapter draws attention to some of the lessons learned in recent decades.

ATTAINABLE AND UNATTAINABLE GOALS

Two criteria for realizing goals are (1) the goal must be expressed in observable and measurable terms in order to inform people of what they should expect to see when the goal is realized and (2) the premise upon which the goal is based must be true.

Two of the goals that Congress sought to achieve with passage of the PRWOA are useful to illustrate the issue. The goals are (1) to provide assistance to needy families so that children may be cared for in their own homes; and (2) to prevent and reduce the incidence of out-of-wedlock pregnancies.

The first goal points to an observable and measurable outcome because whether children remain in their own homes can be measured. However, the premise that parents will actually use funds for food, clothing, adequate shelter, medical care, and other basic needs is not necessarily true. Goal attainment is beyond the control of policymakers because some parents may not use their benefits for the good of their children, and some parents may not provide a safe environment for their children regardless of the amount of money they have, causing the state to remove children from the care of their parents.

The second goal also points to an observable and measurable outcome because the number of teen pregnancies can be counted, and the marital status of new parents can be ascertained. However, there is no empirical support for the premise that a teenager, in deciding whether to get pregnant and carry a child to term, will undertake a cost-benefit analysis, taking account of the fact that she may not receive benefits and that even if she does they will be time limited, and decide based on this analysis against having a child. Thus, withholding financial assistance is not a reasoned solution and cannot be expected to have the desired result.

GOALS AND WORKABLE INTERVENTIONS

A third criterion for realizing goals is that there must be some empirical support for the proposition that the intervention that is expressed or implied in the policy can affect the issue that the policy seeks to address.

Most of you who are reading this text are familiar with the concept of an intervention but in all likelihood think of interventions as micro-level actions, for example, as steps taken when working with individual clients or small groups. However, social policy is a macro-level intervention that is geared toward solving problems of larger social groups.

Social policy as an intervention has two aspects. First, the enactment of any policy, regardless of its substance, sends a message that action is to be taken to reduce or eliminate a social problem. The second and more important aspect of policy as an intervention focuses attention on the method embodied in the policy to reduce or eliminate the problem. When policy is not successful, it is important to look at the intervention the policy prescribes and to ask the question, "Why was it assumed that the action that was chosen would reduce or eliminate the problem toward which it was directed?" We have already considered this issue in our discussion of teen pregnancy and the availability of welfare benefits. The change in the law was made because it was assumed that the availability of cash assistance, which was previously meant as an intervention to reduce poverty, in fact acted as an inducement to young women to have children out of wedlock. If this assumption were true, it follows that withholding financial aid would reduce the rate of out-of-wedlock teenage pregnancy. Consider another example.

In 1962, Congress amended the Aid to Dependent Children Program (ADC) to provide a cash grant to a dependent child's caretaker and renamed the program the Aid to Families with Dependent Children Program (AFDC). The 1962 amendments made federal funds available to the states to enable state agencies to provide services by "trained social workers [who would] help families and individuals . . . become self-supporting" and whose services would help to eliminate the problem of an increase in "illegitimate" births and in the rate of divorce, desertion, and separation.[42] The message that was contained in the new policy was clear: Congress intended to reduce dependency on public welfare. The 1962 amendments rested on the assumption that social casework services were an intervention that

> Experience has shown [when provided] by highly trained welfare personnel can help these situations. These social services, usually provided by trained social workers, are designed to help families and individuals to become self-supporting rather than dependent upon welfare checks.[43]

What the "experience" consisted of is not clear. There were no data to support a hypothesis that the casework services would reduce welfare dependency. Moreover, there were not enough workers trained to provide the required services. In 1960, approximately 89 percent of public assistance workers had no graduate training, and only 13 percent of casework supervisors working in public assistance had completed two years of graduate social work education.[44] By 1967, welfare roles had increased from a 1962 low of 3.5 million recipients to a high of 5 million recipients.[45] In 1967, Winifred Bell, an expert on the AFDC program and head of the Demonstration Projects Group in the Department of Health, Education, and Welfare (renamed the Department of Health and Human Services) provided testimony to Congress. Ms. Bell said that she regretted playing a role in the passage of the 1962 service amendments. Discussing her review of reports from demonstration projects whose goal was the identification of methods to ameliorate poverty, she said that most projects held little promise but were nonetheless funded year after year. The studies were of no consequence, and "hard facts were difficult to locate and when located were rarely useful due to poor original conceptualization, inadequate methodology, failure to include or control sufficient variables, or inability to write clearly and concisely. [Efforts to improve projects in recent years have] met with indifferent success."[46]

UNINTENDED CONSEQUENCES

All the consequences that a law will have cannot be anticipated, and some of the consequences exacerbate rather than resolve the problem that the policy seeks to address. Such was the outcome of a New York City law passed in 1988 that required the city to stop using welfare hotels as placements for homeless families by April 1993. As the city began moving families into public housing, a curious result happened. As more and more families moved into permanent housing, the demand for housing increased. Whereas the city planned for placement of 2,732 families by June 30, 1990, the number for which housing was needed increased to 4,120 by June 1991.[47]

On close examination, the reasons for the surge in demand became clear. In addition to the needs of homeless families, the demand for public housing by the non-homeless population in New York City was great. For example, in 1992 there were approximately 240,000 families wait-listed for public housing, a number that was nearly equal to the total number of housing units available in the city. Each year, approximately 8,000 housing units became available, and it was estimated that, absent any factors that would "bump" one to the head of the list, the wait for housing was approximately twenty years.[48]

Families who had been doubling up with other family members as they waited their turn for public housing quickly figured out that access to such housing was best achieved by becoming homeless. The Mayor's Commission on the Homeless concluded that an unintended consequence of the policy was to increase by thousands the number of families entering the city's shelter system in order to move to the head of the public housing list. The report made clear that families came to see the shelter system as offering them the best chance to move into adequate permanent homes. Consequently, "the City fostered a greater demand and, ironically, a continuation or exacerbation of the crisis."[49]

Summary

Social policy (1) is an expression of social values, (2) is arrived at through a process of debate and decision making, (3) produces a framework for the allocation of social resources to defined categories of people for the purpose of resolving or eliminating social problems, (4) often seeks to affect the future behavior of members of society, and (5) has the force of law.

The social policies that concern us in this text either provide concrete benefits such as income or food assistance or offer protection from discrimination based on individual characteristics such as race and gender. Regardless of the benefit provided, social policy creates a framework that affects social work practice.

Social policy, whether enacted by a legislature, through a public initiative, ordered by a court, or ordered by the executive branch of government, has been defined to include both process and product. Process involves the debate that precedes the passage of policy. Product refers to the provided benefit, the categories of people who are deemed eligible to receive the provided benefit, and the social objective to be achieved by providing the benefit.

The values of a society provide a context for the study of social policy, and a society's values determine the role that the institution of social welfare will play. Americans tend to place great store on self-sufficiency and individual responsibility and on the role of family, community, and church in helping people in need. To a degree, Americans fear that the providing welfare benefits will rob people of the incentive to be self-sufficient, that the availability of welfare will act as an incentive for people to rely on government largesse rather than their own efforts.

The model of social welfare that is most compatible with these values views the social welfare institution as residual, meaning that it comes into play as a corrective when a social problem of major proportions occurs, for example, when a recession or natural disaster creates a need for state action. In a residual model, it is assumed that the problem will be corrected and the role played by the social welfare institution will diminish. When programs are based on a residual model of welfare, benefits are available on a selective basis, meaning that eligibility is contingent on membership in a category defined, for example, by age, disability, or low income.

The residual model stands in contrast to the institutional model, in which the existence of the social welfare institution is seen as permanent, made necessary by the needs of certain populations such as children and the elderly and by certain realities of life such as cyclical recessions and the unemployment that accompanies recessions. In the institutional model, the existence of the institution of social welfare is not a reflection of social dysfunction but a reality of modern life.

Eliminating barriers to employment, housing, accommodation, and services, where barriers are based on personal characteristics, is the corrective that is provided by civil rights policies. A sense of fair play, meaning that a person should not be denied an opportunity based solely on gender, race, or physical ability, is the dominant value that supports civil rights policies. Public support for civil rights policies diminishes when people perceive a shift from providing equal opportunity, as with outreach and recruitment, to determining the outcome, as with preferences and quotas.

The goals of social policy are most likely to be attained when they are expressed in observable and measurable terms, rest on true premises, and employ interventions that research has shown to be effective in reducing or eliminating the problem identified in the policy.

Social Workers and Social Policy

The Historical Context

Many of you who are reading this text may have a general understanding that public policy affects the practice of social work in public agencies. You may know that certain programs exist only because a legislative body has passed a policy that mandates the creation of a program. Examples of the programs created through legislation and supported by public funds include those that serve abused and neglected children in their own homes, children in foster care, and the families of these children. Many of the tasks to be performed and, by implication, the skills that are necessary to perform the tasks in serving clients are described in a series of federal and state statutes.

The effect of policy directives on social work practice is not limited to public agency workers; the directives can affect social work practice in any setting where the provided service is paid for with public funds. In New York City, a significant percentage of children in foster homes are served by voluntary, not-for-profit agencies, many of which are operated by religious organizations under contract to the city of New York. If services are supported by public funds, the agency is acting as an agent of the state, and it must adhere to the same rules and regulations imposed on public agencies.[1] Clients are entitled to the same benefits that they would receive if served directly by the public agency. Thus, agencies operated by the Catholic Church cannot for reasons based on religious convictions deny to foster children the right to family planning information and contraceptive devices.

In some settings, such as schools, outpatient health and mental health clinics, and inpatient settings such as medical and psychiatric hospitals, the extent of control that policy exerts over the day-to-day tasks performed by social workers varies. Nevertheless, social work practice is affected by policies that (1) govern eligibility for service; (2) set rules that a social worker must follow in providing services; (3) guarantee to children with disabilities the right to an education and to all the right to service regardless of personal characteristics such as race or gender or physical ability; and (4) address problems with personal relationships, such as sexual harassment, that develop in the workplace.

Social workers in private practice are also affected by public policy, albeit to a lesser extent than an agency-based worker. Private practitioners must be concerned with the policies that govern licensing and certification and the use of professional titles that exist in all states (see chapter 3). Public policies concerning confidentiality will govern the conditions under which confidential information *may* be disclosed or *must* be disclosed. All social work practitioners are required to report known or suspected cases of child abuse or neglect; in a number of states, practitioners have a duty to warn of threats made by a client to harm a third party; and in all states, practitioners are obligated to serve clients in a nondiscriminatory manner. Policies established by the courts in each state and by state and federal laws determine the conditions under which a practitioner is vulnerable to being sued for malpractice. In addition to recognizing the force of law of these policies, the Code of Ethics of the National Association of Social Workers reminds us that our ethical obligation as professionals includes activities such as monitoring and evaluating policies and programs and providing testimony to legislative bodies to try and ensure that policies being considered will benefit clients.[2]

This chapter and the next address in detail the relationship of social work practice to social policy. In the following pages, social policy as used by social workers as a tool to create change for clients is the topic addressed. We begin this chapter by stepping back to the nineteenth century. After considering briefly some of the ways in which the causes of poverty were viewed, we focus on the individuals and groups engaged in social work, with a primary focus on those social workers whose concern was social reform.

Poverty in the Nineteenth Century

In the nineteenth century, two distinct views of the causes of poverty prevailed in the United States. The first view rested on the assumption that since there were endless opportunities in America, poverty had to be the result of an individual's unwillingness to work, laziness, and moral failure. The second view of poverty focused less on individual deficiencies and more on the social conditions in which the poor lived, such as inadequate housing and the unsanitary living conditions associated with inadequate housing, the lack of education, unsafe and unhealthy working conditions, and low wages, that limited the opportunities available to the poor, whose numbers swelled between 1815 and 1860 when 5 million immigrants entered the United States.[3]

The view that poverty was the result of moral failure was supported by the writings of Herbert Spencer, a social theorist. Spencer applied Charles Darwin's theory of evolution to social behavior and concluded that "the whole effort of nature is to get rid of [the poor], to clear the world of them, and make room for the better."[4] Taken to its logical conclusion, efforts to educate poor people and provide them with the skills that were needed for gainful employment were fruitless and worse because they would weaken humanity by encouraging the poor to reproduce.

These divergent views of poverty produced three very different approaches to assisting the poor. The first, which is addressed in chapter four, was an increase in the use of almshouses or poorhouses where the able-bodied or "unworthy poor," who were those able to work but seemingly unwilling to do so, would be institutionalized—their behavior monitored and controlled—and where good work habits would be learned.[5] The second approach to assisting the poor is found in the formation of "benevolent societies" that saw the elimination of poverty in the improvement of the character of the poor.[6] The third approach is found in the work of the settlement house workers and their concern with effecting change in the environments in which poor people lived and worked.

Benevolent Societies, the Charity Organization Movement, and the Friendly Visitor

Poverty increased early in the nineteenth century, a result of different factors that included an increase in immigration from Europe, a financial "panic" in 1819, and a depression in the 1830s. According to Trattner (1989), "Destitution was widespread; beggars and vagrants stalked the streets."[7] The agencies that existed to provide relief were not able to respond to the magnitude of need.

To learn why charitable groups were not able to alleviate the suffering around them, an investigation was undertaken in New York in the early 1840s. The investigators concluded that the efforts of the benevolent societies were "undisciplined and indiscriminate." The groups lacked the means to ensure that relief efforts were not being duplicated by different groups nor that recipients were worthy of the relief provided. Rather than reducing poverty, the uncoordinated efforts of charitable groups caused poverty to increase.[8]

In 1843, the New York Association for Improving the Conditions of the Poor was formed in response to these conclusions. The mission of this association and of the charity organization societies that came into being in the remaining years of the nineteenth century was not to provide relief but to organize the relief efforts of others. The problems of giving to the unworthy poor and of duplicative efforts would be resolved through "investigation, registration, cooperation and coordination," coupled with adequate relief. These activities promised the end of pauperism and the salvation of urban cities.

But this organized effort was not enough. Convinced that "human beings were naturally inclined to laziness" and that the granting of relief was "suicidal," the "friendly visitor," and later the paid agents of the charity organization societies, focused on the individual case and the moral roots of dependency.[9] Poverty was to be rooted out through the moral example set by friendly visitors, who were intelligent and kind friends and whose job it was to counsel the less fortunate.

THE PROGRESSIVE ERA AND SOCIAL REFORM

The view that the inequality between the friendly visitors and those with whom they worked could be instrumental in reducing or eliminating poverty was not universally held. Despite the efforts of the charity organization societies and their friendly visitors, poverty was increasing along the East Coast. This increase was partly due to a rise in immigration and partly to the cyclical depressions that occurred in the nineteenth century. A depression occurred from 1873 to 1878, followed five years later by the depression of 1883, and then by a three-year depression that lasted from 1893 through 1896. It was difficult to sustain the thinking of Social Darwinists in the face of ongoing economic downturns that seemed to have little to do with nature and much to do with the behavior of corporate tycoons. Not only did the tycoons fail to usher in an era of general prosperity, but their activities in firing workers, shutting down plants, and suppressing union activity through the use of violence caused "widespread disenchantment" on the part of the public with both government and business leaders.[10] Some sought to channel this disenchantment into social reform.

Like the charity organization societies, social reformers thought that compiling data was central to their work. But whereas the societies' data were used for such administrative purposes as creating a registry of recipients and monitoring who received aid, social reformers used their data by presenting it to legislative bodies and the courts to argue that new rules had to be created and some existing rules changed to provide greater opportunities for the poor. The social reformers of the nineteenth century saw social policy as a tool for change. They were the forerunners to modern day social workers for whom lobbying, advocacy, policy analysis, and other forms of research are tools to create social change. In a similar way, friendly visitors of the charity organization societies were the forerunners to modern day clinical social workers.

SETTLEMENT HOUSES, THE PROGRESSIVE ERA, AND SOCIAL REFORM

The era of the settlement houses began in England in 1884 with the opening of Toynbee Hall and in the United States in the late 1880s. Settlement houses grew in number from a handful in Boston, New York, and Chicago to more than 400 settlements by 1910. The overarching goals of many of the settlement house workers were to improve the conditions in which poor people lived and to work for the social and economic reforms that were seen as necessary to allow people to fulfill their potential.[11]

The core group of reformers consisted of women whose names consistently appear in association with social change in the Progressive Era. Some of these women, such as Grace and Edith Abbott, Florence Kelley, and Julia Lathrop, began their association at Hull House, which was established in Chicago by Jane Addams in 1889. These women were joined by Lillian Wald and Sophonisba Breckinridge and by a group of men, including Paul Kellog and Edward Devine, to form the nucleus of the settlement house reformers.

Settlement house workers were well educated and had masters and doctoral degrees in different disciplines.[12] Some had taken courses in social work at the summer institutes that preceded the first university-affiliated schools of social work.

Others held degrees in economics, political science, law, medicine, and sociology. Others were artists and journalists.

These early social workers viewed urban poverty and the effects of industrialization on the health of urban dwellers in pragmatic terms. As such, their interventions included the provision of child care and kindergarten classes for the children of working women, vocational training to help residents develop the skills that were sought after by the businesses in the communities in which they lived, and English language classes for newly arrived immigrants.[13]

In addition to addressing matters of everyday living, settlement house workers focused their attention on the deplorable conditions in slum housing, the effects of poor sanitation on the health of tenement dwellers, the conditions under which children and women worked, and juvenile crime. Settlement house workers learned quickly that the matters that they sought to address had to be resolved through legislation. They lobbied and advocated for change by working with groups to select candidates who would forward their agenda, participating in the development of political platforms, advising officials, serving on public boards, and working with lawyers to litigate for change.[14] Hull House was also a center for social research. Settlement house workers wrote books, which often provided the only information that was available on various aspects of urban living. There was an emphasis on fact-finding, albeit from an advocate's point of view and thus not always objective, concerning the social conditions that the residents wanted to change.

SETTLEMENT HOUSES AND AFRICAN AMERICANS

In 1900 in New York City, African Americans constituted 2 percent of the population, compared to foreign-born white people, who comprised about 40 percent. In Chicago, African Americans represented less than 5 percent of the population at that time. These statistics are said to be representative of population figures for African Americans in northern cities in this period of history.[15]

The conditions under which African Americans worked and lived in northern cities was studied. W. E. B. Du Bois focused his attention on Philadelphia, and Mary White Ovington, the daughter of an abolitionist, and Frances Kellog, a settlement house worker, separately studied the living and working conditions of African Americans in New York. The work of these and others, taken together, produced a picture that showed that "large numbers of northern Negroes [were] living under incredibly bad conditions" that were exacerbated because of the difficulty that African Americans had in finding work and because of the exclusion of African Americans from labor unions.[16]

In 1905, Ovington reported that "colored churches" were the mainstay of charity for African Americans who received very little relief from mainstream institutions.[17] Some settlement houses welcomed black people and insisted that there be no discrimination. Others had special branches in black neighborhoods, whereas some reflected the racist attitudes of their time and ignored the needs of African Americans. In 1910, there were ten settlements specifically for African Americans across the country.[18]

REFORM THROUGH LEGISLATION AND THE COURTS

Throughout American history, legislative and judicial bodies at federal and state levels have been the fora to which reformers have turned in their efforts to create social change. A theme that was played out in the nineteenth century, and that echoes through policy debates today, asks, "What is the proper balance between state governments and the federal government in providing assistance to people in need?"

During and after the Civil War, the federal government was involved in activities (1) that touched upon the social welfare of African Americans, such as the passage of civil rights legislation to ensure that the states would not abridge the rights of newly freed slaves (chapter 4), and (2) that concerned Native Americans, whose tribal lands were sold off by the federal government to non-natives after small allotments were reserved to individual native families.[19] As these examples suggest, federal action in the nineteenth century consisted of activities that were directed at groups, not individuals. Additionally, Washington was developing the agency structure and regulatory framework that had little if anything to do with providing direct aid to the needy. For example, in 1887, Congress passed the Interstate Commerce Act for the purpose of regulating interstate railroads and ensuring fairness in interstate business transactions by preventing monopolies that destroyed competition. Other federal agencies were formed in the early twentieth century, including the Bureau of Chemistry, predecessor to the Food and Drug Administration; the Federal Trade Commission in 1914; the Federal Tariff Board in 1916; and the Commodities Exchange in 1922.[20] Despite these agencies, whose purpose it was to protect consumers from unsafe products and ensure equity across states in business dealings, the federal government was not a friendly arena for the efforts of social reformers in the eighteenth and early nineteenth centuries. To understand why a federal structure to provide for the needy was not created, we must step back in time to 1848, approximately forty years before the settlement house movement began.

DOROTHEA DIX AND THE CARE OF THE INSANE

In the early nineteenth century, one of the ways in which the federal government provided assistance for worthy causes was through the granting of lands for the construction of schools, railroads, and mines. Dorothea Dix was a social reformer who conducted research and wrote about the conditions in prisons and mental hospitals. In studying the care provided to the insane, Dix traveled more than 60,000 miles and visited 27 states to compile data. On June 23, 1848, she presented her findings to Congress and made a plea for a land grant to be used to create asylums for the care of the insane. Congress granted her request and set aside 10 million acres, with an additional 2.5 million acres for the education of the deaf.[21] On May 3, 1854, President Franklin Pierce vetoed the land grant because if Congress "has the power to make provisions for the indigent insane . . . it has the same power to provide for the indigent who are not insane, and thus to transfer to the federal government the charge of all the poor in all the States."[22]

The conviction that the federal government had no role in the provision of welfare to individuals and that the federal government should not set national standards governing labor, whether of adults or children, was pervasive. Federal legislation was passed in 1916, the Keating-Owens Bill, to prohibit child labor on goods in interstate commerce. Two years after its passage, the Supreme Court declared Keating-Owens unconstitutional because it usurped state powers.[23] Again in 1922, the Supreme Court declared unconstitutional a federal tax on the labor of children.[24] The sentiment behind the Pierce veto would echo directly and indirectly through Supreme Court decisions until after the depression of 1929. Not until 1941 did the High Court support limits on child labor when it upheld the Fair Labor Standards Act, which proscribed from interstate commerce goods produced by children.[25]

STATE LEVEL EFFORTS

The success of social reformers occurred at the state level. In New York and other cities, for example, settlement house workers were instrumental in the passage of the laws of 1901 that mandated improved sanitary conditions in tenement housing,[26] and they defeated an effort by New York City to create an elevated structure in an already blighted, congested urban district in favor of a subway system.[27]

In 1910, workmen's compensation laws were passed and within a decade were adopted by more than forty states. Workmen's compensation provided a cash grant to a worker who was injured on the job. This law was attractive to employers because workers traded their right to sue for on-the-job injuries for the certainty of the provided grant. Mother's pension laws and workmen's compensation laws were the "first social insurance measures to be adopted in the United States."[28]

Likewise, efforts to regulate child labor met with greater success at the state level. In 1904, the National Child Labor Committee, whose membership included Florence Kelley of the National Consumers League, Jane Addams of Hull House, Lillian Wald of the Henry Street Settlement in New York, and Edward Devine and Robert DeForest of the New York Charity Organization Society, was formed. The committee set standards to limit the employment of children in manufacturing to those fourteen years and older and those in mining to a minimum age of sixteen, to provide for an eight-hour workday, and to prohibit night work. By 1914, thirty-five states had a fourteen-year age limit and an eight-hour workday for those under sixteen. Thirty-six states employed factory inspectors to enforce the law. However, enforcement was a problem because states with child labor laws saw those without such laws as having an economic advantage.[29]

Despite these gains, there was no regulation of children working in agriculture, canneries, domestic service, street trades, and sweatshop labor, and there were also exemptions for children of widows. In addition, some state efforts to protect the welfare of workers met with defeat. New York passed a law in 1897 limiting the number of hours that a person could be required or allowed to work in a bakery to a maximum of sixty hours each week or ten hours each day. In 1905, the Supreme Court declared the law unconstitutional because it infringed on the individual's right, under the Fourteenth Amendment to the United States Constitution, to contract for their labor.[30] It would be thirty years before the court overruled itself when, in *West Coast Hotel v. Parish*, the Court held that the right to contract was not absolute but could be constrained by "reasonable regulations and prohibitions imposed in interests of the community."[31]

However, another state statute, enacted in 1903 by Oregon to limit to ten hours per day the number of hours that women in certain industries could work, was found to be constitutional by the Supreme Court. Florence Kelley and Josephine Goldmark of the National Consumer's League, an advocacy organization that emphasized use of the law to resolve social problems, wanted equality for women, but theirs was an equality based on gender differences, not on gender neutrality.[32] The league hired Louis Brandeis to argue for upholding the Oregon law before the Supreme Court. Brandeis filed a lengthy brief that was filled with statistics and sociological data compiled by Kelley and her colleagues, who believed that social problems often required legal solutions. The brief detailed the negative effects of long work hours on women's health. The league did not argue for overruling the Supreme Court's earlier decision concerning the number of hours that bakery workers could be employed. It chose instead to defend the Oregon statute based on women's greater physical frailty. The court agreed with Brandeis' argument and upheld the Oregon statute by stating that the difference between the sexes justified a different rule for women than for men.[33]

THE JUVENILE COURT

Until the latter part of the nineteenth century, children convicted of crimes were sometimes incarcerated in a house of refuge designed specifically for minors guilty of criminal offenses,[34] but often they were incarcerated in prisons with adult offenders.[35]

Toward the latter part of the century, the view that delinquent behavior was the result of free choice shifted to a concern about environmental influences and their effects on such behavior. Two conclusions followed from the notion that environmental factors influenced delinquency. First, incarcerating children with adults would exacerbate, not alleviate, the problem; and second, if rehabilitation was an objective, children should be placed in settings where they could be influenced to be good.

The first juvenile court was established in Chicago in 1899. The philosophy of the court was rehabilitation, not establishing guilt. A hallmark of this approach was the absence of due process; children were not seen as needing legal representation because it was assumed that all parties were acting in the best interests of the child and that the adversarial process that characterized proceedings affecting adults would not be helpful. The preferred disposition for juvenile offenders was to return them to their own homes under the supervision of a probation officer.[36]

The Beginning of Federal Involvement in Social Welfare

In 1908, James West, an attorney in the District of Columbia, suggested to President Theodore Roosevelt that he convene in Washington a conference on the care of dependent children. With the backing of Homer Folks of the Children's Aid Society of Philadelphia, Lillian Wald, Jane Addams, Florence Kelley, and others, the President invited 216 child welfare workers to attend a conference.[37]

The Conference on the Care of Dependent Children, the first White House conference on children and families, was significant for social welfare. First, many of the conferees were convinced that public assistance programs should be established to provide financial assistance so that children could be maintained in their own homes. The first Mother's Pension Laws, precursors to the Aid to Dependent Children provisions in the Social Security Act of 1935, were passed in 1911 in the State of Illinois as a direct outgrowth of the conference.

Second, the conference brought to fruition a goal that Lillian Wald and Florence Kelley had been working toward since the early 1900s, when they had begun a lobbying effort for the creation of a federal bureau to compile data on various matters concerning the welfare of children. After a decade of advocacy, the Children's Bureau was created in 1912 and is today a part of the United States Department of Health and Human Services. The bureau's mandate was straightforward: "To investigate and report upon all matters pertaining to the welfare of children and child life among all classes of our people."

Under the stewardship of Julia Lathrop, who headed the bureau from its inception until 1921, the bureau focused its data-gathering efforts on the availability and use of prenatal care services, on infant and maternal mortality, and on child hygiene. In 1921, when Grace Abbott took over from Julia Lathrop as bureau chief, the Maternity and Infancy Protection Act, commonly known as the Sheppard-Towner Act, was passed. Abbott was charged with administering the act, which provided for federal matching grants for states that chose to establish programs for mothers and babies with the goal of reducing maternal and infant mortality. Its passage signaled a high water mark for the bureau as "a highly significant new venture into social welfare under federal auspices . . ."[38]

THE END OF THE SETTLEMENT HOUSE MOVEMENT

By 1914, when World War I started in Europe, settlement house workers had accomplished a number of objectives, including the passage of legislation to improve tenement housing, mother's pension and workers' compensation laws, laws governing workplace safety, creation of juvenile courts, and the creation of the children's bureau.

The onset of World War I signaled the end of this period of social reform known as the Progressive Movement. National attention turned to the events in Europe. The fear that the war had put and end to reform activities was expressed by Lillian Wald, who said that "War is the doom of all that has taken years of peace to build up."[39] Davis (1967) points out that the social reformers did work to preserve the gains that had been made at the outbreak of the war, but the attention of some in the reform movement turned to assisting the war effort by collecting money for war relief, working with the selective service system, and organizing neighborhood defense councils.[40]

Ironically, the war itself yielded some of the gains that had been sought by social reformers. For example, the National War Labor Board, the War Labor Policies

Board, the United States Employment Service, and other agencies acknowledged the right of all workers to receive a minimum wage that paid enough to provide for the subsistence of the worker and the worker's family, to engage in collective bargaining, and to limit the workday to eight hours. The war effort resulted in the construction of the first public housing that promised to satisfy the wish of the settlement workers to improve the housing conditions of low wage earners.

THE EMERGING PROFESSION OF SOCIAL WORK

A series of events mark the emergence and recognition of social work as a profession. First, in the last quarter of the nineteenth century, the National Conference of Charities and Corrections provided a chance for social workers to gather and exchange information about their work. The opportunity to exchange information was enhanced with the founding of specialized journals and magazines in the 1890s that provided the opportunity for a continuing exchange of information between meetings of the National Conference. During this same period of time, many acknowledged that good intentions alone were not sufficient to accomplish the goals of social workers. Specialized knowledge and skills were required, and the required knowledge and skills could be taught by teachers to students.[41] In 1899, a summer program offered by the New York Charity Organization Society became the first "school" of social work. It was followed in 1903 in Chicago by the Institute of Social Science and in 1904 by the Boston School of Social Work, both of which were founded to train social workers.

The establishment in 1920 of the Association of Training Schools of Professional Social Work, which became the Council of Social Work Education in 1952, strengthened the drive to bring schools of social work under the aegis of a university, which would increase the claim to professional status. In 1935, the association decreed that any school desiring membership had to be part of an institution approved by the Association of American Universities. A model of social work education "based largely on social science theory and research" that had been advocated by Edith Abbott now became the norm.[42]

The formation of professional associations also advanced this movement toward professionalization. These included the American Association of Hospital Social Workers (1918), which became the American Association of Medical Social Workers (1946); the American Association of Social Workers (1920), which would become the National Association of Social Workers in 1955; and the American Association of Psychiatric Social Workers (1926).

Trattner (1989) states that in the 1920s, the majority of social workers had neither the time for nor the interest in social reform, and efforts to help those in need focused on the individual case method that had been favored by the friendly visitors. Social workers assumed that those in need had strength and inner resources, and when these individuals were freed from the shackles of fear, inhibition, and other psychological impediments, they could overcome their difficulties.[43]

THE SCHOOLS OF SOCIAL WORK

When the first schools of social work opened their doors in Chicago in 1907 and in New York in 1910, there were divisions in thought as to the proper training for the

newly emerging social worker. The curriculum of the New York School of Philanthropy, which would become the Columbia University School of Social Work, was
associated with the casework of Mary Richmond, which grew out of her earlier
advocacy for the value of friendly visiting and its emphasis on one-on-one efforts
to change individuals. In contrast, the developing Chicago School of Civics and
Philanthropy, later to become the School of Social Service Administration at the
University of Chicago, developed a curriculum that was influenced by the work of
social reformers such as Julia Lathrop and Edith and Grace Abbott, who believed
that research, social policy, and public administration were the proper domain of
social workers.[44]

Despite their differences, Richmond, Lathrop, and the Abbotts believed that the
distinguishing characteristics of the new profession should include the systematic
compilation of facts and other forms of evidence upon which an intervention would
be developed and applied to alleviate a problem.[45] And despite her focus on the
casework method, Mary Richmond believed firmly in the value of social reform:

> I have spent 25 years of my life in an attempt to get social casework accepted as
> a valid process . . . now I shall spend the rest of my life trying to demonstrate to
> social caseworkers that there is more to social work than . . . casework.[46]

Summary

In the nineteenth and early twentieth centuries, there were two schools of thought
about how best to help the poor. The first, reflected in the work of the friendly
visitors, saw poverty as a consequence of moral deficiencies. Change would be
accomplished on a case-by-case basis from the moral example set by friendly visitors
and their persuasive talents.

Rejecting this view of assistance and change, social workers who were associated
with Progressive Era reform saw poverty as a consequence of educational deficits,
lack of job skills, and poor health from living and working in unsanitary and unsafe
conditions. These early social workers pursued change by providing English classes
for newly arrived immigrants and other educational and job training opportunities,
advocating for the passage of laws to improve the unsanitary conditions in tenement
housing and the unsafe conditions in factories, and advocating for labor laws to
shorten the work week. Compiling data that described and documented the deplorable living and working conditions of the poor and using these data to persuade
legislators that change was needed were key strategies for social reformers.

Settlement house workers achieved their early success at the state level with the
passage of the laws that (1) required the improvement of unsanitary conditions in
tenement housing, (2) regulated the working conditions of women and children,
(3) provided compensation for workers who were injured on the job, and (4) created
the first juvenile courts.

After the turn of the century, attention turned to the federal government, where
some progress was made. The first White House conference on children and families
was held in 1909 and contributed to the passage of Mother's Pension Laws, the

creation of the Children's Bureau, and the passage of the maternity and infancy health legislation.

World War I brought an end to the Progressive Era, yet change continued. Minimum wage laws were passed, workers gained the right to engage in collective bargaining, working conditions improved with the eight-hour workday, and the first public housing was constructed to replace tenement housing.

The end of the nineteenth century and the early decades of the twentieth century saw the practice of social work transformed from a vocation into a profession. National conferences were held and professional journals were published. In the early years of the new century, paid workers began to replace friendly visitors, and summer educational programs in social work made their appearance, soon to be replaced by the first schools of social work established in Chicago in 1907 and in New York in 1910.[47] As the Progressive Era drew to a close, the emphasis on social reform and social change gave way to an emphasis on change at the individual level as the social work profession increasingly adopted the practice of social casework to effect change.

CHAPTER 3

Social Work and Social Policy
The Present Context

Professional status confers privileges but carries costs. The privileges include (1) the recognition and respect that society will accord you as a member of a profession with a specialized body of knowledge and skills; (2) the recognition by other professionals, such as members of the legal and medical professions, who need the unique knowledge and skills you possess and who may ask you to assist them in their work; (3) the right of those who pass a state licensing exam to exclusive use of a professional title such as "clinical social worker" or "psychotherapist"; (4) certain legal protections that shield you from suit for errors of judgment that are made while acting in good faith; and (5) the personal pride that comes from attaining professional status.

The costs of professionalization are in the form of controls—rules that govern your responsibility to protect the confidentiality of client information, that require that otherwise confidential information be disclosed, and that require you to provide services to eligible clients without regard to personal characteristics such as race, gender, and physical disability.

The material in this chapter covers some of the privileges and some of the costs that come with professional status. But first, we will look at the way in which social services are organized in the United States, after which we will continue our discussion of the relationship of social work practice to social policy that was begun in chapter 2.

SECTION 1: THE ORGANIZATION OF SOCIAL SERVICES

The public and the private sectors provide social services. The private sector includes not-for-profit agencies and for-profit entities that offer a range of services, such as educational, health, and mental health services, in an array of settings, including social service agencies, schools, hospitals, and the offices of private practitioners.

Using the 1995 membership database of the National Association of Social Workers (NASW), Gibelman and Schervish (1997) provide data on the primary settings in which 88,544 social workers, of the 153,814 NASW members, are employed.[1] Eighty percent of these members work in agency settings, and 20 percent are in private practice. Approximately 34 percent are in the public sector (state, local, and federal agencies); 38 percent in the private, not-for-profit sector; and 28 percent in the for-profit sector. There is no information on the percentage of workers in the private sector whose work is supported by public funds.

In descending order, the primary practice settings are health care settings (34%); social service agencies (21%); schools and residential facilities (approximately 7% each); college/university settings (4%); mental health settings (3%); and private practice (20%). The remaining 4 percent practice in miscellaneous settings.

Public Agencies

Public agencies in each state administer a variety of social welfare programs, including but not limited to those that determine a client's eligibility for financial, food, or medical assistance and those that provide protective services, foster care services, and adoption services for children; counseling and shelter to victims of domestic violence; treatment to individuals addicted to alcohol or drugs; and assistance in obtaining housing and job training.

The authority of social service programs is described in state statutes that identify the organizational unit within the state or local government that is responsible for administering programs and providing direct services. For example, the New York State Office for the Prevention of Domestic Violence was created by statute. The statute grants to this office diverse responsibilities, such as (1) advising the governor and the legislature on how best to respond to the problem of domestic violence; (2) developing and implementing policies and programs to assist victims of domestic violence and their families; (3) disseminating information concerning this social problem; (4) developing and coordinating outreach and educational programs across New York State; and (5) developing and delivering training to professionals working in the field of domestic violence.[2] In addition, the office awards contracts for "batterers' programs" to private sector agencies to provide services to victims of domestic violence.

Not-for-Profit Agencies

Not-for-profit agencies are generally organized as corporations chartered by the secretary of state. Charters identify the purpose of the agency with regard to services offered and clients served, specify its organizational framework, and name its officers.

To provide certain services such as child care and adoption services, not-for-profit agencies must obtain a license from the state in addition to their charter. The granting of a license requires that the agency meet certain standards, for example, standards for fire safety and teacher-to-student ratios.

Historically, not-for-profit agencies have been supported by endowments, the interest earned from endowments, fees for service, contributions from the general public, and corporate gifts. In 1962 and again in 1968, Congress amended the Social Security Act (see chapter 9) to allow public agencies to enter into contracts to purchase from not-for-profit agencies services the public agency had themselves provided. The New York law through which "batterers' programs" are established provides that the New York State Office for the Prevention of Domestic Violence enter into contracts with community agencies to provide this service. Today, government is the single largest source of funding for not-for-profit social service agencies, providing approximately 50 percent of agency income for employment, training, social services, and mental health services.[3]

For-Profit Entities

For-profit entities include corporations, partnerships, and solo practitioners who are licensed to provide services such as medical services, counseling, or day care. Rules governing the formation of a business vary by state. As a general rule, corporations and partnerships register with a designated state office and identify, among other things, the purpose of their business and the services they will offer. In contrast, licensed social workers conducting solo practices usually practice on the basis of their professional license alone. If, however, a partnership or corporation is formed, the practice will probably be required to register.

Privatization

When the Social Security Act was amended in the 1960s to allow public agencies to enter into contracts with not-for-profit agencies, the movement to "privatize" services—to shift service provision from the public to the private sector—began. The movement gained momentum in the 1980s when President Reagan established a series of commissions and charged each with studying ways to reduce federal expenses and to increase the role of the private sector in performing functions traditionally performed by government.[4] Today, legislative support for privatization is found throughout federal law. For example, the welfare reform legislation that was enacted in 1996 (see chapter 10) provides that the states may administer and provide services themselves or they may contract with charitable, religious, or private organizations for services for recipients of the Temporary Assistance to Needy Families Program (TANF), the Supplemental Security Income Program, and the Food Stamp Program.[5] Further evidence that the federal government hopes to increase the role of the private sector in service provision can be found in the Federal Activities Inventory Reform Act of 1998.[6] This act encourages governmental contracting with the private sector except for matters of concern to national security and for functions that are inherently governmental, meaning that the service has traditionally been carried out as a government function, unless better value can be obtained by direct government provision or where the private sector lacks the capacity to provide the goods or services required.[7]

PRIVATIZATION: PRO AND CON

Various reasons are offered for and against privatizing government services.[8] Proponents of privatization think that the size of government should be limited; thus, government should not undertake activities that can be performed by the private sector. In addition, they claim that (1) the private sector can offer services of higher quality in a more efficient manner at less cost than the public sector can; (2) private sector offerings provide greater flexibility, involve less red tape, and offer innovative approaches lacking in public sector provision; (3) there are not enough state personnel with the expertise required to provide quality service; and (4) program implementation will be more efficient under private sector control.

Opponents of privatization argue that (1) cost savings are not realized; (2) there is no guarantee that the competition necessary to yield cost savings exists; (3) privatization diminishes the accountability of governmental officials; (4) service quality is compromised in favor of profits; and (5) privatization threatens the jobs of public sector employees.

The evidence concerning the efficiency and effectiveness of private sector services compared to public sector services is mixed, as is the evidence concerning financial savings. With certain services, it is reasonable to conclude that privatization is more cost effective than public provision. For example, with the exception of Veteran's Administration hospitals, the federal government is not in the business of providing direct medical services to the population at large, and state- or city-run public hospitals are not numerous enough to meet the demand for medical service. Thus, relying on the private sector to deliver medical services that are available under the Medicaid and Medicare programs is a more reasonable response than would be the government building or taking over hospitals and hiring all of the medical personnel needed to provide services. Likewise, if a social service agency that does not routinely provide mental health services requires a mental health evaluation of a client, contracting with a private provider is more reasonable than hiring an additional staff person.

According to O'Looney (1993) and Bartly (1996), there is no conclusive evidence that private sector services are more efficient or more effective.[9] The mixed picture produced by two other studies conducted by the United States General Accounting Office (GAO) in 1996 and 1997 supports their conclusion. The first GAO study asked, "Are privately run prisons more cost efficient than those run by government?"[10] Data compiled in four states showed no cost differences in two states, a 7 percent savings in favor of private prisons reported by one state, and another state reporting that private prisons were more costly.

The second GAO study reviewed privatization efforts in Georgia, Massachusetts, Michigan, New York, and Virginia as well as in the city of Indianapolis. From their data-gathering efforts, we learned that contracting with private bidders is the most common form of privatization. Contracts provide for the successful bidder to render the contracted-for service and for the government to retain management and policy control over the provided service and to control the quality of the provided service.

The GAO reports that government agencies estimated that there would be savings from "outsourcing" of highway maintenance services, physical security at military facilities, child support enforcement collection, and other aspects of fiscal management for social services.[11] However, data to evaluate the "reliable and complete cost" of privatization efforts and to inform decision making were not available at any site.[12]

In 1997, the Council of State Governments surveyed state respondents (auditors, budget directors, and comptrollers) and agency respondents (social services, mental health, education, and transportation) to learn about state privatization activities and the cost effectiveness of state privatization.[13] Twenty-nine states provided information concerning cost savings. Of these states, 24 percent reported savings in excess of 15 percent, and 40 percent reported savings between 6 and 10 percent.[14] These savings were realized through the privatization of administrative and general services such as custodial services, pest control, building inspection, and snow removal.

When actual human services are at issue, such as social services, corrections, mental health, secondary and post-secondary education, and juvenile rehabilitation, the savings are more modest. With fewer than half of the states responding and fewer still providing cost information, savings rarely exceeded 5 percent for these kinds of services. Of human service agencies, only mental health reported higher savings, but very few agencies reported. For example, twenty-eight states responded and fourteen provided costs savings information. Of the fourteen, fewer than half reported savings in excess of 15 percent.[15]

The private agency or private practitioner who contracts to serve public sector clients surrenders a degree of autonomy because the provider must adhere to all government rules that regulate the provision of a given service.

At times, the control that is given up may be minimal. For example, a private agency that contracts to conduct mental health assessments of public agency clients will have to adhere to contract terms that may specify the precise information that is required, the form in which it is to be presented, and the time frame for providing a report. Some of the agreed-to terms may differ from the private agency's usual procedures but are not likely to result in too great a loss of autonomy. At the other end of the spectrum is the situation, referred to in chapter 2, where I reported that a court held that agencies operated by the Catholic Church cannot for religious reasons deny to foster children the right to family planning information and contraceptive devices. From the standpoint of the religious agency, such a requirement may represent an extreme and possibly unacceptable degree of government intrusion.

In general, not-for-profit private social service agencies may have lost some of their unique distinctions as of a result of their reliance on government funding. For example, free of government restraints, these agencies can accept whatever clients they choose to serve and serve clients in whatever manner they deem appropriate. This freedom gives agencies the flexibility to experiment with novel approaches to service provision. Experimentation is difficult when operating under restrictions established by federal or state statutes because the service provided to a client cannot vary solely on the basis of whether the client is served by the public or the private sector.

Other issues are of concern when a decision is being made to privatize a public service. For example, the United States Justice Department changed its initial decision to contract with private groups to operate portions of federal prisons because it was not able to reduce the possibility of a strike or walkout of correctional officers who are employed by private firms.[16]

A 1997 decision of the United States Supreme Court may pose a significant barrier to efforts to privatize public services. In *Richardson v. McKnight,* Ronnie Lee McKnight, a prisoner at a private correctional facility in Tennessee, sued the firm that operated the prison, including two prison guards in its employ, claiming that his constitutional rights had been violated by the use of "extremely tight physical restraints."[17] The issue addressed by the Supreme Court, discussed at greater length in the following paragraphs, concerned the subject of immunity from suit for monetary damages that is conferred on public employees for actions taken in the course of their employment.

Traditionally, public employees are immune from suit as long as their actions do not violate clearly established statutory or constitutional rights that the employee was aware of or should have been aware of. In *Richardson,* the Supreme Court was asked to extend qualified immunity to prison guards employed by a private firm. The Court held that the two guards were not entitled to qualified immunity for these reasons: (1) there was no historical precedent for extending the principle of immunity to privately employed prison guards; (2) the private firm received little governmental supervision in its operation of the prison; (3) the task of running the prison had been undertaken for profit; and (4) the purpose of a qualified immunity defense is to protect public officials acting in their official capacity from being sued for civil damages.

According to the Council of State Governments, unionized state employees have been the source of the "most persistent opposition to privatization in some states."[18] Fearful of the loss of jobs and benefits, prison guards in Illinois were successful in having legislation passed that banned the privatization of prisons.[19] In 1996, Boston City Hospital, a public institution, merged with a private university hospital. The newly created Boston Medical Center resisted the efforts of residents and interns to have the center recognize its collective bargaining unit. The medical center agreed to recognize the collective bargaining unit only after months of "adamant opposition to [the] union for interns and residents, after 78 percent of the 162 residents and interns indicated by signing cards that they favored representation."[20]

In 1997, the administration of Governor Weld in Massachusetts sought to privatize a variety of public services. State workers argued that the Weld administration was engaging in "union busting," that privatization was costly to taxpayers, and that it had a disproportionately negative effect on minority workers. As a result of these claims, the legislature passed an act to control privatization based in part on its findings that "using private contractors to provide public services formerly provided by state employees does not always promote the public interest." The newly enacted law requires a cost-benefit analysis of any privatization effort that results in a contract with an aggregate value of at least $100,000. The agency seeking to privatize must show that the overall cost of having the private sector perform the service will be less than the cost of performance by public employees. Moreover, it must be demonstrated that the quality of the service provided will not decline. If a public service is privatized, there must be assurances that private contracts provide for health insurance, hiring of qualified agency employees, nondiscriminatory hiring, and affirmative action. The state auditor to whom the plan for privatization must be submitted is to determine whether the provisions in the statue have been satisfied.[21]

Forms of Privatization and Services Privatized

In the 1997 survey by the Council of State Governments mentioned earlier, two other questions were addressed: first, what form does privatization take? and second, what services are most often privatized? (Table 3.1). The use of contracts with private firms is the major form of privatization, accounting for approximately 80 percent of privatization. When grants and subsidies from private sources are added to contracting, both account for close to 86 percent of privatization activities for health services, 92 percent for mental health/mental retardation services, and 84 percent for social services. Privatization of educational services is almost always accomplished through the use of contracts (93 percent of the time).

SECTION 2: POLICY AND PRACTICE

Policy may affect your practice in three ways. First, a series of policies affects the practice of all social workers, including policies that (1) govern professional certification and licensing and the use of professional titles; (2) address your responsibility to maintain information as confidential and permit or require you to disclose otherwise confidential information; and (3) dictate the terms under which social workers who practice in public and private agency settings may be held liable for malpractice. Second, some policies delineate the tasks that you must perform in serving clients. These policies are specific to areas of practice, such as child welfare and substance abuse treatment. Third, other policies concern the conferring of benefits, such as income support, food, housing, or medical services, that are available to your clients. The remainder of this chapter is concerned with policies of the first kind. Policies that dictate tasks and those that confer benefits on clients are discussed in parts II and III.

Professional Certification and Licensing

In 1995, the United States Bureau of Labor Statistics reported that there were 660,000 employees with the job title of social worker, 484,000 of whom had either a bachelor's degree (BSW) or a master's degree (MSW) in social work.[22] Only those

TABLE 3.1. Forms of Privatization by Percentage of Use for Seven Privatized Services: 1997

Form	Administration (n = 31)	Corrections (n = 35)	Education (n = 24)	Health (n = 29)	M.H./M.R. (n = 28)	Social Services (n = 27)	Transportation (n = 38)
Asset sale	.3	.3	0	1.2	.5	.3	0
Contracts	86.7	82.8	92.5	60.2	82.7	68.1	91
Franchise	.3	.3	0	.4	0	2.2	.7
Grants and subsidies	0	3.4	3.2	24.5	9.4	16.1	3.2
Private donations	0	.3	0	1.2	0	1.3	.2
Public-private partnership	4.5	5.2	1.1	8.3	5.4	6.3	1.8
Service shedding	7.4	4.5	2.2	2.5	0	.3	.7
Volunteerism	.6	3.1	1.1	1.2	.5	1.6	2.3
Vouchers	0	0	0	0	.5	3.8	0

Source: Keon S. Chi and Cindy Jasper, *Private Practices: A Review of Privatization in State Government* (Lexington, Ky.: Council of State Governments, 1998).

Note: It was reported that privatization occurred for the following services; there was no information reported as to form or percentage of use: (1) juvenile rehabilitation, (2) higher education, (3) labor, (4) natural resources, (5) parks and recreation, (6) public safety and police, and (7) treasury.

Definitions: (1) Asset sale means the sale of state assets to private firms; (2) Contracting is used in the everyday sense; (3) Franchise occurs when the state gives a monopoly to a private firm; (4) Grants and subsidies refer to awards made to provide a service; (5) Private donation occurs when personnel, facilities, or equipment are loaned to the public sector; (6) Partnerships refer to cooperative projects that rely on private resources rather than public resources; (7) Service shedding occurs when the state "drastically reduces" the level of service so that the private sector can assume the function using private resources; (8) Volunteerism refers to reliance on volunteers to provide the service; and (9) Vouchers are used to allow eligible clients to purchase services on the open market from private firms. Deregulation defined as changing government regulations to favor the private sector was used but its use was reported only for health services (0.4%).

who hold a master's degree from a school of social work or social welfare that is accredited by the Council on Social Work Education are eligible for one of the credentialing programs administered by the National Association of Social Workers (NASW).

The NASW Office of Quality Assurance sets and promotes standards and confers credentials for the professional who has met minimum educational and practice standards. Four programs are administered by the office, each of which confers a different credential, including ACSW, conferred by the Academy of Certified Social Workers; SSWS, school social work specialist; QCSW, qualified clinical social worker; and DCSW, diplomate in clinical social work.

In addition to an earned master's degree from an accredited school of social work, applicants to the NASW programs must have at least two years of post-MSW supervised professional experience, and they must successfully complete an examination. Certain credentials require that applicants pass a special test. For example, to be credentialed as SSWS, applicants must pass the School Social Worker Specialty Area Test. To retain the credential, the social worker must participate in continuing professional education and earn a minimum of 30 hours of continuing professional education every three years. The applicant for the QCSW must also hold a valid state social work license or certificate. Those applying for the diplomate must have three additional years of advanced clinical practice, in addition to the two years of practice experience required for all credentials. Holders of the diplomate must also have the highest level of social work license or certification available in their state, and they must successfully complete the NASW Diplomate Clinical Assessment Examination.

Certificates that are issued by professional organizations are not to be confused with state-issued licenses. Licenses are not necessary for the social worker who chooses to practice in an agency under the agency's license. Individual licenses confer the right to engage in private practice and the exclusive right to use designated professional titles. For example, in Minnesota and Florida only state-licensed social workers, and those whom they supervise, may call themselves "psychotherapists," and only licensed social workers are deemed to be qualified mental health professionals. Colorado and Alabama restrict the "private, independent practice of social work and the right to use the title licensed social worker, independent social worker and social worker" to holders of state licenses.[23]

Requirements for state licenses vary, but in general states set a minimum age for the applicant, who must hold a master's or doctoral degree from an accredited institution, have a minimum number of hours of practice experience, and pass a state-administered examination. A number of states require a state-issued license as a basis for the practitioner to receive third-party payments from insurance companies.

It is your individual responsibility to be familiar with the licensing laws of the state in which you practice, because misuse of a professional title may subject you to legal liability.[24]

Confidentiality

Social workers and other providers of social services have a statutory obligation to maintain the confidentiality of client information. Clearly, a client's confidential records may be released with consent of the client, but otherwise, release of information is governed by a series of federal and state statutes and court rulings.

Before proceeding you should note that "confidentiality" should not be confused with "privilege." Privilege refers to the right to withhold confidential information in a court of law. Privilege is conferred by the legislature or the courts. A social worker cannot refuse to testify in court by claiming that the requested information is confidential: to do so is to place yourself at risk of being held in contempt of court. You can withhold information only if the privilege to do so is granted to you. Most states extend privilege to social workers, although the privilege may be limited to certified or licensed social workers. In 1996, the Supreme Court extended to licensed social workers the privilege to withhold testimony in federal court. Previously, such privilege had been granted only to psychologists and psychiatrists.[25]

Statutes contain exceptions to privilege. For example, you cannot claim that privilege exempts you from reporting known or suspected child abuse or neglect, nor can you refuse to testify in court if a client, whose disclosures are at issue, waives his right and chooses to reveal otherwise confidential information. Moreover, in any judicial proceeding, a judge may decide that society's need for full disclosure overrides the client's right to claim confidentiality of information.[26]

Guidelines for maintaining client records in a confidential manner are found in the NASW Code of Ethics, federal and state statutes, and constitutional provisions that protect a client's right to privacy in health and mental health records. The code admonishes social workers to safeguard the "confidentiality of all information obtained in the course of professional service, except for compelling professional reasons."[27] However, this guideline is too general to provide direction for release of information in specific cases. To learn what can and should be done in specific cases, workers must refer to state and federal statutes to learn when and under what conditions they may release client information.

Statutes that govern confidentiality vary by state. Some states have adopted versions of the Federal Privacy Act (see next section), and some have adopted the *Uniform Health-Care Information Act,* a model law promulgated by the Conference of Commissioners on Uniform State Laws that seeks to establish national standards for the maintenance of and the release of confidential health and mental health information.[28]

A review of the various state statutes that govern confidentiality is beyond the scope of this book. What follows is a brief overview of federal rules and a discussion of your obligation as a service provider to maintain client confidentiality and under certain circumstances to release otherwise confidential information without a client's consent.

FEDERAL STATUTES AND CLIENT CONFIDENTIALITY

The provisions in federal statutes that require service providers to maintain client records in a confidential manner and that concern the conditions under which information in client records may be released range from the very general to the very specific and are spread across a series of statutes. For example, the Ryan White Comprehensive AIDS Resources Emergency Act (CARE Act) requires each state receiving federal funds to provide for the confidentiality of information concerning a patient's health status, but it is left to the states to develop specific laws concerning records maintenance and release of information.[29] The Americans with Disabilities Act (ADA) contains somewhat greater detail. The ADA provides that medical information acquired in the course of a pre-employment medical examination cannot be disclosed and requires further that an employer maintain such information on separate forms in a separate medical file and treat the information as confidential.[30] The most restrictive federal rules governing release of information concern clients who have received treatment for alcohol or drug abuse. Federal rules are detailed to the point of providing a form that may be used when information is requested. Information is not to be released unless the voluntary consent form (1) names the program or person permitted to release information; (2) names or provides the title of the person or organization to which disclosure is to be made; (3) names the patient whose signature and date of signature is required, unless the patient is not competent to give consent, in which case consent must be given by a person designated to act on behalf of the patient; (4) states the purpose for which the disclosure is to be made; (5) identifies with specificity how much and what kind of information is to be disclosed; (6) states that the consent may be revoked at any time prior to the time that the program or person to whom the information was released relied on the information to make a treatment decision; and (7) states a date, event, or condition upon which the consent will expire if not revoked beforehand. The law specifies also that consent forms cannot last any longer than is reasonably necessary to serve the purpose for which consent was given.[31]

The Federal Privacy Act protects individual privacy with regard to information maintained by federal agencies, but the conditions for sharing information are broad and provide less protection than the title of the act suggests. Records, which are defined to include any item of information, such as a person's educational, financial, medical, criminal, or employment history, are to be disclosed "pursuant to a written request by, or with the prior written consent of, the individual to whom the record pertains."[32] Nevertheless, there are numerous exceptions to this provision. For example, records may be disclosed under a variety of circumstances, including disclosure to personnel who work in the agency that maintains the record and who need the record in the performance of their duties. Thus, medical records could be disclosed to persons responsible for determining whether a patient is entitled to insurance payments, to a colleague with whom one is sharing case-management responsibility, or to a supervisor or group of supervisors who are responsible for supervising the record keeper or the person described in the record. Records are also accessible for law enforcement activities and pursuant to a court order.[33] Of the various exceptions in the privacy act, the "routine use" exception is the most troublesome. For example, the Veterans Administration has created no fewer than thirty-eight "routine" uses, some exceedingly broad, for its patients' medical records.[34]

Moreover, there is potential for conflict between the federal Freedom of Information Act (FOIA) of 1966,[35] which establishes rules for accessing records that are maintained by the federal government, and the privacy act. The FOIA allows access to any information maintained by a federal agency that is not covered by one of nine enumerated exemptions. Of the nine exemptions, the only records of concern to the providers of social services that are expressly exempted from disclosure are medical records. Another exemption provides that an agency may refuse an FOIA request when the sought-after materials are exempted from disclosure by another statute. On its face, this exemption implies that records protected under the privacy act are automatically exempt from FOIA disclosure. However, because this provision is not specific as to the protected records, ongoing court interpretation is required to determine whether in any set of circumstances records are protected or must be disclosed.[36]

The Health Insurance Portability and Accountability Act of 1996[37] requires Congress to enact privacy protections within three years. Congress directed the Department of Health and Human Services to propose security standards and a "universal patient identifier" that could link a patient's files throughout the nation's health care system. Commenting on this requirement, the National Research Council of the American Academy of Sciences stated that the use of a patient identifier had to be balanced against patient privacy and that such use had to be backed by policies that define proper and improper access and impose sanctions against abusers.[38] The act admonishes health care providers, defined to include insurance companies and "clearinghouses,"[39] who maintain or transmit health information to

> Maintain reasonable and appropriate administrative, technical, and physical safeguards to ensure the integrity and confidentiality of the information; to protect against any reasonably anticipated—threats or hazards to the security or integrity of the information; and unauthorized uses or disclosures of the information.[40]

Disclosure of Confidential Information

Sharing personal information, especially in large bureaucracies, is unregulated. Even when protections exist, such as those found in the Federal Privacy Act, people may be unaware of the extent to which their personal information is shared with others. The National Research Panel of the American Academy of Sciences reports that individuals might be surprised at the "electronic access now available to doctors, hospitals, insurers, prescription plans and state health agencies."[41] The panel urged that providers adopt a series of practices to reduce unauthorized access to information, including the use of unique passwords for any employee authorized to access a patient's record, systems that are programmed to shut down if a work station is left idle for a set period of time, routine audits to track all accesses to confidential information, and a zero-tolerance policy for violators in light of the fact that at present most hospitals allow doctors and nurses to access the files of all patients, including those not under their care.

Countering this position are those who argue that the provision of high quality health care services might be seriously impaired by rules limiting access since proponents of such rules "fundamentally" fail to recognize that health care today occurs in an "integrated marketplace" where sharing of information in multiple directions is a day-to-day occurrence. Patients are ultimately put at risk if privacy provisions require that the patient decide to whom their information should be available. They argue that current proposals concerning privacy will hinder the provision of health care and increase its costs.[42]

These general concerns aside, there are a variety of circumstances in which confidential information may be disclosed without the consent of the client. In general, when the state can demonstrate a need for information that overrides an individual's right to privacy and confidentiality, the state's need will trump the individual's right. Thus, in *Whalen v. Roe*, the United States Supreme Court—responding to a challenge to a New York statute that provided for the creation of a centralized databank for storing personal identifying information on individuals receiving prescriptions for drugs such as opium, cocaine, and amphetamines, and after finding that the Fourteenth Amendment confers on the individual an "interest in avoiding disclosure of personal matters"—ruled that the patient-identification system was a reasonable exercise of state power and that there was no evidence to sustain the allegation that the plaintiffs' constitutional rights to privacy were threatened.[43] In addition, most states require that physicians, laboratories, or both report confirmed cases of sexually transmitted diseases (STDs) to public health officials so that the sex partners of the infected person can be notified of potential STD exposure, be tested, and receive any necessary treatment. All states permit disclosure of otherwise confidential information when disclosure is ordered by a court.

Duty to Warn

Thus far we have considered situations in which disclosure of otherwise confidential information is permitted. There are circumstances in which disclosure is required. For example, all states require all professionals who come into contact with children to report known or suspected child abuse to state officials. In this section, the obligation of a social worker or other mental health provider to warn a third party who is not a client that their life has been threatened by a client is considered.

The issue arose first in California in the late summer of 1974 when Prosenjit Poddar, a voluntary outpatient who was receiving mental health services at Cowell Memorial Hospital at the University of California at Berkeley, told his therapist that he was going to kill his girlfriend. Although Poddar did not identify the young woman by name, he provided enough information so that her identity could be easily ascertained. Poddar's therapist, after consulting with superiors, decided to commit the young man for observation in a mental hospital. The campus police took Poddar into custody then released him when they became convinced that he was rational and were given his promise to stay away from his girlfriend. Poddar killed his girlfriend Tatiana Tarasoff shortly after her return from summer vacation.

Tarasoff's parents brought suit against the university, arguing that their daughter should have been warned of the threat that was made against her life. The Supreme Court of California agreed with the Tarasoffs. The court ruled that when a doctor or a psychotherapist determines, or through the exercise of reasonable professional judgment should determine, that a patient poses a danger to another, who is not a patient, a duty arises obligating the professional to warn the person who is endangered (*Tarasoff* I).[44]

The *Tarasoff* ruling raised concern among mental health professionals who resisted the notion that they were able to predict who was and who was not dangerous. They were concerned that therapists, rather than face a lawsuit, would engage in defensive practices by issuing unnecessary warnings and that the therapist-patient relationship would be severely undermined if the client knew that her or his disclosures could be made public.

The outcry from the professional community caused the California Supreme Court to reconsider *Tarasoff*. In July 1976 the court vacated its 1974 ruling and after rehearing, clarified the duty that therapists owed to third parties who are the subject of a patient's threat (*Tarasoff* II).[45] The therapist's duty is to act reasonably under the circumstances, the court said. This duty may be discharged in several ways, including warning the person threatened or informing others who are likely to apprise the person, notifying the police in the vicinity where the threatened person lived, committing the patient, or taking other steps that are reasonable under the circumstances.

In the summer of 1980, the California Supreme Court had occasion to revisit and further clarify its *Tarasoff* ruling in *Thompson v. Alameda County*.[46] *Thompson* concerned an incarcerated juvenile offender who said that when he was released he would kill a child in his neighborhood. While on leave he did so. California's High Court distinguished *Thompson* from *Tarasoff* and dismissed the suit brought by the murdered boy's parents. Unlike the victim in *Tarasoff*, there was no "readily identifiable" victim in *Thompson*. The victim could have been any one of the children in the neighborhood where the patient lived. Not only would warnings be difficult to give, but they would serve little purpose since parents could do no more than exercise the ordinary vigilance over their children that is expected of them.

Concerning the relationship between therapist and client, the court recognized that the nature of the therapeutic relationship encourages candor. Clients may express their intent to commit acts of violence, the court noted, but these are rarely carried out. A therapist should not reveal these threats as a routine matter, since doing so would clearly disrupt the relationship between client and therapist. Therapists have a duty to maintain the confidentiality of their communications with their clients unless doing so creates a danger to others. Even when disclosure is necessary, the therapist should take precautions to preserve a client's privacy to the fullest extent possible in light of the need to prevent the threatened harm.

> Thus, we [make] clear that the therapist has no general duty to warn of each threat. Only if he . . . determine[s], or under applicable professional standards reasonably should have determined, that a patient poses a serious danger of violence to others, does he bear a duty to exercise reasonable care to protect the foreseeable victim of that danger. . . . the intended victim . . . need not be specifically named, he must be readily identifiable.[47]

Since the *Tarasoff* ruling, a majority of states, through statute or court decisions, have established rules that address the issue of a professional's duty to warn. The majority of states use the phrase "mental health professional" in discussing who is obligated to provide a warning; states using this phrase include social workers in their definition of mental health professional, although in some states the duty to warn is limited to "licensed social workers,"[48] suggesting that social workers providing clinical services under the license of the agency for whom they are employed may not be liable for a failure to warn.

Although there are several exceptions (discussed in the following paragraphs), the rules established by the states have in common that (1) the client must make an explicit threat to an identified or identifiable victim; (2) the therapist has no express duty to warn the threatened victim, but a general duty to warn that may be satisfied in the same ways spelled out by the California court in *Tarasoff* II; and (3) the professional is immunized against suit for disclosing confidential information.[49]

Texas and Wisconsin do not require that a specific victim be identified, but that the therapist warn everyone within the "zone of danger" who may, depending upon the threat that is made, include all members of a person's family or all who work with the client.[50]

The kind of warning required by California and other states with rules similar to *Tarasoff* rests on the assumption that the special relationship that exists between therapist and client extends to third parties who are threatened by the client. Courts in New York, Florida, Virginia, and Kansas[51] have not been willing to expand the notion of special relationship in so broad a manner. Thus, New York's High Court allowed the parents of an infant to sue a pediatrician and the manufacturer of polio vaccine for injuries suffered by the infant's father who was exposed to the virus in providing personal care to the infant. The risk of parental "contact" polio was well known, and the court found that a special relationship between the parents and physician who knew or should have known that the parents relied on his special medical expertise and should have warned them of the risk of exposure.[52]

In contrast, a New York court rejected a wife's claim against her husband's physician in which she argued that the physician was negligent because he failed to warn her that her husband had tuberculosis.[53] The court held that a physician's duty is owed to the patient. The wife was a member of the community-at-large. She may also be a member of that class of people whom the physician knew or should have known were relying on him. However, the court reasoned that if it extended a duty of care, there would be no line of demarcation. Stated otherwise, there is no point where that duty would end. If there is a duty to a patient's spouse, why not extend the duty to other individuals with whom the patient had close contact, such as other relatives, co-workers, or even fellow commuters.

New York relies on the "professional judgment rule," whereby physicians or mental health professionals will not be held liable if they have used their best judgment in making treatment decisions, and courts will not find professional liability for simple errors of judgment.[54] Thus, the professional judgment rule has been used to exculpate psychiatrists from liability for diagnostic decisions,[55] treatment decisions,[56] decisions to release hospital patients who later harm themselves or others,[57] and decisions denying hospital admission.[58] New York courts will not apply the professional judgment standard to immunize psychiatric decisions where there was a failure to evaluate the condition of potentially dangerous patients before discharging them from the hospital[59] or where there was a failure to keep detailed and proper medical notes, and, consequently, it could not be established whether any evaluation of the patient's suicidal propensities had been made by a qualified psychiatrist.[60]

Social Worker Liability and the Doctrine of Qualified Immunity

Individuals who occupy social worker positions, regardless of whether they hold a degree in social work, are liable to being sued for monetary damages when clients allege that the worker's practice has caused the client to suffer an injury. However, the doctrine of qualified immunity protects public employees performing discretionary functions from being sued for civil damages. The shield of qualified immunity applies as long as the employees' conduct "does not violate a clearly established statutory or constitutional right of which a reasonable person would have known."[61] Thus, a social worker who reports suspected child abuse or who warns a third party that his or her life is endangered based on a threat made by a patient will be immune from suit as long as the report was made in good faith.

Qualified immunity furthers an important public policy goal by encouraging social workers and other public officials to use the discretion their jobs require without fear of being sued and to enhance the likelihood that qualified people will not turn away from public service because of a fear of lawsuits.

Qualified immunity may extend to social workers in private agencies who are performing a public function. Recall the earlier discussion of the case of *Richardson v. McKnight* where the Supreme Court ruled that prison guards who were employed by a private corporation were not entitled to claim immunity from suit. In 1998, in *Bartell v. Lohiser*,[62] a federal judge ruled that social workers employed by a not-for-profit social service agency who were working under contract with a public agency were entitled to qualified immunity. The Court referred to the reasoning of the Supreme Court in distinguishing *Bartell* from *Richardson*. In *Richardson*, even though the prison guards were performing a public function, they were employed by a private firm with no direct and ongoing supervision by the state. Moreover, private firms who wish to have their contracts renewed have an incentive to hire and retain the most qualified personnel, do not operate under the constraints of a civil service system, and thus can readily discharge unsatisfactory staff and provide fiscal incentives to those who perform well. Finally, private firms are shielded by the insurance that they are statutorily required to carry.

The *Bartell* court decision said that the private, not-for-profit agency employed its workers to perform a public service task at the express direction and under the close supervision of governmental officials. Moreover, the public agency purchased the service only when it could not meet the particular needs of an individual child. As such, the private agency was serving as an adjunct to the state agency in performing an essential government activity of protecting wards of the state. The *Bartell* court was concerned that without immunity, workers in the private agency would not undertake to make the difficult decisions that their jobs required, which in this case involved recommending whether a parent was fit to resume care of a child. Faced with liability, not-for-profit firms would not be likely to enter into contracts with state agencies. If not-for-profit organizations refused to contract with the public sector, this would only increase the pressure on a system whose resources were already strained.[63]

Summary

Two topics have been covered in this chapter: the organization of social services and, continuing the discussion begun in chapter 2, the relationship of social work practice to social policy.

Social services are provided by the public and the private sectors. The private sector includes not-for-profit agencies and for-profit agencies. The services provided by public agencies are described in the statutes that create them. Those provided by private agencies are described in documents that each agency files with its home state. Public agencies typically purchase a broad array of services, such as counseling services, medical and mental health services, and foster care services, from not-for-profit agencies. Beginning in the 1980s, the movement to privatize social services and provide services from for-profit agencies gained momentum; today legislative support for privatization is found throughout federal law.

The evidence is mixed as to whether the gains that were hypothesized about privatization—reducing the size of government, improving service quality, and delivering service in a more efficient and flexible manner with less red tape and greater innovation—have been realized. States have not done well in compiling reliable and complete cost data that are needed to evaluate privatization efforts. Focusing on the provision of social services, corrections, mental health, secondary and postsecondary education, and juvenile rehabilitation, reported savings are modest, rarely exceeding 5 percent. Moreover, because the provider agency, whether public or private, must adhere to whatever government rules regulate the provision of a given service, it is not clear why there would be less red tape, more efficient service delivery, and greater innovation.

Most privatization is accomplished by the state contracting for particular services with private firms or through the use of grants and subsidies. Taken together, these methods account for between 84 percent and 92 percent of privatization activities.

Public policy affects social work practice in different ways. In this chapter, we have considered policies that control professional certification and licensing; policies that control confidentiality of client information; and policies that dictate the terms under which social workers who practice in public and private agency settings may be held liable for malpractice.

The National Association of Social Workers offers several credentials, all of which require the applicant to possess a master's degree from an accredited school of social work and a defined minimum of practice experience. Licenses that are issued by state governments confer the right to engage in private practice and the exclusive right to use designated professional titles, such as state-licensed social workers.

Professional ethics and diverse policies set by legislative bodies and by the courts require social workers to maintain the confidentiality of client information; and the Supreme Court has ruled that individuals have a constitutionally protected interest in preventing disclosure of personal matters.

The Federal Privacy Act is the main federal statute governing the release of information that is held by federal agencies, and a number of states have adopted their own versions of this statute. The act contains exceptions that allow otherwise confidential information to be shared with others who work in the agency that maintains the record and with law enforcement personnel. The act also provides an exception when information is required for "routine use," but its failure to define this phrase precisely creates a broad loophole for disclosure. Finally, any otherwise confidential information may be disclosed when ordered by a court.

There are situations where policy mandates disclosure without client consent, including a social worker's obligation to report known or suspected child abuse or neglect and, in some states, to warn a third party who is not a client that his or her life has been threatened by a client.

The final topic reviewed in this chapter addressed immunity from suit for actions taken in the course of a social worker's duties as long as the social worker was acting in good faith. The general rule is that social workers will receive immunity in a suit for monetary damages if they act in good faith. However, the immunity that is enjoyed by workers in public agencies and in not-for-profit agencies may not apply to social workers who are employed by proprietary private sector firms.

PART

In chapter 2, you were introduced to the ways in which social workers of the nineteenth century used social policy as a tool for social reform. The material in the first chapter of part II (chapter 4) is also historical but broader in its focus. Two topics occupy our attention: first, the development of social policy in the early colonies and subsequently in the newly created United States; second, with the ways in which social policy was used as a tool to support discrimination against minorities as well as to rectify some discriminatory acts. The role of the United States Supreme Court in sustaining discriminatory treatment is addressed.

Chapters 5 and 6 are concerned with the policymaking process, and chapter 7 is concerned with the process of creating the federal budget and allocating funds for social programs. Chapter 5 asks the question "Of the myriad issues that concern the public-at-large, such as domestic violence, health care, and housing, how do some capture the attention of policymakers such that a policy to address a given problem is passed? In chapter 6, we turn our attention to the processes followed by the legislative, judicial, and executive branches of government as well as by the public-at-large in crafting social policy. In chapter 7, we turn our attention to the creation of the federal budget and the allocation of public funds to support social policy.

Social Welfare Policy in the Colonies and Early Nineteenth Century and the Discriminatory Treatment of Racial Minorities

Colonial America

The early colonists carried forward the feudal traditions that they brought with them from Europe. Society was organized around a system of wealthy landholders and those who labored for them. A shortage of labor in the early colonies ensured ongoing employment, and it was possible for those without land of their own to acquire it.[1]

But employment and the possibility of an average laborer acquiring land should not be confused with the acquisition of wealth. The difficulties of life in the new colonies forced many to live if not in poverty, then at the edge of it. Moreover, half the people who migrated to the New World were indentured servants who had to serve a term of four years or more before they became free. When their term of indenture ended, most were too poor to buy land, so they worked the land of others. Thus, the earliest colonies had to develop the means to deal with the needy, who were assisted informally, either by their neighbors or by the church with monies tithed by parishioners.

THE ENGLISH POOR LAW OF 1601

The Poor Law of 1601 was the first formal social welfare policy adopted by the colonists.[2] The Poor Law was significant in several respects. Its adoption was an acknowledgment of the principle that government had a role in providing for the poor. Funds were raised through taxation, rather than the earlier practice of relying on voluntary contributions to the church. Under the poor laws, family members had reciprocal responsibilities of support. The responsibilities of a parent to a child extended to grandparents, and children were obliged to support these adults.

Responsibility for administering the poor laws fell to the parish and town council, which was the smallest unit of government. Overseers of the poor determined, on a case-by-case basis, both the need for aid and the worthiness of recipients to receive aid. Those considered "worthy poor" were children, who were indentured to families who provided for their material needs and were responsible for training them in a useful trade accomplished through work performed on the family farm or the family cottage industry. Also worthy were the lame, the blind, and those who were not at fault for their unemployment. The latter group received "outdoor relief," which was provided to people in their own homes in the form of cash or food assistance, or "indoor relief," which was provided in almshouses, also called poorhouses, where the sick or the elderly received medical care as well as shelter. The "unworthy poor," who were vagrants, drunkards, the shiftless, and the lazy not willing to work, were sent to workhouses and forced to do menial labor in exchange for the necessities of life, or they were "auctioned off" to families who provided food and shelter in exchange for work.

Residency requirements, called Laws of Settlement, were established under the poor laws. The poor were "encouraged" to move on to the next town or they were simply returned to the town from which they came. During this time, the concept of "less eligibility," meaning that the poor should not receive more financial assistance than the lowest wage paid to a laborer, came into being and remains with us today.[3]

AMERICAN REVOLUTION

The American Revolution had little effect on the policy framework for assisting the needy, although, as is the case with any war and the destruction it brings, the Revolution increased the number of people in need. The colonial poor laws were retained by the newly existing states and adopted by the legislatures of subsequently created states.[4] From the standpoint of assisting the needy, the most significant effect of the War of Independence was the assumption by state governments of responsibility for administering welfare due to the financial inability of local units of government to respond to the demand created by the war.

For the student of social policy, the most significant events of the late eighteenth century are the creation, beginning in 1775, of state constitutions and the United States Constitution of 1787. The state constitutions and the federal Constitution created our system of government by establishing the executive, judicial, and legislative branches of government and articulating the separation of powers among these branches of government. The bills of rights that accompanied the state and federal constitutions are the source of many of the rights that we enjoy today.

SLAVERY

Slavery was brought to the Caribbean Islands in the fifteenth century and to the early colonies to meet the demand for labor on farms and to build roads.

The early English colonies did not have a systematic body of law concerning slavery, which was created from nothing and was simply assumed to be lawful without precedent or rationale.[5] For example, a Maryland statute of 1638 without explanation stated simply that "all Christians—except slaves" shall have the full rights of Englishmen. A statute adopted by Rhode Island in 1652 referred to the practice of buying and selling slaves and provided that Englishmen should have a right to their service forever. In the 1600s, slaves in South Carolina were granted freedom of religion for as long as they remained slaves, and the developing constitution of that state granted to freemen "absolute power and authority over Negro Slaves, of whatever upbringing or Religion."[6] The laws that governed slavery developed in a piecemeal manner until the late 1700s, at which time a court in England ruled that there was no basis for slavery absent a statute that sanctioned it.[7] Based on this ruling and not finding an authorizing statute, the English court freed a slave who had been brought to England from the colonies and confined in preparation for being sent to the West Indies.

Subsequently, slavery in the colonies would be regulated though statute. The Fugitive Slave Act of 1793 was passed by Congress to provide a means for enforcing the Fugitive Slave Clause of the federal Constitution. This clause authorized slave holders to pursue and recover their "property," even if a slave escaped to a state that did not recognize slavery.[8]

At the time that the Fugitive Slave Act was passed, all of the Northern colonies had outlawed slavery except for New Jersey and New York, where slavery would be legal until 1799 (New York) and 1804 (New Jersey). The abolition of slavery in the North caused many Northern states to rebel against the Fugitive Slave Act of 1793. Judges would not hear cases that were brought under the act, and the legislatures of many states prohibited their state officials from enforcing it.[9] To counter this resistance, Congress passed a second Fugitive Slave Law in 1850.[10] Under terms of the 1850 act, federal commissioners were appointed throughout the country and charged with enforcement. Federal marshals were authorized to assist in the capture of fugitive slaves and, if necessary, to call upon federal troops to assist them.

The Fugitive Slave Law encouraged kidnapping of escaped slaves and returning them to their "owners." To put an end to this practice, some states enacted Personal Liberty Laws to prevent anyone from kidnapping African Americans, whereas in other states, courts refused to return free slaves. For example, in 1836 in *Commonwealth v. Aves*, a Massachusetts court refused to return a slave because to do so was against "natural rights" and the laws of the Commonwealth.[11]

In 1842, the United States Supreme Court issued its first ruling concerning the constitutionality of the Fugitive Slave Clause and the Fugitive Slave Act of 1793. In *Prigg v. Pennsylvania*,[12] a slave owner was convicted of violating Pennsylvania's Personal Liberty Law after he kidnapped Margaret Morgan, a black woman, and removed her from Pennsylvania to Maryland for the purpose of selling her as a slave. The Supreme Court overturned Prigg's conviction and upheld the constitutionality of the Fugitive Slave Act. The Court held that the act prohibited any state from freeing fugitive slaves, and it affirmed a slave owner's right to have his property returned.

The Nineteenth Century

Poverty increased early in the nineteenth century. In chapter 2, we reviewed nineteenth century approaches to dealing with poverty and the different factors that played a role in increasing poverty, including increased European immigration, a financial "panic" in 1819, and a depression in the 1830s. In addition, the economy was making a transition from mainly agricultural to industrial, and this transition gained significant momentum after the Civil War. The demand for aid increased, but the laissez-faire philosophy of the time was antagonistic to the provision of assistance, which was considered by some to be immoral since it interfered with the "natural" right to accumulate wealth (see the discussion of Social Darwinism in chapter 2).

Laissez-faire thinking assumed that efforts to interfere with the supply and demand forces of the market (for example, to control wages or otherwise regulate industry) would undermine the economic order. Outdoor relief, which you will recall provided aid to people in their own homes, was said to exacerbate the problems of poverty by robbing individuals of their sense of individual responsibility.

In 1824, John Yates, then Secretary of State in New York, produced a report that was critical of outdoor relief. To provide relief without requiring that individuals modify their behavior was, according to two reports, hurtful and a waste of taxpayer money.[13] If relief was necessary, it was better provided in institutional settings such as workhouses and almshouses, where the poor could be observed, their behavior controlled, and good work habits encouraged.[14] Moreover, the communities in which the poor lived provided bad influences because of the bars and gambling parlors located there. The poor would be better off if they were removed from their communities. The criticisms contained in the Yates report were echoed in reports that were issued in Massachusetts and Pennsylvania.

The New York legislature responded to the Yates Report by requiring that almshouses, where the poor would receive indoor relief, should be erected and that outdoor relief should be all but abandoned. Refusal to go to an almshouse resulted in the denial of relief. The conviction that relief should be provided in an institutional setting spread in Northeastern and Midwestern states but not in the South, where outdoor relief continued to be used.[15] Providing for the poor in institutional settings and the charity organization societies' efforts to reform the poor through the moral example of friendly visitors (see chapter 2) were the normative approaches to assisting the poor in the years preceding the Civil War.

ABOLITION

A number of forces contributed to the abolition of slavery. As the United States gained new territory, there was sentiment among abolitionists that slavery, if not altogether abolished, should not be allowed in newly acquired territories. Thus, provisions in the Northwest Ordinance of 1787 prohibited slavery in the newly acquired territory, which would become the states of Ohio, Indiana, Illinois, Michigan, Wisconsin, and part of Minnesota. The Missouri Compromise of 1820 allowed Missouri to enter the union as a slave state on the condition that Maine, which had petitioned for statehood, would be a free state. Moreover, the Missouri Compromise prohibited the spread of slavery north of Missouri's Northern boundary, but it was repealed in 1854. In the Northern states, slavery was abolished on a state-by-state basis, and civil disobedience, manifested in the creation of the Underground Railway, sought to undermine slavery in slave states.

Two events in the mid-nineteenth century, the Fugitive Slave Law of 1850 and the Supreme Court's decision in the case of *Dred Scott v. Sandford*, laid the groundwork for the Civil War and the end of slavery. Recall that the Fugitive Slave Law created a federal role in the capture and return of runaway slaves. The law angered abolitionists and legislative bodies in the Northern states because it undermined their authority to provide a safe haven for runaway slaves and made the states subservient to the federal government. The 1850 law gave "teeth" to the Supreme Court's 1842 decision in *Prigg v. Pennsylvania*, because it not only affirmed a slave owner's right to have property returned but provided a means for enforcing this right without relying on state-by-state efforts.

The decision of the United States Supreme Court in 1857 in the case of *Dred Scott v. Sandford* hastened the movement toward the conflict of these interests.[16] Scott, a slave, was brought by his owner into Illinois where slavery was prohibited. After his return to Missouri, Scott sued for his freedom, arguing that he was free by reason of having resided in free territory. The Supreme Court ruled that Scott was not a citizen of the United States and that the descendants of slaves could not become citizens of the United States. His tenure in a non-slave territory did not confer upon him the status of United States citizen. Moreover, the Court ruled that the Missouri Compromise was unconstitutional because, if its provisions applied, slave owners could be deprived of their property without due process of law.

In 1860, Abraham Lincoln was elected president. At the time of Lincoln's election, seven states had already seceded from the Union. One year after Lincoln's election, the Civil War began and lasted until 1865. In 1863, President Lincoln freed, by an executive order known as the Emancipation Proclamation, all slaves in those parts of the United States that were in rebellion against the federal government.[17] He did so without congressional authority and despite constitutional provisions supporting slavery. Two years later, slavery was permanently abolished when the states ratified the Thirteenth Amendment to the Constitution.

CIVIL WAR

The causes of the Civil War are many and complex but had much to do with economic issues that, for the South, were inextricably linked to the maintenance of slavery. Some Southerners saw Lincoln's election as signaling the end of slavery and the loss of their wealth that slaves represented. The loss of slave labor would weaken the bargaining power that slave owners had to keep down the wages of white laborers, whose ability to negotiate for higher wages was restricted by the threat that they would be replaced by slaves. The desire of Southern states to secede increased, and on April 12, 1861, the Civil War began.[18]

The Civil War created a great need for relief; and individuals could not be blamed for the problems they encountered. Laws were passed allowing localities to raise funds for relief for the sick and poor, for wounded soldiers and their families, and for the founding of homes for disabled veterans.

Direct public aid was normative. Concern that soldiers would die unnecessarily due to the filth and disease in battlefield situations led to the creation of the United States Sanitary Commission, the first national public health group.[19]

RECONSTRUCTION

Newly freed slaves were confronted with a variety of problems, some stemming from being denied an education and the opportunity to develop work skills other than those needed on plantations, others from the difficulties that followed from their change in status, and still others from the resistance by many in the South to emancipation. Resistance to their advancement took different forms, ranging from the guerilla war waged by the Ku Klux Klan and the extraordinary violence committed against African Americans[20] to the Jim Crow laws (named for an antebellum minstrel show character) of the late nineteenth century that created a caste system based on race. The caste system was maintained by a Supreme Court that was not sympathetic to the plight of African Americans (see later section on the Supreme Court).

The federal government countered Southern resistance in several ways. In 1865, Congress established the Bureau of Refugees, Freedmen and Abandoned Lands, commonly referred to as the Freedman's Bureau, for the purpose of providing relief for black and white refugees of the Civil War.[21] The bureau, which was to operate for one year after the end of the war, was charged with providing clothing and fuel for impoverished refugees and freedmen from Southern states and with acquiring and later selling up to forty acres of abandoned land to any refugee or freedman. A report of December 1865 detailed the bureau's activities on behalf of freedmen who benefited from programs that provided education, regulated labor and land distribution, resolved real estate disputes, supervised civil and criminal justice systems through Freedmen's Courts, registered marriages, aided orphans, and provided medical care.

In 1866, Congress extended the life of the bureau, which remained in force until 1872. In the later years of its existence, providing for the education of African Americans was a major thrust of bureau activity. More than a dozen institutions of higher education, including Howard University, were established.

RECONSTRUCTION CIVIL RIGHTS STATUTES

The activities of the bureau were significant, but the bureau could not provide for the equality promised by emancipation. Efforts to attain this goal would fall to the federal government. However, up to this point in American history, the states, not the federal government, were considered the guardians of individual rights. The task that confronted Congress was to enact a statute that would provide for the federal government to step in when states failed to act.

In 1866, Congress passed the Civil Rights Act, codified in 1868 as the Fourteenth Amendment to the Constitution.[22] Congressional intent in passing the Civil Rights Act was to provide a means for African Americans to enforce their individual rights under the authority of the federal government. Thus, Congress sought to close the gap that the Supreme Court referred to when it had ruled that the federal Constitution could not be used to control state action.[23]

The Civil Rights Act of 1866 sought to protect the rights of an individual to buy, own, rent, and sell property and enter into employment contracts and to protect African Americans from discriminatory treatment by police and state courts. It was Congress's intent that the same conditions that applied to white citizens would apply to black citizens.[24] The act opened the door of federal courts to protect African Americans from the "corrupt law enforcement practices that allowed crimes against them to go unpunished, and subjected them to arrest, trial, and conviction of crimes by hostile and prejudiced sheriffs, judges, and juries."[25]

Violence against African Americans continued after the war ended. In 1870, Congress passed the Enforcement Act[26] that provided for criminal sanctions against anyone who interfered with a person's efforts to vote and that prohibited private conspiracies that might result in a violation of civil rights. In 1871, Congress passed the Ku Klux Klan Act. This act provided a means whereby an individual or group could bring suit in federal court on a showing that an act of violence was inflicted as the result of a conspiracy intended to deprive the individual or group of equal protection under the law.[27]

The Fifteenth Amendment to the Constitution, adopted in 1870, provides that citizens of the United States, excluding women, have a right to vote and that right "shall not be denied or abridged by the United States or by any State on account of race, color or previous condition of servitude."[28] Nevertheless, a number of states established rules for voting that denied the vote altogether to "paupers" or those who resided in poorhouses and that limited the right of African Americans to vote through use of poll taxes, literacy tests, and grandfather clauses, which precluded a freedman from voting if he was a lineal descendent of a person not entitled or able to vote. Voting rights legislation that was part of the Enforcement Act of 1870 was repealed because qualifications for voting were deemed to be in the control of state, not federal government. Barriers to voting would remain in place until the Voting Rights Act of 1965 abolished them.[29]

THE SUPREME COURT

Nineteenth century decisions of the Supreme Court favored the segregationist cause. As noted earlier, the Supreme Court ruled that the Fugitive Slave Clause was constitutional (*Prigg v. Pennsylvania*), that slaves could not become United States citizens (*Dred Scott v. Sanford*), and that the federal Constitution did not confer on the national government the right to secure the fundamental rights of citizens within the states (*Barron v. City of Baltimore*). In addition, in a series of cases known of as the Civil Rights Cases, the Court held that the Civil Rights Act of 1875, which prohibited race-based discriminatory acts by individuals who denied African Americans access to places of public accommodation, public conveyances, and places of public amusement, was unconstitutional.[30] Congress could act to invalidate discriminatory state laws and the actions that followed from them, but Congress lacked the authority to legislate against actions of individuals. Moreover, the Court recognized that Congress has the right under the Thirteenth Amendment "to enact all necessary and proper laws for the obliteration and prevention of slavery with all its badges and incidents,"[31] but found that barring African American people from places of public accommodation did not place upon them "badges" of slavery.

In 1896, in the case of *Plessy v. Ferguson*,[32] the Supreme Court legitimized segregation. Plessy posed the question, "Was a Louisiana statute that provided separate accommodations for blacks and whites constitutional?" After discussing the fact that some states had separated African Americans from whites in schools and places of public accommodations, the majority of the Court held that such legislation could pass constitutional muster. The Court held that the act of separating the races did not violate the constitutional rights of African Americans and did not deny to African Americans the Fourteenth Amendment's guarantee of equal protection under the law. Once again addressing itself to what constituted a "badge" of slavery, the Court reasoned that race-based segregation did not constitute a badge of inferiority. The separate but equal doctrine of *Plessy* would remain the law until 1954 when, in *Brown v. Board of Education*, it was found to be unconstitutional.

Immigration from China

In search of a better way of life, Chinese people, the first Asians to immigrate to the United States, began their journey in the 1840s to participate in the California gold rush. Migration continued throughout the nineteenth century when Chinese laborers were recruited for work on railroads.

An original spirit of welcome changed to one of hostility as the Chinese population grew in size. McClain (1984) tells us that the Chinese were resented because they worked too hard, often for less pay than others were willing to accept; saved too much; and spent too little in shops operated by non-Chinese people.[33]

To limit immigration by and work opportunities for Chinese people, the state of California (1) enacted tax laws, such as the Capitation Tax of 1852, that required owners of ships entering California ports to post a $500 bond for each passenger or make a fixed per-passenger payment[34]; (2) enacted employment licensing laws, for example, the Foreign Miner's License Tax Laws of 1850 and 1852, that required foreign-born people who wished to work in state mines, a source of employment for Chinese people, to purchase a license to do so[35]; (3) imposed residency taxes, such as the Chinese Police Tax, formally entitled "An Act to Protect Free White Labor Against Competition with Chinese Coolie Labor, and to Discourage the Immigration of the Chinese into the State of California," that imposed a tax of $2.50 per month on all Chinese people who resided in the state, except those who were operating businesses, had licenses to work in the mines, or were engaged in the production or manufacture of sugar, rice, coffee, or tea[36]; and (4) enforced, only against Chinese people, municipal regulations that set standards for buildings in which laundries were operated.[37]

Some tax laws were abated when district associations, formed by leaders in Chinese communities, convinced legislators that Chinese people did not represent an economic threat to the white community and that it was best to tread softly because of trade agreements that existed between the United States and China. In fact, trade agreements between the United States and China were cited by California courts as the reason for enjoining the state from imposing a fishing tax because the tax violated a treaty with China[38] and from enforcing a law that forbid California corporations from employing Chinese people.[39]

Immigration from Japan

Immigration from Japan did not begin in earnest until the late nineteenth century. The immigration of Japanese people was not regulated, as was the case with people from China. However, in 1907 President Theodore Roosevelt entered into a "Gentlemen's Agreement" with the Japanese government whereby the president agreed not to seek an exclusionary law in exchange for the Japanese government's agreement to limit immigration to the United States by passport controls.[40]

INTERNMENT OF JAPANESE PEOPLE

At the beginning of the war with Japan, Congress enacted a series of orders, such as curfew laws, that required Japanese people in designated parts of the West Coast to remain in their homes from 8 P.M. to 6 A.M. Curfew laws were followed in 1942 by an executive order and then by an act of Congress that provided for the removal and exclusion of Japanese people from certain parts of the West Coast and their internment in camps for the duration of the war.[41]

The Supreme Court ruled this act of Congress was a legitimate exercise of its war power, despite the fact that two-thirds of the Japanese people who were interred had been born in the United States and thus were United States citizens whose loyalty to the United States was not questioned. The Court ruled that the onset of the war with Japan sanctioned whatever precautions against espionage and sabotage were deemed necessary, and it reasoned that its decision was not race-based but due to the impossibility of separating the loyal from the disloyal Japanese. Citing congressional hearings, the Court justified its reasoning on the finding that more than 5,000 Japanese would not swear unqualified allegiance to the United States nor renounce their allegiance to the Emperor of Japan.[42] Three justices dissented in part by recognizing that the decision to exclude Japanese, but not Italian or German Americans, was a race-based extension of the prejudice that Japanese citizens had repeatedly faced.

The injustice of the internment was acknowledged in 1988 when Congress passed the Civil Liberties Act. An apology was extended to Japanese Americans and funds were appropriated for public education with the hope of preventing similar events. Financial compensation was offered to individuals of Japanese ancestry in the amount of $20,000 for their loss of liberty and the destruction of their property.[43]

Citizenship

The first statutes concerning naturalization, the process by which one becomes a citizen of a country, were enacted in 1790 and conferred the right to pursue naturalization to "any alien, being a free white person."[44] In 1870, by amendment,

Congress extended the right of citizenship to African Americans but retained the word "white" in the statute for the express purpose of preventing Chinese and Japanese people from becoming citizens.[45]

In 1876, Congress formed a special committee to investigate and report on the nature and extent of the problems posed by Chinese immigrants.[46] Chinese immigrants were said to be dangerous, undesirable, and uninterested in becoming citizens. Since most did not learn to speak English, granting them citizenship and the right to vote was considered dangerous because the Chinese population was almost equal in size to the population of all adult voters, and the Chinese votes would be controlled by community leaders. The result would be the destruction of republican institutions because Chinese immigrants were accustomed to authoritarian governments. The report of the committee set the stage for the Chinese Exclusion Acts of 1882, 1892, and 1902.[47] Under the terms of the 1882 act, immigration of Chinese people was suspended for ten years, certificates of residence were required, and Chinese people who left the United States temporarily had to show their certificates proving prior residence to regain entry to the United States. Chinese immigrants were ineligible by their race to become naturalized citizens.[48] The act was amended in October 1888 to deny reentry to any Chinese person who left the United States. The Chinese Deportation Act of 1892[49] extended the exclusion of Chinese people for 10 years and required that any Chinese laborer who was arrested for not having the required certificate had to prove, at risk of deportation, that he was entitled to be in the United States. In 1902, the prohibition on immigration of Chinese was extended indefinitely.

Chinese people challenged the exclusion acts on two occasions and lost both times when the United States Supreme Court held that the acts were a constitutionally permissible exercise of congressional power,[50] even though the act of 1882 abrogated the provisions of a treaty between the United States and China providing that citizens of each country had reciprocal rights of immigration and emigration.[51]

Also withstanding challenge was the requirement that Chinese people obtain certificates showing that their residence in the United States was lawful and that failure to produce the required certificate was grounds for deportation. The Court found this requirement to be a permissible exercise of congressional power.

In 1943, when China was allied with the United States during World War II, the exclusion laws were repealed and Chinese people became eligible for citizenship. The right of citizenship was extended in 1946 to people from the Philippine Islands and from the Indian subcontinent. However, barriers to citizenship for Japanese people would not be removed until 1952, when the Immigration and Nationality Act was passed.[52]

THE ALIEN LAND LAW

Under the terms of California's Alien Land Law, residents who were not eligible for United States citizenship were not permitted to own or use agricultural lands. When the law was passed, it applied to Chinese as well as Japanese people, but the prohibition against Chinese people was lifted in 1943 when they became eligible for citizenship. The California law, and a similar law in Washington State, survived

Supreme Court scrutiny when the Court held that any state could deny to any alien the right to own land within its borders.[53]

Land Acquisition by the United States

The acquisition of land was critical to the growth of the United States, but westward expansion was limited by land claims of Native Americans and of Spain, France, and Mexico. In the Louisiana Purchase of 1803, the United States acquired from France land that extended north from the Mississippi River to the Rocky Mountains. As the nineteenth century progressed, territorial expansion was supported by the notion, captured in the phrase Manifest Destiny, that God had ordained that white men extend American institutions into new territory. Manifest Destiny justified the appropriation of Native American lands, the Mexican-American War of 1846, the Alaska Purchase of 1867, and the Spanish-American War of 1898, all of which resulted in territorial gains for the United States.

The annexation of the Republic of Texas in 1845 was the catalyst for the United States to go to war with Mexico the following year. In 1848, the Treaty of Guadalupe Hidalgo defined the conditions for ending the war.[54] Mexico ceded California, New Mexico, other southwestern territories, and portions of Colorado and Wyoming to the United States. The acquired land represented approximately one-half of the territory of Mexico, and the treaty "created a new ethnic minority group, the Mexican-Americans."[55] The treaty conferred citizenship on Mexican people who chose to stay in the territory acquired after the war.[56] The Protocol of Queretaro (1848) provided that land grants that had been perfected by the government of Mexico within the newly acquired areas would be honored by the United States and that territorial disputes would be resolved in American courts.[57] However, the land claims of many Mexican people were not perfected when the war ended, meaning that their land claims would be difficult if not impossible to substantiate. This situation was known to both the Mexican and American officials who negotiated the treaty,[58] and was, in large measure, the result of the instability of the government of Mexico. From 1821, when Mexico gained its independence from Spain until 1850, the country had fifty governments, almost all the result of military coups.[59]

To settle land disputes, Congress passed the Land Act of 1851. The act established a board of land commissioners who were charged with settling private land claims in California.[60] The board adjudicated 813 claims, of which 604, involving about nine million acres, were confirmed. Nevertheless, del Castillo (1998) reports that most Mexican American landholders lost their lands due to the costs of litigation coupled with falling cattle prices and high interest rates.[61]

The need for cheap agricultural labor has traditionally strained the relationship between the United States and the people of Mexico who have been permitted to come to the United States when labor needs have dictated and who have been summarily deported when the need for labor waned. For example, the Immigration Act of 1917 imposed a literacy requirement and a head tax as conditions for migration.[62] Agricultural employers, concerned that the requirements would severely reduce their immigrant labor supply, successfully lobbied Congress to exempt Mexican people from the literacy requirement and head tax. Between 1931 and 1934, when jobs were scarce due to the Depression, the United States deported more than 300,000 Mexican people. World War II created labor shortages, and once again the United States looked to Mexico to increase its labor force. In 1942 and again in 1943, American and Mexican officials entered into a "contract," creating the Bracero Program that permitted Mexican people to work in the United States.[63] But mass deportations were the order of the day in the early 1950s when, under the "Operation Wetback" program, one million people were deported.

Native Americans

The legal relationship between Native American people and the colonies was established in 1775 when the Continental Congress divided Indian country into three departments and appointed commissioners to oversee treaty negotiations with Native tribes.[64] The Articles of Confederation of 1781 established the principle that relationships with Native American people were the province of the national government, not of the states, and the Northwest Ordinance of 1787 stipulated that relationships with Native people were to be conducted in "good faith [so that] their lands were never to be taken from them without their consent; and that laws were to be made to ensure the preservation of peace and friendship."[65]

Agreements between the United States and Native people were in the form of treaties, which are compacts between two or more independent nations. Their use to formalize relationships between the United States and Native American people was in recognition of the sovereignty of Native Americans and the fact that they were not subjects of the United States.[66] Between 1778 and 1871, approximately 400 treaties were signed, chiefly for the purpose of gaining land concessions from Native Americans and to regulate trade. Hirschfelder and de Montano (1993) report that some of the negotiated treaties were agreed to on the basis of equality between parties, but many were dictated to already-defeated tribes. Moreover, in some cases only portions of a tribe participated in treaty negotiations that bound the entire tribe.[67]

The assumption of Native American sovereignty notwithstanding, the relationship between the United States and Native Americans was at the sufferance of the Supreme Court and the Congress. The equality implied by the use of treaties was often a fiction because treaties were not honored, and the terms of treaties were more often than not dictated by the United States.[68] Moreover, the federal government frequently enacted laws that conflicted with treaty provisions, and white people often violated treaty terms and thereby provoked many of the nineteenth century Indian wars.

Between 1823 and 1832, two cases came before the United States Supreme Court that asked, "Could the State of Georgia impose its law within the territory belonging to the Cherokee Nation and could the state incorporate the Cherokee lands into the territory belonging to the State of Georgia?" The Cherokee argued that it was a foreign state that did not owe allegiance to the United States.[69]

In writing for the Court, Chief Justice Marshall diminished the sovereignty of the Cherokee nation to that of a "domestic dependent nation," whose relationship to the United States was that of a ward to a guardian. According to Justice Marshall, Indian nations were "independent political communities" of limited sovereignty, because they could not enter into agreements with nations outside the United States. The tribes had not surrendered their independence and power of self-government, the Court held; they had simply placed themselves under the protection of a stronger sovereign. Thus, Native American tribes having relinquished their external powers retained the ability to govern their own internal affairs.

The Indian Removal Act of 1830 diminished further the autonomy of Native Americans.[70] The act provided for the removal of Native Americans from their lands. Between 1830 and 1840, Native people were moved from all sections of the country to the Oklahoma territory. By its terms, the act guaranteed that the new land would forever belong to the tribes. However, in the mid-1850s, the reservation system was established under which Native Americans were displaced once again and relocated onto much smaller tracts of land than those originally promised to them.[71]

As the nineteenth century progressed, Native American sovereignty was further eroded. In an act of March 3, 1871, Congress stated its intention to honor treaties made before that date, but also said that

> No Indian nation or tribe, within the territory of the United States, shall be acknowledged or recognized as an independent nation, tribe, or power, with whom the United States may contract by treaty.[72]

After 1871, acts of Congress became the tool for regulating the relationship between Native American people and the United States. The doctrine that Congress had absolute power over laws affecting Native tribes began to develop.

In 1887, Congress signaled its intent to abolish tribes and reservations and to eliminate the tribes as independent nations and powers. Toward this end, the General Allotment Act of 1887, the Dawes Act, was passed providing for the redistribution of Native American lands. The Dawes Act intended to assimilate and "civilize" Native American people by turning them into land-owning farmers.

As the nineteenth century drew to a close, the Supreme Court issued a series of rulings that diminished further the sovereignty of Native Americans.[73] In 1886, the High Court found that the United States had the authority and right to govern Native Americans by acts of Congress, rather than by treaty, because they were within the territorial limits of the United States and were thus subject to the laws enacted by Congress for their protection and for the protection of the people with whom they come in contact. Indeed, the Court claimed that Congress had the absolute power to legislate matters concerning tribes subject only to any limits imposed by the United States Constitution.[74] Moreover, the Court held that Congress was not bound by treaties that have been made with tribes but could supersede them or unilaterally abrogate them.[75]

In 1934, Congress passed the Indian Reorganization Act,[76] which put an end to the federal government's policy of forced assimilation and encouraged Native governments to adopt constitutions and to develop or adopt court systems. Provisions in the act created the reservation system.

Tribal Government

Despite the loss of sovereignty, Native tribes remain semiautonomous nations. For example, the federal Constitution does not apply to the relationship between a tribal government and Native people who are living on the reservations under its auspices. The federal Constitution is designed as a compact between the federal government and the governments of the separate states; Native tribes are not considered states and they did not ratify the Constitution.[77] In 1968, Congress enacted the Indian Civil Rights Act,[78] which applies some provisions of the Bill of Rights to tribes, for example, protecting freedom of speech and religion, precluding warrantless searches, and providing certain due process guarantees in court.

Implementation of the Indian Reorganization Act was left to the Bureau of Indian Affairs (BIA), which is housed in the United States Department of the Interior.[79] As a general matter, the BIA is responsible for carrying out relations between the government of the United States and the governments of recognized Native American tribes.[80] Today, the BIA's responsibilities include providing funds to tribal governments for education, disaster relief, health, repair of buildings and for employment of physicians, Indian police, Indian judges, and other employees.[81]

After passage of the Indian Reorganization Act, the BIA encouraged tribal governments to adopt constitutions, which it frequently drafted for them, and to establish court systems.[82] Tribal councils, whose membership includes a chair, a vice-chair, and a set number of council members, are the legislative bodies that set policies for the reservations through the adoption of resolutions, ordinances, or laws. The tribal court is a creation of the tribal council and for this reason is subject to political influence.[83]

Most tribal court systems consist of a trial court and at least one level of appellate review, but some have a three-tier system with two levels of appellate review. Problem solving in native courts range from the use of traditional dispute resolution methods, where matters are resolved in private, to those that have established court systems that blend Anglo procedural safeguards with traditional cultural beliefs and practices.[84]

Tribal courts have both criminal and civil jurisdiction. Criminal jurisdiction does not extend to the acts of non-Indians, and it is limited by provisions in the Major Crimes Act under whose terms serious felonies such as murder, manslaughter, and kidnapping committed by Native Americans against Native Americans are within the jurisdiction of United States courts even if committed on native territory.[85] Civil matters such as divorce and child custody are adjudicated by tribal courts. In civil matters, tribal courts may adjudicate issues involving non-Indians.

Despite having semiautonomous status, the BIA exercises a considerable amount of supervision over internal tribal matters. A constitution that was developed after passage of the Indian Reorganization Act may allow the BIA to supervise a tribe in a variety of ways. Lyttle (1993) reports that BIA approval may be required for certain actions taken by the tribal council, including (1) changes in criteria for tribal membership including the conditions for excluding tribal members; (2) development of a tribal budget; (3) borrowing of money; (4) establishment of tribal courts and law enforcement departments; (5) rules for adoption of minor children; (6) rules to regulate domestic disputes; (7) approval for constitutional amendments; and (8) approval to pass a law and order code.

The ability of tribal courts to function effectively was enhanced by the passage of the Indian Tribal Justice Act of 1993, which authorizes annual appropriations for the operation of tribal courts and which establishes the federal Office of Tribal Justice in order "to provide the funds and technical assistance to the tribes as well as to promote cooperation between the tribal systems and the federal and state judicial systems."[86]

Summary

The first formal social welfare policy adopted by the American colonies was the English Poor Law of 1601. Adoption of the Poor Law was significant because it embodied principles of social welfare that are with us to this day: These are that (1) government, not simply churches and nonsectarian groups, have a role in providing assistance to the needy; (2) raising funds through taxation, rather than relying on voluntary contributions to aid the poor, was acceptable; (3) the poor were to be categorized with reference to their worthiness to receive aid, and those deemed unworthy were to receive harsh treatment; and (4) the poor should not receive more financial assistance than the lowest wage paid to a laborer. In 1969, the Supreme Court struck down residency requirements that had been part of the poor laws because they interfered with a citizen's constitutionally protected right to move freely within the United States.[87]

In this chapter as well as in chapter 2, I addressed the laissez-faire philosophy that evolved in the nineteenth century as America became industrialized. This worldview supported the notion that the acquisition of wealth and the existence of poverty were "natural" conditions, from which it followed that aiding the poor was, to a degree, immoral because it interfered with the "natural" order of things. Consequently, the practice of providing aid to people in their own homes was all but abolished in favor of providing aid in institutional settings where the poor could be observed, their behavior controlled, and good work habits encouraged.

The desire to expand the American frontier and the need for a supply of cheap labor on Southern plantations, in Northern factories, and in the new western territories ran hand-in-hand. Beginning with the fifteenth century practice of enslaving people of African descent, America embarked on shameful periods of history that continued through the eighteenth and nineteenth centuries, when laws codified discrimination against people of Asian descent and when the appropriation of Native American lands was sanctioned by law, to the twentieth century practice of inviting people of Mexican descent to work in agricultural industries and then forcibly deporting them when their labor was no longer needed. Legislative bodies enacted race-based laws to limit the opportunities available to non-white people, and time and again the United States Supreme Court has supported race-based discriminatory policies. The Court's 1896 ruling in *Plessy v. Ferguson* sanctioned the racial segregation that would last until the mid-twentieth century.

But there is another side to the need for labor, which is that it provided the opportunity for some people, seeking a better way of life, to emigrate to the United States. In addition, efforts at the end of the Civil War to rectify the mistreatment of African Americans by the passage of civil rights legislation and amendments to the federal Constitution laid the foundation for the civil rights policies and constitutional safeguards that exist today.

CHAPTER

Issues, Problems, and Agenda Setting

The focus of this chapter is on agenda setting, which refers to the process by which social issues are transformed into social problems and considered for possible remedy by a branch of government or by the public-at-large. At any given time, a number of issues compete for a place on the agenda of the persons or groups in a position to propose a policy solution. Evidence of this competition is seen in the number of newspapers and news magazines, television news and talk shows, professional journals and other information sources that seek to convince you that society must fund medical research; provide health insurance, housing, and jobs to those in need; care for children who are abused and neglected; reduce or eliminate the illegal use of controlled substances; reduce welfare dependency; eliminate discriminatory practices in business and education; improve public education; rebuild the infrastructure of major cities; respond to the needs of people in poorer nations; and address other matters that disrupt people's lives. Of these myriad issues, only some will find their way onto the policy agenda.

This chapter is divided into two sections. Section 1 contains a general discussion of agenda setting and focuses on the role played by the media in the agenda setting process. The material in section 1 applies mainly to agenda setting by the legislative and executive branches of government and to the voter initiated agenda. Little is known about the media's ability to influence the judicial agenda, although members of the bench who hold elective office may be more vulnerable to media influence than tenured judges.[1] Although it would be naive to assume that judges are immune to public opinion, the discussion of the media's role will not refer to judicial agenda setting. In section 2, we turn our attention to consider the agenda setting process in the legislative, executive, and judicial branches of government and by the public through the process of voter initiative.

SECTION 1: AGENDA SETTING

A "social issue" is a topic of discussion that develops out of a concern or a dispute between people and/or groups of people. A social issue becomes a "social problem" when the public discussion of it raises questions or unveils difficulties that must be resolved for the good of society. The generic term "agenda" means a list, outline, or plan of things to be done or matters to be acted upon. "Social policy agenda" has a more specific meaning, as defined and discussed by Cobb and Elder (1972).

Cobb and Elder divide the policy agenda into two categories.[2] The "formal agenda," also referred to as the institutional or governmental agenda, consists of items that have been placed for consideration on the policy agenda by Congress or the executive branch. The "systematic agenda" or "agenda of controversy" consists of issues that have received enough attention to ensure public awareness, that reflect a concern shared by some members of the public that action is required, that are seen as appropriate for redress by government, or that are subject to resolution by citizen initiative. The systematic agenda concerns us in this chapter. The fact that an issue is placed on the systematic agenda does not mean that a remedy will be produced, but simply that the issue will be considered for a possible remedy. What happens once an issue is placed on the agenda is the subject of chapter 6, which is concerned with policymaking. Here, we are considering only *how* the agenda is set.

The Media and Agenda Setting

The list of social problems that "compete" for public attention is long, and the process by which an issue comes to be defined as a social problem is not self-evident.[3] As a first step in setting the systematic agenda, some individual or group must "take on" the issue and begin the process of translation that results in framing the issue as a social problem. The more controversial the issue, the greater the need to inform the public and to gauge public reaction to the proposed change.

No one would seriously question the proposition that the role of the media in disseminating information to the general public is crucial, because few people have access to alternative sources of information concerning world events. Information that is disseminated by the media tells us what to think about and how to think about issues and thus sets the terms of any debate over controversial matters.[4]

There is empirical support for the proposition that the media play a crucial role in shaping public opinion. McCombs and Shaw (1972) interviewed 100 voters and then analyzed the information reported by the mass media that served the voters whom they interviewed. They concluded that the media are the primary source of information on national political matters, and they found a high correlation between the events deemed important by voters and the events covered in the media.[5] In a series of experiments, Iyengar, Peters, and Kinder (1982) asked participants to review news stories that emphasized different issues. One group saw stories focusing on inadequacies in American defense preparedness, and another group saw stories with no content concerning defense preparedness. Pre- and post-test results supported the hypothesis that "by ignoring some problems and by attending to others, television news programming profoundly affects which problems viewers take seriously."[6] Page and Shapiro (1992) studied foreign issues that were covered by television news during a fifteen-year period of time. They concluded that television news coverage influenced public opinion as to the importance of an issue but, more importantly, that predictions could be made concerning changes in public opinion based on the shifting focus of news coverage.[7] A national survey that was conducted in 1995 confirms this view. Respondents cited television twice as often as newspapers as their major source of information on acquired immunodeficiency syndrome (AIDS), and television was twenty-five times more likely to be an information source on this health issue than was a physician.[8] Shephard (1998) reports that the news media have had a significant effect on the development of public policy concerning youth crime. He argues that there has been an increase in the number of juveniles remanded to adult court from a low of 7,000 in 1988 to more than 12,000 in 1994. This increase occurred despite the fact that juveniles were responsible for just over 30 percent of all crime in 1974, compared to approximately 22 percent in 1994, and were responsible for approximately 12 percent of violent crimes in 1974, compared to just over 14 percent of violent crimes in 1994. Shephard attributes the shift toward trying juveniles as adults to the increase in homicides committed by youth and, most importantly, "[to] the public and political perception that youth crime has become epidemic and is a major threat to the peace and order of society."[9]

A federal judge in Missouri, discussing federal sentencing guidelines and the extreme penalties applied for possession of crack cocaine compared to powder cocaine, argued that Congress' perception of the danger of crack cocaine was media driven. According to Judge Cahill in 1994, Congress relied on continued media coverage of the dangers posed to society by users of crack cocaine in its decision to impose harsh penalties.[10]

Nelson (1984) studied how the agenda was set for child abuse reporting laws. She reported that newspaper and news magazine coverage was critical to sustaining public interest in this topic.[11] Likewise, Hacker (1998), in his investigation into the Health Care Reform Act proposed by President Clinton in the early 1990s, stated that editorials in the *New York Times* were the "main cause of heightened interest" in this subject.[12]

Is the relationship between the media and public opinion one-way or is it reciprocal? Stated otherwise, do the media report a story without taking into account public response or, after reporting, are polls taken to gauge public response and used to judge how much attention to pay to an issue and how to frame issues to sustain public interest? McCombs and Shaw (1972) suggested that the media do more than react to audience interest, implying a linear relationship between media presentation and public opinion. Hacker (1998) questioned this view, suggesting that the relationship may be reciprocal. He reported that in 1990, fewer than ten articles on health care appeared in the *New York Times*, the *Christian Science Monitor*, and the *Wall Street Journal*, yet public opinion polls taken in 1991 showed that 90 percent of Americans believed that fundamental reform of the health care system was called for. Between 1991 and 1992, in the same three newspapers, the number of articles on health care reform jumped from approximately thirty-five in 1991 to ninety-five in 1992. Further supporting his suggestion of a reciprocal relationship, Hacker reported that shortly after President Clinton introduced his Health Care Reform Act in 1993, polls showed that the public found confusing the terms used by experts to explain the president's health care plan. "Public relations managers" went to work and devised a new terminology, examples of which include changing the phrase "managed competition" to "a uniquely American solution to an American problem." The phrase "universal coverage" was dropped out of a concern that the public might associate this concept with coverage for the poor, and the phrase "health security" appeared in the hope of addressing the public's concern about losing health insurance.[13]

The process of agenda setting may begin when a public official, such as the president or a member of Congress, names an issue in a public forum. For example, in his 1992 presidential campaign, candidate Clinton promised to "end welfare as we know it." In 1994, when the Republican party gained control of Congress, Representative Newt Gingrich introduced the American public to the "Contract with America," which dealt with a variety of issues, including welfare reform.[14] Although efforts to reform welfare programs have a long history, this issue was "staked out" in the 1990s by both Democrats and Republicans, and the process of agenda setting for reform of the welfare system began anew.

Agenda Setting and the Use of Symbolic Devices

When an issue is controversial enough to be recognized as a problem, those with a position or interest cast the issue in terms that are designed to convince the public that their perception of the problem is accurate and their proposed solution appropriate. The welfare system in the United States is not popular with the general public, and there is little doubt that efforts at reform would find public support. Capitalizing on the unpopularity of welfare, candidate Clinton, in his 1992 presidential campaign, promised welfare reform. However, after the election, health care reform took center stage and provided an opportunity for the Republican party to define the issue of welfare reform after the party's 1994 electoral victory in the United States Congress. The reform that was proposed by the Republican majority in 1994 was to end the sixty-year-old Aid to Families with Dependent Children Program (AFDC), with its guarantee of some income security to dependent children and their caretakers. The proposal was radical in nature, and selling it to the public to win support was essential. Those who wish to control the agenda often make use of numbers and symbolic devices such as personal stories and metaphor.[15]

STORIES

Every story has a theme. For both Democrats and Republicans the theme of welfare reform was family values, which is convenient because the phrase has no commonly understood meaning. Thus, Democrats could claim to be the party of family values, while supporting a woman's right to choose to continue or terminate a pregnancy and arguing for inclusiveness that extended to lesbians and gays. The conservative wing of the Republican party could also claim to be the party of family values, but refer to abortion and homosexuality as forces contributing to the family decline.[16]

Stories follow a pattern that includes (1) problem identification, (2) reference to a period of time when things were "good," and (3) tales of decline, including identification of victims and villains. Tales of decline set the stage for tales of control. Tales of control are compelling because they remind us that we have the freedom to control our lives and to remedy the identified problem.[17]

PROBLEM IDENTIFICATION Both Democrats and Republicans agreed that "disintegrating families" were the key issues in the welfare crisis if not central to other social problems. In the words of Democratic Senator Daniel Patrick Moynihan, decaying family structure was the source of "the drug crisis, the education crisis, and the problems of teen pregnancy and juvenile crime."[18] Republican Representative Clay Shaw, Chairman of the House Ways and Means Committee, said that out-of-wedlock births to poor people result in homes where "mothers struggle, and children suffer . . . 64 percent of children born to single parents live in poverty, while just 8 percent of children born to two-parent families live in poverty. . . . the best thing we can do to fight poverty is to encourage marriage and to discourage out-of-wedlock births."[19]

WHEN THINGS WERE GOOD To many who believe that the American family is threatened, the 1950s provide a baseline against which current behavior is measured. Where the family is concerned, the media have a nostalgia for this period of history during which the "breadwinner father and homemaker mother" were decreed to be the only acceptable family form.[20] According to Representative Newt Gingrich, the country is "longing for the good old days. . . . so that we can come back to who we used to be . . . when we talk about family values and oppose multiculturalism, that's pure 1950s Midwestern tradition."[21]

THE TIME OF DECLINE—THE 1960S AS VILLAIN Every story evokes a period of time when decline from the ideal state began, and in our story the 1960s are presented as the period of turnaround for the American family. For social conservatives, the 1960s portray an image of moral decline, licentiousness, and social experimentation that was threatening to traditional values and social institutions. Testifying before the Senate on behalf of the Christian Coalition in 1996, Heidi Stirrup said that "there has been a steady decline . . . even destruction . . . of the family unit over the last thirty years."[22] According to Representative Gingrich, "Things went off track with Johnson's Great Society Programs."[23]

Using narratives is a political strategy whereby storytellers may exaggerate the issue and may not take account of facts that contradict their position. Nor is it necessary to consider alternative views, including the view that the issue itself is not a problem. The narrative is meant to appeal to raw emotions, not to engender critical debate. For example, Skolnick (1991) tells us that family life in America has gone through a series of changes in the twentieth century, beginning with the sexual revolution of the 1920s and the divorce rates that accompanied that revolution.[24]

The storyteller need not acknowledge this view, nor need she or he recognize that the 1950s may have been a historical anachronism rather than a norm. The referred-to stability of family life is somewhat mythical, since the rising divorce rate began in the decade of the 1950s. The view that the conservatives present of the 1960s is one-sided, since the rebellious children of the 1960s came from the idealized families of the 1950s. Skolnick tells us that the "tensions and discontents simmering underneath the seemingly bland surface of life in [the decade of the 50s] fueled the cultural revolts of the 1960s."

VILLAINS AND VICTIMS   Any good story requires villains and victims. To some, the welfare system is the villain, since it is said to trap many young people in a cycle of dependency that de-emphasizes work and independence, rewards young mothers for violating the rules, and consigns millions of children and their families to a lifetime of poverty.[25] Others saw parents whose behavior did not conform to social expectations as the villains. Senator Joseph Lieberman of Connecticut said that "welfare makes it feasible for a man to father a child without worrying about being a parent. It makes it possible for a young woman (too often a teen-age girl) to have a child, move away from home, get an apartment and survive—without working. It makes it easier for millions of families to get by, but virtually impossible for them to get ahead."[26]

The victims may be named as the children whose intellectual development was said to be negatively affected by dependence on welfare, thus increasing the likelihood of school failure and adversely affecting future earnings. Moreover, children who are born out of wedlock and reared without fathers were viewed as more likely to engage in early sexual activity, fail in school, commit crimes and end up on welfare as adults.[27]

Finally, society itself may be presented as a victim, because welfare dependency burdens the taxpayer. This view was expressed by Charles Murray of the American Enterprise Institute, who testified before Congress that throughout human history a single woman with a small child has not been viewed as either a viable economic unit or as a legitimate social unit. In small numbers, they must be a net drain on the community's resources. In large numbers, they must destroy the community's capacity to sustain itself.[28]

METAPHORS AND NUMBERS

For those who are trying to set the policy agenda, the status quo is viewed as less of a problem than changing social conditions. Thus, advocates must talk about change, which they emphasize through the use of numbers or the use of metaphor. Numbers play an important role in trying to convince people that there is a problem that has to be solved. For example, the number of births to unmarried teenage mothers increased almost fourfold between 1960 and 1996. But, however compelling numbers may be, they are "dry" and often fail to provide a point of reference in the experience of the listener. Thus, the statement that in 1996 more than 300,000 children were born to unmarried teenagers may have more impact with the use of metaphor, which applies a dramatic or extreme term to a subject that does not have literal meaning for that subject. For example, when we are told that "illegitimacy rates are skyrocketing,"[29] or that the "sky really is falling,"[30] or that there is an "epidemic of illegitimate births," we know that skyrockets are not really flying, the sky is not really falling, and that births—illegitimate or not—are not really a disease. However, these terms do evoke the loss of control and heightened sense of need for change that the reformers want to impart.[31]

THE RESOLUTION

The advocate who wishes to move an item onto an agenda must be prepared to offer a resolution to the identified problem. In 1995 and 1996, at the height of the debate on welfare reform, there was consensus among Democrats and Republicans that births to unmarried teenagers were a problem that had to be addressed. However, each party offered a different resolution. The welfare reform proposal advanced by the Democratic party would have required teen parents on welfare to live in adult-supervised environments and to complete high school.[32] The Republican proposal would have denied benefits to teen mothers under the age of eighteen.[33] The result was a compromise, the details of which are found in chapter 10.

Agenda Setting and Windows of Opportunity

Reform of the welfare system was a strategic part of the Democratic and Republican electoral campaigns in 1992 and 1994. The agenda setting strategies used by both parties were crafted to advance the proposals that reflected the political platform of each party. An alternative approach to agenda setting occurs when events, rather than speeches made by presidents and legislators, trigger media scrutiny and focus public attention on an issue of concern to a special interest group.[34] Events may open a "window of opportunity," allowing interested parties to advance their agenda and seek the public support necessary to convince policymakers to adopt a resolution, even a controversial one. For example, forty states plus the District of Columbia enacted hate crimes legislation that provides for increased penalties for persons who are convicted of a crime that is animated by bias based on the victims' race, religion, color, or national origin. Twenty-one of these statutes also cover sexual orientation. Groups that are concerned with the rights of lesbians and gay men have advocated to have sexual orientation included in the statutes of the nineteen jurisdictions that do not include it, and they have advocated for federal legislation covering hate crimes.[35]

In the fall of 1998, a young gay man named Matthew Sheppard was brutally murdered in Wyoming. Sheppard's sexual orientation was said to be a contributing factor, if not the actual reason why he was chosen as a victim. Wyoming does not have any hate crimes legislation. Within seven days of Sheppard's murder, 352 newspaper articles appeared across the United States describing his murder, at times in graphic detail, and discussing the issue of hate crimes and hate crime legislation.[36] Newspaper coverage included President Clinton's call for the passage of hate crimes legislation. The *Christian Science Monitor* reported statistics, compiled by the Federal Bureau of Investigation, showing that while violent crimes in general decreased across the United States, hate crimes implicating the victim's sexual orientation had increased from 8.9 percent in 1991 to 11.6 percent in 1996.[37]

Newspaper accounts reflected the polar opposites that frequently accompany debates on controversial issues. One side called for Wyoming, other states, and the federal government to enact hate crimes legislation, arguing that the absence of such laws increased the likelihood of bias-motivated crimes. The other side argued that hate crime laws punish "thoughts" and that judges already have the power to enhance penalties for crimes that are especially egregious; because hate crime laws punish speech, i.e., what one says when committing a crime, they violate a person's first amendment rights to free speech.

On October 12, 1999, four days after Matthew Sheppard's murder, the governor of Wyoming, whose legislature had rejected three hate crimes bills since 1994, said, "I ask for a collective suggestion for anti-bias, anti-hate legislation that can be presented to the Wyoming Legislature for their consideration in January."[38] In February 1999, the Wyoming legislature again rejected hate crimes legislation.[39]

Media interest peaks and wanes as new issues surface to command attention. Matthew Sheppard's murder is a prime example of what Downs (1972) refers to as the media's "issue-attention cycle," during which events trigger media scrutiny that is invariably short lived. Sensing boredom on the part of the public, the media shifts its focus to other issues.[40]

Media Agenda Setting and Worthy Causes

However important media attention may be, it is not always a necessary first step in moving the agenda along. In discussing the passage of federal legislation dealing with child abuse, Nelson (1984) refers to agenda setting that takes place within organizations, whereby officials with the power to make decisions propel an issue onto the legislative agenda because they deem the issue worthy of attention. When the organization is a federal agency, such as the Childrens' Bureau as was the case in Nelson's research, agenda setting may be especially efficient because officials in the organization have direct access to legislators whom they can lobby to propose legislation that favors their issue. It is noteworthy that the media did not come into play when child abuse first reached the agenda of the bureau in 1955, but the media would attend to the issue after the summer of 1962 when Dr. C. Henry Kempe's article on the "battered child syndrome" was published.[41] Thus, the ease or difficulty with which an issue is defined as a social problem and proceeds onto the policy agenda may depend on the source that lays claim to the issue. The power, authority, or influence of a source may lessen the media's role in setting the initial agenda.

In describing how the United States Children's Bureau, which is located in the executive branch, "adopted" the issue of child abuse, Nelson draws attention to another aspect of agenda setting: timing. The political climate and public receptivity often force policymakers to consider issues that they can ignore at other times. Child abuse was adopted as an issue by the Children's Bureau at the beginning of the Civil Rights era when some segments of society were focused on matters of individual rights and social rearrangements that redressed past abuses. At this time, there was a receptivity to conferring certain rights on children that recognized them as people separate from their parents, and this receptivity set the stage for transforming the issue of child abuse into the problem of child abuse.

Thus far, the discussion of the media has implied that media attention may force an issue onto the policy agenda, but media attention does not always ensure this outcome. Consider the following.

In June 1981, the Centers for Disease Control reported that a rare form of pneumonia had been diagnosed in five homosexual men. These men had what would come to be known of as AIDS. There were no stories reported in the *New York Times* on this subject in 1981 nor, for that matter, in any national newspaper in the United States. In 1982, when approximately 300 people had died of AIDS,[42] the *New York Times* reported four stories on this subject.

As shown in Figure 5.1, with the exception of the intervals between 1983 and 1984 and 1988 and 1989, when the number of news stories decreased, there was a continual rise in coverage by the *New York Times* throughout the decade of the 1980s. Coverage peaked in 1988 with the publication of 1,304 stories and, after a decline to 666 stories in 1989, rose again in 1990 to 1,206 stories. Despite the attention that AIDS was receiving in the media in New York and elsewhere,[43] AIDS did not find its way onto the agenda of either Congress or the executive branch of government

FIGURE 5.1. Number of articles in the *New York Times* concerning human immunodeficiency virus and acquired immunodeficiency syndrome in 1981–1990.

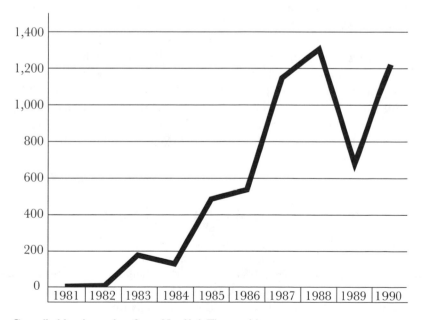

Source: Compiled by the author from *New York Times* archive.

during the 1980s, although there was ongoing criticism reported in the media of the federal government for its failure to assume a leadership role in combating the epidemic.[44]

If media attention were sufficient to guarantee a place on the systematic agenda, AIDS would have taken its place there long before 1990, the year in which the first federal legislation to deal with the epidemic, the Ryan White Comprehensive AIDS Resources Emergency Act (CARE Act), was passed. Other factors must be taken into account to understand why, despite extensive media coverage, despite the fact that by 1990 more than 48,000 Americans had developed AIDS, and despite the fact that an estimated 750,000 Americans were infected with human immunodeficiency virus (HIV), the issue did not achieve a place on the agenda of the federal government.[45]

First, from the beginning of the epidemic, AIDS was associated with sexual behavior and later with intravenous drug use. Information that was presented in the media took on, either expressly or by implication, a moral tone.[46] Hays and Glick (1997) suggest that policies that concern moral issues are especially difficult to enact[47] because they touch on and at times threaten deeply held convictions that are often rooted in religious beliefs about the way that human beings should conduct their relationships. The moral dialogue concerning AIDS was especially clear in the lines that were drawn between "innocent victims" and others who, by implication, were responsible for contracting the disease. In addition to the fact that AIDS focused a spotlight on sexual behavior, the view of policymakers and the general public toward gay men and later toward intravenous drug users must be taken into account. Representative Henry Waxman from California went so far as to say that had AIDS "appeared among Americans of Norwegian descent, or among tennis players, rather than gay males, the responses of both the government and the medical community would have been different."[48]

Nowhere was the indifference of elected officials to the plight of gay men and intravenous drug users more evident and the inability of the media to force the issue of AIDS onto the policy agenda more obvious than in the dedication to the Ryan White Comprehensive AIDS Resources Emergency Act. The members of Congress needed someone they could cast as an innocent victim on whose behalf legislation could be passed. Thus, the legislation was dedicated to the memory of Ryan White, a child and hemophiliac who contracted AIDS through a contaminated blood transfusion. White was introduced to people across America and across the world as a face of AIDS that caring human beings could not turn their back upon.[49]

SECTION 2: LEGISLATIVE AGENDA SETTING

Proposals reach the legislative agenda in a variety of ways. Any member of Congress may introduce a bill that supports the agenda of her or his party or of a special interest group that successfully lobbies for the introduction of legislation. Congress may enact legislation to overturn a decision of the United States Supreme Court when members of Congress think that the Court has misinterpreted Congress's intent in enacting a statute. [50] The president influences directly some of the legislation that is introduced by members of the president's party. For example, in June 1996, four democratic representatives introduced President Clinton's version of welfare reform, the "Work First and Personal Responsibility Act of 1996,"[51] as a counter proposal to the legislation that was introduced by the Republican party. The executive branch also moves issues onto the legislative agenda through its agencies by working with members of Congress, as was the case when the Children's Bureau developed the proposal that would become the Child Abuse Prevention and Treatment Act. Presidents and members of Congress also take advantage of opportunities to urge reconsideration of legislation previously introduced but not enacted. For example, since 1997 various members of Congress have been urging the passage of hate crimes legislation. In the fall of 1998, after Matthew Sheppard was murdered, in light of the media scrutiny of his murder and because of the degree of public sympathy and outrage at the brutality of what appeared to be a bias crime, President Clinton revived the issue of federal hate crimes legislation and urged Congress to pass the Federal Hate Crimes Protection Act, which would provide for enhanced penalties for crimes motivated by the sexual orientation, gender, or disability of the victim.[52]

An item on the legislative agenda originates as a bill. A bill is a proposal that is made to enact new legislation, amend existing legislation, or appropriate funds and authorize their expenditure. A bill is introduced into either the House or Senate. Every year, legislators introduce thousands of bills, only a fraction of which will become law. For example, between January 4, 1995, and October 4, 1996, the House of Representatives was in session for 289 days. In this brief time period, 5,329 bills (an average of approximately eighteen bills per day), were introduced. Of the 5,329 introduced bills, only 488 (9 percent) were passed by the House.[53]

Some of the legislation that is introduced each year is commemorative, seeking to establish, for example, Dessert Day or National Grapefruit Month.[54] Some bills are introduced by legislators primarily to gain the attention of or to appease pressure groups who are their constituents. For example, in 1995, almost identical versions of legislation entitled the Parental Rights and Responsibilities Act (PRRA) were introduced in the House and in the Senate.[55] Congressional supporters of the bill thought that some states had gone too far in limiting parental rights to control the upbringing of their children. Proponents argued that parents were excluded from decisions concerning school curricula; they were against granting to youth the right to make certain medical decisions without parental notification or consent, and they opposed proscriptions against corporal methods of discipline. The PRRA promised to restore parental rights in these areas.[56]

Opponents of the legislation argued that the PRRA would shift control over family matters from the states, whose laws traditionally have controlled family matters, to the federal government; that schools would have to negotiate all aspects of curriculum with parents[57]; and that the bill would result in protracted litigation[58] because its language was ambiguous and contradictory. For example, the bill provided that parents had the right to use corporal methods of discipline with their children but provided also that a state's child protective laws were not to be undermined. Not addressed in the proposal was the question of how far does a parent's right to use corporal methods of discipline go and at what point does the use of corporal methods of discipline cross the line and become abuse.

From the time that it was introduced, the likelihood that the PRRA would pass was low. This bill was partisan, supported in both houses of Congress by 156 Republicans but only eight Democrats. Moreover, as earlier noted, the issues that the PRRA addressed are traditionally within the control of state government. Because reducing the size of the federal bureaucracy and returning control to the states were at the heart of the Republican platform in 1995, the same year that the PRRA was proposed, the likelihood was slim that a sufficient number of Republican legislators would vote to give the federal government supremacy over the states in these matters. Introducing and discussing the bill gave proponents the arena they wanted to appease their constituents, but it was introduced without their belief that it would actually pass.

In any given year, most legislation deals with routine matters, although, as the welfare reform legislation of 1996 makes clear, legislation that dramatically alters the relationship between citizens and the government may be enacted. Nevertheless, in most years, the majority of bills passed by Congress deal with government operations. Consider bills passed by the House of Representatives in 1996. Slightly more than 50 percent of legislation that passed was in the form of amendments (27 percent) and appropriations bills funding government operations (28 percent).

Of the 72 percent of bills not covering appropriations, defense spending accounted for approximately 3 percent; welfare reform, including bills affecting income support programs and social service programs, approximately 4 percent; other social matters, including health care, education, and housing, 7 percent; bills affecting trade, including reducing the volume of federal regulations, 8 percent; matters concerning the environment, energy conservation, and national parks, 20 percent; commemorative legislation, 11 percent; and Native American/Alaskan Native affairs, approximately 3 percent. The remaining 16 percent consisted of a variety of issues such as bills concerned with copyright protection, consumer affairs, federal sentencing guidelines, transportation, abortion, defense of marriage, campaign finance, English as an official language, and the 2002 Winter Olympics.[59]

Minority Agenda Setting

Racial minorities have historically been outside of the political process. For this reason, drawing the attention of legislators to matters that concern minority groups is especially difficult. There is a "mobilization of bias," according to Bachrach and Baratz, which they define as a "set of predominant values, beliefs, rituals, and institutional procedures that operate systematically and consistently to the benefit of certain groups and to the exclusion of others."[60] McClain (1993), in her discussion of how the majority may keep matters that concern minority groups from the agenda, refers to majoritarian tactics that include the use of "existing power relationships" to block the introduction of legislation favorable to minorities and the use of terrorism to prevent black people from developing their concerns into full-fledged issues.[61]

Minority Agenda Setting and the Voting Rights Act

Prior to passage of the Voting Rights Act of 1965, some state and political subdivisions imposed literacy tests and required the payment of poll taxes as a way of reducing the likelihood that black citizens would exercise their right to vote. Passage of the act put an end to such practices by making the imposition of rules and procedures that deny citizens the right to vote based on race or color a violation of federal law.[62]

Meacham reports that once voter registration laws and procedures that discriminated against racial minorities were out of the way, minority registration and the election of black and Hispanic officials increased dramatically, especially in Southern states. By 1988, more than 6,000 racial minorities held elected offices, in contrast to fewer than 500 before passage of the act. In this period of time, the racial makeup of state legislatures increased "from a few in Eastern and Midwestern states to 400 blacks and 123 Hispanics throughout the country. Scores of minorities became mayors; hundreds were elected to city councils and school boards."[63]

Miller studied the effects of the act and judicial decisions enforcing compliance with the act on the creation of black caucuses in seven Southern states and on setting of the legislative agenda by the newly formed caucuses.[64] In addition to commemorative legislation to honor Martin Luther King Jr. and anti-apartheid bills, much of the agenda setting of the caucuses was on substantive matters that would (1) affect minority economic development; (2) increase the number of black officials; (3) enhance institutions of higher education that served mainly minority populations; (4) effect judicial reform; and (5) provide human services.

When minority groups have not been able to elect officials to advance a group's agenda, action by groups at the community level provides an alternative mechanism. In his discussion of community organizing in Mexican American barrios in Texas, Marquez describes the work of the Industrial Areas Foundations (IAF), neighborhood organizations that advocated for the concerns of Mexican American people.[65] Marquez documents the success of the IAFs, whose work resulted in the reallocation of state funds to equalize educational funding across the state, the acquisition of millions of dollars for capital improvements in housing and sanitation, the creation of new jobs, and the prevention of private firms from disposing of toxic waste near poor communities. Marquez writes that the ability of the IAFs to attract media attention forced local politicians to take account of their concerns in their ongoing decision making.

Agenda Setting by the Executive Branch

The executive branch of government tries to influence the policy agenda in different ways. The brief discussion of the role played by the Children's Bureau in moving the subject of child abuse onto the legislative agenda is one example, and the introduction of President Clinton's version of welfare reform is another.

A president whose party holds a majority in Congress should have an advantage in agenda setting because the president's agenda and that of the congressional majority should overlap. This overlap, coupled with party loyalty and an obligation to advance the president's agenda, should increase the likelihood that any differences in approach to achieving policy objectives will be smoothed over for the sake of achieving consensus. But, although the power of the office of the president is sufficient to ensure public attention to issues that are raised, it is not sufficient to ensure passage of desired legislation. When the president proposes change that is dramatic, public opinion plays a role in the fate of the proposal, and there may be significant disagreements between the president and members of Congress even when they share party affiliation.

For example, in the 1992 presidential campaign, candidate Clinton promised to end unconditionally the ban against lesbians and gays serving in the military.[66] The promise proved to be much more controversial than anticipated, and despite the fact that the Democratic Party controlled both houses of Congress in 1993, the president met significant resistance when he tried to fulfill his promise.[67] As Commander and Chief of the Armed Forces, the president could have lifted the ban by executive order had he chosen to do so (see chapter 6). But executive orders can be overturned by Congress, and some members of Congress threatened to do so if the president acted unilaterally.

The differences between the president and Congress reached an impasse that resulted in Congress holding hearings on the subject of lifting the ban against gays in the military. Senator Dan Coates of Indiana, testifying before the Senate Committee, said that the president was wavering in his promise to lift the ban because of the polls; mail received from the public showed a lack of support for the president's position, which was opposed also by the Joint Chiefs of Staff and rank-and-file soldiers who said that a change in policy would seriously undermine the effectiveness, the normal discipline, and the good order of the armed services.[68] One member of the House claimed to have five boxes of documents with 21,000 signatures of Americans who were vehemently opposed to changing the ban. It was said that the ban was supported by active duty reserves and retired members of the Navy, Marines, and Coast Guard and that the Senate Task Force on Military Personnel, after conducting a survey of "hundreds of generals and admirals," found that all were overwhelmingly against any compromise and any change in the ban.[69]

On July 19, 1993, President Clinton issued a compromise directive, commonly referred to as the "Don't Ask, Don't Tell, Don't Pursue" rule. The president's directive maintained the ban on active homosexuals serving in the military but prohibited recruiters from asking questions about the sexual orientation of a person seeking to enlist in the armed forces; the directive also purports to limit the freedom of commanding officers to conduct investigations into alleged homosexual conduct.[70] On July 29, 1993, Congress codified the president's directive.[71]

Discussion about President Clinton's failure to lift the ban on homosexuals serving in the military suggested that public support opposed lifting the ban, but there was disagreement on this point. For example, in July 1992, one year before President Clinton issued his directive, *New York Newsday* reported that 81 percent of Americans were opposed to the military's policy of firing lesbians and gays.[72] In the earlier discussion of AIDS, I stated that moral concerns can affect whether a policy is passed to address a social problem. That discussion is applicable here. The moral nature of the ban on gays in the military is clear in the language of the statute passed by Congress in the summer of 1993 that states, "The presence in the armed forces of persons who demonstrate a propensity or intent to engage in homosexual acts would create an unacceptable risk to the high standards of morale, good order and discipline, and unit cohesion that are the essence of military capability."[73]

Another way in which the president can influence the policy agenda is derived, in part, from Article II, Section 2 of the federal Constitution (the Appointments Clause). This clause provides that the president, with the advice and consent of the Senate, appoints officials to run federal agencies, such as the Department of Health and Human Services and the Department of Education, which, as we shall see in chapter 6, play a significant role in setting social welfare policy. The president also nominates people to fill vacancies in the federal courts. Although the agenda setting role of the judiciary is discussed in a later section, an example of the president's ability to influence the court's agenda through power to appoint judges is in order.[74]

Between 1969 and 1972, President Richard Nixon appointed four Supreme Court Justices who produced a conservative majority on the Court. Discussing the agenda setting power of the court, Freedman (1996) reports that a public "outcry" against pornography and "permissive" decisions of the Supreme Court under the stewardship of Chief Justice Earl Warren coincided with the emergence of the new conservative majority who gave state and local units of government greater freedom than in the past to govern the world of adult entertainment. Supreme Court decision making was influenced by the chief executive—both his campaign against "permissiveness" and his power to appoint justices—and by the public's concern as raised and reported by the media.[75]

The Public Role in Agenda Setting

The public may play a direct role in setting the policy agenda in two ways. First, as discussed later, the public affects the civil agenda of trial courts by the cases that it brings to the courts with the criminal agenda affected by prosecutorial decisions. In addition, the public may create policy through the voter initiative. To use the voter initiative, members of the public must acquire a specified number of signatures to a petition (see chapter 6). If the requisite number of signatures is acquired, the issue is set forth for public acceptance or rejection in a general election.

Although it is discussed in detail in chapter 6, the voter initiative is important to this chapter's discussion because it is a unique approach to agenda setting. Unlike other forms of agenda setting, the discourse concerning the merits of any initiative proposal is carried on by members of the public with each other; it is not controlled by elected officials.

> Average citizens must invest substantial effort and resources in getting the attention of others including government officials and the media but unlike government agencies and officials who can reach the public through press releases or news conferences, and leaks, ordinary people must identify and define their

issues as problems worthy of concern and requiring immediate attention and they must find a way to capture media attention.[76]

The words and phrases used to define a particular issue are crucial in convincing people that the issue is a problem, in ultimately getting the requisite number of signatures to place the issue on the political agenda, and in gaining the votes necessary to enact policy. A brief example will serve to illustrate this issue.

In November 1996, Californians voted to amend the state constitution to end affirmative action in programs operated by state and local government. The California Civil Rights Initiative, or Proposition 209 as it was popularly known, was placed on the ballot by voter initiative. Proposition 209 received a great deal of media attention, as did the topic of affirmative action in general, at the time it was proposed. Fueling the discussion was a ruling in March 1996 by the 5th Circuit Court of Appeals that the use of racial preferences in university admissions violated the federal constitution.[77] This decision appeared to contradict directly an earlier decision of the Supreme Court ruling that use of race as one of the factors in the admissions process was permissible.[78] The decision of the Appellate Court, plus the fact that the chairman of the Proposition 209 committee was African American, guaranteed press attention. Between January 1, 1996, and the November election, more than 400 articles were published in California newspapers.[79]

Proponents and opponents of Proposition 209 framed their arguments according to what they believed to be the reasons why people support and oppose affirmative action programs. Those who wanted to continue affirmative action programs appealed to a basic sense of fairness by framing their argument in the language of opportunity; and they made clear that they were trying to protect opportunities for qualified individuals. According to these people, who opposed the proposition, the law in California that provided opportunities for women and minorities through tutoring, mentoring, outreach, recruitment, and counseling to *ensure equal opportunity* would be eliminated. They said that Proposition 209 would put an end to outreach and recruitment programs that encourage applicants for government jobs and contracts and to programs designed to encourage girls to study and pursue careers in math and science.

Supporters of the proposition, knowing that some members of the public viewed affirmative action programs with reference to imposing outcomes rather than providing opportunities, framed their debate accordingly. Proponents urged a yes vote in order to eliminate affirmative action programs for women and minorities that give *preferential treatment*. Acknowledging that the initial impulse behind affirmative action was a noble one, proponents went on to say that "special interests [had] hijacked the civil rights movement. Instead of equality, governments imposed quotas, preferences, and set-asides." Using the language of reverse discrimination, supporters of the measure argued that government was discriminating against students, job applicants, and contractors who were losing opportunities because of their race was not "the preferred RACE" [capitals in the original].[80]

Agenda Setting—The Courts

To understand agenda setting in the courts, you should have a general understanding of the court hierarchy and the role that each court in the hierarchy plays. I use the federal court system for purposes of illustration.

THE HIERARCHY OF COURTS

The federal court system has three tiers, consisting of ninety-four district courts, eleven midlevel appellate courts, and one Supreme Court. District courts are trial courts where criminal and civil matters are heard. Each of the eleven midlevel appellate courts serves a specified number of states, with an appellate court for the District of Columbia. Appeals from judgments of a district court are taken by the appellate court serving the state in which the district court is located. The United States Supreme Court is the final court of appeal. Agenda setting in trial courts differs from agenda setting in appellate courts because appellate courts have a great deal of discretion in choosing the cases that they will hear, whereas trial courts do not. After briefly discussing how the agenda is set for district courts, we will consider how the agenda is set for the United States Supreme Court.

DISTRICT COURT AGENDA SETTING

A district court judge cannot turn away a proper case that is filed by a proper party and that is within the jurisdiction of the court. Courts cannot entertain hypothetical cases nor can they address academic questions. Thus, a proper case is one involving specific and concrete issues that affect the legal relations of the involved parties. A proper party is a person with standing to bring suit, which means that the party bringing suit must have been injured or must be threatened with injury. District courts have jurisdiction over all civil actions that arise under the federal Constitution or federal law. Thus, if you think that you have been discriminated against—denied a job or an educational opportunity because of your race, color, gender, religion, or national origin—it takes very little to establish that you are a proper party with standing to bring suit under the Civil Rights Act of 1964 and that a federal district court is the proper forum to hear your complaint.[81]

Because district courts cannot turn away proper cases, they do not set their own agenda as can appellate court judges who, with few exceptions, have discretion in choosing the cases they will hear. District court judges may, however, delay scheduling civil cases because the caseload of federal courts is high and because criminal cases have priority over civil matters.

The civil agenda of district courts is set by individuals suing on their own behalf and by special interest groups suing on behalf of classes of people who claim a common injury and request a common remedy. The activities of the National Association for the Advancement of Colored People (NAACP) in turning to the courts, when political units of government would not act to end state-sanctioned segregation, is a prime example of how special interest groups set the court's agenda.

Congress may also affect the agenda of district courts, which it did in 1996 when it prohibited legal aide lawyers from bringing class action lawsuits.[82] Poor people often rely on legal aide lawyers for assistance, and legal aide services are funded in large part by the federal government. When a legal aide attorney is confronted with a problem that affects a significant number of people, she or he may find it more efficient to tackle the problem via a class action lawsuit, brought on behalf of all who are experiencing the problem and to seeking relief for all affected parties, than it would be to sue on a case-by-case basis. Bringing suit on a case-by-case basis is time consuming, the required actions are repetitive, and the ultimate remedy of declaring the law unconstitutional may be more difficult to realize. For example, under provisions of the welfare reform law of 1996 (see chapter 10), certain welfare benefits are denied to noncitizen legal immigrants. Given the number of people affected, a class action suit would be the most efficient approach to challenging this rule. However, in 1996, Congress amended the law that provides funds for the Legal Services Corporation, thereby prohibiting legal aide lawyers from bringing class action lawsuits.

Supreme Court Agenda Setting

> Anyone who suggests that this is an objective institution is just wrong; the notion that we are objective is just fallacious.
>
> *Unnamed Justice of the United States Supreme Court*[83]

As already noted, appellate courts have discretion in choosing the cases they will review and thus are provided with a degree of agenda setting freedom not found at the trial court level. The United States Supreme Court enjoys even greater, almost exclusive discretion in choosing what cases it will hear.

The first step in setting the Court's agenda occurs before cases reach the Court, through a filtering process by practicing attorneys who decide what cases to appeal. The second step occurs when the Court decides to grant or refuse a petition for certiorari (literally meaning "to be informed of"). The majority of cases that come to the attention of the Court come forward on a petition for certiorari. If the petition is granted, the Court inspects the proceedings of the lower court whose ruling is on appeal. The Court receives as many as 5,000 petitions each year, no more than 5 percent of which will be granted review. The decision not to accept a case for review is an agenda setting action, because it allows the appellate court rulings to stand.

When petitions for cert reach the Court, they are directed to law clerks who review the petitions and who write memos summarizing the "issues, facts, and opinions of the lower court." Memos contain a brief analysis and a recommendation to grant or deny review. A "discuss list" is created from written memos. Exclusion of a case from the discuss list is equivalent to a denial of cert. Next, the justices hold a conference, discuss the cases on the list, and vote whether to grant review. Four votes are needed for a grant of cert. In setting its agenda, the Court takes into account legalistic and strategic concerns.

LEGALISTIC CONCERNS

Rule 10 of Title 28 of the United States Code provides that review by the Court is discretionary.[84] The rule tells us that a grant of cert should be for "compelling" reasons and that the issue that is presented for review should concern an "important" federal matter. Perhaps for these reasons, review is likely to be granted when the federal government is the party seeking review; when there is a conflict between lower appellate courts, such that the law on a given question must be settled to give direction to future decisions; or when amicus, meaning friend of the court, briefs are filed because they signal to the court that the matter under consideration is important.[85] Some cases are granted cert because the issue has social as well as legal importance. For example, overturning the law that allowed African American children to be segregated racially had great legal significance as well as social significance for the children who were being denied educational opportunities because of their race.

STRATEGIC CONCERNS

Strategic concerns have to do with nonlegal matters that affect a vote to grant or deny cert, for example, whether it is the right time to address a particular issue and whether a justice thinks that she or he can achieve the outcome that is desired. Cases involving issues such as abortion, affirmative action, or hate speech are more likely to be outcome oriented and to trigger strategic voting.

There are many examples of cases that are selected for cert on strategic grounds. In 1955, shortly after the court decided *Brown v. Board of Education,* it was asked, in *Naim v. Naim,* to strike down Virginia's antimiscegenation statute.[86] The Court denied cert and avoided dealing with the issue of interracial marriage for 12 years until 1967, when the Court deemed Virginia's antimiscegenation statute unconstitutional.[87] The Court denied review because it did not think that the South was ready, immediately following the desegregation decision in *Brown,* for another decision invalidating its race-based policies. H. W. Perry interviewed a justice about the Court's refusal to address the issue presented in *Naim.* "I was convinced," the justice said, "that what motivated [the court to deny cert] . . . was that they thought that this was just not the right time to deal with the matter in this case and they just passed making a decision no matter how important it was."[88]

"Defensive denials" refers to a tactic that justices may use to deny cert based on a belief that the desired result is not attainable. For example, in 1991, Mississippi enacted a statute requiring (1) physicians to inform any woman who was requesting an abortion of the medical risks involved and (2) a waiting period of 24 hours after the information disclosure before an abortion could be performed.[89] In 1992, the Court of Appeals for the 5th Circuit upheld the statute as constitutional, and the Supreme Court refused to hear the case on appeal. Justice Harry Blackmun, an advocate of a women's right to choose to continue or terminate a pregnancy, concurred in the decision to deny review. Levinson (1993) argues that the only way to understand Justice Blackmun's denial is to view it as a defensive denial, given his support of a woman's right to choose and since the waiting period required by the statute was apt to have a negative effect on poor women since it might necessitate unaffordable back-and-forth travel or an overnight stay near a clinic.[90] Stated otherwise, Justice Blackmun may have concluded, based on the composition of the Court at the time, that a grant of cert would result in setting a Court precedent upholding the Mississippi statute. If Justice Blackman had believed that the Court might overturn the Mississippi statute, he may have voted to grant review.

The defensive denial has been used in other issues. According to Supreme Court law clerks interviewed by Perry, gay rights issues were the area of review most frequently "ducked" by the justices. Those justices who thought that gay rights issues deserved a hearing voted against granting cert because they believed that the outcome of any review would be negative for gay and lesbian people. Others justices avoided the issue because they thought it "messy, controversial, perhaps doing reputational damage to the Court when no one was being prosecuted under Sodomy statutes."[91]

Summary

The question addressed in this chapter is, "How are social issues transformed into social problems and, once transformed, how do social problems find their was onto the policy agenda?" The media play an important role in advancing the agenda of the legislative and executive branches of government as well as that of private parties seeking to resolve a problem by means of the voter initiative. The role of the media in affecting the agenda of the judicial branch is less well known.

Print and visual media keep the public informed about ongoing events. The media frame issues by choosing the language to describe events and the context in which to present events. The relationship between the media and the public is not a simple one by which the media teach and the public learns. Evidence suggests a reciprocity where the media, after presenting information, gauge public reaction through polling and shape future stories to the interest of their audience.

At times, the role played by the media is shaped by carefully crafted political campaigns and other special interest groups. At other times, the media respond to spectacular events as they occur, such as natural disasters and horrific crimes, when the story that is forthcoming is shaped less by strategy than by minute-to-minute reaction to the events surrounding the reported tragedy. Finally, although media attention may focus public attention on an issue, it is not sufficient to ensure that an issue will find its way onto the agenda of governmental bodies. The media reported extensively on the AIDS epidemic for years before Congress took up the issue.

Each branch of government sets its agenda differently. The agenda of legislative bodies is set with the introduction of a bill by a member of the House or Senate. The executive branch advances its agenda in different ways: Executive level agencies may work with members of Congress to draft legislation, and congressional members of the president's party will introduce legislation that reflects the priorities of the executive branch. The president may act unilaterally by issuing an executive order, but when the subject matter evokes strong emotions, as when President Clinton sought to lift the ban against gays serving in the military, Congress may thwart the president's efforts. However, as we shall see in chapter 6, many executive orders become law with little or no reaction by Congress.

As to the judicial system, agenda setting follows two tracks. The civil agenda of trial courts is set by individuals and special interest groups when they bring suits that challenge the status quo or that try to enforce existing laws. Appellate courts have a great deal of discretion in selecting the cases they will hear on an appeal. The highest appellate court, the United States Supreme Court, agrees to review only 5 percent of the cases submitted for review each year. Both legal and strategic concerns affect the decisions to review appealed cases. Legal concerns focus on the role of the court in reviewing cases that address important federal matters; thus, cases where the United States is a party are likely to be reviewed, as are cases where the High Court must resolve disputed questions of law. When lower level appellate courts interpret the law in different ways, the High Court is likely to grant review. Strategic concerns focus attention on desired outcomes. Strategic decision making influences the vote according to a justice's prediction of achieving the outcome she or he desires.

In a number of states, the public-at-large is able to set its own policy agenda through the mechanism of the voter initiative. Here, the ability of a group to place an issue on the ballot is contingent on convincing a percentage of the voting public to sign a petition supporting the initiative.

It is important to bear in mind that although the branches of government may act independently to place items on the policy agenda, the legislative, executive, and judicial branches often interact in the agenda setting process. The brief discussion of the role played by the Children's Bureau, an agency of the executive branch, in setting the policy agenda for passage of the Child Abuse Prevention and Treatment Act was one example. The fact that Congress may affect the Supreme Court's agenda when it overturns a High Court decision because it does not agree with the Courts' interpretation of a federal statute is another. The president's power to appoint federal judges and heads of government agencies and the limits placed on the president by the constitutional requirement that the Senate approve the appointments made is a further example.

This chapter would not be complete without raising the issue of public access to information via the Internet and without asking, but not answering, the question of whether this medium of communication will affect agenda setting in the future. Unlike the print media and television, where information is directed to a passive audience and shaped by editorial policies, the interactive nature of the Internet creates the potential for influencing public opinion in ways not previously imagined. For example, some news organizations conduct polls on their Web sites immediately after a story is presented. The reader is asked to advance an opinion concerning the subject matter of the story. The news provider has continual and rapid feedback as to public interest in the story as well as public opinion of how the story was told. We know that public opinion polls influence how the media shape stories, and there is little reason to believe that data compiled from polls conducted through the Internet will be treated differently.

In addition, Internet chat rooms provide a forum for ongoing dialogue between people around the globe, thus providing access to diverse points of view that the average person would not have had access to in the past. Finally, the almost instant dissemination of governmental information and the availability of source documents on the Internet are significant (see Guide to Online Research). For example, very soon after Kenneth Starr, the Independent Counsel for the Whitewater Investigation, issued a report on President Clinton's involvement with Monica Lewinsky, Congress made the report available to the public via the Internet. Shortly thereafter, depositions of various witnesses were made available. Mr. Starr is a prosecutor and his report, like that of any prosecutor, reflects the stance of an advocate. A reader cannot determine the degree, if any, to which the facts are slanted by the context in which they are portrayed or whether the information represents a full accounting. However, when depositions and other source documents from the report were made available, any person with access to the Internet was in a position to review these documents and form her or his own opinion on the accuracy and thoroughness of Starr's report. In the same way, congressional laws and committee reports and testimony are available via the Internet and allow the student of social policy to review new statutes immediately and, by reading committee documents, to gain insight into the positions taken by advocates for and against the policy and the intent of those members of Congress participating in committee deliberations.

6

Policymaking

This chapter continues the discussion begun in chapter 5. As discussed there, the fact that an issue is placed on the policy agenda does not mean that a policy will be enacted, simply that the issue addressed by the policy will be considered. This chapter is divided into four sections, each of which deals with policymaking. In section 1, our attention will be focused on the legislative branch of government, and in section 2 we focus on the executive branch. Policymaking by the public-at-large is the topic covered in section 3, and policymaking by the judiciary is covered in section 4.

SECTION 1: THE LEGISLATIVE PROCESS

Legislative proposals reach the United States Congress when a bill is introduced in either the House or the Senate. The legislative bodies of forty-nine of the fifty states also consist of two chambers; only one state, Nebraska, has a unicameral legislature whose single body is called the State Senate. A discussion of each state is beyond the scope of this text, because there is considerable variation in the operations of state legislative bodies.[1]

Introducing Legislation

Members of the United States Congress may introduce bills of interest to themselves or bills that have been proposed by the executive branch or by their constituents or special interest groups that have successfully lobbied for the introduction of a bill. Members seek support from others, who may become co-sponsors of the proposed legislation. Whether a bill originated in the House or the Senate can be

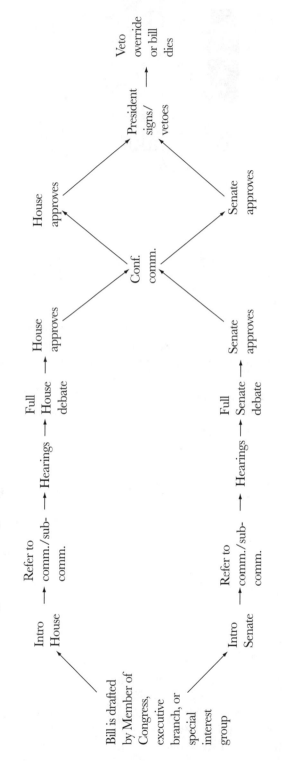

FIGURE 6.1. Flow of legislation through the House and the Senate.

determined by the alpha-prefix assigned to the bill number: HB is used to designate House bills and SB to designate Senate bills.

The path a bill follows after introduction is depicted in Figure 6.1. The process is the same in the House and the Senate. Different versions of the same legislation may be introduced into either chamber or simultaneously introduced into both chambers. If a bill is introduced into only one chamber and the bill is supported throughout the process, it is then submitted to the other chamber, where the same process is repeated. If simultaneously introduced and supported throughout the process, differences in the House and Senate versions are worked out in a conference committee (discussed in the following paragraphs). When legislation is proposed in the House or the Senate, it is "read into" the *Congressional Record* of the House or the Senate (the *Record*). The *Record*, published each day Congress is in session, is the first place in which the text of a newly proposed bill appears. The *Record* often contains opinions about the bill that are expressed by members of Congress and not found elsewhere.

The first step after a bill is introduced is assignment to an appropriate committee, which may in turn assign the bill to a subcommittee. There are nineteen standing committees in the House and seventeen in the Senate; each body also has subcommittees, more than 100 in the House and more than ninety in the Senate. Committees have specific areas of jurisdiction to which bills are assigned accordingly. Bills introduced in the Senate that address social welfare matters are assigned to the Committee on Health, Education, Labor and Pensions, and those introduced in the House are assigned to a subcommittee of the House Ways and Means Committee.

Bills receive a great deal of attention in committee, where the cost of proposed legislation is calculated. Standing committees have the power to "kill, alter, or report unchanged" the bills assigned to them[2]; these committees include staff who are subject-matter experts able to "fine tune" legislative proposals. When hearings occur, they are held before committees. The testimony that is offered may result in a bill's modification and may affect the bill's chances of passage, as does the estimated cost of implementing the legislation.

If a bill is voted out of committee, it is then subject to floor debate in the chamber in which it was first introduced. As noted above, if the bill if supported by a majority of that chamber, it is then submitted to the other chamber, where the process is repeated. If both chambers support a bill without change, it is sent to the president for signature. If a bill is supported by either chamber but with modifications, a conference committee comprised of members of both the House and the Senate is convened and charged with ironing out the differences between House and Senate versions. Assuming that differences are resolved, the revised bill is subject to reconsideration by both chambers independently. If approved, it is sent to the president. If signed by the president, it becomes law. If vetoed by the president, it becomes law only if a two-thirds majority in each chamber votes to override the veto.

Influences on Policymaking

To describe the process by which a bill is introduced and to follow a bill through the legislative bodies where it becomes policy leaves unanswered the question, "Why are some policies passed and others not?" For example, in chapter 2, I reported that in the mid-nineteenth century President Franklin Pierce vetoed a congressional grant of land for the creation of hospitals for the mentally ill because he was concerned that such a grant would lead to federal involvement in caring for all poor people. In 1935, with passage of the Social Security Act, the federal government became the major actor in setting social policy and providing funds to care for the poor, thus undertaking to do exactly what Pierce sought to avoid (see chapter 9). In 1996, with passage of the Personal Responsibility and Work Opportunity Act (PRWOA), the federal government put an end to a program that had guaranteed some income to support poor children and their caretakers for 60 years. How can this history of rejecting, creating, revising, and overturning the same kind of policy be explained? Before exploring why some policies are passed and others not, bear in mind that, as reported in chapter 5, most legislation considered by Congress is concerned with routine matters. The kind of policy discussed here involves the small number of bills that dramatically affect the relationship between citizens and the government.

There are models of decision making that seek to explain how legislators make policy decisions. Rationale choice theory, also called "social choice theory," "positive political theory," and "public choice theory," assumes that policymaking can be explained by the use of economic models whereby decision makers conduct a cost-benefit analysis to select from available options the one that maximizes goal attainment while minimizing cost. There is little proof that public policymakers make decisions in this manner.[3] In chapter 1, I reported that the PRWOA seeks to make government sponsored financial support for able-bodied adults unattractive by requiring that most recipients work within twenty-four months of the time they begin to receive benefits. Before the PRWOA was passed, Congress had good reason to believe that the work requirements were not attainable. This conclusion was reached in 1995 by the General Accounting Office (GAO), which conducts investigations at the request of members of Congress who are seeking information concerning policy. The GAO conducted a study of the Job Opportunities and Basic Skills Training Program (JOBS), which was part of the program to be ended when the PRWOA passed. The GAO informed Congress that maximum monthly enrollment in work related activities under the JOBS program did not exceed 13 percent of potential enrollees despite the promise of child care and a rich array of services.[4] In July 1996, one month before the new law passed, the Congressional Budget Office (CBO), which provides cost data to congressional committees in order to assist them in their deliberations on proposed legislation, reached the same conclusion.[5] If rational choice guided decision making, the logical prediction using the data provided by the GAO and the CBO would not lead to a requirement that recipients of financial support go to work within twenty-four months of the time they become recipients of benefits.

Lindblom (1968) argues that the policymaking process is best understood as one where change occurs slowly.[6] Policymakers avoid risk taking and preserve the status quo by making incremental changes to existing policy. Reduction of risk increases the likelihood that consensus will be achieved among policymakers and that the various federal bureaucracies whose task it is to assist in policy implementation will support the proposed change since preserving the status quo is the sine qua non of bureaucratic decision making.

In discussing legislative agenda setting (chapter 5), I reported that between January 4, 1995, and October 4, 1996, an average of eighteen bills a day were introduced into the House of Representatives. In any year, many of the introduced bills deal with minor matters; nevertheless, the volume argues against the cost-benefit approach posited by proponents of a rational choice decision making model. An incremental model is more useful for describing what legislators do and how they do it than for explaining why they make choices and why, as was the case in 1996 when the PRWOA was passed, radical departures are sometimes taken.

SPECIAL INTEREST GROUPS

Policymaking is influenced by special interest groups, although their influence does not fit within any particular model of policymaking. Special interest groups consist of so-called "think tanks," lobbyists, and political action committees (PACs), which can be any group that receives contributions in excess of $1,000 in a calendar year or that spends in excess of $1,000 during a calendar year to influence a federal election.[7]

The PACs provide funds to candidates for public office and to political parties. All PACs must register with the Federal Election Commission, and federal law limits the amount of money that individuals can contribute to PACs and the amount of money that certain PACs can contribute to individual candidates and committees.[8]

According to the Federal Elections Commission, the number of PACs increased significantly between 1977 and 1995, with the greatest growth occurring in PACs that represent big business. Big business PACs increased from less than 600 to approximately 1,800; PACs that represent trade groups, membership groups and health groups doubled in number from 400 to 800; and PACs representing labor increased from 200 to approximately 375.[9]

In an eighteen-month period of time in 1997 and 1998, PACs contributed more than $292 million to political campaigns. Corporations led with contributions in excess of $90 million and were followed (in descending order by amount of contribution) by trade, membership, and health groups; nonconnected groups; and labor.[10] Each contributed in excess of $60 million. Not surprisingly, the influence of PACs on the voting behavior of elected officials is said to be a function of the sums of money contributed. The groups that make the largest contributions wield the greatest amount of influence.[11]

THINK TANKS

Think tanks include conservative groups, such as the American Enterprise Institute and the Heritage Foundation, and liberal groups, such as the Center on Budget and Policy Priorities and the Urban Institute. Think tanks attempt to influence policymaking through the preparation of reports containing analysis of the effects of alternative approaches to achieving policy goals. The mission of the Heritage Foundation is

To formulate and promote conservative public policies based on the principles of free enterprise, limited government, individual freedom, traditional American values, and a strong national defense. [The foundation] pursues this mission by performing timely accurate research addressing key policy issues and effectively marketing these findings to its primary audiences: members of Congress, key congressional staff members, policymakers in the Executive branch, the nation's news media, and the academic and policy communities.[12]

The Center on Budget and Policy Priorities

Was founded to provide information about the impact of the Reagan Administrations' proposed budget reductions on low income families and to counter the rhetorical images and sound-bites, such as the phrase that a "safety net" would be maintained for the "truly needy," rather than on solid analysis. The Center specializes in research and analysis oriented toward practical policy decisions faced by policymakers at federal and state levels. The Center examines various data and research findings and produces solid analytic reports on a timely basis that are accessible to public officials at national, state, and local levels, to nonprofit organizations, and to the media.[13]

LOBBYING AND INDIVIDUAL ACTION

Lobbying groups, such as the National Association of Social Workers or the American Association of Retired Persons (AARP), may or may not produce reports that analyze alternative policy proposals. Lobbying groups seek to influence policymakers by face-to-face contact with members of Congress or their staff who are working on legislation of significance to their constituents and by urging direct constituent participation. For example, at their Web site, the AARP (1) lists legislation of concern to their members, (2) identifies the legislative committee and its meeting schedule for considering the legislation, (3) provides the name of House and Senate representatives, (4) encourages individuals to voice their opinions, and (5) provides direct E-mail links for sending messages to representatives.[14]

Individuals may influence the policymaking process in a variety of ways. In addition to expressing their point of view, as encouraged by groups such as the AARP, individuals in some states participate through use of the voter initiative, they support lobbying groups and PACs that advance their interests, and they vote, but the percentage of registered voters who cast their ballots in federal elections has been decreasing since 1960. In that year, 63 percent of the voting age population turned out at the polls, compared to 49 percent in 1996.[15] Voting behavior varies considerably by age. In 1996, young people aged eighteen to twenty had the lowest turnout, with 31 percent voting, compared to voters older than sixty-five, with 67 percent voting.[16]

I began this section by posing the question, "Why are some policies passed and others not?" I do not think that any rational answer can be drawn from the preceding material about the social welfare arena and policies affecting the so-called "unworthy poor." Although models of policymaking have been developed, it is not clear that any single model allows us to predict the voting behavior of members of Congress. Descriptive models such as incrementalism are useful to observe what happens and to make predictions concerning the speed of policy change, but they are of limited value in understanding the conditions that support major policy shifts.

Policymaking is influenced by multiple factors, including the values of the individual policymaker, the interests of the policymaker's constituents, the influence of special interest groups, public opinion (see chapter 1 and the discussion of President Clinton's health care proposal), and the social context in which a policy is proposed. These factors are not mutually exclusive, and identifying any single factor may not be possible.

There have been several dramatic shifts in public policy in the twentieth century. A brief overview of two such shifts may provide some insight into the question, "What factors influence major shifts in policy?"

Take as a first example the passage of the Social Security Act in 1935. The Depression of 1929 provides a social and economic context for the act's passage, which, as earlier noted, was significant because it marked the entry of the federal government into the public policy arena and created a permanent federal role in assisting the poor. During the Depression, 13 to 15 million people lost their jobs, and there was a great deal of social unrest that the government sought to quell by providing some assistance to those in need. These social conditions made acceptable the type of federal involvement that President Pierce disdained. Moreover, most of the provisions in the Social Security Act of 1935 assisted the so-called "deserving poor," those who were out of work through no fault of their own.

Consider next the enactment in 1996 of the PRWOA. The PRWOA eliminated the sixty-year-old cash entitlement provided by the Aid to Families with Dependent Children Program (AFDC). Its passage was a watershed for a conservative movement that dates back to the 1950s and that was especially strong in the 1980s when Ronald Reagan was president. The overall goal of what is referred to as the "new federalism," a term that refers to the balance of authority between the federal government and the states, is to reduce the federal presence in funding and regulating social welfare activities and restoring to the states the control over social welfare matters that was lost when the Social Security Act was passed. In addition to the philosophical concerns that federalism represents, elimination of the AFDC program was desirable because of a conviction that the program created the dependency it was meant to alleviate and because its recipients were mainly the undeserving poor.[17]

President Reagan's efforts in the 1980s to significantly reduce the federal role in social welfare were not completely successful because he lacked bipartisan support for his programs. By 1996, support for a significant change in the AFDC program came from different quarters.[18] First, as noted in chapter 5, in his 1992 presidential campaign, candidate Clinton promised to "end welfare as we know it," thus adding Democratic support to the sentiment expressed by the Republican party. At the same time, public opinion supported modifying the welfare system for several reasons, including (1) the belief that the system was subject to abuse and was actually being abused; (2) unemployment rates, the lowest since the 1960s, lent support to the proposition that work was available for those seriously in search of it[19]; and (3) the longer hours, harder work, and dual-income households experienced by many who resented those on the public dole.[20] The social context in 1996 when the AFDC program was reformed was diametrically opposite to the conditions in 1935 when the policy was enacted.

SECTION 2: THE EXECUTIVE BRANCH

At the federal and state levels, the executive branch of government participates in policymaking in three ways. The first, already referred to, occurs when the executive branch proposes a bill to the legislative branch. Second, the president or a state governor engages directly in policymaking by issuing executive orders. Third, executive agencies such as the United States Department of Health and Human Services and the United States Department of Education issue administrative laws, referred to as regulations or rules (both of these terms have the same meaning), to guide those who are responsible for implementing legislation. Rules are issued to ensure that the intent of the legislature is carried out in a uniform manner across the states.

Administrative law is of central importance to human service providers because the rules spell out and govern day-to-day matters, such as a client's eligibility for services and a worker's responsibilities. The focus in this section is on executive action at the federal level, and we begin with administrative law.

Administrative Agencies and Administrative Law

Starting with the creation of the Interstate Commerce Commission in the late nineteenth century, administrative agencies such as the Social Security Administration and the United States Department of Health and Human Services have been formed to address a variety of specific issues concerning the operation of government programs. Administrative agencies set rules that govern the behavior of states in administering programs that are funded in whole or in part by the federal government. Federal agencies may audit state behavior to ensure that the states are complying with acts of Congress and with the regulations issued by the administrative agency.

THE DELEGATION DOCTRINE

The Constitution reserves to the Congress the authority to make laws. In 1892, the Supreme Court ruled that a congressional delegation of its legislative power to an agency of the executive branch was not constitutional,[21] but the Court held that Congress does not abrogate its role as lawmaker when it delegates to the executive branch the authority to make rules that do no more than secure the result that was intended by the law.[22] In modern times, a congressional delegation of authority to an agency of the executive branch to make rules will withstand constitutional scrutiny as long as it is possible "to ascertain whether the will of Congress had been obeyed."[23]

THE ADMINISTRATIVE PROCEDURES ACT

Administrative agencies are vested with the powers otherwise reserved to the legislative, executive, and judicial branches of government. Administrative agencies do make law, a task assigned by the constitution to the Congress; they investigate violations of the law, a task assigned to the executive branch; and, along with the judiciary, they adjudicate disputes, as when clients claim that they have been denied benefits to which they are entitled. For example, the Social Security Administration operates the Supplemental Security Income (SSI) program, through which cash benefits are available to eligible people with disabilities. The Social Security Administration makes law because it creates the list of conditions that define disability and establishes the rules for determining whether a client is eligible for benefits. The Social Security Administration also has the power to investigate whether their rules are being applied in a uniform manner. And the agency acts as judge and jury when its administrative law judges hear a client's appeal of benefit denials. [24]

The extensive grant of authority by the legislative branch to the executive branch can be understood as arising from two factors. First, acts of Congress often use general terms and leave to experts in federal agencies the task of defining the terms used. Thus, when Congress passed the Americans with Disabilities Act, it declined to create a definitive list of the conditions, diseases, or infections that might constitute disabilities.[25] If a human services provider has to determine whether a client's condition, disease, or infection is a legal disability, he or she would look to federal regulations for guidance.[26]

The second factor for granting authority to the executive branch has to do with the flexibility of the regulatory process. Regulations can be changed more easily than legislation can be amended. For example, a definitive list of disabilities that was created in the late 1970s would not have identified Human Immunodeficiency Virus as a disabling condition. If adding newly discovered conditions to a list were subject to the process of congressional amendments, clients would be denied benefits until Congress had the time to go through the lengthy process described at the start of this chapter in order to amend the law. But the authorized agency was able to add Human Immunodeficiency Virus and Acquired Immunodeficiency Syndrome as disabling conditions through its regulatory powers.

When Congress creates an administrative agency, the statute that authorizes the agency to perform its functions generally contains a provision for the agency to issue rules and regulations to effectuate the agency's purpose. Administrative agencies derive their authority primarily from the Administrative Procedures Act (APA) of 1946[27] and similar statutes that exist in a majority of states. The APA establishes the framework for an administrative agency to carry out its rulemaking and adjudicatory functions. The Freedom of Information Act is part of the APA.[28]

Section 553 of the APA describes the procedures that administrative agencies must follow when they make rules that are defined as agency statements "designed to implement, interpret, or prescribe law or policy."[29] Proposed rules must appear in the *Federal Register,* which is published five days a week, at least thirty days before the rule is to take effect, and the adopted rule is published in the *Code of Federal Regulations,* which contains all administrative rules. The notice that appears in the

Federal Register identifies by name the statute that the rule is meant to implement and informs the public of any hearings that are to be held for the purpose of receiving public commentary.[30]

Advocacy groups, such as the National Association of Social Workers, the American Public Welfare Association, and the Child Welfare League of America, monitor the *Federal Register* for rules that may affect their constituents. The APA requires that the administrative agency proposing the rule provide to interested parties the chance to "participate in the rule making through submission of written data, views, or arguments with or without opportunity for oral presentation."[31] Administrative agencies are required to consider public commentary and to include in the adopted rule a brief statement of the purpose the rule is to achieve and why, in light of the feedback provided, the rule took its final form. Some statutes require that rules for implementing the statute be made "on the record," meaning that a full hearing must take place where interested parties have the opportunity to present evidence and cross examine witnesses.[32]

JUDICIAL REVIEW

Judicial review refers to the power of state as well as federal courts to determine whether acts of the legislature or the executive branch of government are constitutional and to overturn those that are not. The APA sanctions judicial review of decisions made by administrative agencies.[33]

Access to judicial review allows individuals and organizations who think that the rules issued by an administrative agency go beyond the intent of a statute to challenge the rule. However, courts will defer to the judgment of administrative agencies to interpret statutes with "broad language." For example, in 1988, the Secretary of the Department of Health and Human Services issued regulations governing the use of family planning grants that are made under Title X of the Public Health Service Act (see chapter 11).[34] The issued regulations prohibited grantees from providing any abortion counseling or referral services to their family planning patients and from engaging in any political or litigation activities designed to promote abortion rights. These regulations were challenged by recipients of Title X funding who argued that the restrictions were not authorized by Title X and that they violated the First Amendment rights of health care providers and their clients. The regulations were upheld because the Supreme Court considered them a legitimate interpretation of the broad language of the statute.[35]

Executive Orders

Executive orders are directives issued by the president or by a state governor for the purpose of making law. Their use has been referred to at several points previously in this text, including the use of such orders to end slavery (the Emancipation Proclamation, see chapter 4) and to intern people of Japanese descent during World War II (see chapter 4). The intention, subsequently discarded, of President Clinton to end discrimination against gays and lesbians in the military through an executive order was discussed in chapter 5.

The public is notified that the president intends to make law when the executive order is published in the *Federal Register,* but only orders designated as executive orders or presidential proclamations,[36] which are meant to have the force of law and which affect the general public, need be published.[37] Executive orders published in the *Register* will, once adopted, appear in the *Code of Federal Regulations.* Thus, by failing to designate a directive as an executive order or presidential proclamation, the president may without notice act in ways that have significant consequences for the public, as was made clear in the "decision making" that controlled the war in Vietnam but was not stated or revealed publicly.[38]

AUTHORITY FOR THE USE OF EXECUTIVE ORDERS

Presidents since George Washington have used the executive order to make law,[39] although nowhere in the Constitution is the president granted lawmaking power. Executives justify their lawmaking power by referring to (1) a statute in which Congress has empowered the president to act unilaterally in times of national emergency, and (2) "the powers vested [in the office of the president] by the Constitution and laws of the United States."[40]

CONDITIONS FOR USE OF THE EXECUTIVE ORDER

Doubtless there are a variety of reasons why a president decides to make law through use of the executive order rather than by proposing that Congress enact legislation. Ending the ban on gays and lesbians in the military must be seen, in part, as fulfilling a campaign promise and, in part, as acting when Congress was unlikely to do so. President Truman's executive order that desegregated the armed forces after World War II and John F. Kennedy's executive order that initiated affirmative action were also motivated by political concerns. Like the rules and regulations of administrative agencies, executive orders can be quickly issued because they bypass the lengthy committee and debate process in Congress. Some executive orders are issued of necessity to conduct the day-to-day business of government.[41]

ENDING EXECUTIVE ORDERS

A president may repeal or modify an order that he has issued, or an order may repealed by a subsequent president. Some executive orders have an expiration date, and others expire when the conditions that caused their issuance have passed. An order may be overturned after judicial review, or Congress may enact a statute that has the effect of overturning an executive order. The Supreme Court, in 1952, overturned an executive order issued by President Truman. While the country was engaged in the Korean War, steelworkers threatened to strike. Basing his order on the perceived threat to the war effort that a strike would cause, President Truman ordered the Secretary of Commerce to take control of and to operate most of the steel mills in the United States. The Court overturned the president's order because the Constitution did not confer on him the power to take control of private property, despite the emergency.[42]

SECTION 3: POLICYMAKING BY THE PUBLIC-AT-LARGE

In twenty-two states and the District of Columbia, the public is able to propose amendments to a state's constitution and to enact legislation through the mechanism of the voter initiative.[43] The voter initiative enables the public to command the passage of legislation when the legislature has not acted. It differs from the voter referendum, which confers on the electorate the power to approve or reject statutes already enacted by the legislature.[44]

Since the voter initiative is found only at the state level, interested advocates must study a state's procedural requirements for placing an initiative on the ballot. In general, states require that petitions to place an initiative on the ballot be signed by a specified percentage of state-registered voters who voted in a recent election. For example, for a proposed statute to go forth in California, the petition must be signed by a number of registered voters equal to 5 percent of those who voted for all candidates for governor at the last gubernatorial election. If the proposal is an amendment to the state constitution, the number of signatures must equal 8 percent of registered voters. If the petition passes muster, the proposal it contains is placed on the ballot at the next general election.[45] The percentage of required signatures in Colorado is the same as in California; however, whereas California determines whether the number of signatures is correct by referring to the last gubernatorial election, Colorado refers to candidates for the office of Secretary of State at the last general election.[46]

The voter initiative was a Progressive Era reform (chapter 2) whose purpose was to prevent special interest groups from unduly influencing legislative bodies and to give the public the power to counteract legislative enactments.[47] It seems, however, that the voter initiative has become the purview of special interest groups with significant amounts of money. Two examples will show why.

In 1998, the *Los Angeles Times* described the effort of Reed Hastings to mount an initiative drive for the purpose of easing the process of establishing charter schools in California. After legislators failed to show an interest in Hasting's plan, the *Times* reported that he turned to experts for advice on how to mount an initiative. He was told that one begins with at least $1 million, and then one

> Hires the best politically connected legal talent to draft the measure, gets a professional signature-gathering firm to circulate the petitions, engages a professional campaign management team and then expects to spend at least $15 million to wage the campaign.[48]

Another example is Proposition 209 in California, which ended affirmative action in that state. A federal judge reported that 693,230 valid signatures were required to get the initiative on the ballot. Since a number of signatures are invariably disqualified, such as when people who are not registered voters sign a petition, the group supporting the initiative tried to increase the number of signatures by 50 percent over the required number. According to the judge, signature gatherers had to obtain up to 7,000 signatures a day. This necessitated hiring "paid signature gatherers." Each obtained signature cost between $0.70 and $1.50. Even with volunteers gathering some of the required signatures, the cost of obtaining the requisite number of signatures and staffing a few offices from which the campaign was run can cost from $500,000 to $1.5 million. In addition, a campaign must be run to convince the voters to support the proposition. Campaigns try to reach voters through television, radio, print advertising, and direct mail. The campaign to support Proposition 209 spent $3.1 million before voting day.[49]

Initiatives are subject to legal challenges and may be overturned. In 1992, voters in Colorado approved an amendment to the state constitution that prohibited any legislative, executive, or judicial action at the state or local level that would provide civil rights protection (for example, protection against discrimination in employment or housing) based on sexual "orientation, conduct, practices or relationships." The Colorado Supreme Court and later the United States Supreme Court found that the amendment was unconstitutional under the Equal Protection clause of the Fourteenth Amendment because it denied lesbians and gays, but no other group, "the fundamental right to participate in the political process." Stated otherwise, lesbians and gays were prevented from petitioning their representatives for legislative action.[50]

As use of the voter initiative has grown so has dissatisfaction by some with this process of policymaking. In 1993, the state of Colorado set rules for use of the voter initiative by requiring that petition circulators (1) be at least 18 years old and registered to vote; (2) wear badges showing their name, their status as volunteer or paid circulator, and, if paid, the name and telephone number of their employer; and (3) attach to each petition section an affidavit showing the petition circulator's name and address. In addition, when proponents of any petition were going to file their initiative with the state, they had to disclose (a) the name, address, and county of voter registration of all paid circulators; (b) the amount of money they paid per petition signature and the total amount paid to each circulator; and (c) on a monthly basis, the names of the proponents, the name and address of each paid circulator, the name of the proposed ballot measure, and the amount of money paid and owed to each circulator during the month. The state justified these requirements as driven by administrative efficiency, a wish to detect any fraud in the initiative process, and the wish to keep voters informed on all aspects of the process from filing onward. A divided United States Supreme Court held that the measures were an unconstitutional infringement on political speech that could not be justified by the interests claimed by the state.[51]

SECTION 4: POLICYMAKING BY THE JUDICIARY

When policymaking is discussed, the judiciary does not usually come to mind as a policymaking body. Yet many of the opinions and orders that judges issue in civil matters have the same effect on the public-at-large as legislative acts, and they are, to all intents and purposes, public policy.

Our concern in this final section is with the tools that judges use to craft social policy. First, the subject of institutional reform through the mechanism of the class action suit is discussed. Next, we turn our attention to the power of state courts, using the common law, to engage in policymaking. Finally, we look at judicial interpretation of constitutional and other statutory provisions as a policymaking tool.

Before beginning, the following should be remembered from chapter 5. The federal court system is three tiered, consisting of (1) district courts, which are trial courts where criminal and civil matters are heard; (2) midlevel appellate courts, each serving a specified number of states; and (3) the Supreme Court. State court systems duplicate this three-tiered structure. States also have lower-tiered courts, such as family or juvenile courts, small claims courts, and town or village courts, but our focus does not include these lower-tiered courts.

Sources of Judicial Authority

Courts derive their authority from the federal constitution and the constitutions of the various states and from a multiplicity of statues that spell out the jurisdiction or power vested in a particular type of court to hear certain types of cases. Some courts have the jurisdiction to hear criminal matters; others, to probate wills, finalize adoptions, adjudicate delinquents, and hear other matters concerning children. Still others are courts of general jurisdiction, meaning that they may hear any type of case.

The power of federal or state courts extends to "cases and controversies,"[52] meaning that courts do not consider academic or philosophical questions nor do they address issues that have already been settled. You cannot, for example, ask a court what would happen if a client sued the federal government after she or he was denied health insurance benefits that the client believed she or he was entitled to receive. Before a court will entertain this question, the client must apply for benefits and be denied these benefits. Since courts deal only with actual events, unlike the legislature, the executive branch, or the public-at-large, they are "reactive" rather than "proactive" bodies and do not have the power to reach out for issues to address.

Institutional Reform Through Use of the Remedial Decree

Courts deal with civil and criminal matters. Civil matters involve disputes between individuals or between individuals and the state that do not focus on criminal wrongdoing. Criminal matters are concerned with determining whether a person charged with a crime is guilty and, if so, determining an appropriate punishment.

In civil matters, trial courts may remedy a wrong by providing monetary relief. When a client asks a court to find that he or she is entitled to receive cash benefits the client is asking for a monetary award. One example of this was briefly referred to earlier in this chapter when discussing the role of administrative law judges.

Trial courts also have extensive powers in equity to correct or remedy injustices. Here, the concern of the party or parties bringing suit is to change government policy and reform the practices of federal or state agents.

Suits that seek to reform institutions are usually filed as class actions, meaning that a small number of named individuals, five or six for example, claim an injury and argue that they represent an entire class of people, all of whom allegedly sustained the same injury. For instance, the named individuals may claim that they have been incarcerated in a state mental hospital under unsanitary conditions and that they have been denied any treatment to justify their incarceration. Class actions seek equitable relief, meaning that monetary compensation alone cannot right the wrong that is alleged. Equitable relief takes the form of injunctions, which are court orders telling the government to act or not to act in a certain way. The power of equitable decrees is that they may be broad, requiring the government to undertake a variety of tasks that are ordinarily delegated by legislative bodies.

Consider the following. In the early 1950s, class action suits were filed against schools in Kansas, South Carolina, Virginia, and Delaware. These suits were filed on behalf of African American children. It was argued that the education African American children received in racially segregated schools was inferior to that provided to white children and that their rights under the Equal Protection Clause of the Fourteenth Amendment were violated.

This matter was litigated over a number of years. In 1954 and 1955, the Supreme Court upheld lower court orders that mandated the desegregation of public schools.[53] Because a number of school districts did not comply with the desegregation plans established by the courts, the Supreme Court sanctioned extensive judicial involvement in restructuring educational systems to achieve the goals that desegregation sought to accomplish.[54] The Supreme Court sanctioned (1) reassignment of teachers to achieve faculty desegregation, (2) the use of white to nonwhite ratios as a starting point for setting integration goals, (3) altering school attendance zones, and (4) busing to achieve integration.

Consider a second example. In 1989, the American Civil Liberties Union sued the state of Connecticut on behalf of all "abused, neglected, abandoned and at-risk children" in the care, custody, or supervision of the State Department of Children and Family Services (DCFS). The suit challenged almost all operations of the DCFS by claiming that the structure and administration of the department violated the children's federal constitutional and statutory rights.[55] The suit resulted in a "consent decree," which is a combination of a contract between the parties and an order of the court, to settle the suit. The consent decree and resulting twelve manuals that contained regulations to guide implementation of the mandates in the decree called for changes that ranged from the creation of a training academy and detailed training requirements for all social workers to budgeting and management of the DCFS. What is important for our discussion is that the decree became the state's policy for child welfare services, as did the court orders in the school desegregation cases. These policies, which may remain in force for decades, are the product of judicial, not legislative action. In addition to court sanctioned policies to govern the operation of child welfare agencies and school systems, courts have sanctioned policies to govern the operation of prisons, mental hospitals, and police departments.[56]

The desegregation cases that began in the 1950s and the child welfare reform cases for the 1980s are examples of public policy created by remedial decrees issued by the courts. Remedial decrees are crafted in different ways. A judge may request the assistance of outside experts, including those in government agencies, in order to set standards of care. Special interest groups may also offer their services. For example, the American Psychological Association, the American Association on Mental Deficiency, and the National Legal Aid and Defenders Association, all of whom had an interest in setting standards for the care of mentally ill people, offered their services to an Alabama court to settle a lawsuit concerning treatment of people incarcerated in a state mental hospital. The court may also (1) allow defendants, such as a state department or agency, or the state legislature to devise a plan for correcting the problems identified; (2) select a remedy from those crafted by plaintiffs' and defendants' attorneys; (3) appoint a master or panel to develop a remedial plan; (4) appoint experts to devise a remedial plan; (5) order litigants to negotiate a remedy with defendants; or (6) impose its own independently arrived-at remedy.

Public notice and a fairness hearing are required before a remedy is approved. At a fairness hearing, those affected by the proposed settlement may voice their objections. The purpose of a fairness hearing is to present information to a judge, who determines whether the settlement proposal is a fair, reasonable, and adequate approach to resolving the problems identified.[57]

Common Law Policymaking

The English Common Law was brought to the early colonies and was to a significant extent the "exclusive source of law" in the states until the twentieth century, when statutory law began to replace common law policymaking.[58] Before discussing the common law and its relationship to policymaking, note that federal courts were created by the Constitution after the Republic was formed and do not have the inherited common law tradition of state courts. Scholars debate whether, outside of narrow limits, there is any such thing as federal common law.[59] The discussion that follows applies mainly to state courts.

The common law is lawmaking and policymaking by judges.[60] The rules that form the common law are derived from the aggregate of human wisdom that have been embodied over time in cases that form a "stable body of rules" for settling disputes and guiding future behavior.[61] This accumulation of rules or precedents, reported in written decisions, restrains a judge from engaging in freewheeling decision making; at the same time, the rules and precedents provide a great deal of latitude to a judge to interpret rules in light of current realities and individual beliefs. A legislative body may enact a statute that overturns a decision based on common law, but absent such statutes the common law provides courts with a significant amount of latitude to make policy.

For example, in 1974 and 1976, when California's Supreme Court decided the *Tarasoff* case (see chapter 3), it established the rule that a therapist has a duty to warn a third party who is in danger. To establish the rule, the Court referred to the common law concept of "special relationship." The Court held that a special relationship existed between a therapist and a third party that imposed on the therapist a duty to act to protect a third party.

The courts may also step in and apply the common law to develop public policy when a state legislature chooses to avoid controversial issues[62] such as the so-called "right to die" cases.[63] These cases pit the state's interest in preserving life against an individual's common law right to refuse medical treatment. New York's Court of Appeals held that a competent adult had the right to elect an appropriate course of treatment and that this right included the right to refuse treatment.[64]

Constitutional Interpretation

Interpretation of constitutional and other statutory terms is another tool used by the judiciary to formulate policy. Constitutional interpretation is the area in which the courts have the greatest degree of policymaking power, because they, and not the legislative or executive branches, have the final say in interpreting constitutions. To overturn judicial interpretation of the constitution, a legislative body has to undertake the extremely difficult and lengthy process of amending the constitution.

Consider the following example. The concept of privacy is not expressly mentioned in the federal Constitution. The right of privacy was first inferred as an aspect of "liberty" in the Due Process Clause of the Fourteenth Amendment in 1965, when the Supreme Court overturned a Connecticut statute that banned the use of contraceptives.[65] The 1965 decision is significant in several respects. First, the Court overturned a law made by elected officials and substituted its judgment for that of the legislature. This decision was not based on a violation of an express constitutional provisions where, for example, a legislature passed a law limiting freedom of speech or religion, but on the Supreme Court justices' understanding of what the concept of liberty means. Second, the 1965 decision had far-reaching consequences because it set the stage for future decisions that rested on an expanded notion of privacy, including a Court decision that overturned a Texas law banning abortions (*Roe v. Wade*),[66] and by implication any other states' laws banning abortion. It would also be used to claim that individuals have a right to privacy in their medical records.[67]

Terms such as liberty and equal protection are not self-defining. The term "liberty" in the Due Process Clause of the Fourteenth Amendment means more than freedom from confinement or physical restraint. Over time, the Supreme Court has interpreted the fundamental right to liberty to include matters as diverse as (1) a parent's right to send a child to a private school[68]; (2) the right to marry, including the right to marry a person of another race[69]; and (3) the right to procreate, use contraceptives to prevent procreation, and terminate a pregnancy.[70]

Some legal scholars think that the role of the Court in constitutional or statutory interpretation should be limited to discerning the intent of the Framers and Ratifiers of the Constitution. From this point of view, the privacy cases were wrongly decided because had the Framers intended there to be a constitutionally protected right to privacy they would have expressly included such a right in the Constitution.[71] Thus, these scholars claim, when judges interpret the Constitution to create new rights and policies for the nation, they are crossing the line into the realm of legislative behavior that the Constitution assigns to elected bodies. There is another point of view holding that discerning the intention of the Framers is not possible, especially with the more general constitutional phrases such as due process and equal protection. This point of view draws attention to the difficulty of identifying the intention of the individual Framers of the Constitution as well as the aggregate intention of all who ratified the Constitution.[72]

Judges who take an expansive view of the language in the Constitution are more likely than others to view the law in "functional" terms, meaning that their task is to ensure that the law achieves social justice rather than to merely interpret existing laws.[73] Judges who apply this point of view are less likely than others to defer to the decisions of legislative bodies, and they are not overly concerned with the idea that policy is being made by nonelected officials. A functional approach to constitutional interpretation was the dominant approach used when the Supreme Court was headed by Chief Justice Earl Warren. The Warren Court was responsible for major civil rights decisions beginning with *Brown v. Board of Education* in 1954, with *Roe v. Wade* a decade later, and continuing into the mid-1980s. By 1986, however, the composition of the Court had changed, as had the view of many justices of their right to overturn state laws that did not violate clearly established constitutional principles.[74]

CHANGING LEGAL PRECEDENT

Judges "are flesh-and-blood human beings, not demi-gods to whom objective truth has been revealed."[75] Rulings issued by judges, therefore, will be influenced by a judge's perception of her or his individual role and of the proper role of the judiciary. I do not mean to suggest that judges do not follow rules. The principle of *stare decisis*, meaning that courts adhere to established precedent, is a guiding principle for judicial action. But this general rule is not an "inexorable command."[76] In 1897, Oliver Wendell Holmes, Justice of the Massachusetts Supreme Court, reminded his brethren that

> History should be used mainly as a critical device to serve reform, allowing the jurist to identify for modification or replacement doctrines, whose original bases in policy no longer hold. . . . It is revolting to have no better reason for a rule of law than that it was laid down in the time of Henry IV."[77]

Having said this, two questions come to mind. First, "When an issue first reaches a court, what guides the creation of precedent?" and second, "What are the conditions for overturning established precedent?"

The first question has been broached. Precedent for some is found by determining what the Framers of the Constitution meant when they used certain terms, and for others precedent is determined with an eye to the social context in which a current question arises and with a wish to achieve social justice. It is important also to recognize bias or prejudice as a factor in court decisions that produce public policy. No reasonable argument could be made that the 1857 ruling of the Supreme Court, holding that the descendants of slaves could not become citizens of the United States (see chapter 4), rested on an unbiased view of citizenship, any more than reason, and not prejudice, dictated the Supreme Court's 1986 decision in *Bowers v. Hardwick*.[78] In *Bowers*, the court was asked to extend the developing privacy doctrine to conclude that a Georgia sodomy statute that had been invoked to criminalize consensual sexual behavior in the privacy of a person's home was unconstitutional. As earlier noted, the composition of the Court had changed by 1986 and no longer reflected the liberal leanings of the Warren Court. The Court refused to strike the Georgia statue and ruled that there is no constitutional right to engage in sodomy. Four justices, in a dissenting opinion authored by Justice Blackmun, stated that the *Bowers* case was not about "a fundamental right to engage in homosexual sodomy," but on "the . . . right most valued by civilized men . . . namely . . . the right to be let alone."[79] However, a majority prejudiced against homosexuality prevailed.

Turning to the second question, it is clear that courts do overturn established law. Kelso and Kelso (1996) suggest that the Supreme Court's departure from precedent can be explained in different ways. Judicial bias or prejudice may cause a judge to conclude that the case that established the precedent was wrongly decided and may influence a judge's decision to support, narrow or overrule the rule of law. Other influences may be a judge's preferences for one of the contesting parties, or for one of the lawyers, the weight a judge assigns to whether or not the precedent has become an integral part of subsequent case law, and the extent to which individuals have relied on a precedent to advance important ends in their lives.[80] Let us consider some examples.

In chapter 4, I referred to the 1896 case of *Plessy v. Ferguson*[81] in which the Supreme Court legitimized racial segregation. The Court found that legislation segregating the races was constitutional because segregation did not constitute a "badge" of slavery, which was outlawed by the Thirteenth Amendment. In 1954, in *Brown v. Board of Education,* the Court overturned *Plessy,* finding that segregated schools were unconstitutional because segregating children on the basis of race violated the Equal Protection Clause of the Fourteenth Amendment.[82] The language of the Constitution was the same in 1896 when *Plessy* was decided as in 1954 when *Brown* was decided, so interpretation alone cannot logically support both decisions, which were diametrically opposed to each other. Thus, the court must reconcile the different rulings with a reasoned argument. When *Brown* was decided, the Court distinguished the case from *Plessy* by referring to the importance of public education in the mid-1950s compared to 1896.[83] The Court's decision that the Equal Protection Clause was being violated by an action of the state was determined by the Court's understanding of changing social conditions, and *Brown v. Board of Education* is not the only example of this.[84]

The issue of sustaining precedent, based on the fact that people have relied on a court ruling, can be illustrated with reference to *Roe v Wade.* Since 1965 when that case was decided, the Supreme Court has heard a number of cases dealing with state laws that have sought, if not to overturn *Roe,* to at least narrow its scope. Through the years, the Court has made clear that (1) due process does not confer a right to governmental aid, thus upholding a ban on the use of federal funds to pay for abortions for poor women[85] and a state ban on the performance of abortions by public employees in public hospitals[86]; (2) parents cannot have an absolute veto over a minor's right to elect an abortion,[87] but a state may require that a minor who does not have parental consent to make use of a judicial bypass procedure where a court must approve the minor's choice[88]; (3) a required twenty-four-hour waiting period and informed consent provisions requiring physicians to provide certain information to a woman seeking an abortion were not constitutional[89]; and (4) a state requirement that a second physician be present at the abortion could not withstand constitutional scrutiny.[90]

In 1992, in *Planned Parenthood v. Casey*, Justice O'Connor explained the Court's unwillingness to overturn the 1965 decision, which at that time some justices thought should be overruled, by noting that

> For two decades people have . . . organized intimate relationships and made choices that define their views of themselves and their places in society, in reliance on the availability of abortion. . . . The ability of women to participate equally in the economic and social life of the Nation has been facilitated by their ability to control their reproductive lives. The Constitution serves human values, and while the effect of reliance on Roe cannot be exactly measured, neither can the certain costs of overruling Roe for people who have ordered their thinking and living around that case be dismissed.[91]

Statutory Interpretation

When the language in a statute is precise and its meaning plain, unless it goes against a state or federal constitution, courts are bound to adhere to the dictates of the legislative branch of government. But judges should

> Not try to make a fortress out of the dictionary . . . [they] must remember that statutes always have some purpose or object to accomplish, whose sympathetic and imaginative discovery is the surest guide to their meaning.[92]

When terms are vague or subject to differential meaning, courts at the federal and state level must interpret the unclear terms. Guidance must be provided to those responsible for implementing the law and to lower courts whose decisions may reflect disagreement over the meaning of key terms. If the legislative branch does not support a judicial decision, it may, rewrite the interpreted legislation to reflect more clearly its intent unless the issue involves constitutional interpretation.

Judge Judith Kaye, the Chief Judge of New York's Court of Appeals, [93] provides an example of statutory interpretation that reflects an effort to remain faithful to the intent of the legislature. In her discussion, Judge Kaye (1995) refers to a case where her court had to interpret the phrase "currently dangerous" in a statute that addressed the question, "Should a person found not responsible for attempted murder by reason of a mental condition remain confined in a secure mental health facility?" The word "currently," meaning "right now, at this moment," is clear, Judge Kaye wrote, but to apply these words strictly supports the illogical conclusion that a person who is restrained and surrounded by armed guards is not currently dangerous. Since this conclusion could not have been what the legislature intended, the court sought to give the term "currently" a meaning that would comport with common sense. The term could not permit an interpretation that current referred to the condition of a person who was confined and not dangerous for that reason.

So literal an interpretation of "currently" would have made it impossible to be faithful to the basic legislative goal of protecting the public from a potentially dangerous person.[94]

When judges undertake the task of interpreting statutes, they seek guidance from other sources. First, rather than delving into the minds of legislators to discern their intent, a court may, as in the example just provided, consider on its own the purpose of the statute and give meaning to its unclear or contradictory terms to carry out that purpose. Next, courts must consider any specific rules of interpretation that are provided by a legislative body. For example, the Americans with Disabilities Act of 1990 (ADA) uses terms similar to those found in the Vocational Rehabilitation Act (VRA) of 1975. In passing the ADA, Congress expressly stated that the body of case law developed under the VRA guides the courts in interpreting the new law in order to provide to disabled people the same standard of protection that had been applied under the VRA.[95]

Legislative history, found in the reports issued by legislative committees and subcommittees, and the minutes of the floor debates that precede passage of a bill are two other sources of information for discerning legislative intent. Some judges argue that legislative history has little value in discovering legislative intent, because it is biased and "unauthoritative."[96] For example, Justice Antonin Scalia criticizes the use of legislative history because

> As anyone familiar with modern-day drafting of congressional committee reports is well aware, the references to the cases were inserted, at best by a committee staff member on his or her own initiative, and at worst by a committee staff member at the suggestion of a lawyer-lobbyist; and the purpose of those references was not primarily to inform the Members of Congress what the bill meant . . . but rather to influence judicial construction.[97]

Nevertheless, a search for legislative intent is necessary when statutory language is vague or, as in the example of the New York state legislature's use of "currently dangerous," would produce an illogical result. Floor debates may not be useful because they are not the forum in which words are "fine tuned," but committees and their reports may be a primary source to which judges turn for a record of efforts to fine-tune language.

As Chief Judge Kaye goes on to say, judges "choose among competing policies in order to fill the gaps" and different considerations of "social welfare" and "public policy" enter into the decisions that they make.[98] In 1989, for example, the New York Court of Appeals held that the term "family" in the noneviction provisions of the New York City rent control statute of 1946 include the deceased tenant's homosexual partner.[99] The legislation did not contain a definition of family nor was there legislative history that addressed the issue of what family meant for purposes of the law, although it is reasonable to conclude that in 1946, the term family referred to people with a legal relationship. The Court reasoned that the term family

> Should not be rigidly restricted to those people who have [legally] formalized their relationship . . . The intended protection against sudden eviction should

not rest on fictitious legal distinctions or genetic history, but instead should find its foundation in the reality of family life. The . . . rent-control statute [seeks] . . . to protect occupants from the sudden loss of their homes and requires the result reached. In the context of eviction, a more realistic, and certainly equally valid, view of a family includes two adult lifetime partners whose relationship is long term and characterized by an emotional and financial commitment and interdependence.[100]

Summary

The subject of policymaking and the policymaking role of the legislative, executive, and judicial branches of government have been the focus of this chapter. Most actions taken by the different branches of government are important because they deal with ongoing government operations and the needs of the country, but they are routine and mundane in nature. However, some government policymaking marks radical shifts in the focus of government policy and affects greatly the relationship between government and the people.

Members of Congress, and the president in the issuance of executive orders, are influenced by diverse factors; much of the decision making that occurs may be explained more as political than rational. There is little proof that reason is a guiding principle in policymaking and, considering the passage in 1996 of the PRWOA, there are data to suggest that other influences have a greater impact, including (1) the personal values of the policymaker; (2) the state of the economy; and (3) the influence of special interest groups, such as PACs that provide funds to support political practices and individual candidates; "think tanks" that supply analysis of different approaches to achieving policy goals; and lobbyists who attempt to influence members of Congress through face-to-face contact.

Liberal as well as conservative groups attempt to influence legislation, and there is evidence that success or failure is tied to the group's wealth. Those groups contributing the most money having the greatest degree of influence. The influence of individuals on congressional action is expressed through contributions to PACs, think tanks, and lobbying organizations and through voting behavior, although the percentage of registered voters who actually vote is not great.

Policy is set also by the executive branch of government when administrative agencies such as the Department of Health and Human Services issue regulations to aid in policy implementation and by the president through the mechanism of the executive order. In addition to lawmaking through the issuance of rules, administrative agencies investigate violations of the law and they adjudicate disputes, for example, when a client claims denial of benefits to which the client is entitled.

Agency rulemaking is subject to the provisions of the Administrative Procedures Act and to requirements in the act that provide for the publication of proposed rules and for public commentary concerning the proposed rule.

In almost half the states the public is able to make state policy through use of the voter initiative. The voter initiative came into being during the Progressive Era of the early twentieth century. Although it was created, at least in part, to prevent special interest groups from unduly influencing legislative bodies by giving the public the power to counteract legislative enactments, the voter initiative may have become the tool of special interest groups with significant amounts of money.

Judges craft social policy by using a variety of tools, including the remedial decree, which has been used to reform institutions and organizations as varied as state child welfare systems, mental hospitals, prisons, and the police. The role of the courts in interpreting constitutions and statutes adds further to a court's policymaking power, and state court judges may use their common law power to engage in policymaking.

Judges are not immune from imposing their personal values on the process of interpreting the Constitution and statutes. They may also consider changing social conditions and not limit themselves to the letter of the law. And judges are not immune to political pressure.

The right to privacy was identified by the United States Supreme Court in 1965, and the application of the privacy doctrine to a woman's right to choose to terminate a pregnancy illustrates the Court's willingness to interpret the language of the Constitution to broaden human rights. The Court's refusal to extend the right to privacy to cover homosexual conduct occurring in the privacy of one's home expresses the limits of the Court's willingness to extend rights. Of central importance here in understanding policymaking by the courts is that neither the grant of privacy nor its limitation is a logical result of constitutional interpretation as much as it is the particular understanding of what the Constitution means by different judges at different points in history. Another example of the subjectivity that is involved in judicial decision making is the dramatic changes in court rulings over time, for example, the constitutionality of segregated schools in one era and the unconstitutionality of segregated schools in another era. Legal scholars hold different views about the role of the Court in interpreting the Constitution and carving out new rights. Some consider it a positive and necessary role, whereas others consider this role best left to legislative bodies.

The effect that a state court has in creating policy through use of its common law power was demonstrated by California's Supreme Court in the 1970s. The Court ruled that a therapist has a duty to warn a third party who is in danger. As discussed in chapter 3, a majority of states have adopted their own versions of the *Tarasoff* ruling, some by statute and some by state courts exercising their common law powers.

In conclusion, be mindful of the fact that the policymaking system described in this chapter is subject to a variety of checks and balances. For example, in chapter 5, I reported that the president nominates officials to run federal agencies as well as members of the federal courts, but that appointments are subject to congressional approval. Congress may thwart a nomination if the ideology of a nominee is not acceptable to members of Congress. Although this topic is not discussed here, note also that many state judges are elected. The decisions they make are open to public scrutiny, and their reelection may be subject to voter approval or disapproval of their decisions.

In addition, we have considered the fact that courts may overrule a legislative act that they find to be unconstitutional, and they may overrule an action of a federal agency if an issued ruling does not reflect congressional intent. Except for court decisions that rest on constitutional interpretation, Congress may overrule an unfavored decision by writing a new statute or revising an existing one. I have reported that in more than twenty states voters may act independently of the legislature through the voter initiative or referendum, but this policymaking power is subject to judicial scrutiny; a policy passed through voter initiative may be overturned if a court finds that it is not constitutional.

Finally, a choice held by Congress is its power to cut the budget of an executive agency whose actions it does not support. The budget process is the subject of the next chapter.

The Federal Budget Process

The federal budget may seem at best a dull topic, but it is of central importance to the student of social policy. The federal budget is the principal policy statement of the president of the United States, because it sets forth the president's priorities for spending and taxation. Because the budget reflects choices made among competing social programs and the values these programs represent, it is as much a statement of policy as it is a financial document. Social programs are implemented, shaped, and directed only after funds are appropriated; and whether a social program will continue is contingent on ongoing funding. The federal budget contains (1) a record of actual receipts and spending levels for the fiscal year just completed; (2) a record of current-year estimated receipts and spending; and (3) estimated receipts and spending for the upcoming fiscal year and subsequent four years.[1]

Each year, different groups compete for funds, and the budget process provides an opportunity for advocates to advance the importance of their programs and the necessity of continued program funding. Congress need not repeal legislation to allow a program to die. Failure to provide funding, at the least, reduces significantly the impact that a social program has and, at the worst, sounds the death knell for a social policy and the programs it supports.

My objective in this chapter is to familiarize you with the budget process, to do so in manner that makes the process accessible, and to acquaint you with the sources of funding for social policy. To meet these objectives, I have endeavored to simplify a very complex process.[2] We begin by considering the sources of revenue upon which the federal government relies. Then we continue with an overview of the expense categories that are found in the federal budget. The section that follows addresses sources of funding for social policy. Next, budget formulation is reviewed by beginning with the role of the executive branch and continuing with the role of

Congress. This chapter concludes with a discussion of the federal deficit and revenue control measures that have been put in place to eliminate the deficit.

Revenue Sources and Outlays

Revenue raised from individual income tax accounts for 48 percent of government revenue. Payroll taxes represent 34 percent of revenue. Payroll taxes include monies that are withheld from individual paychecks as well as employer contributions for old age retirement benefits, Medicare, and unemployment insurance. Corporate income tax represents 10 percent of revenue. Excise taxes, for example, taxes raised on alcohol, tobacco, and transportation fuels, account for 4 percent. Other sources, such as custom duties and earnings of the Federal Reserve, account for another 4 percent.[3]

As shown in Table 7.1, the lion's share of the federal budget for fiscal year 2000 (68 percent) is to be spent on mandatory programs. Mandatory programs are those whose funds are authorized by permanent laws. They include interest on the federal debt (11 percent) and spending on entitlement programs, such as Social Security (22 percent), Medicare (11 percent), Medicaid (6 percent), other programs such as the retirement program for federal employees, unemployment insurance and farm subsidies (6 percent), and means-tested entitlement programs, which include food stamps, supplemental security income, child nutrition, veteran's pensions, and the

TABLE 7.1. Estimated Federal Expenditures by Category: Fiscal Year 2000

Category	Percent of budget	
Mandatory program spending		
Social Security	22	
Interest	11	
Medicare	11	
Medicaid	6	
Other mandatory*	6	
Means-tested entitlements†	6	
Reserve pending Social Security Reform	6	
Subtotal percent mandatory spending		68
Discretionary spending		
National defense	15	
Nondefense discretionary‡	17	
Subtotal percent discretionary spending		32

Source: Office of Management and Budget, *Budget of the United States Government: Fiscal Year 2000* (Washington, D.C., March 1999).
*Federal retirement and insurance, unemployment insurance, farm subsidies.
†Food stamps, SSI, child nutrition, earned income tax credit, veteran's pensions.
‡Education, training, science, technology, housing, foreign aid, transportation.

earned income tax credit. Funding for mandatory programs is not subject to the budget process (described in the next section) and can be affected only by changes in the laws that create the programs.

For fiscal year 2000, discretionary funding accounts for approximately one-third of the federal budget (Table 7.1), and almost one-half of discretionary funds (15 percent) are allocated to national defense. Nondefense discretionary funding is allocated to a variety of programs, including social services, education, training, science, technology, housing, foreign aid, and transportation.

The president and Congress may choose how to spend discretionary funds, but these funds are capped through the year 2002, with a fiscal cap for the year 2000 set at approximately $592 million out of an approximate budget of $1.8 trillion.[4] Any changes to current legislation that would result in increases in mandatory spending or decreases in current revenue sources must be offset by spending cuts in other parts of the budget or by revenue increases. The provision in the law, called "pay-as-you-go," is designed to prevent increases in the deficit as a result of new legislative enactments.

Sources of Funding for Social Policy and Programs

Funding for policies and programs comes from different sources, including employer and employee contributions to the Social Security Trust Fund and federal and state revenues.

THE SOCIAL SECURITY TRUST FUND

Taxes that are withheld from an employee's paycheck and contributions that are made by employers are placed in the Social Security Trust Fund. The employer and employee pay a tax of 6.2 percent of the employee's income on the first $68,400 earned each year. These monies, together with interest earned on trust fund investments, support the Old Age, Survivor and Disability Insurance program (OASDI), which makes payments to eligible individuals when they retire and to certain people with disabilities.[5] A portion of the trust fund is also set aside to create the Medicare trust funds that provide health care benefits to eligible retirees (see chapter 12).

Funds that are collected from those currently employed are used to pay benefits for retirees. At the present time, it is projected that benefits will exceed income some time around the year 2013.[6]

FINANCING PROGRAMS THROUGH FEDERAL AND STATE REVENUES

Social programs may be federalized, meaning that the entire cost of the program comes from federal revenues, or program costs may be shared by government at the federal and state level.

The Supplemental Security Income program (SSI) that provides cash benefits for eligible disabled, aged, or blind people is an example of a federalized program. Created in 1972, the costs of SSI are borne by the federal government.[7] Some states supplement the basic federal grant but they are not required to do so as a condition for program participation.

In contrast, the costs of the Medicaid program, and the former Aid to Families with Dependent Children program, are shared by the federal government and the states. Unlike the SSI program, state cost-sharing is a condition for state participation in this program. The federal share is based on a state's per capita income, with the poorest states receiving the most funds. Federal reimbursement ranges from a low of 50 percent of program costs to a high of 83 percent. Under the Temporary Assistance to Needy Families Program (TANF), the program that replaced AFDC, the funding formula changes. The TANF is a capped block-grant program. Each state receives a sum of money determined by funds that the state received in recent years for the former AFDC and related programs. Supplemental grants are available to certain states (see chapter 10).[8]

Under legislation that was passed in 1995, the Congressional Budget Office analyzes proposed legislation to determine whether it contains an "unfunded mandate," meaning a requirement that is imposed by the federal government on the states without funds provided, whose cost is estimated to exceed 50 million dollars per year.[9] Any such mandate may be subject to an objection by a member of Congress and will not be passed unless a majority supports the provision. There are, however, numerous exceptions to the limitation on unfunded mandates.[10]

FUNDING FOR CIVIL RIGHTS LEGISLATION

The benefits of civil rights legislation, such as the Civil Rights Act of 1964 or the Americans with Disabilities Act, are indirect. As reported in chapter 1, unlike SSI or Medicaid policies that confer concrete benefits in the form of cash or payments for medical care, civil rights policies confer "status," because their goal is to place all members of society on an equal footing by eliminating discrimination based on personal characteristics such as race or gender.

Funding for civil rights legislation is directed to programs that seek to enforce the law on behalf of individuals and groups, for example, legal aid services and law school clinics that assist individuals such as battered women, people with Acquired Immunodeficiency Syndrome and prisoners, and to the Equal Employment Opportunities Commission (EEOC). States may also have their own agencies charged with enforcing state civil rights legislation.

The EEOC was created by the Civil Rights Act of 1964 and is charged with enforcing that act as well as the Age Discrimination in Employment Act of 1967, the Equal Pay Act of 1963, and the employment provisions of the Americans with Disabilities Act of 1990 (ADA) and the Vocational Rehabilitation Act of 1973. Enforcement activities include investigation of complaints and trying to settle complaints without litigation.

The enforcement activities of the EEOC are limited by its budget, the amount of which reflects the importance that the executive branch places on enforcement of civil rights litigation. For example, the EEOC's budget was severely restricted in the 1980s and early 1990's because of the low priority assigned to civil rights enforcement by the Reagan and Bush administrations. The EEOC lost staff during these years and has yet to recoup close to 1,000 positions that were lost. Staff losses took place during the time when the EEOC was also given an expanded mandate to enforce the 1990 ADA and the 1991 amendments to the 1964 Civil Rights Act. Complaints to the EEOC increased from approximately 72,000 in 1992 to close to 81,000 in 1997. The EEOC's enforcement activities are also limited because approximately 90 percent of the agency's budget is allocated to fixed costs, including employees' salaries and benefits and rent for office space, with only 10 percent going for litigation, technology, and staff training.[11]

FUNDING FOR JUDICIAL REFORM

When, as discussed in chapter 6, a court orders busing to enforce a school integration order a complete overhaul of a state social service system, or the deinstitutionalization of a mental hospital or prison reform, it relies on the legislative and executive branches of government to allocate the funds necessary to enforce its orders.

For example, in January 1991, the state of Connecticut settled a class action lawsuit that was brought against the State Department of Children and Family Services. The settlement required an extensive overhaul of the state system that served children and their families. Almost immediately after the settlement was approved by the court, the state legislature provided $800,000, which was used to hire staff at a juvenile detention facility, and then appropriated $6.3 million for the first full year of implementation of the settlement.[12]

The funds needed to implement a court order may be obtained by increasing taxes, through the sale of state bonds or property, and from the federal government. Unless state revenues increase, the funds that are needed to implement a court order are likely to be shifted from funds for one population to another, for example, from the elderly to children. There are limits to the amount of money that can be shifted across programs, and shifting of funds is guaranteed to meet resistance from those whose programs are cut.

To secure funds for implementing a court order requiring broad changes in Alabama's mental health system, plaintiffs asked the court to direct state agents to "sell or encumber portions of its landholdings."[13] While not ruling on this request, the judge indicated his willingness to take the necessary steps to ensure that the order was implemented. He urged the state legislature to go into special session for the purpose of appropriating funds. The judge subsequently directed defendants "to attempt to qualify its facilities and programs for Medicare and Medicaid funds and other appropriate grants."

The court may "compel some expenditures indirectly by giving the state the option of implementing the needed reforms, closing a facility, or otherwise reducing services." Pressure can be brought to bear on the legislature from special interest groups who support the reform effort, and the court may obtain commitments from defendants to seek resources from the legislature.[14]

The Budget Process: The Role of the Executive Branch

Formulation of the federal budget is a four-step process that begins in the executive branch where the budget is developed. Step two takes place when the president submits the budget to Congress for consideration. Step three is concerned with execution of the budget, and step four with the audit and control of the budget.[15]

The federal government did not have a formal system for creating the budget until 1921, when the Budget and Accounting Act was passed.[16] The act created the Office of Management and Budget (OMB) to assist the president in developing the budget, and it provides that each year the chief executive develop and forward a budget to Congress.

Each budget is named for the calendar year in which it ends, and budgets are prepared on a tight timetable shown in Figure 7.1. In preparing the president's budget, the OMB submits instructions, policy guidelines, and tentative budget ceilings to agencies and departments of the executive branch, such as the Department of Health and Human Services, the Department of Housing, and the Department of Education, to help them assemble their budgets for submission to the OMB. Agencies request funds for existing programs and for new programs, and each agency and department will advocate for the programs under its control at budget hearings held by Congress. The OMB has the authority to adjust up or down the budget requests submitted by agencies.[17]

Neither the president nor Congress has total discretion in establishing budget priorities. More than 50 percent of the budget consists of "direct spending" or mandatory spending (see Table 7.1) for the food stamp program; for entitlement programs, such as Social Security, SSI, Medicare, Medicaid, federal retirement programs, veteran's benefits, agricultural price supports, and previously made contractual commitments; and for interest payments on the federal debt.

Even where there is discretion in funding, the president and Congress must deal with various advocates. For example, in the realm of national security, communities where employment depends on governmental contracts and the existence of military bases are staunch advocates, if not for increasing budgets in the areas that affect them, then at least for maintaining budgets at current levels.

The Budget Process: The Role of Congress

Although the federal budget may be the principal policy statement of the president, the federal Constitution provides that only Congress has the power to raise taxes

FIGURE 7.1. Federal budget timetable.

Budget Name	The Budget of the United States Government for FY 1999
Period Covered	October 1, 1998 to September 30, 1999
Submitted to Congress	February 1998

and to authorize spending for the defense and general welfare of the United States, thus precluding unilateral action by the president to allocate funds. Congress may accept, reject, or modify the president's budget, which is, in the final analysis, a request to Congress for funds.[18]

To understand the congressional budget process, we must first consider the authority of congressional committees. Recall that in chapter 6 I said that when a bill is introduced in either the House or the Senate, it is assigned to an appropriate committee. The proposed legislation may be assigned to a subcommittee. I noted also that committee deliberations take account of the cost of proposed legislation. Legislation that survives the committee process will contain a section *authorizing* funds to carry out the purpose of the legislation. The section authorizing funds may set a ceiling; for example, legislation providing grants to the states for certain child welfare services contains the following authorization language:

> For the purpose of enabling the United States, through the Secretary, to cooperate with State public welfare agencies in establishing, extending, and strengthening child welfare services, there is authorized to be appropriated for each fiscal year the sum of $325,000,000.[19]

As an alternative to a ceiling, the section that authorizes funding for education of children with disabilities provides that

> For the purposes of carrying out the provisions of this section, there are authorized to be appropriated such sums as may be necessary.[20]

But because funds are authorized does not mean that funds will be *appropriated*. Despite the fact that the authorizing section is a piece of legislation, a program may not be funded, or it may be underfunded. Congress must support a program through *appropriations* that are made in the budget.

The structure of the congressional budget process is found in the Congressional Budget Act of 1974.[21] After Congress receives the president's budget, it is reviewed and analyzed by the Congressional Budget Office (CBO), which provides a report on the budget to the House. The budget act requires that the House and Senate adopt a concurrent budget resolution on or before April 15 of each year.[22] The concurrent resolution does not require the president's signature and it does not have the force of law.

The concurrent budget resolution is a directive that establishes a framework for spending for the current fiscal year and the next four years, specifies anticipated revenues, and identifies any budget surplus or deficit.[23] The resolution may specify spending targets for each committee charged with reviewing and recommending funding levels. Targets seek to achieve specified levels of savings to ensure that spending conforms to anticipated revenues. The instructions that are contained in the resolution provide a means for directing committees to make changes in mandatory programs.

The House Appropriations Committee refers the budget to appropriations subcommittees that undertake their work pursuant to the directives in the budget resolution. Subcommittees hold hearings at which agency officials, interest groups, and others testify about increases or decreases in spending and make their budget recommendations to the House Appropriations Committee. As a rule, the House Appropriations Committee adopts subcommittee recommendations, and the full House usually accepts without change the recommendation of the House Appropriations Committee.

The budget is divided into twenty budget functions, seventeen of which focus on broad areas of national need. Three functions deal with interest, receipts, and allowances for future budgets and do not directly address any specific national need.[24] Functional categories include health; transportation; income security; and education, training, employment, and social services. Functional categories may be subdivided. For example, the functional category of health includes the subfunctions of health care services and health research and training.[25]

The Senate Appropriations Committee receives appropriations bills from the House. The Senate review does not involve an in-depth examination of the overall budget, but focuses instead on items in dispute and on "appeals" from agencies whose budgets have been cut and who are seeking restoration.[26] As is the case with any legislation, differences between House and Senate versions of the budget are resolved by conference committee (see chapter 6).

PRESIDENTIAL ACTION

After Congress adopts a budget resolution, it is sent to the president who may veto the budget and cause Congress to make revisions if it cannot override a presidential veto. If the president signs the budget, it is enacted as law and creates the legal authority to obligate and ultimately spend funds. Typically, the total amount appropriated by Congress does not deviate from the budget originally submitted by the president by more than 3 or 4 percent.

Failure of the Congress and the president to reach a budget agreement before the end of the fiscal year results in the shutting down of federal agencies, with the exception of those whose work involves protection of human life or the protection of property, unless Congress passes a continuing resolution that allows the agency to operate on the basis of the previous year's budget or some other agreed-upon level.

BUDGET EXECUTION AND AUDIT AND CONTROL

Budget execution involves the distribution of funds to agencies and departments and is the third step in the budget process. The fourth step, audit and control, holds each federal agency responsible for complying with the provisions in the statutes that created the programs for which the agencies bear responsibility.

Audit and control are carried out under two laws. The Inspector General Act of 1978 establishes "agency inspectors general" to provide policy direction and to conduct, supervise, and coordinate audits and investigations related to agency programs and operations. The Chief Financial Officers Act of 1990 establishes "agency chief financial officers" to oversee all financial management activities related to agency programs and operations.[27] The OMB also oversees agency efforts to obtain program objectives, and the United States General Accounting Office audits, examines, and evaluates government programs.

Federal Expenditures and the Federal Deficit

The federal budget was in balance in 1940 and remained so through the mid-1960s, except when the costs associated with World War II and the Korean War resulted in deficits. As shown in Table 7.2, defense spending increased from $1.6 million in 1940 to $83 million in 1945. This increase was followed by a significant drop in 1948 to $9.1 million, with a dramatic increase in the early 1950s to $52.8 million when the United States became involved in the Korean conflict.

Except for a drop in defense spending between 1953, when such spending was close to $53 million, and 1960, when it dropped to $48 million, spending on national defense increased steadily after 1960, with a sharp jump from $79 million in 1972 to $134 million in 1980, almost doubling between 1980 and 1985 to approximately $253 million in the latter year.

Deficit spending began in the late 1960s and early 1970s. The rise coincided with increases in military expenditures and was helped along by an increased role by the federal government in funding social programs (see Table 7.2). The deficit continued to grow with only slight deviations until approximately 1990, when it reached approximately $300 billion.

Increases in federal expenditures for social programs began after 1965 for the following reasons:

> The federal programs that provide medical assistance to the elderly, Medicare, and to the poor, Medicaid, began in the mid-1960s. Their costs steadily increased. For example, the Medicare program began modestly with outlays of less than 1 billion dollars in fiscal year 1966, growing to 7.5 billion dollars in 1972, more than quadrupled to 32 billion dollars in 1980, and more than doubled to 66 billion dollars in 1985.

> The Supplemental Security Income Program (SSI) that provides cash assistance to individuals with disabilities was established in 1972 and began to make payments in 1974 when program costs were 5.2 billion dollars. By 1995, program costs had risen to $27 billion. [28]

Federal costs for the AFDC that provided income to dependent children and their caretakers increased from $2.7 million in 1970 to $7.1 million in 1980 to $13.7 million in 1995.[29]

> Individuals who are eligible for SSI and who were eligible for AFDC were automatically eligible for medical benefits under the Medicaid Program. In 1995, the latest year for which data is available, 87 percent of AFDC households also received food stamps, as did 50 percent of SSI households. Increases in SSI and AFDC created automatic expenditures in other programs categories.[30]

TABLE 7.2. Federal Expenditures for Selected Budget Functions—Selected Years (1940–1998) and Estimates for 2000.

Function	1940	1945	1948	1953	1960	1966	1972	1980	1985	1990	1995	1998	2000 (Estimate)
Defense	1.6	83.0	9.1	52.8	48.1	58.4	79.1	134.0	252.7	299.3	272.0	268.5	274.0
Education and social services	2.0	0.1	0.2	0.4	1.0	4.4	12.5	32.0	29.3	38.8	54.2	55.0	63.3
Health*	0.06	0.2	0.2	0.3	0.8	2.5	8.7	23.2	33.5	57.7	115.4	131.4	152.2
Medicare		—	—	—	—	0.06	7.5	32.1	66.0	98.1	159.8	192.8	216.6
Income security†	1.5	1.1	2.5	3.8	7.3	9.7	27.6	86.6	128.2	147.0	220.4	233.2	258.0
Social Security	0.03	0.3	0.6	2.7	11.6	20.1	40.1	118.5	189.0	248.6	335.8	379.2	408.6
Veteran's benefits	0.6	0.1	6.5	4.5	5.4	5.9	10.7	21.1	26.2	29.0	37.0	41.8	44.0
Physical resources‡	2.3	1.7	2.2	4.0	8.0	13.4	19.5	66.0	57.0	126.0	59.2	74.7	84.8
Interest on debt	0.9	3.1	4.3	5.2	6.9	9.4	15.5	52.5	129.5	184.2	232.2	243.4	215.1
Other functions§	0.8	4.4	5.9	5.8	7.8	17.0	18.8	45.0	68.2	60.8	73.0	80.0	94.4
Undistributed offsetting receipts‖	−0.3	−1.3	−1.6	−3.6	−4.8	−6.5	−9.6	−20.0	−32.7	−36.6	−44.5	−47.2	−45.6
Total	9.5	93.0	29.8	76.0	92.1	134.4	230.4	591.0	946.9	1,253.0	1,515.0	1,652.8	1,765.4

Source: Data from Office of Management and Budget, *Budget of the United States Government: Fiscal Year 2000* (Washington, D.C., March 1999).

Note: In millions of dollars.

*Includes Medicaid.

†Includes supplemental security income, AFDC, food stamps, unemployment insurance, and federal employee retirement benefits.

‡Includes energy, natural resources and environment, commerce, transportation, and community and regional development.

§Includes international affairs, general science, space and technology, agriculture, administration of justice, and general government.

‖Includes rents and royalties from the Outer Continental Shelf, sale of major assets, and employer share of employee retirement payments. Separately listed by the OMB because this income does not belong to any one functional category.

Balancing the Budget

Balancing the federal budget and reducing the federal deficit requires the will to do so. Congress is free to reduce spending or to increase taxes and to apply a budget surplus to deficit reduction. Motivated by an interest in appeasing various special interest groups (see chapter 6), Congress has been reluctant to take the required actions. Instead, members of Congress have tried to create mechanisms that force them to balance the budget. The mechanisms include amending the federal constitution to require a balanced budget, granting to the president the line-item veto so that the president can unilaterally reduce the budget, and enacting statutes to force Congress to produce a balanced budget.

AMENDING THE CONSTITUTION TO ACHIEVE A BALANCED BUDGET

The first proposal to amend the Constitution to require that Congress balance the federal budget was made in 1936 by Representative Harold Knutson of Minnesota. Proposals to amend the Constitution have been repeated many times since then, with Congress nearly achieving its goal in 1995, when for the first time in history, the House of Representatives passed the Balanced-Budget Amendment. The amendment went down to failure in the Senate by a single vote.[31]

THE LINE-ITEM VETO

Article I, Section Seven, of the Constitution (the Presentment Clause) provides that when the president receives a bill from the Congress, the president may (1) sign the bill; (2) veto the bill; (3) fail to act for 10 days, after which the bill becomes law; or (4) dispose of the bill with a "pocket veto," which occurs if congressional adjournment prevents the return of the bill.

In 1996, Congress passed the Line-Item Veto Act, which empowered the president to cancel items of discretionary spending and, in so doing, to reduce the amount of federal budget. In the spring of 1998, the Supreme Court, in *Clinton v. City of New York*,[32] ruled that the line-item veto violated the Presentment Clause, because it would allow the president to make law by selectively supporting some portions of a bill while vetoing other portions and to do so without congressional approval in violation of the lawmaking power given to Congress in Article I of the Constitution.

STATUTORY MEANS TO REDUCE THE DEFICIT

In December 1985 Congress adopted and the president signed the Balanced Budget and Emergency Deficit Control Act (commonly referred to as the Gramm-Rudman-Hollings Act (GRH)).[33] Passage of GRH was motivated by a desire to balance the budget, on the one hand, and by an unwillingness to voluntarily make the spending cuts or to raise the taxes that would be required to do so, on the other. The GRH set targets for reducing the deficit and specified automatic deficit reduction procedures, if the targets were not met. By the late 1980s, it became clear that the deficit reduction targets would not be met.[34]

The Budget Enforcement Act of 1990 (BEA) amended the GRH.[35] The BEA (1) substituted spending caps for deficit targets for discretionary programs; (2) established the "pay-as-you-go" requirement under which spending increases for entitlement programs or legislation that decreases revenues must be offset with legislation that cuts other statutory entitlements or raises revenues elsewhere; and (3) did not promise to produce a balanced budget. The BEA provides for spending increases in the event of an emergency, such as a war or natural disaster. Under emergency conditions, the budget is exempt from the budget caps and sequestration, meaning the cancellation of discretionary programs that is otherwise required, is suspended.[36]

The logic of the BEA was straightforward: if Congress and the president complied with their own rules and stayed within the spending caps and the "pay-as-you-go" requirements, outlays would stay within prescribed limits and a sequester would never be necessary.[37] As Table 7.2 shows, the budget was balanced in fiscal year 1996 at a time when the economy was especially strong. The Bureau of Labor Statistics reports that from 1997 to 1998, the rate of unemployment was 4.5 percent, the lowest rate that the nation experienced since 1969.[38] What will occur if the economy moves into a recession with an increased demand for social welfare benefits remains to be seen.

Summary

The federal budget is a policy statement of the executive branch of government, but the final federal budget reflects a compromise between the executive and legislative branches, with only Congress constitutionally permitted to raise taxes and to authorize expenditures.

Two-thirds of the federal budget is allocated to mandatory programs, and these funds cannot be controlled by either the president or the Congress absent a change in the legislation that authorized the program. Advocates for social programs compete for the one-third of the budget that is set aside as discretionary funding. Finally, existing legislation mandates that the federal budget be balanced, and this goal was accomplished in 1996.

PART III

Many of the benefits that social policy makes available require that applicants demonstrate that they are poor. Thus we begin this section with a discussion of poverty, with a definition of the concept; a discussion of how it is measured, and a review of who is poor (chapter 8). A major goal of social policy is the prevention, reduction, or elimination of poverty and the alleviation of some of poverty's harshest effects, such as hunger, homelessness, and lack of medical care. The policies that seek to remedy these problems are discussed in part III. Chapter 9 begins with an overview of the events that led to the passage of the Social Security Act and continues with a review of four programs that provide cash to workers at retirement or in the event of disability, who become unemployed through no fault of their own, who sustain on-the-job injuries, and whose earned income is low enough to entitle them to a tax credit.

Chapter 10 covers several cash assistance programs that provide aid unrelated to a recipient's work history. Included are the Temporary Assistance to Needy Families Program and its predecessor, the Aid to Families with Dependent Children Program; the Supplemental Security Income Program that assists people with disabilities; and general assistance programs that the states operate to provide aid to able-bodied adults who do not have children.

Some of the benefits provided by social policy are called "in-kind," meaning that the benefits may be used for a specific purpose, for example, food stamps that can be redeemed only for a specified range of food items and assistance with housing (chapter 11) and payments for medical services that are made through the Medicare and Medicaid programs (chapter 12).

In chapter 13, we turn our attention to civil rights statutes that were enacted to eliminate discrimination in employment, housing, and education and to ensure nondiscriminatory access to services by providing avenues of legal redress for people who are subject to discrimination. Unlike policies that confer cash and in-kind benefits, civil rights policies confer "status," because their goal is to place all members of society on an equal footing by eliminating race- or gender-based discrimination and, in some instances, discrimination that is based on sexual orientation.

CHAPTER 8

Poverty

Many of the clients served by social workers and other human services providers are poor. For some people, their sole reason for going to a social service agency is to alleviate their poverty by applying for government support in the form of cash assistance, food stamps, medical aid, and other types of concrete assistance. Others who are poor may be receiving all of the government benefits for which they are eligible, and still others, although poor, may be employed and not eligible for any government benefits. For people who are not seeking concrete aid, poverty may exacerbate the problems for which they are seeking help, such as marital problems or parent-and-child problems, or personal matters such as depression and loneliness.

Because poverty is central to the lives of many social work clients, it is important to understand how poverty is defined and measured, to know who is poor, and to be familiar with that factors that are said to cause poverty.

The concept of poverty can be rendered simple or complex depending upon how it is defined. A simple definition begins with agreement on what constitutes the necessities of life. These would include food, clothing, and shelter. Other items such as the costs of child care and employment-related transportation may be included. The cost of necessities and other items must be ascertained, and whether to make adjustments for cost-of-living differences around the country and for family size and age of family members must be decided. This decision-making process yields a figure that poverty analysts call the "threshold," "poverty line," or "need standard," which is a sum of money necessary to sustain a minimum standard of living. Poor people are those whose lack the money to obtain the necessities. Using information solicited from the public-at-large, the number of people who are poor can be calculated by determining the number whose income falls below the threshold. The threshold sum can be routinely adjusted for inflation.

The concept of poverty becomes complex when people attempt to take into account psychological factors or what are often considered to be quality-of-life matters. For example, can and should a poverty threshold account for the toll that is exacted on people who live in neighborhoods where the crime rate is high, where one cannot go out alone after dark, or where one is fearful of allowing children to play outside unattended at any time? How does one calculate the costs of knowing that a child's future is compromised because the school she or he attends offers an inferior education relative to that received by children who live in neighborhoods where family income is high? And what of the toll exacted by not having the means to fill medical prescriptions or visit a primary care physician, or by having to choose whether to buy food or to pay rent on time when one has missed a few days of work?

Ultimately, the way that a society chooses to define poverty and the methods that are used to count the poor are "political" decisions in the sense that they are influenced by concerns about the social and personal consequences that would result from any definition or measurement tool that is chosen. For example, in chapter 4 I referred to the concept of "less eligibility," meaning that the poor should not receive more financial assistance than the lowest wage paid to a laborer. This kind of decision making reflects the dual concern that able-bodied people should not be rewarded for their decision to not work and that people will forgo paid employment if welfare benefits exceed employment-based wages.

Consider another example. In the early 1970s, a decision was made to adjust social security payments to the elderly to reflect changes in the cost of living (a process called "indexing"). Also in the early 1970s, the Supplemental Security Income Program (SSI), which supplements the income of certain elderly people, was enacted by Congress. Indexing combined with the additional income available from the SSI program resulted in a significant decrease in poverty among people aged sixty-five and older. The percent of elderly people in poverty was reduced from approximately 19 percent in 1972 to 15 percent in 1982 to 10.5 percent in 1999. By contrast, payments to poor children under the Aid to Families with Dependent Children Program (AFDC) were not indexed. The percent of children younger than eighteen years of age living in poverty increased from 15 percent of children in 1972 to 23 percent in 1982, with a drop to 18.9 percent in 1998.[1] The decision not to index payments to children and their caretakers, like the decision to keep welfare payments below what a wage earner would make, reflects a concern that higher payments will reward people for behavior that is deemed socially undesirable, such as having children without benefit of marriage and thereby reinforcing men for not supporting their children coupled with the concern that people will forgo paid employment if welfare benefits exceed employment-based wages.

The organization of this chapter is as follows. We begin with a series of questions, including "How is poverty defined and measured?" and "Are the data that describe the poverty status of the American population accurate?" Some of the definitions that are used by the United States Census Bureau when it gathers and reports data are then discussed and followed by the question, "What are the characteristics of poor people in the United States?" Next, we look at the relationship between employment and poverty; and then some theoretical explanations for poverty are reviewed.

Defining Poverty

Poverty may be defined as "fixed" or "relative." We start with the meaning of "fixed poverty" because that is the standard used in the United States. Poverty is defined by the government as economic deprivation, meaning the poor are those who lack the resources to meet basic needs.[2] The Social Security Administration first published poverty statistics in the early 1960s and used a poverty measure that was developed by a staff economist named Mollie Orshansky.[3]

At the time the formula was developed, approximately one-third of income was spent on food. To determine the poverty threshold, the United States Department of Agriculture calculated the cost of a minimum adequate diet for a "reference family," which was a family of four. This figure was adjusted for families of different size; the food needs of children under eighteen and of adults over sixty-five were taken into account, and adjustments were made to reflect the economies of scale that occur in large families. The cost of this "food basket," as it is commonly called, is annually adjusted to reflect changes in the Consumer Price Index. The resulting figure was multiplied by three to determine the poverty threshold.

The poverty threshold, in addition to providing a baseline figure against which income is measured and the number of poor people determined, is used also to determine eligibility for means-tested programs such as food stamps, Head Start, legal services, and maternal and child health.

"Relative" as opposed to "fixed" definitions of poverty establish a poverty threshold in relation to either family expenditures or family income. Although the fixed measure currently in use is expenditure based, it considers only food expenses and assumes that the factor of three by which the food costs are multiplied will take account of other expenses. Unlike a true expenditure model, the Orshansky formula is not routinely updated to take account of actual expenditures.

A more realistic expenditure model would be based on data that are gathered from the public instead of from a "reference family" model and would be adjusted on a regular basis to take account of the shifting percentage of family income spent on various expenditures. For example, such a model would take account of the fact that food now represents only one-seventh of a family's budget in comparison to the one-third it represented in the mid-1900s, and it would reflect the relative portions of income spent on different goods and services. Relative thresholds would be updated each year with reference to actual expenditures, thus reflecting real changes in patterns of consumption.[4]

A poverty measure that is income based rather than expenditure based views individual or family income in relation to the income of others and sets a cutoff point in the income distribution that defines poverty for families of different size. Consider the data in Figure 8.1, which show the percent of aggregate income that is received by the population divided into quintiles for six time periods between 1947 and 1998. From a relative perspective, the purchasing power represented by

FIGURE 8.1. Shares of aggregate income received by top and bottom fifths of the population.

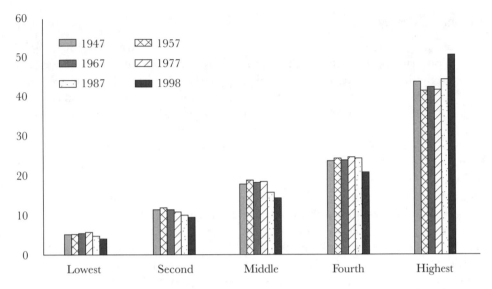

Source: U.S. Census Bureau, *Money Income in the United States,* (Washington, D.C.: U.S. Department of Commerce, 1999).

income stands, to some degree, for the place or status that an individual holds in society, especially in a society where status is often linked with consumption of goods and services.

As the data in Figure 8.1 show, the percent of aggregate income received by the top-fifth of the population is disproportionately high and has grown at a rapid pace since 1977. The percent of aggregate income received by the lowest fifth grew slightly until 1977, after which time it dropped from a high of approximately 5.2 percent to a 1998 low of 4.2 percent. For those in the second quintile, the percent of aggregate income has dropped steadily since 1957; and for those in the middle and fourth quintiles, there were fluctuations in the years until 1977, since which time the percentage of aggregate income has dropped. In 1998, the share of aggregate income received by the top fifth increased dramatically to 49.2 percent of income received.

Those supporting a relative view of poverty argue for establishing the poverty threshold as a percentage of the median family income, thereby judging poverty in relation to the resources of other members of society. This approach assumes that those members of society with resources significantly below the resources of others are poor, even through they may have sufficient income for food, clothing, and shelter. They are poor because they are not able to participate fully in society.

A relative approach is highly subjective because selection of a cutoff point is arbitrary and not based on knowledge of patterns of expenditure. It poses difficulties in standardizing a poverty rate, because median family income is subject to significant shifts in the business cycle and periodic recessions. Income shifts may be attributable to whether teenagers are working and are subject to fluctuations in a second wage-earners salary.[5]

Gathering Data to Determine How Many People Are Poor

Since 1947, answers to questions such as "What is the median family income?" "How has it changed?" "How many people are in poverty?" and "What impact, if any, have government programs had in reducing poverty?" have been derived from information that is compiled by the United States Census Bureau (CB) when it conducts its Current Population Survey (CPS).[6] The survey is conducted in March of each year. Field representatives of the CB interview, personally or by phone, a sample of approximately 50,000 households across the nation. A household is defined as a housing unit with all of its residents, whether or not they are related. Questions are asked about participation in the labor force, income earned in the year preceding the survey (questions asked in March 1999 concern income in March 1998), health insurance status, and participation in government programs during the prior year.

Data are collected from the civilian, noninstitutionalized population living in the fifty states and the District of Columbia and from members of the armed forces who are living in the United States not on a military base unless they are living on base with their families.

Each person in the sample who is fifteen years or older is asked about before-tax income from a variety of sources, including (1) earned and unearned income from interest, dividends, rents, royalties, and estates and trusts; (2) unemployment compensation; (3) workers' compensation; (4) social security payments, other retirement income, and veteran's benefits; (5) any form of public assistance including income from the Temporary Assistance to Needy Families Program (TANF), disability income, or general assistance; (6) educational assistance; (7) alimony; (8) child support; (9) financial assistance from outside the household; and (10) any other income. Questions do not include information concerning noncash benefits received, such as food stamps, health insurance benefits, rent-free housing, and goods produced and consumed on the farm. Also, employer payments for retirement, medical care, and educational expenses are not counted, nor are capital gains, borrowed money, tax refunds, gifts, and lump-sum inheritances.

With these data in hand, the number of people who are living in poverty is calculated by comparing resources with the baseline threshold derived from the poverty index developed by Mollie Orshansky.

DO POVERTY DATA ACCURATELY MEASURE POVERTY?

The CPS was designed primarily to compile data on employment and unemployment. Compiling accurate information concerning income and other measures of wealth is a secondary purpose and, in the opinion of some analysts, the CPS does not provide accurate and reliable information concerning the resources that define income, wealth, and poverty.[7] Acquired information concerning money income and earnings is considered "relatively good" when judged against other measures, but this is not so for income from transfer programs such as SSI, which are said to be underestimated by as much as 20 percent, and for property income, approximately 55 percent of which is not identified. The CB is experimenting with alternatives to the CPS.[8]

Dissatisfaction with the way that poverty is measured goes beyond the use of the CPS to gather data to include the continued use of the food-basket formula as a baseline against which resources are measured and the number of people in poverty is determined. As already mentioned, food now represents only one-seventh of a family's budget, not the one-third that it represented in the 1950s, and continued use of the one-third multiplier grossly underestimates the cost of living.[9]

Additional concerns are that (1) the need standard yielded by application of the Orshansky formula does not take into account differences in the cost of living in different regions of the country[10]; (2) the definition of poverty rests on assumptions about needed income that do not take into account patterns of expenditure and will count as poor anyone whose income is below the threshold even if their consumption, through such practices as borrowing, depleting savings, or using credit cards, is high; (3) benefits such as food stamps, housing subsidies, and health insurance are not counted as income, nor are other resources such as credit, savings, and gifts; (4) child care costs are not considered in the multiplier nor are child support payments made by a noncustodial parent; (5) lifestyle differences are not taken into account, for example, a retired couple with an annual income of $15,000 whose mortgage is paid off and without work-related expenses is given the same determination as a single parent with children whose income is similar.[11]

AN ALTERNATIVE APPROACH TO MEASURING POVERTY

An alternative approach to measuring poverty first requires that a decision be made as to how to define family resources: whether to focus on income or expenditures. The National Academy of Sciences argues that patterns of expenditures and consumption provide a better measure of material wealth and deprivation than does knowledge of income.[12] Data on expenditures are available from the Department of Labor's Consumer Expenditure Survey (CES), which compiles data each year on the spending patterns of a sample of American households. However, the United States General Accounting Office (GAO) has concluded that CES data are not adequate for measuring poverty because of the small sample size and low response rate. Also, the costs of administering the surveys and analyzing the data are high because participants are interviewed and required to keep diaries with detailed records of items they purchase, such as food, household supplies, and medicines.

Adopting an alternative approach to measuring poverty also requires consensus on what constitutes necessities beyond food, clothing, and shelter. For example, child care may be a necessity for a majority of American families, and, unless provided by government, out-of-pocket expenses such as this would probably have to be taken into account in ascertaining a family budget.

The Panel on Poverty and Family Assistance of the National Academy of Sciences has proposed an alternative to the Orshansky model (Table 8.1). With the

TABLE 8.1. Proposed and Alternative Measures for Calculating a Poverty Threshold

Element	Proposed measure	Current measure
Standard of need	Budget for food, clothing, shelter (includes utilities) and an added amount for other needs (e.g., household supplies, personal care, non-work-related transportation)	Food times a large multiplier for all other expenses
Method for calculation	Consumer expenditures, updated annually	Food basket as a baseline updated annually
Geographic	Adjusted for region of the country	No adjustment
Family resources*	Sum of money from all sources plus in-kind benefits minus expenses including taxes, child care, and other work-related expenses (in families with no stay-at-home adult), child-support payments and out-of-pocket medical costs, including health insurance premiums	Gross (before tax) money income from all sources
Economic unit	Families (including cohabiting couples) and unrelated individuals	Families and unrelated individuals

Source: Panel on Poverty and Family Assistance, Committee on National Statistics of the National Research Council, *Measuring Poverty: A New Approach* (Washington, D.C.: National Academy Press, 1996), 40–41, 66.

*Calculate as follows: (a) estimate gross money from all public and private sources for a family or unrelated individual (this is income in the Orshansky measure); (b) add the value of near-money nonmedical in-kind benefits, such as food stamps, subsidized housing, school lunches, and home energy assistance; (c) deduct out-of-pocket medical care, including health insurance premiums; (d) deduct income taxes and Social Security payroll taxes; (e) for families in which all parents work, deduct actual child care costs, per week worked, not to exceed the earnings of the parent with the lower earning or a cap that is adjusted annually for inflation; (f) for each working adult, deduct a flat amount per week worked (adjusted for inflation, not to exceed earnings) to account for work-related transportation and miscellaneous expenses; and (g) deduct child support payments from the income of the payer.

academy's model, poverty would be calculated by using patterns of expenditures but with the addition of items, such as household supplies and personal care items, to the standard of need. Differences in the cost of living based on geographic variation are taken into account, and the definition of family resources is broadened. Rather than defining resources as before-tax income, the proposed model adds in-kind benefits (e.g., food stamps and housing allowances) and deducts expenses (e.g., child care, child support payments, and out-of-pocket medical costs). Finally, the definition of family is broadened by taking into account the combined resources of cohabiting couples.

Proponents of reformulating the approach to defining poverty have difficulty in agreeing on how to factor in health care benefits provided by Medicaid and Medicare programs.[13] A family that receives food stamps, for example, has more disposable cash from a TANF or SSI benefit than a family without food stamps. Because the value of food stamps is constant, varying only by family size, their value is easily taken into account (see chapter 11). By contrast, medical benefits are not directly fungible except for those that replace out-of-pocket expenses. For example, health insurance that would pay for prescription medication or a doctor's visit, which might otherwise come from available cash, have a direct bearing on available cash in the same way as food stamps do.

The difficulty in taking medical benefits into account is how to allow for high-cost care. For example, if an individual had surgery costing $40,000, despite the enormous value of such a benefit, it would make little sense to add $40,000 to the individual's income, since that money is not otherwise available. A further difficulty with calculating medical benefits is that they are not used by all families in any year.

THE EFFECT OF DIFFERENT MEASURES ON POVERTY STATISTICS

The data in Table 8.2 show how the number of people in poverty will fluctuate when different factors are taken into account. In considering these data, bear in mind that the current definition of poverty counts gross wages as income and therefore includes monies that will be deducted as taxes and that are not available for consumption.

Definition one is the 1997 official poverty measure. In 1997, 13.3 percent of the population was poor. This datum provides a baseline to which different factors are added or subtracted, and the fluctuations in the number and percent of people in poverty are shown. From this official measure, the second definition subtracts from income government cash benefits, such as social security and workers' compensation. The poverty rate increases significantly, from 13.3 percent to 21 percent, reflecting the value of government transfers. Definition three adds capital gains and the value of an employers' contributions for health insurance, resulting in a decrease in the poverty rate to 20.3 percent. The next three definitions differ in the application of taxes. Definition four increases the population in poverty to 21.4 percent by excluding from income social security payroll and federal income taxes. Definition five takes account of the earned income tax credit and decreases the percent of people in poverty to 20 percent. In definition six, state income tax is deducted, increasing the percentage in poverty slightly to 20.1 percent.

TABLE 8.2. The Cumulative Effect of Taxes and Transfers on Poverty Estimates: 1997 (in Thousands)

	Income definitions	Number below poverty	Poverty rate
Definition 1	Current measure	35,574	13.3
Definition 2	Definition 1 less government cash transfers*	56,390	21.0
Definition 3	Definition 2 plus capital gains and employee health benefits	54,573	20.3
Definition 4	Definition 3 less social security payroll and federal income tax	57,520	21.4
Definition 5	Definition 4 plus the earned income tax credit	53,601	20.0
Definition 6	Definition 5 less state income tax	54,036	20.1
Definition 7	Definition 6 plus government cash transfers	35,849	13.4
Definition 8	Definition 7 plus the value of Medicare and school lunch	34,748	12.9
Definition 9	Definition 8 plus the value of Medicaid and other means-tested government noncash transfers	26,940	10.0

Source: U.S. Census Bureau, *Current Population Survey Reports: Poverty in the United States: 1997* (Washington, D.C., 1998).
*Includes non-means-tested transfers such as social security payments and unemployment compensation.

The last three definitions add back government benefits. Definition seven adds in government cash transfers and brings the poverty rate almost back to the rate under the current definition (13.3 percent compared to 13.4 percent). Definition eight adds the value of school lunches and an assigned value for Medicare, decreasing the percent of the population in poverty to 12.9 percent. Definition nine assigns a value for Medicaid and other means-tested noncash transfers, such as food stamps and housing subsidies, reducing the percent of the population in poverty to a low of 10 percent.

Census Bureau Definitions

Information compiled by the CB is the source of data reported in this chapter. The CB reports income data for families, individuals, and households. Interpreting CB data requires that the reader be familiar with the definitions of family, individual, and household used by the bureau.

The CB defines a family as two or more people residing together who are related by birth, marriage, or adoption. Cohabiting couples who combine their income, as families do, are counted as individuals. Married couples fare better financially than their single counterparts (see Figure 8.4 later in this chapter). However, ignoring the fact that a cohabiting couple's combined income may be on a par with that of married couples probably has the effect of overestimating the number of people who are poor. For example, two unmarried individuals sharing a home will, if their individual incomes are below the poverty level, be counted as two poor people. However, their combined income may be outside of the poverty range, and if counted as family income, the number of people in poverty would decrease.

In addition, the CB reports the income of "households" defined as all of the people who occupy a single housing unit. There are two types of households, family households and nonfamily households. Family households consist of a family, as defined in the previous paragraph, and unrelated "subfamily" members, for example, a foster child, lodger, or employee. A nonfamily household is defined as a person living alone as well as a person living with others to whom she or he is not related. Household data are difficult to interpret, and comparisons between family and household data should not be made. For example, a household may consist of a highly paid professional and her housekeeper, but no meaning can be assigned to their household income since the resources of the highly paid professional cannot, beyond the salary paid, be deemed available to the housekeeper. However, the live-in housekeeper may enjoy a better standard of living than would be the case if rent had to be paid from her or his income. By the same token, two or more families may, for reasons of economy, share an apartment or house and as with the housekeeper, their standard of living may exceed what either family alone would have. Nevertheless, combining their incomes may greatly exaggerate their wealth if it is mistakenly assumed that the income of each family is available to the other.

Poverty Threshold and Number and Characteristics of People in Poverty

The data in Table 8.3 show the poverty threshold for individuals and families of two or more for 1998. For a single person, the poverty level was $8,316, with an adjustment for age over and under sixty-five, and for a family of two it was $10,634, again with an age adjustment.

In ascending order, the poverty threshold was $13,003 for a family of three; $16,600 for family of four; $22,228 for a family of six and $28,166 for a family of eight.

In 1998, 12.7 percent of the population lived in poverty, down from 13.7 percent the previous year (Figure 8.2). This translates to 34.5 million people with incomes at or below the poverty line, almost equal to the number of poor in the late 1950s and considerably up from a low of approximately 24 million in the mid-1970s.

The percent of people in poverty by selected characteristics is reported in Figure 8.3. In 1998, 11.2 percent of poor people lived in families, and 48.8 percent lived in unrelated "subfamilies." Individuals represented 19.9 percent of the poor. Of people in poverty, 8.2 percent were white, 26.1 percent were black, 25.6 percent were of Hispanic origin, and 12.5 percent were of Asian or Pacific Island ancestry.

TABLE 8.3. 1998 Poverty Thresholds by Family Size (in Dollars)

Size of family unit	Poverty threshold
One	8,316
Under 65	8,480
Over 65	7,818
Two	10,634
Under 65	10,972
Over 65	9,862
Three people	13,003
Four people	16,660
Six people	22,228
Eight people	28,166

Source: U.S. Department of Commerce, U.S. Census Bureau. "Poverty in the United States," 1999.

FIGURE 8.2. Number of poor and poverty rate: Selected years—1959 to 1998.

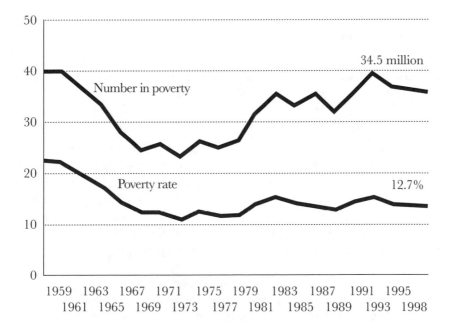

Source: U.S. Census Bureau, *Poverty in the United States,* (Washington, D.C.: U.S. Department of Commerce, 1999).

FIGURE 8.3. Percent of people in poverty by selected characteristics: 1998.

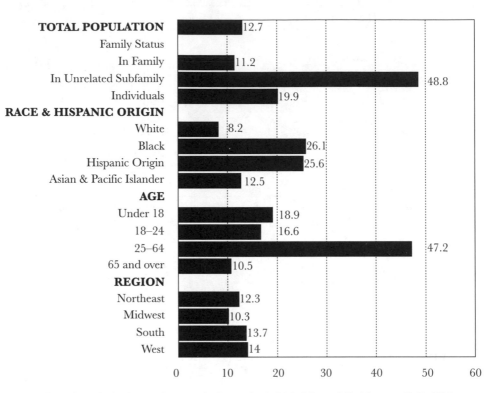

Source: Data from U.S. Census Bureau, in *Poverty in the United States*, (Washington, D.C.: U.S. Department of Commerce, 1999).
Families are two or more people related by birth, marriage, or adoption who reside together. Subfamilies consist of two or more people related to one another but not related to the person in whose name the home is owned or rented. Two brothers who are in foster care in the household of an unrelated foster parent would be a subfamily.

Whites comprise close to 83 percent of the United States population. With 8.2 percent in poverty, white people are the only group that is underrepresented in poverty statistics. The poverty rate for other groups, relative to the percent of the population that the group represents, is considerably higher. Black people comprise 12.7 percent of the population, but they represent 26.1 percent of the poor; people of Hispanic origin make up 11.3 percent of the population but represent 25.6 percent; and people of Asian and Pacific Island ancestry comprise 4 percent of the poor but represent 12.5 percent.[14]

People under the age of eighteen and those between the ages of twenty-five and sixty-four are the groups most likely to be poor, with 18.9 percent of the former group and 47.2 percent of the latter group so classified. People aged eighteen to twenty-four have a poverty rate of 16.6 percent, and those over age sixty-five have a poverty rate of 10.5 percent, the lowest poverty rate of any age group.

There is some geographic variation in the percent of poor people. The Midwest, where 10.3 percent of people are poor, has the lowest poverty rate of any region of the country, followed by the Northeast with a poverty rate of 12.3 percent. Southern states, where the poverty rate is 13.7 percent, are next followed by Western states, with a poverty rate of 14 percent. There are city-by-city variations. Some cities have poverty rates that are significantly above the national average. For example, in 1995, when the national poverty rate was approximately 13.5 percent, the rate in the District of Columbia was 20 percent; New Orleans, 34 percent; St. Louis, 30 percent; Richmond, Virginia, 25 percent; Philadelphia, 24 percent; and Miami, 43 percent.[15]

As shown in Figure 8.4, the rate of poverty among families headed by women dropped considerably from a rate of 42.6 percent in 1959 to a low of 30 percent in 1979, rose in the early 1980s to approximately 35 percent, and fell to 29.9 percent in 1998. By contrast, the poverty rate in 1997 for families headed by men was considerably lower but had increased from its 1974 low of less than 10 percent. The lowest rate of poverty is found among married couples, 5.3 percent of whom were poor in 1998, the same percent as in 1973. As shown in Figure 8.4, the poverty rate fluctuates more for female- and male-headed families than it does for married couples, due, no doubt, to the ability of a second wage-earner's salary to offset any income losses that are caused by cyclical recessions.

Education and Income

The relationship between education and income is shown in Figure 8.5. Before discussing these data, bear the following in mind. The CB definition of income includes income from a variety of sources, including earnings, government benefits such as Social Security and SSI, interest and dividends, alimony, and child support.[16]

At every educational level, men have a higher income than women with a comparable level of education. The income of women hovers at approximately 70 percent of that of men except for those with less than a ninth-grade education, where women's earnings are approximately 76 percent of men's earnings.[17]

Regardless of gender, there is a significant income differential for those with a college education compared to those for whom a high school diploma is a terminal degree. Women with a college education have a median income in excess of $35,408, which is more than 60 percent higher than the income of women with a high school diploma. For men, the difference between groups is almost as great. College-educated men have a median income in excess of $49,982, compared to men with a high school diploma, whose income was $30,868. Income continues to decrease as education decreases. Men who have less than a high school diploma have a median income that is close to $23,438; where women with a comparable level of education have a significantly lower income of about $15,847. The income of men drops to $18,553 for those with less than a ninth-grade education and to $14,132 for women with a similar level of education.

FIGURE 8.4. Percent of female-headed, male-headed, and married couple families in poverty: 1998. Asterisk indicates that datum is for 1997.

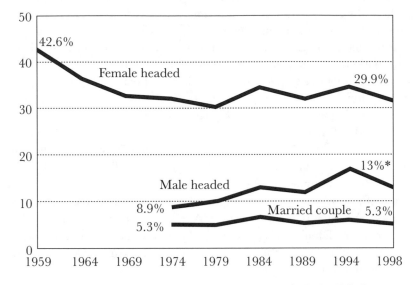

Source: U.S. Census Bureau, *Poverty in the United States*, (Washington, D.C.: U.S. Department of Commerce, 1999).

Family and Household Income

The purchasing power available to a family consists of income from a variety of sources, including wages and salaries, government benefits, interest, and dividends and other sources. Available income varies by gender, marital status, and race.

Married couples living together fare better economically than do families headed by women or men who do not live with a spouse (Figure 8.6). In 1998, approximately 62 percent of married women were in the paid labor force, compared to less than 23 percent in 1951. The median income of married couples in 1998 was in excess of $54,000 per year compared to $39,414 for male-headed families with no spouse present and $24,393 per year for female-headed families with no spouse present. In Figure 8.4 we saw that relative to other household types, female-headed families have consistently experienced the highest poverty rate. Although the percent of female-headed families in poverty has decreased from a 1959 high of 42.6 percent to 29.9 percent in 1998, the percent of poor female-headed families in 1998 is more than twice the rate for male-headed families and close to six times the rate for married couple families.

The median household income by race and Hispanic origin is shown in Figure 8.7. Asian and Pacific Islanders with a median household income in 1998 of $46,637 have consistently had the highest household income. In contrast, the median family income for white households was $40,912; Hispanic households, $28,330; and black households, $25,351.

FIGURE 8.5. Median earnings of men and women by educational level: 1998.

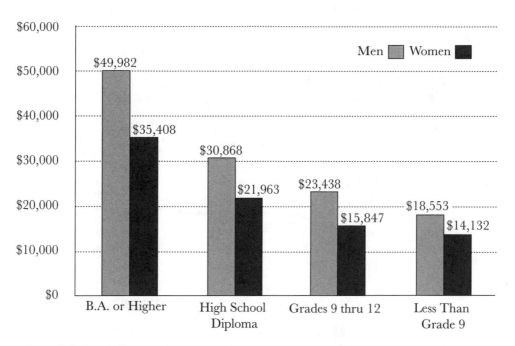

Source: U.S. Census Bureau, *Money Income in the United States,* (Washington, D.C.: U.S. Department of Commerce, 1999).

Income, Poverty, and Labor Force Participation

Labor force participation is no guarantee of an income above the poverty line. Of the more than 34.5 million poor people in the United States in 1998 (see Figure 8.2), the CB classified one in five, (7.4 million) people, as "working poor,"[18] meaning they spent at least twenty-seven weeks in the labor force and had incomes below the official poverty threshold.

The relationship between part-time compared to full-time work and poverty for people sixteen years of age and older is shown in Table 8.4.

In 1997, of the 92 million full-time workers, more than 2 million (2.5 percent) had incomes below the poverty line, compared to slightly more than 7 million (13.8 percent) of the 51 million part-time workers.

RACE AS A FACTOR

Differences in poverty rates for working women and men without taking race into account were negligible in 1997. For full-time workers, the percent in poverty was 2.5 for men and 2.6 for women; the difference was larger for part-time workers, where almost 12.3 percent of men and 14.5 percent of women had incomes below the poverty line. The within-race gender disparity for white people is likewise neg-

FIGURE 8.6. Median income of married couple families and single male- and female-headed families: 1998.

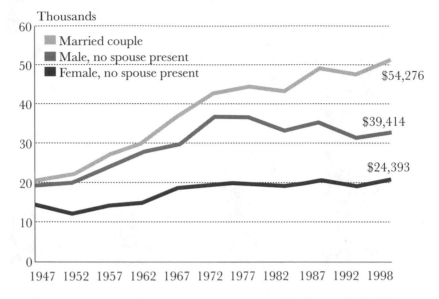

Source: U.S. Census Bureau, *Money Income in the United States*, (Washington, D.C.: U.S. Department of Commerce, 1999).

ligible. Of full-time workers, slightly more than 2 percent of women and men had incomes below the poverty level (2.3 percent for men and 2.1 percent for women); for those working part time, 11.8 percent of men and 12.1 percent of women had below poverty-level incomes. The within-race gender disparity is much greater for people of African descent. Of full-time workers, 3.5 percent of men compared to 5.3 percent of women had incomes below the poverty line; for part-time workers the disparity was even greater, with approximately 21 percent of men and 31 percent of women earning below the poverty line. For people of Hispanic origin, the gender gap narrowed compared to people of African descent. Of full-time workers, 8.5 percent of Hispanic males and 6.9 percent of Hispanic women had incomes below the poverty level; for part-time workers, 24.6 of men compared to 25 percent of women had incomes below the poverty level. Three-fourths of the working poor were employed in one of three groups: service workers; technical, sales, and administrative support positions; or operators, fabricators, or laborers.

FAMILY WORKFORCE PARTICIPATION AS A FACTOR

In 1997, close to 4.3 million families lived below the poverty level, even though at least one family member was in the labor force for twenty-seven weeks or more. Of these families, nearly one-half were headed by women. Families with just one member in the labor force had a poverty rate that was seven times greater than families

FIGURE 8.7. Median household income by race and Hispanic origin: 1967 to 1998.

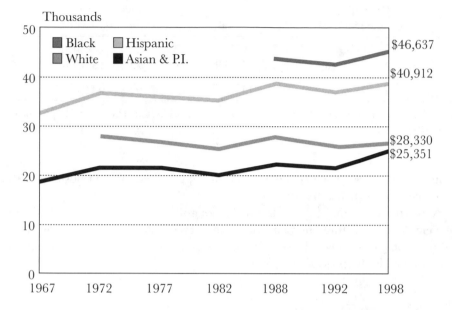

Source: Data from U.S. Census Bureau, in *Poverty in the United States*, (Washington, D.C.: U.S. Department of Commerce, 1999).
Note: 1998 was the first year in which data were reported for Asian and Pacific Islander households. 1972 was the first year in which data were reported for Hispanic households.

with two or more members in the labor force. When the working family was female-headed, the poverty rate was double that of male-headed families.

CHILDREN IN THE FAMILY

When the female-headed family contained children under the age of eighteen, the rate of poverty exceeded 26 percent compared to a poverty rate in excess of 13 percent for male-headed families.

JOB LOSS AND POVERTY

Job loss, depending on the length of time unemployed, may add to the number of working people in poverty, even when new employment at comparable pay is found. Between January 1995 and December 1997, the United States Department of Labor (DOL) reports that 3.6 million workers lost jobs that they had held for at least three years (called long-term workers by the DOL), with an additional 4.4 million workers losing jobs that they held for less than three years, for a total of 8 million "displaced" workers. A displaced worker is a person at least twenty years of age who loses a job due to (1) the closure or move of their plant or company (47 percent of workers);

TABLE 8.4. Poverty Rates for Employed Workers Sixteen Years of Age and Older by Full-Time Compared to Part-Time Work: 1997 (Number in Thousands)

Percent of time worked	Total	Income below poverty level
Full time	92,631	2,345 (2.5%)
Not full time	51,336	7,096 (13.8%)
Total	143,967	9,441 (6.6%)

Source: U.S. Census Bureau, *Poverty in the United States* (Washington, D.C.: U.S. Department of Commerce, 1999).

(2) insufficient work (21 percent of workers); or (3) abolition of their position or shift (32 percent of workers).[19]

About three-fourths of those classified as long-term displaced workers had found new employment within one year, with more than one-half of those displaced from full-time jobs re-employed in jobs with earnings that were the same or higher than those earned in the previous employment.

Theories of Poverty

There are theories that purport to explain why some people are poor and others not. Theories of poverty are important, not because they provide full and satisfactory explanations of poverty, but because social policy contains interventions that are expected to reduce or eliminate poverty and these interventions follow from the views that are held by policymakers concerning the causes of poverty.

Before the discussion of two of these theories that follows, it is helpful to acknowledge that certain conditions associated with poverty do not need a theoretical explanation. For example, it is not difficult to understand why children, who cannot control their level of income, are more likely to be poor than adults. Also, the fact that part-time workers, unless they are professionals working at high hourly rates, are more likely to be poor than full-time workers does not need a theoretical explanation.

CULTURE OF POVERTY

Culture-of-poverty theorists occupy two camps, agreeing only that there are aggregates of people who are socially and geographically isolated from the mainstream. Isolation is said to perpetuate a system of norms and values that are different from those generally held and that are inimical to self-help.

Groups negatively affected include people who live in urban ghettos as well as people who live in geographically isolated rural communities. Culture-of-poverty theorists argue that values that are passed from generation to generation perpetuate poverty and intergenerational dependency on government assistance.[20] Moreover, they argue that in urban ghettos where educational opportunities are limited, where crime is high and success is associated with criminal behavior and not hard work, and where welfare benefits are available, the person who works is seen as a "chump," and the community-at-large condones its own behavioral norms, which are seen as deviant rather than adaptive.[21]

Wilson (1997) argues that despite extensive poverty, black residents of inner-city ghettos do not undermine traditional American values concerning individual initiative. Instead, these residents reinforce them, although they may have a difficult time living up to a mainstream code of behavior. Poverty in inner cities, according to Wilson, is due mainly to the lack of work opportunities.[22]

Earlier I said that culture-of-poverty theorists occupy two camps. The conservative view sees the availability of welfare itself as a cause of poverty, because, as they argue, knowledge that one can rely on the welfare system is said to reinforce dependency. This point of view animated the debate that surrounded passage of the Personal Responsibility and Work Opportunity Act (PRWOA) of 1996.[23] Some of the requirements found in the PRWOA seek to break the cycle of poverty by mandating that most recipients be employed within two years of receiving benefits and by imposing a sixty-month lifetime limit, after which benefits are cut off (see chapter 10).

The liberal perspective takes issue with the notion of a culture of poverty, which is seen as "blaming the victim" rather than the "system." Racism and other forms of characteristic-based discrimination, coupled with the lack of educational and work opportunities in inner cities, are seen as having created nearly insurmountable barriers to achievement, and interventions would seek to increase educational and work opportunities.

Both conservative and liberal views are to an extent defeatist. The former fails to account for gender- and race-based privilege as factors in gaining access to educational and employment opportunities, taking it as a given that hard work is necessary and sufficient to access. The liberal point of view, in striving to highlight systemic deficiencies so as not to blame the victim, may have created a situation were people see themselves as victims of social and environmental conditions that they cannot control.

STRUCTURAL POVERTY

A structural view of poverty sees poverty as entrenched within the system and includes class "exploitation," where poverty is seen as serving an economic function because it keeps available a class of workers willing to work for low wages. In this view, government systems operate to restrict eligibility for welfare programs when the economy requires an increase in workers, necessitated, for instance, by increased tourism or agricultural needs at harvesting time, thus increasing the pool of people available for work. Eligibility rules are relaxed when the economy can no longer provide jobs.

A structural view takes account also of barriers to self-sufficiency, such as racism, sexism, and homophobia, that limit opportunity. Several examples have been provided in previous chapters. For example, in chapter 1 I discussed a lawsuit that was brought by black employees of Duke Power Company. The workers alleged that the power company limited the advancement opportunities of black employees by creating barriers to career advancement through imposition of job requirements that were not related to job performance, and the Supreme Court supported the employees' claim. No amount of individual initiative can overcome a barrier such as this. Nor can the barriers that were erected after the Civil War to prevent African Americans from voting, and thus gaining the access to the power that comes from having elected officials, be surmounted by individual initiative. Thus, viewing poverty within a structural framework suggests (1) that simply increasing opportunity will not affect poverty rates because of discrimination and (2) that policies, for example, the Civil Rights Act of 1964 and the Americans with Disability Act of 1990, are needed to counter the misbehavior of some members of society.

A significant structural change that has been taking place in the United States and elsewhere is the shift from a manufacturing to a service economy. In the last third of the twentieth century, a great deal of manufacturing began to shift from the United States to out-of-country production, causing the loss of tens of thousands of jobs. For example, in the early 1970s the domestic textile industry employed 1 million workers, and the apparel industry employed 1.4 million. In 1995, textile industry employment had decreased to 667,000 jobs, and in 1996, apparel industry employment decreased to 863,000. According to the CB, textile and apparel establishments declined from 31,021 in 1982 to 28,935 in 1992.[24]

While work in these areas decreased, service sector employment increased. In April 1999, the DOL reported that service industries that provide information services, educational services, and health care services, for example, added 131,000 jobs relative to the prior year. The financial, engineering, and management sectors also added jobs, but employment in manufacturing continued to decline, showing a cumulative loss of 26,000 in the first quarter of 1999 compared with 35,000 for all of 1998.[25]

The changing nature of work in America and other industrialized countries is undeniable. Increasingly, work opportunities are tied to education and advanced skills training. For example, in the United States more than 17 million full-time jobs were created between 1988 and 1998, two-thirds of which were professional, managerial, and technical. In contrast to the 1950s, when only 16 percent of United States' workers were professionals, managers, or technical workers, the proportion in 1996 had changed to one in three.[26]

The shift toward a service economy is such that the DOL is revising its sixty-year-old system for classifying industries, eliminating 60 percent of the previous listings and adding 358 new industries, many of which are service related and included information services; health care and social assistance; professional, scientific, and technical services; and educational services.[27]

This changing nature of work was highlighted in the earlier presented data on the relationship between education and income. Although a number of service sector jobs may pay little more that the minimum wage (e.g., jobs in "limited service restaurants" and convenience stores),[28] many jobs will, as just noted, require a higher level of education or skills training.

At the present time, there are retraining programs for displaced workers. Focusing on changed employment opportunities, programs such as the North American Free Trade Agreement (NAFTA)–Transitional Adjustment Assistance program retrains workers whose jobs were lost when their plants or companies closed or moved, and the program provides extended unemployment payments. Between early 1994 and spring of 1997, about 133,000 workers were assisted by this program.[29]

Summary

The poverty threshold in the United States is determined by ascertaining the cost of food for a family of four and multiplying by three the cost of providing a minimally adequate diet. Adjustments are made for family size and age of family members. Critics of this approach to setting a poverty threshold argue, among other things, that (1) the cost of food, which represented one-third of a family's budget when the formula was developed in the 1950s, now represents only one-seventh, thus continued use of the one-third multiplier grossly underestimates the cost of living; (2) the poverty threshold should be adjusted to take into account geographic differences in the cost of living; (3) allowance should be made for costs such as child care that were not historically a part of the budget of most families; and (4) the poverty threshold should take into account the standard of living in society, and the poverty rate should be set relative to the resources of other members of society.

The number of poor people in the U.S. is determined using data that are gathered each year by the CB in their yearly survey of a sample of approximately 50,000 American households. In 1997, 13.3 percent of the population, or slightly more than 35 million people, had incomes at or below the poverty line.

Data from 1998 show that almost one-half of poor people lived in unrelated subfamilies, with slightly more than 11 percent in families. Individuals accounted for close to 20 percent of poor people. By race or origin, white people, 8 percent of whom were poor, had the lowest rate of poverty when compared to black people and people of Hispanic origin, where approximately 26 percent of each group were poor, and people of Asian or Pacific Island ancestry, of whom more than 12 percent were poor. By age, those under eighteen and those aged twenty-five to sixty-four were the groups most likely to be poor, with close to 19 percent of the former group and 47 percent of the latter group so classified. The lowest rates of poverty were found in the Midwest (10 percent) and the Northeast (12 percent), with higher rates in the South and West, where close to 14 percent of the population were poor.

Single female-headed families, with a 1998 poverty rate of close to 30 percent, had the highest rate of poverty of any family type. The poverty rate for single male-headed families was significantly lower at 13 percent with the lowest poverty rate found among married couples at 5.3 percent.

At every level of education, the income of males exceeds that of females with a comparable level of education. The income disparity is smallest between college-educated women and men where the income of women is approximately 70 percent of that of men.

Gender aside, there is a significant income differential for those with a college education compared to others. Women with a college education have a median income in excess of $35,408, more than 60 percent the income of women with a high school diploma, and college-educated men have a median income close to $50,000, compared to the approximate $31,000 income for men with a high school diploma.

Approximately 20 percent of working people are poor, and close to 14 percent of part-time workers compared to 2.5 percent of full-time workers have incomes below the poverty line. Gender differences are slight; 2.5 percent of men and 2.6 of women who work full time have incomes below the poverty level.

Within-race gender disparity for whites is negligible, where slightly more than 2 percent of women and men who work full-time have incomes at or below the poverty level. For blacks the gender disparity is greater, where 3.5 percent of men compared to 5.3 percent of women have incomes below the poverty line. For people of Hispanic origin, 8.5 percent of men and 6.9 of women had poverty level incomes.

Scholars seek to explain poverty with reference to different theories. Culture-of-poverty theorists locate the causes of poverty in the value systems of the poor who lack a work ethic and come to depend on government assistance. Structural theorists argue that systemic causes, such as racism, sexism, and other forms of discrimination, prevent access to opportunity and access to advancement and that these barriers must be broken down by government interventions.

A conservative or culture-of-poverty point of view seeks to resolve poverty by breaking the cycle of intergenerational poverty by mandating that able-bodied welfare recipients work for their benefits and by limiting the amount of time that welfare benefits are available to individuals. A liberal or structural perspective finds solutions in increased government intervention to improve public schools and to fund child care, housing, health care services, work training, and job readiness opportunities.

Regardless of one's position on the political spectrum, the changing nature of work in America, from manufacturing to service, is undeniable, as is the fact that work opportunities are increasingly tied to education and advanced skills training.

CHAPTER 9

Social Insurance

The most direct way to alleviate poverty is to provide cash to people in need. Proposals to do so give rise to several concerns. The first concern is expressed conceptually in the division of the poor into the categories of worthy and unworthy (see chapter 4). This labeling reflects a concern that people should be self-sufficient and that the availability of public assistance will rob people of the incentive to work.

Accepting the proposition that some form of public assistance will be provided, two additional concerns arise. Framed as questions, these ask, "What role should be played by government, as compared to the private sector?" (see chapter 3) and, if there is a role for government, "What is the proper division of responsibility between the states and the federal government?" (see chapter 2) The latter concern was captured in President Franklin Pierce's veto message of 1854 that justified his denying federal grants for the care of the insane:

> If Congress has the power to make provisions for the indigent insane . . . it has the same power to provide for the indigent who are not insane, and thus to transfer to the federal government the charge of all the poor in all the States.

We begin with an overview of events of the nineteenth and early twentieth centuries that led to the creation of the American welfare state. This is followed by a review of policies that provide income support to retirees, injured workers, the unemployed, and to the working-poor. As discussed in chapter 2, in the second decade of the twentieth century a number of states assumed some responsibility for aiding the poor. Aid took the form of cash assistance provided through Mother's Pension laws and Workers' Compensation laws. From 1911, when Illinois established the first Mother's Pension law and Wisconsin the first Workers' Compensation law, to the latter years of the Great Depression of 1929, responsibility for aiding the poor remained primarily at the state level.

The Depression and the Role of the Federal Government

The stock market crash of 1929 signaled the beginning of the Great Depression. Unemployment and poverty associated with job loss created an emergency that was national in scope. Between 1929 and 1936, an average of 10 million people were unemployed, peaking at times to a high of 16 million.[1]

Efforts to resolve the problems created by mass unemployment included federally sponsored employment programs, such as the Works Progress Administration and the Public Works Administration, and proposals for providing income assistance that ranged from Senator Huey Long's "Share Our Wealth" program, calling for redistribution of wealth from the very rich to those of modest means, to the Townsend Plan, proposed by a physician from the Pacific Northwest,[2] that called for the creation of a pension system to be financed through a tax on commercial and financial transactions. Under the terms of the Townsend Plan, $200 per month would be provided to people sixty years of age and older who were not convicted felons and who, if employed, would agree to retire and to spend their stipend within thirty days of its receipt. The popularity of the plan was reflected in a petition of support to Congress signed by more than twenty million people.

Efforts by the federal government to intervene and alleviate the problems created by the Depression met with resistance from the Supreme Court.[3] The Court deemed unconstitutional two major pieces of Depression era legislation that were passed in 1933. The first, the National Industrial Recovery Act (NIRA), was the cornerstone of President Roosevelt's strategy to alter the course of events.[4] The NIRA delegated to the president the discretion to make whatever laws he thought necessary to begin the process of rehabilitating American industry and expanding trade. The NIRA was unconstitutional, the High Court said, because it delegated to the president the power to make laws, a role that the Constitution expressly delegated to the Congress (see discussion in chapter 7).[5]

Congressional passage in the same year of the Agricultural Adjustment Act (AAA) marked a further attempt to alleviate the distress caused by the Depression. The AAA provided for a subsidy to farmers who agreed to limit the amount of acreage in production. If production could be limited, the price of food could be controlled and, it was assumed, farming could be returned to profitability. In *United States v. Butler,* the Supreme Court ruled that the AAA was unconstitutional.[6] It infringed on the power of state government to control agriculture and, as such, it violated the Tenth Amendment to the federal constitution that provides that all powers the Constitution does not expressly grant to the federal government are reserved to the states.[7] Clearly, there was nothing in the Constitution that gave to the federal government the power to control agriculture within the states.

The justification offered by the federal government for intervening in matters otherwise left to the states rested on a provision in Article 1 of the Constitution that allows Congress to raise revenues to provide for the "general welfare of the United

States."[8] A key issue that the Court grappled with during the Depression was whether relief provided to individuals in the form of pensions, for example, was for the general welfare or was too particularized to survive constitutional scrutiny.

In 1937, the Supreme Court finally conceded that the unemployment problems created by the Depression were of national significance and that federal intervention to promote the general welfare was constitutional. The case at hand, *Steward v. Davis*,[9] involved a challenge to the tax-based system of unemployment insurance that was part of the Social Security Act of 1935. Those opposed to the tax argued that the federal government had no right to impose it, and they asked the Court to declare the legislation unconstitutional. The Court disagreed. Its reasoning had less to do with any change in the law than with the pragmatic necessity of dealing with the significant problems created by the Depression that were beyond the ability of the states to handle. There was, the Supreme Court found, a

> Need of help from the nation if the people were not to starve. It is too late today for the argument to be heard with tolerance that in a crisis so extreme the use of the moneys of the nation to relieve the unemployed and their dependents is a use for any purpose narrower than the promotion of the general welfare.[10]

This new interpretation of the federal role lay the groundwork for the American welfare state. Justice Cardozo articulated the reasoning for allowing Congress to spend money in aid of the general welfare.

> Needs that were narrow or parochial a century ago may be interwoven in our day with the well-being of the nation . . . The purge of nation-wide calamity that began in 1929 has taught . . . [us that there is a] . . . solidarity of interests that may once have seemed to be divided. Unemployment spreads . . . from state to state [and] is an ill not particular but general, which may be checked, if Congress so determines, by the resources of the nation. . . . [11]

The national response to the Depression was significant. Between January 1933 and July 1936, the

> States incurred obligations of $689,291,802 for emergency relief; local subdivisions an additional $775,675,366. In the same period the obligations for emergency relief incurred by the national government were $2,929,307,125, or twice the obligations of states and local agencies combined. According to the President's budget message for the fiscal year 1938, the national government expended for public works and unemployment relief for the three fiscal years 1934, 1935, and 1936, the stupendous total of $8,681,000,000.[12]

The Selling of Social Security

In the spring of 1934, President Roosevelt announced his intention to create a program of social security. In a message that he delivered to Congress on June 8, 1934, he said:

> Security was attained in the earlier days through the interdependence of members of families upon each other and of the families within a small community upon

each other. The complexities of great communities and of organized industry make less real these simple means of security. Therefore, we are compelled to employ the active interest of the Nation as a whole through government in order to encourage a greater security for each individual who composes it . . . This seeking for a greater measure of welfare and happiness does not indicate a change in values. It is rather a return to values lost in the course of our economic development and expansion. . . .

By executive order, the president formed the Committee on Economic Security (CES), charging its members with studying the problems produced by the Depression and with recommending a way to resolve these difficulties that might serve as the basis for forming legislation. Before the year was out, the CES produced a draft legislative proposal that was presented to Congress in January 1935.

Before the Social Security Act could be passed, legislators and the general public had to be convinced that a federal role in providing assistance to needy individuals was appropriate. A two-pronged approach was taken. First, borrowing from the rhetoric of Wisconsin Senator Robert LaFollette Jr., Roosevelt defended his proposals against a conservative attack by making reference to the American history of providing relief from natural disasters. Why, LaFollette had asked, is a national response appropriate to a natural disaster but inappropriate to an economic disaster? No one would question the responsibility of the federal government if the Depression had been an earthquake—a fast and generous response would be expected. However, because the unemployed and their dependents are the victims of an "economic earthquake," resulting from the failure of leadership of American industry, finance, and government, efforts to provide aid by the federal government are discredited by calling it a dole.[13] The temporary nature of disaster relief compared to the permanent federal role that the act would create in providing for the needy was not addressed in their argument.

A major part of selling the act was to convince people that its benefits were not a "handout" but were owed to recipients. This was done by drawing parallels between the benefits that the act would provide and commercial insurance. The decision to emphasize insurance was a pragmatic one, and insurance became "the central symbol" in marketing of the act.[14] The public was familiar with the concept of insurance and was likely to accept the argument that benefits provided under the act were a return on an investment made during one's working years. People had "old age insurance accounts" that they created to protect themselves.[15] This line of thought safeguarded the self-respect of those who would reap the benefits of the act. The language of insurance (e.g., premiums paid and contributions made) was used in lieu of reference to taxes. The fact that social insurance differs from the actuarial principles on which commercial insurance is based was not generally discussed, nor was the reality that the goals of the act were achieved by a "pay-as-you-go" system where income collected from those currently employed and their employers was redistributed to retirees, that is, from higher-income to lower-income members of society.[16]

The proposal submitted by the CES was subject to several months of congressional hearings. The Social Security Act was passed by Congress and signed into law by President Roosevelt on August 14, 1935.[17]

The original act contained provisions that did not fit within the insurance concept, such as the Aid to Dependent Children Program and benefits to workers who lost their jobs, and these were looked on as inferior programs because of the wish to maintain a focus on a set of principles that fit within the insurance framework. These principles required a focus on the following: (1) the program rested on contributions made by people who would later qualify for benefits based upon the taxes they paid; (2) having made contributions, the individual had a legal entitlement to benefits; and (3) no demonstration of financial need would be required.

Other provisions of the act were that (1) benefits would be tied to wages earned; (2) the program would be national in its scope; (3) the program would be operated by the federal government; and (4) participation would be compulsory for workers in commerce and industry,[18] which included approximately 60 percent of the 1935 workforce.[19] Those not covered included employers with fewer than eight employees, the self-employed, domestic workers, and agricultural workers.[20] With the passage of time, originally excluded groups were brought into the system. By 1997, approximately 97 percent of all workers were covered, as were the self-employed. However, approximately 6.6 million workers do not currently participate in the Social Security system. These are mainly employees of local, state, and federal government who participate in alternative retirement systems; clergy who choose not to be covered; certain religious sects; college students who work at their academic institutions; household workers who earn less than a certain amount per annum ($1,100 in 1998); those under age eighteen; and self-employed workers with annual net earnings, set at $400 in 1998.[21]

To organize the initial program, the Social Security Board was formed. In 1939, the board became a part of the president's cabinet. In 1946, the Social Security Administration (SSA) was formed and given the responsibility of managing some of the programs created by the act, with unemployment insurance transferred to the Department of Labor in 1946. Today, the SSA is an independent agency within the federal government.

The Social Security Act

The various titles of the Social Security Act, including the year in which each was enacted and the chapters in which each will be discussed, is shown in Table 9.1. The act of 1935 contained 11 titles, five of which (VI through IX and XI) did not provide benefits directly to individuals. Four of the five titles addressed administrative matters (VII through IX and XI) and the other, Title VI, provided grants to the states to establish and maintain public-health services. As to the titles concerned with administrative matters, Title VII established the Social Security Board and charged its members with operating the various programs created by the act. The amount of employment-related tax to be paid was set forth in Title VIII, and the fact that the act applied only to employers with eight or more employees was set forth in Title IX. Title XI, the final administrative title, contained a variety of

TABLE 9.1. Titles of the Social Security Act, Year Enacted, and Text Chapter Where Title Is Discussed

Title	Title name	Passed	Covered in chapter
I	Grants* for Old Age Assistance†	1935	10
II	Old Age Survivors	1935	
	Old Age Disability Insurance (together OASDI)	1956	9
III	Grants for Unemployment Comp.	1935	9
IV‡	Grants for Aid to Dependent Children	1935	10
V	Grants for Maternal and Child Health	1935	11
VI	Public Health (repealed)	1935	—
VII	Administration of the Act	1935	—§
VIII	Employment Taxes	1935	—
	(transferred to Internal Revenue Code)		
IX	Miscellaneous Provisions Relating to	1935	—
	Employment Security		
X	Grants for Aid to the Blind†	1935	10
XI	General Provisions	1935	—
XII	Loans to the States for Unemployment Benefits	1944	9
XIII	Unemployment for Seamen (repealed)	1946	—
XIV	Grants for the Permanently and Totally Disabled†	1972	10
XV	Unemployment for Federal Workers	1954	—
	(transferred to Title V of the U.S. Code)		
XVI	Supplemental Security Income‖	1972	10
XVII	Grants for Action to Combat Mental Retardation	1963	—
	(inactive)		
XVIII	Medicare	1965	11
XIX	Medicaid	1965	11
XX	Social Service Block Grant	1975	—‖
XXI	State Children's Health Insurance Program	1997	11

Source: Compiled by the author.
*All grants are to the states.
†Applicable only to Puerto Rico, Guam, the Virgin Islands, and American Samoa.
‡Later modified to include a caretaker grant and for services to families and children.
§Reference to administrative issues is made in several chapters.
‖Limited to the fifty states and the District of Columbia. The Northern Mariana Islands are the only jurisdiction outside of the United States authorized to operate an SSI program.

miscellaneous provisions, such as rules governing the promulgation and issuance of regulations, the confidentiality of certain information provided to the Internal Revenue Service, and provisions concerning cooperative research endeavors between the federal government, state governments, and other agencies.

The six remaining titles (I through V and X) were benefit conferring, providing (1) grants to the states for old age assistance (Title I)[22]; (2) the Old Age, Survivors, and Disability Insurance program (Title II)[23]; (3)grants to the states for unemployment insurance (Title III)[24]; (4) grants to the states to provide for children under 16 who had been deprived of parental support (Title IV)[25]; (5) grants to the states for maternal and child health (Title V)[26]; and (6) grants to the states for aid to the blind (Title X).[27]

Titles I and X, together with Title XIV, which was enacted in 1972, provided financial aid for people with disabilities. In 1972, when the Supplemental Security Income Program (Title XVI)[28] was passed, Titles I, X, and XIV were repealed in the fifty states and the District of Columbia but remain as benefit programs for Puerto Rico, Guam, the United States Virgin Islands, and American Samoa. Title XVI is not applicable to these jurisdictions.

The remainder of this chapter is concerned with Titles II (Old Age, Survivors, and Disability Insurance), III, and XII, each addressing a different aspect of unemployment insurance, and with the Earned Income Tax Credit, part of the Internal Revenue Code, which has a direct bearing on efforts to reduce poverty.

Title II: Old Age, Survivors, and Disability Insurance

The Old Age, Survivors, and Disability Insurance program (OASDI) provides monthly benefits to retired and disabled workers, their dependents, and their survivors. The OASDI is the largest social program in the United States, providing coverage for approximately 97 percent of workers. In March 1999, the program paid out $32 billion[29] to 44,247,000 beneficiaries. Thirty-nine percent of retirees derive all their income from social security, with an additional 11 percent deriving more than 90 percent of their income from this source. Thirty-three percent of retirees derive between 50 and 89 percent of their income from social security, with only 17 percent deriving less than 50 percent of their income from this source.[30]

In 1999, retired workers received an average monthly benefit of $781, disabled workers received $733, and widows and widowers received an average monthly benefit of $751. Since 1972, benefits have been annually adjusted to reflect increases in the cost of living.

The data in Figure 9.1 show the number of program beneficiaries by the type of benefit received. Of the 44,247,000 beneficiaries, 62 percent were retired workers 10.7 percent were disabled workers, 6.8 percent were the spouse of a retired or disabled worker, 11.6 percent were the spouse or parent of a deceased worker, and 8.7 percent were the children of retired, disabled or deceased workers.[31]

SOURCE OF REVENUES AND THE TRUST FUNDS

Social Security revenues include funds for the OASDI program and for the Medicare program (see chapter 12.) Funds are derived from three sources: (1) payroll taxes, representing about 90 percent of revenues; (2) income taxes paid by beneficiaries whose income exceeds certain amounts; and (3) interest earned on United States Treasury Securities in which funds are invested.

For each employee, the first $72,600 in earnings is taxed for the OASDI program, but there is no ceiling on taxable earnings for the Medicare program. Employer

FIGURE 9.1. Number of social security beneficiaries by type of benefit: March 1999.

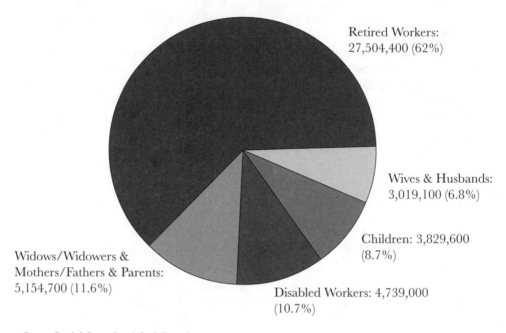

Retired Workers: 27,504,400 (62%)

Wives & Husbands: 3,019,100 (6.8%)

Children: 3,829,600 (8.7%)

Widows/Widowers & Mothers/Fathers & Parents: 5,154,700 (11.6%)

Disabled Workers: 4,739,000 (10.7%)

Source: Social Security Administration.

and employee each pay a tax of 7.65 percent, 6.2 percent of which is allocated to OASDI and 1.45 percent to Medicare. The tax rate for self-employed workers was 15.3 percent in 1999.

Revenues are credited to four trust funds: the Old Age Survivors Insurance Fund (OASI), the Disability Insurance Fund (DI), and within the Medicare Program, the Medicare Hospital Insurance Trust Fund and the Supplementary Medical Insurance Trust Fund. Revenues do not literally go into fund accounts; rather, they become a part of the government's pool of available cash (Treasury funds). Revenues "appear" in trust accounts through bookkeeping entries. Since funds go into the government's pool of available cash, it follows that beneficiaries are paid from the federal government's general revenues, and the trust funds are debited accordingly. The government spends surplus Social Security funds as it does any other income, but the credit to the trust fund accounts creates an obligation on the part of the government to workers.

BENEFITS ARE PROGRESSIVE

The formula for determining benefits is progressive, meaning that workers with lower wages have a higher portion of their earnings replaced than do workers with higher earnings. This approach to setting benefit levels sacrifices equity, where the return received by an individual would approximate the contributions she or he were made into the system, and instead seeks "income adequacy" to ensure a minimum standard of living for all beneficiaries. For example, the full retirement benefit payable to a minimum-wage worker who retired in 1996 was $467 a month, replacing 48 percent of monthly earnings, compared to an average wage earner's benefit replacing 37 percent of average monthly earnings and a high wage earner's benefit of approximately 28 percent of earnings.[32] The progressive nature of the program redistributes income to ensure some measure of income adequacy at retirement that would be absent if benefits were determined solely on the basis of actual taxes previously paid.

RETIREMENT AGE, CONTINUED WORK, AND BENEFITS

Workers may retire at age sixty-two and, since 1985, the majority have done so.[33] However, the benefits received by an early retiree are reduced on average by 20 percent. Full benefits are available to fully insured workers, defined as workers with 40 quarters of covered employment before reaching age sixty-five. The age of full retirement will increase in the early years of this century to age sixty-six (for those born after 1943) and to age sixty-seven (for those born after 1959).

Retirees may continue to work, but until a worker reaches full retirement age, these earnings affect benefits. In 2000, for those under retirement age, maximum earnings were $10,080, with a loss of $1 for every $2 over that limit. On April 7, 2000, President Clinton signed into law the Senior Citizens Freedom to Work Act.[34] This legislation eliminates the earning penalty that applied to people aged 65 to 69 who lost $1 in benefits for every $3 earned over $14,500. Beginning in January 2000, there will be no loss in benefits for people who continue to work beyond the age of full retirement.

TAXATION OF BENEFITS

The Social Security Act Amendments of 1983 and the Omnibus Budget Reconciliation Act of 1993 required beneficiaries to report a part of their benefits as taxable income. Effective in 1994, individuals whose income exceeds $34,000 and married couples whose income exceeds $44,000 are required to report up to 85 percent of their benefits as taxable income. Revenues raised pursuant to the 1983 and 1994 amendments are credited to the OASDI trust fund and the Medicare trust fund.[35]

SOCIAL SECURITY BENEFITS FOR NONCITIZENS

The Personal Responsibility and Work Opportunity Reconciliation Act of 1996 (see chapter 10) together with the Immigration Responsibility Act of 1996 affect the payment of benefits to noncitizen residents of the United States. Effective December 1, 1996, noncitizens who apply for benefits under the OASDI program must provide proof that they have attained citizenship or are otherwise lawfully present. A lawfully present alien is a person who was admitted under an immigration quota, as a refugee, or asylee; or a person who is awaiting approval of an application for political asylum or who belongs to any class of aliens permitted to reside in the United States for humanitarian or other reasons.[36]

Disability

Unlike the Old Age Assistance Program, eligibility for benefits under the Social Security Disability Insurance Program (SSDI) are not age based. However, applicants must establish that they are disabled and unable to engage in "substantial gainful activity" (SGA) due to a physical or mental impairment that is likely to result in death or that has lasted or can be expected to last for at least 12 months.[37] The applicant must also accept a referral for and offer of vocational rehabilitation services. Failure to accept an offer of service is grounds for disqualification.

As of July 1, 1999, a disability claimant whose earnings exceeded $700 per month (or $1,050 per month if blind) was presumptively engaging in SGA and would be denied disability-based benefits.[38] If individuals are not disqualified on the basis of earnings, they must establish that they have a covered disability. To do so, claimants present medical evidence that describes their symptoms, signs of illness, and laboratory findings. This information is compared with disability listings maintained by the SSA. If the applicant's condition "matches" a condition on the list, the applicant is deemed disabled and eligible for benefits. If the applicant's condition does not match a listed condition, whether the condition is equivalent to a listed condition is determined.

Equivalence may be medical. For example, the applicant may have the signs, symptoms, and laboratory findings associated with a listed condition, but the diagnosis may not fit precisely with a listed diagnosis, or the applicant may have a functional equivalence. A condition is functionally equivalent to a listed condition when the question "Is the applicant's ability to function limited as if the condition were medically equivalent?" can be answered affirmatively. A finding of medical or functional equivalence will result in the granting of benefits. Applicants who receive adverse rulings, including a termination of benefits previously granted, may request that their applications be reconsidered. Subsequent denial is subject to appeal before an administrative law judge (see chapter 6), then to the SSA's Appeals Council, and ultimately to a federal district court.

PERIODIC REVIEW

Except for those deemed to be permanently disabled, the SSA conducts eligibility reviews every three years if it has been determined that the individual's medical condition may improve. Otherwise, review is conducted every seven years. Benefits may be terminated if it is found that the person's condition has improved such that she or he can engage in an substantial gainful activity.[39]

WAITING PERIOD

There is a five-month waiting period before one receives SSDI benefits. Benefits become payable beginning with the sixth full month of disability. However, benefits may be payable in the first full month of disability to a worker who becomes disabled within sixty months of termination of SSDI benefits from any earlier period of disability.

INCENTIVES TO WORK

Disabled beneficiaries may "test" their ability to work without losing all of their benefits. The test period consists of a "trial work period" during which a disabled beneficiary may work for up to nine months without adversely affecting disability or Medicare benefits. This is followed by an extended disability period of five and one-half years in which cash disability benefits are suspended for any month in which the individual is engaged in SGA; however, Medicare coverage continues so long as the individual is otherwise eligible for disability benefits.

To encourage work, impairment-related work expenses paid for by the person with a disability are deducted from gross earnings before it is decided whether earnings imply SGA, or work may be subsidized if the subsidy will improve the worker's chances of increasing, through additional supervision or training, his or her ability to perform the job satisfactorily.[40] Impairment-related work expenses include medical devices, attendant care, and, for those who work at home, structural modifications, such as a wheelchair ramp or enlargement of a doorway.[41]

Status of the Old Age, Survivors, and Disability Insurance Trust Funds

Social Security taxes were first collected in 1937. From that date until the early 1970s, payments made into the system exceeded payments that were made to retirees. The situation changed in the early 1970s. At that time, Congress provided for automatic cost of living increases (COLAs) but a flaw in the method of determining the amount of the COLA coupled with high inflation caused double-digit benefit increases. For example, benefits increased by 15 percent in 1970 and by 20 percent in 1972.[42] In addition, a weak economy in the 1970s negatively affected trust fund reserves. Beginning in 1973, payments into the system fell behind payments made to retirees, and trust fund reserves declined.

Congress acted a number of times during the 1970s and early 1980s to prevent trust fund insolvency. The flawed indexing formula was corrected in 1977. Major changes were made in 1983, at which time the economy improved and increased trust fund reserves. The 1983 changes included (1) a gradual increase in the age for receiving full retirement benefits, (2) subjecting benefits to taxation, and (3) bringing previously excluded groups into the social security system. Once again, income began to exceed payments made, and the trust funds grew, resulting in a 1990 surplus of $200 billion and an expected surplus of $967 billion by the beginning of 2001.

The changes that were made in 1983 were an attempt to eliminate the long-run problems that confronted the system. In fact, projections made at that time showed that income would exceed expenditures until the year 2025, after which surpluses would be exhausted and there would be an indefinite period of deficits.

PROBLEMS IN THE OLD AGE, SURVIVORS, AND DISABILITY INSURANCE SYSTEM

Expenditures for the OASDI programs projected through the year 2007 are shown in Figure 9.2. Program costs increased more than fivefold between 1975 and 1996,

FIGURE 9.2. OASDI outlays through 1996 and projections through 2007.

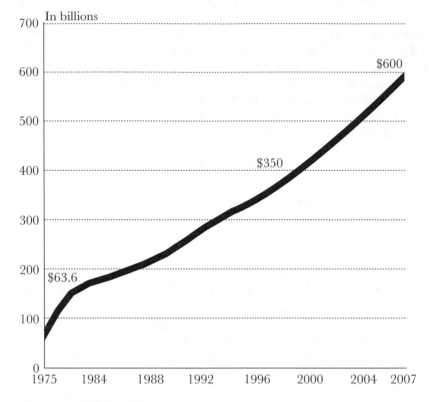

Source: Congressional Budget Office.

from $63.6 billion to $350 billion. In 1996, program costs for OASDI represented 22.4 percent of the total United States' $1.56 trillion budget. Costs are expected to increase to approximately $600 billion in the year 2007.[43]

In 1997 and 1998, the solvency of the trust funds were assessed by the funds' Board of Trustees and by the Congressional Budget Office. Both groups predicted that the funds would be solvent into the second decade of the twenty-first century. This prediction rested on two assumptions: First, that the 76 million "baby boomers" (born between 1946 and 1964) would be at their peak earning years for the next two decades, thus increasing the funds' cash reserves; and second, that retirees born in the Depression era, who were the major group of beneficiaries when the predictions were made, were relatively small in number, yielding a ratio of retirees to workers that allowed the pay-as-you-go operation of the system to function smoothly.

However, long-range predictions are a cause for concern. The cash flow into the trust funds is expected to turn negative in 2013, following which reserves will be drawn down as the baby boom generation retires in large numbers. It is projected that funds will be exhausted in 2026. As the data in Table 9.2 show, the number of beneficiaries will grow by 17 million between the year 2000 and 2020, and the ratio of beneficiaries to workers will fall from 3.3 in 2000 to 2.4 in the year 2020. The decrease will continue, so that by 2040 there will be only 2 workers for each program recipient.

Overall, the population of people aged sixty-five and older is expected to grow from a 1998 figure of 35 million to 61 million in 2025, an increase of 75 percent.[44] The number of workers will grow by only 15 percent.

FIXING THE PROBLEM

Once revenues are not sufficient to meet payments, interest will begin to fall significantly because the securities in which funds were invested will have to be redeemed to help pay benefits. Recommendations for making the trust funds solvent include traditional approaches, for example, (1) changing the formula for calculating retirement benefits[45]; (2) increasing the age of retirement to 70; (3) reducing cost-of-living increases; (4) mandating the participation of workers who are not currently in the system; (5) raising the payroll tax; (6) increasing the income tax on social security benefits; (7) taxing some nonwage compensation, such as employer-provided health insurance and pension contributions; (8) eliminating or reducing some benefits; for example, in 1997 spousal, survivor, and dependent child benefits accounted for more than 25 percent of program expenditures, but a needs test has never been applied to these benefits; and (9) means-testing all benefits.

More novel approaches include creating retirement accounts (called "personal security accounts" or "individual accounts" that would be under the control and management of the individual) or maintaining the current system but investing social security taxes in the stock market (perhaps by splitting investments, with a portion going toward securities and a portion toward market investments).[46]

The argument for allowing investment choices is both philosophical and practical. The philosophical argument is based on an individual's responsibility for ensuring that he or she has an adequate retirement income. The practical argument is based on recognizing that government investments have a low rate of return. The government currently invests social security withholding taxes in government bonds for which the rate of return is less than 2.5 percent, compared to a rate of average

TABLE 9.2. Covered Workers, OASDI Beneficiaries, and Worker Beneficiary Ratios, Selected Years 1960 to 2040

Work force measure	1960	1980	2000	2020	2040
Covered workers (in millions)	73	112	149	166	171
OASDI beneficiaries (in millions)	14	35	46	69	86
Worker/beneficiary ratio	5.1	3.2	3.3	2.4	2.0

Source: House, Committee on Ways and Means, "Section 1: Social Security: The Old-Age, Survivors, and Disability Insurance (OASDI) Programs," *Green Book* (Washington, D.C., 1998).

rate of return on investment in business and industry of 7 percent.[47] Moreover, a system of personal accounts that belong to a worker could, as with other assets, be willed to a person of choice. At present, the benefits of a single worker who dies before or shortly after collecting remain a part of the fund and cannot be left to an heir.

A strength of the present system is that it is risk free, meaning that the government has a fixed obligation to the retiree. Any approach to financing that provides for market investment promises a greater rate of return than government securities, but increases risk to the individual. Market investments that are based on individual choice could result in a more equitable return, but without a government guaranteed income. They may not provide income adequacy for all participants.

One option would be for the government to "split" retirement benefits into a guaranteed benefit that is based on a progressive formula and supported by payroll taxes with a supplemental benefit from investments. The risks inherent in investing in the stock market and the lack of knowledge of how to invest are arguments that are made against turning over control to individuals, and it is possible that absent a mandatory system to ensure that monies are invested, individuals could use their monies for present needs. In addition, since the monies paid to retirees come from the taxes paid by those currently working, any change in the system would have to take account of how the government will continue to meet its obligations to those currently retired as well as to those close to retirement who do not have enough working years left to benefit from private investment accounts. If large numbers of those currently working pulled out of the system, the government would have few options for meeting its obligations. Alone or in combination (1) other spending would have to be curtailed, (2) benefits would have to be reduced, (3) taxes would have to be raised, (4) money would have to be borrowed, and/or (5) the conditions for receipt of benefits would have to change. Finally, the effects of privatization on the SSDI program and on survivor's benefits have not been clearly examined.[48]

Unemployment Insurance: Basic Program Definition and Operation

Unemployment insurance (UI) provides to an eligible claimant a part of the wages lost due to recent involuntary unemployment. By replacing a portion of lost wages, UI seeks to stabilize the economy during periods of recession. There are several unemployment insurance programs, including the "regular" federal-state program authorized under Title III of the Social Security Act (Table 9.1), plus two federally operated programs: the Unemployment Compensation for Federal Employees program that provides benefits to unemployed civilian federal employees and the Unemployment Compensation for Ex-Servicemen program that serves members of the armed service following their discharge from active duty. The discussion that follows is concerned with the "regular" UI program.

Unemployment insurance is a joint federal and state program.[49] At the federal level, the program is housed in the Department of Labor with each state, defined to include the District of Columbia, Puerto Rico, and the Virgin Islands, responsible for operating a state employment security agency (SECA) where claims are made.

Each state (1) finances its own benefit program, with administrative costs borne by the federal government and the costs of the extended benefit program (see next section) shared equally by the federal government and the states; (2) administers its own program within a regulatory framework that is set by the federal government; (3) collects payroll taxes; (4) determines who will and who will not receive benefits; (5) sets the benefit amount and benefit duration; and (6) sets the conditions for disqualifying individuals from the program. The states maintain accounts in the United States Treasury, in which funds are deposited from payroll taxes and from contributions from state and local government and some nonprofit employers who are reimbursing the fund for benefits paid to their former employees.[50] If a state runs low on money, due, for example, to a high and prolonged rate of unemployment, federal loans are available under Title XII of the Social Security Act (Table 9.1).

The Federal Unemployment Tax Act (FUTA) requires covered employers to pay a tax of 6.2 percent on the first $7,000 of yearly wages that are paid to each employee.[51] The federal government reduces this tax by 5.4 percent for states with no delinquent federal debts, resulting in a net tax rate to the states of 0.8 percent. The typical FUTA tax per worker is $56 since most earn more than $7,000 per year ($7,000 × 0.8 percent).

COVERED WORKERS AND BENEFICIARIES

In 1996, approximately 97 percent of all wage and salary workers were covered by the UI program.[52] Workers who are deemed eligible for benefits may receive them for up to twenty-six weeks (thirty weeks in Massachusetts and Washington) after which they may be eligible for an additional thirteen weeks of benefits under the Federal/State Extended Unemployment Compensation program of 1970, referred to generally as the Extended Benefits (EB) Program. The EB program is not automatic; rather, it is triggered by one of several formulas established in federal law. One formula used by a majority of states triggers the EB program whenever the unemployment rate for insured workers reaches 6 percent.

In 1996, approximately 36 percent of unemployed workers were receiving UI benefits. There are many reasons why the percent of beneficiaries is low, including (1) all workers are not covered by the UI system; (2) some of the unemployed may have exceed the twenty-six week benefit period or the EB period; (3) the statewide unemployment rate may be too low to trigger the EB period; (4) unemployment may have been voluntary or due to work-related misbehavior; (5) claimants may be unavailable for work or unwilling to accept an offered position; (6) some unemployed workers may not have worked for the required state-established "base period" or may not have the required base-period earnings, ranging from a low of $130 in Hawaii to $3,400 in Florida[53]; or (7) some workers may be unemployed due to a labor dispute.[54]

THE READY, WILLING, AND ABLE TO WORK REQUIREMENT

In all states, throughout the benefit period, claimants must be ready, willing, and able to work. Most states require that the applicant for benefits register for work at a local employment office, that an applicant be pursuing employment or making a reasonable effort to find work, and that the applicant accept "suitable" employment. Refusing, without good cause, an offer of suitable employment is a basis for denying or terminating benefits.

Suitable employment is employment that (1) does not pose a threat to the claimant's health, safety, and morals; (2) does not exceed what the claimant is physically fit and trained to perform; and (3) is geographically proximate to the claimant's residence. In considering whether to grant or deny benefits, UI programs generally take account of the likelihood that applicants will find customary work that is close to their places of residence. As the length of unemployment increases, the SECA expects claimants to broaden their definitions of suitable work.

The EB program requires that states deny extended benefits to applicants who are unwilling to accept jobs that are offered in writing or are listed with the state employment office. In addition, EB may be denied when applicants do not apply for jobs to which they are referred by the state, if the work (1) is within the person's capabilities, (2) pays a wage that is equal to the minimum wage, (3) pays a gross weekly wage that exceeds the person's average weekly unemployment benefit plus any supplemental unemployment compensation, and (4) is in other respects consistent with the state's definition of suitable work.[55]

If there is not a fit between the applicant and an available job, the states must refer those claiming EB to any job that satisfies these requirements. However, a state has discretion not to make such a referral if the state determines that a claimant's chances of finding work in her or his customary occupation within a short period of time are good.

There are exceptions to the rule requiring claimants to accept offered work. A job may be turned down if (1) the position is vacant due to a strike, lockout, or other labor dispute; (2) the wages, hours, or other conditions of the work offered are substantially less favorable to the individual than those prevailing for similar work in the locality; or (3) if, as a condition of being employed, the individual would be required to join a union or to resign from or refrain from joining any bona fide labor organization.[56]

Each state determines the amount of the unemployment benefit, which replaces between 50 and 70 percent of lost pretax wages. However, because there is an inverse relationship between earnings and benefits, where the highest wage earners receive lower replacement rates, the average benefit received in 1996 was approximately 35 percent of lost wages. As noted earlier, benefits are available for up to twenty-six weeks, with the possibility of a thirteen-week extension.

The average weekly benefits paid by ten highest paying and ten lowest paying states are shown in Table 9.3. The minimum and maximum weekly benefits are also shown. The range of benefits paid in the states with the highest benefit ranges from $270 per week in Hawaii to $213 per week in Illinois. The range in the lowest paying states is $94 in Puerto Rico to $170 in Arkansas. The minimum weekly benefit in 1997, not counting those states that provide a benefit for dependents, ranged from a low of $5 in Hawaii to $60 in New Jersey. In the same year, the

TABLE 9.3. Amount and Duration of Weekly Benefits for Total Unemployment
Paid by the Ten Highest Paying and Ten Lowest Paying States: 1996 and 1997

State	1996 average weekly benefit*	1996 average weekly wage	1997 weekly benefit amount	
			Minimum	Maximum
Hawaii	270	501	5	351
New Jersey	255	684	60	374
Massachusetts	254	656	14–21	362–543
District of Columbia	236	773	50	309
Minnesota	234	549	38	314
Rhode Island	228	496	41–51	336–420
Delaware	224	594	20	300
Connecticut	222	707	15–25	353–403
Pennsylvania	219	547	35–40	362–370
Illinois	213	602	51	257–341
Puerto Rico	94	NI	7	152
Louisiana	128	475	10	193
Mississippi	141	409	30	180
Alabama	142	471	22	180
South Dakota	150	382	28	187
Virgin Islands	150	NI	32	231
Arizona	151	499	40	185
California	152	601	40	230
New Hampshire	153	535	32	228
Arkansas	170	418	49	273

Source: Compiled by the author from data in House, Committee on Ways and Means, "Section
4: Unemployment Compensation," *Green Book* (Washington. D.C., 1998).
*States showing a range pay a dependent's benefits.

maximum benefit ranged from a high of $374 in New Jersey to a low of $152 in
Puerto Rico.

EXHAUSTING BENEFITS

The assumption that workers who claim unemployment benefits will be re-
employed within a relatively short time period can be inferred from the fact that
UI benefits are available for no more than thirty-nine weeks if the rate of unemployment is high enough to trigger an EB period. The regularly employed worker
who is temporarily laid off during slow business cycles is the kind of the person for
whom the program was created. Benefit exhaustion is more likely to occur during
extended periods of recession, during which spells of unemployment increase.[57]

For a significant number of workers, the thirty-nine-week benefit period is not
sufficient. In 1996, 2.7 million workers (33 percent of those who received benefits in
the twelve months ending March 1996) exhausted their benefits.[58] Those most likely

to return to work before exhausting benefits are workers referred to by the Department of Labor as "job attached" meaning that they are laid off and recalled to work before their benefits run out. A significant number of workers whose jobs are terminated and those with low skill levels exhaust their benefits.[59]

PROBLEMS IN THE UNEMPLOYMENT INSURANCE PROGRAM

There are several significant problems in the operation of the UI system. As earlier noted, the system benefits mainly the so-called "attached" workers who experience periodic layoffs between extended periods of employment.

The unattached include those who have lost their jobs and who have difficulty finding new work. (Recall the reference in chapter 8 to the estimated 1 million manufacturing jobs lost.) The unattached include also seasonal workers, for example, those in the tourist industry who may be unable to fulfill the requirement for four consecutive quarters of work.

The EB program has two problems. First, it is subject to ongoing "tinkering." Rather than make a statutory provision that mandates automatic extensions of the twenty-six-week program when periods of recession result in protracted periods of unemployment, piecemeal programs are put in place.[60] Congress may do this by voting to extend the period for unemployment benefits during periods of recession. An example of this is the Temporary Emergency Unemployment Compensation Program, operated from November 1991 through April 1994. This temporary program provided either seven or thirteen additional weeks of benefits. In 1992, the federal government provided for a new "optional trigger" that would have added seven weeks of benefits, but no more than seven states have adopted this trigger.

A second and more serious problem is the use of the statewide unemployment rate as a trigger for extended benefits, since the state rate may mask within-state pockets of high unemployment. The cost of such strict limits on extended benefits is high. The Center on Budget Policies and Priorities reports that during the height of the 1993 recession in California, the long-term unemployed constituted 25 percent of the total unemployed, resulting in approximately 50,000 California workers per month who exhausted their regular UI benefits without finding work.[61]

Workers' Compensation

Wisconsin passed the first workers' compensation law in 1911. Today, workers' compensation programs are operated by all the states, including the District of Columbia, Puerto Rico, and the United States Virgin Islands.[62] With the exception of several federal programs discussed in this section, workers' compensation programs are state run. Private employers purchase insurance coverage for their workers from private insurance companies.

Workers' compensation programs provide cash payments to replace lost wages, and they cover medical expenses for injury or death sustained in the performance of a work-related service. The claimant must demonstrate that the injury arose out of the performance of a work- related service, meaning that a causal connection between the task performed and the injury sustained must be established. If a worker cannot make the requisite showing and is deemed ineligible for benefits, he or she may have recourse to SSDI or to cash assistance through the Supplemental Security Income Program (see chapter 10.)[63]

The theory behind workers' compensation programs is that injured employees promptly receive cash benefits for which they give up their right to sue for work-related injuries. State statutes preclude litigation-based awards to injured employees unless they can demonstrate that the employer intended to cause harm.[64] Thus, workers' compensation is the exclusive remedy for work-related injury or death. State statutes typically protect a worker from retaliatory discharge for filing a workers' compensation claim.

Each state sets the amount of benefit as a percentage of wages. States use as a baseline either the national average weekly wage or the state's average weekly or monthly wage. The majority of states provide a benefit equal to or greater than two-thirds of the baseline wage up to a weekly maximum. In 1998, Mississippi's weekly benefit of $279.78 was the lowest of the fifty states, with only Puerto Rico's maximum of $65.00 per week paying less. Iowa, with a weekly payment of $903, was the highest paying state.[65]

Most states provide benefits for the duration of the work-sustained disability, although some states have a maximum benefit. For example, Kansas sets a limit of $100,000, and Tennessee sets a limit of $196,800. States commonly offset the benefit against other received benefits, such as those obtained from an employer's pension or disability plan, unemployment insurance, or Social Security disability benefits.

The Office of Workers' Compensation Programs (OWCP) in the United States Department of Labor was established in 1916 to administer workers' compensation claims under three programs:(1) the Federal Employees' Compensation Act provides benefits to more than three million federal employees, including members of the Peace Corps, Vista volunteers, Reserve Officers Training Corps Cadets, Job Corps, Youth Corps enrollees and, under limited conditions, to nonfederal law enforcement officers who sustain injuries involving crimes against the United States; (2) the Longshore and Harbor Workers' Compensation Act of 1927 provides coverage to maritime workers who sustain injury or who are killed on the navigable waters of the United States as well as workers on "adjoining piers, docks and terminals" (Compensation under this act is paid by employers who are self-insured or through insurance policies provided by private insurers to employers); and (3) the Black Lung Benefits Reform Act of 1977 provides monthly payments and medical treatment to coal miners totally disabled from pneumoconiosis (black lung disease) arising from their employment in the nation's coal mines and monthly payments to their surviving dependents.[66]

Earned Income Tax Credit

Thus far we have discussed the provision of cash to individuals who have retired; become disabled or unemployed; or have had work-related injuries. The reviewed programs provide assistance by transferring cash, either from a unit of government or an insurance carrier to an individual in need.

Income from other sources is also available to individuals and families. Some of these sources are reviewed in subsequent chapters. Here we are concerned with a specific benefit that is available though the United States Tax Code. Although not further discussed, you should know that many tax code benefits accrue mainly to middle- and upper-income people. For example, the ability to deduct mortgage interest and property taxes reduces the overall costs of home ownership, making more of one's wages available for consumption, and the same is true for employer-paid health insurance and pension benefits. In this concluding section, we are concerned with the Earned Income Tax Credit (EITC).

The federal government first made the EITC available to low-income working taxpayers with children in 1975 and extended the program to low-income working taxpayers who do not have children in 1994. In addition, in 1998, ten states were operating EITC programs to alleviate the burden of state and local taxes. The federal program has a dual goal of countering the impact of Social Security taxes on low-income families and of encouraging low-income families to seek employment rather than welfare.

Taxpayers access EITC benefits by filing an income tax return. The amount of any tax rebate varies by income, by whether the claimant has children and, if so, by the number of children. In 1997, the maximum credit available to a taxpayer with one child and an income of $6,500 was equal to 34 percent of earnings, which translated into a rebate of $2,210. The corresponding figures for a taxpayer with two children was a maximum income of $9,140, yielding a credit of 40 percent of earnings and a rebate of $3,656. As income increases, the amount of the credit decreases, and there is no additional benefit for families with more than two children. In 1997, the credit phased out completely at $25,750.[67] The Personal Responsibility and Work Opportunity Act of 1996 (see chapter 10) modified the EITC program by making ineligible those taxpayers with investment income exceeding $2,200, regardless of their earned income, and denied the credit to taxpayers without valid Social Security numbers.[68]

The EITC is available only to those whose earnings indicate financial need, and, as such, it is a means-tested program. However, it is an atypical means-tested program because the amount of a rebate may exceed the amount of taxes withheld, resulting in a transfer of funds from the general treasury.[69] The EITC is a therefore a negative income tax. The EITC, unlike other means-tested programs that are reviewed in the next chapter, operates through the Internal Revenue Service (IRS). The IRS, while conducting compliance reviews to uncover fraud (for example, by checking the validity of Social Security numbers),[70] assumes good faith on the part of the taxpayers who are not forced to jump through hoops to receive their benefits. Because the entire transaction is carried out on paper, the stigma that may result from going to a welfare office is absent. Finally, taxpayers may elect to receive their EITC through an advanced payment program where they receive their credit in their paychecks and do not have to wait until they file a return to receive their rebate. Consider the following example of how the EITC works.

A single parent with one child, working full time throughout the year at a wage of $8 per hour, earns $16,600 per year. This worker owes $342 in 1998 federal income taxes which are withheld from the paycheck during the year. The family also qualifies for an EITC of $1,577. The EITC allows the family to get back the $342 it paid in income taxes and to receive an additional refund of $1,235. The EITC refund serves to offset some of the worker's $2,540 in payroll taxes that also were paid during the year.[71]

For those who claim children, there is a test for relationship, residency, and age. The claimed child must be a natural child, grandchild, stepchild, foster, or adopted child of the taxpayer, and the child must reside with the taxpayer in the United States for more than one half of the tax year. Moreover, the child must be younger than nineteen years of age, unless the child is a full-time student, in which case the child may be claimed until age twenty-four, or the child must be permanently and totally disabled.

The staff of the Committee on Ways and Means of the House of Representatives estimated that more than 18.5 million wage earners were expected to take advantage of the EITC in 1997. Direct payments were expected to be close to $22 billion, which exceeds the benefits paid by the Aid to Families with Dependent Children Program in 1996. The average credit per family in the year 2000 is estimated to be $1,557.[72]

According to the Center on Budget and Policy Priorities, in 1996, the EITC lifted 4.6 million people, including 2.4 million children, out of poverty. The EITC is said to help more working families out of poverty than any other government program.

Summary

The passage of the Social Security Act of 1935 marked the entry of the federal government into the welfare arena. The act was part of the federal response to the national emergency that was created by the Great Depression of 1929. The emergency it created was of such magnitude as to preclude its resolution by the states acting alone. Thus, the constitutional wall that had maintained a separation between federal and state government in providing for the general welfare of the public fell, and it was acknowledged that the effort to rebuild the American economy required federal leadership and federal funds.

To convince policymakers and the public that the Social Security Act was necessary, it was portrayed and "sold" as a form of insurance. Workers were to invest a portion of their earnings in government controlled old age insurance accounts, and in return, they would receive a measure of financial security should they become disabled or when they retired. Provisions of the act that did not fit within the insurance concept, such as Aid to Dependent Children and unemployment benefits, were downplayed as was the fact the system operated as a "pay-as-you- go" system where income collected from those currently employed and their employers was redistributed to retirees.

In this chapter, three titles of the act were reviewed as was one portion of the United States Tax Code that provides for income to low wage earners.

Financial assistance is available to eligible disabled workers, their dependents, and survivors and to retirees through the OASDI program. Program revenues come mainly from taxes that are withheld from employees, from an employer's matching contribution, and from payments directly made by the self-employed. To ensure an adequate income at retirement, the program provides for low wage earners to have a higher portion of their earnings replaced than high wage earners.

Since the Social Security system operates on a "pay-as-you-go" basis, the ratio of workers to retirees must yield sufficient income to support retirees lest taxes be raised, funds borrowed, or other social programs cut. The ratio of workers to retirees has been steadily decreasing and will fall dramatically as the 76 million "baby boomers" retire in large numbers in the second decade of this century. Recommendations for restoring solvency to the program include traditional measures, such as advancing the age of retirement or increasing the payroll tax, as well as novel approaches that allow some or all of a worker's contributions to be invested in funds of the worker's choice or with investment decisions shared by the worker with the federal government. The latter options are expected to yield a rate of return in excess of the 2.5 percent return on the securities in which the government currently invests social security taxes.

The act UI program is funded by a tax that is levied on employers, and certain program costs are paid by the federal government. A program participant receives a portion of lost wages for up to twenty-six weeks, and there is a possibility of an additional thirteen weeks of assistance when statewide unemployment reaches a specified percent. Only a small percent of the unemployed receive UI benefits. Not all workers are covered by the program, some who were covered exceed the maximum benefit period, others leave their jobs voluntarily or are dismissed for work-related misbehavior, and others may not have worked the required period of time before losing their jobs.

The program serves best the laid-off worker who experiences episodic periods of unemployment punctuated by prolonged work periods. The system's weaknesses are most apparent (1) for the seasonal worker who does not maintain a job long enough to establish eligibility for the program; (2) when the economy moves into a recession with lengthy periods of unemployment; and (3) when unemployment rates are differential within a state such that the state rate does not go high enough to trigger the program.

The workers' compensation program was the last of the three programs created under the 1935 act that are reviewed in this chapter. Workers' compensation programs replace a portion of lost wages to workers who are injured in the performance of their work and to the families of a worker who is killed on the job. In exchange for a guaranteed benefit, workers forgo their right to sue for on-the-job injuries except for those rare cases where workers can demonstrate that their employers intended to cause them harm.

Under provisions contained in the United States Tax Code, low wage earners may be eligible for the EITC. The EITC exists to counter somewhat the impact of Social Security taxes and to encourage work rather than welfare. The benefits of the EITC are accessed by filing an income tax return. If wages fall below a set amount (in 1997, $6,500 for a taxpayer with one child), the taxpayer receives a rebate. The EITC is unique relative to other programs that are means tested. Operating through the filing of a tax return, the recipient does no more than what is required of all wage earners, and because the benefit is received as a tax refund, the program does not carry the stigma often associated with welfare programs.

CHAPTER **10**

Programs of Public Assistance

In this chapter we continue our review of government programs that provide cash assistance to people in need. Unlike those programs reviewed in chapter 9, the ones covered here do not bear any relationship to a claimant's work history. The reviewed programs are referred to collectively as public assistance, and they are the programs that usually come to mind when reference is made to "welfare."

Five of the six reviewed programs are part of the Social Security Act (see Table 9.1). The authority for these programs is found in Title IV (Aid to Families with Dependent Children/Temporary Assistance for Needy Families Program) (AFDC/TANF), Title XVI (Supplemental Security Income for people with disabilities), and Titles I, X, and XIV that provide grants for old age assistance (Title I) and disabilities (X and XIV) but apply only to Puerto Rico, Guam, the United States Virgin Islands, and American Samoa. Finally, general assistance programs that are created by state law with no federal involvement are reviewed.

Of the original public assistance titles, AFDC affects the greatest number of people and has been the most controversial of the act's original programs. The controversial nature of public assistance programs was recognized in 1935 when, as noted in chapter 9, these titles were downplayed relative to the insurance titles. Concern that the availability of cash assistance to women raising children on their own would provide an incentive for them to have "illegitimate" children and for men to desert their families was voiced immediately after the passage of Mother's Pension laws in the early nineteenth century (chapter 2) and has echoed through the twentieth century.[1] This chapter begins with a brief discussion of the original Aid to Dependent Children (ADC) program and a review of some of the amendments to the law that governs aid to needy children and their caretakers. The events that led up to the demise of what Martha Derthick (1979) has referred to as the "despised alternative" to the insurance titles of the act are also discussed.[2] Next, income support programs for people with disabilities are reviewed, as are general assistance programs.

SECTION 1: AID TO DEPENDENT CHILDREN AND EFFORTS TO CONTROL CASELOAD SIZE

The ADC program was built on the foundation laid by the Mother's Pension programs of the early twentieth century and provided financial assistance only to children, with no cash grant for the child's caretaker. The ADC program, like its predecessors, was grounded in a basic mistrust of those in need, and from the beginning efforts were made to control the size of the ADC caseload and to ensure that benefits went only to those deemed worthy of help.

From the program's inception in 1935 through the 1960s, the worthiness of a child to receive cash assistance was determined (1) on the basis of the mother's marital status when she gave birth, with "illegitimacy" providing the grounds for deeming the home unsuitable and for denying aid; (2) by whether a woman had a man, not her husband, living in her home; (3) by whether the mother fostered religious training; and (4) on the basis of her race, with African American families unlikely to receive any assistance.[3] A variety of methods were used and rules imposed to limit access to public assistance, including unannounced home visits to determine the suitability of the home, residency requirements that denied aid to people who moved across state lines, barriers erected to deny a fair hearing to anyone who was denied benefits or who lost their grant, and "employable mother rules" that denied aid to an applicant "as long as [her labors] were needed in the cotton fields."[4]

When the act was passed in 1935, its objective was to provide financial aid to needy dependent children so that they could be maintained in their own homes.[5] There were no provisions to help families become self-sufficient and to move off of the welfare rolls. A 1940 policy statement issued by the federal Bureau of Public Assistance referred to "services" to improve the conditions in a child's home, but services were not defined nor was their provision mandated.[6] In 1956, the objective of Title IV was modified when the phrase "and other services" was added, so that its purpose became "to provide financial assistance and other services" to needy dependent children and the parents or relatives with whom they live to help to strengthen and maintain family life. However, these services were not defined.[7]

The 1960s saw other changes to the ADC program. Judicial rulings brought an end to the practice of making unannounced home visits and of denying aid to families who were not residents of the states in which application was made. In 1961, the program was modified to allow for the provision of aid to families where there was an unemployed father in the home, and in 1962, a caretaker grant was added and the program was renamed Aid to Families with Dependent Children.

Also in 1962, the "service amendments" to Title IV were passed.[8] Their purpose was to encourage the states to create and provide social services and to hire case-workers who would assist welfare recipients with the ultimate goal of reducing the number of people receiving aid. For reasons discussed in chapter 1, the 1962 amendments did not result in helping people attain self-sufficiency. In fact, the welfare rolls increased. Between December 1960 and February 1969, more than 800,000 families were added, an increase of 107 percent.[9] By 1967, disenchantment with the idea that social casework was an intervention that could reduce welfare dependency was widespread, and in that year Congress addressed the subject of moving AFDC recipients off the rolls and into paid employment.

The first mandatory work requirement for AFDC recipients was written into law in 1967.[10] The Work Incentive Program (WIN was the acronym used) was created. "Employable" persons older than age sixteen were required to sign up for job training or work as a condition for AFDC eligibility. The WIN program required AFDC recipients to register for work but did not require participation in a work program. In 1986, there were 1.6 million AFDC clients registered with WIN, but only 220,000 were receiving services. In 1988, Congress acted again. The Family Support Act replaced WIN with the Job Opportunities and Basic Skills Training Program (JOBS).[11] Federal law required each state to operate a JOBS program, and most able-bodied parents had to participate except for those whose youngest child was younger than age three.[12] States were required to guarantee care for an AFDC child younger than age thirteen if care was a necessary condition for a parent to participate in the program. In 1992, the states were exempting more than one-half of the adult caseload from JOBS requirements, including women with children younger than age three, women with disabilities, and those with problems in finding transportation or appropriate child care. In some states, 70 to 80 percent of a state's caseload was exempt from work requirements.[13]

The fact the 1962 service amendments and work programs did not reduce the size of the welfare rolls explains only the maintenance of the status quo, but it does not cast light on the question, "Why did the number of people receiving AFDC increase?" To answer this question, we must look elsewhere.

In his inaugural address, President John F. Kennedy issued a "call to arms" in which he asked Americans to confront head-on the problems of poverty. A conservative Congress blocked Kennedy's efforts to enact antipoverty legislation, but after his assassination the Johnson administration was successful in getting legislation passed that would launch the programs of the "Great Society" or "The War on Poverty," as they were commonly known. The Economic Opportunity Act (EOA) was passed in August 1964, and the Office of Economic Opportunity (OEO) in Washington was assigned responsibility for administering the programs that were to be developed under it.[14] The objective of Great Society programs was to reduce poverty by encouraging the "maximum feasible participation" of people in poor communities to develop and operate programs created under the EOA. Education and work training were to help people develop the skills necessary for them to exit the welfare rolls.[15]

The Great Society is significant to this discussion because of the effect it had on the growth of the AFDC rolls. Specifically, social workers and attorneys working at community service programs that operated out of local OEO offices informed people of their eligibility for public assistance and assisted people in applying for welfare benefits. In addition, attorneys brought suits that resulted in overturning a variety of restrictive eligibility rules, such as residency requirements, and in bringing a stop to such practices as unannounced home visits.[16]

The National Welfare Rights Organization (NWRO) was an outgrowth of the Great Society. Social workers, participants in the Volunteers in Service to America Program (VISTA), a domestic Peace Corps, and attorneys participated in local NWROs where the process of informing people of their entitlement to welfare continued. The NWROs provided also a forum for organizing groups to demonstrate against restrictive eligibility rules. In 1967, there were 200 welfare rights groups in seventy cities. By 1972, the AFDC roles more than doubled, with an annual average growth of 16.9 percent.[17]

By the end of the 1960s, America was retreating on the War on Poverty. Great Society programs had to compete for funds with the war in Vietnam, there was some evidence of corruption and mismanagement of program funds by local groups, and there was growing disenchantment on the part of bureaucrats with programs that were using government funds to fight the government.[18] The ascent of Richard Nixon to the presidency in 1969 marked the demise of Great Society programs. However, the number of individual AFDC recipients continued to increase from 7,429,000 in 1970, to 10,597,000 in 1990, and to an estimated 14,226,000 in 1994.[19]

Neither the service amendments nor work programs reduced the number of AFDC recipients, but numbers and program costs were not the only forces driving the demand for welfare reform. There was little public support for the AFDC program, and recipients themselves found it degrading and demoralizing. The welfare system was not only blamed for discouraging workforce participation but also for encouraging out-of-wedlock births. For example, the majority of women on welfare had their first child as a teenager; more than two-thirds of all out-of-wedlock childbearers ended up on welfare; and 84 percent of teen mothers who were not married when their first child was born became welfare recipients.[20] Just over one-half of teen mothers completed high school during adolescence and early adulthood, and of those who did, most had few basic skills. Thus, their earning potential was low, increasing the likelihood of remaining on welfare. Moreover, only 20 percent of the fathers of children born to teens were ordered to pay child support, and of those so ordered only a small fraction paid the award amount.[21] Also, welfare was seen as perpetuating intergenerational poverty (see chapter 8 and the discussion of the culture of poverty.), and the length of time that families spent on welfare was a matter of great concern. Determining the length of time that families remain on the AFDC rolls is a complicated task, and the picture produced by different researchers is often contradictory.[22] Using data compiled by the United States Census Bureau from the National Longitudinal Study of Youth, we learn that people moved on and off of the welfare rolls. In an "average" year, one-half of the caseload left, due mainly to finding work, but many returned when a recession hit or when their seasonal work came to an end. Those who departed were replaced by new entrants and by returning recipients.[23] Additionally, approximately one-half of the persons on the rolls at a given time had received benefits, counting repeat spells, for more than six and one-half years, and close to 35 percent of new enrollees were expected to receive benefits for six years.[24]

SECTION 2: WELFARE REFORM AND THE TEMPORARY ASSISTANCE TO NEEDY FAMILIES PROGRAM

Efforts to reform welfare programs have a long history and include the 1962 service amendments and the WIN and JOBS programs discussed previously. In 1994, when the Republican party gained control of Congress, the momentum to reform welfare was strong. The AFDC caseload was the highest that it had ever been, with an average of 5 million families, or one in seven American families, served by the program, at a cost of $14.2 billion in federal funds in addition to $11.9 billion in state and local funds.[25] Reform had played a role in the 1992 presidential campaign when candidate Clinton promised to "end welfare as we know it," and it was a central part of the Republican parties "Contract With America." In early 1995, a debate began in Congress and between Congress and President Clinton on the subject of reforming the AFDC program.[26] The debate was about reducing federal expenditures for welfare, and it was also about ideology. The latter covered a range of issues, including the proper means for achieving policy goals; the responsibility of government for assisting people in need; and the proper balance of responsibility between the federal government and state governments in establishing policy goals, devising methods to achieve policy goals, and controlling access to public assistance. The issue of federal versus state control is captured in the term "devolution," which refers to a reduced federal role in setting all the regulations that govern the operation of social welfare programs in favor of an increased decision-making role for people and units of government that are closest to the problem that is being addressed. As you will see from the following discussion, when Congress passed the TANF program, state decision-making authority increased relative to state authority under the AFDC program. However, the federal government still sets regulations within which the state decision making occurs. Because the states have always had autonomy in making certain decisions that control the operation of the AFDC program, devolution is best understood as a shifting balance in federal versus state authority, not as an abrogation of control by the federal government.

In August 1996, the Personal Responsibility and Work Opportunity Reconciliation Act (PRWOA) was signed into law by President Clinton. The PRWOA created changes in the Supplemental Security Income Program (SSI) (see section 3) and the Food Stamp Program (see chapter 11), and it repealed three federal programs: AFDC, Emergency Assistance for Needy Families,[27] and JOBS. These programs were replaced by the Title I TANF program. The states had until July 1, 1997, to implement TANF.

Temporary Assistance to Needy Families Compared to Aid to Families with Dependent Children

Similarities and differences between the AFDC and TANF programs are shown in Table 10.1. As was the case with AFDC, TANF is funded jointly by the federal government and the states. The federal share of program costs is inversely related to a state's per capita income, with poorer states receiving a greater share of program costs. In 1996, federal matching funds varied from 50 percent to 78 percent of benefit costs and was set at 50 percent of the costs of program administration.[28] The TANF program requires states to continue their contributions (referred to as the "Maintenance of Effort" requirement) to the program at a rate equal to 75 percent of the funds allocated in fiscal year 1994, the year in which caseloads peaked, or 80 percent if a state fails to meet TANF's mandatory work requirements.

Native American tribes, including some Native Alaskan groups, may design and operate their own cash benefit programs for needy children. By April 1999, sixty-two Native American and Alaskan groups located in twelve states had chosen this option.[29] When programs are operated directly by a tribal organization, funds are taken from a state's TANF Block Grant. Native American recipients who live in Indian reservations or an Alaskan Native village, with a population of at least 1,000 and an adult unemployment rate of 50 percent, are exempt from the sixty-month benefit time limit.

The AFDC program identified categories of people that states were obliged to serve as long as an applicant's income was below state-set limits. Under TANF, states are free to determine who is eligible, but the requirement that an eligible family is one with at least one minor child or a pregnant women is still used. Unmarried teens must live with a parent or other responsible adult. Teenagers who have not completed high school or its equivalent may meet their work obligation if they remain in school, attend a program leading to an equivalence certificate, or attend an educational program that is directly related to employment.[30]

Individuals convicted after August 22, 1996, of a drug-related felony are ineligible for federally funded assistance as is anyone who fraudulently misrepresented their residence to obtain food stamps or Medicaid. States may elect to disqualify anyone who fails to assign child support or spousal support rights to the state. A parent who will not cooperate with the state in establishing paternity and in obtaining an order for child support may have his or her benefit reduced or terminated, but states may establish "good cause" exceptions to this rule, for example, for victims of domestic violence whose compliance would make it difficult for them to escape domestic violence or would unfairly penalize individuals who are or have been victimized by domestic violence.[31] States determine the income level below which an applicant may be eligible for benefits and the amount of the benefit to be paid.

The passage of TANF ended the open-ended entitlement that existed under AFDC. An entitlement program is one in which all who met a state's eligibility requirements receive benefits. Under AFDC, there was no ceiling on the costs that the federal government would pay. When TANF was passed, a capped-block-grant program replaced the open-ended entitlement. With capped block grants, each state

TABLE 10.1. AFDC Compared to TANF on Several Dimensions

Dimension	AFDC	TANF
State funding	Match required for each federal dollar	States must spend 75% of "historic" levels
Categories eligible	Children with one parent or with an incapacitated parent or unemployed second parent	Set by state
Income limits	Set by state	Set by state
Benefit levels	Set by state	Set by state
Federal funding	Unlimited	Fixed block grant
Entitlement	States had to assist all eligible families	No entitlement to aid
Work trigger	None	Work required within two years of receiving benefits
Time limit for benefits	None	Sixty months with hardship exemption for 20% of caseload
Work requirement	JOBS program required participation but not work	Fifty percent of each state's caseload must be engaged in specified work activities by 2002
Exemptions from work	Parents with children under age three or under age one at state option	None. States may exempt single parents caring for child under age one year.

Source: House, Committee on Ways and Means, 105th Cong., 2nd sess., "Section 7: Aid to Families with Dependent Children and Temporary Assistance for Needy Families (Title IV-A)," *Green Book: Background Material and Data on Programs Within the Jurisdiction of the Committee on Ways and Means* (Washington, D.C., 1998), Table 7.1.

knows in advance the amount of money it will receive. If the number of program applicants exceeds the appropriated funds, assistance is denied, or if granted, assistance is paid for by the state entirely from its own revenues. The TANF program provides for the federal government to make a yearly lump-sum payment to each state whose share of the TANF Block Grant is based on the combined amount of money received by the state for AFDC, Emergency Assistance for Needy Families, and the JOBS program, in fiscal year 1994, fiscal year 1995, or the average of funds received for fiscal years 1992 through 1994, whichever is highest.[32]

Because the amount of the grant received by each is based on years when case-loads were high, TANF has produced an economic windfall for a number of states. The combination of the additional funds provided by the federal government and the state's share under the "Maintenance of Effort" requirement (which, like the federal share is fixed and not dependent on the number of beneficiaries) produced economic gains in 1997 for forty-five states that were eligible to receive more funding under TANF than they received under AFDC in 1996.[33] As of early 1999, New York, for example, built up a $500 million surplus in federal welfare that was expected to grow to $1.4 billion in the next year. Some of these funds would be allocated to helping TANF recipients make the transition from work to welfare, with about $400 million to be left in the United States Treasury as a hedge against an economic downturn.[34]

A supplemental block grant is available for four years for states that experienced a 10 percent population growth between 1990 and 1994 and for states whose baseline year grant was 35 percent below the national average. In the event of a recession or other emergency, there is a loan fund and a contingency fund that provides matching grants to states that require assistance.[35] States may also save any portion of their TANF grant for future use by leaving revenues in the United States Treasury. Most states have their own "rainy day" fund for use in the event of emergency.

Unlike AFDC, TANF contains a "trigger" requiring beneficiaries to participate in work (defined later) within two years of receiving benefits and precludes the receipt of assistance beyond sixty months. The sixty months need not be consecutive; thus, a family may move on and off the rolls over a period of years as long as the total time does not exceed sixty months. But states may cut recipients off in less time. Connecticut, Massachusetts, and Louisiana have short time periods (discussed later) and have dropped between 5,000 and 19,000 families from their welfare rolls. Wisconsin, which implemented its welfare reform program before required to do so by federal law, has been extending benefit periods for those reaching the state-imposed maximum, and Connecticut, as discussed later, has a "safety net" program that allows exemptions and extensions under certain circumstances.[36]

Under federal law, the sixty-month time limit applies only to "assistance" defined as "cash, payments, vouchers, and other . . . benefits designed to meet a family's ongoing basic needs [for] food, clothing, shelter, utilities, household goods, personal care items, and general incidental expenses."[37] Aid that may be provided for more than sixty months includes (1) nonrecurring benefits provided to resolve a short-term crisis that is likely to be resolved within four months; (2) one-time assistance that is provided through a diversion program (discussed later); (3) payments that subsidize employment of a TANF recipient; (4) TANF funds that an individuals saves in an individual development account (discussed later) (5) support services such as child care and transportation for employed families; (6) an earned income tax credit refund (see chapter 9); (7) services including counseling, case management, peer support, child care information and referral, transitional services, job retention, job advancement, and other employment-related services that do not provide basic income support; and (8) transportation benefits provided under a Job Access or Reverse Commute project (discussed later) to an individual who is not otherwise receiving assistance. In addition, child-only cases, such as families in which a parent is receiving Supplemental Security Income (discussed later) or a child is being cared for by a relative who is not a TANF recipient, are exempt, as are cases supported by state funds.

Federal law provides that the states may exempt up to 20 percent of their TANF caseload from the sixty-month time limit for reasons of "hardship," which the states are free to define. Exemptions may include people with disabilities or an individual who has been battered or subjected to extreme cruelty.[38] From their evaluation of experimental programs that were implemented in seven states before the passage of TANF, all of which set time limits for receipt of benefits (see the later discussion of waiver programs), the Manpower Demonstration Research Corporation (1999) reported that states exempted "child-only" cases, where there was no caretaker grant, and cases where the adult recipient was older than age sixty. Incapacitated adults and those caring for an incapacitated child were also exempt, but problems were created because of the vague definition of children's incapacity, because adults whose disability made it difficult to work were not considered incapacitated, and because some adults could not obtain medical documentation of their incapacitating condition.[39]

Goals of the Temporary Assistance to Needy Families Program

The TANF program and the AFDC program it replaced share the goal of providing financial support to families to allow children to be raised in their own homes or in the home of relatives. However, TANF seeks also to modify the behavior of current or soon-to-be parents through a series of objectives intended to (1) reduce welfare dependency, (2) increase work opportunities for parents, (3) control welfare spending, (4) restore the American family, and (5) reduce out-of-wedlock pregnancies.

Program Operation

All states participate in TANF, although federal law does not require that they do so. Each state submits a TANF plan to the Department of Health and Human Services (DHHS), whose approval of the plan is a condition for receipt of federal funds. The state plan is a written document that outlines how the state will (1) operate a state-administered or state-supervised program of financial aid for needy families, with or expecting children, that provides job preparation, requires participation in work, and provides support services to parents[40]; (2) require financially assisted caretakers to engage in work as defined by the state when the state determines that they are ready to do so, but no later than twenty-four months after a caretaker first receives TANF support; (3) maintain the confidentiality of recipient information collected using federal funds; (4) prevent and reduce the incidence of out-of-wedlock pregnancies, especially teenage pregnancies, including setting numerical goals for reducing the rate of illegitimate births, providing education concerning statutory rape, and involving men in the education program. In addition, the plan must (5) report whether the state will assist noncitizens; (6) establish objective criteria for delivering benefits, determining eligibility, and allowing applicants whose benefits have been terminated or who have been denied benefits a chance to appeal; (7) certify that the state will operate a child support enforcement program and a foster care and adoption assistance program and will ensure that children served by a foster care or adoption program will receive medical assistance under the Medicaid program; (8) identify the state agency or agencies responsible for administering and supervising the TANF program; and (9) at state option, certify that standards and procedures are in place to identify individuals with a history of domestic violence and to make referrals for counseling and other services where appropriate.

PARTICIPATION IN WORK

The percentage of a state's TANF caseload that must engage in work is set by federal rules. Rates of participation began at 25 percent in 1997 and will rise to 50 percent in 2002 and thereafter, with a required 90 percent participation rate in 2002 for two-parent families. States may exempt from work requirements single parents who are caring for a child younger than one year. A state's required rate of participation is lowered by the secretary of DHHS if the state's caseload is reduced below its fiscal year 1995 level.[41] In December 1998, thirty-six states reported to DHHS that they met the work requirements for 1997, but ten of these states met the requirement by reductions in their welfare caseloads.[42]

"Engaged in work" means involved in an acceptable work activity for thirty hours a week. Women caring for children under age six need not work for more than twenty hours per week. States may define work to include (1) employment in a subsidized or unsubsidized job in the private or the public sector; (2) involvement in a work-experience program; (3) job search, job readiness, or on-the-job training; (4) involvement in a community service program; (5) education directly related to employment, including vocational education or job-skills training; (6) secondary school attendance or involvement in a program leading to a certificate of general equivalence; and (7) the provision of child care services to an individual who is participating in a community service program.[43]

In calculating whether a state is meeting its mandatory participation rates, time limits are set on job search and job readiness activities (which may count for no more than six weeks per recipient unless the state's unemployment rate rises above the national average, in which case the number of weeks is extended to twelve), vocational education and training (which cannot count for more than twelve months), and education other than high school or its equivalent (which counts only if it is directly related to employment.)[44]

Block grants may be reduced for states that fail to meet required rates of participation. Penalties range from 5 percent in the first year, rising yearly at a rate of 2 percent to a high of 21 percent. But grant reductions are based "on the degree of noncompliance," and the secretary of DHHS may reduce the penalty if noncompliance is due to "extraordinary circumstances," such as a natural disaster or regional recession.

If an adult recipient refuses to engage in required work, the state must reduce the family grant. States are free to eliminate the grant for all family members or to provide a "child only" grant to ensure some measure of income for children. States may not eliminate food stamp or Medicaid benefits for children due to a parent's unwillingness to participate in work activities. Single parents caring for a child under age six may not be penalized for failure to engage in a work activity if they demonstrate that appropriate and affordable child care is unavailable and that they cannot arrange for informal child care.[45]

For each TANF recipient who is at least eighteen years old or has not completed high school, received a high school equivalency certificate, or is not attending secondary school, the states must, within thirty days of the time an individual is deemed eligible for TANF assistance, develop in writing an "Individual Responsibility Plan" after assessing the recipient's skills, prior work experience, and employability. Among other requirements, the plan must (1) state an employment goal, including a plan for immediately moving the recipient into private sector employment; (2) describe what the recipient must do, for example, attend school and maintain certain grades to obtain and retain private sector employment; and (3) describe the services the state will provide to assist the recipient obtain and retain private sector employment. Failure without good cause to comply with the plan that the recipient has signed may result in a reduction of assistance.[46]

Benefit Levels

By January 1, 1998, forty-eight states had TANF plans in effect. The maximum benefit level to families in all but four jurisdictions equaled the benefit paid under the AFDC program. Changes were made in Maryland and Vermont, where benefit levels increased, and in California and the District of Columbia, where they were reduced.

As discussed in chapter 8, each state determines a "need standard" defined as the amount of money required for families of different sizes to obtain food, clothing, and housing and to meet other basic needs, such as purchasing furniture and winter clothing. States need not pay the full need standard, and as the data in Table 10.2 show, only six jurisdictions (Delaware, Guam, Kansas, Massachusetts, New Mexico, and New York City) do so. The majority of states provide a grant that is well below the standard of need.

All TANF recipients are automatically eligible to receive food stamps. Before the AFDC program ended, recipients were automatically eligible for Medicaid, but TANF severed this link. Under the new law, states must continue Medicaid coverage for those who were or would have been eligible for AFDC on July 1, 1996, as if the program were still in effect. For others, the states have flexibility in setting eligibility rules for Medicaid. As shown in Table 10.2, adding the value of a food stamp grant to the AFDC/TANF grant increases significantly the benefits that are available, as does adding the value of a housing subsidy. However, in 1995, fewer than 25 percent

TABLE 10.2. Need Standard and Maximum AFDC/TANF and Food Stamp Benefits for a One-Parent Family of Three: January 1997

State	Gross income limit to be eligible	100% of need	Maximum AFDC grant*	Food stamp benefit	Combined benefits	Combined benefit as a percent of 1997 poverty guideline†	AFDC benefit as a percent of 1997 poverty guideline
Alabama	$1,245	$673	$164	$315	$479	43	15
Alaska	1,955	1,057	923	323	1,246	90	66
Arizona	1,783	964	347	315	662	60	31
Arkansas	1,304	705	204	315	519	47	18
California	1,360	735	565	261	826	74	51
Colorado	779	421	356	315	671	60	32
Connecticut	1,613	872	636	239	875	79	57
Delaware	625	338	338	315	653	59	30
D.C.	1,317	712	398	311	709	64	36
Florida	2,002	1,082	303	315	618	56	27
Georgia	784	424	280	315	595	54	25
Guam	1,245	673	673	434	1,107	100	61
Hawaii	2,109	1,140	712	472	1,184	93	56
Idaho	1,833	991	317	315	632	57	29
Illinois	1,830	989	377	315	692	62	34
Indiana	592	320	288	315	603	54	26
Iowa	1,571	849	426	302	728	66	38
Kansas	794	429	429	302	730	66	39
Kentucky	973	526	262	315	577	52	24
Louisiana	1,217	658	190	315	505	45	17
Maine	1,023	553	418	305	723	65	38

Maryland	956	517	377	315	692	62	34
Massachusetts	1,045	565	565	261	826	74	51
Michigan							
Wastenaw Cty	1,151	622	489	292	752	68	41
Wayne Cty	1,084	586	459	284	722	70	84
Minnesota	984	532	532	271	803	72	48
Mississippi	681	368	120	315	435	39	11
Missouri	1,565	846	292	315	607	55	26
Montana	1,032	558	438	299	737	66	39
Nebraska	673	364	364	315	679	61	33
Nevada	1,423	769	348	315	663	60	31
New Hampshire	3,210	1,735	550	265	815	73	50
New Jersey	1,822	985	424	303	727	65	38
New Mexico	720	389	389	314	702	63	35
New York							
New York City	1,067	577	577	257	834	75	52
Suffolk Cty	1,301	703	703	219	922	83	63
North Carolina	1,006	544	272	315	587	53	24
North Dakota	797	431	431	301	732	66	39
Ohio	1,758	950	341	315	656	59	31
Oklahoma	1,193	645	307	315	622	56	28
Oregon	851	460	460	292	752	68	41
Pennsylvania	1,136	614	421	304	725	65	38
Puerto Rico	666	360	180	NA‡	180	16	NA
Rhode Island	1,025	554	554	264	818	74	50
South Carolina	999	540	200	315	515	46	18
South Dakota	938	507	430	301	731	66	39

Continued

TABLE 10.2. Need Standard and Maximum AFDC/TANF and Food Stamp Benefits for a One-Parent Family of Three: January 1997 (*Continued*)

State	Gross income limit to be eligible	100% of need	Maximum AFDC grant*	Food stamp benefit	Combined benefits	Combined benefit as a percent of 1997 poverty guideline†	AFDC benefit as a percent of 1997 poverty guideline
Tennessee	1,252	677	185	315	500	45	17
Texas	1,389	751	188	315	503	45	17
Utah	1,051	568	426	302	728	66	38
Vermont	2,226	1,203	639	238	878	79	58
Virgin Islands	555	300	240	405	645	58	22
Virginia	727	393	354	315	669	60	32
Washington	2,281	1,233	546	266	812	73	49
West Virginia	1,833	991	253	315	568	51	23
Wisconsin	1,197	647	517	275	792	71	47
Wyoming	1,247	674	360	315	675	61	32
Median AFDC		377		315	692	62	34

Source: House, Committee on Ways and Means, 105th Cong., 2nd sess., "Section 7: Aid to Families with Dependent Children and Temporary Assistance for Needy Families (Title IV-A)," *Green Book: Background Material and Data on Programs Within the Jurisdiction of the Committee on Ways and Means* (Washington, D.C., 1988), Table 7.8.

Note: In most states these amounts apply also to two-parent families (where the second parent is unemployed or incapacitated). Some states do increase benefits for two-parent families.

*Some states vary the amount of benefit by geographic region. The amount shown here is the highest benefit paid for each state.

†The 1997 poverty guidelines for a family of three are $1,111 per month for the forty-eight contiguous states and the District of Columbia, $1,389 for Alaska, and $1,278 for Hawaii.

‡Puerto Rico does not have a food stamp program. Instead, a cash nutritional assistance payment is provided.

of AFDC recipients lived in public housing (11.6 percent) or received housing subsidies (12.9 percent),[47] thus an adjustment to each state's benefit level to account for
a housing subsidy is not possible nor, for reasons discussed in chapter 8, is it possible
to assign a constant value to Medicaid benefits that most TANF recipients receive.
Returning to the combined benefit provided by AFDC/TANF and food stamps,
and assuming that a poverty level income is necessary to live adequately within any
state, it is clear that few states provide a sufficient benefit. Only in Guam is the
combined benefit equal to 100 percent of the poverty level. A majority of jurisdictions provide a benefit that is significantly below the poverty level. Nationally, the
median AFDC/TANF benefit provides a sum equal to 34 percent of the poverty
level, and the combined benefit is equal to 62 percent.

Unlike payments made under the Old Age, Survivors, and Disability Insurance
program (chapter 9), AFDC payments were not routinely adjusted for inflation. The
purchasing power that was available to an AFDC beneficiary fell over the years.
The value of benefits peaked in fiscal year 1970, with an average monthly benefit
per family of $178, equivalent in 1996 dollars to $734.[48] In 1996, the average monthly
benefit paid was $374; 51 percent of the purchasing power of the 1970 grant.

STATE DISCRETION IN PROGRAM OPERATION

States have discretion in the way they operate their TANF programs within a broad
regulatory framework set by the federal government. Each state must meet minimum work participation rates, and work requirements must be imposed on adult
recipients within twenty-four months of the time their grant begins, but states
may require recipients to participate in work activities at an earlier time.[49] Nine
states require work "immediately" upon application. Some set varying lengths of
time, requiring work within forty-five or ninety days of application, whereas others
adhere to the twenty-four-month time period that is set by federal law. As noted
earlier, states may terminate benefits in less than sixty months. New York, California,
and Connecticut provide a "safety net" program. Connecticut, for example, sets a
benefit time limit of twenty-one months but provides a safety net that allows families
to receive an exemption and have their benefits extended when the needy caretaker
is (1) incapacitated, (2) caring for a family member who is incapacitated, (3) elderly,
(4) pregnant or postpartum and has a physician's statement that work is contrain-
dicated, (5) deemed to be unemployable, (6) a minor who is attending and performing satisfactorily in high school or a high school equivalency program, or (7) deemed
to have made a good faith effort to comply with program requirements but is unable
to do so.[50] Safety net programs may provide cash and in-kind assistance, such as
food and clothing or vouchers to pay rent. Such programs may blunt the harsh
effects of TANF's sixty-month time limit, its disqualification of a teenager not living
with a responsible adult, and its exclusion of families headed by noncitizens.[51]

Nineteen states have imposed a family cap that precludes a family from obtaining
increased benefits if they have an additional child or that provides for reduced
benefits if the family has an additional child. Also, federal funds may not be used
to aid newly arrived immigrants until they have been in this country for seven years,
excepting new arrivals who are in the United States under a grant of political asylum

and anyone whose deportation has been withheld. In addition, benefits may be provided to noncitizens who are honorably discharged veterans or active-duty personnel and to their spouses and dependent children.[52] States are free to continue or deny TANF benefits to noncitizens who were living in this country on August 22, 1996, when TANF was passed. The majority of states have chosen to continue benefits. American-born children of noncitizens become citizens at birth, and these children, but not their parents, are eligible to receive a grant.

Applying for Benefits

Before welfare reform, the AFDC applicant's eligibility was judged on the basis of income, assets, and family composition. These criteria still apply, but since the passage of TANF states are enforcing more stringent rules, such as requiring a parent to cooperate in obtaining child support from a noncustodial parent (see chapter 15) and hastening an adult recipient's movement into the work force. The General Accounting Office (GAO) (1998) reports that some applicants decide to not apply for benefits after they learn about the stringent work requirements and rules about cooperation in obtaining child support.[53]

STRATEGIES TO REDUCE APPLICATIONS FOR ASSISTANCE-DIVERSION PROGRAMS

Thirty states have in place diversion programs that seek to direct families from welfare, if they can be helped through other means. These programs may include one-time cash payments to avoid eviction or to enable a family to repair an automobile needed for transportation to work.[54] Some states require families who receive one-time assistance to agree to not apply for TANF for a specified time period or provided funds may be subject to repayment. In some states, parents may be required to work off the provided payment. Diversion programs also provide support services, such as child care, transportation, health benefits, or assistance in finding work, and an applicant's compliance may be a condition for later applying for TANF. Texas, for example, requires applicants for TANF to attend workforce orientations before they are approved for TANF benefits, and in Oregon applicants must engage in a job search for thirty days before they are screened for TANF eligibility.

An effort to demonstrate that work pays is shown in Figure 10.1 which depicts a sign on the doors of the Portland, Oregon, welfare office that says, "A request for assistance in Oregon is a request for jobs services and services to help move to self-sufficiency." Income comparisons show the advantages of work by comparing the net monthly income of a TANF recipient to that of a minimum wage worker whose income is increased by the Earned Income Tax Credit (EITC) (see chapter 9) and by a child support payment of $210. The income of the family with earned income, supplemented by food stamps, the EITC, and child support payments is above the poverty level, whereas the income of the TANF recipient, despite the benefit afforded by food stamps, is not. Even if the family is unable to enforce a child support order, their income of $1,247 ($1,457 minus $210) is still above the poverty level.

FIGURE 10.1. A comparison of net monthly income: receiving cash assistance versus working (family of three), April 1998.

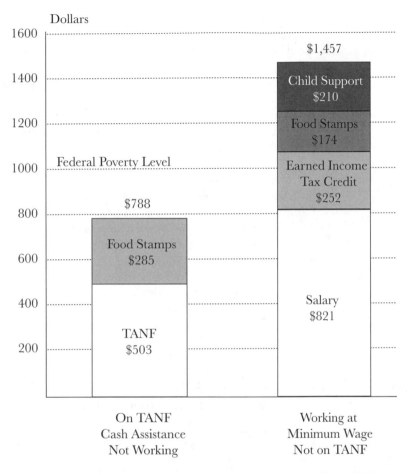

Source: U.S. General Accounting Office, *States Are Restructuring Programs to Reduce Welfare Dependency,* GAO/HEHS-98-109 (Washington, D.C., 1998).

What the chart fails to show is the effect on family income of work-related expenses, such as child care and transportation and other costs. Oregon does provide medical coverage through the Oregon Health Plan for low-wage families who do not qualify for Medicaid, and child care is available to participants in Oregon's Jobs-Plus Program.[55]

In Wisconsin, families enrolled in TANF are assigned to one of four program components, as show in Table 10.3. All components include case management, defined as a process of assessing an applicant's needs for employment, training, and supportive services and for assisting the person in obtaining services to achieve self-sufficiency and support services such as child care, job training, and health insurance.[56]

TABLE 10.3. Wisconsin Works Program Components, Percent of TANF Applicants Assigned to Each, and Conditions for Assignment: February 1998

Component and percent assigned	Conditions for assignment and benefits provided
1. Transition, 25.1%	Unable to obtain unsubsidized work due to severe barriers Assigned to appropriate activity, given recipient's limitations, up to twenty-eight hours per week (such as mental health and substance abuse counseling) and twelve hours per week of education and training Receive a monthly cash allowance, case management and support services
2. Community service work, 47.9%	Poor work habits or low job skills Assigned to a job serving a useful public purpose Receive a monthly cash allowance, case management, and support services, up to thirty hours per week in work training activities and ten hours per week in education and training activities
3. Trial jobs Subsidized employment, 1.7%	Lack enough work experience to be "job ready" Provided a subsidized job Receive at least minimum wage, case management, and support services
4. Unsubsidized employment, 25.4%	Judged "job ready" Assigned to job search Receive case management and support services but not eligible for monthly cash assistance

Source: Data from U.S. General Accounting Office, *States Are Restructuring Programs to Reduce Welfare Dependency,* GAO/HEHS-98-109 (Washington, D.C., 1998), 62.

The differences between the program components lie in the work expectations. Twenty-five percent of recipients are in the transitional component; they receive a monthly cash allowance and are assigned to an activity that may include counseling for mental health or substance abuse problems. Those who are assigned to components two through four participate in some work activity that includes community work, subsidized by a cash allowance, for approximately 48 percent of recipients who lack the work habits or skills to find employment and subsidized employment at the minimum wage for the approximately 2 percent of participants who are deemed to be job ready; one-quarter of participants are assigned to job search, and no cash assistance is provided.

Diversion programs have yet to be fully evaluated. Preliminary data from Oregon and Wisconsin suggest that approximately 40 percent of applicants were diverted who were likely to have qualified for benefits. It is important to note that diversion programs may reduce direct cash benefits, but they do not necessarily reduce overall program costs, since the provided services are costly. Wisconsin's diversion program is reported to have increased its spending per family from $9,700 to approximately $15,700.[57]

STRATEGIES TO HASTEN A FAMILY'S MOVEMENT INTO THE WORKFORCE: WORK FIRST PROGRAMS

The TANF program emphasizes putting applicants and recipients to work at the earliest possible time and de-emphasizes "human capital development" approaches that stress education and training as precursors to work. Work First programs assume that "any job is a good job and that the best way to succeed in the labor market is to join it, developing work habits and skills on the job rather than in a classroom."[58] There is no single Work First model. Work First programs may include (1) an individual assessment to determine if barriers, such as the lack of child care or problems in transportation, hinder an applicant's ability to engage in job search; (2) job clubs in which a facilitator works with recipients to ensure that they understand the purpose of job search, discuss whether part-time work is acceptable, what wage to expect, and where the expectation that employment will be found is addressed; (3) telephone rooms where participants contact prospective employers; and (4) an in-depth assessment for those unable to find employment to identify additional supports such as education, job training, or subsidized employment that will help a participant move into work as quickly as possible. In addition, (5) support services, such as child care and transportation, for those who find employment are routinely offered,[59] as are (6) activities to help participants retain their jobs. To increase the number of available jobs, some states involve the private sector to develop welfare-to-work plans. They ask businesses to report job openings directly to the welfare department, or they ask private industry to participate in providing classroom training, internships, and job opportunities.[60]

When education occurs, it is likely to take the form of on-the-job training, unpaid work experience, or work in a community service program. In addition, a participant may be involved in short-term skills development classes, usually lasting no more than four to six weeks, where the focus is on developing a specific set of skills, such as typing or computer skills, and where English language training to require the vocabulary needed for a work environment may be provided. Job readiness services, such as learning how to prepare a resume, participate in a job interview, and how to dress appropriately for a job interview, may be included. There is little emphasis on the development of job skills through vocational training programs.[61] Exceptions to Work First activities are made for pregnant women, teens who are in school, parents who are ill or incapacitated, the caretakers of ill or incapacitated family members, older participants, and those residing in rural areas. Also, assuming that resources such as child care are limited, a program may target its resources to new applicants with a recent work history or conversely to long-term recipients who need the greatest help.

In keeping with the Work First focus, some states have transformed their welfare offices into job placement centers and redefined the tasks performed by case workers to support a work focus. Case workers may be responsible for (1) screening applicants and making referrals to a Work First program or for other services; (2) offering employment assistance by providing resource information and making job referrals; (3) motivating clients to seek work; (4) sanctioning noncompliant clients; (5) exploring the potential for diversion away from TANF; (6) collecting information about applicants and recipients to define what they need to facilitate self-sufficiency; and (7) monitoring client involvement in work-related activities. A number of states help clients obtain work-related transportation by enlisting volunteers and by providing funds for vehicle repair.[62]

Some states sanction adults who do not participate in required work activities by terminating the grant to the entire family, rather than reducing the family's grant by the amount attributable to the noncomplying adult.[63] And states are less likely than they were under the AFDC program to exempt adults with physical and mental impairments and those with small children. A Work First approach has increased the percent of TANF recipients assigned to job placement rather than to job readiness activities. In 1994, California placed 23 percent of recipients in job placement activities, compared to 47 percent in 1997. Connecticut reported a shift from 15 percent to 68 percent; Louisiana, from 12 percent to 51 percent; and Maryland, from 35 percent to 90 percent.[64]

INCENTIVE TO WORK

Table 10.4 shows for seven states the amount of earned income, savings, and other assets that a family who is receiving TANF may have without losing their eligibility for all TANF assistance. The horizontal line at the bottom of the table compares these data to limits that were set under the AFDC program.[65] Each of the states has increased countable assets, which refers to the value of a family's assets that will be disregarded in determining eligibility, and the vehicle allowance. Six of the seven states have increased the amount of earnings that a recipient may keep without affecting TANF benefits. In addition, three of the states allow TANF recipients to invest in Individual Development Accounts in which a family may accumulate assets for education, home purchase, or starting a business. The value of these accounts is not considered in determining eligibility for aid.

Additional incentives, not shown in Table 10.4, include continuing child care and Medicaid for families no longer eligible for TANF participation. Thirty-five states are offering some form of case management to help people retain their jobs or find new jobs should they lose work.

WELFARE-TO-WORK GRANTS

The Balanced Budget Act Amendment of 1997[66] amended the 1996 TANF legislation by providing for a program of welfare-to-work grants (WTW). The WTW grants provide matching funds to the states to assist welfare recipients who do not have the work skills, education, and employment experience to find work and to assist those who reside in high poverty areas to move into unsubsidized employment. At least 70 percent of grant funds must be directed toward assisting TANF eligible

TABLE 10.4. Asset Limits and Earnings Disregard Policies: Seven States

State	Countable asset limit	Vehicle allowance	Individual development accounts	Monthly earned income disregard*
California	$2,000	$4,650	Yes	$225 plus 50% of the remainder up to the minimum basic standard of adequate care†
Connecticut	$3,000	One vehicle	No	All earnings up to the poverty level until time limit is reached
Louisiana	$2,000	$10,000	Yes	$120; up to $900 for the first 6 months of work
Maryland	$2,000‡	One vehicle	No	26% up to the maximum income limit
Oregon	$10,000 or $2,500§	$10,000	Yes	50% up to the maximum income limit
Texas	$2,000	$4,650	No	Unchanged
Wisconsin	$2,500	$10,000	No	All income up to 115% of the poverty calculation
Prior limits under AFDC	$1,000	$1,500	No	$90; $30 plus one-third of the first 4 months and then $30 for the next 8 months.

Source: U.S. General Accounting Office, *States Are Restructuring Programs to Reduce Welfare Dependency*, GAO/HEHS-98-109 (Washington, D.C., 1998), Table 2.3.
*Exclusive of disregards for child care expenses.
†The minimum basic standard of care is determined on the basis of the number of eligible people in the family with adjustments for regional variations in cost of living.
‡In addition, each dependent child may save up to $2,000 from earnings without it counting against the family's asset limit.
§The upper limit is for those participating satisfactorily in the states welfare-to-work program; the lower limit is for nonparticipants.

individuals who face two of three labor market "deficiencies," defined to include (1) lack of a high school diploma or general equivalency certificate and low reading or math skills, (2) a substance abuse problem, or (3) a poor work history, meaning that the individual has not worked for more than three consecutive months in the past twelve calendar months.[67] The program may also serve (4) families who have received AFDC or TANF assistance for at least thirty months, (5) those at risk of being terminated from TANF within twelve months, (6) those who would be long-term recipients but for the fact that they have exceeded their time limits for receiving benefits, and (7) noncustodial parents if the custodial parent is a long-term TANF recipient, or if a minor is a long-term recipient in a case where a grant is being provided only to a child. The remaining 30 percent of grant funds may be spent on recent TANF recipients or noncustodial parents who have characteristics associated with long-term welfare dependence—such as school dropout, teen pregnancy, or poor work history.

The WTW grants may be used to fund (1) job readiness, placement, and post-employment services; (2) community service or work experience programs; (3) job creation by subsidizing public or private sector employment; (4) on-the-job training; and (5) job retention or support services if such are not otherwise available. These work-related activities are not further defined, and they allow grant recipients maximum flexibility to develop and implement programs. Additional training funds are available through the Community Services Block Grant (CSBG) whose funds must, as of fiscal year 2000, be used to support TANF's work requirements.[68]

Trutko and colleagues studied implementation of WTW grants in eleven states. Implementation was more difficult than expected. Some states had yet to serve any clients, and others were serving only 30 percent of those eligible for the program. When programs were operational, (1) some adopted a Work First approach, requiring or encouraging individuals to find employment; (2) others served clients who were not successful in finding work, with some moving participants directly into on-the-job training programs and subsidized employment; and (3) others provided support services including child care, transportation, housing, and referrals to substance abuse programs. Some states were using WTW funds to target noncustodial parents of TANF-supported children to enable them to work and support their families, but states reported difficulties in locating and serving this population and acknowledged that specific outreach efforts would have to be developed. State administrators stressed that it was too early to draw any conclusions about the success of WTW in helping people find and retain employment.[69]

CHILD CARE AND DEVELOPMENT BLOCK GRANT

When TANF was passed, Congress ended three child care programs and expanded the Child Care and Development Block Grant (CCDBG) to replace the terminated programs.[70] The three terminated programs had provided (1) guaranteed child care for welfare recipients who were participating in the JOBS program or other state-approved education and training activities; (2) transitional child care for a maximum of twelve months to families that lost their AFDC eligibility because their work-related income increased; and (3) child care for low-income families who were not

AFDC recipients but who were at risk of becoming so because the lack of child care threatened their ability to work.

The CCDBG authorized $1 billion annually for child care for fiscal years 1996 through 2002. Each state receives a fixed sum equal to the funds received under the three discontinued programs in 1994 or 1995, or the average of fiscal years 1992 through 1994, whichever is greater. States may transfer up to 30 percent of TANF Block Grant funds to the CCDBG, but these funds must be spent according to CCDBG rules. States are allowed to use TANF funds for child care without a transfer to the CCDBG, in which case CCDBG rules do not apply.

States must allocate 70 percent of their child care block grant funds to provide child care services for TANF recipients or for families at risk of becoming TANF recipients with children younger than thirteen years of age who reside with the parent. The remaining funds may be used to provide child care to any family whose income does not exceed the state's median income by 85 percent.

No less than 4 percent of received funds must be spent on activities that promote parental choice. For example, consumer education helps parents make informed decisions concerning the kind of child care that best serves the needs of their families and on activities to improve the quality and quantity of child care. Parents are free to place their child in a child care program that is operated under a grant or contract with a state or municipal agency or to receive a child care certificate that the parent may use to select a provider of choice.[71]

Under the Title XX Social Services Block Grant Program, each state receives a fixed sum of money that is determined by the state's population (see chapter 14). States are not required to provide matching funds, and the federal government does not establish eligibility rules for services funded under Title XX. In fiscal year 1995, the Congressional Research Service reported that states spent approximately 14 percent of their Title XX funds on child day care.[72] In addition, the Head Start Program (see chapter 15) provides part-day or full-day child care for three- and four-year-olds from low income families.

A seven-state study conducted by the United States GAO (1998) reported that California, Connecticut, Louisiana, Maryland, Oregon, Texas, and Wisconsin expected to meet the child care needs of families who were required to work as well as those of families who were making the transition off of welfare for fiscal year 1997, with some exceptions.[73] However, the states questioned their ability to expand child care to meet future needs, were concerned that efforts to increase child care could result in providing child care of unknown quality, and doubted they would be able to offer child care to nonwelfare, working-poor families.

In 1999, the GAO surveyed child care administrators and education departments in the fifty states and the District of Columbia, they surveyed 537 child care resource and referral agencies, and they conducted on-site visits to four states. Investigators were told that child care for three- and four-year-olds was generally not difficult to obtain. However, child care for infants, toddlers, and children with special needs was difficult to find. For all children, there were problems of accessibility, especially for people in rural areas, and child care during nonstandard hours was lacking.[74]

The Effects of Welfare Reform: What Do We Know?

Nationally, the AFDC/TANF caseload has dropped considerably, and for this reason TANF has been hailed a success.[75] However, establishing a relationship between a decline in caseload size and the implementation of TANF legislation is not an easy matter. As the data in Figure 10.2 show, caseloads peaked in January 1994 and began their decline after that time, more than thirty-two months before TANF was enacted and more than three and one-half years before the states were required to implement their TANF programs. But caseloads dropped dramatically after passage of TANF, with a 32 percent reduction between January 1997 and January 1998,[76] suggesting an association between the passage and implementation of the new legislation and caseload reduction. A number of factors may explain these reductions, including (1) a strong economy that generated work for 741,000 never-married moth-

FIGURE 10.2. Number of AFDC/TANF recipients by family and individual recipient status in January for six years.

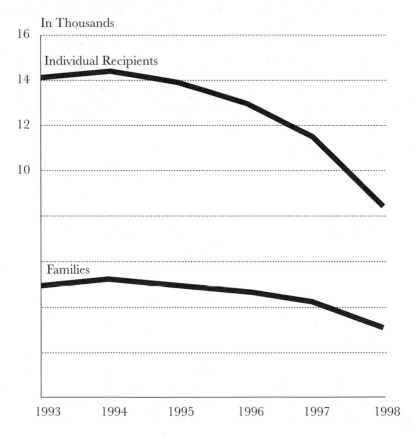

Source: U.S. Department of Health and Human Services, *Change in Welfare Caseloads as of June 1998* (Washington, D.C., 1998).

ers who sought employment between the first quarter of 1996 and the second quarter of 1998[77]; (2) the TANF "message" that welfare recipients would be required to work, which may have reduced applications for benefits; (3) implementation of diversion programs, which may have had a similar effect; and (4) the Section 1115 Waiver Program, which was underway in forty-six states before TANF was enacted. We turn our attention to waiver programs, which are important to a discussion of TANF.

SECTION 1115 WAIVER PROGRAM

Since 1962, the Section 1115 Waiver Program has allowed the states to request that the secretary of HHS "waive" the regulations that the Social Security Act imposed on operation of the AFDC Program at the state level.[78] Waivers allowed the states to experiment by implementing projects that promoted the purposes of the AFDC program as long as the experiments did not increase program costs to the federal government. Some of these waiver programs contained provisions that would be incorporated into TANF, such as time limits for receipt of benefits, mandatory work requirements, limiting to thirty or sixty days the amount of time that job search activities would be counted as work-related, elimination of benefits for all family members for failure of an adult recipient to comply with work requirements, benefit reductions for failure to cooperate with child support enforcement offices, and incentives, including an increase in the amount of earned income that a recipient could retain without a reduction in benefits.[79] States were allowed to continue their waiver programs when TANF was passed and to request new or additional waivers until July 1, 1997. Any conflict between state law that governed the operation of a waiver program and federal law governing operation of TANF were to be resolved in favor of the states.[80] Waivers were granted for a period of five to eleven years from the date of approval; thus, some state waiver programs may remain in effect until 2008.

However, caution must be exercised in attributing the caseload decline to waiver programs. Some were in effect when the rolls were climbing in the early 1990s, and others were in various stages of design and implementation when TANF was enacted. In their study of the decline of welfare caseloads, Martini and Wiseman (1997) go so far as to argue that waivers do not "cause" caseload reduction but follow them, because reductions in caseload free up the resources that are needed to engage in experimentation.[81]

FAMILIES WHO LEAVE WELFARE AND FIND WORK

The question, "What is the employment status of adults who head households that were recipients of AFDC?" can be framed in one of two ways: a researcher can ask a former recipient, "Do you have a job today?" (a point-in-time study), or a researcher may ask about a recipient's employment history over time (a tracking study).

Two studies conducted by the GAO asked the first of these questions. In the first study, data from waiver programs in Massachusetts, Michigan, and Utah were reviewed.[82] Work participation rates increased between the fall of 1995 and the fall of

1996 from 19 percent to 36 percent in Massachusetts, from 21 percent to 42 percent in Michigan, and from 42 percent to 57 percent in Utah, with a majority of recipients in Massachusetts and Michigan finding unsubsidized employment. In its second research endeavor, the GAO visited seven states.[83] The data compiled confirmed the findings from the earlier study. In five of the seven states, there were significant increases in the number of AFDC recipients who found work. California, Louisiana, and Maryland reported a doubling in job placement rates, and Oregon and Wisconsin reported increases of more than 70 percent.

Investigators at the GAO (1999) and Brauner and Loprest (1999) of the Urban Institute reviewed a series of studies that tracked the employment history of welfare recipients. The reviewed studies overlapped for eight states, with some additional studies viewed by one team and not the other. Regardless of whether the studies were duplicative, the central findings were similar, and the following information is a compilation of findings from both studies.[84] The length of follow-up after families left the AFDC rolls varied by state and ranged from short periods of several months to studies that followed up two years after exit.

The families on whom information was reported left the AFDC/TANF rolls during or after 1995. The GAO cautions that differences in the composition of the studied families, sampling limitations, and differences in the time periods when families were tracked were such that only seven of the seventeen studies they reviewed provided data that could be generalized and then only to families within the studied states. From both studies we learn that

1. Most of the adults were employed at some time after leaving welfare, but the percentage of those ever employed differed from the percent employed at follow-up. In Washington, South Carolina, Indiana, and Wisconsin, between 82 percent (Wisconsin) and 87 percent (Washington) were ever employed. At the time of follow-up, 62 percent of recipients in Wisconsin and South Carolina were employed, as were 71 percent in Washington. Data reported from a follow-up study of Connecticut's work program produced similar figures. Of those employed at the end of their last benefit month, 72 percent were employed when contacted at three and six month intervals.[85]

2. Between 19 percent and 30 percent of families returned to the welfare rolls, and many families whose cash assistance stopped received Medicaid, food stamps, housing assistance, and aid from other programs, such as the School Lunch Program and the Women, Infants, and Children (WIC) food supplement program, indicating that earned income was low enough to qualify the family for these benefits.

3. Between 13 percent and 35 percent of families received child support payments, and 11 percent to 65 percent received help from their families and friends. Whether a family is financially better off after leaving welfare was difficult to answer because specific information concerning total household income, such as earnings from a second worker or the amount of financial assistance from families or friends, was not available. In addition, the reviewed studies did not provide comprehensive information on employment-related expenses, including child care and transportation.

4. Employment was found in a variety of settings, including hotels and restaurants; industries such as agriculture, forestry, and mining; and different occupations, including clerical and health and personal care service providers. Hourly earnings ranged from the minimum wage of $5.15 per hour to $8.09 per hour.

5. None of the studies reported on changes in family composition due to marriage or pregnancy after leaving welfare, and there was no indication of increases in homelessness or separation of parents and children.

6. Data concerning family well-being are limited. In three states, 54 to 77 percent of recipients reported that "life was better" after leaving the welfare rolls, and approximately sixty percent of respondents in two states reported "feeling" that they would not return to welfare. Some of the reported negative effects came from 60 percent of families in two states who said that they "were barely making it," from 17 to 33 percent of families in four states who reported problems in providing enough food for their families, from 11 to 47 percent of families in five states who reported problems in paying utility bills, and from 29 to 39 percent of respondents in three states who reported problems paying rent.

In her study of families who leave welfare, Pamela Loprest (1999) compared a representative sample of 1,289 families who left welfare between 1995 and 1997 with a sample of working-poor families who have not recently been on welfare. Sixty-one percent of those leaving welfare were employed when interviewed. Approximately one-third had returned to welfare and were receiving benefits in 1997. The hourly and monthly earnings and job characteristics of those leaving welfare were the same as those of the comparison group.[86]

In a series of studies, the Manpower Demonstration Research Corporation, an independent research group that studies the effects of welfare-to-work projects, informs us that waiver programs in Florida, Delaware, Indiana, and Vermont reported employment increases in the experimental compared to control group participants. Differences ranged from a low of 2.5 percent in Vermont to a high of 11 percent in Delaware.[87]

Comparing Labor-Force Attachment (LFA) programs, a Work First type of program, with Human Capital Development (HCD) programs in Georgia, Michigan, and Riverside, California, showed that "mixed" programs maintaining an employment focus but also providing short-term education, training activities, and unpaid work experience yield greater increases in the number of people employed and in earnings than job search programs alone.[88] Two-year findings showed that the LFA approach compared to the HCD approach increased the number of employed participants by 24 percent, reduced the number on AFDC by 16 percent, and increased earnings by 26 percent. Still, 57 percent of the LFA group remained on AFDC, with average earnings of $285 monthly compared to LFA.

The MDRC (2000) evaluated the effects of Minnesota's Family Investment Program (MFIP). The MFIP increases the welfare grant of those who go to work by up to 20 percent, and the earned income disregard is increased so that recipients retain 38 cents of each welfare dollar for each dollar earned.[89] Participants in MFIP are eligible to receive welfare benefits until their income is 40 percent above the poverty line.

The MDRC's evaluation included 14,000 families who were randomly assigned to MFIP or traditional AFDC. The source and amount of income of each group was compared. Families were followed for up to 36 months. Close to 50 percent of MFIP single parents on welfare for two out of the three years preceding the project, compared to almost 37 percent of a similar group receiving AFDC, were working; approximately 85 percent of the former group compared to 81 percent of the latter were receiving some welfare benefits; and close to 25 percent of the MFIP group had earnings above the poverty level compared to close to 15 percent of the AFDC group.[90] The MFIP added approximately $2,000 per year to government costs for each family.[91]

The work program in Portland, Oregon, encourages participants to seek "good" jobs, which are defined as full-time work with pay above the minimum wage, benefits, and the potential for advancement. Portland's program provides recipients with short-term education, vocational training, work experience, and life-skills training to increase their employability. There was an 11 percent gain in employment levels for those in the experimental group compared to those assigned to the control group, and two-year earnings for experimental group participants showed an increase of $1,800 per participant, an increase of 35 percent over control group earnings.[92]

Issues in the Implementation of Temporary Assistance to Needy Families

Ultimately, the success of TANF will be judged by whether those who leave the welfare rolls maintain employment, especially when the economy enters one of its cyclical periods of recession. Reduced caseloads are not a proxy for program success, since caseloads can be reduced by discouraging people from applying for benefits, by moving applicants into diversion programs, or simply by making eligibility rules more stringent. Moreover, as discussed earlier, in an average year, one-half of the caseload leaves the welfare rolls. Therefore, some percentage of those finding work may have become employed without any change in the law. As employable recipients move off of the welfare rolls, state officials have expressed their concern that caseloads will be reduced to those who are hardest to place.

Zedlewski (1999) surveyed 1,564 TANF recipients. Twenty-three percent reported that they did not confront any "significant" obstacles in finding work, whereas others reported two or more obstacles as follows: (1) 41 percent had less than a high school education, (2) 43 percent had not worked for three or more years, (3) 19 percent cared for a child who was less than one year of age (15 percent) or a child with a disability (4 percent), (4) 7 percent did not speak English, (5) 10 percent did not have an automobile and did not live in a metropolitan area, and (6) 48 percent reported physical or mental health problems, many of which were severe.[93]

There are no data to inform the question, "How will states respond to an increased demand for assistance in a recession?" In a weak economy, some who lose their jobs will be eligible for unemployment insurance. When their unemployment insurance runs out, they may reapply for TANF or general assistance (discussed later), and those not eligible for unemployment insurance may apply for cash assistance immediately after losing their jobs. The funds available through the TANF

Block Grant are fixed, and the extent to which states will make use of any reserve funds, borrow from the TANF loan fund, or appropriate additional state funds is not known. States may choose to increase the number of people who receive aid by reducing the size of a cash grant, or they may make it difficult to access benefits by imposing restrictive eligibility rules.[94]

But loss of employment is not the only issue. Some families will reach the state-imposed maximum time period for receipt of benefits. To illustrate the different ways in which states may respond to such a future situation, consider the following. Both Connecticut and Florida limit the duration for receipt of benefits to two years or less. Both states provide for extensions for those reaching time limits. In one Florida county, almost all participants who reached the time limit had their benefit canceled, whereas in Connecticut, approximately one-half of participants who reached their time limit were found to have made a good-faith effort to find work and were granted at least one six-month extension.

The Manpower Demonstration Research Corporation reports that this disparity seems to be the result of differences in the way the two states designed and implemented their programs. In Florida, the program was heavily staffed and required participant involvement in an array of activities. Recipients were closely monitored. The irony of the program is that as the number of services increased, so did the demands that were placed on recipients to participate, with the increased chances that recipients would "slip up" and have their benefits cancelled for failure to comply. By contrast, the Connecticut program was understaffed, and the participants were required to engage in fewer activities. Understaffing precluded the close monitoring that characterized the Florida program, and it was rare for recipients to have their grants reduced or canceled for failing to meet a program requirement.[95]

There are two final issues to consider in predicting the success of welfare-to-work programs. These are barriers to work that are created by the lack of transportation and the lack of child care. Approximately 75 percent of welfare recipients live in central cities or rural areas, but two-thirds of newly created jobs are located in the suburbs, many in areas where there is no public transportation or where transportation is not routinely available on weekends or evenings.[96]

In 1998, Congress enacted the Transportation Equity Act for the Twenty-first Century, which authorizes the Access to Jobs and Reverse Commute Program.[97] Congress authorized $750 million for fiscal years 1999 through 2003. The Department of Transportation makes grants to local organizations, not-for-profit groups, and transit authorities to increase options for transporting people to work. In its first year of operation, the majority of grants were made to existing transit authorities who had the capacity to expand transportation into unserved or underserved areas. Approaches to increasing the availability of transportation included expanding the hours of operation or the locations reached by existing transportation systems and implementing new systems through the use of vans, shuttles and "demand-responsive" systems that respond to requests for transportation rather than operating on a fixed route or schedule.

The lack of child care has historically plagued efforts to place welfare recipients in jobs. Based on a survey of officials operating JOBS programs, the GAO concluded that inability to locate a sufficient number of child care slots was a major factor in limiting participation rates.[98]

To illustrate the difficulties that cities and states may confront in obtaining child care, the GAO estimated that by the year 2002, when states are expected to have 50 percent of their TANF caseloads participating in work activities, the city of Chicago would have available infant care for approximately 12 percent of those requiring this service, a deficit of close to 24,000 slots.[99] In Baltimore, slots would be available for 30 percent of families with infants. Moreover, within-city availability can be expected to vary by poor compared to nonpoor neighborhoods. In Chicago, for example, child care slots can be found for 22 percent of those needing care for infants who live in nonpoor neighborhoods, but for only 11 percent of children in poor neighborhoods. Comparable figures for Baltimore are 48 percent for nonpoor and 32 percent for poor.

SECTION 3: SUPPLEMENTAL SECURITY INCOME

The Supplemental Security Income Program (SSI) is Title XVI of the Social Security Act of 1935.[100] The SSI program, like the Social Security Disability Program discussed in chapter 9, provides a cash grant for a disabled child or adult. When enacted in 1972, SSI replaced three titles of the act: Title I, Grants for Old Age Assistance; Title X, Grants for Aid to the Blind; and Title XIV, Grants for the Permanently and Totally Disabled (see Table 9.1) Title XVI is applicable to residents of the United States, defined to include the fifty states, the District of Columbia, and the Northern Mariana Islands. Supplemental Security Income is not available to residents of Puerto Rico, Guam, the United States Virgin Islands, and American Samoa (the Territories), where the titles that were replaced by SSI remain in effect and provide a grant-in-aid program for people with disabilities.[101]

People with disabilities are considered "worthy" of the assistance they receive, and this consideration of "worthiness" is reflected in differences between SSI and TANF. First, unlike TANF, SSI is an entitlement program, so all applicants receive assistance if they meet the program's eligibility standards. Second, the costs of the SSI program are borne solely by the federal government, meaning that recipients of SSI are ensured a basic grant of uniform value regardless of the state in which they live, although a number of states supplement the basic federal grant. Each of the Territories sets its own benefit level. Finally, unlike AFDC/TANF, SSI payments have been adjusted to reflect increases in the cost of living. The monthly payment to an individual in 1997 was $484, up from $140 in 1974; in 1997, a couple received $726 per month, up from $210 in 1974. In 1997, the basic individual SSI benefit provided an amount equal to 77.2 percent of the poverty level, which is in excess of the percentage of the poverty level paid by the AFDC/TANF program in a majority of states (see Table 10.2). The federal benefit, combined with a state supplement where available, plus food stamps, is significant. In 1997, Alaska supplemented the federal benefit of $484 for an individual recipient with a state benefit of $362. When coupled with a food stamp benefit of $99, a disabled individual living alone received a total monthly benefit of $945.[102]

Characteristics of Recipients

In March 1999, there were more than 6.6 million recipients of SSI (Figure 10.3) receiving federal payments that totaled nearly $29 billion. Slightly more than 5 percent of SSI recipients also received benefits from the Old Age, Survivors, and Disability Insurance Program (chapter 9) because they were elderly (1.8 percent) or blind and disabled (3.6 percent). The ratio of elderly to disabled recipients—which was nearly equal in 1975 at 53 percent elderly and 47 percent disabled—shifted, so that 80 percent were disabled and 20 percent were elderly in March 1999. Of the nonelderly, the SSI program saw a dramatic growth in the number of recipients under eighteen years of age. Between 1985 and 1995, the number quadrupled from 227,000 to 917,000, respectively. This growth was the occasion for modifications to the SSI program for children, discussed later, that were made when the PRWOA was passed in 1996.

RECIPIENTS AND ELIGIBILITY RULES

Supplemental security income provides a subsistence level of income to disabled adults and children. A disabled adult is one who cannot continue to do previous work or other work in the national economy because of a "medically determinable physical or mental impairment which [is likely] to result in death or which has lasted or can be expected to last for [at least] 12 months."[103] A disabled child is an individual under the age of eighteen who, like the adult, has a medically determinable physical or mental impairment. The child's impairment must "result in marked and severe functional limitations," and as with the adult, the disability must be expected to result in death or must have lasted or be expected to last for a continuous period of not less than twelve months.

The eligibility rules for SSI parallel in most ways the rules for the Social Security Disability Insurance Program (SSDI) discussed in chapter 9, except that applicants for SSI bases their claims on their disabling condition and lack of income, not on their disabling condition and work history. The means test for SSI takes into account the applicant's income, including the income of a nondisabled spouse. In the same manner, the income of a parent who resides with the child applicant is deemed to be available to the child.

There is a monthly resource limit of $2,000 for an individual and $3,000 for a couple. In determining whether the resource limit has been met, certain items are excluded from consideration, such as a home, household goods, personal effects, and an automobile.[104] Also, food stamps, housing subsidies, the value of social services and income that is set aside for the purpose of helping the recipient become self-sufficient are not counted as income for the purpose of determining eligibility.[105]

EVALUATION PROCESS

Whether an adult is eligible for disability benefits is determined through a five-step evaluation process. A child's eligibility is determined on the basis of the first three steps.

Steps 1 and 2 require a determination of (1) whether the adult or older child is

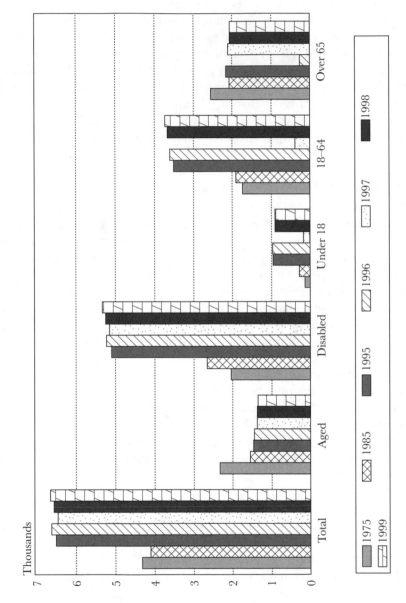

FIGURE 10.3. Number of SSI recipients by category and age: 1975 to 1999 (in thousands).

Source: Social Security Administration.

presently working or the younger child is engaged in age-appropriate substantial gainful activity (an affirmative answer disqualifies the individual) and, if not, (2) whether the applicant's impairment(s) is severe enough to limit significantly the ability to perform basic work-related or school-related activities (if not, the applicant is disqualified). If an applicant is earning in excess of $700 per month, or $1,050 per month if blind, he or she is considered able to engage in a substantial gainful activity and will not be eligible for benefits.[106] At step 3, evidence in an applicant's medical file describing symptoms, signs of illness, and laboratory findings is compared with disability listings compiled by the Social Security Administration for a direct match or for a finding of medical or functional "equivalency."[107]

Medical equivalence exists when the applicant has the signs, symptoms, and laboratory findings associated with a listed condition, but does not have a diagnosis that matches directly a listed condition. Functional equivalence means that the applicant's ability to function is limited as if his or her condition were medically equivalent.

If the applicant has certain conditions, such as Acquired Immune Deficiency Syndrome (AIDS) or symptoms of equal severity to those of a person diagnosed with AIDS, the applicant is considered likely to receive benefits and will be categorized as "presumptively" eligible, meaning that benefits may be paid for up to six months before the full application process is complete. In addition, the law permits an emergency payment to a presumptively eligible person that is paid in advance of a final determination of eligibility. An emergency payment is repaid through proportional deductions from benefit checks. In March 1996, the rules for eligibility for SSI were changed to disqualify from coverage individuals whose alcohol or drug use was the "contributing factor" material to their disability.[108]

For the adult whose eligibility cannot be finalized at step 3, the inquiry continues. In Step 4, applicants are asked whether they are able to do work that they have done in the past and, if not, Step 5 asks whether applicants are able to engage in any other substantial gainful activity given their age, education, and work experience.[109] These steps are a "vocational analysis," and benefits will be denied if the answer to either inquiry is affirmative.

Eligibility for SSI is limited to United States citizens, refugees or asylees, and noncitizens who were SSI recipients as of August 22, 1996, or who were living in the United States on that date and later became disabled.[110] Residency in the United States or the Northern Mariana Islands is also required, but children of military personnel stationed outside the United States and students who are temporarily abroad are eligible. Applicants for SSI must, before receiving benefits, apply for all other benefits to which they may be entitled, and they must accept vocational rehabilitation services if they are offered. The Social Security Administration reimburses state vocational rehabilitation agencies for reasonable costs associated with providing services to disabled persons to assist them in becoming self-sufficient.

Disability in Children

Before passage of the PRWOA, a child applicant was subject to a fourth step in the eligibility determination process, referred to as an individual functional assessment

(IFA). An IFA was comparable to the vocational analysis conducted for adults. An IFA asked whether the child was able to engage in normal everyday activities of living, such as " . . . speaking, walking, washing, dressing and . . . going to school, etc." Children whose impairment significantly reduced their ability to engage in everyday activities, acquire the skills necessary to assume an adult role, or "grow, develop, or mature physically, mentally or emotionally and thus to attain developmental milestones" were judged to have an impairment and passed the IFA test.[111] Passage of the PRWOA ended the use of IFAs. Henceforth, children would be eligible to receive SSI only if their condition matched a listed condition or was the medical or functional equivalent of a listed condition.

Congress eliminated the IFAs because of the growth in the number of children receiving SSI which, as noted earlier, quadrupled between 1985 and 1995 (see Figure 10.3). Recipient growth was said to be caused by a lax definition of disability, which resulted in children with modest conditions or impairments receiving assistance. When the PRWOA was passed, the definition of childhood disability was amended so that only children with "marked and severe" disabilities would receive benefits. "Maladaptive behavior," which refers to behavior that is destructive to oneself, others, property, or animals, was eliminated from the listed conditions used to determine eligibility, because some members of Congress thought that children were being coached by their parents to "fake" mental impairments. The PRWOA required that the Social Security Administration make a one-time redetermination of a child's continuing eligibility. In June 1999, the GAO reported that the SSA had completed 98 percent of these reviews, finding about 115,300 children, 42 percent of the 273,600 whose cases were reviewed, ineligible for continued aid. One-half of these cases were under appeal at the time the GAO issued its report. The SSA estimated that approximately 100,000 children would be found to be ineligible when all appeals were exhausted.[112]

CONTINUING DISABILITY REVIEWS

As with the SSDI program (chapter 9), reviews are conducted every three years if it has been determined that medical improvement is possible. Otherwise, review is conducted after seven years.[113] The person subject to review must present evidence from a physician, psychologist, or other professional who has provided treatment or conducted an evaluation and any other evidence that will support the claim for ongoing disability.

Supplemental Security Income, Medicaid, and Food Stamps

States treat SSI recipients in relation to Medicaid in one of three ways. In thirty-two states and the District of Columbia, an application for SSI is an application for Medicaid, and the approved SSI applicant automatically receives Medicaid. Seven states provide Medicaid for all SSI recipients but require the SSI applicant to file separately for health benefits. The last option allows the states to impose stricter standards for Medicaid eligibility than for SSI. Nationally, approximately 80 percent of SSI recipients automatically receive Medicaid.

Recipients of SSI may be eligible for food stamps. Eligibility is automatic for the individual living alone and for a household where all members receive SSI. Other households must meet the income requirements that are set for the Food Stamp Program (see chapter 11).

INCENTIVES TO WORK

The SSI program provides a variety of incentives for people with disabilities to work. Some are the same as those reviewed in chapter 9 where I discussed the SSDI program; others are unique. As with SSDI, impairment-related work expenses are deducted from gross earnings before a determination is made as to whether an applicant is engaging in a substantial gainful activity. Expenses may include medical devices, attendant care, or structural alterations to an automobile that enable the person to drive to work and residential modifications, such as a wheelchair ramp, or enlargement of a doorway for a person who works at home.

Two additional features are common to SSI and SSDI. First, the applicant for SSI must accept a referral for vocational rehabilitation services if these are deemed appropriate. Acceptance of a referral is a condition for receiving a grant, unless the applicant has good cause to refuse to participate in a referred to program. Benefits will continue for individuals who are engaged in an approved vocational rehabilitation program, if program completion is likely to enable the person to work permanently. Second, subsidized employment may be available for an individual whose skills are not as fully developed as those of a nondisabled worker. Subsidies may support providing the disabled worker with more supervision than others who are doing the same job, or they may support task simplification, which is accomplished by assigning some task-related responsibilities to another worker.

Under the Earned Income Exclusion, the first $65 of each month's earnings are deducted, plus one-half of remaining earnings, before the amount of the SSI benefit is calculated. For a student in regular school attendance who is under 22 years of age, up to $400 of earned income per month is excluded, up to a yearly maximum of $1,620.

A participant in the SSI program may set aside income as part of a Plan for Achieving Self-Support (PASS). The written PASS must set a work-related goal that the person is capable of performing and may include the acquisition of additional education or vocational training or plans to start a business. A timetable for attaining the goal must be specified and assurances provided that the set-aside funds will be used to achieve the PASS. The PASS must be approved by the SSA and is subject to ongoing review.

Additional work incentives are found in the "set aside" for property that is essential for the SSI recipient to achieve self-support. For example, the total value of tools or equipment needed for work is excluded. Up to $6,000 in nonbusiness property may be excluded when eligibility is determined, if the property is used to produce necessary goods or services. This property may include the value of land used to grow vegetables or keep livestock for consumption by the beneficiary's household.

The Section 1619 Work Incentive program allows recipients of SSI to receive benefits even if gross earnings are above the substantial gainful activity level, as long as there is no medical improvement in the individual's disability.[114] Finally, under legislation enacted in December 1999, states may continue Medicaid coverage for SSI beneficiaries who return to work even if their earnings become too high to receive a cash benefit if they remain disabled. In addition, federal funds became available for demonstration programs to provide Medicaid coverage to people with "potentially disabling conditions." A person who is positive for Human Immuno-deficiency Virus but does not have symptoms of AIDS is potentially disabled, but not actually so, and is not eligible for SSI cash benefits; however, under a demonstration grant, this person could become eligible for Medicaid benefits.[115]

SECTION 4: GENERAL ASSISTANCE

General Assistance (GA) is a program of last resort for those in need of financial assistance but do not qualify for aid under any of the programs reviewed in this and the previous chapter. Forty-two states operate GA programs. Thirty-three programs are available throughout the state, with the remaining programs operating in some but not all of a state's counties or local jurisdictions.[116] A GA recipient may be eligible for food stamps and Medicaid.

General Assistance programs are funded entirely by state, county, or local units of government. In twenty-eight states, GA provides cash assistance, and in eleven, it provides vendor payments or vouchers for rent or utilities. Three states pay a combination of cash and vendor payments or provide vouchers. On average, GA cash benefits average 39 percent of the poverty level.[117]

Those who may be eligible for GA include children, childless individuals and families, the unemployed who are not eligible for unemployment insurance or those who have exhausted their unemployment benefits, individuals with disabilities whose disability is expected to last fewer than twelve months, and families who have lost their AFDC/TANF benefits.

Because GA is a state- or locally run program, benefit levels and eligibility requirements vary. Eighteen of the forty-two states with GA programs do not impose a time limit for receipt of benefits, but others do; some states impose work requirements. New York, for example, limits cash assistance to two years and requires GA recipients to accept offered employment. California limits assistance for employable people to nine months out of a twelve month period and reserves the option to require nondisabled individuals to work.[118] In Connecticut, GA is denied to persons who are deemed to be employable,[119] and in Illinois recipients over the age of sixteen who are not in school are required to accept "bona fide offers of employment."[120]

The Refugee Assistance Act is a federal program that provides cash assistance to eligible refugees. Refugees are noncitizens who are not able to return to their country of origin because of persecution or a well-founded fear of persecution due to their race, religion, nationality, membership in social group or political opinion.[121]

Summary

In this chapter, we reviewed three public assistance programs: AFDC/TANF, SSI, and GA. Financing of public assistance programs comes solely from federal and/ or state funds and are therefore distinguished from social insurance programs (reviewed in chapter 9) that are funded partly by employment-based contributions made by individuals.

The passage of TANF was animated by concern that the availability of welfare encouraged out-of-wedlock births, discouraged the formation of two-parent families, and perpetuated a cycle of dependency on governmental support. In addition, it was assumed that the growth of the AFDC caseload, which hit a historical high two years before the passage of TANF, was best controlled if the federal role was diminished in favor of increased state authority for setting program rules and by limiting an unmarried teenager's access to income support.

The TANF program ended the sixty-year-old AFDC program and the entitlement that ensured a measure of income security for needy children and their caretakers and replaced it with a capped block grant. Henceforth, if the number of program applicants exceeded block grant funds, aid would be denied, or if granted, paid for entirely by the state. In addition, financial assistance would be linked to mandatory work requirements for adult beneficiaries who would also be required to participate in establishing paternity and collecting child support. With few exceptions, program participation for parents and children would be limited to no more than sixty months in a lifetime.

Each state sets the amount of the TANF grant. The majority of states pay a grant that is less than the amount of money required for families of different sizes to obtain food, clothing, and housing and to meet other basic needs within the state. TANF recipients are eligible to receive food stamps and Medicaid, and when the value of food stamps is added to the TANF grant, the benefit increases significantly. But on a national basis, the median grant is equal to only 34 percent of the poverty level, and the combined TANF and food stamp benefit is equal to 62 percent of the poverty level.

Because of the discretion that TANF provides to the states, generalizations concerning program operation cannot be made. For example, some states require the adult recipient to engage in work activities "immediately" upon application, others require work within forty-five or ninety days, others adhere to the 24-month-time period set by federal law, and some states terminate benefits in less than the sixty month limit set in federal law. Family caps that exist in nineteen states preclude additional payments for children born after the family enters the TANF rolls, and states are free to grant or deny benefits to newly arrived immigrants.

More than one-half of the states have put in place "diversion programs" that seek to redirect applicants from applying for benefits by providing temporary assistance in the form of, for example, emergency cash grants or support services such as child care, and other states have implemented Work First programs that emphasize putting applicants to work at the earliest possible time. Work First programs assist applicants by helping them identify and overcome barriers to employment through the provision of support services, including child care and transportation. In addition, work incentives have been put in place, such as increasing the amount of earned income that a family may have before its TANF benefits are reduced and that encourage people to save without losing their eligibility for all assistance.

The AFDC/TANF caseload decreased significantly after it peaked in 1994, but the decrease cannot be attributed solely to the new law. Contributing factors include a strong economy and the jobs generated by it, experimental work programs existing in a number of states prior to the passage of TANF that enabled some families to find work, and strategies that were implemented after passage of TANF that have discouraged or diverted families from applying for aid.

The success of TANF will be judged by whether those who leave the welfare rolls maintain employment, but available data are limited to a small number of states and by methodological problems that preclude in-state generalizations for all but a handful of studies. With these caveats in mind, we have information indicating that 60 to 70 percent of families are still employed when follow-up information is gathered; 19 to 30 percent of families return to welfare; and of those who do not receive cash assistance, other supports are obtained such as Medicaid or food stamps, indicating that the family's earned income was low enough to qualify for these benefits. Few families receive child support payments (13 to 35 percent), and some (11 to 65 percent) are helped by their families and friends.

Because AFDC had no time limit for receipt of benefits, recipients who left the rolls for work and later lost their job could, as a rule, rely on re-entry to AFDC. The TANF program's sixty month time limit eliminates this guarantee, and there are no data to inform the question, "How will states respond to an increased demand for assistance in a recession?" Whether states will provide assistance by using their own reserve funds or whether they will borrow from the TANF loan fund is not known. Finally, the lack of child care has been a barrier to the success of work programs in the past, and whether states will develop ways of increasing the supply of needed child care remains to be seen.

Individuals with disabilities may be eligible for financial aid under the SSI program, Title XVI of the Social Security Act. Supplemental Security Income is an entitlement program, so all applicants receive assistance if they meet the program's eligibility standards, and SSI is funded entirely by the federal government. The benefit levels under SSI are more generous than those available under TANF and provide a benefit equal to approximately 77 percent of the poverty level.

In addition to establishing financial need, adult applicants who file disability-based claims rests their case on their inability to engage in productive work (defined as work that produces an income of more than $700 per month or $1,050 per month for a person who is blind), and child applicants base their claims on their inability to engage in age-appropriate activities, such as attending school. The adult or the child must support a claim of disability with medical evidence, and the disability must be one that is expected to last for twelve months or more or to result in death.

Of the more than 6 million SSI recipients in March 1999, 80 percent were eligible due to a disability and 20 percent due to age. The number of child recipients grew dramatically between 1985 and 1995, quadrupling from 227,000 to 917,000 and causing Congress to modify the eligibility rules for children, restricting eligibility to those with severe disabilities and eliminating from eligibility children whose claim was based on the child engaging in behavior that was destructive to self, others, property, or animals. It is expected that about 100,000 children will lose their SSI benefits as a result of these changes.

The SSI program encourages work and does so by (1) providing incentives, such as an allowed deduction for work-related expenses made necessary by the applicant's disability, before a determination is made as to whether an applicant is financially eligible to receive SSI; (2) providing vocational rehabilitation services where appropriate; (3) through the earned income exclusion, where the first $65 of each month's earnings are deducted plus one-half of remaining earnings before the amount of the SSI benefit is calculated; (4) by allowing SSI recipients to set aside income as part of a PASS; and (5) through the Section 1619 Work Incentive program that allows recipients to receive benefits even if gross earnings would otherwise disqualify the individual, as long is there is no medical improvement in the individual's disability. Medicaid coverage is continued for most working SSI beneficiaries under age sixty-five when their earnings become too high to allow an SSI cash payment if they remain disabled or require medical services in order to work and if gross earned income is insufficient to replace SSI and Medicaid.[122]

State programs that provide cash assistance through GA programs were the last type of program reviewed in this chapter. General assistance is available in forty-two states but is not necessarily operated statewide. Although some GA programs provide cash assistance, others provide instead for vendor payments to be used for rent or utilities, or they provide vouchers for the recipient's use. The average GA cash benefit is equal to 39 percent of the poverty level. Some states limit the amount of time that a recipient may participate in a GA program, and some states require that the recipient work in exchange for benefits.

Food and Housing

Programs that provide cash assistance to people in need were reviewed in chapter 10. The purchasing power of individuals and families who receive cash assistance is increased by food and housing benefits because their receipt leaves more disposable cash.

In section 1 of this chapter, policies that provide food assistance to individuals and families are reviewed. Following a brief description of hunger in America and the history of the federal response to it, our attention turns to the (1) Food Stamp Program (FSP); (2) Emergency Food Assistance Program; (3) School Lunch and School Breakfast Program (SLSB); (4) Supplemental Nutrition Program for Women, Infants and Children (WIC); and (5) programs that provide food service to the elderly.

Section 2 addresses housing and the federal policies that provide for housing construction and rehabilitation, subsidies for rent, and a series of programs that serve specific populations such as the homeless, people with Acquired Immune Deficiency Syndrome (AIDS), Native Americans, and youth.

Before beginning, a cautionary note is in order. Programs such as the Supplemental Security Income Program (SSI), which was reviewed in chapter 10, and the FSP, which is reviewed in this chapter, provide a single benefit: cash in the former program and coupons redeemable for food in the latter. If you understand how a program defines "beneficiary" and if the benefit is clearly defined, reported information describing the number of program participants is easily interpreted. For example, in chapter 10 I reported that in 1995, 917,000 individuals under the age of eighteen received SSI benefits. This means that a check was provided to that number of people. However, starting in this chapter and continuing in later chapters, some of the reviewed programs offer a range of benefits, and how many of these are received by each beneficiary may not be readily apparent. For example, a participant in the WIC program may receive a referral for nutrition and health services, vouchers or checks that can be redeemed for food items, or infant formula. Programs that provide a range of services may report the number of participants but not link the number reported to any specific program component. You will see later in this chapter that the WIC program served in excess of 90 percent of eligible infants, but you will not know what particular service was provided.

SECTION 1: FOOD PROGRAMS

Hunger in America

Data concerning the availability of food and relationship between diet, health, and hunger are compiled by the Centers for Disease Control's National Center on Health Statistics, the Census Bureau's Current Population Survey (see chapter 8), and by the Department of Agriculture (DOA). In 1996, the Centers for Disease Control and the DOA began to gather data through interviews with and physical examinations of individuals in 1,900 geographic areas in the fifty states and the District of Columbia. Within each area, a random sample was selected, yielding approximately 43,000 households with more than 100,000 individuals.[1]

The compiled data were reported in 1998. The number of households experiencing hunger or "food insecurity," meaning that the household did not having the means to acquire enough food to meet basic needs, was increasing. The number of children lacking food increased from slightly over 10 million in 1997 to approximately 14 million in 1998, while the number of adults lacking food increased from 15.7 million in 1997 to 22 million in 1998.[2]

Another 1998 report, issued by the United States Conference of Mayors, informs us that 67 percent of thirty surveyed cities reported that requests for emergency food assistance from families with children increased by an average of 14 percent, and requests by the elderly increased an average of six percent. Approximately 21 percent of requests could not be met. Of families requiring help, 37 percent of the families requesting help were employed.

THE FEDERAL RESPONSE TO HUNGER

The first federal effort to address the problem of hunger in the United States was undertaken in 1935 when excess farm commodities were distributed by the federal government to the states, who, in turn, distributed food to people in need.[3] Reducing food surpluses that depressed the farm economy, not the nutritional needs of people, was the driving force behind the program; the program was criticized because the distributed commodities did not produce a nutritionally balanced diet.[4] Commodities distribution continued under the Agriculture Act of 1949, which added dietary guidelines and a list of commodities to be purchased by the government for distribution. However, the commodities that were purchased were chosen less out of a concern for nutritional requirements than to continue the practice of providing price supports for farmers.[5]

The Food Stamp Program

The FSP began in 1961 when President Kennedy issued an executive order that allowed a demonstration project to go forth in which "coupons" could be purchased to acquire food and "bonus" stamps were provided for additional food purchases.[6] In 1964, Congress codified the executive order when it enacted the Food Stamp Act. The states were given the option of replacing their commodities distribution program with coupon distribution. In 1974, the FSP became mandatory across the county; and in 1977, the requirement to purchase coupons was eliminated. Relative to the commodities distribution program, the provision of stamps increased both the food choices available to program participants as well as their disposable income since money previously spent on food was now available for other necessities.

The FSP is operated by the U.S. Department of Agriculture (DOA) through its Food and Nutrition Service (FNS) in cooperation with the states. Assisting low-income participants acquire food in order to have a nutritionally balanced diet is its purpose. The program is an entitlement program that is operated in all fifty states, the District of Columbia, Guam, and the Virgin Islands. Puerto Rico, the Northern Mariana Islands, and American Samoa operate a Nutrition Assistance Program that is funded through a block grant.[7] The federal government pays 100 percent of the costs of the provided stamps and approximately 50 percent of the costs of program administration. Participants receive coupons that can be used to purchase food products.[8] An FSP participant is a "household" defined as one or more individuals who live together, purchase food together, and prepare meals together.

NUMBER OF RECIPIENTS AND DECLINING CASELOADS

In the first six months of 1999, the FSP assisted an average of 18.5 million recipients each month, down from a monthly average of 25.5 million recipients in 1996, for a reduction in caseload size of 27 percent over three years. Program costs for fiscal year 1998 were $16.9 billion.[9]

Reasons cited for the caseload decline include (1) a stronger economy with more people at work, resulting in a decreased demand for food stamps; (2) the exclusion of noncitizens from the program; (3) a new work requirement for able-bodied adults without children may have caused some people not to apply for the program; (4) failure by some city and state agencies to inform people that they may still be eligible for food stamps after they lost their cash benefits when the Temporary Assistance to Needy Families Program (TANF) was implemented or when regulations to the SSI Program were changed; and (5) state-implemented barriers to participation in the FSP, some of which violate federal law.[10]

Officials in a number of states discussed declining caseloads with investigators from the General Accounting Office (GAO), and GAO investigators reviewed reports concerning this matter. Information from state officials emphasized that confusion concerning ongoing eligibility for food stamps despite loss of cash assistance was a contributing factor in caseload decline. For example, a report concerning food stamp participants in Wisconsin noted that 51 percent of former recipients still eligible did not receive food stamps, and 34 percent did not know that they might be eligible. The Wisconsin study revealed also that 32 percent of former recipients had no way to buy food for some period of time after they left welfare, with 13 percent relying on food pantries. A report from South Carolina informs us that 40 percent of former and still eligible recipients did not receive food stamps, and 22 percent did not know that they might be eligible. Thirteen percent of former welfare recipients had no way to buy food for some period of time after they left welfare, with 17 percent of these people turning to shelters or food pantries. Similar results were produced by studies conducted in Massachusetts and Texas.

Concerned with declining caseloads, the FNS investigated applications practices in several states. The investigation was also prompted by advocates reporting illegal practices, such as clients being misinformed about their right to apply for stamps. Two examples speak for themselves.

EXAMPLES OF FNS INVESTIGATIONS

New York City. In 1998, New York City began converting welfare offices to job centers where applicants for welfare were diverted from government programs by requiring them to find employment or other private sources of assistance. To be eligible for TANF and food stamps, applicants first had to search extensively for a job and explore alternate resources, such as private food pantries, family, or friends. In 1998, the FNS reviewed New York City's Food Stamp Program and found that New York City was in violation of federal law because caseworkers (1) did not permit households to apply for food stamps during their first visit, (2) did not inform applicants about the availability of food stamps if the applicants either were denied TANF benefits or accepted a diversion payment, and (3) frequently denied food stamp benefits to applicants for failure to participate in a job center's employment-related activities. In addition, caseworkers refused to accept food stamp applications because it was "too late" in the day, and they encouraged applicants to withdraw their food stamp applications. State and city officials said that some job center practices help end government dependency, prevent fraud, and protect applicants' rights and that city officials believed they have the right to interpret the Welfare Reform Act and develop policies and procedures on the basis of their interpretations because regulations to implement the Welfare Reform Act's revisions had not been issued. Nevertheless, the state submitted a plan for corrective action. The FNS notified New York State officials that if the corrective action plan was not implemented by May 1999, it would institute a fine of $5 million every three months. The plan was implemented in April 1999.

Portland, Oregon. In Oregon, FNS investigated the practices in welfare offices and learned that food stamp applicants' rights were being violated. Those applying for food stamps were forced to return on a second day before meeting with an eligibility worker who was available for one hour each day between 7:30 a.m. and 8:30 a.m. Applicants arriving after 8:30 a.m. were given an application form and asked to return for an appointment on another day. It should not be surprising that the number of applicants that appeared at the welfare office in the one-hour time period exceeded the number of people that could be served in a single day. Hence, an applicant could wait all day, only to be told at the close of business to return on another day. At the direction of FNS, Oregon submitted a corrective action plan.

Source: U.S. General Accounting Office, *Food Stamp Program: Various Factors Have Led to Declining Participation,* GAO/RCED-99-185 (Washington, D.C., 1999), 35–36.

On July 14, 1999, President Clinton announced that the DOA would undertake a nationwide public education campaign to inform families about the FSP and that an expanded, toll-free information hotline for those wishing to learn about the program would be implemented.

Food Stamp Eligibility and Characteristics of Recipients

An applicant for food stamps applies at a local welfare office, usually the same office at which application for cash assistance under TANF or the General Assistance Program (GA) is made. All household members must apply together, and the income and assets of all are combined to determine eligibility. To ensure that homeless people are not denied stamps, assistance cannot be made contingent upon an applicant providing a fixed mailing address or permanent residence.

If all members of a household are receiving cash assistance through TANF, SSI, or GA, they are not subject to an income test. Households where only some members participate in one of these cash assistance programs and households whose members do not participate in any publicly assisted cash program must establish that they are income eligible, except those with an elderly resident.[11]

Applicants must satisfy a gross income test and a net income test. Deductibles that are subtracted from monthly gross income include (1) the cost of child care for a dependent child, if care is required for work, training, or education, in an amount not to exceed $200 for each child under two years of age and no more than $175 for others; (2) child support payments provided under a legal obligation; and (3) shelter costs that exceed one-half of household income, but are not more than $275. In the fall of 1999, the gross monthly income for a family of four could not exceed $1,783 per month nor could the net income exceed $1,271 a month. Households may have other resources, such as savings not in excess of $2,000, except for households with at least one person sixty years of age or older, which may have savings of $3,000. In addition, the cost of an automobile is not counted if the vehicle is used for long-distance travel for work, but is counted for daily commuting, as a home, or to transport a person with a disability. Otherwise, the value of a vehicle in excess of $4,650 is counted against eligibility.[12] Eligibility for food stamps must be recertified every three to twelve months.[13]

Children who are receiving food stamp benefits are automatically eligible for free school meals and for the Special Supplemental Nutrition Program and WIC, which are discussed later. Federal law requires that eligibility determinations be made within thirty days of application and that food stamps be provided at that time unless a household is deemed ineligible. Applications may be expedited and stamps provided within seven days of application for people with no cash or with extraordinarily high living expenses. In a number of states, the long-standing practice of providing coupons for use in purchasing food is being replaced by debit cards with electronic benefit transfers.

The data in Table 11.1 show categories of FSP participants in 1996 and 1997 and the decline in participants attributable to the welfare reform amendments of 1996. The number of people participating in the FSP declined in every category for which data was available. Able-bodied adults without dependents, with close to 25 percent losing their food stamp benefits, experienced the greatest decline. Sixteen percent of preschool-age children lost their food benefits, and close to 14 percent of adults with dependents lost benefits.

Recipients may be sanctioned for failure to adhere to the rules of the FSP or to the rules of another public assistance program. For example, the failure of one person to cooperate with child support enforcement rules may result in disqualifying all members of a household for up to 180 days, as may failure of the head of household to comply with the program's work requirements. The length of a period of disqualification may increase for a participant who has been previously sanctioned.[14]

FOOD STAMPS AND NONCITIZENS

The Personal Responsibility and Work Opportunity Reconciliation Act of 1996 (PRWOA) denied food stamps to noncitizens, except for certain categories of ref-

TABLE 11.1. Selected Demographic Characteristics of Food Stamp Participants: 1996–1997 (in Thousands)

Categories	Fiscal year 1996	Fiscal year 1997	Change in number of participants	Percent change
Children*	13,212	11,868	−1,344	−10.2
Preschool age	4,815	4,046	−769	−16.0
School age	8,397	7,825	−574	−6.8
Adults with dependents	7,582	6,549	−1,033	−13.6
Able-bodied adults without dependents	1,107	833	−274	−24.8
Permanent resident aliens	1,463	4,023	−440	−0.31
Elderly†	1,895	1,834	−61	−3.2
Disabled	NA	2,278	NA	NA

Source: U.S. General Accounting Office, *Food Stamp Program; Various Factors Have Led to Declining Participation,* GAO/RCED-99-185 (Washington, D.C., 1999).
Note: NA, not available.
*Children are individuals aged 0–17. Preschool children are less than age 5, and school children are aged 5 to 17.
†Elderly are individuals 60 years of age and older.

ugees,[15] for immigrants with at least forty quarters of work, and for active-duty and retired members of the armed forces.[16] The Balanced Budget Act of 1997 and the Agricultural Research, Extension, and Education Reform Act of 1998[17] restored benefits to three groups of people who were legally in the United States on August 22, 1996. Benefits were restored to (1) children under eighteen years of age, (2) those over the age of sixty-five, and (3) people with disabilities. In addition, benefits were restored to people from Laos who assisted the United States war effort in Vietnam and to Native Americans who are legally entitled to move back and forth between the U.S., Canada, and Mexico.[18] States may choose to purchase food stamps from the federal government and to provide them to ineligible noncitizens at state expense. As of June 1999, thirteen states had chosen to do so.[19]

FOOD STAMP BENEFIT LEVEL

Food stamp benefit levels are based on the Thrifty Food Plan (TFP), developed by the DOA in 1965 and adjusted only slightly since that time. The TFP reflects the cost of maintaining a family of four at minimum levels of nutrition. The food stamp benefit is indexed for inflation. The DOA assumes that a typical household will spend 30 percent of available cash on food and that the value of the provided food stamps will make up the difference between the 30 percent and the cost of an "adequate low-cost diet." Given the low benefit level provided by the Aid to Families with Dependent Children (AFDC) program and its successor, TANF (see chapter 10), plus the percentage of income that families pay for rent, it is questionable whether the assumption that low-income families can afford to spend 30 percent of their discretionary income on food is accurate.

The "dollar" value of food stamps varies by household size and net monthly income. The benefit level is the same in the forty-eight contiguous states and the District of Columbia, with a slightly higher benefit provided in Alaska, Hawaii, Guam, and the Virgin Islands. Benefit levels are shown in Table 11.2.

TABLE 11.2. Maximum Monthly Food Stamp Allotments, Fiscal Year 1998

Household size	48 States and D.C.	Alaska	Hawaii	Guam	Virgin Islands
1 person	$122	$154	$197	$180	$157
2 people	224	283	361	331	288
3 people	321	405	517	474	413
4 people	408	514	657	602	525
5 people	485	611	780	715	623
6 people	582	733	936	858	748
7 people	643	810	1,035	948	827
8 people	735	926	1,183	1,083	945
Each added person	+92	+116	+148	+135	+118

Source: House, Committee on Ways and Means, "Section 15: Other Programs," *Green Book* (Washington, D.C., 1998), 935.

USING STAMPS

Food stamps may be used to acquire (1) food that will be prepared and consumed at home, but not food sold by a vendor for immediate consumption, nor alcohol or tobacco; (2) seeds and plants to grow food for personal consumption; (3) meals prepared and served through communal dining programs for the elderly and for people with disabilities or home-delivered meals for the same populations; (4) meals prepared and served in institutional settings; and (6) hunting and fishing equipment such as nets, hooks, fishing rods, and knives for people living in certain remote areas of Alaska.

PARTICIPATION IN THE FOOD STAMP AND OTHER PROGRAMS

Approximately 80 percent of food stamp recipients participate in a government cash assistance program, either TANF, SSI, or GA. Table 10.2 showed the combined value to recipients of the benefits provided by the AFDC program and the FSP and highlighted the fact that the addition of food stamps increased significantly the purchasing power of families in both programs.

Food stamp recipients participate also in other federal programs, as the data in Table 11.3 show. In 1995, close to 49 percent of food stamp recipients also received AFDC, approximately 28 percent received SSI, nearly 26 percent received Social Security retirement benefits, 2.5 percent received unemployment benefits, and 22.5 percent received Medicare.

Food Stamp Work Requirements

Recipients of food stamps are required to satisfy the program's work requirements, but this requirement is more form than substance. This is so because more than

TABLE 11.3. Percent of Recipients Participating in Cash Assistance Programs and the Medicare Program and in Selected Food and Housing Programs: 1995

Cash assistance programs	Food and housing programs			
	Food stamps	WIC	Free or reduced school meals	Public or subsidized rental housing
AFDC	48.9	41.7	30.3	28.7
SSI	27.6	9.3	11.9	22.0
Social Security	25.6	9.9	11.4	37.6
Unemployment compensation	2.5	3.6	3.8	1.8
Medicare*	22.5	5.8	6.8	36.2

Source: House, Committee on Ways and Means, "Section 15: Other Programs," *Green Book* (Washington, D.C., 1998), 921.
*Data were not reported separately for the Medicaid program.

one-half of FSP recipients will not be expected to work because they are elderly recipients of Social Security (25.6 percent) or disabled recipients of SSI (27.6 percent). Moreover, close to 50 percent of FSP participants in 1996 were also participating in the AFDC program and are already required to work under provisions in the TANF program that were discussed in chapter 10. The FSP work requirements will affect any TANF recipient who loses TANF benefits, but whose income is low enough to qualify for food stamps. In addition, a number of groups are exempt from work requirements, including (1) people with physical or mental disabilities that render them unable to work; (2) those under sixteen years of age or over sixty years of age; (3) an adult who is caring for a dependent who is disabled or one who is under six years of age; or (4) an adult with a child aged six to twelve, if adequate child care is not available; (5) residents of drug addiction and alcoholic treatment programs; and (6) others whom a state elects to exclude from mandatory work requirements. Finally, states with an unemployment rate in excess of 10 percent and those without enough jobs to provide employment for food stamp recipients may request that DOA waiver the work requirement. As of June 1998, thirty-eight states and the District of Columbia had received waivers from the DOA.[20]

The work requirement of the FSP can be met by (1) registering for work; (2) participating in an employment or training program, if assigned by the state; (3) reporting to an employer to whom the state makes a referral; or (4) accepting suitable employment.[21]

Able-bodied adults with no dependents are limited to a maximum of six months of food stamps in any thirty-six month period, unless the adult is employed at least half time. Food stamps are denied to (1) workers who are on strike, unless they were eligible for stamps before the strike; (2) students in post-secondary educational programs; and (3) to people who live in institutional settings except for those in group homes that are approved residences for recipients of SSI, in drug addiction or alcohol treatment programs, in shelters for battered women, or in shelters for the homeless.

FRAUD AND ABUSE

In 1998 and 1999, the GAO conducted three studies that asked whether those receiving food stamps were entitled to their benefits. The GAO reported that 26,000 deceased people were counted as household members for purposes of determining benefits, that approximately 20,000 people were receiving benefits in two states at the same time, and that 3,000 individuals who had been disqualified from the program were receiving benefits.[22] The GAO attributed these problems to laxness on the part of state officials, such as failure to remove disqualified and deceased people from the rolls or to check the database maintained by the DOA to determine whether an individual was simultaneously collecting in more than one state. However, the GAO acknowledged that the DOA database is incomplete and contains errors.[23] Retail store owners have been charged with food stamp fraud for accepting stamps for ineligible items and for buying stamps from customers at discount prices. For example, 331 merchants were charged with purchasing food stamps valued at $13,500 for $6,900.[24]

In the fall of 1999, the federal government filed charges against a number of nonprofit groups across the country and charged forty-four people with claiming millions of dollars in funds for meals never served to children in day care centers.[25]

Emergency Food Assistance Program

In the early 1980s, federal law authorized the Emergency Food Assistance Program (TEFAP) to distribute surplus food to the states and to local groups that feed the hungry.[26] The states turn over surplus commodities to "feeding organizations," defined as any public or nonprofit organization that enters into an agreement with the state to provide nutrition assistance to needy persons by distributing the provided commodities. Feeding organizations include soup kitchens, food banks, hunger centers, and similar groups.[27]

Each state receives a share of excess food commodities. Sixty percent of each state's share is determined by the number of individuals in households with incomes below the poverty level; the remaining 40 percent is based on the number of unemployed persons.

Guidelines for eligibility are set at state discretion, and in a number of states eligibility guidelines for commodities are more restrictive than for food stamps. In 1997, an estimated 3.8 million households were served by the TEFAP program, which distributed more than 117 million pounds of food valued at more than $140 million.[28]

School Lunch and School Breakfast Programs

Meals for children in primary and secondary school and for those in child care are authorized by the National School Lunch Act. The act authorizes the School Lunch and School Breakfast Program (SLSB) and the Child and Adult Care Food Program (CACFP). The SLSB program provides meals free of charge or at a reduced cost to low-income children in primary and secondary schools and in residential treatment centers,[29] and CACFP provides meals to children in nonresidential child care centers.[30]

The enrollment of school districts in the SLSB program is voluntary. The federal government provides funds and food commodities to enrolled public and not-for-profit private elementary and secondary schools and to residential child care institutions. Children whose family income is less than 130 percent of the federal poverty level receive free meals, and those whose family income is between 130 and 185 percent of the federal poverty level receive meals at a cost not to exceed 40 cents for lunch or 30 cents for breakfast.

In fiscal year 1996, approximately 26 million children per day, or 57 percent of the children enrolled in participating schools and residential centers, were beneficiaries of the SLSB program at a cost to the federal government of approximately $5.5 billion. Fewer students participate in the breakfast program. In fiscal year 1996, 6.6 million children, or 20 percent of eligible children, participated.

CHILD AND ADULT CARE FOOD PROGRAM

Meals for children attending public or private nonresidential child care centers, including Head Start centers, may be provided through the CACFP. Federal funds subsidize the cost of breakfast, lunch, supper, and snacks. In fiscal year 1998, 2.4 million children received meals, at a cost of $1.7 billion. [31] The CACFP subsidies may be used to feed children younger than twelve, migrant children younger than fifteen, and handicapped children regardless of age.

Meals and snacks are free to children from families with an income below 130 percent of the federal poverty level and are also served at a reduced price to children with family income between 130 and 185 percent of the poverty level. A small Summer Food Service Program subsidizes meals for approximately 2 million children who participate in summer recreational programs.

Supplemental Nutrition Program for Women, Infants, and Children

Low-income pregnant women often suffer from health-related conditions, such as iron-deficiency anemia, and more than one-half suffer from being overweight or underweight. Women who are underweight and those who smoke and consume alcohol during pregnancy are at risk for giving birth prematurely, and the newborn is at risk for the health problems attendant to premature birth.[32]

The WIC program of 1972 (1) provides screening to assess nutritional risk; (2) makes referrals for health, welfare, and social services; (3) provides vouchers or checks to purchase specific nutritional items; (4) distributes food commodities, such as milk, cheese, eggs, or infant formula; and (5) provides education concerning nutrition. The WIC program operates in all of the states, in the District of Columbia, at thirty-three Native American tribal organizations; and in Puerto Rico, the United States Virgin Islands, American Samoa, and Guam.

Services provided by WIC are delivered at WIC agencies, which include county health departments and hospitals, mobile vans, schools, Indian reservations and Indian Health Service facilities, migrant health centers, and public housing sites. Women who are employed outside of the home have expressed difficulty in accessing WIC benefits due to conflicts between their hours of work and the hours that a WIC agency is open. To accommodate the needs of working women, some agencies allow women to schedule appointments, rather than taking women on a first-come, first-serve basis, whereas others allow someone other than the participant to pick up her check or food vouchers. Few WIC agencies are open on Saturdays, and few provide for early morning or evening appointments. Approximately one quarter of WIC participants who work do not have access to a WIC agency during the working day.[33]

Services are available to low-income pregnant and postpartum women and their infants, to breastfeeding women up to one year postpartum, and to low-income children up to five years of age.[34] When food commodities are provided, they are tailored to the food needs of recipients according to (1) the age of infants and children, that is, birth to three months; four to twelve months; one to five years; (2) the special dietary needs of women and children; and (3) whether a women is pregnant, nursing, or a postpartum non-nursing mother.

The WIC program is not an entitlement program, and the number of participants is limited by annual federal appropriations, supplemented by state funds and the participation of manufacturers who provide rebates on infant formula. The FNS reports that 98 percent of eligible infants and 60 percent of eligible children were served in 1998.[35]

Eligible families have an income at or below 185 percent of the poverty level and a medically determinable nutritional risk. An applicant's nutritional risk must be established by medical evidence showing an abnormal physical condition attributable to nutritional deficiencies; dietary deficiencies that place the applicant at risk or conditions that predispose the applicant to inadequate nutrition or nutritionally related medical problems. Families and households that are eligible for TANF, food stamps, or Medicaid have met WIC's financial eligibility test; and a pregnant woman who satisfies any of the program's financial requirements may be deemed "presumptively" eligible to receive assistance until the nutritional risk evaluation is complete.

The costs of the WIC program vary according to the commodities provided, differences in retail store prices when vouchers are used, and administrative costs, including the cost of nutrition risk screening, breastfeeding support, and nutrition education programs. In fiscal year 1996, the average cost of a WIC food package was $31 a month to the federal government, with administrative costs averaging $11 a month. In the same year, the federal government spent in excess of $3.5 billion to provide WIC services to approximately 7.2 million women, infants, and children.

Participation in WIC is time limited. Pregnant women may participate throughout their pregnancy and for up to six months after childbirth. The eligibility of nursing mothers must be recertified every six months, and participation ends when the infant turns one year of age. As noted, children are eligible for up to five years of age.

In 1992, WIC began its Farmer's Market Nutrition Program (FMNP). The FMNP is a very limited program that provides vouchers to WIC participants and to those who are on a waiting list to be certified as eligible for WIC. Vouchers, whose value does not exceed $10 to $20 per recipient per year, can be used to acquire fruits and vegetables from farmers' markets. At state option, participation may be limited to certain groups, such as pregnant and breastfeeding women. In the fall of 1999, FMNP programs were operating in thirty-three states, the District of Columbia, and Guam.[36] In fiscal year 1998, there were approximately 1.4 million participants.

Food for the Elderly

The American Academy of Family Physicians, working with the American Dietetic Association and the National Council on the Aging, reports that

> Older Americans, due to many environmental, social, economic and physical changes of aging, are at disproportionate risk of poor nutrition that can adversely

affect their health and vitality. Nutrition-related health problems cause considerable dysfunction and disability, decreased quality of life, and in many cases, increased morbidity and mortality. Malnourished older Americans get more infections and diseases; their injuries take longer to heal; surgery on them is riskier; and their hospital stays are longer and more expensive.[37]

Nutrition services for the elderly are provided mainly under the authority of the Older Americans Act (OAA) of 1965, enacted as part of President Johnson's Great Society programs (see chapter 5). Administered by the Administration on Aging (AOA) in the Department of Health and Human Services, the OAA is the primary vehicle for providing community-based supportive and nutrition services to elderly persons.[38] The AOA distributes funds to designated state agencies by using a formula grant that is based on the number of state residents older than sixty years of age. In addition, the DOA distributes food commodities to the designated state agency or, at state discretion, cash in lieu of commodities. If a state chooses the cash option, it is required by federal law to "promptly and equitably" disburse the received funds to the agencies providing food services to the elderly. Funds can only be used to purchase agricultural commodities for nutrition programs. The cash option allows agencies discretion in meal planning, for example, to meet the special dietary needs of the elderly, which commodities distributed by the government may not satisfy.[39]

The OAA has seven titles. Our interest is in Title III. It authorizes a variety of social services, including the Elderly Nutrition Program that provides congregate meals served at community centers, churches, schools, and the like and the "meals-on-wheels" program that serves elderly people in their own homes. (See chapter 14 for a discussion of other provisions in the OAA).[40] In addition, Title III funds may be used for nutritional screening, assessment, education, and counseling to assist the elderly in identifying individual nutritional problems and working out ways of solving identified problems, including education to develop the skills needed to plan for and prepare nutritionally balanced meals.[41]

Title III nutrition programs are the OAA's largest program. Funding for fiscal year 1998 for both the congregate and at-home meals program was $486.4 million, representing 56 percent of the AOA's budget.[42] In 1995, 242 million meals were served to over 3.4 million older persons. Fifty-one percent of meals were served in congregate settings and 49 percent to people at home.[43] Participation rates by low-income minorities has been low in part because meals were not culturally appropriate, outreach did not take account of language differences, and publicity in minority communities was limited.[44]

There is no means test for Title III services, but an effort is made to target services to the elderly in greatest economic or social need, especially low-income minority individuals. Services may also be provided to (1) the spouse of an eligible recipient regardless of age, (2) disabled people under sixty years of age who accompany an elderly person to meals, (3) disabled people who live in housing facilities occupied mainly by the elderly if congregate meals are served, and (4) nutrition service volunteers. Tribal organizations are free to provide services to people under the age of sixty.

Programs may require participants to pay a fee on a sliding scale, referred to as an individual's "contribution" to the program.[45] To help preserve the dignity of the elderly, fees are set on the basis of an individual's self-declaration of income, and services cannot be denied due to an inability or unwillingness to pay. Cost-sharing requirements may not be imposed on persons whose income is less than 150 percent of the federal poverty level.

A 1992 evaluation of the OAA's nutrition programs found that relative to the elderly population, those participating in nutrition programs tended to (1) be older, (2) be poor, (3) live alone, (4) belong to a minority group, and (5) to have health and functional limitations that placed them at nutritional risk. Hospitals and nursing homes are the common sources of referral for home-delivered meals, and more than 40 percent of programs had waiting lists that are likely to increase as population of elderly people grows.

The services provided through the OAA are important but reach only a limited number of people in need. This limitation is clear from the percentage of people on waiting lists for services and is evident in the fact that federal funds pay for only 37 percent of the costs of meals provided in congregate settings and 23 percent of the cost of home-delivered meals. Regardless of the program, each meal served costs slightly over $5. In addition to federal funds, additional support comes from state and local government, private donations, and participant contributions, which yield $1.70 for each $1 of federal funds spent on the congregate care program and $3.35 for each $1 spent on the at-home meals program.[46]

SECTION 2: HOUSING

Federal involvement in providing housing assistance began in 1937 when the United States Housing Act was passed. The 1937 act authorized partnerships between the federal government and state and local units of government. The act, as amended by the Cranston-Gonzales National Affordable Housing Act of 1990 and the Quality Housing and Work Responsibility Act of 1998, is an umbrella policy covering a range of housing programs.

The United States Department of Housing and Urban Development (HUD) administers the majority of federal housing programs. [47] Public Housing Authorities (PHAs) receive federal grants to build and operate housing for low-income individuals and families.[48] Low income is defined as a percent of the poverty level or as a percent of the median income in the community that receives a grant. For example, in 1999, Section 8 housing vouchers (discussed later) were awarded to families with an income below 30 percent of the median income in the area where the applicant resided. Unlike the great majority of social welfare programs, federal funds flow mainly to city or county housing authorities, bypassing state government.

The act, as amended by the National Affordable Housing Act of 1990, seeks

(1) to ensure that every resident of the United States has access to decent shelter or assistance in avoiding homelessness; (2) to increase the Nation's supply of

decent housing that is affordable to low-income and moderate-income families and accessible to job opportunities; (3) to improve housing opportunities for all residents of the United States, particularly members of disadvantaged minorities, on a nondiscriminatory basis; (4) to help make neighborhoods safe and livable; (5) to expand opportunities for home ownership; (6) to provide every American community with a reliable, readily available supply of mortgage finance at the lowest possible interest rates; and (7) to encourage tenant empowerment and reduce generational poverty in federally assisted and public housing by improving the means by which self-sufficiency may be achieved.[49]

Over time, a complex array of programs have developed in response to the housing needs of diverse low-income groups, including families, the elderly, people with disabilities, battered women, and the homeless. In addition, a home buyer may be eligible for a federally guaranteed mortgage, where the government will pay the lender should the home owner default, and the federal government subsidizes home purchases for middle- and upper-income individuals and families by providing tax breaks that allow home owners to deduct from their income tax returns mortgage interest and property taxes. In some states, local government provides tax incentives to support "gentrification," which refers to the process of renovating run-down housing stock in decaying inner-city neighborhoods. Gentrification results in increasing the supply of high cost housing while decreasing the availability of housing for low-income individuals and families.[50] The programs that are of interest to us are those that serve people with low incomes. Except for programs directed toward the homeless, most give preference to families over individuals, and all share the objective of increasing access to safe housing.

From the standpoint of the recipients, housing assistance is probably second only to cash assistance in importance. The tangible benefit provided by a program that puts a "roof over one's head" cannot be underestimated. But housing programs, unlike cash assistance programs, reach only a small number of people in need because of low funding levels and the fact that housing programs are not entitlement programs. The HUD estimates that there are close to 15 million very low-income families in the United States, defined as families with an income less than 50 percent of the median income in the area where the family resides.[51] Although all of these families qualify for housing aid, fewer than 5 million receive any assistance. Consider that of all families on AFDC/TANF, only 20 percent receive a housing benefit: 8 percent live in public housing, and 12 percent receive rent subsidies.[52]

Housing programs are subject to yearly appropriations; and fluctuations in funding result in long waiting lists for access to housing assistance. Moreover, HUD appropriations have been declining. In constant dollars, funds decreased from a 1978 high of $77.6 billion to a 1989 low of $11.6 billion. The budget for HUD in fiscal year 1999, set at $24.5 billion, was the "best budget in a decade."[53] Each year new commitments are made to assist with rent payments. Between 1977 and 1997 approximately 2.9 million new commitments were made, but the number of new commitments has been steadily declining.[54]

Rent subsidies, which are discussed later, are based on income as is the amount of rent charged in publicly owned buildings. At the time of this writing, the effect of TANF's work requirement on public housing is unknown. The Quality Housing and Work Responsibility Act of 1998 (QHWRA) provides a safeguard for residents of public housing by disregarding earned income to determine rent for twelve months after new employment is found. Rent increases will be phased in after that time.[55] Recipients of TANF who receive housing assistance and live in privately owned homes may be subject to rent increases as their income increases. The loss of cash benefits for some TANF recipients may increase pressure on PHAs for access to public housing and on HUD for additional housing subsidies,[56] especially for families with housing subsidies who are more likely than others to be long-term welfare recipients. As a group, they may be less likely to find and retain employment and most likely to create a need for higher subsidies if cash benefits are lost at the end of sixty months. In 1994, the median cumulative period of welfare recipiency for those who also received HUD assistance was fifty-seven months compared to thirty-seven months for those not receiving HUD assistance.[57]

Table 11.4 lists in alphabetical order a series of federal initiatives through which programs to help shelter low-income individuals and families are funded. The statutory authority of each is shown. Discussion of some of the major programs follows. Note in the discussion the degree of overlap across programs in populations served. This is a common occurrence when social policy evolves in a piecemeal manner in response to emerging social problems. For example, people with AIDS are disabled under the law and may receive services from several programs that serve people with disabilities as well as services from the Housing Opportunities for People with AIDS Act that was enacted by Congress to address the housing needs of this population.

Housing Programs

State and local housing authorities are eligible for Housing Act grants based on their submission to HUD of a five-year plan that details, among other things (1) the housing needs of people with low and moderate incomes, as well as the needs of the elderly, people with disabilities, and the homeless; (2) the available housing stock, including its condition; (3) the strategies the community will use to meet identified housing needs; and (3) how funds provided under the act will be coordinated with funds provided under Community Development Block Grant, the Stewart B. McKinney Homeless Assistance Act, and the Housing Opportunities for People with AIDS Act (all of which are discussed later in this section).[58]

The federal government's role in providing housing assistance has shifted over time from the construction of new housing to a role that favors rehabilitating existing housing stock. To support new construction, the federal government through the Low Income Housing Tax Credit provides tax incentives to private developers who agree to construct housing and reserve a percent of newly constructed units for low-income individuals and families.[59]

TABLE 11.4. Federal Housing Programs

Program	Purpose	Statutory authority
Battered Women's Shelter Program	To provide immediate shelter and related assistance to victims of domestic violence and their dependents	42 U.S.C. §10401
Community Development Block Grant	To develop viable urban communities by providing decent housing and a suitable living environment and to expand job economic opportunities	42 U.S.C. §5301
Housing Assistance for Native Americans	Grants to Native tribes to acquire land, construct and rehabilitate housing, subsidize rents and create utilities	25 U.S.C. §4101
Low Income Housing Preservation	Part of the National Affordable Housing Act. Seeks to preserve affordable housing for low-income families	42 U.S.C. §12702
Housing Opportunities for People with AIDS	Part of the National Affordable Housing Act. Grants to state and local government to meet the housing needs of people with AIDS	42 U.S.C. §12901
Low Income Housing Tax Credit	A tax credit to private-sector housing developers to encourage their investment in low-income housing	26 U.S.C. §42
Stewart B. McKinney Act	Grants to state and local government, Indian tribes, and private, not-for-profit groups to provide shelter for homeless peoople; includes the Emergency Shelter Grant Program	42 U.S.C. §11381

(continued)

TABLE 11.4. Federal Housing Programs (*Continued*)

Program	Purpose	Statutory authority
National Affordable Housing Act	A series of discrete programs including the HOME and HOPE Programs and Housing for the Frail Elderly. The purpose of the act is to increase the supply of safe and affordable housing, provide shelter, and facilitate home ownership	42 U.S.C. §12702
Quality Housing and Work Responsibility Act of 1998	Part of the U.S. Housing Act. Funds are available to assess the cost effectiveness or rehabilitating or demolishing public housing; amends portions of the Section 8 housing program and provides for private ownership of public housing authority units	42 U.S.C. §1434
Runaway and Homeless Youth Act	Grants to public and private groups to provide shelter and other assistance to runaway and homeless youth outside of the law enforcement system, child welfare system, mental health system, and juvenile justice system	42 U.S.C. §5701
Section 8 Project Based Housing and Rent Subsidies	Subsidizes the rent of low-income households	42 U.S.C. §1437f
Shelter Care Plus	Provides rent assistance to house the mentally ill and chronic substance abusers	42 U.S.C. §11403
Single Room Occupancy Rehabilitation Program	Part of the Housing Assistance for People with AIDS Act to rehabilitate housing to provide single room occupancy units	42 U.S.C. §12906
Supportive Housing Program	Provides capital for housing projects and project rental assistance for the elderly and people with disabilities, including funds for supportive services	12 U.S.C. §1701q 42 U.S.C. §8011
U.S. Housing Act	Authorized federal grants to state and local government PHAs to build and operate public housing	42 U.S.C. §1437

THE HOME INVESTMENT PARTNERSHIP PROGRAM

The Home Investment Partnership Program (HOME) provides block grants to local communities who decide how best to meet local needs for affordable rental housing. The program is targeted to low-income individuals and families, meaning those whose income is at or below 60 percent of the median income in the geographic area receiving the grant, with a focus on those in distressed urban areas.[60] Those who receive HOME grants are encouraged to test different approaches to meeting program goals. For example, a model program may provide funds to developers to construct, acquire, or rehabilitate rental housing properties; fund the rehabilitation of privately owned rental housing; support a "sweat-equity" program where low-income families themselves purchase and rehabilitate housing; or fund a program to create a home repair service to aid older and disabled homeowners make needed home repairs.[61] The HOME funds cannot be used for emergency shelters, but they may be combined with funds that are available through the Stewart B. McKinney Homeless Assistance Act to pay for the acquisition of rehabilitation of housing for the homeless.[62]

In the summer of 1996, the Urban Institute interviewed program officials in thirty-eight states and learned that most HOME funds have been used to construct or rehabilitate rental housing. Those interviewed expressed the concern that the 1996 welfare reform act would increase pressure to use HOME funds to subsidize rental assistance in order to ease the transition from welfare to work.[63]

FEDERALLY SUPPORTED HOME OWNERSHIP FOR LOW-INCOME FAMILIES

The transfer of publicly owned housing to private ownership is permissible under the Housing Act of 1937. And HUD has reported some success in transferring to private ownership publicly owned single family homes under the Housing Opportunities for People Everywhere Program of the Cranston-Gonzales National Affordable Housing Act of 1990, popularly called the HOPE III program.[64] In 1995, HUD reported that 1,234 HOPE III homes with an average value of $56,000 had been sold to families, one-third of whom were public housing residents. The median income of HOPE III home buyers was $19,374.[65]

The latest federal initiative to transfer public housing units to private ownership became effective on October 1, 1999, under provisions in the QHWRA of 1998.[66] The QHWRA provides for the sale of housing units owned by a PHA to low-income families for use as their principal residence.[67] When a PHA decides to sell housing units, it may establish requirements for purchasers, including proof of income, record of employment, or participation in an employment or training program, and rules may be set that concern the effect on ownership of involvement in criminal activity. The occupant or occupants of a housing unit has a right of first refusal. Those who decide not to purchase their unit must receive ninety days notice that they will be relocated, and they must be offered comparable housing in a location that is comparable to the area where the displaced tenant lived. Rental assistance in the form of Section 8 tenant-based assistance or project-based assistance may be offered (see later discussion). The actual or reasonable costs of relocation must be paid for and ownership of the occupied unit cannot be transferred until the tenant is relocated.

HOUSING FOR THE FRAIL ELDERLY AND FOR PEOPLE WITH DISABILITIES

Between 20 and 30 percent of the elderly who live in publicly supported housing are "frail," requiring special services that housing authorities are not equipped to provide. The Congregate Housing Service Program seeks to provide for the housing needs of the frail elderly and of people with disabilities. Program funds may be used to modify buildings and units within buildings to meet the needs of eligible applicants or to create congregate space to accommodate services that enhance independent living. In addition, funds may be used to provide support services to assist the frail elderly and others with disabilities to live independently.[68] Also fundable are health, mental health, and other services needed by people with disabilities, tenant-based rental assistance, and assistance to private, nonprofit organizations to expand the supply of supportive housing for persons with disabilities.[69]

Project-Based Housing and Rent Subsidies

In the late 1970s and early 1980s, between 50 and 70 percent of federal housing funds went to construction. Since that time, the production of new housing has been cut back in favor of the less costly subsidy programs.

The blighted condition of many public housing projects has led to their demolition. By early 1996, more than 23,000 units in high-rise projects had been demolished, and some demolished projects were replaced with townhouses.[70] To further HUD's goal of replacing decaying inner-city public housing, provisions in the QHWRA provide that PHAs that operate housing projects with more than 300 units and a 10 percent vacancy rate must determine if the cost of housing rehabilitation exceeds the costs of demolition plus the costs of providing Section 8 vouchers to relocate tenants; if so, the project is to be demolished within five years and its tenants provided with Section 8 vouchers.[71] The HOPE VI program funds demolition. Originally, HOPE VI required replacement of demolished units on a one-to-one basis, but this is no longer so. And HUD expects to replace approximately 40 percent of demolished units with the expectation that the private sector will be encouraged through the provision of tax incentives to replace the remaining 60 percent.[72] In July 1999 there were approximately 1.3 million public housing units supported by the national government at an annual cost of $6 billion.[73]

Public Housing Authorities establish written policies for tenant admission. These include criteria and procedures to select tenants, grant "special admissions," and create waiting lists and remove people from a waiting list. For example, one's name may be removed from a waiting list for failing to provide updated information on family composition or income. Waiting lists may be closed when a PHA determines that there is a sufficient pool of applicants in relation to available funding. If a waiting list is reopened, public notice is required, including time and place for applying and criteria defining what families may apply.

Selection criteria may give preference to those with a history of timely payment of rent and may take into account the need to safeguard the health, safety, and welfare of other tenants by excluding applicants whose conduct suggests a threat to others. If an applicant has a record of conduct that might threaten the health or safety of others, PHAs are to consider whether there is any evidence of the applicant's participation in or willingness to participate in rehabilitation programs.

Criteria for being placed on a waiting list must conform to the Fair Housing Act's requirements for nondiscriminatory access to housing (see chapter 13), but there is no legally enforceable right to be placed on a waiting list. Preference may be given to the elderly, people with disabilities, or families with children, and criteria may be reasonably related to creating a tenant body with mixed incomes, as long as these criteria do not result in prohibited discrimination.

Families may be "special admissions" if, for example, they were displaced from a demolished public housing facility or were residents in a facility whose units are being sold under a contract to privatize public housing.[74] As discussed in chapter 1, a court order may give a family not on a waiting list preference over one on a waiting list. These special considerations aside, program participants must be selected from a waiting list.[75]

Tenants of public housing projects may be subject to eviction for engaging in criminal activity that threatens other tenants. President Clinton's "One Strike and You're Out" of public housing policy was signed into law in March 1996. Under the terms of this policy, leases for new public-housing tenants must specify that any criminal violation that involves the use of guns or drugs is a basis for eviction, and tenants are subject to eviction for the drug-related activity of their guests or of a person residing in the apartment under the tenant's control. A person evicted for drug-related activity is not eligible for public housing for three years.[76] Courts have been divided on the question of whether the tenant's knowledge of illegal drug activity is a precondition for eviction. For example, a New York court ruled that a tenant could not be evicted because her baby-sitter had used drugs because the tenant was not aware of the use, but courts in California and Louisiana ruled that knowledge was not a precondition for eviction and allowed the eviction of a tenant when narcotics were found in her son's bedroom.[77]

RENTAL SUBSIDIES

The HUD operates two Section 8 housing assistance programs. In one, assistance is tenant-based, meaning that rent subsidies allow participants to find housing in the private housing market. The second program provides project-based assistance, meaning that the family lives in housing developed by the government or with government support.[78] Because HUD guarantees repayment of the mortgages on many housing developments built by the private sector, the project-based rental assistance program provides a means for tenants to pay their rent, ensuring that project developers have a stream of funds to meet mortgage payments.[79]

Preference for the Section 8 program is given to families (1) who are involuntarily displaced, for example, due to the sale or demolition of public housing projects; (2) who pay more than 50 percent of their income for rent; and (3) who reside in substandard housing.[80] Rent is based on an applicant's income and is subject to yearly predeterminations.[81] Provisions in QHWRA give preference to low-income families. Tenant-based vouchers will go to families whose income is less than 30 percent of the area median, and 40 percent of newly available units in a project-based Section 8 facility will be reserved for families with similar incomes. In 1997, these programs provided over $16 billion in rental assistance payments to approximately 1.4 million low-income households.[82]

Section 8 programs reduce the amount of money that recipients pay out-of-pocket for rent to 30 percent of their adjusted income. Gross income may be adjusted by excluding (1) $400 for each elderly and disabled person; (2) unreimbursed medical expenses that exceed 3 percent of any family's annual income; (3) child care expenses that are necessary to enable a family member to work or further her or his education; and (4) child support payments that do not exceed $480 for each child.[83] The difference between the actual rent as charged by the property owner and the 30 percent paid by the tenant is paid for by the Section 8 program.

The tenant-based program participant receives either a rent voucher or a rent certificate. In the certificate program, property owners agree to accept HUD's fair market payment and cannot charge more for the housing unit. In the voucher program, if the rent exceeds the fair market value of the rental unit, the household pays the excess cost. The voucher program is more useful to families in cities where rentals are difficult to find and where property owners may be unwilling to enter into agreements to accept HUD's fair market value.[84] The certificate program operates a Family Unification Program under which rental assistance is available to a limited number of families—16,000 in 1999—to prevent children from being separated from their families because the family's housing does not meet health or safety codes. Certification by a public welfare agency that children are at risk of being placed in foster care is a condition for eligibility for this program.

Housing Assistance for the Homeless

Twenty-three federal programs operated by four agencies provide housing assistance to the estimated 2.3 million adults and children who are homeless at some point in time each year. An additional twenty-six programs provide other forms of assistance such as food and nutrition services and health care.[85]

Of the various policies that benefit the homeless, the Stewart B. McKinney Act of 1987 (McKinney act) is the largest. It was the first comprehensive federal law to provide shelter and support services for people without homes.[86] In passing the McKinney act, Congress intended to bring together a variety of programs for the homeless under a single umbrella. For purposes of eligibility, the McKinney act defines as homeless people without a "fixed, and adequate nighttime residence, a nighttime residence that provides temporary living accommodation, or a person who resides in a place that was not designed as a sleeping accommodation for humans."[87] Note that the McKinney act requires each state to guarantee equal access to public education for children of homeless families and for homeless children[88] (chapter 16).

THE EMERGENCY SHELTER GRANT PROGRAM

The Emergency Shelter Grant Program (ESG)[89] of the McKinney act makes grants to state and local government to prevent homelessness by renovating, rehabilitating, or converting buildings for use as emergency shelters or transitional housing and by providing necessary social services.

The grant applicant must submit a five-year plan to HUD that describes the needs of the homeless and how the described needs will be met in a coordinated and integrated manner.

The ESG funds cannot be used to construct new buildings nor may funds be used to develop or lease permanent housing. Grantees must ensure that any building using ESG funds will continue to be used as a homeless shelter and that the rehabilitated structure will be safe and sanitary. The five-year plan must describe how the confidentiality of victims of domestic violence will be maintained, and it must conform to civil rights policies concerning equal access and nondiscriminatory access to shelter. Grantees are also required to supplement the grant with funds from other sources.

THE SINGLE-ROOM OCCUPANCY (SRO) REHABILITATION PROGRAM

Funds are available to rehabilitate single-room occupancy (SRO) dwellings and to subsidize the rent for homeless people. The SRO buildings are designed mainly for individual occupancy. Many do not contain food preparation or sanitary facilities. Because SROs are small and because they lack cooking and sanitary facilities, they provide a low rent option for housing the homeless, but they yield a low rate of return on the investment of the property owner. Subsidies from HUD are available if the agency determines that the property owner is unlikely to convert the property without a subsidy. The tenants' subsidy is the difference between the rent, which cannot exceed fair market rent, and 30 percent of the beneficiary's adjusted income.

SHELTER PLUS CARE PROGRAM

The Shelter Plus Care Program (SPC)[90] aids homeless people who are mentally ill, have chronic substance abuse problems, or other disabilities. The SPC program makes available (1) tenant-based rental assistance, (2) sponsor-based rental assistance, (3) project-based rental assistance, or (4) SRO assistance. The program requires that participants receive other support services but does not fund support services that are provided through other programs.

SUPPORTIVE HOUSING PROGRAM

The Supportive Housing Program assists the homeless, the elderly, and people with disabilities. Grants are made to not-for-profit organizations that provide supportive housing and associated services (Table 11.5) or supportive services without housing. The program for people with disabilities provides assistance to help people make the transition to independent living. Funds may be used to provide (1) for homeless people, transitional housing for a period of time not to exceed twenty-four months, with six months of follow-up services to support an adjustment to living independently; (2) for people with disabilities, permanent housing; (3) supportive services for homeless persons not provided in conjunction with supportive housing; (4) innovative programs to meet the long-term needs of homeless persons; and (5) safe havens for homeless individuals with serious mental illness who reside on the streets and who may not be willing or able to avail themselves of supportive services. Program funds may not be used to develop or operate emergency shelters, although the funds may be used to provide supportive services at shelters.

Those who are eligible for service include homeless individuals and families with children and homeless people with disabilities. The Supportive Housing Program will also assist a homeless person whose sole impairment is alcoholism or drug addiction.

Homeless Youth

Operating outside of the juvenile justice and child protective service system, the Department of Health and Human Services (DHHS) provides grants to public and private agencies to operate shelter programs to assist homeless youth.

Three grant programs exist. The Runaway and Homeless Youth Basic Center Program funds emergency shelter, food and clothing as well as outreach and aftercare services. The Runaway and Homeless Youth Education and Prevention Program makes grants for the purpose of preventing sexual exploitation of runaway youth. These grants fund "street-based" outreach and include funds for emergency shelter, counseling, educational activities and follow-up. Long-term residential services are available through the Runaway and Homeless Youth Transitional Living Program. Young people aged sixteen to twenty-one are eligible for up to eighteen months of service to help them make the transition to independent living. In addition to shelter, the transitional living program provides physical and mental health service, career counseling, and education in basic life skills such as budgeting and seeking employment.

Housing Opportunities for People with AIDS

The Housing Opportunities for Persons with AIDS (HOPWA) is Title VII of the National Affordable Housing Act. This program provides grants to state and local units of government to devise strategies to meet the housing needs of people with AIDS and their families. The HOPWA grants may be used to (1) provide information about housing; (2) coordinate efforts to expand housing; (3) purchase, lease, renovate, repair, or convert housing; (4) provide short-term shelter; (5) provide short-term financial aid to pay rent for homeless people or to prevent homelessness; (6) make utility payments; and (7) provide support services including health, mental health and substance abuse treatment and counseling, day care, and nutritional services. Funds may also be used to develop SRO dwellings and to provide low cost community-based residential alternatives to institutional care.[91]

Most HOPWA funding is used for rental assistance programs and to fund housing rehabilitation, repair, and conversion. Funds may also be used to provide rental assistance to prevent homelessness.[92]

Housing Assistance for Native Americans

Housing assistance for low-income Native Americans is available through the Native American Housing Assistance and Self-Determination Act of 1996 (NAHASDA).[93] Native tribes, following submission and approval of a housing plan to the Secretary of HUD, are eligible to receive block grant funds for use in finding affordable housing in "safe and healthy environments on Indian reservations, in Indian communities, and in Native Alaskan villages."[94]

Fundable activities include acquiring land, constructing housing, rehabilitating housing, and demolition of housing that cannot be rehabilitated. Funds may be used for the costs associated with new housing and upgrading existing housing such as developing utilities. Funds may also be used to subsidize rents and to manage housing projects.

Community Development

Community development refers to efforts made by both the public and private sectors to "stimulate financial, social, and human capital investment in low-income neighborhoods."[95] Community development activities are funded by both the private and the public sectors.

The federal government supports efforts to revitalize inner cities through the Community Development Block Grant Program (CDBG).[96] The CDBG funds may be used to provide housing and to expand economic opportunities for poor people in the nation's cities. The acquisition or rehabilitation of shelters and the costs of operating shelters and of providing services such as counseling, training, and treatment are legitimate uses of CDBG funds, which may also be used to construct temporary shelters and transitional housing, such as halfway homes for people with chronic mental health problems.

Community Development Corporations (CDCs) are another force in reshaping inner-city areas. The CDCs are community based and resident run self-help groups. Working with members of the business community, CDCs strive to solve community problems by creating housing; providing job training, child care, health services; and through advocacy for community needs, and they exist in most American cities. They are funded through a combination of public and private resources.

To increase the ability of CDCs to improve conditions in their communities, the National Community Development Initiative (NCDI) was started in 1991. Funding was provided by foundations and was later supplemented by corporate funds and by funds provided by HUD. In addition to funding the start-up of CDCs, the NCDI provided funds to enable small CDCs to grow and existing CDCs to expand. Creating new housing by purchasing and rehabilitating dilapidated buildings is a major CDC/NCDI effort. Between July 1991 and June 1997, more than 90,000 units of housing were developed for low-income residents in addition to commercial, office, and industrial space.[97]

Shelters for Battered Women

The DHHS makes grants to nonprofit groups to establish projects in local communities to "coordinate intervention and prevention of domestic violence."[98] Funds may be used to provide shelter and related assistance such as outreach, legal services, health services, and counseling to victims of domestic violence and their dependents. Funds are limited, however, with no more than $400,000 authorized for fiscal year 2000.

Social Services and Housing

Many of the reviewed housing programs, especially those serving the elderly, people with disabilities, and the homeless, allow funds to be used to provide support services. The GAO reports that approximately one-third of homeless people have problems with alcohol or drugs and 25 percent have a lifetime history of mental illness.[99] Despite these problems, Shinn and Weitzman (1998), based on interviews with 266 homeless families, concluded that the availability of housing subsidies, not mental or physical problems, predicted housing stability for families.[100]

Table 11.5 shows services that may be made available by program. Education is the most common service. Although listed as a separate category, education may encompass outreach to educate eligible populations concerning the availability of a program and criteria for program eligibility, and education may also include job training. In the Runaway Youth Program and Supportive Housing Program, education is directed toward the development of skills for living independently. Case management services that seek to coordinate the services received by program participants, to make referrals for needed services, and to help participants gain access to needed services are available in some of the listed programs as are primary health and mental health services.

Summary

In this chapter, we reviewed a number of programs that assist low-income individuals and families to acquire food and housing. Neither food nor housing programs reach all of the people in need of the services they provide.

The FSP serves low-income individuals and families who receive coupons that can be exchanged for food products. Households whose members are receiving cash assistance through TANF, SSI, or a state's GA program are eligible for food stamps. Others must establish income eligibility.

Food stamp benefit levels are based on the "Thrifty Food Plan" developed by the DOA. The DOA assumes a household will spend 30 percent of available cash on food and that the provided stamps will make up the difference between the 30 percent and the cost of an "adequate low-cost diet." The benefit level is the same

TABLE 11.5. Housing Programs and Support Services

Program	Outreach	Case management*	Child care	Clothing	Education	Food	Job training	Primary health	Mental health	Substance abuse treatment	Life skills training	Transportation
CDBG†		X			X	X						X
HOPWA‡	X	X	X		X	X	X	X	X	X		X
Runaway Youth§	X			X	X	X		X	X			
McKinney Act	X	X	X		X	X	X	X	X		X	
Shelter for Victims of Domestic Violence	X	X	X		X			X	X	X	X	X
Supportive Housing	X	X	X		X	X	X	X	X	X	X	X

Source: Compiled by the author using data reported in U.S. General Accounting Office, *Homelessness: Coordination and Evaluation of Programs Are Essential* (Washington, D.C., 1999).
*Case management involves assessment of need and linking clients to services that can meet identified needs.
†Community Services Block Grant
‡Housing Opportunities for People with AIDS
§Other services include outreach, education to prevent sexual exploitation and aftercare

in the forty-eight contiguous states and the District of Columbia, where a one-person household receives food stamps valued at no more than $122 each month. Benefit levels are higher in Alaska, Hawaii, Guam, and the Virgin Islands. For example, the individual beneficiary living in Alaska would receive an allotment of stamps valued at $154.

To fulfill the objective of assisting recipients to have a nutritionally balanced diet, the use of food stamps is limited mainly to acquiring food for home preparation and consumption. Exceptions are made to accommodate recipients in rural areas who grow their own food or who hunt for their food. In these limited cases, food stamps may be used to acquire seeds and plants or hunting and fishing equipment. Food stamps may also be used to pay for meals prepared and served through communal dining programs that serve the elderly and people with disabilities, and they may be used to pay for home-delivered meals for either population.

In addition to the FSP, food assistance is available through (1) TEFAP, which distributes surplus food to groups that feed the hungry such as soup kitchens and food banks; (2) SLSB, which provides meals free of charge or at low cost to children in primary and secondary school; and (3) CACFP, which provides meals for children attending public or private nonresidential child care centers, including Head Start centers.

The WIC program serves pregnant and postpartum women, their infants, and their children up to five years of age. Eligible families are low income and at a medically determinable nutritional risk. Families that are eligible for TANF, food stamps, or Medicaid are eligible for WIC and a low-income pregnant woman may receive immediate assistance while awaiting the results of the required nutritional risk evaluation. The WIC program provides a range of services, including (1) screening to assess nutritional risk; (2) referrals for health, welfare, and social services; (3) vouchers or checks to purchase specific nutritional items; (4) distribution of food commodities; and (5) education concerning nutrition.

Nutrition services for the elderly are provided mainly under the authority of Title III of the OAA of 1965. The act authorizes the Elderly Nutrition Program that provides congregate meals served at community centers, churches, and schools and the meals-on-wheels program that serves people in their own homes. There is no means test for Title III services. Programs are allowed to charge a fee on a sliding scale, but a cost-sharing requirement cannot be imposed on an elderly person as a condition for participation in a nutrition program.

Federal priorities for housing people in need favor the rehabilitation of run-down housing over the construction of new housing. To the extent that there is support for new construction, it is in the form of tax credits to private developers who agree to construct housing and reserve a percent of newly constructed units for low-income individuals and families.

Housing assistance that is available is funded through an array of programs that are targeted to low-income groups, including families, the elderly, people with disabilities, battered women, and the homeless. Each program specifies the purpose to which its grants may be put, such as the rehabilitation of existing housing under the HOME program, and many of the programs specify also the populations to be served. Programs exist to rehabilitate housing and to provide shelter for (1) the homeless under the Steward B. McKinney Act; (2) the elderly and people with disabilities under the Housing for the Frail Elderly Program; (3) people with AIDS under the Housing Opportunities for People with AIDS Program; (4) victims of domestic violence under the Battered Women's Shelter Program; (5) Native Americans under the Housing Assistance for Native Americans Program; (6) the mentally ill through the Shelter Care Plus Program of the Stewart B. McKinney Act; and (7) homeless and runaway youth through a series of programs including the Runaway and Homeless Youth Transitional Living Program.

Additional housing support is found in (1) the HOPE programs and programs funded under the QHWRA, both of which support the transfer of publicly owned housing to private ownership, with an emphasis on the sale of housing units to low-income families for use as their principal residence; (3) the HOPE VI program that funds the demolition of decaying public housing and the replacement of some of the demolished housing units with new housing; and (3) the Section 8 housing assistance program that subsidizes the rent of low-income individuals and families by providing a rent subsidy that allows participants to find housing in the private market or that subsidized the rent of people who live in housing that was developed by the government or with government support.

Many of the reviewed housing programs, especially those serving the elderly, people with disabilities, and the homeless, allow funds to be used to provide support services, including outreach, education, job training, case management, primary health, and mental health service.

CHAPTER

Health Policy

This chapter is about the health care system in the United States. Health care is paid for through a mix of private and public funds that totaled $988.6 billion in 1995. Funds are spent on direct services ($878.8 billion), including physician services, hospital services, dental services, and other health care services, and on indirect costs that include program administration, operation of the United States Public Health Service, funding medical research, and hospital construction ($109.8 billion) (Table 12.1).

In 1995, 56 percent of American health care was paid for with private funds, such as out-of-pocket expenses for health insurance and direct payments for medical care (Table 12.1). Public funds, which support an array of programs including Medicare, Medicaid, the State Children's Health Insurance Program, and programs operated by the Indian Health Service and by the Veteran's Administration, accounted for 44 percent of spending.

Spending $3,462 per capita on health care, the United States spends more than any other country, exceeding by more than $1,000 the per capita health care costs of Switzerland and Germany, the countries that rank second and third in per capita health care spending (Table 12.2). Health care represents 14.1 percent of the United States gross domestic product, compared to 10.3 percent and 9.5 percent in Germany and Switzerland, respectively. In the United States, the public sector pays for less than 45 percent of the nation's health care bill, compared to more than 70 percent in Germany and Switzerland and close to or in excess of 80 percent in some European countries.

Before 1965 when the Medicare and Medicaid programs were enacted, government involvement in the health care arena was limited to caring for veterans and to supporting programs of limited scope such as the Title V Maternal and Child Health Care provisions of the Social Security Act (see later discussion) and to sup-

TABLE 12.1. Sources of Funding for Personal Health Care and National Health Expenditures by Spending Category: 1995

Source	Amount (in billions)
Private health insurance	$276.8
Out-of-pocket	182.6
Other private funds	27.3
Total private funds	$486.7 (56%)
Federal	303.6
State and local	88.5
Total public funds	392.1 (44%)
Total personal health expenditures	$878.8

Spending-Direct Service	Amount (in billions)
Hospital care	350.1 (40%)
Physician services	201.6 (23%)
Dental services	45.8 (5%)
Other professional services	52.6 (6%)
Home health care	28.6 (3%)
Drugs and other medical nondurables	83.4 (9%)
Vision products and other medical durables	13.8 (2%)
Nursing home care	77.9 (9%)
Other personal health care	25.0 (3%)
Subtotal	$878.8

Spending-Indirect Service	
Program administration and net cost of private health insurance	47.7
Government public health activities	31.4
Research and construction of medical facilities	30.7
Total national health expenditures	$988.6

Source: House, Committee on Ways and Means, "Appendix C: National and International Health Care Expenditures and Health Insurance Coverage," *Green Book* (Washington, D.C., 1998), Tables C1 and C4.

porting employer-provided health insurance through the United States Tax Code, which allows employers to deduct from their income tax the cost of health insurance they provide. In 1999, tax deductions cost the government approximately $76 billion, making the Tax Code the third most expensive government health care program after Medicare and Medicaid.[1] Since passage of Medicare and Medicaid, programs affecting health have grown in a piecemeal manner in relation to defined

TABLE 12.2. Per Capita Health Care Expenditures in Dollars, as a Percent of the Gross Domestic Product and Percent Paid by Public Funds: United States Compared to Twenty-three Countries: 1995

Country	Per capita costs ($)	Percent of gross domestic product (%)	Percent paid by public funds (%)
Australia	1,609	8.4	68.5
Austria	1,573	7.8	76
Belgium	1,653	8.1	87.9
Canada	2,005	9.9	71.8
Denmark	1,344	6.6	83.4
Finland	1,289	7.9	74.8
France	1,868	9.7	78.4
Germany	2,020	10.3	78.4
Greece	634	5.5	76.2
Iceland	1,571	8.1	84
Ireland	1,201	7.6	80.7
Italy	1,559	8.4	70.6
Japan	1,454	6.9	76.8
Luxembourg	1,962	6.5	91.8
Netherlands	1,643	8.8	77.7
Norway	1,754	8.0	83
New Zealand	1,151	7.1	76.8
Portugal	939	7.8	63.4
Spain	992	7.3	78.6
Sweden	1,339	7.6	83
Switzerland	2,280	9.5	71.9
Turkey	272	5.2	50
United Kingdom	1,213	6.9	84.1
United States	3,462	14.1	44.8

Source: House, Committee on Ways and Means, "Appendix C: National and International Health Care Expenditures and Health Insurance Coverage," *Green Book* (Washington, D.C., 1988), Table C31.

issues, ensuring, for example, that children are vaccinated and that people with specific illnesses such as Acquired Immune Deficiency Syndrome (AIDS) have their medical needs met.

Despite the existence of publicly funded health care, most Americans derive their health insurance from their employment. Approximately 60 percent of the population that has medical coverage at any point in time is covered by employment-based insurance, with an additional 13 percent covered through the Medicare program, for which eligibility is linked to employment history.[2] However, the role of business in proving health insurance has been diminishing, increasing the numbers of uninsured and creating a demand for government to fill the gap created by loss of employment-based insurance.[3]

This chapter is divided into three sections. In section 1, the two largest publicly funded health care programs, Medicare and Medicaid, are reviewed, as are several programs that exist to provide health care to children. Section 2 contains an overview of a series of specific and limited health policies, for example, policies guaranteeing emergency room care regardless of ability to pay and policies that require nondiscriminatory access to health care. Health care reform is the subject of section 3. You should know that a complete understanding of the American commitment to health care would take into account activities of the Veteran's Administration, the United States Public Health Service, and the role of the federal government in financing medical education, medical research, and hospital construction. However, these topics are beyond the scope of this text. Because the topic of health care policy is rife with its own language, a glossary is presented.

HEALTH CARE GLOSSARY

Capitation	A fixed sum that is paid to a provider to cover all medical services. If costs exceed the capitated sum, the provider absorbs the extra costs. If costs are less than the capitated sum, the provider keeps the difference.
Co-payment	A part payment made by the service recipient.
Coordinated Care Plans	HMOs, PSOs, and PPOs (described below).
Deductible	A yearly amount that the recipient must pay before any insurance coverage is provided.
Fee-for-Service Programs	Each physician that is seen and other medical services provided are paid for at a rate set by the health care program.
Fee-for-Service, Private	A policy with capitated payments to the insurer who reimburses contract providers on a predetermined rate. If a participant chooses an outside provider, the plan reimburses the provider at the Medicare rate.
Gatekeeper	Role assigned to a primary care physician who controls access to specialized services.
Health Maintenance Organization (HMO)	An HMO is an insurer who hires or contracts with physicians and other medical providers to serve its members generally on a capitated basis.
Managed Care Plan (MCP)	A generic term embracing institutional arrangements that have in common an effort to integrate the dual roles of service payer and service provider. Capitated service provision and the use of primary care physicians as gatekeepers are common plan elements.

Medical Savings Account (MSA)	A participant purchases a catastrophic health insurance plan, with a deductible not to exceed $6,000, and establishes a tax-free MSA. The positive difference between the government's capitated contribution to the premium and the actual cost is deposited in an MSA.
Point of Service	An option in a coordinated or managed care plan that allows participants to use services outside of the plan with some cost-sharing responsibilities.
Preferred Provider Organization (PPO)	A medical entity formed by doctors and hospitals who contract with an insurer to serve its members. Services are provided on a fee-for-service basis.
Provider Sponsored Organization (PSO)	Similar to HMOs except that they are owned and operated by providers, not insurers. Services are provided on a capitated basis.
Risk Plan	Any capitated plan where the provider is at risk of losing money when the cost of service exceeds the capitation.

SECTION 1: MEDICARE, MEDICAID, AND CHILDREN'S HEALTH INSURANCE

Medicare

The Medicare Program of 1965, Title XVIII of the Social Security Act, is an entitlement program.[4] The Health Care Financing Administration (HCFA) housed within the Department of Health and Human Services (DHHS) is the federal agency responsible for administering the program, including overseeing the Medicare Hospital Insurance Trust Fund that covers Medicare Part A and the Supplementary Medical Insurance Trust Fund that covers Medicare Part B. Operating nationwide, Medicare provides health insurance for almost all people who are over the age of sixty-five, for some younger people who have received Supplemental Security Disability Income for two years (see chapter 10), and for most people who need a kidney transplant or renal dialysis. People aged sixty-five and older whose employment history does not make them eligible for Medicare may purchase Medicare insurance by paying the actual cost, which was $311 per month in 1997.[5] The Medicare program is comprised of Parts A, B, and C, which are discussed next.

PART A—BENEFITS

Part A is financed through a payroll tax of 1.45 percent that is paid by employers and employees on all earnings. Part A covers (1) inpatient hospital services, (2) nursing care in a skilled nursing care facility (SNCF), (3) home health services, and (4) hospice care. Patients pay an annual deductible, which was $768 in 1999 for the first sixty days of inpatient hospital care.[6]

As shown in Figure 12.1, the number of program enrollees nearly doubled between 1975, from approximately 24 million to an estimated high of 39 million in 1999. The number of beneficiaries has also increased, but at a slower rate, from just over 5 million in 1975 to an estimated high of 8.5 million in 1999. Health care costs have soared from $10.6 billion in 1975 to an estimated $144.6 billion in 1999.

INPATIENT HOSPITAL SERVICES   Medicare pays for costs usually associated with inpatient care such as room and board, diagnosis, operating and recovery room, intensive care, nursing services, medications, supplies, appliances, and equipment. Part A does not pay for physicians' fees unless the beneficiary is receiving services in a teaching hospital where the costs of services provided by a physician, psychologist, nurse-midwife, and nurse anesthetist are covered.[7]

Coverage is for a "spell" of illness. A spell begins on the first day of hospitalization and ends on the sixtieth consecutive day. If a patient remains in the hospital for an additional thirty consecutive days, he or she is responsible for a co-payment. A new benefit period begins with the next hospital admission. Medicare beneficiaries are entitled to an additional sixty days of inpatient care in a lifetime. Inpatient psychiatric treatment is limited to 190 days in a lifetime.[8]

FIGURE 12.1. Number of enrollees and beneficiaries receiving services and average annual benefit per enrollee and fiscal outlays. Selected years, 1975 through 1999, Part A. Data for fiscal years 1997 through 1999 are estimated.

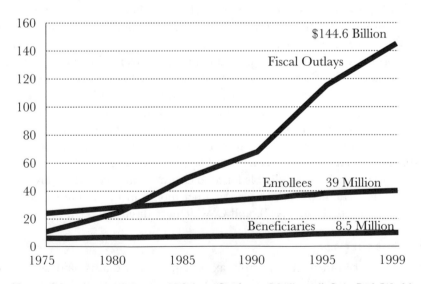

Source: House, Committee on Ways and Means, "Section 2: Medicare," *Green Book* (Washington, D.C., 1998), Tables 2.1 and 2.2.

SKILLED NURSING CARE IN A SPECIALIZED FACILITY   Medicare pays for care in a SNCF for up to 100 days after hospitalization for those who are transferred to a SNCF within thirty days of hospital discharge and contingent upon a physician certifying the need for such care. The SNCF program provides for the costs of room and board plus nursing care and may include specialized services such as (1) physical, occupational, or speech therapy; (2) pharmaceuticals; (3) medical equipment and appliances; (4) medical social services; and (5) the costs of services provided by interns and residents in training. Patients requiring skilled nursing care are subject to a coinsurance charge.

HOME HEALTH CARE   Medicare provides for home health visits for patients who require skilled nursing care, physical therapy, social work services, or speech therapy, but not on a daily basis. Eligible patients are homebound, are under a physician's care, and have a written care plan. The duration of coverage is not limited nor are the number of home health visits. Deductibles and coinsurance do not apply accept for durable medical equipment. Available services are provided on a part-time basis, meaning that they are furnished for less than eight hours in a day and twenty-eight hours in a week. Services may include those provided by a (1) nurse; (2) home health aid; (3) physical, occupational, or speech therapist; (4) medical social worker; or (5) intern or resident. Medical supplies and equipment may be provided. By 2003, a portion of the costs of home health visits will be transferred from Part A to the voluntary Part B program, discussed later, making them available to some but not all Medicare recipients.

HOSPICE CARE   Hospice services are provided mainly in the home. The emphasis is on pain reduction and supportive social and counseling services for terminally ill patients and their families. A terminally ill patient is one whose physician certifies a life expectancy of six months or less. Available services are described in a written care plan that is developed and regularly reviewed by an attending physician. Services may include (1) physician care, nursing care, and the services of a home health aide; (2) physical, occupational, or speech therapy; (3) medical social services; (4) homemaker services; (5) medical devices including the cost of drugs; (6) short-term inpatient care; (7) respite care not to exceed five consecutive days for a terminally ill patient's primary caregiver; and (8) other services that are specified in the care plan. Drugs and respite care are subject to co-payments.

PROSPECTIVE PAYMENT SYSTEM   Until 1983, Medicare reimbursed providers for the reasonable cost of services provided. In 1983, the Social Security Act was amended, and Medicare began to pay for (1) inpatient and outpatient hospital services; (2) home health services; (3) skilled nursing facility services; and (3) outpatient rehabilitation services on the basis of a prospective payment system, meaning that a predetermined rate is paid for the provided service.[9] For example, reimbursements for the care of a hospitalized patient are based on the patient's diagnosis, which must match one of 500 diagnosis-related groups (DRGs). Each group refers to a particular medical condition and related treatment. Payments for DRGs represent the national average cost per case for treating the particular diagnosis. In a prospective payment system, if the cost of service is less than the payment made to the provider, the provider keeps the difference. Conversely, if the cost of service exceeds the payment, the provider absorbs the loss. Certain types of hospitals, for example, those providing psychiatric care, physical rehabilitation, alcohol and drug abuse hospitals, children's hospitals, long-term hospitals, and hospitals that are disproportionately involved in the treatment for and research on cancer, are paid of the basis of the reasonable costs of care.[10]

PART B—SERVICES AND PROVIDER

Medicare Part B is a voluntary program that is financed by participants' monthly premiums, which were $44 per month in 1998. By 2002, under the Specified Low Income Medicare Beneficiary Program (SLIMB), the states must pay the cost of Part B premiums for beneficiaries whose income is up to 135 percent of the poverty level. The SLIMB program is operated under the Medicaid program, not Medicare. Medicaid may also provide coverage for qualified Medicare beneficiaries whose income is low and who have few assets.

Part B pays for approximately 80 percent of the approved fees and charges for out-of-hospital services after the recipient pays an annual deductible of $100. Physicians are paid on the basis of a fee schedule that takes into account the skill and time required to provide the service, practice expenses, and malpractice fees. Nonphysician providers receive a percentage of the fee paid to a physician. For example, certified nurse-midwives are paid at 65 percent of the fee schedule. If physicians do not accept the Medicare payment as payment in full, the patient must pay the difference between the Medicare fee and the physician's charges.

Part B services include (1) hospital outpatient services, including emergency room services, and the costs associated with laboratory testing, physical therapy, ambulance services, and operating room services; (2) physician services as well as the services of physician assistants, certified midwives, clinical psychologists, clinical social workers, and physical and occupational therapists; (3) durable medical equipment; and (4) preventive services such as mammograms and screening for diabetes. As a rule, outpatient prescription drugs are not paid for by Medicare but there are exceptions, including immunosuppressive drugs provided after an organ transplant and certain oral cancer drugs. Flu shots, pneumonia vaccines, and hepatitis B vaccines are covered for those at risk. Routine physical examinations, eyeglasses, and cosmetic surgery are not covered. In addition, the secretary of the DHHS may decide that any service or item provided is not "reasonable and necessary for the diagnosis or treatment of an illness or injury" and exclude an item from coverage.[11]

PART C—MEDICARE PLUS CHOICE PROVIDER PLANS

Recall the discussion in chapter 9 of the need to ensure the solvency of the Old Age, Survivors, and Disability Insurance trust fund, which is threatened by the number of people expected to retire in the first decades of this century and the reduced ratio of workers to retirees. The solvency of the Medicare trust fund is of concern for the same reasons, added to which are the escalating costs of health care (see Figure 12.1). In an effort to ensure solvency through the first decade of the twenty-first century and to increase the range of provider options from which participants may choose, Congress amended the Medicare program in 1997 when it passed the Balanced Budget Act. Congress added a new Part C, the Medicare + Choice Program, which offers a variety of capitated payment plans as a cost control measure.[12] Congress also authorized a reduction in reimbursement rates to hospitals and physicians under Parts A and B and increased the Part B premium.[13] Medicare + Choice offers two fee-for-service options; three coordinated care plans, which are (1) health management organizations (HMOs), (2) provider sponsored organizations (PSOs), and (3) preferred provider organizations (PPOs); and medical savings accounts (MSAs).

Traditional fee-for-service has always been a part of the Medicare program. The participant in the traditional program chooses a provider who is reimbursed at the program's provider rate. If the charged fee exceeds the reimbursement rate, the beneficiary pays the difference. The new private fee-for-service arrangement pays physicians on a capitated basis.

There are three types of coordinated care plans, differing in their organizational arrangements. Health management organizations have been a permissible provider option since 1982 and have been synonymous with the concept of managed care.[14] In March 1999, about 6.7 million people, or 17 percent of Medicare's 39 million Part A beneficiaries, were enrolled in 300 managed care plans (MCPs), 90 percent of which were HMOs. Most HMOs operate as capitated plans using a gatekeeper model where a physician, usually a primary care physician, controls access to specialized services. Capitated plans are referred to as "risk" plans because the provider must absorb any service costs that exceed the capitated rate. Capitated plans should encourage an increase in preventive care to reduce the higher costs associated with disease, but they may deliver less care than needed as a cost-saving measure. Health maintenance organizations may be owned by physicians, insurance companies, or a combination of the two.

The PSOs and PPOs expand the range of managed care options in the hope of bringing MCPs to the 25 percent of Medicare beneficiaries who live in areas where such plans are not available.[15]

A PPO is a medical entity owned by doctors and hospitals who contract with an insurer to provide services on a fee-for-service basis. Thus, unlike traditional HMOs, PPOs are not paid on a capitated basis and there are no gatekeepers. Beneficiaries are served by physicians in a network of providers. Full coverage is provided when services are obtained from one of the network's physicians, with partial coverage provided if services are sought from a physician outside of the network. Unlike physicians in an HMO, those in a fee-for-service PPO have no financial incentive to voluntarily minimize access to services.[16]

A PSO is similar to an HMO in that services are provided on a capitated basis. A PSO is owned by a health care provider or group of providers who themselves or through contracts with others provide most of the health care needed by beneficiaries.[17]

Medical savings accounts (MSAs) are available on a demonstration basis until

January 2003. People who select this option have an MSA, which they open in a bank of their own choosing, and a Medicare MSA Health Policy for which premiums are paid by the Medicare program. Each year, Medicare deposits a sum of money into the MSA, and the sum varies according to the services that the policy covers and the area in which the participant lives.

The MSA policies must provide for all of the coverage that a Medicare participant is entitled to receive after the enrollee pays a deductible, which may be as high as $6,000 annually. An example offered by the HCFA will be helpful to understand MSAs.

> In 1998, Jane chooses an MSA Plan and sets up an account. She chooses a policy with a $5,000 deductible. . . . Jane receives a $1,200 yearly deposit from the Medicare program into her account . . . on January 1. During 1999 Jane has a routine check-up, dental check-ups and fills her regular prescriptions (benefits not covered by the Original Medicare Plan). She pays for these services using the $1,200 in her account. At the end of the year, Jane has $900 in her Account. On January 1, 2000 another $1,200 deposit is added to her account. Now, Jane has $2,100 in her account for medical expenses.[18]

Note that Jane's medical costs suggest that she is healthy. Should a costly illness occur or should she require a special procedure, she would have to pay the difference between the $1,200 in her account and her $5,000 deductible. In addition, her policy may set a ceiling on certain procedures. For example, Jane may require a hip replacement. The cost of the procedure may be $8,000 but her policy may pay only $6,000 for this procedure. In addition to paying $3,800 ($5,000 deductible minus the $1,200 in her MSA), Jane would be responsible for the $2,000 difference between her policy's payment and the hospital's fee. The MSA plans do not permit the purchase of supplementary insurance to cover the deductible. In addition, Medicare requires that MSA participants maintain their Part B insurance, thus this monthly premium must be taken into account.

The monies in the savings account may be used for any "qualified medical expense," which includes hospitalization, doctor visits, dental exams including the cost of dentures, prescription drugs, vision care including the cost of corrective lenses, laboratory fees, preventive care such as mammograms, medical equipment, and premiums for policies covering long-term care and coverage while receiving unemployment benefits. Any funds in the account in excess of 60 percent of the deductible ($3,000 or 60 percent of Jane's $5,000 deductible) may be used for non-medical expenses, but monies so used are subject to income tax.

Medicare + Choice contains a series of consumer protections that require the provider to ensure (1) access to medically necessary services round-the-clock, seven days a week, without prior authorization; (2) access to procedures to appeal decisions denying service[19]; and (3) implementation of quality assurance programs to monitor the effectiveness of consumer protections.[20] These protections are not required for those insured under Medicaid even though the Medicare and Medicaid beneficiary may be served by the same MCP.

MEDIGAP INSURANCE

Some who participate in the Medicare program may purchase supplemental insurance from a private insurer.[21] There are ten variations on Medigap coverage which by law must be labeled options A through J to facilitate consumer comparison of the offered benefits.[22] Plan A provides a basic supplemental benefit that covers certain items such as the hospital coinsurance payments that Part A Medicare requires after the sixty-first day of hospitalization and coverage for a part of the coinsurance payments required by Part B.

The benefits of Medigap Plans increase as one moves up the alphabet from A to J. For example, all Type C plans cover coinsurance that is associated with skilled nursing care, plus deductibles that are required by Medicare Parts A and B. Medigap Plan D provides for some of the costs associated with recovery at home.

Medigap policies are expensive, costing $95 or more per month. Coverage may not be denied because of a preexisting condition if the applicant has at least six months of continuous coverage under another policy. Thus, a person who has had employment-based insurance for at least six months at the point of retirement cannot be denied a Medigap policy because of a preexisting condition, but the cost of a policy may be higher than for another who does not have a preexisting condition. Medigap policies that offer a prescription drug benefit may require an annual deductible of $250 plus a co-payment that averages 50 percent of medical costs with a ceiling on such payments.

Finally, you should know that Medicare provides funds to hospitals (1) for graduate education, which is the part of a physician's education that follows medical school; (2) that serve a high proportion of low-income patients; (3) for "outlier" cases that involve a high cost when compared to others with the same DRG, and (4) via the Medicare Incentive Payment Program, which pays a 10 percent bonus to physicians that serve Medicare patients in areas where there is a shortage of primary care physicians. However, the annual bonus, which averages $341, is not sufficient to recruit and retain physicians, and most bonuses go to specialists, not primary care physicians.[23]

Medicaid

The Medicaid Program of 1965, Title XIX of the Social Security Act, is an entitlement program for poor people who are categorically eligible due to age, disability, membership in a family with dependent children and to pregnant women who meet the program's need standard.[24] In addition to the categorically eligible, forty states extend Medicaid coverage to the "medically needy" who are categorically eligible but whose income is too high to qualify for coverage. States may set higher income or resource standards, allowing people to qualify for the medically needy program, or a person may qualify because their medical expenses deplete their income and assets. In 1996, Medicaid provided health care coverage to approximately 12 percent of the population, excluding those in institutions, and close to 45 percent of people with incomes below the poverty level.[25] Medicaid is the major source for health coverage for individuals who are dependent on publicly supported health care.

The number of people eligible for Medicaid benefits remained relatively constant from 1975 through the mid-1980s. There were approximately 22 million program participants in 1975; 21.6 million in 1980, and 21.8 million in 1985 (Figure 12.2). In 1985, an upward trend began, and the number of participants reached 25 million in 1990 and 36 million in 1995.[26] The latter increase corresponds to the increase in the size of the Aid to Families with Dependent Children (AFDC) caseload that was discussed in chapter 10 and the fact that Medicaid eligibility was automatic for AFDC recipients. As was the case with the Medicare program, costs have soared from a 1975 low of $12.6 billion to a 1998 high of $184.7 billion.

Medicaid is operated in a joint state-federal partnership. Each state designs and administers its own program within a regulatory framework that is set by the federal government. Federal funds are provided to the states to defray program costs, including the costs of program administration. The federal share is based on a state's per capita income and varies from approximately 50 percent to 80 percent of program costs.

ELIGIBILITY

Eligibility for Medicaid is contingent on membership in a category (see previous discussion) and on low income and lack of assets. Medicaid eligibility is complex,

FIGURE 12.2. Number of Medicaid recipients: selected years, 1975 through 1995, and program outlays: selected years, 1975 through 1998. 1995 is the last year for which data describing the number of recipients is available.

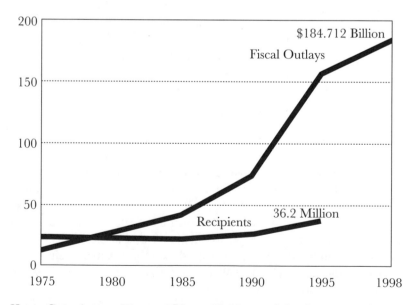

Source: House, Committee on Ways and Means, "Section 15: Other Programs," *Green Book* (Washington, D.C., 1998), Tables 15.13 and 15.14.

and states are said to rely on its complexity to discourage applications.[27] In general, a person whose resources exceed $2,000 or a couple whose resources exceed $3,000 is not eligible. Before the welfare reform amendments of 1996 (chapter 10), Medicaid eligibility was automatic for recipients of cash assistance through the AFDC program, but this is no longer true. The 1996 amendments gave states the option of establishing different income and asset tests for Medicaid than for cash assistance programs. However, states must continue Medicaid coverage for those who were or would have been eligible for AFDC as of July 1, 1996, as if the AFDC program were still in effect.[28] Others must apply separately for medical coverage. To encourage states to enroll low-income families who lose their eligibility for cash assistance in the Medicaid program, Congress created a $500 million fund with federal matching funds increased to as much as 90 percent of costs.[29]

Recall the discussion in chapter 10 concerning the eligibility of noncitizens for financial assistance under the Temporary Assistance for Needy Families Program (TANF). The conditions for receipt of Medicaid are essentially the same. Newly arrived immigrants are not eligible for coverage for five years (the time period for TANF is seven years), but coverage is continued for those who were in the United States on August 22, 1996, as it is for honorably discharged veterans, active duty military personnel, their spouses, and dependent children.

In almost all states, recipients of Supplemental Security Income (SSI) are automatically eligible for Medicaid. Those not automatically eligible must satisfy income and resource standards that are linked to the monthly income limits of the SSI program. Medicaid coverage cannot be discontinued for children who lose their SSI benefits,[30] and as reported in chapter 10, states may continue coverage for people with disabilities who return to work.

MEDICAID REIMBURSEMENT RATES

As with the Medicare program, Medicaid reimburses hospitals on a prospective payment system, and reimbursement rates for health care providers are set by the states. Reimbursement rates are low, providing a disincentive for medical providers (including insurance companies) to serve Medicaid clients.[31] Low reimbursement rates jeopardize access to office-based primary care. For example, some physicians report that low rates of reimbursement cause them to limit the number of Medicaid patients they treat or to forgo payment for services rendered because the reimbursement rate is so low that it is not worth the time it takes to complete the paperwork. Moreover, the unwillingness of some physicians to treat Medicaid patients causes some poor people to rely on hospital emergency rooms or "Medicaid mills,"[32] which are small clinics that provide primary care. In general, Medicaid mills provide a low level of care. For example, 40 percent of the physicians working in New York's Medicaid mills are not listed in the New York State Medical Directory, and many are not board certified.

SERVICES PROVIDED

Federal law identifies a minimum service package that the states must provide to all who are categorically eligible, including (1) inpatient and outpatient hospital care;

(2) laboratory and X-ray services; (3) nursing and facility services; (4) home health services; (5) physician's services; (6) early periodic screening, diagnostic and testing services (EPSDT) for youth under the age of twenty-one (discussed later); (7) medical and surgical dental services; (8) family planning services and supplies; and (9) pediatric and family nurse practitioner services.[33] Prescription drug coverage is not mandated, but it is provided by all states,[34] although it may be limited as to the number of prescriptions a person may obtain within a given time period and the total costs that the states will pay. At their option, the states may support rural health clinics, home health care services, private duty nursing services, clinic services, dental services, and physical therapy. The federal government will share in the cost of such services.[35]

States that serve the medically needy must offer, among other things (1) prenatal care and delivery services; (2) ambulatory services to individuals under the age of eighteen and to individuals entitled to institutional services; and (3) home health care if an individual is entitled to care in a nursing facility. Some states add to the menu of services an "optional service package" that includes (1) clinic services; (2) services in a nursing facilities for individuals under the age of twenty-one; (3) vision care; (4) dental care; and (5) prosthetic devices. States determine both the amount and the duration of service, but services must be offered for a length of time likely to achieve the purpose of the service.

Finally, states may experiment with different approaches to meeting the goals of the Medicaid program by receiving a Medicaid waiver from the DHHS. States have used Medicaid waivers to provide special services to help individuals avoid hospitalization through the provision of home- or community-based services, such as (1) case management services, (2) homemaker services, (3) home health aide services, (4) personal care services, (5) adult day health services, (6) habilitation services, (7) respite care services, and (8) day treatment or "other partial hospitalization services, psychosocial rehabilitation services and clinic services."[36]

LONG-TERM NURSING HOME CARE

Long-term care refers to a range of services, including medical, social, and personal care services that may be provided to people in their own homes or in long-term care facilities. Approximately 70 percent of spending for long-term care goes to the cost of nursing home care, and 30 percent goes to home care.[37] The demand for long-term care services is expected to increase in this century as the population ages, particularly the population over the age of eighty-five.

The Medicare service package does not include long-term nursing home care. Thus, a person needing publicly supported service must turn to the Medicaid program, which paid for approximately 38 percent of nursing home care in 1995; 47 percent of costs were paid for out-of-pocket.[38] An individual in need of nursing home care may be eligible for Medicaid because they are categorically or medically eligible, as discussed earlier, or they may meet the "300 percent rule," under which Medicaid benefits can be provided to individuals in need of care whose income does not exceed 300 percent of the basic SSI cash benefit.[39] The individual who is not eligible for Medicaid must pay for their own care until they "spend down" their resources to qualify.

In 1988, Congress passed the Medicaid Catastrophic Coverage Act to protect the assets and income of a noninstitutionalized spouse, referred to as the "community spouse," (CS) when one member of a couple requires Medicaid-assisted long-term nursing home care.[40] Protected assets include the value of (1) a home; (2) household goods, personal effects, and an automobile; (3) burial space; and (4) other property that is necessary for the self-support of the CS.[41] The rule of thumb is that after calculating the value of a couple's nonprotected resources, the CS is allowed to keep one-half, subject to a minimum and maximum amount. In 1998, a state could not require the CS to deplete resources below $16,152 nor allow retention of resources in excess of $80,760. After the resources of the CS have been set aside, the spouse who requires institutionalized care must reduce her or his resources to the $2,000 maximum allowed by the Medicaid program, although states have flexibility to increase this amount. In addition, the CS may retain some monthly income. In 1999, a state was precluded from requiring the CS to reduce monthly income below $1,356 nor to keep more than $2,049, after which a contribution to the care of the spouse in the nursing home is required. The value of retained resources and income may increase if the CS is caring for a minor or dependent child or another who relies for support on the CS,[42] and resource amounts are annually adjusted for inflation.

Medicaid law punishes individuals who transfer assets to become Medicaid eligible. At the time of application, federal law instructs the states to "look back" for period of 36 months or more to see if assets were transferred. The applicant who has transferred assets for less than their market value within the look-back period is barred from receiving Medicaid for a period of time that is calculated by dividing the value of the transferred assets by the monthly cost of nursing home care in the community where the couple resides. Thus, if assets valued at $72,000 are transferred and the monthly cost of nursing home care is $2,000, Medicaid will not provide assistance for 36 months.

Children's Health

Health care coverage for children is found in a mix of programs. Children are covered under Medicaid's Early and Periodic Screening, Diagnostic, and Treatment Program, and services are available through the Maternal and Child Health Program. Federal law requires the states, through Medicaid, to provide coverage for pregnant women and children so that by 2002, health coverage will be available for children and youth up to age eighteen whose family income is up to 100 percent of the federal poverty level.[43] Health care coverage is found also in the 1997 amendments to the Social Security Act that created the Title XXI Children's Health Insurance Program, and health-related services are found in the Title X Family Planning Program and the Newborn and Mother's Health Protection Act of 1996.[44]

EARLY AND PERIODIC SCREENING, DIAGNOSTIC AND TREATMENT PROGRAM

The EPSDT program is part of the Medicaid program. States must provide EPSDT services to all children who are categorically eligible for Medicaid, to pregnant women, and to children who are medically needy. Services include (1) outreach to inform eligible families that services are available; (2) comprehensive health, mental health, and developmental history; (3) medical examinations, including vision, dental, and hearing examinations and all necessary immunizations; (4) treatment to remediate physical health problems; and (5) transportation to and from medical appointments. One of the most important features of the EPSDT program is it makes preventative services available, a benefit not routinely provided by publicly funded programs. Federal law requires the states to provide any necessary service that federal law allows even if the service is not a part of the state's Medicaid plan.[45]

There are connections between the EPSDT program and other federal programs serving children and their families, and the HCFA directs the states to use EPSDT case managers to coordinate efforts across programs. For example, many states use some of their Title XX Social Service Block Grant funds to provide information and referral services that may be used to accomplish the required outreach (chapter 14). And there is an overlap in the population of children served by the EPSDT program with children served under the Title V Maternal and Child Health Care Block Grant. Title V funds (1) support services to reduce infant mortality and the incidence of handicapping conditions in newborns; (2) support rehabilitation services for blind and disabled children under 16 years of age; and (3) may be used to develop community-based health care systems and to provided community-based health care.[46]

STATE CHILDREN'S HEALTH INSURANCE PROGRAM

Congress enacted the State Children's Health Insurance Program (SCHIP) as Title XXI of the Social Security Act in 1997 to provide health insurance to some of the approximately 11 million uninsured children under the age of eighteen and to their parents if this is cost effective.[47] Congress authorized $24 billion for the first five years of SCHIP, an amount sufficient to provide health coverage for 6 million of the 11 million uninsured children.[48] The costs of SCHIP are shared between the federal government and the states, which receive a higher federal match for SCHIP, averaging 70 percent of costs compared to 57 percent of costs under the Medicaid program. To ensure that states do not shift Medicaid-eligible children into SCHIP, states must first assess a child's eligibility for Medicaid and enroll the child in that program if eligible.

The program serves children whose family income is too high to qualify for Medicaid but is below 200 percent of the poverty level, which was $32,900 for a family of four in 1998. States that had expanded Medicaid coverage for children under a waiver program before passage of Title XXI may provide coverage for children in families whose income exceeds the 200 percent level. For example, New York's Title XXI plan provides for serving children in families with an income up to 222 percent of the poverty level, and Oklahoma has set its ceiling at 250 percent of the poverty level.[49] Implementation of SCHIP accelerates the requirement that all children under the age of eighteen with incomes up to 100 percent of the poverty level be covered by health insurance.[50]

States may implement SCHIP by (1) expanding their Medicaid program; (2) developing a new program; or (3) a combination of these options. Approximately one-half of the fifty-one state and territorial programs approved by early 1999 were Medicaid expansions, and the remaining programs were variations of options two and three. Strategies must be implemented to ensure that children who are covered under private insurance are not disenrolled and moved to SCHIP, but states may subsidize the cost of enrolling a child in an employer-sponsored health care program.

States that expand Medicaid have the advantage of using an existing structure at the cost of accepting all of the regulatory constraints imposed by the Medicaid program, including the fact that Medicaid is an entitlement program that must serve all who meet its eligibility rules, and the benefits package is fixed. A newly developed SCHIP may operate as a block grant with an enrollment cap, the benefit package may offer less than is required by Medicaid rules, eligibility may take into account age and access to other forms of health insurance, and co-payments that are not allowed under Medicaid for most children's services are permissible.[51]

Because experience tells us that program eligibility does not equate with program enrollment, outreach to educate parents concerning the SCHIP program and efforts to help parents enroll their children are critical to program success. In 1996, the General Accounting Office estimated that approximately 23 percent of children eligible for Medicaid were not enrolled, and uninsured children were most likely to be in working-poor families, Hispanic, and either born in the United States to foreign parents or eligible foreign-born children. Failure of parents to enroll their children occurs for a variety of reasons, including ignorance concerning eligibility, confusion over continuing eligibility once the link between AFDC and automatic Medicaid eligibility was broken, avoiding the program because of the stigma associated with it, language barriers, and complex enrollment procedures. The program encourages the states to develop outreach programs but restricts the amount of SCHIP funds that may be used for this purpose in order to preserve the bulk of funding for service provision. States are advertising the existence of SCHIP through direct mailings to potential beneficiaries; involving community groups in educational efforts; providing pamphlets to drug stores, day care centers, and churches; and providing information through school districts. In the first six months of 1999, nationwide enrollment increased from 834,790 children to 1,310,959 children. The process that states must follow by determining first a child's eligibility for Medicaid is resulting in one Medicaid enrollment for each SCHIP enrollment.[52]

NEWBORN AND MOTHER'S HEALTH PROTECTION ACT OF 1996

Concerned that health care plans were limiting the duration of hospital stay after childbirth, Congress enacted the Newborn and Mother's Health Protection Act of 1996.[53] Congressional intent was that decisions concerning the duration of post-delivery hospital stay be made on a case-by-case basis, taking into account the "health of the mother, the health and stability of the newborn, the ability and confidence of the mother and the father to care for their newborn, the adequacy of support systems at home, and the access of the mother and her newborn to appropriate follow-up health care." The appropriate time for discharge is to be made by the attending provider in consultation with the mother. The act applies only to plans that offer hospital benefits in connection with childbirth. It does not require that such protection be offered.

SECTION 2: OTHER POLICIES AFFECTING HEALTH

In this section, we consider (1) a series of policies that affect health care directly through the provision of services, (2) indirectly by conferring on patients certain civil rights protections, and (3) policies that protect the right of those leaving their employment to continue at their own expense their employment-based health insurance.

Title X Family Planning

In 1970, Congress amended the Public Health Service Act with a new Title X. Title X provides federal funds to the states to establish, provide, and evaluate family planning services, which are defined as services to inform people of how they may prevent pregnancy.[54] Low-income families receive priority when services are in short supply, and they may not be charged for services. Educational materials that are developed using Title X funds must be developed for the population or community to whom the service is addressed. Title X funds may not be used to give advice concerning abortion nor may they be used to make referrals for or to advocate for abortion as a method of family planning.[55]

The Emergency Medical Treatment and Active Labor Act

The Emergency Medical Treatment and Active Labor Act (EMTALA) provides that hospitals with emergency departments that receive federal funds must provide medical screenings and stabilizing treatments to any individual requesting assistance regardless of ability to pay.[56] Once stabilized, patients may be transferred to another hospital if the required care is not provided by the hospital at which the patient sought help, but a hospital may not delay screening or providing needed treatment to inquire about the individual's ability to pay. Service must be provided even if the hospital knows that the patient's insurance will not pay because preauthorization was not obtained.

The Ryan White Comprehensive AIDS Resources Emergency Act

The Ryan White Comprehensive AIDS Resources Emergency Act (CARE act) provides funds to the states for certain health services for people with AIDS. The CARE act complements Medicaid's inpatient service benefit by allowing funds to be used to prevent unnecessary hospitalizations. Outpatient services include health and mental health services, plus support services such as home health, homemaker, respite care, transportation, and nutritional services.

The CARE act funds may be used to provide inpatient services if the purpose is to prevent unnecessary hospitalization or to expedite hospital discharge, and they may be used to provide financial assistance to low-income individuals to maintain their health insurance.[57] Medications for people with AIDS are paid for in part through the AIDS Drug Reimbursement Program, which is part of the CARE act.

The CARE act funds are available also for early intervention services that include referrals for health services and to programs offering experimental treatments, counseling, and testing for Human Immunodeficiency Virus, with special funding for primary health care centers and migrant health centers that serve the homeless.[58] A program of services for women, infants, children, and youth is also funded through the CARE act. Outpatient health services for women and their families must include case management, transportation, child care, and other support services needed to enable women and their families to participate in research programs. Referrals for inpatient hospital services, substance abuse treatment, and other needed support services are required where appropriate.[59] Grants for Special Projects of National Significance[60] are made for projects that, among other things, (1) serve low-income clients; (2) support respite care services in minority communities; and (3) provide health care and support services to underserved populations such as minorities, including Native Americans, people in rural areas, the homeless, and prisoners.

Indian Health Services

The federal government, through the United States Public Health Service, is responsible for funding health care for Native Americans, including Alaska Natives.[61] But shortages of physicians and other health care professionals, outdated medical facilities, and inadequate funds have posed continuing difficulties in providing needed care. For people living on reservations, health problems are exacerbated by the lack of proper waste disposal systems, inadequate water supplies, and the health dangers that these conditions create.

In 1976, Congress passed the Indian Health Care Improvement Act to increase access to medical care and to improve the health status of Native Americans "over a seven-year period, to a level equal to that enjoyed by other American citizens."[62] Funds are available through the act for training physicians, nurses, and paraprofessionals who are willing to serve Native communities and for outreach to identify Native families with health problems, refer them to needed health services, and ensure that Native Americans know of their eligibility for existing health care programs such as Medicare and Medicaid.

Patient Self-Determination Act

The Patient Self-Determination Act of 1990 was passed because some people are not able to participate in medical decisions that affect the course of their treatment and because people do not always consider in advance of hospital admission the need to make their wishes known about extraordinary care measures or to provide for another to make decisions for them.[63] The PSDA addresses such situations in a limited context. Hospitals, nursing homes, home health agencies, hospices, and prepaid health care organizations that participate in the Medicaid or Medicare programs are required to provide at the time of admission written information describing a patient's rights to create a living will or advance directive that will inform medical providers of the patient's wishes concerning his or her health care if the patient is unable to participate in decision making. The information provided must be specific as to the laws of the state in which the institution is located and about institutional practices so that patients can select an institution that will honor their wishes.

Civil Rights Policies and Access to Medical Care

Access to medical care requires access to physicians' offices, clinics, and hospitals. Provisions in the Vocational Rehabilitation Act provide that recipients of federal funds cannot deny medical care to a person based on the patient's disability, and the Americans with Disabilities Act provides the same protection against discriminatory treatment by private practitioners. These acts are discussed in detail in chapter 13.

Continuing Private Health Care Coverage

Loss of employment has traditionally meant a loss of health insurance, and some workers lose health insurance when their work hours are reduced. The Consolidated Omnibus Budget Reconciliation Act of 1985[64] (COBRA) provides that an insured worker and the employee's divorced or widowed spouse have the right to continue at their own expense the insurance received under an employment-based group plan for up to 36 months.[65] The cost of continued coverage may not exceed 2 percent of the group insurance premium. The 1990 amendments to COBRA allow a state to use Medicaid funds to pay for continuation coverage when it is cost effective to do so. An added concern for a person who loses employment-based coverage is an inability to acquire new insurance due to a preexisting medical condition. An estimated 81 million Americans have some type of preexisting medical condition.[66] The Health Insurance Portability Act (HIPPA) of 1996 adds to the protections found in COBRA by limiting the ability of an insurer to deny coverage to an employee leaving a group plan on the basis of a preexisting condition.[67] Under HIPPA, individuals are allowed to continue their insurance coverage, or insurance must be made available through "risk pools," where insurance companies share responsibility for providing coverage.

Under HIPPA, an insurer is not required to offer any particular benefit package. The law does not limit the premiums that may be charged nor the deductibles and coinsurance payments required. Whether persons with preexisting conditions continue their employment-based policy or join a risk-pool, they are likely to pay a premium that is on average 200 percent higher than what would be paid by persons without preexisting conditions.[68] However, HIPPA does not allow an insurer to charge a premium that is greater than the premium paid by others with the same condition.[69]

Mental Health Parity Act

An employer who provides health insurance is not required to provide coverage for mental health services. However, if a group plan provides coverage for medical and mental health services, it may not impose different standards for receipt of either type of benefit.[70] Thus, if there are annual limitations or aggregate lifetime benefits that apply to medical coverage, the same rules may apply to coverage for mental health. The law does not apply to benefits for the treatment of substance abuse or chemical dependency problems. When Congress passed the Mental Health Parity Act, it included a "sunset clause," meaning that the provisions of the act are applicable only until September 30, 2001, but they may be extended.

SECTION 3: HEALTH CARE REFORM

Health care reform was a major political issue in the last decade of the twentieth century due to (1) rising health care costs; (2) increases in the number of retirees who would increase the demand for Medicare and Medicaid coverage, making cost control difficult; and (3) increases in the number of working-age people without health insurance. The latter supported a demand for the government to fill the gap left by the loss of employment-based insurance and fueled the concern that publicly supported health programs could not remain fiscally solvent.

Controlling costs through capitated MCPs with gatekeeper access to services was a major reform of the last decades of the twentieth century. However, this reform met with some resistance from consumers and health care providers that supported a movement for government regulation of MCPs. Implementing and enforcing regulations are costly, producing an ironic situation where controlling the remedy meant to control costs increases the cost of care.

Consumers were concerned that (1) they might have to change primary care providers if their physician of choice was not a participating provider in an MCP, (2) their autonomy to see specialists would be curtailed by "gatekeepers," (3) decisions concerning whether their health services would be provided were arbitrarily made by a "faceless" decision maker working for an MCP, and (4) those handling an appeal of an adverse decision would act as arbitrarily as the person who denied the requested care.

Care providers have a dual concern with MCPs and with other government efforts to control the costs of health care. Physicians see their professional autonomy undermined and their livelihoods threatened when MCPs implement cost control mechanisms that result in denying a physician's request for procedures considered medically necessary and in reducing provider fees. The concern of the medical community was such that in June 1999, the American Medical Association laid the groundwork for a "national labor union" for physicians to increase their bargaining power with MCPs.[71] Then, the government lowered reimbursement rates to MCPs, causing a number of them to withdraw from the Medicaid and Medicare markets. In the fall of 1998, citing mainly reasons of financial loss, about 400,000 Medicare beneficiaries lost their MCP coverage when their plans stopped serving Medicare clients,[72] and about 100 MCPs announced their intentions to not renew their Medicare contracts or to reduce the areas of the country served.[73] In addition, in September 1999, the DHHS reported that some MCPs intend to control prescription drug costs by charging co-payments, capping drug coverage at $500 per year, or discontinuing drug coverage.[74] Twenty-three percent of Medicare participants who lost coverage from MCPs transferred to the Medicare fee-for-service program. Others relied upon employer-sponsored health insurance, Medicaid, or other insurance arrangements.[75]

Financial concerns have cause nursing homes to retreat from the Medicaid market and to transfer patients to other nursing homes. Problems caused by the latter led President Clinton to sign the Nursing Home Resident Protection Act in March 1999, which prohibits nursing homes who withdraw from the Medicaid program from transferring or discharging nursing home residents.[76]

In the remaining pages of this chapter, the following issues are reviewed (1) program solvency; (2) the uninsured; (3) the aging of the American population; (4) medical technology; (5) regulation of managed care; and (6) options for further health care reform.

Solvency

The problem of escalating health care costs was graphically illustrated in Figure 12.1 (Medicare) and Figure 12.2 (Medicaid). The Medicare Hospital Insurance trust fund has been running a cash deficit since 1992, which is expected to reach more than $20 billion in fiscal year 2010. In 1999, payroll taxes paid for only 89 percent of hospital insurance spending.[77]

Some of the costs of medical care are due to the use of unnecessary medical procedures, and some are the result of fraudulent billing by medical providers. Some physicians practice "defensive medicine," where tests and specialists are overutilized to avoid or limit the damages from malpractice suits. The DHHS estimates that overpayments due to "billing errors, fraud, medically unnecessary services, and other problems" were $12.6 billion in fiscal year 1998. Efforts to overcome these problems are found in provisions of HIPPA and the Medicare Integrity Program. Before approval of claims, five program checks are to be made, including (1) a medical review of all claims; (2) determinations of whether primary responsibility for claims fall on the Medicare program or on another insurer; (3) routing audits of cost reports; (4) identification and investigation of potential fraud cases; and (5) provider education and training.[78]

The Uninsured

The number of people lacking health insurance varies across time for several reasons. First, the link between employment and health insurance is such that the number of uninsured will vary with periods of economic recession and growth. Even when unemployment is low, the number of people without health insurance may remain high because the number of employers providing health insurance is decreasing. The smaller the business, the greater the likelihood of not having employment-based health insurance; close to 50 percent of uninsured workers are employed in businesses with fewer than twenty-five employees.[79]

That a person is legally entitled to continue her health insurance after job loss is significant but limited by the financial ability of an unemployed person to pay insurance premiums. Exacerbating the situation is the fact that eligibility rules for the Medicaid program may shift over time causing the number of uninsured to increase or decrease. Recall the decrease in the number of Medicaid enrollees in the early 1980s that was illustrated in Figure 12.2. This was a result of changes in AFDC eligibility rules that reduced the size of both the AFDC and the Medicaid programs.[80] In 10 states, 1.3 million individuals whose receipt of Medicaid was TANF-related lost their health insurance benefits between June 1997 and June 1999.[81] In 1998, the United States Census Bureau estimated that 44.3 million Americans lacked health insurance.[82]

Despite the fact that Medicaid provides health insurance for poor people, poverty—more than any other characteristic—is associated with the lack of health insurance. In 1998 (Figure 12.3), slightly more than 32 percent of poor people, compared to 16.3 percent of non-poor people lacked health insurance. Whether working full- or part-time, low-wage workers have uninsurance rates in excess of 40 percent and are far more likely to lack insurance than non-poor full- or part-time workers, who have rates of uninsurance at 16.9 percent and 23.2 percent, respectively. The association between poverty and lack of health insurance holds true regardless of race and age; 28.8 percent of poor black people, 33.8 percent of poor white people, and 44 percent of poor people of Hispanic origin lack health insurance, and poor people between the ages of eighteen and sixty-four have high rates of uninsurance. Considering citizenship and its association to health care, we see that the relationship between poverty and the lack of health insurance holds true whether an uninsured person is native born, a naturalized citizen, or a person born in another country.

The Aging of the American Population

In the late 1990s, the elderly represented approximately 13 percent of the total population; by 2030, they will comprise 20 percent. Growth in the Medicare program is measured by the number of enrollees and by the rising costs of health care. Cost is associated with the number of enrollees but is fueled by new technologies that may increase costs even when enrollment remains constant. When viewed from the perspective of the entire budget and the economy, the growth in Medicare is

FIGURE 1 2.3. Percent of all persons and of poor persons never covered by health insurance during the year 1998.

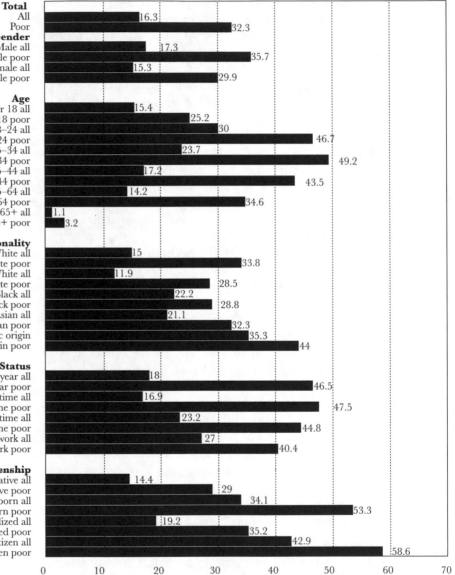

Source: Jennifer A. Campbell, *Current Population Survey.* U.S. Census Bureau.

not sustainable over time. In addition to the costs of the Medicare program, the elderly, together with people with disabilities, consume a disproportionate share of Medicaid expenditures. Taken together, these groups account for one of four Medicaid beneficiaries, but they receive two of every three Medicaid dollars.[83] The effects of an aging population and rising health care costs are further illustrated in Table 12.3, which shows the average annual growth in skilled nursing care (14.8 percent) and home health care (13.4 percent), services most likely to benefit older segments of society, compared to inpatient care (7.7 percent).

MEDICAL TECHNOLOGY AND HEALTH CARE COSTS

Medical technology that increases the chances for survival of premature newborns and treatments that sustain life at the opposite end of the age spectrum, together with other procedures that rely for their effectiveness on advanced technologies, drive up health care costs. Eighty-one percent of health economists responding to a 1995 survey concerning health care costs agreed with the statement: "The primary reason for the increase in the health sector's share of the gross domestic product over the past 30 years is technological change in medicine."[84]

Some new technologies may reduce the cost of individual procedures by allowing them to be performed on an outpatient basis or by hastening hospital discharge, but at the same time, the availability of less intrusive technologies that require less time in the hospital increases the demand for specific procedures. It has been suggested that reducing health care costs will require limiting the availability of new technologies.[85]

In April 1999, the HCFA announced its intention to bring order and cost control to the process of deciding what services are "necessary and reasonable" for Medicare beneficiaries through the use of "evidence based decision making." The HFCA will consider (1) whether there is demonstrable evidence, such as data from controlled clinical trials, that supports applying a technology because it will result in improved patient management or health outcomes, for example, a reduction in mortality or morbidity; (2) that the recommended technology is the most appropriate way of treating the illness and that it is provided by qualified personnel; and (3) the cost of the service in comparison to other treatments for the same condition.[86]

TABLE 12.3. Benefit Payments by Service Under Medicare Parts A and B During Selected Fiscal Years: 1985–1998 (in Millions)

	1985	1990	1995	1998*	Average annual growth
Inpatient	$45,218	$59,285	$87,441	$109,299	7.7%
Skilled nursing home	550	2,821	9,104	13,779	14.8
Home health	1,908	3,297	14,995	21,879	13.4
Hospice	34	318	1,854	2,214	6.1

Source: House, Committee on Ways and Means, "Section 2: Medicare," *Green Book* (Washington, D.C., 1998).
*Estimate.

Managed Care

Managed care is attractive to some consumers. For example, prescription drug coverage costs approximately $600 per elderly person per year. Some MCPs pay for prescription drugs as well as other services not provided for in fee-for-service plans, such as routine physical examinations, hearing aids, and eyeglasses. The United States General Accounting Office concluded that the availability of prescription drug coverage may be the most important reason why Medicare beneficiaries enroll in MCPs.[87] In addition, co-payments and other out-of-pocket expenses may be lower than those in a traditional fee-for-service plan.[88]

The characteristics of MCPs that make them attractive to policymakers, mainly the use of gatekeepers to limit access to specialists and cost containment through capitation, may make them unattractive to beneficiaries with chronic illnesses whose medical needs require access to specialists and who are not served well in a commercial model whose viability is related to limiting medical costs.[89] And many physicians have a low opinion of MCPs. From a nationwide survey conducted in 1999, we learn that 87 percent of 1,053 physicians reported that their patients were denied some health care service and that the majority of denials resulted in a "serious" decline in patient health. Almost one-half of the 768 nurses surveyed agreed with this conclusion, and one-quarter of all provider-respondents reported that they have exaggerated the severity of a patient's condition in order to obtain needed service. On the plus side, 47 percent of doctors said that MCPs helped them manage a patient's care.[90]

REGULATION OF MANAGED CARE PROGRAMS

Consumers have expressed dissatisfaction with MCPs by suing them, and the courts have shown a receptivity to consumer-initiated litigation against MCPs.[91] To appease consumers and reduce litigation, states have addressed consumer concerns by issuing regulations to govern the operation of MCPs. Issues commonly identified by consumers as problematic are reported in the left-hand column of Table 12.4 and the solutions adopted by some states are shown in the right-hand column.

The issues of greatest concern to consumers fall into the categories of access, information, and appeals. To prevent the use of hospital emergency rooms for routine medical care while providing necessary access, states have adopted the "prudent person" rule, which asks whether another faced with a similar situation would have gone to a hospital emergency room. Thus, if a child is bleeding from a injury and a parent using ordinary measures cannot stop the bleeding, emergency room use might be considered prudent, whereas such use may be unwarranted if a child has been running a low grade fever for a short time period.

One of the tasks of "gatekeepers" in a managed care model is to control costs through prudent use of specialized services and access to specialists. However, complaints have been voiced regarding difficulties in gaining access to specialists when there are none with the needed expertise among an MCP's providers or when a specialist in obstetrics or the treatment of a chronic illness is needed as a primary care physician. Some states have dealt with this issue by requiring MCPs to authorize multiple visits to specialists, to pay for the cost of visiting a specialist if the plan does not have a provider with the needed expertise, and to allow pregnant women and people with chronic illnesses to use specialists as primary care physicians. Two additional access concerns arise when a physician withdraws from an MCP and the plan requires the beneficiary to go to a participating provider or when an MCP's list of acceptable medications does not contain a needed or effective medication. Some states are dealing with the first issue by requiring that an MCP allow patients whose health would be seriously threatened by a change in provider to continue with their nonparticipating physician and with the second problem by requiring MCPs to allow access to needed medications.

Choosing an appropriate MCP requires information on a variety of issues concerning benefits, appeals procedures, costs to the consumer, and procedures for seeing specialists, but some MCPs have not been forthcoming and have penalized physicians who provided full disclosure to patients as well as physicians who advocated for their patients during an appeal. States have enacted legislation that prohibits an MCP from taking adverse action against medical providers who alerts their patients to these issues or who take on the role of advocate at an appeal. Finally, some MCPs have created barriers to appeals by failing to provide to patients information describing the basis of adverse decisions, by failing to notify patients of the procedures to be followed in filing an appeal, and by delaying a decision on an appealed matter, possibly contributing to a patient's worsening condition. A number of states require full disclosure on all matters concerning the process of filing an appeal, and some required expedited appeals with decisions within forty-eight to seventy-two hours. In addition, the appeals process in some states is triggered by a verbal complaint, and some states require that an appeal be heard by providers with expertise in the matter, excluding from the review people involved in the original service denial.

Health Care Options

A variety of options have been considered to provide health insurance to the uninsured at a reasonable cost. Some proposals are relatively simple, for example, calling upon the government to subsidize the cost of health insurance through vouchers or tax credits. Three proposals are briefly reviewed.

MANAGED COMPETITION

President Clinton's proposed Health Security Act was referred to in chapter 1. The proposal called for the provision of medical insurance and the delivery of medical care through "managed competition."[92] Health insurance purchasing cooperatives would be formed and charged with contracting with medical providers for health care.[93] Employers would pay the cost of insurance for full-time workers, and the federal government would pay for others. The cooperatives, offering a federally defined health benefit package, would be competitive. It was argued that competition would keep down health care costs, but the plan did not deal adequately with the absence of competition in small metropolitan areas and in rural areas, nor did

TABLE 12.4. Issues in Managed Care Plans and Solutions Implemented by Some States

Issue	Solutions available in some states
Access	
Emergency room use	If a "prudent person" faced with the same facts and circumstances would have used the emergency room, the MCP should pay for its use.
Access to specialists	Primary care providers are authorized to refer to specialists for more than one visit without plan approval.
Out-of-network referrals	Plans must permit referrals outside the plan's network when the plan does not have network providers available to meet medical needs.
Specialists as primary care physicians	Plans must allow enrollees with chronic, disabling, or life-threatening conditions to use specialists as primary care providers and pregnant women to use obstetric physicans as primary providers.
Continuity in care	Plans must pay for treatment when a provider's contract is not renewed unless nonrenewal was due to problems with quality of care provided. Continuity of care must be medically necessary, such as when the enrollee has a life-threatening disease or condition, degenerative and disabling disease or condition, or an acute condition. Most laws limit the duration of continued care to 90 or 120 days.
Access to nonformulary drugs	Plans are required to allow enrollees to obtain nonformulary prescription drugs without financial penalty when the formulary equivalent is ineffective or when the equivalent causes, or might cause, an adverse or harmful reaction.

Information

Full disclosure/gag rules

Full disclosure, including information describing (1) benefits available; (2) prior authorizations required; (3) procedures for filing appeals; (4) premiums, coinsurance, co-payments, deductibles, or other charges to the subscriber; (5) how to select and access specialists; (6) information concerning all possible treatment options; and (7) advocacy for patients who appeal adverse decisions.

Appeals

When a service is denied, reduced, or terminated, written notice must be provided that includes the reason(s) for the denial or change in care and that provides information on how to appeal. Some states require that appeals be resolved within specified time frames, such as 30 days, and expedited appeals require resolution within 2 business days or 72 hours. Some states require that verbal complaints trigger an appeal process and some that the appeal be heard by providers with expertise in the clinical area under review who were not involved in the original decision.

Source: Compiled by author.

it take into account the ability of competing groups to set a "bidding floor" below which no group would go in order to sustain high profits.[94]

SINGLE-PAYER SYSTEMS

Policymakers have looked north to Canada and considered adopting a "single-payer" system like the one used in that country. In a single-payer system, a unit of government pays for all of the costs of a defined health care package. Single-payer systems can be contrasted with all-payer systems that exist in some countries of Western Europe, where health care is paid for by both private and public "payers" who negotiate fixed-rates with providers, and with a "socialized" system such as Great Britain's National Health, where the government by employing physicians and hospital ownership is the provider of service. Universal coverage, a common benefits package, and cost containment are common to all three approaches.

In Canada, the national government funds directly health programs that are operated in each province. Physicians negotiate their fees through professional associations. Proposals for single-payer systems were made twice in the 1990s, first by Representative Marty Russo of Illinois in 1991 and again by Senator Paul Wellstone in 1993. Under Senator Wellstone's proposal, the federal government would be the single-payer for universal health insurance. The system would be financed through a progressive tax on businesses and individuals. Each state, through a grant-in-aid program, would administer its own program and negotiate provider fees.[95]

From the consumer's viewpoint, the advantages of Senator Wellstone's proposal were (1) universal coverage; (2) similar benefits for all; (3) greater emphasis on preventive care; and (4) administrative simplification. However, it is not clear that the administrative simplification and the emphasis on prevention would yield the anticipated savings. In Canada as in the United States, the costs of health care have escalated, and the Canadian government is considering cost control mechanisms similar to managed care.[96]

THE OREGON HEALTH PLAN

Rationing health care is another approach to providing universal coverage. Health care is, of course, rationed, albeit in an informal manner. Obvious examples include (1) the number of people with no health insurance; (2) the loss of coverage when eligibility rules for public programs change; (3) the limitations on provided services when government establishes a service "package" as it has for both Medicare and Medicaid; (4) the limited care options for people who live in underserved areas of the country; and (5) the requirement for preapproval for certain procedures, which may result in granting or denying coverage. In the opinion of some, an objective system of rationing is a necessary step if the goal of providing universal coverage is to be achieved because it promises a way of reducing health care costs.[97]

The state of Oregon implemented the Oregon Health Plan, a program that rationed health care, in 1993 after receiving a Medicaid waiver.[98] The state's objective was to provide universal health insurance by rationing health care to Medicaid recipients. Rationing would allow the state's Medicaid program to expand to cover all residents with incomes below the poverty level. The state has achieved the latter goal but has not been successful in providing universal coverage because employer mandates were successfully resisted by the business community.

The rationing scheme was produced by a health care commission formed by the state. The commission was charged with creating a list of services and prioritizing those listed according to the benefit each produced. A line was drawn, below which services were not available.[99] The plan gave priority to (1) treatments that prevent death and are likely to lead to a complete recovery, (2) maternity care, (3) treatments that prevent death but do not promise full recovery, and (4) treatments that do not improve the quality of life. Within each of these categories, treatment procedures are prioritized on the basis of outcome data that include a quality of life component.[100]

Jacobs and colleagues (1999), writing about the Oregon plan, state that the rationing system was never fully realized due to a combination of within-state politics coupled with federal regulations that limited the state's flexibility, despite the state having received a Medicaid waiver. Program costs were financed from general revenues and the imposition of a cigarette tax, not from savings realized by rationing, and the "list" was as much a description of a benefit package as it was a guide to control access to service.[101] It was not possible, for example, to limit service to those "above the line" because some that were "below" were a medically necessary part of an "above the line" treatment regime.

Summary

A number of policies that provide for health care and issues concerning access to health care have been the subject of this chapter. Medicare is a three-part program that provides health insurance for almost all people over the age of sixty-five. Part A covers (1) inpatient hospital services, (2) nursing care in a SNCF, (3) home health services, and (4) hospice care. Part B is a voluntary program that pays a percent of the costs of outpatient services, for example, physicians' fees, the services of clinical social workers and psychologists, and the costs of durable medical equipment, and for some preventive services such as mammograms and screening for diabetes. Part C describes provider options, which include fee-for-service plans and MCPs. There is an emphasis on MCPs that control the costs of care through capitation, where a fixed sum is paid to the provider to serve all of the participant's medical needs, and through the use of gatekeepers who control access to specialized care and specialized procedures. Some Medicare participants purchase Medigap supplemental insurance to pay for deductibles and coinsurance charges required by the Medicare program and for services not provided by Medicare, such as home health care and prescription drug benefits.

Medicaid is a health insurance program that is operated in a joint federal-state partnership. Medicaid is the major source for health coverage for individuals who are dependent on publicly supported health care. Coverage is available for poor people who are categorically eligible due to age, disability, membership in a family with dependent children and for pregnant women who meet the program's financial

276 I *Part III*

need standard. Some states cover the "medically needy" who are categorically eligible for Medicaid but whose income is too high to qualify for coverage.

Both Medicaid and Medicare pay hospitals and use a prospective payment system where the cost paid by the government varies according to the patient's diagnosis. Both Medicaid and Medicare encourage participants to enroll in MCPs to control health care costs. Medicaid reimburses health care providers at a lower rate than Medicare, and some health care providers have expressed a reluctance to service Medicare patients due to low rates of reimbursement.

Medicare pays for a variety of services, including (1) inpatient and outpatient hospital care and the costs associated with hospital care; (2) nursing home care; (3) physician's services; and (4) special services for children. Prescription drug coverage is provided by all states.

Because Medicare does not pay the costs of long-term nursing home care, many elderly who require such care turn to the Medicaid program. Elderly persons who are not married and require nursing home care must "spend down" their assets until they are financially eligible for Medicaid assistance. Medicaid law makes special provisions for the spouse of a person requiring long-term nursing home care to retain assets and income.

Several programs provide health care coverage for children. Medicaid's EPSDT program requires states to inform families who meet financial standards that their children are eligible to receive comprehensive health, mental health, and developmental screening and treatment to remediate physical health problems. Additional services are available through the Maternal and Child Health Care Block Grant, and health insurance is available to children whose family income is too high to qualify for Medicaid coverage through SCHIP, which Congress enacted in 1997 to provide health insurance to some of the approximately 11 million children who lack health insurance.

Other policies affecting health care include (1) the Title X Family Planning program, which provides information to help people prevent pregnancy; (2) the Emergency Medical Treatment and Active Labor Act, which guarantees medical screenings and stabilizing treatments to any individual requesting assistance from a federally supported hospital emergency room regardless of ability to pay; (3) the Ryan White Comprehensive AIDS Resources Emergency Act, through which health services are provided for people with AIDS; (4) the Indian Health Care Improvement Act, which seeks to increase access of Native people to medical care and to improve their health status; (5) the Patient Self-Determination Act, which requires federally supported hospitals and other care facilities to provide information to patients on their rights to participate in medical decisions by informing medical providers in advance of hospital admittance of their wishes if they are unable to participate in decision making; (6) civil rights policies, which protect individuals in need of medical care from discriminatory treatment by medical practitioners; (7) policies that provide for individuals to continue their health coverage at their own expense after leaving a place of employment regardless of the presence of a preexisting medical condition; and (8) the Mental Health Parity Act, which provides that if a group insurance plan provides coverage for medical and mental health services, it may not impose different standards for receipt of either type of benefit.

At the conclusion of this chapter, the discussion of health care reform included (1) the conflict that exists between rising health care costs due to the aging of the American population and the demands that this places on the Medicare system; (2) the number of people who lack health insurance, which creates pressure on the government to expand coverage; and (3) the efforts by government to control the spiraling costs of health care.

The government's major cost-containment efforts are found in the move to managed care, for reasons discussed at the beginning of this summary, and in reduced rates of reimbursements to care providers. Because of difficulties that some have experienced with MCPs, a number of states have adopted regulations such as those that ensure patient access to necessary emergency room care without prior plan approval, that allow use of specialists as primary care providers for certain populations, and that require streamlined appeals procedures for those who believe that they have been wrongly denied care. We concluded with a review of options for further reform of the health care system, including (1) managed competition, (2) single-payer systems, and (3) explicit rationing of health care, which was tried when the state of Oregon adopted the Oregon Health Plan.

Civil Rights

Civil rights refer to personal freedoms guaranteed by the United States Constitution and by the constitutions of the various states. Civil rights statutes implement and give force to guaranteed rights by providing a means for an individual to seek a legal remedy if he or she believes that his or her right to equal treatment under the law has been violated. Civil rights were discussed briefly in chapter 4 where I referred to the Civil Rights Act of 1866 that addressed the relationship between newly freed slaves and state government. The act of 1866 provided a means for African Americans, under the protection of the federal government, to enforce their right to buy, own, rent, and sell property and to enter into employment contracts, and it included safeguards against discriminatory treatment by police and state courts.

The focus of the 1866 act was on discrimination by officials working for or acting on behalf of state government. In an effort to end discrimination against African Americans by individuals not acting on behalf of the state, Congress passed the Civil Rights Act of 1875 to prohibit individuals from denying access to places of public accommodation and the use of public transportation. In a series of cases known of as the Civil Rights Cases, the United States Supreme Court found the act of 1875 unconstitutional because Congress lacked the authority to enact legislation that controlled the actions of individuals who were not acting as state agents.

The Supreme Court's rejection of the Civil Rights Act of 1875, together with the Court's ruling in *Plessy v. Ferguson* that sanctioned race-based segregation, legitimized racism in states that chose to legislatively mandate the "separate but equal" doctrine of *Plessy* (see chapter 4). Civil rights proceeded at a snail's pace after 1875. In 1946, President Harry Truman appointed a committee to review this subject. The committee issued a report in 1947 and recommended that states enact laws to guarantee equal access to places of public accommodation. In 1948, by executive order, President Truman integrated the armed forces and in 1955, the Supreme Court, in *Brown v. Board of Education,* held that segregated public schools violated the federal constitution. The Court's decision in *Brown* was a major blow to the Jim Crow system of racial segregation that had been sanctioned by the Court's earlier ruling in *Plessy v. Ferguson.* By 1964, thirty-two states had passed laws guaranteeing nondiscriminatory access to places of public accommodation.

Events Leading Up to Passage of the Civil Rights Act of 1964

The "modern" civil rights movement began in the 1950s when an African American woman named Rosa Parks refused to move to the back of the bus to make room for a white passenger. Parks' action sparked a bus boycott by the black community in Montgomery, Alabama, that lasted for more than a year, ending in 1956 when the Supreme Court struck down laws segregating public transportation.[1]

The movement for civil rights continued in the early 1960s with lunch-counter sit-ins in North Carolina, voter-registration drives elsewhere in southern states, and public demonstrations calling for civil rights for people of color. In 1963, the March on Washington took place, at which several hundred thousand people heard Dr. Martin Luther King give his famous "I Have a Dream" speech.[2] The Civil Rights Act of 1964 was passed one year later, followed by passage of the Voting Rights Act in 1965.[3] The act of 1964 was a "pledge [to] the full use of the power, resources and leadership of the federal Government to eliminate discrimination based of race, color, religion, or national origin."[4]

This organization of this chapter is as follows. After a brief discussion of congressional authority to enact civil rights legislation, we will turn our attention to a series of Civil Rights Acts and the issues they address, including prohibitions against discrimination (1) in employment, and the related topics of affirmative action and workplace harassment; (2) in access to services; (3) in wages based on gender; and (4) in access to housing. You should know that the states have their own civil rights laws that cover many of the same issues, affecting the behavior of employers, property owners, and those who control access to places of public accommodation. A discussion of state specific statutes is beyond the scope of this text.

Congressional Authority to Enact Civil Rights Legislation

The actions that Congress may take to control the behavior of individuals within the states is an important topic for the student who is interested in the use of civil rights legislation to remedy social problems. Congressional actions that affect the behavior of individuals within the states raise questions of "federalism" that are concerned with the balance of authority in legislative and judicial matters between federal and state government.

The American system of government grants to the states a general "police power," which refers to the authority vested in state government to enact legislation to protect the health, safety, and welfare of the public. This power is subject to the Fourteenth Amendment, which means that a state cannot enact a law that expressly violates a right enumerated in the federal constitution. Thus, a state cannot deprive citizens of their right to free speech or their right to elect to continue or terminate a pregnancy. The Constitution does not grant a general police power to the federal government. Thus, when Congress acts to control the behavior of state officials or of public citizens acting for themselves, it must justify its actions. Congress finds justification in its powers under the federal Constitution to regulate interstate commerce and to enforce "by appropriate legislation [the Fourteenth Amendment's guarantee that] no State shall . . . deny to any person within its jurisdiction the equal protection of the laws."[5]

An example will be helpful in understanding this issue and in understanding how the Supreme Court has interpreted congressional power over time. In the introduction to this chapter, I reported that Congress passed a civil rights act in 1875 that banned race-based discrimination in access to places of public accommodations such as inns, restaurants, and theaters. The Supreme Court held that the act was unconstitutional because Congress lacked the authority to ban discrimination by individuals who were not acting as agents of the state. Stated otherwise, the High Court said that Congress had no authority to regulate purely private conduct. This decision ended federal efforts to eliminate race-based discrimination by individuals until the Civil Rights Act of 1964 was passed. Shortly after passage of the 1964 act, a motel in Georgia asked a federal court to prevent its implementation making the same argument that had been made against the act of 1875.[6]

The Court found that the motel advertised in media designed to attract patrons who lived outside the state of Georgia and that approximately 75 percent of the motel's guests came from out of state. The Court said that Congress may affect the behavior of individuals who are not agents of the states through the Commerce Clause of the federal Constitution that authorizes Congress to regulate commerce "with foreign nations, and among the several States, and with Indian Tribes."[7] Distinguishing its 1875 ruling from its current position, the Court said that the world had changed since 1875:

> Certain kinds of businesses might not in 1875 have been sufficiently involved in interstate commerce to warrant bringing them within ambit of [Congress'] commerce power . . . conditions of transportation and commerce have changed dramatically . . . and there was overwhelming evidence that discrimination by hotels and motels impeded interstate travel.[8]

The Commerce Clause was a source of extensive power for Congress. Between the Depression of 1929 and 1995, the Supreme Court struck down only one act in which Congress evoked the Commerce Clause as a source of authority. However, since 1995, the Court has handed down several decisions that narrow Congress' Commerce Clause power, and a once arcane subject of interest to legal scholars and historians is now a matter of concern to social workers and others in the helping professions who advocate for client rights.[9]

For example, in 1999, the Fourth Circuit Court of appeals in Virginia held that Congress lacked the authority under the Commerce Clause to enact portions of the Violence Against Women Act (VAWA) that provides that "all persons within the

United States [have a right] to be free from crimes of violence motivated by gender."[10] Specifically, the Court struck down that portion of the act that allows a victim of gender-based violence to sue a perpetrator in federal court (see chapter 14 for a discussion of the VAWA). In May 2000, the Supreme Court affirmed the decision of the Fourth Circuit Court of Appeals.[11] Because of this decision, other civil rights statutes, for example, the Americans with Disabilities Act (ADA) (discussed later) that affects private behavior, may be deemed to be beyond the control of the federal government.

The Civil Rights Act of 1964

The Civil Rights Act of 1964 contains ten titles.[12] Title I provides that the right to vote in national elections cannot be denied on the basis of race, and this title provides for prompt review by the federal courts of challenges to state laws affecting voting. Ensuring access to places of public accommodation such as hotels and restaurants without regard to race is the focus of Title II.[13] Titles III and IV authorize the justice department to file suits to desegregate public facilities (Title III) and to desegregate schools (Title IV). The United States Civil Rights Commission, established in 1957, was made permanent under Title V. The commission was charged with (1) investigating allegations concerning civil rights violations, (2) compiling and disseminating information concerning civil rights, and (3) educating the public on this subject.[14]

Employment discrimination is prohibited by Titles VI and VII; Title VI addresses discrimination in programs that receive federal funds and Title VII addresses discrimination in employment by private and public entities[15] regardless of whether they receive federal funds. Title VII authorizes the formation of the Equal Employment Opportunity Commission (EEOC) (see later discussion). Title VIII authorizes data gathering describing registration and voting behavior, Title IX addresses the role played by the courts in enforcing the act, and Title X contains miscellaneous provisions.

We begin our review with the employment provisions of the Civil Rights Act of 1964 and employment protections found in other statutes, such as the Vocational Rehabilitation Act (VRA) of 1973, the ADA, and the Age Discrimination and Employment Act (ADEA) of 1967. This focus is important to social workers and other human service providers for several reasons. First, any barrier to employment or to promotion that is based on personal characteristics of the individual rather than on qualifications for a job are a type of "structural barrier" that was referred to in chapter 8. Structural barriers may hinder a person's efforts to move themselves out of poverty and may thwart a person's efforts to comply with the work requirements found in various provisions of the Personal Responsibility and Work Opportunity Act (PRWOA). In addition, some of you will work with people with disabilities, and you should be familiar with the provisions in the VRA and the ADA that protect a disabled person from discrimination in employment due solely to a disability. Finally, the authority for affirmative action programs and for laws preventing workplace harassment are derived from the employment provisions of the Civil Rights Act of 1964.

Employment

The laws that prevent employers[16] from denying an individual a job or a promotion based solely on a personal characteristic are shown in Table 13.1. Title VII of the Civil Rights Act of 1964 provides a general prohibition concerning employment discrimination that makes it illegal for an employer "to fail or refuse to hire or to discharge any individual, or otherwise to discriminate against any individual with respect to compensation, terms, conditions or privileges of employment because of such individual's race, color, religion, sex or national origin."[17] The quoted phrase

TABLE 13.1. Federal Laws That Protect Individuals Against Discrimination on the Basis of Personal Characteristics

Law	Characteristic(s) covered	Statutory authority
Civil Rights Act of 1964—Title VI*	Race, sex, color, national origin, and religion in programs receiving federal funds	42 U.S.C. §2000d
Civil Rights Act of 1964—Title VII	Race, sex, color, national origin, and religion in programs in general	42 U.S.C. §2000e
Educational Amendments of 1972—Title IX	Sex	20 U.S.C. §1681
Vocational Rehabilitation Act—Section 501-1973	Disability	29 U.S.C. §794
Americans with Disabilities Act—Title I	Disability	42 U.S.C. §12111
Equal Employment Opportunity in Federal Government	Race, color, religion, sex, national origin, handicap, age, or sexual orientation	Executive Order No. 11478
Age Discrimination in Employment Act	Age 40 and over	29 U.S.C. §621
Equal Pay Act	Sex	29 U.S.C. §206(d)

*Discrimination claims concerning admissions to educational institutions rely in part on Title VI and on the Equal Protection Clause of the Fourteenth Amendment.

in Title VII[18] became a model for later enacted civil rights legislation concerning employment and for the executive order that is listed in Table 13.1.

Except when courts order affirmative action to remedy documented discrimination, an employer cannot justify a hiring or promotion decision that favors one race over another. There are exceptions for gender. An adverse employment decision based on gender is not illegal if it can be shown that the requirement is justified by the nature of a business or what is referred to as a "bona fide occupational requirement" (BFOQ). For example, the number of jobs available to women in a men's prison may be limited by the potential for violence against women when a high percentage of inmates are imprisoned for violent sex crimes against women,[19] and the gender of personal care attendants in a nursing home may be specified as may the gender of fashion models or actors. In addition, an airline may require a pregnant flight attendant to take a leave of absence since passenger safety is essential to the airline's business, and the ability to respond to emergency situations is a BFOQ for a flight attendant.[20] However, under the Pregnancy Discrimination Act, an adverse employment action that is not justified by a BFOQ would be illegal discrimination.[21]

The EEOC was created under Title VII. The commission's original mandate was to enforce the employment provisions of Title VII. The EEOC's mandate has been expanded to include responsibility for enforcing the employment provisions of all of the statutes listed in Table 13.1, except for the executive order, as well as the Equal Pay Act, which is discussed later. In addition to the enforcement role that is played by the EEOC, the Department of Labor's Office of Contract Compliance studies the employment practices of government contractors. The compliance office has an agreement with the EEOC whereby information concerning workplace practices that may be in violation of the provisions of any statute over which the EEOC has authority are shared.[22]

Proving in court a claim of employment discrimination is a complex procedure, a thorough discussion of which is beyond the scope of this text. In general, the person making the claim charges that the only reason why a job or promotion was denied was due to a personal characteristic such as sex, race, disability, or age that is unrelated to the ability to perform the job in question. To defend against a claim, an employer must offer a nondiscriminatory reason for its actions.

Job discrimination may be intentional, although it is very difficult to prove that an employer intended to discriminate. An alternative explanation focuses on the result of a neutral policy where there is an adverse impact on racial minorities or women. Recall the discussion in chapter 1 of the lawsuit by African American workers against Duke Power Company. The workers claimed that the requirement that applicants for promotion possess a high school diploma and pass a test had a discriminatory impact on them since data showed that they were less likely than white applicants to pass the test and to have a high school diploma. The Supreme Court stated that employment tests are permissible and that the test used by the power company was neutral, meaning that women or men of any race could pass. However, the Court ruled that "neutral" job requirements could survive a court challenge only if they were shown to be necessary to job performance. The power company failed to demonstrate that its employment criteria were necessary.

The simple classification of discriminatory acts as intentional or unintentional but adversely affecting a protected class does not embrace all conduct that violates the law. Some adverse employment decisions reflect what the courts call "mixed motives." Consider the following example.

Ann Hopkins was employed by Price Waterhouse, a nationwide firm that provides financial management services. Hopkins was a candidate for partner, but she was turned down. No one disputed the fact that she had made significant contributions to the firm; her record of procuring contracts was unequalled by any of the firm's partners, and her clients were "very pleased" with her work. Nevertheless, eight of thirty-two partners recommended that she be denied a partnership. Both supporters and detractors referred to her as "overly aggressive, unduly harsh, difficult to work with and impatient with staff. She swore at times and seemed insensitive to others."[23]

Hopkins resigned from the firm. The question before the court was whether the firm's concerns about her interpersonal skills constituted a legitimate and nondiscriminatory reason for the denial of a partnership or whether they were a pretext to disguise sex discrimination.

Hopkins set out two arguments to support her claim of discrimination. First, that the criticisms of her interpersonal skills were false; and second, that the criticisms of her interpersonal skills rested on sexual stereotyping by men and that she was not evaluated as a manager, but as a "women manager." The firm denied that discrimination was at the heart of its decision. Denying Hopkins a partnership was a proper business action, they said, because the firm feared that having an abrasive partner would threaten company morale.

A firm is free to evaluate a candidate's interpersonal skills, the Court ruled, since an "inability to get along with staff or peers is a legitimate, nondiscriminatory reason for refusing to admit a candidate to partnership."[24] But the court found merit in Hopkins' claim of sexual stereotyping because of those in the firm who commented on her bid for partnership, one said that by being assertive she was "overcompensating for being a woman," another suggested that she needed to take a "course at charm school," while another advised her to "walk more femininely, talk more femininely, dress more femininely, wear make-up, have her hair styled, and wear jewelry."[25] There was additional evidence that Hopkins was judged harshly due to her sex. For example, one of her supporters reported that although she did have a difficult personality, many of the men in the firm were "worse" and that her language and personality came into focus "because it's a lady using foul language."[26]

The Court ruled in Hopkins' favor, finding that the decision not to admit her to partnership was tainted by discriminatory evaluations that were the direct result of the firm's failure to address the problem of sexual stereotyping in the way partners evaluated Hopkins. The Court said that "where sex discrimination is present, even if a promotion decision is a mixture of legitimate and discriminatory considerations, uncertainties must be resolved against the employer so that the remedial purposes of Title VII will not be thwarted."

ADVANCEMENT WITHIN A FIRM

In the early days of the civil rights movement, access to entry-level employment opportunities was a central focus of those concerned with implementation of civil rights legislation. As women and racial minorities gained access to jobs, issues concerning advancement came to the fore. Sex stereotyping of the kind experienced by Hopkins as well as racial stereotyping act as barriers to advancement. The term "the glass ceiling" was coined in a 1986 article in the *Wall Street Journal* to describe a "transparent" barrier to promotion that prevents qualified women and minorities from reaching high levels of achievement.[27]

The Civil Rights Act of 1964 was amended in 1991. The amendments included the Glass Ceiling Act, which was passed after Congress found that despite the increased presence of women and minorities in the workplace, both groups were underrepresented in management and decision-making positions in business due to the existence of "artificial barriers" to advancement.[28]

The Glass Ceiling Commission was established in 1991 and authorized to operate for four years.[29] Congress charged the commission with studying the procedures that businesses use to (1) fill management positions; (2) foster staff development; and (3) compensate and reward employees. Data were gathered at public hearings; papers were commissioned; corporate executives were surveyed; and focus groups were held during which Asian and Pacific Islanders, African Americans, and Hispanic/Latino executives were asked to express their views on these matters. The commission issued its final report in November 1995.[30] Some of the identified barriers to the advancement of women and minorities included (1) failure to engage in outreach; (2) a corporate climate that isolates women and minorities; (3) lack of mentoring; (4) lack of management training; (5) clustering minorities and women in positions with little opportunity for advancement; and (6) workplace harassment.

The commission report increased awareness of the existence of the glass ceiling and recommended that data describing diversity in American business be published by the government. Awards for diversity and excellence in corporate management were made. In 1995, the Bureau of Labor Statistics reported that progress had been made for women. There were 7.3 million women employed in management and executive positions, an increase of 31 percent since 1988. The positions were most likely to be in fields dominated by women, such as the service industry. Women were not likely to be managers in industries concerned with manufacturing, construction, transportation, and utilities.[31]

AFFIRMATIVE ACTION

Affirmative action is an imprecise term. It includes a range of initiatives such as outreach where a job announcement states that applications are welcome from "people of color, women, veterans, people with disabilities, and lesbians and gays" and includes efforts to advertise in media likely to reach members of the sought-after groups. Affirmative action includes also (1) voluntary programs to increase workforce or educational diversity; (2) federal requirements that government sponsored programs "ensure that applicants are employed . . . without regard to their race, color, religion, sex or national origin;" (3) set-asides in government contracts; and (4) court-ordered remedies to address documented discrimination.

The roots of affirmative action lie in an executive order issued by President Kennedy in 1961 in which he required government agencies to take affirmative action when entering into contracts. This commitment was reaffirmed by President Johnson in 1967 and by President Nixon in 1969. In 1973, when Congress enacted the VRA, it codified the requirement that federal contractors take affirmative action to employ and promote qualified individuals with disabilities.[32] By 1991, the Supreme Court and the general public were developing a conservative view of affirmative action that is reflected in the 1991 Amendments to the 1964 Civil Rights Act. The amendments state that the act shall not be construed to require or encourage an employer to adopt hiring or promotion quotas on the basis of race, color, religion, sex, or national origin, and private firms cannot be required to incorporate affirmative action programs into their employment strategies unless ordered to do so by a court, after a finding that a private employer has engaged in intentional discrimination.[33]

In 1995, the Supreme Court dealt a severe blow to affirmative action programs when it ruled that all racial classifications imposed by any unit of government would be subject to the strictest standard of review, meaning that the government actor that imposes the race-based scheme must offer a "compelling" reason for the classification and the remedy taken must be limited to addressing the offending behavior.[34] It is almost impossible for government to justify a law that divides people into groups on the basis of race, and at this point in American history it is very likely that the Supreme Court will deem unconstitutional affirmative action programs unless they address a specific and limited history of discrimination by the entity that devised the remedy. [35]

The discussion that follows covers (1) justifications offered for affirmative action programs; (2) the conditions under which affirmative actions programs are permissible; and (3) class-based affirmative action.

JUSTIFICATION FOR AFFIRMATIVE ACTION—COMPENSATION OR DIVERSITY?

The Equal Protection Clause of the Fourteenth Amendment provides that all citizens of the United States will be treated equally under the law. Any affirmative action program that favors a particular group over another creates a conflict with the Equal Protection Clause, and the preference afforded must be justified. Two arguments have been offered in favor of affirmative action programs: affirmative action as compensatory and affirmative action to promote diversity.

The compensatory rationale argues that affirmative action programs are necessary to remedy past discrimination. Diversity is concerned with the present and focuses on the value that is said to adhere from exposure to different groups in the workplace and in educational settings.

House and Senate reports issued prior to passage of the Civil Rights Act of 1964 leave no doubt that compensation for historical discrimination against African Americans was what Congress had in mind when the act was passed.[36] The act originally did not contain any reference to sex, which was added "as a joke" the day before the act was passed. Its addition by Representative Howard Smith, a conservative representative and opponent of civil rights legislation, was meant to derail the entire civil rights bill. Because "sex" was added at the last minute, there is no legislative history to explain the position of Congress on gender-based issues. As to race, Congress said that

> Today, more than 100 years after their formal emancipation, Negroes, who make up over 10 percent of our population, are by virtue of one or another type of discrimination not accorded the rights, privileges, and opportunities which are considered to be, and must be, the birthright of all citizens.[37]

Over time, the compensatory argument has lost some of its moral force. Some people believe that they should not be made to "pay for the sins of their fathers,"[38] and more than thirty-five years after passage of the 1964 act, the compensatory argument leaves open the possibility that this "debt" will be never ending. In addition, a focus on compensation gives rise to disputes about who should benefit from affirmative action programs. For example, compensatory claims made by straight white women and by gays and lesbians do not have the moral force of arguments made by African Americans. There is no question that there has been historical discrimination against women, gays, and lesbians, but when the pie is small as it often is with educational and employment opportunities, compensatory arguments often reduce to issues of who has suffered more or to whom the lion's share of compensation is due.

Diversity as a rationale for affirmative action was first advanced by Justice Lewis Powell in his 1978 decision in *Regents of the University of California v. Bakke*.[39] Alan Bakke was a white male applicant for the university's medical school. Bakke's grades and test scores were above average for the class admitted to the medical school in the year in which he applied. After being denied admission, he sued, alleging "reverse discrimination." Bakke argued that the admission practice of setting aside sixteen of 100 seats for minorities violated his right to equal protection under the Fourteenth Amendment.

Justice Powell voted in favor of racial preferences, though not quotas, if used to "obtain the educational benefits that flow from ethnically diverse student body."[40] Justice Powell stood alone on his position on diversity. Justices Brennan, White, Marshall, and Blackmun supported diversity only if used to "remedy the lingering effects of past discrimination," but Justice Powell said that

> Universities must be accorded the right to select those students who will contribute the most to the "robust exchange of ideas," . . . an otherwise qualified medical student with a particular background—whether it be ethnic, geographic, culturally advantaged or disadvantaged—may bring to a professional school of medicine experiences, outlooks, and ideas that enrich the training of its student body and better equip its graduates to render with understanding their vital service to humanity.[41]

However, Justice Powell concluded that the university's medical program did not further the goal of diversity since race was the only factor considered.

As attractive as the diversity argument may be, it too has its shortcomings that again focus on limited opportunities and raise questions about how to divide the pie. Using a compensatory scheme, and considering the House and Senate Reports with their focus on remedying historical discrimination, it could be argued that the only people of African ancestry who should benefit from affirmative action programs are African Americans. From the standpoint of diversity, however, Africans recently immigrated from the Caribbean and directly from Africa would be as eligible as any other group.

Consider the following and its implications for diversity. In 1996, Cheryl Hopwood, a white women, and three white male applicants to the law school at the University of Texas sued the school for denying them admission, arguing that they were discriminated against on the basis of race.[42] In the recent past, women were "favored" by affirmative action programs operated by law schools because their presence in entering classes was small. In 1965, for example, the percentage of women entering law school was approximately 4 percent. By 1986, the percentage had increased to over 40 percent.[43] The first of two lessons to be learned from *Hopwood* is that a group that is "favored" today may be out of favor tomorrow. It is worth noting that Hopwood's grades on the Law School Admissions Test were high, and that as a "returning student," in her thirties, who was raising a severely handicapped child, she had much to offer from the standpoint of diversity. The second lesson that *Hopwood* teaches is best approached as questions that ask, "If diversity is meant to reflect current demographics and recognizing the extraordinary diversity of the American population at this point in history, how many 'slots' are saved for members of each group?" and "What is the effect on civil society of 'balkanizing' its members and formally announcing that opportunity is limited?"[44]

WHAT KIND OF AFFIRMATIVE ACTION PROGRAMS ARE LEGALLY PERMISSIBLE?

The Fifth Circuit Court of Appeals in the *Hopwood* case ended the use of affirmative action in public institutions in Texas, Louisiana, and Missouri, the three states covered by the Circuit Court. Affirmative action has been ended in California and Washington as a result of voter initiatives. Elsewhere in the country, an affirmative action program is not likely to survive a legal challenge, whether the challenge is on constitutional or statutory grounds, unless it is demonstrated with specificity that the business, educational institution, or other entity has a past record of discrimination.[45] Reference to discrimination in society at large will not salvage the program, and three federal circuit courts covering twelve states have ruled that achieving a diverse workforce or student body is not an acceptable rationale for an affirmative action program.[46] Even when the entity is private and not a recipient of federal funds, its affirmative action program will survive challenge only if the plan: (1) eliminates a conspicuous racial imbalance in jobs that have historically been segregated; (2) does not erect an absolute bar to the interests of white employees; and (3) is temporary, intended to achieve racial balance rather than to maintain racial balance.[47]

The means chosen to remedy the problem must be narrowly tailored to achieve the goal.[48] For example, when there is evidence of past discrimination, courts have broad power to remedy past injustices. The Civil Rights Act provides that

> If the court finds . . . [evidence] of . . . an unlawful employment practice . . . the court may [stop the entity] from engaging in [the] unlawful employment practice, and order such affirmative action as may be appropriate, which may include, but is not limited to, reinstatement or hiring of employees, with or without back pay or any other equitable relief as the court deems appropriate.[49]

To illustrate the extent of permissible relief, consider the following. The Alabama Department of Public Safety engaged in a "blatant and continuous pattern and practice of discrimination in hiring in the Alabama Department of Public Safety, both as to troopers and supporting personnel."[50] The Supreme Court sanctioned a quota system to remedy the blatant discrimination. The department was ordered to undertake a program that required a one-to-one ratio in promotions where one black officer would be promoted for every white officer promoted. The program was necessary, the Court ruled, to remedy prior discrimination.

CLASS-BASED AFFIRMATIVE ACTION

In the late 1970s, Antonin Scalia, then a professor of law at the University of Chicago, noted that recently arrived white immigrants are "to a disproportionate degree . . . the competitors with urban blacks and Hispanics for jobs, education and housing" and these groups of the "unknown, unaffluent, and unorganized" suffer the most for the efforts to correct historical racial injustices.[51]

Others have echoed this concern and have noted that affirmative action programs have benefited mainly the black middle class. Stephen L. Carter, reflecting on his experiences as an "affirmative action baby," makes the point that middle class blacks are the beneficiaries of affirmative action or, stated otherwise, that the greatest benefits go to those with the least need. William Julius Wilson argues that "minority individuals from the most advantaged families tend to be disproportionately represented among those of their racial group most qualified for preferred status, such as college admissions, higher-paying jobs, and promotions." Affirmative action policies, Wilson points out, "enhance opportunities for the more advantaged without adequately remedying the problems of the disadvantaged." Importantly, affirmative action does not open up broad avenues of upward mobility for the masses of disadvantaged blacks. Like other form of "creaming," they provided opportunities for those individuals from low socioeconomic backgrounds with the greatest educational and social resources.[52] Thus, it is argued, that class, not race, should be a basis for preferential admissions, especially in institutions of higher education. In a class-based system, economic disadvantage would replace race or gender as a basis for preferred treatment. A class-based system would, as Kahlenberg states in his book *The Remedy: Class, Race and Affirmative Action*, acknowledge that opportunity in America is not "equal" and that "privilege tends to perpetuate itself."

A class-based system would open doors to economically disadvantaged people regardless of their race or gender and counteract the perpetuation of privilege. And, since "class" is not protected by the Constitution, programs that provide class-based preferences are on stronger grounds than those that base preference on race or gender.

SEXUAL ORIENTATION AND AFFIRMATIVE ACTION

With the exception of President Clinton's executive order banning discrimination based on sexual orientation by federal agencies, sexual orientation protection is not covered under any other federal laws (Table 13.1). The Employment Non-Discrimination Act, which would have extended to lesbians and gays the same employment protections that exist in the 1964 Civil Rights Act, has been introduced in Congress repeatedly but has gone down to defeat each year.[53]

Eleven states cover sexual orientation in their antidiscrimination laws, and there are executive orders in five states that offer the same protections for public employees. In addition, a number of cities and counties protect against discrimination based on sexual orientation.[54] A measure passed by voters in Colorado that denied to lesbians and gays the right to petition elected officials for protective legislation was deemed unconstitutional by the United States Supreme Court.[55] Writing for the Court's majority, Justice Kennedy likened the Colorado legislation that would deny political access based on class membership to the nineteenth century ruling in *Plessy v. Ferguson* and to the dissent of Justice Harlan, who admonished the court that "the Constitution neither knows nor tolerates classes among its citizens."

SEXUAL HARASSMENT

Workplace harassment involves conduct that is perceived as harmful or offensive by the person who is targeted by a co-worker(s) or a supervisor. The offending conduct may involve sexual harassment where the employee is pressured to engage in unwanted sexual contact in exchange for a favorable work rating, promotion, or pay raise (quid pro quo harassment), or the offensive conduct may create a "hostile work environment" by unreasonably interfering with an individual's work performance[56] because of sex,[57] race,[58] or sexual orientation.[59] The offending conduct need not involve "sexual desire" to support a claim of discrimination on the basis of sex. For example, a female office manager may think that clerical work is not appropriate for men and may harass a male employee because of his sex with no implication that she is sexually interested in him. Thus, a lesbian or a gay man may be denied a job based on sexual orientation and have no recourse under Title VII but, once employed, is protected from sexual harassment.[60] The EEOC reports that the number of sexual harassment charges increased from 6,883 in 1991 to 15,618 in 1998. The number of racial harassment charges rose from 4,910 to 9,908 charges in the same time period.[61]

The Supreme Court distinguishes "innocuous conduct, such as teasing, offhand comments, and isolated incidents, that may reflect normative workplace interactions, from conduct that is both objectively and subjectively offensive, [to] a reasonable person."[62] In determining whether an environment is hostile or abusive, courts look at all of the circumstances, including "frequency of discriminatory conduct, its severity, whether it is physically threatening or humiliating or a mere offensive utterance, and whether it unreasonably interferes with an employee's work performance."[63] In essence, the behavior of concern must be so severe as to make it extremely difficult if not impossible for the person who is being harassed to perform her or his job, but the law does not require evidence of "concrete psychological harm."[64]

The employer who fails to take reasonable care to prevent and correct harassment may be liable for the misconduct of an employee.[65] Reasonable care may be demonstrated by disseminating and enforcing antiharassment policies and by putting in place complaint procedures. Effective implementation of policies and procedures is critical. According to the EEOC, the "best policy and complaint procedure will not . . . satisfy the burden of proving reasonable care if . . . the employer failed to implement its process effectively."[66]

Title IX of the Higher Education Amendments of 1972

Title IX prohibits sex discrimination, defined to include employment discrimination and discrimination against women in funding athletic programs, by educational institutions that receive federal funds.[67] Additionally, courts have ruled that Title IX provides a basis for a suit against an educational institution for sexual harassment, which includes harassment by teachers, colleagues, and peers.

Educational institutions include public or private preschools, elementary or secondary schools, trade schools, professional schools, and colleges and universities. Educational institutions that are run by religious organizations are exempt if the provisions of Title IX are inconsistent with the institutions' religious principles.

The Vocational Rehabilitation Act and the Americans with Disabilities Act

Section 501 of the VRA of 1973 and Title I of the ADA of 1990 protect against disability-based discrimination in employment. The VRA and the ADA differ in the following ways: (1) the VRA's prohibition against discrimination is limited to entities receiving federal funds, whereas the ADA protects people with disabilities from discrimination by employers regardless of whether they receive federal funds; (2) protection against discrimination by the executive branch of the federal government is found in the VRA, whereas the ADA protects from discriminatory acts by the Congress, a corporation wholly owned by the federal government, an Indian tribe, or a bona fide private membership club (other than a labor organization)[68]; and (3) the VRA requires affirmative action for the disabled but the ADA does not, because Congress could not impose an affirmative action requirement on private businesses.[69]

The definition of disability is the same under the ADA and the VRA and under the Fair Housing Act (FHA), discussed later, and provisions for determining the rights of the disabled are essentially similar under the VRA and the ADA. Disabled persons are those with a physical or mental impairment that limits significantly their ability to undertake a major life activity that the average person can perform with little or no difficulty, such as "caring for ones-self, performing manual tasks, walking, seeing, hearing, speaking, breathing, learning, and working."[70] The definition also includes those who have a "record" of an impairment. A record may be found where an individual has a history of an impairment or has been misclassified as having a mental or physical impairment that substantially limits one or more major life activities.[71] Covered also are people who are "regarded" as having an impairment.[72] The latter category covers those who have (1) physical disabilities that do not substantially limit a major life activity but who are treated as though they are so limited; (2) physical or mental disabilities that substantially limit a major life activity only as a result of the attitudes of others toward the disability; or (3) no impairments but who are treated as having a substantially limiting impairment.

Anyone who is convicted of illegally manufacturing or distributing controlled substances or who is illegally using or addicted to controlled substances, except for recovering drug abusers who are in treatment programs and not currently using illegal drugs, is not covered by the VRA, ADA, and FHA. The exemption does not affect anyone who is using drugs that are prescribed by a physician.[73]

Court rulings made under the VRA are precedent setting for the ADA, meaning that with few exceptions judges interpret the ADA by referring to cases decided under the VRA.[74] The following discussion is focused mainly on the ADA.

As noted earlier, the employment provisions in the ADA were modeled after Title VII of the Civil Rights Act of 1964. The language of Title I, as with Title VII, states that an employer may not discriminate against qualified individuals with disabilities in the "terms, conditions, and privileges of employment."[75] Title I prevents an employer from (1) using selection criteria that screen out disabled individuals unless the criteria are shown to be job related; (2) conducting medical examinations or making inquiries of applicants or current employees as to whether they have a disability; and (3) administering tests in a manner that highlights disabilities to the detriment of the applicant's abilities.[76] Title I protects from discrimination persons who are excluded from consideration because of their association or relationship with a disabled person.

A disabled person must be "otherwise qualified" to perform the job. An otherwise qualified person is one who has the knowledge and/or skills, experience, education, and other job related requirements so that she or he can perform the essential functions of the job. Essential job functions are the basic duties that define the job. A function may be considered essential if (1) the position exists to perform the function; (2) there are a limited number of employees available to perform the function; or (3) the function is highly specialized.[77]

An employer is required to make reasonable accommodation for the employee who requires accommodation.[78] Reasonable accommodation may include (1) making existing facilities used by employees readily accessible to and usable by individuals with disabilities; (2) restructuring jobs, including part-time or modified work schedules; (3) reassigning individuals to a vacant position; (4) acquiring or modifying equipment or devices; (5) adjusting or modifying as appropriate examinations, training materials, or policies; (6) providing qualified readers or interpreters; and

(7) making other similar accommodations for individuals with disabilities. Whether an accommodation is reasonable is calculated by taking account of a number of factors, including the nature and cost of the accommodation balanced against available resources and the effect of the accommodation on the overall operation of the business.[79]

An example will illustrate how courts determine whether an accommodation is reasonable. In *Nelson v. Thornburgh*,[80] blind income maintenance workers employed by the state of Pennsylvania sued the state. The workers were not able to perform their job, which involved extensive paperwork, without the aid of readers. The workers had hired readers, whose fees they paid themselves, and whose assistance enabled them to meet the requirements of their job as well as their sighted colleagues.

The workers asked the Court to order the state to pay the reader's fees, arguing that this was a reasonable accommodation to their disability. The Court agreed, finding that it would not be an undue hardship for the state of Pennsylvania to pay the fees, which ranged from a low of $1,000 per year to a high of $5,000 per year. This cost was a fraction of the $300 million budget of the department and would not be an undue burden for the department.

An employer is not required to hire a person who poses a direct threat to the health or safety of others, and an employee who contracts a contagious or communicable disease that creates such a risk may be reassigned to a position that reduces or eliminates risk to others.[81] For example, courts have ruled that medical personnel positive for Human Immunodeficiency Virus whose job requires them to perform invasive medical procedures that may pose a threat to others may, as a reasonable accommodation, be reassigned to a position that does not involve patient contact.[82]

ACCESS TO SERVICES

Title II of the Civil Rights Act of 1964 prohibits places of public accommodation from denying access to individuals based on their race. Titles II and III of the ADA provide similar protections for a person with a disability. Title II of the ADA states that qualified individuals with disabilities should not be excluded because of their disability from "services, programs or activities of a public entity."[83] Title III offers the same protection from discrimination by private entities, for example, hotels, places of entertainment, shops, and private providers of social, mental health, and medical services. A qualified individual is one who meets the eligibility criteria for the service or program they are seeking.[84] For example, children in foster care cannot be excluded from adoption programs due solely to their disabilities, nor can a provider of medical services deny service to disabled persons solely on the basis of their disability.

Public entities that are covered by the ADA include state or local government, those acting to achieve governmental ends, and the National Rail Road Passenger Corporation. These entities are obliged, when necessary, to accommodate people with disabilities, including the removal of architectural, communications, or transportation barriers or the provision of auxiliary aids and services.[85] The removal of architectural barriers is required by Title III when removal is "readily achievable."[86] Readily achievable means "easily accomplishable and able to be carried out without much difficulty or expense."[87] The legislative history of the ADA shows that Congress was concerned that the barrier removal provisions in the law not result in businesses closing and loss of jobs and community services if compliance necessitated significant monetary investment. This problem was anticipated in depressed or rural areas where business might operate "at the margin or at a loss."[88] In each case, factors to be considered in determining whether barrier removal is readily achievable involves balancing the nature and cost of the action against the financial resources, number of employees, and business size of the affected entity.

The VRA requires that all of the programs of a recipient of federal financial assistance be available to persons with disabilities. This statute requires major structural changes in existing facilities, if other means are ineffective in achieving program access, thus imposing a higher standard than the ADA's "readily achievable" requirement.

The ADA sets standards for both public and private transportation systems (exclusive of airlines, which are covered by the Air Carrier Access Act)[89] that govern accessibility for new, used, and remanufactured vehicles[90] operated on fixed route systems, which are systems that travel a standard route on a regular schedule, for (1) paratransit systems that public entities must, absent a financial hardship waiver, operate as a complement to fixed route systems to provide transportation to people whose disability precludes use of a fixed route system, and (2) for demand responsive systems, which are any systems that do not meet the definition of a fixed route system.

Age Discrimination in Employment Act

The ADEA provides that employees who are at least forty years of age cannot be refused a job or fired based solely on "arbitrary employment practices," such as establishing age requirements that are not related to the skills that are required for the job. When passed in 1967, the ADEA's protections extended to people age forty to sixty-five. Amendments of 1978 extended the upper age limit to seventy, and in 1986, the upper age limit was eliminated.[91] In addition to preventing arbitrary firing or job denial, the ADEA's preclusion against firing workers over the age of seventy meshes with the pragmatic objective, discussed in chapter 9, of making the Old Age Retirement Program solvent by increasing the age of retirement, which increases funds that are paid into the system by those still working and reduces the benefits paid out. The ADEA also has a social goal, which is to address the problem created when increasing numbers of older workers are not able to find employment after losing their jobs; it reduces the deterioration in skills and the lowering of morale.[92]

Reasonable age limits may be set if they constitute BFOQ, and retirement ages are not arbitrary if they are bona fide. Courts have held, for example, that mandatory retirement ages as low as age fifty for police work are not arbitrary, nor is a mandatory retirement age for bus drivers.[93]

Equal Pay Act

The Equal Pay Act of 1963 prohibits gender-based discrimination in the payment of wages for equal work on jobs requiring equal skill, effort, and responsibility, performed under similar working conditions. Congress passed the act after finding that gender-based wage differentials affected interstate commerce. There are exceptions to the equal pay requirement, where pay differentials may not be discriminatory when they are based on a seniority system or a merit system.[94]

Equal pay should not be confused with the movement for "comparable" pay, which Congress rejected because of the "impossible task of ascertaining the worth of comparable work." Although equal pay assumes equivalent positions, comparable pay requires classifying jobs on objective criteria and determining that the skill necessary to perform jobs "A" and "B" are the same even though the jobs themselves are not.[95]

The Fair Housing Act

The FHA of 1968 proscribed housing practices that discriminated on the basis of race, color, national origin, or religion. The FHA was amended in 1974 by adding gender as a protected class and again in 1988 when protection was extended to disabled individuals and to families with children, including foster families. The FHA's protections extend beyond the disabled individual to protect also those who reside with or associate with the individual who has a disability.[96]

The FHA prohibits discrimination (1) in the sale or rental of a building or part of any building that is used, designed, or intended to be a residence for one or more families, and any vacant land that is offered for sale or lease for the construction of a residential building[97]; and (2) in activities associated with the rental and sale of housing such as advertising, financing, and the provision of brokerage services.[98] Precluded also are actions that coerce, intimidate, threaten, or interfere with the rights of any person covered by the FHA, or of a person who assists another in exercising their rights.[99]

Exempt from coverage are (1) noncommercial buildings that are owned or operated by religious organizations; (2) private clubs whose facilities are not open to the public; (3) housing for older persons; and (4) single-family housing sold or rented by an owner, if the owner does not own more than three single-family houses at the same time.[100]

The law sets standards for construction of new multifamily dwellings to increase the supply of housing for people with disabilities. Multifamily dwellings are buildings with four or more units with elevators or ground floor units in nonelevator buildings. The law requires that residential units be accessible and adaptable. For example, doors and hallways must be wide enough to accommodate wheelchairs, and light switches must be in convenient locations. A disabled person should be able to make changes easily by installing grab bars in the bathroom, if needed, without major renovations or changes in the structure of the dwelling.[101]

A property owner's obligation to a prospective tenant does not extend to the person whose tenancy creates a direct threat and substantial risk of harm to the health and safety of others because of current conduct or a history of overt acts. However, generalizations about people and assumptions, subjective fears, and speculation are not enough to establish that a person poses a direct threat. The property owner must obtain references to aid in evaluating an applicant as a candidate for tenancy. Inferences that a recent history of a physical or mental illness or disability or treatment for such illnesses or disabilities constitutes proof that an applicant will be unable to fulfill his or her tenancy obligations may not be drawn.[102]

Moreover, the proviso that a property owner need not rent to a person who poses a direct threat does not give the property owner a grant to query prospective tenants about matters that are unrelated to their ability to meet requirements for tenancy. Permissible questions include those regarding a person's rental history or inquiries that focus on whether a person has acted in a manner that would pose a direct threat to the health or safety of other tenants, but blanket questions about whether an individual has a disability are illegal. A property owner may not make inquiries that would require the individual to disclose or waive his or her right to confidentiality concerning his or her medical condition or history. The only exception is that a prospective tenant may be asked about current illegal abuse of or addiction to controlled substances.

Summary

Provisions in the Civil Rights Act of 1964 that protect against discrimination in employment on the basis of race, color, sex, national origin, and religion have been the focus of our attention. In addition, we have explored affirmative action programs that courts sanction under the employment provisions of the Civil Rights Act, and we have looked at protection against workplace harassment based on sex, race, and sexual orientation.

Since passage of the Civil Rights Act in 1964, a range of civil rights statutes have been acted. These statutes protect (1) people with disabilities from discrimination in employment, and they require that people with disabilities have access to places of public accommodation; (2) people over the age of forty from adverse employment decisions based on age; (3) young women from funding schemes that deny monies to women's athletic programs and that protect students and teachers from sexual harassment by colleagues and peers; (4) against illegal discrimination in the rental or sale of property due to a person's race, color, sex, national origin, religion, or disability; and (5) against gender-based discrimination in the payment of wages for equal work when jobs require equal skill, effort, and responsibility and are performed under similar working conditions.

The Civil Rights Act of 1964 does not afford any protection for lesbians and gay men who claim employment discrimination based on their sexual orientation, and efforts to enact federal legislation offering this protection have failed. Ironically, although a lesbian or gay man is not protected from a discriminatory job action, she or he is protected against sexual harassment in the workplace. Limited protection against discrimination based on sexual orientation is found in an executive order issued by President Clinton prohibiting employment discrimination by federal agencies and by the laws of some states, cities, and towns.

Affirmative action programs were discussed at length. Such programs were developed to compensate for discrimination that denied to people of color and women the opportunity to receive an advanced education and to work. Over time, the compensatory rationale has given way to a focus on diversity, with its emphasis on creating an educational workforce whose profile resembles the community-at-large. Since affirmative action programs favor people based on race or gender, they must be reconciled with the constitutional mandate that people be treated equally under the law without regard to such personal characteristics.

In 1995, the Supreme Court dealt a severe blow to affirmative action programs when it ruled that government-imposed racial classifications would be strictly scrutinized by the Court, making it highly unlikely that any affirmative action program will survive a legal challenge unless there is a clear record of past discrimination by the entity whose program is challenged. In addition, voter initiatives have severely restricted the use of affirmative action programs in California and Washington, and three federal circuit courts have severely circumscribed their use in other states.

Opponents of affirmative action argue that preferences given should rest on "class," not race or gender. This position stems from a combination of experience and conviction that people from the middle class have been the prime beneficiaries of affirmative action and that the cost of the advantage given has fallen on students of minorities and women who come from economically disadvantaged backgrounds.

PART

IV

Social services refers to both organizational arrangements and to forms of problem-solving assistance. The organization of social services through the private and public sectors was discussed in chapter 3, where "privatization" was reviewed and where some distinctions were drawn between public and private sector social service agencies.

For the sake of convenience, I use the term social services to embrace all forms of helping of concern to social workers and other mental health professionals that do not involve the provision of cash, coupons, or vouchers that can be used to obtain goods and services or direct payment by a unit of government to a service provider, as with the Medicaid or Medicare programs.

Social services take a variety of forms ranging from the simple to the complex. When a unit of government funds day care for a child, the provided service is relatively simple in that it can be described with reference to (1) whether the program is custodial or educational, (2) the number of hours per day or per week that the child receives care, (3) the activities in which the child is engaged, and (4) whether related services such as nutritional services are provided. Other social services are more complex. Foster care, for example, is a service for children whose parents cannot or will not care for them. The complexity of the provided service compared to the day care example lies in the following: the provision of foster care services involves multiple actors, such as a protective service worker who conducted an investigation into a report of neglect or abuse and who recommended the child's placement after a finding of neglect, a home-finding worker who locates a foster family for the child, and a foster care worker who provides services to the child, the birth family, and to the foster family and who must answer the question, "Can this child safely be returned to the care of the parents?" In addition, the provision of foster care frequently involves actors from different systems, for instance, the juvenile or family court judge who approves the child's placement and reviews the child's case on a regular basis, attorneys for the public agency and often for the child, and parents as well as medical providers and social workers in private agencies who, working under a purchase-of-service contract with a public agency, provide services such as family counseling.

From a client's perspective, the value of social services cannot be understated. Discharge services provided by a hospital-based social worker who arranges for homemaker and visiting nurse services may make the difference between a person having to enter a long-term care nursing facility or being able to remain at home. Other services, such as job training or assistance in job search, transportation services, and child care may make the difference between attaining independence or remaining on welfare.

Social services are funded mainly, but not exclusively, through the use of block grants, which were discussed in previous chapters, for example, in chapter 9 where the Temporary Assistance for Needy Families (TANF) Block Grant was reviewed, in chapter 11 where block grants for food and housing were discussed, and in chapter 12 where block grants to provide health care were described.

Block grants are attractive to policymakers for both practical and political reasons. At a practical level, government officials may favor them because program costs are predetermined. Recall the discussion in chapter 10 of the TANF program, which ended the cash entitlement that had existed under the Aid to Families with Dependent Children Program (AFDC). The open-ended nature of AFDC meant that program costs could vary considerably in relation to the employment rate and the increased demand for aid when unemployment was high. With a block grant, government officials know in advance what a program will cost, and this is a significant advantage in budgeting. Some block grants are limited use, for example, providing a specific service to a targeted population; the Maternal and Child Health Block Grant described in chapter 12 is an example. Funding for other block grants is flexible, meaning that state and local officials have discretion in deciding how the grant will be spent. Flexible grants may be used to fund a variety of programs that take into account local need.

Block grants have another practical aspect that lies in the permission granted by Congress to local officials to transfer funds from one grant to another. This was referred to in chapter 10, where I reported that states may transfer up to 30 percent of funds from the TANF block grant to the Child Care Development Block Grant. Finally, block grants are politically attractive because they send a message to recipients that there is no entitlement to government assistance, and they reduce the federal role in deciding what services are most helpful by transferring decision-making authority to state and local units of government that are better able to make decisions concerning local need.

As you read the material in this part, recall the cautionary note in chapter 11 where I said that if you understand how a program defines "beneficiary" and if the benefit is clearly defined, as with a program that provides cash assistance or food stamps, you know exactly what was provided to program participants. Programs that provide social services often provide a range of services, and how many of the available services were received by each beneficiary may not be readily apparent. For example, a participant in the Supplemental Nutrition Program for Women, Infants, and Children (WIC) may receive a referral for nutrition and health services, vouchers or checks that can be redeemed for food items, or infant formula. Programs that provide a range of services may report the number of participants but not link the number reported to any specific program component.

There are three chapters in this part of the text. Chapter 14 is general in that it describes funding sources for a broad range of social services. Chapter 15 focuses on child welfare services, including prevention and protection, foster care and adoption services, and child support. Education is the subject of chapter 16, where policies that support education for disadvantaged children and the social services provided by some educational programs are discussed.

CHAPTER 14

Social Services

Social services to assist clients move from welfare to independence, aid in problem solving, and improve physical health and sustain physical well-being have been referred to at several points in this text, including chapter 1, where reference was made to the provision of casework services to help families become self-supporting; chapter 9, where job-related services for adult recipients of aid under the Temporary Assistance to Needy Families Program (TANF) were reviewed; chapter 11, where services to assess nutritional risk to pregnant women and assist with medical and nutritional needs were discussed, and where services to assist the elderly, people with disabilities, and the homeless meet their housing needs were covered; chapter 12, where medical services provided by physicians, nurses, and other health care providers were identified; and chapter 13, where civil rights statutes and the prohibitions they contain against denying services to people on the basis of race, sex, or disability were reviewed.

Social services in the United States are provided by the public sector, the voluntary not-for-profit sector, and for-profit agencies. The public sector administers a variety of programs, such as those organized to determine a client's eligibility for financial assistance, medical or food assistance, or any of the social services. The voluntary sector consists of "mainstream" agencies, particularly those operated by faith-based groups and other philanthropic organizations and by grass-roots groups that address problems that public agencies and mainstream organizations do not address. For example, recall the discussion in chapter 5 of the Acquired Immune Deficiency Syndrome (AIDS) epidemic and the fact that the federal government did not act to assist people with AIDS until 1990, almost a full decade after the first cases of AIDS were diagnosed. The service gap was filled by grassroots activity, including fund raising and service provision.[1]

The federal government was not involved in funding social services for welfare recipients until 1956.[2] From 1956 until 1962, services funded with federal dollars were available only through public agencies. In 1962 and again in 1968, Congress amended the Social Security Act to allow public agencies to enter into contracts to purchase from not-for-profit agencies services the public agency had previously provided. Some public agencies are including performance goals in their contracts, where payment for services is contingent upon achieving preset targets. For example, North Carolina pays private adoption agencies for their work with adoptive parents. Sixty percent of the per case fee is paid when children are placed in an adoptive home; 20 percent, when an adoption decree is issued; and the final 20 percent, after one year of uninterrupted placement.[3]

Table 14.1 lists by name and purpose a series of block grants that fund services, the amount of money allocated to each block grant in fiscal year 1999, and the source of statutory authority for each. For the listed grants, funds are provided to the states, which in turn distribute monies to local units of government and, in some cases, directly to voluntary agencies that provide services under contract to the state. In limited cases, the Ryan White Comprehensive AIDS Resources Emergency Act (CARE act), for example, funds bypass the state government and go directly to local units of government.

In addition to funding specific social services such as treatment for the mentally ill or those with a substance abuse problem, the federal government undertakes "initiatives" where a social problem is identified, and the states are encouraged to use block grant funds to develop and implement programs that address the problem identified. Alternatively, a federal agency may directly fund demonstration programs that seek to identify ways of resolving the problem that is the focus of the initiative. For example, in 1997, President Clinton announced that the Department of Health and Human Services would support an initiative to prevent teen pregnancy. Toward this end, some states use block grant funds, for example, funds allocated under the Title XX Social Services Block Grant, even though prevention of teen pregnancy is not referred to in the statute that authorizes the grant.

As shown in Table 14.1, significant sums of money are provided through the various grant programs, and it is difficult to gain a perspective on what exactly the billions of dollars in program funds provide. How much service is purchased for the involved sum? A simple example will be helpful to put this matter into perspective. The Ryan White CARE Act funds the provision of prescription medication for people with AIDS through the AIDS Drug Assistance Program (ADAP). In 1998, federal funds combined with state funds were in excess of $510 million. In June 1998, ADAP programs served 53,765 clients at a monthly cost of $747 per client for a monthly bill of more than $40 million. Despite the sum of money involved, eleven states had to cap enrollment for their programs and create a waiting list of more than 2,500 people; six states limited access to the most expensive medications; and fourteen states reported that they would run out of money before the end of the fiscal year.[4] In reviewing the material in this chapter, you will see that this shortfall is not unusual.

In the following pages we will review the block grants that are listed in Table 14.1. Other block grants that provide services are not discussed, including (1) the

TABLE 14.1. Social Services Grants by Title, Purpose, Allocated Funds in 1999 and Statutory Authority

Name	Purpose	Funding	Statutory authority
Title XX Social Service Block Grant	To provide at state discretion a range of social services whose purpose is the reduction of economic dependency and the prevention of problems such as child abuse and supporting home-based over institutional care	$2.4 billion	42 U.S.C. §1397
Ryan White CARE Act	Financial assistance to state and local units of government to provide a range of services for people with HIV and AIDS	$1.5 billion	42 U.S.C. §300ff
Community Mental Health Services Block Grant	To provide comprehensive community mental health services to adults with serious mental illness and to children with serious emotional disturbance. Demonstration project funds are available for counseling for people who learn that they are HIV positive and to assist mentally ill homeless people make a transition from homelessness	$466 million	42 U.S.C. §300x
Substance Abuse Prevention and Treatment Block Grant	To support primary prevention services, treatment and rehabilitation services for individuals with alcohol and drug abuse problems; special services must be provided for pregnant women and women with dependent children	$1.58 billion	42 U.S.C. §290bb
Older Americans Act	To develop and implement comprehensive community-based services provided at home and at senior centers	$300 million	42 U.S.C. §3001
Violence Against Women Act	To reduce the incidence of gender-based violence, provide police training, coordinate law enforcement efforts, and provide public education services to victims of domestic violence and to fund demonstration programs to reduce domestic violence	$1.6 billion for 1994 through 1999	42 U.S.C. §13981

Source: Compiled by the author.

Low-Income Home Energy Assistance Block Grant that provided slightly more than $1 billion in 1999 to aid the elderly and people with disabilities pay the costs of home heating and that provided grants for use in paying for home weatherization; (2) the Safe and Drug Free Schools and Communities Grant that provided approximately $566 million in 1999 to prevent illegal drug use among students and violence in and around schools as well as funding educational, cultural, and recreational activities before and after school; and (3) the Preventive Health and Health Services Block Grant, funded at $1.5 million in 1999, to support local health departments in their efforts at rodent control and to fund studies to test ways to provide emergency medical services for children and for victims of sex offenses as well as to prevent sex offenses.

Title XX Social Services Block Grant

In 1956 when the federal government became involved in funding social services, Congress offered to assist the states by paying for 50 percent of the costs of provided services, but few states accepted this offer. Convinced that social services were essential to reducing welfare dependency, Congress increased the incentive in 1962 by agreeing to pay for 75 percent of the costs of services. Funding was open-ended, meaning that the federal government would fund 75 percent of the costs of whatever services the states chose to provide. A number of states responded aggressively to the increased federal contribution, and federal costs soared from $281.6 million in fiscal year 1967 to $1.688 billion in fiscal year 1972.[5] In 1972, as a cost-control measure, Congress capped the federal share of social service expenditures at $2.5 billion. This sum was to be divided among the states based on their relative populations. In 1996, the average state received $50 million.[6]

In 1975, Congress established the Title XX Social Service Block Grant Program as part of the Social Security Act.[7] The $2.5 billion cap was retained as was the formula for allocating funds. Title XX is an entitlement program where the beneficiary is the state, not the individual, which was the case with entitlements such as Medicaid and Supplemental Security Income (SSI). States are not required to match federal funds. Yearly appropriations for Title XX have fluctuated, and the value of the Title XX funds decreased in constant dollars by 67 percent between 1977 and 1997. Title XX funds for fiscal year 1999 were $1.9 billion. Congress has reduced authorizations to $1.7 billion for fiscal year 2002 and thereafter, signaling a significant decline in the federal commitment to this social service block grant.[8]

Federal funds may be used to assist individuals and families (1) achieve or maintain economic self-support to prevent, reduce, or eliminate dependency; (2) achieve or maintain self-sufficiency, including reduction or prevention of dependency; (3) prevent or remedy neglect, abuse, or exploitation of children and adults, or preserve, rehabilitate or reunite families; (4) prevent or reduce inappropriate institutional care by providing for community-based care, home-based care, or other forms of less intensive care; and (5) secure referral or admission for institutional care when other forms of care are not appropriate, or to provide services to individuals in institutions.[9]

Services that will meet federal goals are suggested by the Department of Health and Human Services and include (1) child care, (2) adult day care, (3) child and adult protective services, (4) services for children and adults in foster care, (5) in-home services, (6) transportation services, (7) family planning services, (8) job training and employment services, (9) information and referral, (10) counseling, (11) food preparation and delivery, (12) health support services, and (13) services designed to meet the needs of children, the aged, the mentally retarded, the blind, the emotionally disturbed, the physically handicapped, and alcoholics and drug addicts. In addition, Title XX funds may be used for administrative purposes such as program planning and evaluation, training and retraining personnel to provide service, and conferences or workshops. In 1993, Congress authorized the Empowerment Zone and Enterprise Community (EZ/EC) Program to fund economic development in "distressed communities." Funds are used for a variety of purposes, such as providing new businesses with start-up monies, financing needed communications services, and expanding employment opportunities. The 1993 authorization allowed the use of Title XX funds to bolster EZ/EC efforts by allowing funds to be used for otherwise prohibited activities such as purchasing and improving land or providing cash to individuals to assist with medical needs.[10]

A state may transfer up to 10 percent of its Title XX funds to the Title V Maternal and Child Health Care Block Grant (see chapter 12), to the Alcohol, Drug Abuse, and Mental Health Services Block Grant (see below) and to certain other limited block grants.[11]

States are required to file an annual Title XX Report with the Department of Health and Human Services in which they identify the provided services, the number of adults and children served, and the amount of money spent on services for children and adults. Eligibility criteria for each service are to be specified, and whether the service was provided by a public or private agency is to be reported.[12] Despite this extensive reporting requirement, there are no data that describe accurately the number of service recipients. States "estimate" how many people were served by Title XX programs using a variety of statistical procedures whose validity may not provide precise estimates. In 1997, an estimated 9.26 million people, 5.5 million of whom were children, received services funded by Title XX.[13]

Table 14.2 lists services offered using Title XX funds by the number of states offering each type of service and the percent of Title XX funds used for each service in 1995, the last year for which data are available. States have discretion in the categories they use to describe expenditures, making direct comparisons across categories impossible.

All states used some funds for child day care, which consumed the greatest percentage of funds expended for any one service. Services that directly support a state's child welfare mission appear in several categories, including adoption services, foster care services for children, and protective services for children. It is likely that some of the child day care funds also support child welfare services and case management services as well as home-based services, which include homemaker, chore services, and home health.

Precisely what services are provided and whether provided services are limited

TABLE 14.2. Title XX Services Offered by Number of States Offering Each Service and Percent of Funds Allocated to Each Service: 1995

Service	Number of states	Percent of funds
Adoption	35	.1
Case management	33	4.3
Counseling	22	1.3
Day care: adults	29	0.8
Day care: children	51	14.8
Education training	18	0.9
Emergency	14	n.i.
Employment	19	1.1
Family planning	20	1.1
Foster care: adults	15	0.7
Foster care: children	41	10.4
Health related	21	0.6
Home based*	45	10.3
Home delivered/congregate meals	22	0.7
Housing services	12	0.2
Information and referral	27	0.8
Legal	12	0.4
Independent/transitional living	21	0.4
Prevention/intervention†	42	6.8
Pregnancy and parenting	n.i.	0.4
Protective: adults	35	2.1
Protective: children	44	11.0
Residential care/treatment	26	3.9
Social support‡	27	n.i.
Special services for children	16	n.i.
Special services for the disabled	33	3.9
Special services for youth at risk	19	2.0
Substance abuse services	12	0.3
Services for unmarried parents	17	n.i.
Transportation	29	0.6
Other§	32	6.1
Administrative	n.i.	12.9

Source: Compiled by the author from data in House, Committee on Ways and Means, "Section 10: Title XX Social Services Block Grant Program," *Green Book* (Washington, D.C., 1998), 719, 720.
Note: n.i., no information.
*Includes homemaker, chore, home health, companionship, and home maintenance.
†Includes investigation/assessment, family-centered early intervention, home evaluation and supervision, preventive and restoration.
‡Includes socialization, recreation, camping, physical activity, living skills (money management), day treatment, family development, social adjustment, community living services, family management services, life skills education, personal and financial management.
§Includes social services in correctional facilities, services to Hispanics, homeless services, Indian reservation services, and refugee minority programs.

to any recipient category, such as children or the elderly, are not clear from many of the categories used. For example, "emergency, employment, health related, housing and counseling" services are not self-defining. The number of states that provide each type of service indicates that one of the objectives of Title XX, namely, to provide discretion to the states in services offered, is being met. Although the number of states that allocate funds to administrative costs is not indicated, it is reasonable to assume that all of the states direct some of their Title XX funding in this way.

Ryan White Comprehensive AIDS Resources Emergency Act

In June 1999, more than 288,000 cases of AIDS had been diagnosed in the United States. Due to the availability of new pharmaceuticals to treat infection by the Human Immunodeficiency Virus (HIV), the number of people whose infection progressed to full-blown AIDS decreased 18 percent between 1996 and 1997, although the rate of decrease slowed after that time. Deaths related to AIDS decreased by 42 percent between 1996 and 1997 and by 20 percent from 1997 to 1998. Along with a reduction in mortality, there has been a 10 percent increase in the number of people whose life has been extended through the use of new medications.[14]

The CARE act of 1990 was the first comprehensive legislation passed to deal with the AIDS epidemic. The act was discussed briefly in chapter 12 in the context of reviewing health care provisions. Federal grants are made to the states and local units of government to assist them in their efforts to help people with the HIV and AIDS. The CARE act funds have increased from $200 million in fiscal year 1991 to more than $1.4 billion for fiscal year 1999.[15]

In the following pages, the titles of the CARE act and the services made available through each title are reviewed in detail. Before beginning our discussion, you should know that assistance for people with HIV/AIDS is available through other programs. For example, the Medicaid program is a major source of funding to meet the medical costs of treating people with HIV/AIDS, and people with AIDS are disabled and eligible for income support under the SSI program that was discussed in chapter 10. In addition, housing assistance is available through the Housing Assistance for People with AIDS act that was reviewed in chapter 11.

TITLE I: CARE ACT EMERGENCY RELIEF GRANT PROGRAM

Title I funds are provided directly to cities or counties that have been hardest hit by the epidemic. Eligible municipalities are those with a population of 500,000 or more who have reported more than 2,000 confirmed AIDS cases to the Centers for Disease Control in the five years preceding the grant application.[16] The municipalities' chief elected official is charged with creating a health services planning council, whose members include representatives of provider groups (i.e., those providing health, mental health, and social services), individuals with HIV and AIDS, and members of the communities affected by the epidemic. Council membership is to reflect the demographics of the epidemic in the area covered by the council.

In selecting members, Congress has directed that special attention be paid to "disproportionately affected and historically underserved groups and subpopulations."[17] Councils develop comprehensive plans for the organization and delivery of services, and they allocate funds according to the priorities they establish. Funds may be granted to public or not-for-profit groups, such as hospitals, community-based organizations, including hospices and health centers, and ambulatory care facilities, to provide health and support services on an outpatient basis. Services may include case management, substance abuse treatment, mental health treatment, and prophylactic treatment for opportunistic infections. Funds may be used to provide inpatient services if their purpose is to prevent further unnecessary hospitalization or to expedite hospital discharge.[18]

TITLE II: CARE ACT GRANTS

Under Title II, funds are provided to the states without restrictions based on the number of AIDS cases or incidence in the population, thus making CARE act funding available for services in small cities and rural areas whose caseloads do not satisfy the eligibility requirements of Title I. Improving the "quality, availability and organization of health care and support services for individuals and families with HIV and AIDS disease" is the general purpose of Title II.[19] Grants may be used to establish and operate HIV-care consortia, which are associations of one or more public providers and one or more nonprofit providers of service who organize to plan, develop, and deliver services. Services are to be delivered through consortia, where possible, or through purchase contracts with organizations that are not part of a consortium. Services may include outpatient health and mental health services and support services, such as home health and hospice care, attendant care, homemaker services, day or respite care, benefits advocacy, transportation, nutritional services, referrals for housing, and foster care and adoption services. Title II provides for HIV testing for pregnant women and newborns and for a range of medical services to prevent hospitalization, including the provision of durable medical equipment; day treatment or other partial hospitalization services; home-based drug therapy programs, including prescription drugs administered as part of therapy; routine diagnostic testing; and, where appropriate, mental health, developmental, and rehabilitation services.

Title II grants may be used to provide financial assistance to eligible low-income individuals to maintain their health insurance. The AIDS Drug Reimbursement Program, which provides financial assistance to procure medications used to treat the HIV, is part of Title II.[20] And Title II funds are used to provide health care services that are not covered by Medicaid and to serve people not eligible for Medicaid.

In addition to the above, Titles I and II require grantees to provide health and support services to women, infants, children, and youth, including treatments to prevent perinatal transmission of HIV. The percent of funds allocated to services for women and their families must equal the percent of women with families with AIDS in the grant area.[21]

TITLE III: CARE ACT EARLY INTERVENTION SERVICES

Title III funds are available for early intervention services, including referrals for health services and referrals to programs offering experimental treatments; counseling and testing for HIV; and clinical, diagnostic, and therapeutic services. Services are to be provided on an outpatient basis, and 50 percent of funds must go to primary health care centers and migrant health centers that serve the homeless.[22] Counseling that accompanies HIV testing must include information regarding the benefits of testing, early diagnosis, and treatment as well as ways to prevent exposure to and transmission of the HIV. Those counseled must be told that medical information is confidential, that anonymous counseling and testing are available, and that they must be given information regarding their rights to protection against illegal discrimination.

TITLE IV: GRANTS FOR COORDINATED SERVICES AND ACCESS TO RESEARCH FOR WOMEN, INFANTS, CHILDREN, AND YOUTH

Through Title IV, grants are available to providers of primary health care so that women, infants, children, and youth will have the opportunity to participate in research that has the potential for producing clinical benefits. Grantees must provide outpatient health care to women and their families and must include case management services, transportation services, child care services, and other support services needed to enable women and their families to participate in research programs. Programs must make referrals for inpatient hospital services, substance abuse treatment, and other needed support services.[23] Grantees must agree that by the end of the second year of a grant, the number of women and youngsters participating in research projects will be significant.

SPECIAL PROJECT OF NATIONAL SIGNIFICANCE

Grants may be made in any fiscal year to projects of national significance.[24] These are projects serving people with HIV and AIDS that have a potential for replication and may include projects that (1) increase the number of health care facilities that serve low-income individuals and families; (2) provide drug abuse and health care services; (3) support respite care services in minority communities to facilitate participation in family-based care networks; and (4) provide health care and support services to underserved populations such as minorities, including Native Americans, people in rural areas, the homeless, and prisoners.

USE OF CARE ACT FUNDS

The CARE act funds have been used for a variety of purposes geared primarily to enable people with HIV and AIDS to remain in their communities by avoiding unnecessary hospitalizations and by receiving help with rent payments. In 1995, the House of Representatives, hearing testimony on the subject of reauthorization of the CARE act, was told that funds were used (1) in Houston, to provide free dental care, day treatment, and nutrition services; (2) in Dallas, to refurbish and upgrade housing to create homes for people with AIDS; (3) in Atlanta, to prepare and deliver meals to people at home; (4) in Florida, Hawaii, Minnesota, and Wisconsin, to pay the health insurance premiums of people with AIDS; (5) in Denver, to expand the capacity to provide primary care services, including an AIDS-specific clinic and on-site pharmacy at a local hospital; (6) in Utah, to develop a system of community-health centers; and (7) in Missouri, to provide primary health care through a network of 116 primary care physicians who served people living in rural areas, including those with no health insurance. In addition, primary health care services have been supported by CARE act funds in Baltimore, Denver, Los Angeles, Maryland, and South Carolina. In New York, CARE act funds have been used for outreach programs that have informed more than 5,000 Native Americans of services available to them. Twenty-six states used Title IV funds to develop health-related services specifically for women, youth, infants, and children and to provide for developed services through 199 clinical sites.[25]

Mental Health and Substance Abuse

The Substance Abuse and Mental Health Services Administration (SAMSHA) was established in 1982.[26] Within SAMSHA are (1) the Center for Mental Health Services, (2) the Center for Substance Abuse Prevention, and (3) the Center for Substance Abuse Treatment.[27] We begin with a description of the objectives Congress sought to achieve when it established the Center for Mental Health (CMH).

THE MENTAL HEALTH PROBLEM

An estimated 15 to 18 percent of the population of the United States experience mental health problems each year,[28] with 5.5 million people experiencing problems so severe as to require inpatient care.[29] Required treatment is paid for in a variety of ways, including (1) out-of-pocket payments, (2) private insurance, (3) employer-provided insurance, and (4) publicly funded programs including Medicaid, Medicare, the Mental Health Block Grant, and the CARE act.

Until the 1960s, the states paid for most of the costs of caring for the mentally ill. Since then, the federal government has shared in the cost through various grant programs and through the Medicare and Medicaid programs. Medicare and Medicaid together provide approximately 40 percent of the revenue of mental health treatment facilities, and some states provide additional mental health services at their own expense.[30] The Mental Health Block Grant provided $466 million in 1999 for community-based services that emphasize outpatient and short-term inpatient care.

Despite the amount of money spent on mental health services, Bachman (1996) reports that four of the six states that she studied had limited resources to provide mental health services. For example, she reports that officials in Tennessee estimated that only 35 percent of their mentally ill population would be served. Officials in New York and Massachusetts estimated that at least "some" services would be provided to all members of the state's priority population.[31]

The locus of care for people with mental illness has shifted from congregate settings located outside urban centers to community-based care provided in psychiatric units in general hospitals, hospitals run by the Veteran's Administration, residential treatment centers for children and youth, community mental health centers, and the offices of private practitioners.

DEINSTITUTIONALIZATION

Over time, the needs of people with mental health problems have been met in diverse settings including, in Colonial times, their own homes, almshouses, and specially constructed "shacks and huts" that were built for people whose problem manifested itself in violence. In the nineteenth century, the "insane" were cared for in large congregate facilities that gave way in the early 1960s to the era of deinstitutionalization.[32] Deinstitutionalization refers to (1) preventing unnecessary institutional admissions, (2) moving people housed in large congregate facilities to community-based placements where their adjustment to life outside of an institution might be hastened, and (3) developing and implementing programs in the community to meet the needs of the mentally ill on an outpatient basis. The population of state mental hospitals in the 1950s was approximately 500,000, which, by 1987, had decreased to approximately 130,000.[33]

Deinstitutionalization was fueled by (1) the Civil Rights movement of the 1960s, which supported the belief that persons not dangerous to themselves and others had a right to choose not to be hospitalized; (2) a philosophy that treatment would be more effective if delivered in the community where a person lived; (3) the availability of Medicaid funds to support care in nursing homes whose population of psychiatric patients over the age of 65 increased from 188,000 in 1963 to 368,000 in 1969 while the population in large congregate institutions fell from 153,000 in 1962 to 78,000 in 1972[34]; (4) the use of antipsychotic drugs such as Thorazine that made it possible to control the symptoms of mental illness; and (5) evidence that documented state mistreatment of the institutionalized mentally ill. The latter included the neglect that was evident in the deteriorating facilities where people were warehoused, the lack of treatment, and the state's abuse of its power to commit mentally ill people.

A series of federal court decisions hastened the movement to community-based care. The Supreme Court acknowledged the power of the state to commit people who cannot care for themselves,[35] but set ground rules that narrowed the conditions for civil commitment of the mentally ill that limited new admissions to mental hospitals. The Supreme Court held that a person has due process protections, such as the right to a hearing if held for more than forty-eight hours, the right to receive notice prior to commitment, and the right to counsel.[36] The state cannot confine a person who has not committed a crime and who is not dangerous, the Court ruled.[37] In addition, a series of lawsuits raised public awareness of and concern about the care and treatment of people in congregate facilities, and courts rendered judgments ordering the closure of facilities and the placement of those housed in facilities in community settings.[38]

Congress supported the move to deinstitutionalize congregate care hospitals when it passed the Community Mental Health Centers Act of 1963, 1976 amendments to the act, and the Mental Health Systems Act of 1980.[39] These acts supported the creation of community mental health centers (CMHCs) by making available federal funds for construction and by requiring that centers provide inpatient, outpatient, partial hospitalization, emergency, and consultation education services.[40] However, regulations did not require that state hospital discharges be directed to community mental health centers nor that CMHCs and state hospitals coordinate their efforts on behalf of the mentally ill.[41] Moreover, the funds that are saved when an institution is downsized are not necessarily directed toward CMHCs.[42] The Community Mental Health Centers Act was repealed in 1981 and was replaced by the Mental Health Block Grant.

A discussion of deinstitutionalization would be incomplete without reference to homelessness. To many people, the homeless population of American cities bears witness to the failure of the movement to provide humane treatment in community-based settings. Many newspapers equate the homeless population with the mentally ill, and no doubt the average citizen does likewise.[43] The association between homelessness and mental illness is fueled by advocates for the mentally ill who, in their quest for funds for treatment and housing, emphasize the connection, and the association is further fueled by "extreme" cases where a homeless person commits a crime or otherwise behaves in a manner disturbing to the community-at-large. Some students of the criminal justice system claim that law enforcement has taken over the role of caring for the mentally ill, citing statistics that 10 to 15 percent of the population of jails and prisons are people with severe mental illness.[44]

There is no way exactly to know how many homeless people live on the streets due to deinstitutionalization nor can it be known how many homeless people would be placed in institutional settings if the legal standards for commitment had not become stringent. Torrey (1997) estimates that on any given day, approximately 150,000 homeless people are mentally ill.[45] We know that some percentage of the homeless population are youth who have committed status offenses that are forms of misconduct only because of young age. Status offenses include behavior such as truancy and behavior that results in a young person being labeled as "incorrigible and beyond parental control." The Juvenile Justice and Delinquency Prevention Act (JJDPA) contains a deinstitutionalization requirement that precludes incarcerating status offenders with young people who have been adjudicated delinquent, and some researchers argue that the JJDPA's deinstitutionalization requirement has forced young people onto the streets.[46]

As noted above, funds that had supported people in institutions did not necessarily follow them into the community to provide a financial basis for treatment and housing, and the professional literature suggests that people were discharged from mental hospitals without an effort to establish connections with community-based facilities. However, these issues alone do not explain the difficulties encountered in providing community-based care. Some communities have reacted negatively to the creation of group homes for the mentally ill, changing zoning ordinances and denying building permits in order to prevent the creation of shelters, and even well-intentioned efforts to create community-based residential facilities have run into bureaucratic roadblocks in an effort to convert one- and two-family homes into group residences.[47] And, as discussed in chapter 11, "gentrification," which refers to the process of renovating run-down housing stock in decaying inner-city neighborhoods, depleted the stock of low-cost housing units, including single-room occupancy dwellings that in the past provided shelter for poor people.

Extreme situations involving the mentally ill, for example, when Russell Weston "invaded" the United States Capitol building in 1998 and killed two police officers, give rise to the question, "What can be done about the homeless mentally ill?" Although some have suggested "reinstitutionalizing" the mentally ill, it is not likely that this will happen because

> The Federal constitution forbids the confinement of a person who is not dangerous and who is capable of "surviving safely in freedom by himself or with the help of willing and responsible family members or friends. The fact that a person is found to be mentally ill cannot justify confinement and an indefinite "hold" in custodial care. The argument that the state will provide a standard of living superior to what a person would enjoy in the community is not a sufficient basis for confinement nor can a harmless person be confined so that others will not be exposed to ways [that] are different.[48]

The New York State Legislature responded to the murder of a women in 1999 by a homeless man in New York City by enacting a bill to (1) increase outpatient treatment, (2) require service providers to report to a "program coordinator" a person's noncompliance with a treatment plan, (3) provide for petitioning a court to request an order for outpatient treatment, and (4) establish other ways to prevent the need for hospitalization.[49] Whether such legislation will be effective remains to be seen. Among other rights retained by the mentally ill is the right to refuse treatment unless the exercise of this right interferes with the state's right to preserve life.[50] This requirement places a heavy burden on the state when seeking a court order for treatment to show that the state's interest trumps a patient's rights.

THE CENTER FOR MENTAL HEALTH SERVICES

The Center for Mental Health Services in SAMSHA administers the Mental Health Block Grant (MHBG). Funds are provided to the states for the purpose of providing comprehensive community-based mental health services to adults with a serious mental illness and to children with a serious emotional disturbance. Enabling individuals to function outside of inpatient or residential institutions to the maximum extent of their ability is the central goal of the MHBG.

To receive funds, each state must file a mental health services plan.[51] The plan must describe how the state will provide for a community-based system of care that includes care for people living in rural areas. Numerical targets that describe the number of individuals to be served in the state must be reported, and how the state will provide a range of mental health and rehabilitation services must be described. The plan must include services that will help individuals maintain their independence; thus, employment and educational services, housing services, and medical and dental care are appropriate uses for MHBG funds. Funds are available also for case management services, community outreach, and services for people who are coping with the knowledge that they are HIV positive.

Funds are available for demonstration projects to develop and test new methods for working with seriously mentally ill adults and children and adolescents with serious emotional and mental disorders. Funds may be used to support demonstration projects (1) for the prevention of youth suicide; (2) for the assessment and treatment of depressive disorders; (3) for programs to prevent sex offenses and to treat the victims of sex offenses; and (4) to provide mental health services to victims of family violence.[52]

MENTAL HEALTH SERVICES AND MANAGED CARE

Beginning in the early 1990s, a number of states took advantage of a provision in federal law under which they could petition the government to waive Medicaid regulations and move some recipients into managed care programs (MCPs) for mental health services. Provisions in the Balanced Budget Act of 1997 allow states to mandate managed care for most Medicaid recipients. Concern with controlling the costs of mental health care provided the impetus for moving service recipients into MCPs just as it has for the use of MCPs for physical health services.

In 1998, the General Accounting Office (GAO) studied implementation of mental health MCPs in Colorado, Iowa, Massachusetts, and Washington. The range of services was expanded, the GAO reported, to go beyond what Medicaid covered to include (1) individual and group therapy, (2) peer counseling, (3) family preservation services, (4) drop-in centers, and (5) early intervention services. Innovations were implemented such as (1) "mobile crisis counseling;" (2) telephone consultation, which is helpful in rural areas; (3) crisis triage centers; (4) residential support for people released from state hospitals; (5) supported community living that may include twenty-four-hour crisis services and counseling, as well as educational services to teach basic living skills such as hygiene, cooking, shopping, and housekeeping; and (6) assertive community treatment, which seeks to help people with serious and chronic mental health problems remain in the community through the use of community support services and intensive treatment by a multidisciplinary team. The studied states reduced or eliminated requirements for prior authorization for community-based mental health services. The use of inpatient services was reduced.

MENTAL HEALTH SERVICES FOR CHILDREN

Two health care programs that were discussed in chapter 12 contain provisions for providing mental health services for children: the State Children's Health Insurance Program (SCHIP) and the Early and Periodic Screening, Diagnosis and Treatment (EPSDT) program, which is a part of the Medicaid program.

The EPSDT program provides for a comprehensive mental health examination for children and youth under the age of twenty-one. Necessary treatment must be provided even if the required service is not a part of a state's service plan.[53]

Recall that in 1997 Congress amended the Social Security Act and enacted SCHIP to provide health insurance to some of the 11 million uninsured children under the age of eighteen. Expansion of an existing Medicaid program is one option available to the states to implement SCHIP. If a state elects this option, it must provide SCHIP children with all of the benefits available to others, thus making children eligible for EPSDT services.

In addition, grants are available through the Child and Adolescent Service System Program (CASSP) to (1) establish mechanisms to enhance collaborative efforts by persons who serve children, (2) coordinate the provision of services to children, and (3) establish a "continuum of care" for the purpose of serving children in the least restrictive setting, but funds may not be used to provide services.[54]

MENTAL HEALTH ADVOCACY

In 1980 when Congress passed the Mental Health Systems Act, a bill of rights and an advocacy system for mentally ill patients was created. The act was repealed in 1981 except for the provisions concerning patient's rights. In 1986, concerned about the lack of advocacy services for the mentally ill, Congress undertook a nine-month investigation into the conditions in thirty-one state facilities for the mentally ill, the developmentally disabled, and the mentally retarded and conducted hearings on the subject of patient rights and advocacy.

Although the visited facilities had written policies and internal systems for patient advocacy, advocates reported that they were not able to thoroughly investigate complaints and that when investigations did occur, effective disciplinary action was not taken against persons known to be abusive to patients. Congress concluded its investigation finding that "mentally ill persons are subject to abuse and neglect and that State systems for monitoring compliance with established rights of such persons are frequently inadequate." [55] Moreover, an advocacy system that was independent of any provider of service was required. Congress then enacted the Protection and Advocacy for Mentally Ill Individuals Act[56] to ensure that individuals who are not able to advocate for themselves had effective advocacy. Federal funds are provided to the states to develop, implement, and administer advocacy systems for the purpose of investigating incidents of abuse and neglect in institutions and to advocate for patient rights. The act does not create any new rights for the mentally ill; rather, it is concerned with enforcing already existing state and federal rights, including constitutional rights.

Substance Abuse

An estimated 6.5 percent of the population over the age of twelve uses illegal drugs, defined as marijuana or hashish; cocaine, including crack cocaine; inhalants; hallucinogens; heroin; and prescription medications that are used for nonmedical purposes. Marijuana accounts for approximately 90 percent of illicit drug use.[57] Congress has expressed its concern with eliminating drug and alcohol abuse in several ways. For example, in 1999, the budget for the Substance Abuse and Mental Health Services Administration allocated $1.58 billion to the Substance Abuse Block Grant compared to $466 million for mental health services. And, as reported in previous chapters, (1) concerned that the government not support an addict's habit, Congress provided that anyone whose alcohol or drug use was the contributing factor to their disability would not be eligible for financial assistance under the Supplement Security Income Program (chapter 10); (2) only recovering substance abusers who are in treatment programs are eligible for civil rights protection under the Vocational Rehabilitation Act, the Americans with Disabilities Act, and the Fair Housing Act (chapter 13); and (3) a public housing tenant is subject to eviction for drug use or for the drug-related activities of their guests (chapter 11).

The Alcohol, Drug Abuse and Mental Health Administration Reorganization Act of 1992 authorized the Substance Abuse Prevention and Treatment Block Grant Program to provide financial assistance to states and territories to support alcohol and other drug abuse prevention, treatment, and rehabilitation activities and to enable the states to provide services to individuals who abuse alcohol and drugs.[58] Grants are made to the states based upon approval by the Secretary of the Department of Health and Human Services of a state plan describing how funds will be used to prevent and treat alcohol and substance abuse. The plan must describe the state's drug and alcohol problem with reference to the number of involved individuals, and it must identify current activities within the state to prevent and treat substance abuse and for each activity and explain why current activities are not sufficient to meet current need. Examples would be the number of people on waiting lists for a residential drug treatment program or the inability, with current resources, to conduct a statewide educational program concerning alcohol or substance. Eligible states must have in effect a law prohibiting the distribution of tobacco products to anyone under eighteen years of age.

States must allocate funds according to a formula that requires that (1) at least 35 percent of a grant is used for prevention and treatment activities related to alcohol; (2) at least 35 percent for activities related to other drugs, (3) at least 20 percent for primary prevention services; and (4) at least 5 percent of the grant to increase (relative to the availability of services in 1994) treatment services for pregnant women and women with dependent children, including prenatal care and child care while drug treatment services are being provided. Programs serving intravenous drug users (IDUs) must engage in outreach to inform individuals of the availability of treatment. When a program that serves IDUs reaches 90 percent of its capacity, this must be reported to a state official and some "interim" service must be made available to the individual within 120 days of the service request. Interim services include programs that decrease the risk of adverse health effects of substance abuse, promote the health of the individual, and reduce the risk of disease transmission. Acceptable services include

> Counseling and education about HIV and tuberculosis (TB), about the risks of needle-sharing, the risks of transmission to sexual partners and infants, and about steps that can be taken to ensure that HIV and TB transmission does not occur, as well as referral for HIV or TB treatment services if necessary. For pregnant women, interim services also include counseling on the effects of alcohol and drug use on the fetus, as well as referral for prenatal care which are to be made available to the individual not later than 48 hours after such request.[59]

Federal funds may not be used to provide inpatient hospital services unless a physician certifies that the person cannot be safely treated on an outpatient basis or in a residential treatment program, and the physician must certify that the service can reasonably be expected to improve an individual's condition. Funds may not be used to support needle-exchange programs that exist in some states as a way to reduce the risk of HIV infection through shared needle use.[60]

States must increase the availability of treatment services for pregnant women and women with dependent children, make special services available for individuals with tuberculosis and HIV, establish and maintain a revolving loan fund to establish group homes for recovering substance abusers, and improve referrals to treatment.

SPECIAL SERVICES FOR WOMEN

In addition to the 5 percent set-aside for service for pregnant women and women with children, states must ensure that pregnant women receive preference in admission to treatment facilities and must provide outreach services to inform pregnant women of the availability of services. This preference requirement is qualified in the statute by language stating that preference is for women who would "benefit from" the service. Nevertheless, regulations provide that programs serving an IDU population must give preference in admissions for treatment to (1) pregnant women who use intravenous drugs, (2) pregnant substance abusers, (3) injecting drug users, and (4) any others.[61]

Domestic Violence and the Violence Against Women Act

There is no national definition of domestic violence and because state, not federal, laws govern the investigation and prosecution of domestic violence, there is state-by-state variation in how such matters are treated by the police and by the courts. The United States Department of Justice defines domestic violence as criminal acts occurring between individuals with an existing or prior close relationship. Some states limit the definition to actions that occur between spouses or between unmarried adults with a child, some include actions between "boyfriends and girlfriends," and some states include acts involving same sex partners.[62]

Until the 1970s, a number of states treated domestic violence as "a private matter, something other than [a] real crime," where failure to investigate complaints was tolerated and to some extent encouraged.[63] In New York, for example, an act of 1962 decriminalized domestic violence and required criminal courts to transfer to family court matters involving domestic violence. The emphasis under the 1962 law was on rehabilitation, not punishment. One judge in New York said that court discretion in deciding whether cases of domestic assault warranted transfer to criminal court combined with "the benign attitude of various police departments in refusing to make arrests in the face of actual ongoing assaults by abusing spouses," might have the effect of "giving an abusing spouse a practical license to continue assaults."[64]

In response to the women's movement of the 1960s and the 1970s, states undertook legal reform to bring domestic violence under control and to create an array

·of legal remedies for victims of domestic violence. Today, all of the states, the District of Columbia, and Puerto Rico provide that a victim of domestic violence may obtain an order of protection, meaning an order issued by a court that limits or proscribes contact between the offender and the victim. In addition, civil remedies and criminal charges may be brought against offenders in all fifty states and the District of Columbia.[65] Courts in many states have the authority to order the abuser into treatment, and a number of states are providing training to law enforcement personnel on how to handle reports and investigations into domestic violence. To give force to protective orders, New York created a new felony charge of criminal contempt for a person who violates an order of protection by threatening, stalking, or harassing the victim, thereby strengthening existing law that allowed felony charges only if the defendant caused physical injury or property damage exceeding $250.[66]

Thirty-five of forty-seven states responding to a 1996 survey conducted by the Department of Justice reported that they compile data concerning domestic violence.[67] States identified a number of problems in data collection, including (1) poor definitions of the crime, (2) lack of funds to compile data, (3) lack of training for law enforcement to discriminate what should and should not be classified as domestic violence, (4) incompatibility between local and statewide information systems that hinder transferring data, (5) no state authority to compile data, and (6) the voluntary nature of reporting requirements that limit cooperation. Given these issues, it should not come as a surprise that data describing the number of victims of domestic violence vary considerably, from 1 million to 4 million victims each year.[68] In addition to problems posed by the listed items, there are other issues, including that (1) the number of reports will likely result in overestimating the incidence of violence if reports are assumed to reflect number of victims since there may be multiple reports for any one victim; and (2) using "incidents" may result in an underestimate of events since domestic violence reports may not be made until a series of incidents takes place. Compounding the problem is the fact that in some states data are categorized as "family violence" and may include child as well as adult victims. Some states compile their data from different "systems," for example, child protective services, health care providers, law enforcement, and victim assistance services, and this is likely to yield an overestimate unless reports include names so that double-counting can be avoided. Moreover, a number of states reported to the justice department that they compile information using different databases, including (1) registries of protective order issues, (2) civil and criminal court databases, (3) service provider databases such as child abuse registries, and (4) data compiled by a state corrections system.

The Violence Against Women Act (VAWA) was authorized in 1994.[69] The act is administered by the Violence Against Women Office in the Department of Justice. The VAWA is a multipurpose statute that provides that "all persons within the United States [have a right] to be free from crimes of violence motivated by gender."[70] As noted in chapter 13, a provision of the VAWA that allows a victim of gender-based violence to sue a perpetrator in federal court has been found unconstitutional by the Fourth Circuit Court of Appeals, and the Supreme Court affirmed that finding. However, the threat to the VAWA is limited to that section of the law and does not affect other provisions, including those that seek to (1) curtail violence against women through training of law enforcement officials, (2) fund community education and prevention programs, (3) support battered women's shelters, and (4) criminalize interstate acts of domestic violence, including interstate violations of protective orders.

Programs funded by the VAWA and their purposes include

The STOP (Services Training Officers Prosecutors) program makes grants to states and territories to develop and strengthen the criminal justice system's response to violence against women and to support and enhance victim's services. Funds must be allocated according to a formula where 25 percent are directed to law enforcement objectives, 25 percent to prosecution, and 25 percent to victim services. Grantees have discretion in allocating the remaining 25 percent. The STOP Violence Against Indian Women Program is comparable in its objective and required allocation of funds.[71]

Grants to encourage state and local government including tribal governments to treat domestic violence as a serious violation of criminal law. Grant funds may be used to implement mandatory arrest programs, train officials in criminal justice agencies to improve tracking of domestic violence cases and create centralized domestic violence units consisting of police, prosecutors, judges, or other criminal justice agencies.

The Rural Domestic Violence and Child Victimization Enforcement Grant Program seeks to improve and increase services and prevent domestic violence against women and children in rural communities. Grants require collaboration by law enforcement, the judiciary, and programs that provide victim services to develop and implement programs designed to reduce and prevent violence against rural women and children.

To increase the availability and effectiveness of legal assistance for victims of domestic violence, the Domestic Violence Victims' Civil Legal Assistance Discretionary Grant Program supports innovative, collaborative programs that reach battered women on a broad range of issues. Grant funds are used to support or provide legal services in civil matters that are related to domestic violence, for example, to obtain, modify, or enforce orders of protection; to assist in obtaining a divorce or legal separation; to obtain and enforce an order of spousal and child support; to deal with matters concerning child custody and/or visitation; and to deal with administrative issues, for example, to gain access to benefits; housing and/or landlord-tenant matters; and matters related to employment, including unemployment compensation proceedings.

In 1999, Congress authorized grants for a program titled Combat Violent Crimes Against Women on Campuses. Grants are made to institutions of higher education so that campus personnel, student organizations, campus administrators, security personnel, and regional crisis centers affiliated with the institution can develop and strengthen strategies to combat violence against women, including domestic violence, sexual assault, and stalking on campuses.[72]

In 1999, the Urban Institute reported the results of a survey on the use of STOP grant funds by 801 agencies.[73] More than one-half of the 801 agencies offered crisis counseling, information and referral, follow-up, and support activity related to the criminal justice system. Primary activities and services offered by the reporting agencies were (in descending order) responding to hotline calls (26 percent); shelter services (25 percent); court advocacy (24 percent); and counseling (18 percent). Other activities included assisting women in obtaining benefits, housing, and employment (6 percent); medical advocacy (5 percent); and working with children (3 percent).[74]

Programs for the Elderly

Policies that enable elderly people maintain their independence were discussed in previous chapters, including policies that provide financial assistance (chapter 9), food and housing (chapter 11), health care (chapter 12), and protections from age-based discrimination in employment (chapter 13). The solvency of the trust funds that contain employer and employee contributions for financial and health care benefits at retirement were reviewed in chapter 9, and health care issues and the effect of the aging population on the demand for services such as skilled nursing care were discussed in chapter 12. In addition, the aging of the American population was referred to in chapter 9. The population of people aged sixty-five and older is expected to grow from 35 million in 1998 to 61 million in 2025, an increase of 75 percent, with the greatest population growth occurring for people over the age of eighty-five.[75]

The United States has made gains in reducing poverty among the elderly. As reported in chapter 8, the percent of elderly people in poverty was reduced from approximately 19 percent in 1972 to 10.5 percent in 1999. Gains have been made in making health care available to the elderly, but the demand for income and health care support can be expected to increase as the population ages, as will the need for assistance in diverse areas of life. In the following pages, services that are available through the Older Americans Act are reviewed.

The Older Americans Act

The Older Americans Act (OAA) was referred to in chapter 10, where nutrition programs were discussed. The OAA is administered by the Administration on Aging in the Department of Health and Human Services, except for employment provisions that are administered by the Department of Labor. The OAA has seven titles. The act's objectives are reported in Title I, which states as its purpose to assist the elderly to remain in their own communities by eliminating barriers to independent living and by providing community-based services. Title II addresses administrative matters. Social services and nutrition services are provided for in Title III, which receives the lion's share of federal funding. In 1997, 65 percent of federal funds went to support Title III programs, with 65 percent of allocated funds supporting congregate and home-delivered meals. Research to expand knowledge of the problems confronting the elderly, fund projects that train providers of service, and test different approaches to assisting the elderly are funded by Title IV.

Title V supports the Community Service Employment Program that subsidizes part-time, minimum-wage community service jobs for unemployed, low-income persons aged fifty-five or older. Approximately 100,000 economically disadvantaged Americans aged fifty-five and older are employed in schools, hospitals, senior citizen centers, and other community service activities.[76]

Title VI provides grants to fund programs for Native Americans and Native Hawaiians, and Title VII funds the Long-Term Care Ombudsman Program; programs to prevent elder abuse, neglect, and exploitation; and legal assistance programs to protect the rights of the elderly and programs that help the elderly gain access to insurance and public benefits.[77]

Federal grants are made to the states contingent upon the states' submission of a plan that covers a two to four year period of time. Plans identify a single state agency to administer programs funded under the OAA, and they describe how the state will assess what services are needed. The plan must describe the extent to which needed services are already being provided and what services will be developed. Depending upon the residential distribution of elderly people across a state, "area agencies" may be created to develop a plan that describes how funds will be used to meet the specific needs of the elderly in the area agencies' geographic locale. The state plan must build upon the separate area agency plans. In 1999, there were 661 area agencies and 222 tribal organizations nationwide.[78]

Each state receives a minimum allotment from the federal government. Funds beyond that minimum are allocated on the basis of the proportion of individuals aged sixty and older residing in each state. Within-state distribution formulas must also reflect the proportion of individuals sixty and over. States must contribute their own funds, and federal law permits charging program recipients for provided services but precludes mandating that participants pay a fee. States may transfer up to 20 percent of funds to a nutrition program for senior citizens. Services are to be provided to individuals with the greatest economic or social need, particularly low-income minority individuals. Despite the broad goals and provisions in federal law, most of the funds that support programs for the elderly come from the states, localities, private contributions, and care provided by family members.[79] There are an estimated 21 million family caregivers, mainly women in their forties, who devote some of their time for an average of eight years to caring for an elderly family member to avoid institutional care; these voluntary services are valued at more than $200 billion.[80]

In addition to the uses of Title funds noted above, Title III monies may be used to acquire or to construct a building that will be used as a senior center, support protective services for elderly victims of domestic violence, and provide transportation that is needed to receive services or to participate in community programs. Funds may support services to enable the elderly to (1) live in suitable housing that meets the special needs of individuals who require assistance to live independently; (2) receive services in their own homes, including those of a homemaker, home health aide, personal care attendant, or from a person who does chores and home maintenance; and (3) participate in social, educational, and recreational activities.[81] Funds may also be used to provide support for an elderly person's family members and others who voluntarily provide care, including training, counseling, and support groups for caretakers. The OAA funds may be used to provide health services not provided by the Medicare program, for example, routine health screening including testing for vision and hearing problems, and funds may be allocated to physical fitness programs such as group exercise, music, art, and dance therapy.

Summary

In this chapter, policies that support the provision of services have been reviewed. The central goal of the reviewed policies is to support programs that assist people to attain or to maintain their independence. Of the policies reviewed, the Title XX Social Service Block Grant Program allows program developers the greatest latitude to create any social service that meets the block grants' broad objectives of assisting people to become independent of government aid. But funds for this program have decreased over time, and future decreases are planned.

The lion's share of funding for social services supports programs that are limited to specific populations, for example, people with HIV/AIDS, the mentally ill, substance abusers, the elderly, and victims of domestic violence. Creating services that address the needs of specific groups or that seek to resolve specific problems is characteristic of the American approach to providing assistance. Programs are developed in a piecemeal fashion when problems emerge and do not reflect a comprehensive or unified approach to meeting the common service needs of the population. This approach to policymaking is a direct result of an unwillingness of government to acknowledge its permanent role in providing assistance, due to a concern that such an acknowledgment would diminish the incentive to self-help. This approach to policymaking is typical of a residual approach to welfare (see chapter 1).

Because services are provided through an array of policies and programs, a social worker or other mental health professional who is seeking to assist a client obtain benefits must know about available services and must have a general knowledge of eligibility requirements. For example, a client who has a disability may be eligible for cash assistance through SSI, for medical insurance through the Medicaid program, for food assistance through the Food Stamp Program, and for housing assistance through a supportive housing program. However, if alcohol or drug abuse is a key factor contributing to the client's disability, he or she may not be eligible for SSI, although the client may be eligible for Medicaid and for cash assistance from a state's General Assistance Program. If clients have a child, they may be eligible for aid through the TANF irrespective of a history of alcohol or drug abuse. Depending on the state in which the client lives, the child may be eligible for aid under TANF even though the client is not.

All countries are limited in their ability to meet the infinite needs of their citizens; thus, despite the sums of money provided for social services, evidence indicates that available services are not sufficient to meet the demand. In addition, the availability of services is affected by competition for limited funds that results, in part, from (1) the emergence of new social problems, for example, HIV/AIDS did not exist before 1980; (2) the recognition that "old" social problems must be addressed, as is the case with domestic violence; (3) changing demographics, especially the aging of the population and the demand that this creates for new services; and (4) the inescapable fact that the existence of services, in and of itself, may increase the demand for service through outreach programs and referrals.

CHAPTER

Child Welfare

    Child welfare services are a subset of all services that government provides for children. Child welfare services are concerned with preventing abuse and neglect and with providing children with permanent homes. Some services and benefits that are available for children have been reviewed in preceding chapters, including income support provided through the Temporary Assistance to Needy Families Program (TANF) or the Supplemental Security Income Program (SSI) (chapter 10), nutritional support provided through the Food Stamp Program and several programs that address the nutritional needs of children in day care and school settings (chapter 11), health care provided through the Medicaid Program (chapter 12), and social services provided through the Title XX Social Services Block Grant and other policies (chapter 13). In chapter 16, federal policies that provide educational opportunities and educational services for children are addressed.

    Child welfare services are funded by the federal government and by the states and local governments, and some funds are provided by foundations and private contributions. Child welfare services receive only a small percent of government funds. Data compiled from thirteen of the most populated states shows that more than 63 percent of federal and state funds go to TANF, food stamps, Medicaid, and the Earned Income Tax Credit, and 8 percent goes to child protection and family services programs.[1] The remaining funds are spent on child care and early development (6 percent), miscellaneous food and nutrition programs (8 percent), and "other" programs (14 percent), including miscellaneous cash programs, juvenile justice, youth services, and non-Medicaid health care.[2]

    The organizational framework within which child welfare services are provided is unique relative to other service and benefit programs. As with programs reviewed in preceding chapters, the federal government sets policy, develops regulations to guide policy implementation, and funds program operation. Within the federally established framework, each state develops and operates programs that serve clients, often contracting with private agencies to assist in service provision. The unique element in child welfare is the role the federal government assigns to state level juvenile courts, or family courts as they are called in some states, to ensure that the states pursue federal objectives.

This chapter begins with a brief discussion of the juvenile court. Next, our attention turns to a review of policies that support programs and services (1) to protect children from abuse and neglect, (2) to provide foster care for children who cannot be protected and for children whose parents cannot or will not care for them, (3) to place in adoptive homes children in foster care who cannot be returned to their biological parents, and (4) to hold noncustodial parents responsible for paying child support.

The Courts and Child Welfare

In chapter 2, I reported that the first juvenile court was established in Chicago in 1899. The court was created to ensure that children charged with criminal acts were not incarcerated with adult criminals by directing children to programs whose objective was rehabilitation, not punishment. Each state has a juvenile court, and federal law requires that juvenile court judges approve certain state actions, for example, the placement of a child in foster care, as a condition for the state to receive federal matching funds to support a child's placement.

In general, juvenile courts have jurisdiction over dependent children and over children who are adjudicated status offenders and juvenile delinquents. The authority of a juvenile court may extend to matters involving child support, child custody, and domestic violence. In addition, juvenile court judges may have the power to terminate parental rights and to order that paternity be established. In most states, juvenile court jurisdiction extends to all persons eighteen years of age or younger, although in ten states sixteen is the upper age, and in three states it is fifteen.

The importance of the juvenile court to child welfare goes well beyond the narrow role assigned by the federal government. Although a review of the relationship between social work practice in child welfare and the courts is beyond the scope of this text, you should know that social workers often turn to juvenile courts to ask a judge to find that parents have abused or neglected their children and to enter an order (1) authorizing a department of social services to supervise children who are left in their own home, (2) ordering parents and children to participate in programs designed to reduce or eliminate the problems that caused them to be brought before the court, (3) placing a child in foster care, (4) continuing a child in care or returning children to their own homes, (5) terminating parental rights, and (6) sanctioning a child's adoption. In addition, juvenile courts often ask social workers to conduct family studies and to file reports with the court that include recommendations concerning parental fitness and child placement.[3]

Technically speaking, status offenders and juvenile delinquents are not served by a state's child welfare system, but this is not always so, especially with status offenders (often referred to as minors, juveniles, or persons in need of supervision). Status offenders were referred to in the previous chapter where deinstitutionalization was discussed. There, I said that status crimes may involve truancy and behavior that results in a young person being labeled as "incorrigible and beyond parental control," which is of concern to the court only because of young age. The Juvenile Justice and Delinquency Prevention Act (JJDPA) precludes incarcerating status offenders with young people who have been adjudicated delinquent. Thus, a juvenile court judge who thinks that placement away from home is in the young person's best interest may refer the case to a state or county child welfare agency and request that the youth be placed in a foster care setting and supervised by a child welfare worker.

Juvenile delinquents are children that have engaged in criminal activity. In this period of history, the earlier emphasis on rehabilitation rather than punishment is giving way to a trend to remand to adult court and to try as adults young persons charged with serious crimes involving death or egregious bodily harm to others. Federal law provides that juveniles may be tried in federal courts if a state court cannot or will not try the case, if the state does not have programs or services needed by the youth, or if the young person is charged with a federal crime, for example, bank robbery or a crime involving controlled substances.[4]

The Child Abuse Prevention and Treatment Act

In the early 1960s, Dr. C. Henry Kempe brought the problem of child abuse to public attention with the publication of his article "The Battered Child Syndrome." States passed laws mandating the reporting of child abuse and neglect, and in 1974, Congress passed the Child Abuse Prevention and Treatment Act (CAPTA). This act provides financial assistance to the states for demonstration programs for the prevention, identification, and treatment of child abuse and neglect.[5] In 1997, child protective agencies investigated reports of abuse or neglect involving 3 million children. For 1 million of these reports (33 percent), there was sufficient evidence to sustain an allegation that a child had been abused or neglected.[6] States use the terms "founded," "substantiated," or "indicated" when referring to reports where abuse or neglect has occurred.

Many factors contribute to low substantiation rates, including (1) the misuse of reporting laws, for example, by a noncustodial parent as a way of "hassling" a custodial parent; (2) ambiguous language, such as defining neglect as a failure to provide proper care, supervision, or discipline or raising a child in an environment that is injurious to her or his health, which invites over-reporting since the behaviors that constitute neglect are not clear; (3) expanding the definition of child maltreatment, specifically by adding cases of family violence to the responsibilities of child protective workers. Florida, for example, has added "threatened harm," which takes into account assault perpetrated on one adult household member by another and which accounts for 17 to 22 percent of all investigations[7]; and (4) insufficient child welfare staff, which, when combined with high caseloads, makes thorough investigations very difficult.

To qualify for federal assistance, states must provide for (1) the reporting of known or suspected child abuse and neglect, including reports of maltreatment of children in state custody; (2) investigating reports, including procedures for protecting children if abuse or neglect are found; (3) the confidentiality of records concerning child abuse and neglect; (4) representation for children in court proceedings; (5) public education concerning child abuse and neglect; and (6) immunity for persons who report in good faith.[8]

In all states, professionals (including social workers, physicians, and teachers) are mandated to report known or suspected child abuse or neglect, and some states accept reports from the lay public. Mandated reporters are subject to civil, and in some states criminal, penalties for failure to report. Professionals who make reports in good faith cannot be sued even if the report turns out to be groundless and worker and client confidentiality rules are waived.

States differ in how they define abuse and neglect. Federal law establishes a minimum requirement that states define as child abuse "any recent act or failure to act on the part of a parent or caretaker, which results in death, serious physical or emotional harm, sexual abuse or exploitation, or an act or failure to act which presents an imminent risk of serious harm."[9] Federal law requires also that states provide for reporting as neglect the withholding of medical treatment from disabled infants with life-threatening conditions if the provision of medical care would ameliorate or correct the child's condition.[10]

All state have rules governing investigations into reports of child abuse or neglect. Statutes typically specify to whom the report is to be made (social services or the police) when the investigation is to begin (for example, within twenty-four hours following receipt of a report), who is to conduct the investigation (child protective service and/or law enforcement personnel), and when the investigation is to end (sixty days to six months), and there are guidelines for determining whether a report should be founded. Caseworkers and casework supervisors exercise discretion in deciding what cases to investigate and whether to found a case.[11]

Because of the rise in criminal prosecutions of persons charged with child abuse, joint social worker/police investigations are becoming common, and legislation that requires child protective agencies to report to the police or to a prosecutor's office serious cases of abuse or neglect or cases that might result in criminal prosecution have been enacted in the majority of states.[12] At the conclusion of an investigation, a determination must be made as whether there is evidence of abuse or neglect, and if so, whether to provide services or refer a case to court.

Required services are not identified by CAPTA, nor are procedures specified that must be followed once a child is found to be abused or neglected. Forty-four states use 11 percent of the funds they receive under the Title XX Social Services Block Grant for child protective services; forty-two states use 6.8 percent of the funds they receive for prevention/intervention services that may benefit children in addition to other services that are funded, including counseling and day care (see Table 14.2). Some states have codified their obligation to provide preventive and family preservation services, but vague statutory language makes it difficult to determine who is eligible to receive services. For example, eligibility may be restricted to those situations where it is "possible and appropriate" to protect the child from separation or by language requiring a determination that the child is "at risk," at "immediate risk," at "imminent risk," in "imminent danger," or at "actual and imminent risk" of out-of-home placement."[13]

The Adoption Assistance and Child Welfare Act

In 1980, the Adoption Assistance and Child Welfare Act (AACWA) was signed into law. The objectives of the AACWA are to prevent the removal of children from their own homes and to facilitate the placement of children who enter substitute care in permanent family homes, either by reuniting them with their families of origin or through placement in adoptive homes. Federal funds are available to the states to develop and implement programs to prevent placement and to facilitate family reunification or adoption. Child welfare services seek to

> Protect and promote the welfare of all children . . . prevent or [resolve] . . . problems which may result in the [maltreatment] or delinquency of children; prevent the unnecessary separation of children from their families by identifying family problems, assisting families in resolving their problems, and preventing breakup of the family where . . . desirable and possible, [reunite] families and children . . . [through] the provision of services . . . place children in suitable adoptive homes . . . where restoration to the biological family is not possible or appropriate, and assure adequate care of children away from their homes . . . where the child cannot be returned home . . . [or adopted].[14]

The AACWA has two titles. Title IV-E funds an open-ended entitlement program under which the federal government contributes to the costs of maintaining eligible children in foster care. Eligible children are those (1) who would have been eligible for financial assistance under the Aid to Families with Dependent Children (AFDC) program as it existed on June 1, 1995, including children who were abandoned before a determination of eligibility could be made; (2) who are placed in the legal custody of the state under court order; and (3) who are placed in a licensed home.[15] The Title IV-B, Child Welfare Services Block Grant, is the second part of Title IV. The block grant provides federal matching funds to the states to operate programs to prevent abuse or neglect and to prevent the placement of children in foster care.[16]

In addition to Title IV-B, CAPTA funds preventive and protective services. The question "What is the difference between these programs?" is difficult to answer because the concepts of prevention and protection are ambiguous. For example, the goals of CAPTA provide for programs to prevent abuse and neglect, and the goals of Title IV-B provide for programs to prevent or remedy the problems that may result in abuse or neglect. Neither CAPTA nor AACWA provide direction to distinguish prevention from protection programs. Some states have separate programs for prevention and child protection, whereas in others these programs are synonymous. The main distinction between programs may be the emphasis in child protection on procedures to investigate reports of maltreatment. Beyond this, program goals are typically similar in stressing family maintenance and the prevention or reduction of possible maltreatment.

ENTRY INTO FOSTER CARE

In 1999, the General Accounting Office reported that there were 520,000 children in foster care in the United States.[17] Children enter foster care on a voluntary or an involuntary basis, and most cases come to the attention of child welfare services through a report of abuse or neglect. Federal funds are available to support voluntary placements if two conditions are met. First, there must be a binding, written agreement between the agency and the child's parent or guardian. The agreement must specify the child's legal status and the rights and obligations of the parent or guardian, the child, and the agency while the child is in placement. Parents must be able to revoke the agreement and request that their children be returned to their home or to the home of a relative. If the agency opposes the request, it must file a petition with the court and request a finding that returning the child would be contrary to his or her best interests. Second, states may claim federal reimbursement after the child has been in placement in excess of 180 days if there is a judicial determination that continuing in placement is in the best interests of the child.[18]

THE GOALS OF THE ADOPTION ASSISTANCE AND CHILD WELFARE ACT AND PROTECTIONS FOR CHILDREN AND PARENTS

The objectives of the AACWA make clear congressional intent to prevent the unnecessary removal of children from their homes and to enhance the likelihood of returning home those children who must enter substitute care. Congress created a means of monitoring state behavior through the reasonable efforts requirement of the AACWA. Except in cases where a child has been abandoned or subjected to torture or ongoing abuse, including sexual abuse, a judicial determination must be made, in writing, on a case-by-case basis, "that the continuation in the home would be contrary to the welfare of the child, and . . . that reasonable efforts were made to prevent or eliminate the need for removal . . . and to make it possible for the child to return home."[19] The required judicial determination must be met as a condition for the states to claim federal reimbursement under Title IV-E.

Federal law does not define reasonable efforts, and state policies are often vague, defining as reasonable (1) the exercise of due diligence to meet the needs of children and their families through the provision of appropriate services to prevent placement and to enable a child to return home[20] or (2) the provision of services described in a case plan.[21]

Once a child is in foster care, planning to facilitate the child's discharge is required. Written case plans, which must be developed no later than sixty days after an agency assumes responsibility for a child,[22] describe what parents must do to regain custody of their children and what social workers and community providers will do to assist parents. To ensure that contact is maintained between parents and children and to increase the likelihood that children will be returned to their own home, to the extent possible, children are to be placed in the least restrictive, most family-like setting, in close proximity to the parents' home, consistent with the best interests and special needs of the child.[23]

CASE REVIEWS

To ensure that states make efforts to reunite children in foster care with their biological families or to find alternative permanent homes for children who cannot be returned to their families of origin, federal law requires that each child's case be reviewed no less frequently than once every six months. The purpose of this review requirement is

> . . . to determine the continuing necessity for and appropriateness of the placement, the extent of compliance with the case plan, and the extent of progress which has been made toward alleviating or mitigating the causes necessitating placement in foster care, and to project a likely date by which the child may be returned to the home or placed for adoption or legal guardianship.[24]

Cases may be reviewed by a court or by an administrative panel. If the latter is chosen, the panel must include a member not responsible for the case management of or delivery of services to either the child or family being reviewed.

In addition to the six-month review, federal law requires a dispositional review no later than eighteen months after the child enters custody, with ongoing reviews thereafter. For children who entered foster care on or after October 1, 1997, the time frame for the eighteen-month review changed to twelve months, and the hearing is referred to as a permanency planning hearing.[25] The purpose of this review is to decide the permanency plan for the child, including whether he or she should be returned home, placed for adoption, or continued in care for a specified period of time or on a permanent or long-term basis.[26] To safeguard parents' rights, the AACWA extends to them the right to be represented by counsel, receive written notification of the hearing, and participate in the hearing. Parents also have a right to an administrative fair hearing if they are denied services under AACWA. Fair hearings provide a mechanism for ensuring that a client's due process rights are protected and that welfare benefits are not capriciously denied.

Adoption

When children cannot be returned to their biological parents, adoption is generally the plan of choice because it offers children the best chance of living in a permanent family setting. When a child is adopted, all rights and responsibilities that existed between the child and natural parents are terminated and transferred to the adoptive parents. Thus, the legal relationship becomes similar to that between a child and biological parents.

Children become free for adoption upon the death of a parent, when a parent voluntarily relinquishes parental rights, or when the state terminates parental rights. All states have laws that permit termination of parental rights, although the conditions may vary across states. Abandonment of a child for a predetermined time period (six or twelve months) may be grounds for termination, and a parent who has murdered or seriously injured another of his or her children may have parental rights terminated. Social changes such as the availability of abortion, improved methods of birth control, and the increased acceptance of unwed motherhood has decreased markedly the availability of infants for adoption. The universe of children who are available for adoption is becoming synonymous with the universe of children in foster home care.

ADOPTION SUBSIDIES

Many children who are available for adoption have special needs. Although each state may develop its own definition of special needs, a general definition is found in federal law, which defines a special needs child as one who because of ethnic background, age, membership in a minority or sibling group, medical condition, or physical, mental, or emotional handicap is not likely to be adopted without some financial assistance to adoptive parents to defray the costs of medical or psychological services.[27] Title IV-E funds may be used to pay part of the cost of subsidizing the adoption of children with special needs who are eligible for subsidies if, in addition to their unique needs, they are eligible for financial support under Title IV-E or under the SSI Program (chapter 10).

TRANSRACIAL ADOPTIONS

Approximately one-third of the 520,000 children in foster care will not be reunited with their birth families. Minority children, who represent more than 60 percent of the foster care population, wait twice as long as white children for adoptive homes.[28] Opposition to placement of children across racial lines, especially the placement of black children with white families, put an end to the practice of transracial adoptions that was common in the 1960s.

In 1994, finding that tens of thousands of children in foster care were awaiting adoption, Congress passed the Howard M. Metzenbaum Multiethnic Placement Act.[29] The act allowed states to consider race and ethnicity in choosing foster and adoptive homes but prohibited states from denying or delaying a child's placement solely on the basis of race or ethnicity. In 1996, finding that the 1994 act had not facilitated the adoption of minority children, Congress passed the Adoption Promotion and Stability Act, which applies to any agency that receives federal funds.[30] Henceforth, any consideration of race, color, or national origin in placing a child for adoption could be considered illegal discrimination under the 1964 Civil Rights Act. Rather than assuming that same-race placements are always in a child's best interests, the 1996 amendments require that an adoption decision that takes account of race has to be justified by showing why a specific child's placement demanded a same-race placement.

However, the 1996 act does not affect placement decisions for Native American children (see later discussion on the Indian Child Welfare Act) nor does it affect provisions in the Social Security Act that require states to consider placing foster children with an adult relative rather than a nonrelated caregiver.[31] In 1997, approximately 36 percent of children in foster care were placed with relatives, and unless a relative dies or elects not to continue as a foster parent, a child placed with a relative is not likely to become available for adoption. Thus, the universe of children available for transracial adoption is smaller than the universe of children available for adoption.

THE ADOPTION AND SAFE FAMILIES ACT OF 1997

Congress amended the AACWA in 1997 when it passed the Adoption and Safe Families Act (ASFA). The ASFA reflects a shift in philosophy away from the family preservation/family reunification theme that has been prevalent in child welfare since 1980 to a focus on achieving permanency through adoption. ASFA's emphasis on child safety arises from a concern that efforts to reunite children with their birth families have gone too far, favoring parental rights over child safety and a child's need for stability in care. This concern has been fed, in part, by lurid newspaper accounts of tragic deaths of children and the implication that lives were lost because social workers were attending too much to family preservation and reunification concerns.

Toward this end, ASFA provides that the child's health and safety must be the primary concerns for juvenile court judges when they determine whether reasonable efforts to reunite parents and children are required. Reasonable efforts are not required (1) if a judge determines that a child has been subject to extreme forms of abuse, including torture and sexual abuse; (2) if a parent is criminally responsible for the death of another of her or his children; or (3) if a parent's rights concerning a sibling have been involuntarily terminated. In addition, as noted above, the time frame for dispositional case reviews has been changed, and ASFA provides that a state may engage in concurrent planning, where efforts to locate an adoptive home occur in tandem with efforts to reunite the child and her family.[32]

A major change effected by ASFA is the mandate that the state petition the court to terminate parental rights or support a petition filed by another party for children in foster care for fifteen of the most recent twenty-two months; for children found by a court to have been abandoned; and for children whose parent or parents have murdered or caused serious bodily harm to another of their children.[33] States must actively recruit adoptive homes, document their child-specific recruitment efforts, act to approve adoptive homes, and act to finalize adoptions. Exceptions apply for children who are in the care of a relative, for children for whom the state can justify in writing why it is not in the child's best interests to pursue adoption, and where the state has not made the required reasonable efforts to reunite the family. Finally, the newly enacted law provides fiscal incentives to states that increase the number of adoptions over the number of adoptions in prior years. Congress authorized $20 million in fiscal year 1999, with the same authorization for fiscal year 2000 for incentive payments that range from $2,000 to $4,000 per adopted child. [34]

Model Adoption Laws

At any one time, about 8,000 children are legally available for adoption and waiting for an adoptive home but have no current prospects for adoption. The number is small because approximately 78 percent of foster children who are adopted are adopted by their foster parents or relatives. The 8,000 children who are legally free but difficult to place are (1) older, (2) children of color, (3) part of a sibling group, or (4) physical or mentally disabled.[35]

The ASFA provides that states may not delay or deny the adoption of a foster child when an approved family is available in another state. However, difficulties may arise in placing children across state lines due to differences in state laws and because interstate placements raise concerns for social workers because they cannot assess the suitability of the home in which the child will live, nor can they directly ensure the provision of services. To overcome some of these issues, the federal government encourages the states to enter into interstate compacts to increase a child's chances of being placed in an adoptive home.[36] The Interstate Compact on the Placement of Children (ICPC), the Interstate Compact on Adoption and Medical Assistance (ICAMA), and the Uniform Adoption Act (UAA) address concerns that are raised by placement of children across state lines. All fifty states, the District of Columbia, and the Virgin Islands have adopted the ICPC, but neither the ICAMA nor the UAA have been uniformly adopted.

The purpose of the ICPC is to increase that chances that children will be placed with individuals and families or in facilities where they will receive appropriate care. Agreements reached under the ICPC provide for authorities in the state where the child will live to evaluate and rule on the appropriateness of the placement and to provide for any child that is placed the same services that he or she would receive in their home state. Authorities in the sending state are given information sufficient to allow them to evaluate a recommended placement before placement occurs. Financial responsibility for the child, including the responsibility to pay for services, remain with the sending state.

The ICPC deals with issues that arise in placing children prior to their adoption. When a special needs child is adopted across state lines, or when a family that has already adopted a special needs child moves to another state, ICAMA comes into play. This compact provides for continuing adoption assistance and medical coverage for out-of-state adoptions. Continuing assistance is provided for in a written adoption assistance agreement that is entered into between the adoptive parents and the state that will provide the adoption assistance. The written agreement identifies the benefits to which the child will be entitled (continuing medical coverage, for example) and provides for continued assistance for the duration of the adoption.

The UAA seeks to standardize adoption practices and to increase the opportunities for a child to be adopted by requiring that (1) information concerning a child's health, genetic history, and social history be provided to adoptive parents; (2) no person be excluded as a possible adoptive parent based solely on their membership in a category; and that (3) foster parents and others acting as a child's de facto parents have the right to petition a court to adopt a child. To standardize procedures for termination of parental rights, the UAA states that if it is in the best interests of a child, parental rights may be terminated if the parent has failed to contribute to the costs of prenatal, natal, and postnatal care for a child less than six months of age at the time an adoption petition is filed, and for this child as well as for children over six months of age at the time of filing, a parent has failed consistently to make child support payment and failed to visit regularly with the child.

The Independent Living Initiatives

Each year, approximately 20,000 children leave foster care because they have reached the age of majority. Concerned that these youths lacked the skills to live independently, Congress amended the Title IV-E program in 1985 by enacting the Independent Living Program (ILP). The ILP requires that when youths reach the age of sixteen, their case plan contains provisions for services to help them prepare to live independently, including the opportunity to complete high school or its equivalent; to plan for future education or vocational training; and to receive services to develop daily living skills, such as budgeting; and locating and maintaining housing.[37] States provide independent living services, but many young people encounter problems after leaving foster care, including dropping out of school, homelessness, unemployment, incarceration, lack of medical care, mental health problems, and early pregnancy.[38] From visits to independent living centers in California, Maryland, New York, and Texas, the General Accounting Office learned that ILPs are not able to provide all of the assistance that young people require. Program limitations included the absence of (1) links with employers to provide job leads, (2) opportunities for youths to practice skills in real-life settings, and (3) opportunities for supervised practice living. The problem is compounded by a lack of data showing what programmatic approaches work best; thus, there is no basis for making concrete recommendations to improve programs.[39]

In December 1999, President Clinton signed the Foster Care Independence Act, doubling funds for ILPs from $70 million to $140 million annually and allowing foster youth to receive Medicaid support until they reach the age of twenty-one. In addition to federal funds, states provide a match of $25 million, and some states report that they raise additional funds from private sources.[40]

Abandoned Babies Assistance Act

In 1988, Congress amended the AACWA to address the problem of infants and young children being abandoned in hospitals. The Abandoned Infants Assistance Act (AIAA) is concerned with "boarder babies," newborns, infants, and young children who have been cleared for hospital discharge but remain in hospitals because there is no home to which they can be discharged. The AIAA funds programs operated by state and nonprofit agencies to serve abandoned infants and children. Hospitals initiate state intervention on behalf of an abandoned child by making a report to the state agency that is designated to receive reports of child abuse or neglect. The state agency searches for the mother, father, or other family member who may care for the child and simultaneously plans for placement of the child in a safe environment when she or he is ready for hospital discharge.

The Indian Child Welfare Act

The Indian Child Welfare Act of 1978 (ICWA) addresses prevention, foster care placement, and adoption of Indian children. The intention of this law is to protect the best interests of Indian children within their tribal culture. Whether the concern is with placement in a substitute care setting or an adoptive setting, preference is given to placing Native American children with extended family members, with tribal members, or in another Native American home or institution rather than a non-Indian home. Tribal courts have decision-making authority over any child custody proceeding involving an Indian child who resides within a reservation, although tribal courts may enter into agreements with state courts, where each has jurisdiction over child welfare matters concerning Native children.[41] Active, rather than reasonable, efforts are required to prevent family break-up. As with the reasonable efforts requirement of AACWA, the law does not define active efforts.

Data on Children Receiving Child Welfare Services

When enacted in 1980, the AACWA contained a provision that required the states to establish statewide information systems containing data on children in care. This goal was never fully realized. In 1986, amendments to the Social Security Act required the Department of Health and Human Services to oversee creation of a national data system, the Adoption and Foster Care Analysis and Reporting System (AFCARS). Under the 1986 amendments, states are required to collect child-specific data on children in foster care under state supervision and on children who are adopted.

The Adoption and Foster Care Analysis and Reporting System was implemented on October 1, 1994.[42] At the time of this writing, the most recent data available on foster care and adoptions were reported by twenty-five states for the period ending September 30, 1997.[43] The majority of children live in foster family homes (79 percent) either with related (36 percent) or nonrelated caretakers (43 percent). Fifteen percent of children reside in a group home or institution, 4 percent in an independent living situation, and 1 percent each are runaways or reside in a preadoptive home.

Eighty-one percent of children fell into three age categories, each with just over 25 percent of children aged 1 to 5, 6 to 10, and 11 to 15. Males represented 59 percent of children and females, 41 percent. Ninety-five percent of children had a case plan, including reunification with parents or relatives (55 percent), adoption (21 percent), long-term care (8 percent), emancipation (6 percent), and legal guardianship (5 percent). Forty-seven percent of the children were black, non-Hispanic; 36 percent were white, non-Hispanic; 2 percent were Hispanic; 1 percent, Asian/Pacific Islander; and 13 percent, Native American or Native Alaskan. The racial or ethnic background of 1 percent of children was not known. Thirty-one percent of children are in care for less than one year, 20 percent for one to two years; 15 percent for two to three years; and 34 percent of children in care three or more years.

Most children leave the child welfare system to return to their biological parents or to the home of a relative (68 percent), and 13 percent are adopted. Reasons for discharge for the remaining children are emancipation (7 percent), guardianship (3 percent), transfer (5 percent), and runaway (4 percent).[44]

The Temporary Assistance for Needy Families Program, Foster Care, and Child Support

The fact that a TANF recipient is limited to sixty months of lifetime benefits gives rise to the question, "Will parental unemployment increase the demand for foster care when public assistance is lost?" There are alternatives sources of income for unemployed parents who lose their TANF grants that could prevent the loss of a home and the need to place a child in care, including receiving assistance from (1) family or friends; (2) a general assistance program (chapter 10), although it is not likely that parents will be able to maintain their own homes unless they receives additional help, especially a rent subsidy; (3) income received from the SSI program; (4) an extended benefit program that states could implement using some of the "windfall" funds that TANF has produced (chapter 10); or (5) a noncustodial parent. In the following pages, child support enforcement is addressed. As will become clear, child support payments are not a dependable source of income and, when made, are unlikely to be sufficient to maintain a household.

CHILD SUPPORT ENFORCEMENT

In 1975, Congress amended Title IV of the Social Security Act, adding a part D, the Child Support Enforcement and Paternity Establishment Program (CSE).[45] Federal law requires each state to provide CSE services for children receiving TANF, Title IV-E foster care, and Medicaid. States may assist others at their request.

Applicants for TANF must cooperate with the state to establish paternity, if necessary, to locate a noncustodial parent unless exempted for "good cause," and they must assign their support rights to the state. Definitions of "good cause" are left to state discretion, but they usually focus on applicants fears that serious physical or emotional harm will come to them or their children if the noncustodial parent is identified and ordered to child support.[46] A parent who fails without good cause to cooperate in child support enforcement efforts risks losing all TANF benefits or, at state option, sustaining a benefit reduction of at least 25 percent. As long as the parent remains on TANF, collected support is shared by the state and the federal government. When a family leaves the welfare roles, collected funds go to the family even if the noncustodial parent owes money to the state for back support payments. A number of states report that they pay out more to operate their CSE programs than they get back. This is due in part to the fact that the states no longer keep recovered elections.[47]

Federal matching funds support state CSE efforts to (1) locate absent parents using the Federal Parent Locator Service that accesses information from motor vehicle registries, tax files including those of the Internal Revenue Service, and employment and unemployment records[48]; (2) establish paternity; (3) obtain and enforce orders for financial and medical support both within and across state lines; and (4) help families not on public assistance to remain self-sufficient.

For the parent who fails to voluntarily meet a support obligation, funds may be collected through withholding (1) wages, (2) income tax refunds, and (3) "intercepting" unemployment compensation benefits. In addition, a state may act against a nonsupporting parent by (1) withholding, suspending, or restricting the use of driver's licenses, professional and occupational licenses, and recreational licenses; and (2) requiring unemployed noncustodial parents who owe child support to a TANF child to participate in work activities.

SUPPORT PAYMENTS ARE UNLIKELY TO PREVENT THE NEED FOR FOSTER CARE

States determine the amount of child support (1) by combining the income of both parents and setting a support payment as a percentage of combined income, (2) as a percentage of the gross income of the noncustodial parent, with the percentage increasing as the number of children increases, or (3) by combining the first two approaches. Regardless of the approach that is used, support payments are likely to be low. For example, if a noncustodial parent earns the minimum wage of $5.15 an hour and works a 40 hour week, his weekly gross will be $206. If he has two children and lives in Wisconsin, his support obligation will equal 17 percent of gross income or $35 per week; if he lives in New York and the child's mother does not have earned income, his obligation will be 25 percent of income or $52 per week.[49]

In 1995, 13.7 million women and men were raising children alone, and women make up the vast majority of single parents. Approximately 60 percent of single parents had a child support award, the same percent who had an award in 1978. Ninety-two percent of parents with an award had a legally binding agreement. As was the case in 1978, nearly two-thirds of parents with agreements did not receive any payments. Of those receiving payments, only 17.8 percent received payment in full, down from 23.6 percent in 1978. Roughly 30 percent of custodial parents had incomes below the poverty line.[50]

The United States General Accounting Office (GAO) studied child support collections in three states with welfare time limits of less than sixty months where benefit terminations began in 1997. Between 47 percent and 69 percent of families did not have orders of support in the year before their benefits were terminated, leading the GAO to conclude that "many TANF families may not be able to count on child support as a steady source of income when welfare benefits expire . . . only . . . 20 to 30 percent of families [had] . . . child support collected . . . in the 12 months before their benefits were terminated." Where support was collected, mean collections for the twelve-month period before benefit termination ranged from $1,065 to $1,388, and most collections were only a percentage of the amount due.

An inability to locate noncustodial parents was cited as a major reason for failure to collect support, and states that aggressively pursue missing parents report a better rate of collection.[51] For example, in Minnesota and Washington about two-thirds of the cases that remained open for five years received some support, but nevertheless, one-third of cases would lose their benefits with no expectation of child support.[52] When families were on welfare for many years and noncustodial parents had not been identified, it was unlikely that absent parents could be located and support orders obtained.

Education and race are related to the likelihood of having an order of support and to the amount of an award. Seventy-three percent of women with college degrees, compared to 60 percent of high school graduates and 48 percent of high school dropouts, have an order for support, and college graduates receive $4,800 per year in support compared with $2,800 for high school graduates and $1,700 for women who do not complete high school. Sixty-five percent of white women, compared to 50 percent of black women and 41 percent of Hispanic women, have an order of support, and white women receive approximately $3,400 per year compared to $2,100 for black women and $2,700 for Hispanic women. Never-married mothers are one of the poorest demographic groups in the nation, with 44 percent having orders of support compared with 73 percent of divorced women, and never-married mothers who receive support get considerably less than divorced mothers, receiving $1,700 per year compared to $3,600 for women who are divorced.

Summary

The Child Abuse Prevention and Treatment Act requires each state to develop the capacity to receive and investigate reports of child maltreatment and to protect children who are abused or neglected. Social services that are necessary to achieve the act's objectives are funded mainly the Title XX Social Services Block Grant and the Title IV-B Child Welfare Service Block Grant.

The AACWA requires states to implement programs to prevent foster care placement and programs to facilitate the placement of children in permanent family homes. To achieve these objectives, states must, with several exceptions, make reasonable efforts to prevent placement and to reunite children with their birth families. In addition, the law requires written case plans and periodic case review to ensure that plans are implemented and progress is made to placing children in permanent homes. Federal law provides for financial assistance to individuals and families who adopt children with special needs and stresses the importance of states adopting laws that ease the process of finding out-of-state adoptive homes.

The AACWA funds programs for children who have been abandoned in hospitals and programs to facilitate the adoption of children with special needs. Changes to federal law in the 1990s reduced somewhat the emphasis on family preservation and family reunification in favor of finding adoptive homes of children by allowing early termination of parental rights when available evidence indicates that children returned to their biological parents will not be safe and by declaring that rules that preclude absolutely transracial adoptions violate the Civil Rights Act of 1964.

The ILP provides funds for development and implementation of programs to assist young people who will not leave foster care until they reach the age of emancipation obtain an education and develop skills to live on their own.

The ICWA seeks to safeguard the cultural heritage of Native American children by providing for their placement in the homes of Native American families. The provisions of the ICWA are similar to those in the AACWA, with the key difference being that the ICWA provides that tribal courts will have jurisdiction over Native children if they choose to exercise this prerogative.

Child support enforcement laws were discussed in the context of asking whether TANF's sixty-month lifetime benefit period might increase the demand for foster care when benefits run out. Available data suggest that child support is not likely to fill the gap that would remain when a family loses TANF benefits. No more than 60 percent of parents raising children alone have an award of child support, and most receive either no payments or only partial payments. Moreover, formulas that are used to determine awards are not likely to yield an amount of child support sufficient to replace lost benefits; for example, in New York a noncustodial parent would have to earn $40,000 annually for the custodial parent of two children to receive an award of $10,000.

CHAPTER 16

Education

Publicly funded primary and secondary education programs are controlled mainly by state law. The federal government acts in the educational arena by funding programs for children who are disadvantaged due to poverty, disability, and limited English proficiency, by supporting programs to educate Native American, Native Alaskan, and Native Hawaiian children,[1] by establishing rules of national scope that govern access to a child's school records,[2] and through enforcement of civil rights legislation that prohibits discriminatory denial of educational opportunities. Throughout the 1990s, a yearly average of $30 billion in federal funds were provided to support preschool, elementary, and secondary education programs[3] that are administered by a number of federal agencies, including the Departments of Education, Health and Human Services; Agriculture; Labor; Defense; and Veteran's Affairs.

In this chapter, the following federal programs and acts are reviewed: (1) the Head Start Program, (2) the Migrant Education Program, (3) the Elementary and Secondly Education Act; (4) the Stewart B. McKinney Program for homeless children, and (5) the Individuals with Disabilities in Education Act (IDEA).

Note that the bulk of material in this chapter is devoted to the IDEA. This is so because Congress has imposed a series of concrete obligations on school districts that accept IDEA funds that are not found in other educational acts. The imposed obligations have given rise to a significant amount of litigation to ensure that children receive the benefits to which they are entitled, and some of this litigation is reviewed to further your understanding of how statute has been implemented.

Head Start

Head Start began in 1965 as a War on Poverty program (see chapter 10).[4] Federal funds that go to local units of government, school systems, nonprofit organizations, and Native American and Native Alaskan tribes pay for approximately 85 percent of program costs. Other sources of funding for Head Start services include the Title XX Social Services Block Grant (chapter 14), the Child Care and Development Block Grant (chapter 10) and state, local, and foundation funds. The goal of Head Start is to improve the social competence of low-income, preschool children in dealing with everyday situations and to prepare children for later school and social responsibilities by developing learning skills and improving their health so that they can begin school on an equal basis with their more advantaged peers.[5]

Head Start services may be delivered (1) at a Head Start Center (church, school, university, community center, parent's work site), (2) at the child's home, (3) at a combination of the two, or (4) at a locally designed option that suits the specific needs of a community. Program staff are to visit the child's home to assess whether any social or medical services are required and to develop a program for family members to support the child's experience in the education program. Parental involvement in Head Start is extensive. Some parents are volunteers and others are employed as staff. Some parents go through a training program to become certified child care workers.

CHILDREN SERVED

At least 90 percent of children served must come from families with incomes at or below the poverty line, and 10 percent of the slots in local programs must be available for children with disabilities. In 1998, 60 percent of Head Start families earned less than $9,000 per year, and 45 percent participated in the Temporary Assistance to Needy Families Program (TANF) (chapter 10). A Head Start program provides both educational opportunities for the child as well as part-time child care that is needed by a parent who is in the labor force, but Head Start is limited as a child care resource because programs typically provide only part-day care for four to five hours and operate on a school-year schedule of nine months. In 1998, 830,000 children from birth to age five were served at 16,000 centers and in 595 home-based programs at a cost in excess of $3.5 billion. Most children begin Head Start at age four.[6] Close to 80 percent of children speak English as their primary language, and 18 percent speak Spanish. Approximately equal percentages of children are black (38 percent) or white (33 percent), 25 percent of children are of Hispanic origin, and the remaining children are classified as "other."

SERVICES PROVIDED

Head Start services are provided to children and may be provided to members of a child's family. In addition to educational services, Head Start arranges for or makes referrals for medical and dental care, social services, nutritional services, and mental health services. Federal regulations require programs to make use of available community resources before using Head Start funds to provide services. For children, services most likely to be delivered and funded directly by Head Start are educational services, social services, child care, meals, and other nutritional services. When any service is provided to members of a child's family, it is almost always provided by others in the community.[7]

EFFECTIVENESS OF HEAD START

Head Start has diverse goals, and those evaluating Head Start programs may ask different questions, for example, "What effect if any does parental involvement have on the social, academic, and health gains of Head Start children?" or "How does the academic and social performance of children who participate in Head Start compare to a similar group of children who did not experience Head Start?"

The Department of Health and Human Services (DHHS) has not identified specific program outcomes despite a congressional mandate that agencies prepare annual plans that link program performance to outcomes. In its 1998 Performance Plan, DHHS reported that it would

> continue to develop goals, objectives, and measures for all of its programs . . . [and it would] . . . resolve issues that are delaying consensus [as to program] . . . outcome[s], customer-oriented performance measures to be used to monitor progress toward . . . goals and objectives.[8]

The United States General Accounting Office (GAO) takes the position that "impact studies" that seek to answer the question "Is involvement in a Head Start program having a positive impact on participant's lives?"[9] are appropriate. Investigators at the GAO concluded that there is a paucity of such studies and that DHHS's research agenda would do little to provide information regarding program impact because the research agenda of DHHS focuses on "descriptive studies; studies of program variations, involving new and innovative service delivery strategies and demonstration projects; and studies of program quality." Such studies have value but they do not provide the impact information needed in today's results-oriented environment.[10]

The GAO reviewed twenty-two evaluations of Head Start that were conducted after 1976 and concluded that existing research does not provide enough information to answer questions concerning program impact because there are no studies that included a nationally representative sample of program participants. This conclusion has been criticized because Head Start programs are designed to address local needs, and the results of individual studies cannot be combined to draw a national picture. However, the GAO also concluded that the reviewed studies had methodological and design weaknesses, such as the use of control groups that were not comparable. According to officials from DHHS, studies conducted before 1997 showed a positive impact for Head Start, but these studies were discounted by the GAO because their investigators concluded that these studies were not applicable to the redesigned programs that existed in the late 1990s.

In 1981, under contract to DHHS, CRS Inc. reported findings from existing impact. The researchers concluded that children demonstrated significant immediate gains in cognitive test scores but that gains were short-lived when Head Start children were compared to others from a similar background who did not attend Head Start. However, data reported by McKey and colleagues (1985) revealed that Head Start children were less likely than other to be held back in grade and less likely to be placed in special education programs.[11] In 1995, Currie and Duncan, using data from the National Longitudinal Survey of Youth and the National Longitudinal Survey's Mother-Child file, examined the impact of Head Start on more than 900 children. They report that Head Start had a positive and persistent impact on cognitive achievement for white students, including white Hispanic students, but not for others, although all students experienced an increase in preventive medical care.[12]

The Migrant Education Program and Migrant Head Start

In 1965, the Department of Education (DOE) created the Migrant Education Program (MEP), and in 1969, the DHHS created Migrant Head Start (MHS).[13] Both programs were developed to address the unique educational problems of the estimated 3 to 5 million children of migrant farm workers whose educational needs stem from limited English proficiency, rural and social isolation, frequent moves across school districts within a school year, and poverty, with the associated health risks.[14] The goals of MHS are similar to those already reviewed for the regular Head Start Program. Children in MHS are somewhat younger, and they are served for a longer period of time, averaging eight to fourteen hours per day, and some programs operate seven days a week.

The goal of MEP is to ensure that the children of migrant farm workers under the age of twenty-one have the same chance as other children to meet a state's educational standards. The MEP funds support outreach to inform families of the program, information and referral to direct families to needed services, and tutoring and counseling services to elementary and secondary school students who comprise 82 percent of MEP children who are served at approximately 17,000 schools located mainly in rural areas across the nation. Priority is given to students who are failing or at greatest risk of failing in school and whose education has been interrupted by moving during the school year.

There are no evaluations of either program, and neither DHHS nor DOE has a system for transferring information as students move between different locations. Because there is no system for transferring credits, children are often assessed twice or placed in inappropriate classes, and services are delayed.

Elementary and Secondary Education Act

The Act to Strengthen and Improve Elementary and Secondary Schools (previously the Elementary and Secondary Education Act [ESEA] of 1965) funds five programs that have in common the goal of increasing the educational opportunities for economically disadvantaged students and for students who lack English-language proficiency.[15] Title I of the act is the major source of federal funds for schools to upgrade their educational programs. In the 1996–97 school year, Title I funds served 11 million students.[16]

In 1994, Congress amended the act and passed the Goals 2000: Educate America Act. Reform of the primary and secondary educational system nationwide was Congress's objective. Congress required that funds be targeted to schools in the highest poverty areas and authorized the use of federal dollars to assist the states to develop and implement programs that would raise academic standards by improving teaching methods, increasing opportunities for classroom learning, and developing and implementing procedures to measure student achievement.[17] For students whose English-language proficiency is limited, achievement is to be measured to the extent possible in the language and form most likely to yield an accurate assessment.[18] More than half of the states exempt students with limited English-language proficiency from some or all of required assessments. Exemptions are time limited and apply to students recently arrived in the United States, those with limited exposure to classroom-based English-language instruction, and those who score poorly on a test of English-language proficiency. Some school districts accommodate students with limited English proficiency in a number of ways, including (1) reading test directions and the test questions aloud; (2) interpreting and repeating directions; (3) allowing the option of an oral rather than a written exam; and (4) translating the exam into the student's native language. Additional accommodations allow students to take exams individually or in small groups or to have the test administered by a person who is familiar to the student.

In 1997, Hannaway and Kimball reported the results of a fifty-state survey in which they asked about progress being made in implementing the changes required by the Goals 2000 act. With 2,700 school districts responding, they stated that some progress was made with smaller districts, and those serving students in high poverty areas reported the greatest difficulty in reforming curricula and establishing academic standards.[19]

Similar results were reported to Congress in 1999 by Alan Ginsburg, Director of Planning and Evaluation for the DOE. Summarizing the results of a national assessment of Title I, he reported that progress was seen in implementing key provisions of the act, especially the requirements that funds be targeted to schools in the poorest districts and that states implement standards to govern curriculum content, but implementation was "highly uneven across States, districts, and schools."[20] Progress in measuring student performance was limited. Less than a dozen states were able to report three years of comparable assessment information for high- and low-poverty schools. In addition, teacher aides were being used inappropriately, and teacher preparation was not adequate. Paraprofessionals made up half of the staff supported by Title I funds, and they spent most of their time teaching without a supervising teacher present, even though they lack the educational background to teach. Use of paraprofessionals was most likely in high-poverty schools, and only 10 percent of paraprofessionals had a bachelor's degree. In addition, lack of parental involvement was cited as a major problem by school principals, who said that it was a major barrier to reform.

EDUCATION LANGUAGE PROFICIENCY

In Chapter 13, I reported that Title VI of the Civil Rights Act of 1964 prohibits discrimination in programs that receive federal funds. Title VI provides that "No person in the United States, shall, on the ground of race, color, or national origin be excluded from participation in, be denied the benefits of, or be subjected to discrimination under any program or activity receiving federal financial assistance."

Children who are not proficient in the primary language of the country in which they live and attend school operate at an educational disadvantage. The question of a school district's obligation to provide English-language instruction to children whose native language was other than English reached the Supreme Court in the 1970s. In 1974, the Court ruled that the failure of the San Francisco school system to provide English-language instruction to non-English speaking Chinese students violated Title VI. "There is no equality of treatment," the Court said, "merely by providing students with the same facilities, textbooks, teachers, and curriculum; for students who do not understand English are effectively foreclosed from any meaningful education."[21]

In the same year, Congress codified the Supreme Court's decision in the Equal Educational Opportunities Act (EEOA), which states that

> no state shall deny equal opportunity to an individual on account of his or her race, color, sex, or national origin, by . . . failing to take appropriate action to overcome language barriers that impede equal participation . . . in instructional programs.[22]

Thus, the approximately 3.5 million children in the United States who have limited English-language proficiency[23] are entitled to language assistance, and programs may be funded using Title I monies from the ESEA. However, the obligation imposed by the EEOA does not require that school districts use any particular method of assisting students. Schools may choose from different approaches, for example, by adopting bilingual education programs that teach primary subjects such as math and social sciences in a student's native language while the student learns English, or English immersion programs that, as the name implies, immerse children in classes where all or nearly all instruction is in English, with the curriculum modified for children who are learning the language.[24] In determining whether a language remediation program is appropriate, courts must ask and answer three questions. First, "Is the program based on sound educational theory or principles?" Second, "Are the resources and personnel needed to translate the theory into a program available?" and third, "Does the program produce the desired result after it has been implemented for a period of time sufficient to give the plan a legitimate trial?" Programs will pass must if these questions are answered in the affirmative.[25]

Homeless Children and the Stewart B. McKinney Act

Without special assistance, school attendance and school success for homeless children may be impossible. The problems confronting homeless parents in sending their children to school and the problems confronting homeless children in obtaining an education are numerous and include (1) rules that limit the length of shelter stays, causing families to move frequently, with each move possibly taking children out of the district in which they were attending class; (2) the difficulties of locating a school and arranging transportation with each move to a new shelter; (3) the barriers to school enrollment when state and local law contain residency requirements and that require a child's birth, medical, and school records as a condition for school enrollment; and (4) the endless difficulties that must exist for the child who tries to study in a shelter and the debilitating effect of having one's learning continually interrupted. Estimates of the percent of homeless children not attending school vary from a high of 50 percent to a low of 14 percent.[26]

The Stewart B. McKinney Homeless Assistance Act, discussed in chapter 11 where programs to develop housing for homeless people were reviewed, requires that states guarantee equal access to public education for children of homeless families, and the McKinney act confers on homeless children a legally enforceable right to an education.[27] Under the McKinney act, grants to local educational agencies are available to facilitate the enrollment, attendance, and success in school of homeless children and youth.

To receive McKinney act funds, state educational agencies submit a plan describing the assistance that will be provided to homeless children and youth. States are expected to revise laws and practices, for example, by eliminating residency requirements for homeless children and youth, so that they will have the same free appropriate public education as other children.

States are to establish the office of Coordinator of Education of Homeless Children and Youth to compile data and submit reports to the secretary of education describing (1) the number of homeless children and youth and the number served with act funds, (2) the problems confronting homeless children and youth in gaining access to education, (3) the special needs of homeless children and youth, (4) progress made by state and local education agencies in addressing problems identified, and (5) whether programs funded with act monies are successful in allowing homeless children and youth to enroll in, attend, and succeed in school. In addition, the coordinator is to facilitate cooperation among the state educational agency, the state social services agency, and other agencies providing services to homeless children and youth. To improve the provision of comprehensive services to the target population, the coordinator must develop relationships and coordinate with other education, child development, or preschool programs; with providers of services to homeless children and their families; and with runaway and homeless youth centers.

McKinney grants may be used to assist homeless youngsters in different ways, including (1) providing tutoring and other forms of supplemental instruction; (2) expediting evaluations to identify educational strengths and needs and eligibility for special programs, for example, those serving gifted students, disabled students, and students with limited English proficiency; (3) assessing the need for any service that is available under Title I of the ESEA and through school-based nutrition programs; (4) referring for medical, dental, health, and mental health services; (5) providing financial assistance to defray excess transportation costs; (6) providing early childhood education that is not available through other programs; (7) providing before- and after-school, mentoring, and summer programs; (8) paying the cost of locating, obtaining, and transferring any records needed to enroll a child in school; (9) educating and training parents about the rights of and resources available to their children; (10) providing school supplies; and (11) providing other assistance to reduce or eliminate extraordinary or emergency situations that hinder school attendance.

Local educational agencies are to select a school in accordance with parental choice to the extent possible and consistent with the best interests of the child or youth. There is a preference for continuing children in the school they attended before becoming homeless or enrolling them in the school district in which they are temporarily living.[28]

The Individuals with Disabilities in Education Act

Despite the importance of a public education, exclusion of "uneducable and untrainable" children from public schools and segregation of children with disabilities in separate classrooms have been normative practice in the United States.[29] The movement to include children with disabilities in educational settings began in 1966 when Congress amended the ESEA. A grant program was established to assist the states in developing and implementing programs to educate children with disabilities. In 1970, Congress enacted the Education of the Handicapped Act, which repealed the ESEA amendments. Despite congressional efforts, little progress was made in providing educational opportunities for children with disabilities. In 1974, Congress mandated that the states embrace the objective of making available full educational opportunities to children with disabilities, and in 1975 the Education for All Handicapped Children Act (EAHCA) was passed, creating an entitlement that guaranteed to eligible children the right to receive a free appropriate public education. The EAHCA was renamed the Individuals with Disabilities in Education Act in 1990.

The problems that the EAHCA was meant to resolve were expressed by Congress as a series of findings that began with the acknowledgment that there were more than 8 million children with disabilities in the United States, more than half of whom were not receiving appropriate educational services.[30] Of these children, 1 million were said to be excluded entirely from a public school education. In addition, Congress reported that some children did not have a successful educational experience because their disabilities were not detected, and families were often compelled to seek services for their children outside of the public school system, frequently at great distances from their homes and at their own expense, due to the lack of adequate services in the school system.

Each state is free to accept or reject federal financial participation in its educational programs for disabled children.[31] If a state elects to receive federal funds, it must comply with the standards that are set forth in the IDEA. However, the IDEA does not impose national standards for educating disabled children. Each state is free to decide the content and methods to be used in educational programs. Nevertheless, the IDEA contains procedural and substantive requirements. After defining disability, these requirements are reviewed.

DEFINITION OF DISABILITY

The IDEA covers children with severe disabilities. The statute and its implementing regulations define as disabled children who are mentally retarded, hearing impaired (including children who are deaf), and who experience speech, language, or visual impairments (including blindness). Children who are seriously emotionally disturbed are protected by the law, as are those who have orthopedic impairments, children who have suffered from traumatic brain injury, and those who have specific learning disabilities and require special education and related services due to their disability.[32]

The phrase "children with specific learning disabilities" means that the IDEA's protections are extended to children who have a disorder that implicates the psychological processes involved in understanding or in using spoken or written language. The child's difficulties may be observed in an "imperfect ability to listen, think, speak, read, write, spell, or do mathematical calculations. . . . [and the act covers children with] perceptual disabilities, brain injury, minimal brain dysfunction, dyslexia, and developmental aphasia."

The concept of specific learning disabilities does not extend to the child whose learning problems are mainly caused by conditions such as visual, hearing, or motor disabilities, nor does it cover children who are disadvantaged due to environmental, cultural, or economic factors.

Note that the IDEA does not protect the child or youth who is denied access to a regular educational program unless denial is based on a demonstrable disability. Protection from discrimination for those who do not meet the IDEA's definition of disability may be provided by the Vocational Rehabilitation Act and the Americans with Disabilities Act (chapter 13). For example, children who are positive for Human Immunodeficiency Virus (HIV) have experienced extensive discrimination in educational settings.[33] Children who are HIV-positive but asymptomatic do not, by definition, have special educational needs as a result of their HIV status. They need only one thing: protection against discriminatory exclusion from educational settings. Their educational rights would be safeguarded by either the VRA or the ADA. The child who develops Acquired Immune Deficiency Syndrome (AIDS), however, has a severe disability and would be eligible for assistance under the IDEA.

Neither the VRA nor the ADA imposes on a school district an affirmative duty to create special programs for children with disabilities. However, federal regulations provide that

> A recipient of federal funds that operates a public elementary or secondary education program shall provide a free appropriate public education to each qualified handicapped person who is in the recipient's jurisdiction, regardless of the nature or severity of the person's handicap . . . that] related services are required . . . [and that a child is entitled to] an individualized education program developed in accordance with the Individuals with Disabilities in Education Act.[34]

STATE PLANS REQUIRED

In return for receipt of federal funds, each state must guarantee a "Free Appropriate Public Education" (FAPE) to all children with disabilities. A FAPE for disabled children is one that addresses the child's special education needs through the provision of special education classes and related services, such as transportation, counseling, and physical therapy, provided at public expense. A FAPE may require an extended school year to permit children with disabilities to benefit from their educational programs.

States must submit a plan to the DOE that specifies the procedures it will follow to ensure that all eligible children receive the educational protections to which they are entitled. States must identify children with disabilities, evaluate all children to determine their educational needs, notify parent(s) or other legal guardian [hereafter, parents] of their findings, and provide parents with the opportunity to participate in planning for their child's education. The plan must spell out how the state will conduct the required outreach services in order to identify, locate, and evaluate children with disabilities. This obligation extends to "highly mobile" children, for example, the children of migrant farm workers and homeless children as well as to children in private schools, including faith-based private schools.[35] For each child, an Individualized Education Plan (IEP) is required, as is mainstreaming to the extent possible. Each state must provide for a fair hearing so that parents who disagree with the school systems' decisions regarding the education of their child can contest the decisions made.

The protections guaranteed by the IDEA apply only to those children who are eligible for a FAPE as defined by the laws of each state, and the IDEA ensures that a child's disability will not disqualify her or him from receipt of that education. States may use federal funds to provide a FAPE for all disabled children between the ages of three and twenty-one. However, the state is not obliged to serve those with disabilities who are aged three to five and eighteen to twenty-one unless doing so is consistent with state law or practice or education for children and youth in these age groups is mandated by a court.[36]

FREE APPROPRIATE PUBLIC EDUCATION AND THE INDIVIDUALIZED EDUCATION PLANS

Each eligible child is entitled to an IEP, and eligible infants and toddlers are entitled to an Individualized Family Service Plan (in subsequent discussion, these plans are both included in the acronym IEP). The IEP is the foundation for the disabled child's educational entitlement. The IEP is a written statement that describes the instructional program that will be put in place to meet the unique educational needs of the child for whom it is developed. The IEP must be reviewed at least once each year and changed if necessary.

In 1982, the Supreme Court was asked to address the question, "What does the entitlement referred to by the phrase 'Free Appropriate Public Education' entail?" The parents of Amy Rawley, who had a severe hearing impairment, had requested that the school district provide Amy with a sign-language interpreter to aid her in her academic classes. The Court found that the assignment of a sign-language interpreter was not mandated by the law. Amy was entitled to an educational program that was "reasonably calculated to enable [her] to achieve passing marks and advance from grade to grade."[37] However, the law does not create an obligation on a school district to maximize a child's potential or to guarantee any particular educational outcome. Amy's performance was better than average, and she was advancing from grade to grade. The Court conceded that her full potential was not realized due to her hearing impairment but found that the statute did not obligate the school district to ensure that she maximize her potential. The purpose of the law "was more to open the door of public education to handicapped children on appropriate terms than to guarantee any particular level of education once inside."[38]

After *Rowley*, lower courts would elaborate on a school district's obligation under the IDEA. In 1983, the Sixth Circuit Court of Appeals held that a FAPE for autistic children is appropriate if the plan provides a reasonable opportunity for the children to acquire skills that would permit them to function in a noninstitutional setting. However, this does not mean that a school must provide any and all services that might be of benefit to the child. Although schools have an obligation to stay abreast of new teaching methods and to implement those shown to be successful, they are not required to experiment with every new teaching technique. Schools need not spend exorbitant sums on any one child at the expense of other children with disabilities.[39]

DEVELOPMENT OF THE INDIVIDUALIZED EDUCATION PLAN

The IEP is to be in effect at the start or each school year. It is to be developed by a multidisciplinary team in a meeting attended by a representative of the educational agency that is qualified to provide or supervise the child's education program, at least one special education teacher or special education provider, the child's regular education teacher, the child's parents, and the child, when appropriate.[40] The IEP is to describe the current educational performance of the child or youth, the responsibilities of each service provider and teacher in meeting the annual and the short-term instructional objectives, educational services that are to be provided, and the extent to which the child will be able to participate in regular educational programs.

If a school board fails to hold the multidisciplinary review, it cannot contend that it determined the child's special educational needs, that the IEP is adequate, and that it has met the statutory requirement of providing each child with a FAPE.[41] A school district that develops a child's IEP without involving a child's parents, classroom teacher, or other school representative is not complying with the IDEA. If a school district conducts an evaluation that is deficient, parents may be entitled to reimbursement from the district for the costs associated with obtaining another evaluation of their child,[42] and schools may not conduct evaluations using inappropriate testing techniques, for example, testing a vision-impaired child with a test not designed for use with children whose vision is impaired,[43] or evaluating children on the basis of classroom performance without use of other evaluative tools.[44]

No later than a youngster's sixteenth birthday and as early as his or her fourteenth birthday, the IEP must describe the services needed by the young person to make the transition to independence. Transition services are similar to the independent living services that were discussed in chapter 15. Transition services are outcome-oriented services that promote a young person's ability to live independently, including services to facilitate the movement from school to afterschool activities, such as advanced academic or vocational training, and skills that are needed to live independently. Services are to be based on an assessment of the student's needs, preferences, and interests.

RELATED SERVICES

The concept of education under the IDEA embodies academic instruction plus a broad range of related services. Related services that must be provided when necessary for a disabled child to attain the benefits of an educational plan may include

> Transportation, developmental, corrective, and other supportive services (including speech pathology and audiology, psychological services, physical and occupational therapy, recreation, including therapeutic recreation, social work services, counseling services, including rehabilitation counseling, and medical services, except that such medical services shall be for diagnostic and evaluation purposes only) as may be required to assist a child with a disability to benefit from special education, and includes the early identification and assessment of disabling conditions in children. [45]

The First Amendment does not prevent a public school district from providing related services or supplemental remedial instruction to disadvantaged children attending parochial school.[46] The provided assistance is available to all children who qualify for service under the IDEA at whatever school they choose to attend. However, the obligation to provide related services at a private school is not an obligation to pay the student's tuition.[47] If a student's needs can be met in a public school and if the parents choose to place the child in a private school, the public school system is not obligated to pay the child's tuition,[48] nor is the school district that provided a severely disabled child with speech therapy, occupational therapy, and physical therapy at a public site under any obligation to provide these services on site at the parochial school where the child had been voluntarily placed by his or her parents.[49] The state's obligation would be different if the child's placement in a private school was made by the state. When parents elect to privately place their child, the school system must still provide special education and related services designed to meet the needs of private school children with disabilities, but the school has discretion in deciding how best to provide services.[50]

EDUCATION IN PUBLIC, PRIVATE, AND RESIDENTIAL SETTINGS

In 1985, the Supreme Court affirmed a ruling of the Court of Appeals for the First Circuit, holding that if a school district's choice of placement is found by a judicial officer to be inappropriate, the district is obligated to reimburse the child's parents for their unilateral decision to re-place their child if the placement selected by the parents is appropriate.[51] In 1993, again considering the question of a school district's obligation to reimburse parents for placing their child in an educational setting of their choice, the Supreme Court held that educational authorities who do not want to be found liable for reimbursing parents for privately educating their child can avoid liability if they provide the child with a FAPE in public setting or place the child in an appropriate private setting chosen by the state.[52] Moreover, a FAPE includes placement in a residential facility where such placement is necessary to meet a child's educational needs.[53] Thus, where a child required intensive psychiatric treatment in a residential facility and where prior efforts to educate the child without provision of psychiatric services failed, parents are entitled to reimbursement for the expenses they incurred while their child was placed at a residential center.[54]

If residential placement is in response to medical or social problems that can be separated from matters that relate to a child's education, the school district is not required to pay for the noneducational services.[55] Where a child was diagnosed with an emotional disorder that caused behavior problems, including "unpredictable and at sometimes violent behavior," residential placement was not required where it was shown that the child was deriving educational benefits despite these problems.[56]

However, where a brain-damaged student requires a full-time residential program in order to receive a FAPE, the school district was responsible for paying for a round-the-clock behavior modification program necessary for the student to benefit from his or her educational program. Visits by a physician, which last less than one hour per month, do not change an educational program into a mental health or medical program. Moreover, services received by the young person, occupational therapy, psychological services, recreational therapy, physical therapy, medical evaluations, and transportation are expressly cited as related services under the IDEA.[57]

MAINSTREAMING

The IDEA stresses but does not mandate "mainstreaming" of children with disabilities who are to be educated in the least restrictive environment.[58] Segregated placements should occur only when the nature or severity of a child's disability prevents the child from participating in regular classes even with the use of supplementary aids and services. The IDEA requires school districts to have in place a continuum of alternative placements that would include a variety of settings including regular classes, special classes, special schools, home instruction, and instruction in hospitals and institutions.

Children with disabilities should be integrated with children who do not have disabilities to the extent that integration is appropriate for the educational needs of the child.[59] Mainstreaming may produce social as well as academic gains,[60] and courts have sought to balance the concern that children be educated in an integrated setting with the need to ensure that children benefit educationally as well as socially from their educational experience. Courts have approached this goal by providing that educational goals may be achieved by integrating children for some but not all of the school day or for some but not all academic subjects.[61] But a program that simply fills the time of children with disabilities by engaging them in activities that have no educational purpose and that limit contact with other students without disabilities fails to meet the requirements of the law.[62] Even though a private residential placement may maximize a child's educational opportunities, such a placement is not required where "mainstreaming" the child satisfies the statutory mandate.[63] The fact that curricula materials have to be modified to accommodate children with disabilities is not a legitimate reason for segregating them without showing that required modifications impair significantly the education of other children.[64] However, mainstreaming does not require that a child be integrated into a regular classroom if doing so would be at the expense of the child's educational needs.[65] For example, mainstreaming is not necessary nor is it appropriate if the result is failure for the child who would succeed if taught in a segregated classroom.[66]

Some parents who do not wish to have their children integrated into regular classroom settings because they think that a child's educational needs can only be met in special, segregated settings have sued school districts for integrating their children into regular classrooms.[67] If children are performing well in regular classrooms, parents cannot remove them to private residential centers and ask the state to reimburse them for the costs of educating the child.[68]

PROCEDURAL SAFEGUARDS

Earlier I said that a child's parent must have the opportunity to participate in development of the child's IEP. Parents have additional rights under the IDEA, including the right to review (1) all records concerning their child, which includes a right to review the evaluations that contributed to the decision that a child requires special education; (2) all records that contain information regarding the selection of a child's educational placement; and (3) all records that describe the way in which the school district will provide a FAPE to a child. A child's parents have a right to obtain an independent educational evaluation of the child if they so choose.

A child with a disability may be removed from an educational setting for up to ten consecutive school days for a violation of school rules if the infractions would result in the removal of a child who was not disabled. Services may be provided to the disabled child during the removal period. Special provisions in the IDEA concerning discipline come into play if the child is removed from the classroom for more than ten consecutive school days or if the child experiences a series of removals that cumulate to more than ten days in a school year.[69]

If removal exceeds ten days, educational services must be provided after the ten-day period to enable the child to advance toward achieving the goals in his or her IEP. School officials may move children to an "appropriate interim alternative educational setting" for up to forty-five days if a child carries a weapon to school or knowingly possesses illegal drugs. [70]

Any change in a child's educational placement must be preceded by written notice to the child's parents, who have a right to a fair hearing. A school district must permit a child to "stay put" in the classroom during the pendency of any procedure instituted to contest a school decision to move the child, unless the student poses an immediate threat to the safety of others or where the student has violated school rules for reasons unrelated to her or his disability.[71] Thus, a school district was allowed to expel a student with a disability for possession of marijuana because the student knew of the school's antidrug policy.[72]

School districts are required to have procedures to protect the rights of any child whose parents are not known or whose parents are not available, including procedures to protect the rights of children who are wards of the state. Under any of these circumstances, a person who is not an employee of any state or local educational agency that is involved in the education or care of the child is to be assigned to act as a parental surrogate.

Adults who are acting for the child, whether parent, guardian, or surrogate, must receive written notice in their native language (unless it is clearly not possible to provide notice in their native language) before any change is made to a child's IEP, including any change in the child's physical placement. The adults must have the opportunity to register any objections they may have regarding proposed changes, and they are entitled to a fair hearing and the right to appeal an adverse decision. The latter right includes the right to bring an attorney and others who have special knowledge or training in the area of childhood disabilities. At a fair hearing, the child's representative has the right to present evidence, to confront and cross-examine witnesses, and to compel the attendance of witnesses. In addition, the adult who is representing the child's interests is entitled to a verbatim transcript of the proceedings and the right to have the final decision, including the facts that supported the final decision, put in writing.[73]

SPECIAL GRANT PROGRAMS

In addition to mandating a FAPE for school-aged children with disabilities, the IDEA provides for the development and implementation of programs to provide special services for children with disabilities through a series of discretionary grant programs. States may apply for grants to provide special education and related service to infants, toddlers, and children from birth through age eight.[74] In addition, institutions of higher education, vocational and training institutions, and state and local educational agencies may apply for grants to develop and implement new programs and strengthen existing programs to provide educational and related services to disabled youth to assist them in making the transition to independent or semi-independent living. Grants are also available to conduct research in the use of educational media and to assist in the production and distribution of educational media such as captioned films to assist hearing impaired children. Finally, public and private institutions may apply for grants for the express purpose of developing approaches, including curricula materials, to enhance the educational opportunities of children and youth with serious emotional problems.[75]

Summary

The federal government acts in the educational arena by funding programs for those who are disadvantaged. Federal funds are available for preschool, primary, and secondary education.

Head Start is a preschool program that serves low-income children. Head Start seeks to accomplish its objective of preparing children for primary school by providing educational experiences to enhance the social and cognitive skills of the children it serves and by making referrals for needed services, including medical and dental services, social services, nutritional services, and mental health services. Involving parents in their child's educational experience is a core element of Head Start. Toward this end, some parents volunteer at Head Start centers, others are employed as staff, and some parents go through a training program and become certified as child care workers.

Whether involvement in a Head Start program has a positive impact on a child's educational experience cannot be answered with any measure of assurance due to a paucity of studies addressing this matter. Existing studies have yielded conflicting results and have been criticized for methodological and design weaknesses. A 1981 review of studies of Head Start children led to the conclusion that children showed significant immediate gains in cognitive test scores but that gains were short-lived when these children were compared to others from a similar background who did not attend Head Start. But, data reported in 1985 showed that Head Start children were less likely than others of similar background to be held back in grade and less likely to be placed in special education programs, and a 1995 evaluation suggested that academic gains were greater for white than for nonwhite students, but that all students experienced improvement in preventive medical care.

Children of migrant workers and homeless children experience difficulties in obtaining an education due to the frequent moves that define migrant work and homelessness, the problems of that parents confront when enrolling children in new schools, and the problems that some students confront due to a lack of English-language proficiency, social and rural isolation, poverty, and the problems of integrating into new schools several times in an academic year.

The MEP, MHS, and the McKinney act serve these children by financially supporting state activities to locate and place the children of migrant farm workers and of homeless families in school.

The goals of MHS are similar to those of the regular Head Start Program. The MEP focuses on children and youth in primary and secondary school and seeks to ensure that children have the same chance as other children to meet a state's educational standards. The MEP funds support outreach, information, and referral to direct families to needed services, and tutoring, and counseling services. Children in the MEP are served at approximately 17,000 schools located mainly in rural areas across the nation. Priority is given to students who are failing or at greatest risk of failing in school and whose education has been interrupted by moving during the school year.

Under the McKinney act, grants are made to local educational agencies to facilitate the enrollment, attendance, and success in school of homeless children and youth. States that receive McKinney act funds are expected to eliminate residency requirements that may make it impossible to enroll a homeless child in school, and each state is to establish the office of Coordinator of Education of Homeless Children and Youth. The coordinator is charged with compiling data describing children served with McKinney act funds, the problems that homeless children encounter in gaining access to education, their special needs, progress in reducing and eliminated identified problems, and whether programs are successful in allowing homeless children to attend school. Funds may be used for a variety of purposes, including tutoring and other forms of supplemental instruction; expediting evaluations that are needed to place a child in the proper grade; serving gifted students, disabled students, and students with limited English proficiency; and assessing the need for any service that are available under the ESEA and school-based nutrition programs.

The ESEA as amended by the Goals 2000 program seeks to increase educational opportunities for economically disadvantaged students and for students who lack English-language proficiency. Federal funds are targeted to schools in the highest poverty areas and are to be used to assist the states to develop and implement programs that would raise academic standards by improving teaching methods, increasing opportunities for classroom learning, and developing and implementing procedures to measure student achievement.

School districts around the country report that they are making some progress in achieving the ESEA goals, but they report difficulties in reforming curricula, establishing uniform standards, and measuring student performance. Among the problems in achieving ESEA goals was the fact that paraprofessionals made up half of the staff supported by federal funds and these staff, who are not trained teachers, spend most of their time teaching without a supervising teacher present.

Failure of a state school system to provide for the special educational needs of children who lack English-language proficiency is a violation of the child's civil rights. Children who are not proficient in English are entitled to language assistance, and programs may be funded using ESEA funds. However, the obligation to provide assistance does not require a school district to use any particular method of assisting students. Schools may choose from different approaches as long as the selected program rests on sound educational theory, the school has the resources and personnel to implement the program and the program produces the desired result after it has been implemented for a period of time.

The IDEA imposes a duty on school districts to accommodate children with severe disabilities. School districts must actively seek out children with disabilities, and they must provide needed educational opportunities to ensure that children can benefit from their educational program. The IDEA confers a range of benefits on eligible children, who are entitled to an IEP that describes the educational program that will be put in place to meet their educational needs and that may include the services of a physician, social worker, or other professional as long as the service is necessary to attain the objectives of the IEP. A school district's obligation is to assist children in their progress through the educational system, but this obligation does not mean that the school district is obligated to support programs that maximize a child's potential.

Children should receive their education in the least restrictive environment. Segregation of children into special classes should occur only when the child's disability prevents him or her from participating in regular classes. However, children require full-time residential programs in order to receive their educational entitlement, the school district is obligated to pay for the program.

The IDEA seeks to ensure that parents are involved in their children's education by providing that parents have the opportunity to participate in development of the IEP and the right to review all of the records that are relied on in developing the educational program.

Disruptive classroom behavior may result in a child's removal from the classroom. The IDEA provides that removal for up to ten consecutive school days is permissible if the behavior would result in the removal of a child who was not disabled. Services may be provided to the disabled child during the removal period. If removal is for more than ten consecutive school days or if there are a series of removals that cumulate to more than ten days in a school year, the school district is obliged to provide services to the child. If a decision is made to change a child's education placement, the child's parent must receive written notice and has a right to a fair hearing before removal occurs. Removal before the hearing is permissible only if the student poses an immediate threat to the safety of others or if the student has violated school rules for reasons unrelated to her or his disability.

PART

In this concluding part, we return to the topic of why the study of social policy is critical to effective social work practice, which was addressed in part I. In two concluding chapters, implementation (chapter 17) and policy practice (chapter 18) are covered.

A number of actors play a role in implementing social welfare programs, including (1) legislators who enact the laws that make programs possible; (2) staff of administrative agencies who issue rules to guide program implementation; (3) judges who, when asked, decide what the words and phrases in the law means, and whether clients are receiving the benefits to which they are entitled; and (4) program administrators and social worker staff on whose day-to-day actions clients rely. The success of any social program is a function of the interaction of the different players. Social workers, although they frequently diminish the importance of the role they play, are key to program success because they bear responsibility for performing the day-to-day activities that define program operations. In chapter 18, the subject of "policy practice" is addressed. Policy practice is an area of social work practice that allows social workers to play a variety of roles, such as advocate, lobbyist, policy analyst, and program evaluator in an effort to influence policy choices and hence client well-being.

CHAPTER 17

Implementation

The enactment of a new law is only the beginning stage in creating change in social welfare programs. The objectives that a policy seeks to achieve cannot be realized until the policy is implemented, which means that the provisions set forth in a policy must be put into practice to create new programs or to modify existing programs.

Implementation has been referred to in preceding chapters. For example, in chapter 10, I reported that the Temporary Assistance to Needy Families Program (TANF), as implemented in Connecticut and Florida, limits the duration for receipt of benefits to two years or less. Both states provide extensions for some families who reach the time limit. As discussed in chapter 10, almost all who reached the time limit in one Florida county had their benefits canceled, whereas in Connecticut approximately half who reached their time limit were granted an extension. The difference between the results observed in the two states is to be found in the way in which the programs were implemented. Florida's heavily staffed program allowed close monitoring of TANF recipients' compliance with the demands placed on them by the array of job-related services in which they were required to participate. As the number of provided services increased, so did the likelihood that recipients would "slip up" and lose their chance to have their benefits extended, because failure to comply with program requirements constituted grounds for denying an extension. In contrast, the Connecticut program was understaffed, and its participants were asked to engage in fewer activities. Understaffing precluded close monitoring, and recipients rarely had their grants reduced or canceled for failing to meet a program requirement.

Other examples were provided, including in chapter 6, a discussion of the importance of regulations as a guide for implementing programs; in chapter 10, issues some states confronted when they implemented welfare-to-work programs to assist

TANF recipients; and in chapter 11, officials in New York City defending their practice of denying households the chance to apply for food stamps during their first visit to a welfare office, because of the failure of the federal government to provide direction for implementation.

This current chapter begins with a general discussion of why scholars have become interested in the subject of implementation. Next, the role played by legislative bodies, staff in executive level agencies, judges, program administrators and program staff, and the general public in the implementation process is addressed.

Scholarly Interest in the Subject of Implementation

Little attention was paid to the subject of implementation until the 1960s. Until that time, policies enacted by legislative bodies were seen as reflecting a series of clear-cut preferences whose implementation could be wholly specified, eliminating the need for critical decision making at the administrative or program level. Implementation, it was assumed, was divorced from politics and was a neutral, rational, and organized process.

In the 1960s, these assumptions were challenged. The decisions made when policy was developed were seen as more complex than previously thought and hence unlikely to result in clear-cut priorities and choices to guide the implementation process. In addition, there was a growing recognition that politics do not stop once policy is developed. Rather, the political nature of the implementation process was recognized, and the fact that political considerations would influence the process was acknowledged.

Perhaps the most significant events spurring interest in implementation stemmed from the changing federal role in the social welfare arena and in actions of the federal judiciary in the mid-twentieth century. As discussed in chapter 1, the federal government became involved in funding social services in 1962 in an effort to reduce welfare dependency; and, in this era, Congress enacted War on Poverty Programs (chapter 10) that held out a promise of ending poverty and improving the quality of life for poor people. Additionally, federal courts sought to desegregate schools and to reform state social service systems, state mental health systems, and state prisons.[1] The 1962 service amendments did not reduce welfare dependency, and War on Poverty Programs did not end poverty. Why these programs did not yield the desired results spurred interest in the subject of implementation, as did questions concerning whether court involvement was successful in reforming institutional practices.

Interest in the subject of implementation was furthered by changes in policy goals.[2] Beginning in 1955 with school desegregation and continuing with War on Poverty programs (chapter 10) and civil rights legislation (chapter 13), policy has sought to achieve qualitative goals to improve the human condition by establishing the existence of certain rights and by describing methods to enforce identified rights. The problems inherent in implementing policies whose goals are qualitative can best be understood by contrasting them with policies of a technical nature. Technical policies seek to achieve goals that can be described in observable and measurable terms. The process of goal attainment can be specified and is not likely to evoke extensive political controversy, since the proposed changes do not, as a rule, pose a strong threat to the norms or beliefs of the organization of community affected. Whether review of applications for welfare benefits occurs in a timely manner illustrates this type of policy. Timely review can be measured by specifying a maximum latency between application and review, and a process for review, including criteria for decision making, can be established. Since eligibility for welfare benefits is often determined by applying a mathematical formula to information describing the assets and liabilities of applicants, subjectivity in decision making is reduced.[3]

Although clearly stated goals are necessary, they are not sufficient to ensure that implementation will proceed smoothly. First, policymakers may ignore questions of implementation and defer all decision making to implementers. The more controversial the reform effort, the greater the chances that individual beliefs, biases, and political considerations will be major forces in shaping implementation decisions (see the later discussion of transracial adoptions). The final product may bear little resemblance to what advocates or policymakers had in mind. Second, although some policies may contain explicit goals and describe procedures for implementation, they nevertheless challenge normative structures and thereby cause efforts to thwart their implementation. School integration through busing is a classic example. Given knowledge of the demographics of a school system, an outcome, expressed as a desired racial balance, can be set forth as can a means for achieving this outcome by mandating a busing plan. The political controversy that busing has engendered and the effects of this controversy on school integration is well documented. Third, policies whose goals are vague create implementation problems. For example, a federal district court ruling in Alabama that hospitalized mental patients had a right to "adequate and effective treatment" was so vague as to not provide any way of determining what programs or services would satisfy this judicial requirement.[4]

Finally, policymakers at the federal or state level often may have different ideas regarding what goals are to be pursued than do program administrators and staff. If the goals of policy are vague or overly broad in their reach, state and local officials cannot be expected to conform to legislative intent unless specific direction is provided or program implementation is monitored, along with suggestions for change if monitoring shows that legislative goals are not being pursued. Recall the discussion in chapter 16 of the Elementary and Secondary Education Act (ESEA). The ESEA was a War on Poverty program that shared with other programs of this era the goal of ending poverty. This goal is laudable, and longitudinal studies that track and compare outcomes for groups of children who experience different educational programs would help us to understand the relationship between specific educational experiences and later income.

However, although the goal of ending poverty can be translated into an observable and measurable outcome, the means of achieving the goal is less clear. Stated otherwise, there were no clear answers to the question, "What educational programs should be provided, in what combination and to what children?" Studies of how federal funds were being used uncovered the fact that educators at the local level saw ESEA funds as a way of improving educational programs in general, not in terms of mounting programs to achieve the congressional objective of ending poverty.[5] Today, almost forty years after War on Poverty legislation was enacted, poverty is still with us (chapter 8). The ongoing debate about how to improve educational opportunities for disadvantaged children and youth is an indication that ESEA-funded programs did not provide information to answer this question.

The Legislative Role in Implementation

Legislative bodies are not directly involved in program implementation, but decisions made by them affect implementation in different ways. Relevant decisions involve (1) funding, (2) limiting the use of funds to achieve political ends, (3) drafting statutes in specific or general terms, (4) establishing methods for monitoring implementation of programs and subsequent agency practices, (5) approving the president's choice of persons to head executive level agencies, and (6) providing a means for beneficiaries to sue units of government when they believe that they have been denied benefits due them.

FUNDING

In chapter 7, I said social programs are implemented only after funds are appropriated. The amount of money that Congress appropriates is evidence of its commitment to pursuing program goals. Underfunding a program is an alternative to repealing disfavored legislation.

In chapter 14 you were introduced to the Title XX Social Service Block Grant. The purpose of the block grant is to support programs at the state level that seek to help individuals attain economic self-sufficiency and programs to prevent problems such as child abuse and neglect. As reported in chapter 14, funds authorized for Title XX have fluctuated over time, with the value decreasing in constant dollars by 67 percent between 1977 and 1997. Funds authorized for fiscal year 1999 were $1.9 billion, with an authorized reduction to $1.7 billion for fiscal year 2002. This reduction signaled a significant decline in the federal commitment to implementing programs that rely on this funding source and on pursuing the goals of the Title XX program through the provision of social services. Administrators at the state level will have to cut back programs that are funded by Title XX dollars or find alternative funding sources.

The discretion of the states to develop and implement programs to address local need is greatest when Congress funds programs through the mechanism of block grants. But it is not always clear to local authorities what programs and services should be implemented to address local problems. Another way in which legislative bodies are able to influence implementation is to provide funds to evaluate existing programs and funds for demonstration projects to develop and test new methods for working with different groups and different problems. If research programs are implemented, research efforts are monitored, and research results are disseminated, others can benefit from the lessons learned, which can, in turn, influence program implementation. An agency's failure to pursue a research agenda may at best leave others ignorant of the effectiveness of existing programs and at worst allow ineffective programs to continue.

LIMITING THE USE OF FUNDS TO ACHIEVE POLITICAL ENDS

Congress may dictate the content of federally funded programs by specifying in statute what problem-solving methods may and may not be supported with federal funds. The methods chosen may be selected because there are data to support their efficacy. Methods may also be chosen for political reasons, meaning that they are selected either to appease a politician's constituents or to support a politician's biases.

For example, federal funds support sex education programs for primary and secondary school students, but federal monies may not be used to support condom distribution nor may they be used to support programs that "promote or encourage" sexual activity.[6] This position rests, at least in part, on a concern that condom distribution programs and programs that engage students in frank discussion of sexual behavior may encourage young people to engage in sexual activity they might otherwise avoid. Available evidence does not support the latter proposition,[7] and this restriction on the use of funds does not take into account that in 1997 approximately 50 percent of all adolescents had had sexual intercourse and only half used condoms.[8] The failure of sexually active teenagers to use condoms contributes to teenage pregnancies, high rates of sexually transmitted diseases, and high rates of Human Immunodeficiency Virus (HIV) infection. Although Congress has an interest in reducing the incidence of teen pregnancies and sexually transmitted diseases, the activities prohibited in federal law suggest that the limitations written into the law are not likely to result in the implementation of programs that will influence teenage sexual behavior; they are influenced more by moral concerns than by a wish to reduce or eliminate the problem that the policy was meant to address.

STATUTORY LANGUAGE

Statutes are often written in general terms but Congress may, if it chooses to attain a certain outcome, use language that is specific and unambiguous. For example, federal law has long required that case plans be developed for children in foster care, but the law was not specific as to either the form or content of plans, nor has it required that plans be in writing. In a series of studies that were conducted from the late 1950s through the mid-1970s, investigators uncovered the fact that case plans for children in foster care were not routinely developed.[9] When Congress passed the Adoption Assistance and Child Welfare Act in 1980 (see chapter 15), it wanted to ensure that the statutory provisions requiring case plans would be implemented and chose, therefore, to limit social worker discretion in developing case plans. Congress pursued its objective with specific words and phrases that provided that a case plan must be in writing and that the plan must be a discrete part of the case record. The written plan was to include at least the following information:

> A description of the type of home or institution in which the child is to be placed, including a discussion of the appropriateness of the placement and how the

agency which is responsible for the child plans to carry out the voluntary placement agreement entered into or judicial determination made with respect to the
child in accordance with (federal law) . . . the plan must ensure that the child
receives proper care and that services are provided to the parents, child, and
foster parents in order to improve the conditions in the parents home, facilitate
return of the child to his or her own home, or the permanent placement of the
child, and addresses the needs of the child while in foster care, including a discussion of the appropriateness of the services that have been provided to the child
under the plan.[10]

SYSTEM FOR MONITORING IMPLEMENTATION AND ONGOING PRACTICE

There are several ways in which Congress can try to ensure that program implementation is monitored to learn whether the provisions in law are being followed
and the policy goals are attained. First, state plans that describe how each state will
use federal funds must be submitted to federal agencies, and they must be approved
as a condition for states to receive federal funds (see chapters 14 and 16). Plans
provide a yardstick against which state programs can be monitored. The secretary
of each federal agency has the authority to deny funds to states whose plans do not
conform to congressional mandates, and federal agencies may audit state programs
to ensure that federal funds are being used according to the provisions in the approved state plan and are in keeping with general statutory requirements. States
may be fiscally sanctioned for failure to implement their programs as required. For
example, in the early 1990s, the Department of Health and Human Services required the state of Connecticut to reimburse the federal government for close to
$750,000 because the state had not implemented the case review system that is
required by the Adoption Assistance and Child Welfare Act (AACWA).[11]

The General Accounting Office (GAO), whose work has been frequently cited
in this text, is an investigative arm of Congress. When a member of Congress wishes
to learn whether programs are being implemented in accordance with congressional
intent, the member may charge the GAO with sending investigators into the field
to review records and to interview administrative and service-delivery staff to answer
questions concerning implementation. Along these same lines, Congress may authorize funds for program evaluation (chapter 18) by which researchers study implementation, program operation, and attainment of goals. Finally, Congress may
authorize an external body to engage in ongoing monitoring of agency behavior,
as it has with the mandatory court review required by the AACWA (chapter 15).

SENATE APPROVAL OF OFFICIALS TO HEAD EXECUTIVE AGENCIES

Agencies of the executive branch of government, such as the departments of Health
and Human Services and Housing and Urban Development, issue regulations that
play a significant role in guiding program implementation at the state level (see
chapter 6 and later discussion). The officials who run federal agencies are political
appointees who can be expected to carry forth the policies of the president who
appointed them; the regulations that they develop will express these policies. For

example, in chapter 6, I reported that in 1988 the Department of Health and Human Services issued regulations governing the use of family planning grants that prohibited grantees from providing any abortion counseling or referral services to their family-planning patients and from engaging in any political or litigation activities designed to promote abortion rights. These rules were consistent with the position of the Reagan administration that viewed with disfavor the right to choose to continue or to terminate a pregnancy.

Since regulations have the force of law and since they play a significant role in shaping programs, the authority given to agency executives could, if unchecked, have the result of granting to the executive branch the power to enact legislation that the Constitution reserves to the Congress. There are checks and balances. For example, we saw in chapter 6 that individuals or groups who believe that regulations are not consistent with congressional intent when a law was passed may go to court in an attempt to have the regulations overturned, and the constitutional requirement that the Senate approve presidential appointments provides another check against "over politicizing" the policymaking process.

THE RIGHT TO SUE

To ensure that programs are implemented as Congress intended, legislation may provide an "implied" or express right for beneficiaries to sue if they believe that they have been denied benefits. In this way, Congress empowers individuals to act as monitors of state behavior in implementing federal law. In the discussion in chapter 15 of the Adoption Promotion and Stability Act, I reported that Congress deemed any consideration of race, color, or national origin in placing a child for adoption illegal discrimination under the 1964 Civil Rights Act. By making consideration of race a civil rights matter, an individual or couple may sue a state agency if they believe that it has engaged in illegal discrimination.

Role of Administrative Agencies in Implementation

In chapter 6 I discussed the role of administrative agencies in issuing regulations and the necessity for administrative agencies to do so because legislation is often written in general terms. Experts working for administrative agencies are expected to define the terms that are used by Congress in order to provide guidance for implementation activities at the state level. Without regulations, those people responsible for program implementation would be free to follow their own dictates with the possible result that clients would be denied access to benefits to which they are entitled. An example of this was provided at the start of this chapter. I reported that New York officials explained their failure to permit households to apply for food stamps during their first visit to a welfare office and to inform families whose application for TANF was denied that they might be eligible for food stamps, because the federal government did not provide detailed guidelines to implement certain provisions of the 1996 Welfare Reform Act. Another example can be found in the preceding chapter. I reported that the Individuals with Disabilities in Education Act (IDEA) requires that "related services" that are necessary to implement a child's education plan be provided. Federal law provides for the use of Medicaid funds to pay for medically necessary services. However, the Health Care Financing Administration, located within the Department of Health and Human Services, has not issued "clear and consistent" guidelines for coordination between the Medicaid program and state programs operated under the IDEA. The GAO reports that school districts are reluctant to make use of Medicaid funding due to the absence of consistent guidelines and a fear that Medicaid funds will have to be reimbursed to Washington due to inappropriate documentation.[12]

Another way that federal agencies affect implementation is by providing technical assistance to the states. Technical assistance, which may be provided directly by federal officials or by consultants under contract to a federal agency, refers to help that is provided to facilitate program implementation. Those providing technical assistance are experts in their fields, such as mental health, education, or child welfare. Experts consult with program administrators and staff to help them understand what federal law requires of them and how best to implement federal rules by taking into account the context in which a programs operates, for example, differences between serving a rural as compared to an urban population or a population comprised mainly of senior citizens as compared to one where families with young children predominate. In addition to technical assistance, federal funds may be available to provide in-service training programs for social work staff and other program personnel.

To facilitate rule making and program implementation, administrative agencies may undertake "negotiated rule making." Negotiated rule making requires that the agency charged with issuing regulations meet with the agency whose programs are to be regulated and others with an interest in the final rule. The purpose of bringing the parties together when rules are being developed is to identify and resolve potential problems and thus to facilitate program implementation and prevent the likelihood that dissatisfied parties will resort to litigation to prevent a rule from being put in place.[13]

Finally, a federal agency may take over the day-to-day operation of a state or local agency, as a state may take over the day-to-day operation of a county or district agency, if a program is poorly managed. This happened in 1995 when the Department of Housing and Urban Development took over operation of the Chicago Housing Authority.[14]

Role of the Courts in Implementation

The courts have had a significant impact on the implementation of social welfare programs, especially since the 1960s when the federal government provided funds for legal aid lawyers to assist welfare clients obtain and retain benefits.[15]

Courts have by-and-large been responsive to claims for fairness. For example, (1) regulations that required unwarranted searches of a client's home were found to be unconstitutional, and an agency could not fire a social worker for refusing to comply with such regulations[16]; (2) rules that resulted in denying assistance to applicants for the Aid to Families with Dependent Children Program (AFDC) because the applicant lived with a person to whom she was not married were not sustained, because they violated provisions of the Social Security Act[17]; (3) regulations must provide for a fair hearing before AFDC benefits are terminated, thus giving a program beneficiary due process rights that include the right to appear alone or with counsel, present evidence, and confront and cross examine witnesses[18]; (4) regulations reducing AFDC payments for women whose disabilities precluded their involvement in a work program were prevented from being implemented[19]; (5) when a state is required by law to pay reasonable shelter allowances to welfare clients and when the state's constitution establishes an obligation for it to provide for the social welfare of its citizens, regulations providing a schedule of inadequate rent allowances had to be changed[20]; (6) New York was not allowed to deny state-funded Medicaid benefits to legal immigrants,[21] although denying aid to legal immigrants does not violate the federal Constitution[22]; and (7) a state cannot establish residency requirements that limit a new resident's TANF benefits to those received in the state from which she moved because such a provision violated the Equal Protection Clause of the Fourteenth Amendment guaranteeing to all citizens a right to travel.[23]

The judicial, the legislative, and executive branches of government and program administrators interact in an ongoing manner when the actions of one branch of government may cause another to react. Until 1992, a number of suits were brought against state child welfare agencies, more than twenty of which were operating under the guidance of federal courts.[24] An example was provided in chapter 6, where I referred to a lawsuit brought against the state of Connecticut challenging the operations of the State Department of Children and Family Service (DCFS).[25] In 1992, the Supreme Court ruled that individuals cannot bring such suits, because Congress had not conferred on them the "right to sue" public agencies.[26] In 1994, Congress overturned the Supreme Court's decision through an amendment to the AACWA, conferring on children and their parents the right to sue for certain violations of their rights.[27]

The programmatic shaping that results from court action may take place over many years as suits are brought, new procedures are implemented, and issues are relitigated with ongoing implementation. This ongoing process was illustrated in chapter 16, where the IDEA was discussed. Statutory provisions requiring a "Free Appropriate Public Education" (FAPE), "related services," and "mainstreaming" are not self-defining. A program administrator, following regulations issued by the Department of Education, may implement an educational program, whose implemented provisions may be challenged, not once, but many times, by parents who believe that their children are not getting the educational program to which they are entitled. Moreover, changing social conditions bring new litigation. When the IDEA was passed in 1975, no one had heard of HIV infection or of Acquired Immune Deficiency Syndrome (AIDS). In the 1980s and as reported in chapter 16, HIV-positive children experienced extensive discrimination in educational settings that resulted in a spate of lawsuits requiring school districts to implement special procedures for accommodating the needs of such children.

372 | Part V

Role of Program Administrators and Program Staff in Implementation

Legislators, staff at administrative agencies, and federal and state court judges may ignore questions of implementation, and thereby defer all decision making to staff at the program level. This is most likely to occur when the language of a statute or a court-ordered remedial decree is vague and hence subject to differential interpretation or when administrative agencies fail to issue regulations in a timely manner. Without guidance and when reform efforts are controversial, the chances that individual beliefs, biases, and political considerations will be major forces in shaping implementation decisions are great. The final product may bear little resemblance to what advocates or policymakers had in mind. In this section, we consider the role of significant actors and the importance of communication in the implementation process.

Implementation involves a number of actors, including "formal implementers, [those] expressly granted the legal authority, responsibility, and public resources to carry out policy directives, and intermediaries."[28] The latter group consists of "individuals and groups that are delegated responsibility by formal implementers to assist in carrying out public policies."[29] Social workers and their supervisors may not be directly charged with implementation responsibilities, but their actions will influence greatly efforts to create change. All those with responsibility for implementation must be identified, and their role in the implementation process and their implementation responsibilities must be spelled out.

Agency personnel may support the principles embodied in a the new policy because they reflect good professional practices and because they think that clients will benefit or that increased resources may be forthcoming. But there is the potential for alienating those responsible for implementation, thereby ensuring that the process will not proceed smoothly.

Whether or not staff, including line workers and supervisors, participate in decisions concerning implementation affects the success of implementation and the durability of reforms. The involvement of social workers and supervisors in the decision stages is seen as a predictor of both acceptance and satisfaction with an innovation, whereas unilateral decision making by administrators is not conducive to staff acceptance of change.[30] Understandably, staff may resent efforts to create change by administrative fiat and be frustrated and angered if regulatory changes do not conform to the realities of practice. For example, we know that the AACWA requires judicial review of cases and establishes time frames for review. Social workers can file papers requesting a court hearing in a timely fashion, but the date of the hearing, and hence full compliance with the statutory time frames, is under control of the courts. Failure to recognize the limits of what a social worker is able to do can result in a finding of noncompliance, and a social worker can be held accountable, because a review is not held in a timely manner.

Also, implementation efforts may be slowed when new policies require changes that do not conform to existing contractual agreements with community agencies. Contracts may be modified, in time, to fit new requirements; however, a considerable period of time may elapse between the time a policy is amended and the point at which contract modification can occur.

Program staff may resist change if it is seen as threatening their belief systems or their autonomy. Consider the following example. In chapter 15, I referred to the subject of transracial adoptions and the enactment of legislation in 1994 and 1996 that makes consideration of race in the placement of children a potential violation of the Civil Rights Act of 1964. The subject of transracial adoption has been controversial since the early 1970s when the National Association of Black Social Workers took the position that black children should be placed only with same-race families and that to place black children with white homes was a form of "genocide."[31] Although transracial placements did not completely stop, the number of children placed across racial lines decreased, and social work embraced the notion of same-race placements for children. When legislation was subsequently enacted to support cross-race placements, it ran counter to prevailing social work values. In 1998, the United States GAO reported the results of an investigation into the implementation of the Multiethnic Placement Act of 1994 and its 1996 amendment. Its commentary highlights the significant role that social workers play in the implementation process, the difficulties of implementing legislation that challenges longstanding practices and belief systems, the importance of clear guidance from administrative agencies to facilitate implementation, and the relevance of in-service training in matters concerning new or amended policies. The GAO reported:

> Translating legal principles into practical advice for caseworkers, and developing compliance monitoring systems are among the challenges remaining for officials at all levels of government in changing placement decision-making. The implementation of this amended act predominantly relies on the understanding and willingness of individual caseworkers to eliminate a historically important factor—race—from the placement decisions they make. While agency officials and caseworkers understand that this legislation prohibits them from delaying or denying placements on the basis of race, not all believe that eliminating race will result in placements that are in the best interests of children, which is a basic criterion for placement decisions. In addition, state and local officials and caseworkers demonstrated lingering confusion about allowable actions under the law. The state training sessions we attended on the amended act, in which presenters offered contradictory views of allowable activities, showed that neither the state nor HHS has provided clear guidance to caseworkers to apply the law to casework practice. Finally, federal efforts to determine whether placement decisions are consistent with the amended act's restrictions on the use of race-based factors will be hampered by difficulties in identifying data that are complete and sufficient."[32]

Staff may resist change because new programs may increase the opportunities for surveillance of staff behavior. The trend to establishing performance goals (chapter 14) where staff are required to demonstrate that their work produces specified outcomes provides for increased surveillance, as do computerized information management systems, external case review systems, and the involvement of legal counsel. Increased surveillance, in turn, portends to reduce worker autonomy.

Communication

Nakamura and Smallwood identify communication linkages as central to successful implementation. In large bureaucracies, directives typically filter down through a chain of command. Because meetings may be difficult to arrange in large organizations, administrators often rely on written directives to communicate their requirements. Communications problems are compounded when successful implementation requires changing the behavior of actors outside of the public system, for example, social workers in nonprofit agencies who provide services under contract to the public agency. For example, in New York City, the voluntary sector plays a significant role in providing foster care; more than half of the city's foster care children reside in homes that are supervised by nonprofit agencies operating under contract to the city.

Sole reliance on written directives is problematic because, first, they must be very specific and detailed. Even the most well-intentioned staff cannot be expected to carry out vaguely worded directives and to achieve the goals others had in mind but did not accurately express. Abstract directions give encouragement to those who do not support change efforts to act according to their own dictates. Second, follow-up procedures for written communications must be in place to ensure that messages are received and interpreted correctly and that required changes are made. The amount of paper flow in large bureaucracies creates a risk that a message will be lost or regarded as just another in a series of interoffice memos.

In 1973, a lawsuit was filed against New York City alleging that foster care settings were selected on the basis of a child's race and that black and Hispanic children were being denied access to quality placement facilities. The lawsuit was settled by a consent decree that required that children be placed in care on a first-come/first-serve basis, meaning that the first child identified as in need of a placement on any given day would be placed in the first foster care setting able to address the child's special needs, if any. The child welfare agency was not to identify children for placement by race unless the information was deemed to be therapeutically necessary.[33] In 1990, thirty of thirty-nine workers responsible for placing children in foster care settings were interviewed to assess implementation of the consent decree. Twenty-four of the thirty interviewed workers made clear that questions about a child's "skin color" had become a proxy for the now impermissible questions concerning "race." Their responses included:

> Questions are always asked about the child's skin color. There are some foster parents who will not accept black children.
> They always ask about skin-shade, they also ask what kind of hair does the kid have, is it kinky, is it straight, is it coarse?
> Foster parents want information on skin-shade. We have to be frank or the child will be returned the next day.
> Agencies have vacancies but not for dark black children.
> Some agencies ask about skin-shade. Questions are asked about is the kid light-skinned or is the kid dark-skinned?

> They always ask for skin-shade and we give it to them. The agencies say that
> the foster parents need the skin-shade because of their neighborhoods, neigh-
> bors will reject children who are too dark. . . .
> We aren't supposed to report skin-shade but I do because if the kid goes to a
> home where they're not wanted the child will feel uncomfortable.
> They always ask about skin-shade. They want to know if child is light brown or
> dark brown. They will refuse children if they think the kid is too dark.
> Agencies ask about skin-shade. Since I've learned about Wilder I don't tell them
> anymore even if they give me trouble.[34]

The issue of skin color and the effect that providing this information had on implementing the first-come/first-serve provisions of a court order were not difficult
to uncover because the number of staff responsible for placing children was small
and all were located in one office. As the number of actors able to influence implementation increases, so do the difficulties in pinpointing the source of implementation problems. Consider the following.

Implementing court orders to deinstitutionalize mental hospitals has been extremely difficult for reasons that include community resistance to locating group
homes in residential neighborhoods and staff resistance to the changes that deinstitutionalization creates. Robert A. Burt assessed efforts to deinstitutionalize Pennhurst State School and Hospital in Pennsylvania.

> Prospects for effective enforcement are especially hard [when] . . . directed against
> institutional bureaucracies. . . . The size and complicated hierarchal structure of
> [which] means that a judge can rarely identify the one or two or three officials
> who, at the stroke of their pens, could assure compliance with an . . . order and
> conversely who should be fined or jailed for contempt of court when that order
> is not carried out. Moreover, because [the effort at] Pennhurst [sought] to change
> the day-to-day continuous functioning of a behemoth bureaucracy, the judge
> could fully monitor compliance only be creating a shadow bureaucracy virtually
> as large as the defendant enterprise itself. In any event, the defendants' capacity
> to undermine compliance by covert resistance in their daily operations is so great
> that the judge must somehow secure their acquiescence, grudging at least, if he
> hopes to have any lasting effective impact on the institutional enterprise.[35]

His comments concerning the ability of program staff to thwart efforts to change is
applicable to a large bureaucracy, regardless of whether the order for change em-
anates from the legislature, administrative agencies, or the judiciary. The roles
played by legislators, employees of administrative agencies, judges in addition to the
host of "significant actors" working in public agencies, members of the community-
at-large defined to include lay-people, and professionals acting in their capacity as
private citizens or as representatives of nonprofit social services agencies may affect
implementation in several ways. First, some statutes require the participation of
affected groups in decisions concerning program development. Thus, the services
to be supported by public funds may be selected by people in the general com-

munity, as was illustrated in the discussion of the Ryan White Comprehensive AIDS Resources Emergency Act in chapter 14. There, I reported that program planning councils must include members of the communities affected by the epidemic and that membership on councils is to reflect the demographics of the epidemic in the area for which planning occurs. Other ways in which members of the community-at-large may affect implementation have been referred to in previous chapters. Although data to ascertain with certainty the role played by the public-at-large are lacking, efforts to shape legislation and the programs created by legislation may occur through lobbying, by the development of position papers by professionals at "think tanks," by participation at fairness hearings before a judge agrees to a plan to settle a class action lawsuit, and by commenting on proposed rules that are published before regulations become law (chapter 6). You should recall also that since courts are reactive, the judicial actions that influence implementation are often initiated by individuals and advocacy groups who often bring matters to the attention of attorneys who initiate the litigation process (chapter 6).

Summary

Implementation refers to the process by which the tenets set forth in policy are put into practice to create new programs or to modify existing programs. Scholars paid scant attention to the subject of implementation until the 1960s when the federal government undertook to fund programs to end poverty and courts became active in protecting civil rights. Programs to end poverty and improve the quality of life for poor people proved difficult to implement. The goals that were set by policy-makers in the nation's capital were (1) often ambiguous, failing to provide the necessary guidance to create programs at the local level that would meet governmental expectations; (2) in conflict with the objectives of program planners and administrators at the local level, resulting in the use of federal funds for purposes that diverged from what members of Congress had in mind; and (3) met with resistance from agency personnel because policy goals ran counter to prevailing values and standards of practice.

A variety of actors may affect implementation, including legislators, staff of administrative agencies, judges, program staff at the state or local level, and the public-at-large. At the state or local level, successful implementation is a function of (1) the funds that Congress appropriates for program implementation, technical assistance, and in-service training; (2) the limits, if any, that Congress imposes on the programs to be developed; (3) the specificity or ambiguity with which policy goals are articulated; and (4) the information that is available from evaluations of programs implemented by others.

Regulations that are issued by administrative agencies are critical to successful program implementation because legislation is often written in general terms that provide little guidance to program planners. The courts play an ongoing role in implementation because they determine whether programs have been implemented according to congressional intent and whether clients are receiving the services to which they are entitled.

Whether programs are implemented in accordance with the law will ultimately be determined by the actions of program planners, program administrators, social work staff, and other agency personnel. Professional support may be conditioned by whether (1) the principles embodied in policy reflect sound professional practice, (2) the decision making process that precedes implementation includes professional staff, (3) the principles to be implemented take into account the context in which practice occurs and do not pose a significant threat to the belief systems of staff or to their autonomy, (4) communications concerning what is expected of staff are clear and unambiguous, and (5) in-service training is provided to help staff develop new skills.

Policy may assign a role to members of the community-at-large when, for example, it requires that program plans be developed by professionals acting with members from communities likely to be affected by new or amended programs, when people outside of the public system lobby for specific types of programs or participate in fairness hearings or institute litigation, or when professionals develop position papers advocating for one or another type of programs.

CHAPTER

Policy Practice

At the beginning of chapter 1, I said that most of you who are reading this text will be planning your careers as direct service providers to one of the diverse groups served by social workers. I stated also that social workers who understand the policymaking process and have knowledge of the social policies in force have an advantage over others because they are able to participate in the policymaking process and to influence the reform and creation of programs that affect their clients.

In this final chapter, we will revisit the relationship of social work practice to social policy by discussing "policy practice," an area of social work practice whereby practitioners endeavor "to change policies in legislative, agency and community settings whether by establishing new policies, improving existing ones, or defeating the policy initiatives of others."[1]

The roots of policy practice can be traced back to the settlement house movement of the nineteenth and early twentieth centuries, but social workers in general showed little interest in this area of practice after the First World War (chapter 2). Interest in policy practice was renewed in the 1980s in response to the Reagan administration's efforts to reduce the role of the federal government in the welfare arena and to cut social welfare programs. Interest has been sustained by the "devolution" movement that began in the 1990s, referred to in chapter 10 and discussed later. The literature on policy practice has been growing,[2] although it is scant relative to other areas of social work practice. Influencing State Policy, a national organization, was formed in 1997 by social worker practitioners and educators to help other professionals learn how to influence policy formation, implementation, and evaluation.[3] This organization publishes a newsletter entitled "Influence" that reports on a variety of issues concerning the actions of social workers who engage in policy practice.

This chapter begins by addressing the question, "Why should social workers engage in policy practice?" and continues with a discussion of the tasks that define policy practice. A comment before beginning. You may pursue a career as a full-time policy practitioner by working for a professional association as a policy analyst or lobbyist, or you may elect to provide direct services. The latter career choice, however, does not preclude undertaking some of the activities that define policy practice, such as participating in professional organizations that seek to influence policy, advocating for clients to ensure that they receive the benefits to which they are entitled, doing volunteer work at election time to support candidates whose platform is consistent with social work values, and participating in public demonstrations to protest policies that are unfavorable to your clients.

Why Engage in Policy Practice?

An obligation to engage in policy practice can be inferred from the *Code of Ethics* of the National Association of Social Workers (NASW). The code reminds us that professionals have an ethical obligation to monitor and evaluate policies and programs and to testify before policymaking bodies to try and ensure that clients will benefit from new and amended policies.[4] A difficulty that you may encounter, if you are providing direct client services and engage in policy practice, is finding yourself in direct opposition to the agency that employs you and/or to the unit of government that pays your salary.

Consider the following example. In chapter 11, I reported that New York City was found to be in violation of federal law because city caseworkers would not allow households to apply for food stamps during their first visit, and they did not inform applicants that food stamps might be available even if cash benefits were not. Assume that you are a caseworker for the city and that you suspect that the rules that you are asked to follow violate federal law. There are a number of things that you can do, including (1) remaining silent; (2) ignoring the directive by informing your clients of their rights; (3) changing jobs; (4) working alone, or with others in your office, informing your supervisor that you believe that the rules violate federal law and asking that the supervisor do something about it; (5) reporting the suspected violation to the federal government; and/or (6) consulting with an attorney to find out if the law offers any recourse to the identified problem.

Options one and two—remaining silent and ignoring directives—are not ethical. Remaining silent ignores the responsibility of social work professionals to act in the best interests of their clients, and ignoring directives involves deception and is not in keeping with high standards of professional practice nor with acting in ways that enhance respect for the integrity of the profession.[5] Option three—changing jobs—is viable, but it is self-serving, and like remaining silent, it ignores your professional obligation to act in the best interests of your clients. Option four—informing your supervisor of violations—is a good place to start, because it seeks to resolve an issue "in house." However, if your supervisor fails to act or if public officials do not change the rules, then you must consider other options. Options five and six—reporting to the federal government and consulting an attorney—involve difficult choices, because either puts you in direct opposition to your employer. In the final analysis, taking action when you know that client rights are being violated and that clients are suffering for lack of income, food, or shelter should be done in a manner that upholds professional standards of practice.

A social worker in New York City pursued option five—reporting to the federal government—based on her conviction that the city was filing false claims with the federal government in which it sought reimbursement for foster care services that were never provided. Court records suggest that the social worker first wrote anonymous letters to her superiors in which she reported her concerns and then met with agency administrators to ask that they take corrective action.[6] She reported her concerns to the federal government after agency administrators failed to act. As a result of her actions, a lawsuit was filed against the city, which refunded approximately $49 million to the federal government.[7] "Whistleblower" laws at the federal and state level protect an employee from disciplinary action based on the employee's report of employer wrongdoing.[8]

Earlier, I said that the devolution movement of the 1990s has contributed to the renewed interest in policy practice. Devolution refers to a decrease in the federal role in regulating social welfare programs in favor of increasing state autonomy (chapter 10). As decisions concerning program content and eligibility rules move to the state and local level, so do the opportunities and imperative for professionals to become involved in policy practice. Local control may provide opportunities for professional input because (1) the seat of decision making may be geographically closer than the nation's capitol, (2) you may believe that your input will have more influence at the local level than at the national level, and (3) local decision making increases the chances that standards for eligibility and program benefits will vary within a state in ways that you deem unfavorable to clients. Close monitoring of legislative and regulatory actions and of program implementation are ways to identify problems and to act to reduce or eliminate those that may be harmful to clients.

The Tasks That Define Policy Practice

Policy practice can be described with reference to a series of discrete tasks. Before discussing them, consider several points: First, whether you engage in policy practice full-time or part-time, the activities that define this area of practice are the same, but all of the tasks do not necessarily come into play in any one action. For example, during a legislative session, you may be proactive by seeking to contribute to the agenda to be considered, or you may react to an already established agenda by seeking to change it. Even if all of the tasks that define policy practice come into play, they are likely to be shared with other people on the basis of time, skills, interests, and subject-matter expertise. Finally, the tasks that define policy practice do not always proceed in a linear fashion. For example, your efforts to lobby a legislator may begin when you educate yourself about current issues, but after your discussions with legislators and their staff you may learn that you need further self-education before resuming your lobbying tasks. The various tasks involved in policy practice will be discussed under the headings of understanding the legislative process, learning about the subject matter of a bill, advocating for change, setting the agenda, assessing the feasibility of change, analyzing policy, testifying, lobbying, demonstrating in public, and studying the impact of policy.

UNDERSTANDING THE LEGISLATIVE PROCESS

To be effective as a policy practitioner you must know how the legislative process works. In chapter 6, I provided an overview of this process at the federal level. Two Internet sites, www.senate.gov and www.house.gov, are useful resources for learning about (1) congressional committees and the issues that they will address in the forthcoming legislative session; (2) the dates and times that congressional deliberations will occur, including the dates and times of scheduled hearings; and (3) the voting record of your representatives.

To engage in policy practice at the state and local level, you must learn about the process followed in the state in which you practice, and you must monitor impending legislation of importance to the profession. There are a number of ways to learn about these matters:

• Join a local chapter of the NASW and participate in the work of committees that address your substantive practice area, for example, children, the elderly, domestic violence. Local chapters stay abreast of legislative developments that affect their constituents, and many publish newsletters and have Web sites for disseminating information to members.

• Obtain a copy of *The Book of the States* at your local library or purchase a copy. The book is published by the Council of State Governments, located at 2760 Research Park Drive in Lexington, Kentucky. A section of the book describes the legislative process, including how bills are introduced, and identifies the standing committees in each state.

• A number of states have Web sites with information relevant to the policy practitioner. Using your preferred search engine, do the following: (1) in the search box, type *state of (insert the name of your state)*. This action should produce a list of topics concerning the identified state. For example, the result of typing *state of California* will be a Web page that contains links to information concerning (1) the state assembly; (2) the state senate; (3) house and senate committees; (4) deadlines for filing legislation; (5) special interest caucuses, such as the Black and Latino caucus; (6) daily updates on bills introduced into either legislative chamber with the full text of bills reported; and (7) a search option that allows you to find a bill by using either the bill number or search terms, such as "adoption" or "child care."

• The university you attend or your place of employment may subscribe to Westlaw (www.westlaw.com) or Lexis (www.lexis.com). Both are subscription sites, meaning you need an access number to use their services. Either site is valuable to the policy practitioner. Each provides access to (1) federal and state statutes, (2) federal administrative regulations and administrative regulations for some states, and (3) federal and state court decisions that interpret the terms and phrases in policies and decisions that set new policies. In addition, you can "track" legislation after its introduction and identify by name the committee(s) to which the legislation was assigned and date(s) of assignment, the current status of assigned bills, and a synopsis of the major points the bill contains. You may also be able to access legislative history, committee reports, and testimony given before congressional committees. In addition, full-text journal articles are available on these sites. Most of the journals are law reviews, but many are interdisciplinary law and social policy journals.[9]

LEARNING ABOUT THE SUBJECT MATTER OF A BILL

Individuals engage in policy practice to help clients and because they have an interest in particular issues. Advocates tend to be passionate about issues that concern them, and this passion can be positive as long as it does not blind you to the weaknesses of your position or prevent you from seeing the strengths of your opponent's point of view.

The problem that arises from failure to understand fully an issue was illustrated in chapter 1, where I reported that Winifred Bell, an expert on the Aid to Families with Dependent Children program (AFDC) and head of the Demonstration Projects Group in the Department of Health, Education, and Welfare, (renamed Health and Human Services), expressed her regret at the role that she had played in the passage of the 1962 service amendments. Her subsequent review of reports from demonstration projects did not provide support for the proposition that the provision of social services would reduce or eliminate poverty. The uninformed advocate risks making himself or herself look foolish by arguing a position for which there is no empirical support; and she or he brings discredit to the profession.

You are no doubt familiar with the ways in which you can learn about social issues, including (1) reading reports that are published in professional journals or prepared by research institutes, such as the Urban Institute or the American Enterprise Institute; (2) attending professional conferences; and (3) studying systematically your own practice and participating in a research project to evaluate an entire program. The policy practitioner has a distinct advantage if she or he is able to do research using the Internet because of the volume of policy material that is online. A guide to Internet sites containing material relevant for policy research appears at the end of this book. The advantage to using the Internet lies in ease of access to a wealth of current information. Unlike articles published in professional journals that may take a year or two after they are submitted for publication to appear in print, materials available online may appear within twenty-four or forty-eight hours of the time a report is completed. The limitation of Internet research is that available documents may not provide a complete picture of an issue because government agencies, advocacy groups, and research organizations may limit what is available online.

ADVOCACY

Advocacy is a process of supporting or recommending a course of action. Advocacy groups may develop an agenda to guide activities during an upcoming legislative session; or, when courts are considering cases of concern to their constituents, they may act as "friends of the court" by filing *amicus* briefs in which they urge the court to consider the issues they deem important. The agenda of an advocacy group will be based on legislation the group is trying to get introduced as well as legislation that will be considered during the session. Decisions must be made concerning the use of limited resources by focusing on issues that the group thinks it can influence.

Advocates may work on behalf of an individual client or groups of clients with similar needs. For example, clients have a right to appeal decisions that deny them benefits, and you may represent a client at an administrative hearing (chapter 6) or refer a client to an attorney. Acting on behalf of groups, advocates lobby legislators, write position papers, testify before legislative bodies, speak to the general public, participate in demonstrations, and represent children or others who are not able to look after their own interests acting as a "next friend." "Next friends" play a critical advocacy role when lawsuits are filed against public agencies and institutions alleging their failure in the treatment of children or other groups. The "next friend" role is important for two reasons: (1) the state against which the suit is brought cannot represent a person in its custody, since there is a potential for a conflict of interest; (2) nor, in the case of a child in foster care, can the child's parent be an advocate since she or he is likely to have been found unfit by a court of law. Therefore, children who are named as plaintiffs are each represented by individuals, denoted "next friends," who are as a rule professionals and others with "standing" or high social status in their communities.

Social workers can also advocate from and with the support of professional organizations. The New York chapter of the NASW, for example, invites professionals to join their Advocacy and Government Relations Committee to identify and work on issues of importance to the profession and its clients. The chapter develops an agenda for advocacy by selecting and ranking issues and setting priorities for action. The NASW stresses that its ability to advance relevant issues is possible only with the help of its members. It focuses on a broad range of policy issues from statutes that govern the licensing of social workers to programs that provide mental health services and child welfare services.

The New York chapter will often generate a letter-writing campaign targeting specific government officials. The letter-writing campaign may provide a sample letter, but it is best to rewrite the letter in your own words, adding personal anecdotes and experiences, as appropriate. In addition, organizations often have full-time lobbyists who advocate directly with legislators, and organizations may produce reports that contain an analysis of alternative policy proposals.

One of the most important professional contributions that you can make is to monitor proposed regulations and to comment on them. As discussed in chapter 6, the Federal Administrative Procedures Act and similar state statutes require that the administrative agency proposing a new regulation provide the opportunity to "participate in rule making through submission of written data, views, or arguments with or without opportunity for oral presentation." Administrative agencies are required to consider public commentary and to include in the adopted rule a brief statement of the purpose the rule is to achieve and why, in light of the feedback provided, the rule took its final form.

AGENDA SETTING

Chapter 5 was devoted to the subject of agenda setting, which refers to the process by which social issues are transformed into social problems and considered for possible remedy by a branch of government. As a policy practitioner you may be involved in setting an agenda or you may join others in advancing an already established agenda. The legislative agenda may be determined out of public view, as was the case when the Children's Bureau adopted the issue of child abuse, or it may be set in the media, as was the case when Matthew Sheppard's murder placed the issue of hate-crimes legislation on the public agenda (chapter 5). When the agenda is set in public, advocacy and agenda-setting are inextricably linked.

Although you may act as an individual catalyst for agenda setting, it is more likely that you will work with others because of the complexity of the tasks involved. Policy practitioners from different disciplines have an array of skills that can be combined for greater success, and an individual working alone will have difficulty in attracting media attention. Recall the discussion in chapter 2 of the settlement house workers who represented a variety of disciplines, including social work, economics, political science, law, medicine, sociology, the arts, and journalism.

ASSESSING THE FEASIBILITY OF CHANGE

When advocates are seeking to create new policy or to amend existing policy, they must assess the feasibility of getting legislation enacted. For example, welfare reform was discussed in chapter 10 where I reported that efforts to reform the welfare system, specifically, the AFDC program, had a long history. In the early 1990s, the political climate was favorable to reform efforts. The AFDC caseloads were the highest they had ever been; unemployment was low, indicating that jobs were available for those who chose to work; and the general public, including welfare recipients, was dissatisfied with the AFDC system. This created a "window of opportunity" (chapter 5) that Democrats and Republicans took advantage of, and the Personal Responsibility and Work Opportunity Act (PRWOA) of 1996 was enacted.

The availability of funding is another feasibility issue. Funding sources have been identified throughout this text, including (1) congressional appropriations for social welfare programs, such as the Social Services Block Grant or the Substance Abuse and Mental Health Block Grant, (2) permission by Congress to transfer funds across block grants (see chapters 10 and 14), and (3) permission by Congress to use funds for activities not sanctioned in a statute if funds are used to further attainment of statutory goals. For example, funds for TANF can be used for family preservation, foster care, and adoption programs authorized under the Adoption Assistance and Child Welfare Act since the this act shares with TANF the purpose of "providing assistance to needy families so that children may be cared for in their own homes or in the homes of relatives."[10]

In addition, advocates should familiarize themselves with funds that are available for projects of national significance (chapters 14) and with funds that become available each year for demonstration projects. The availability of funds for demonstration programs is announced in the *Federal Register,* which is published each business day. The *Register* can be accessed online at www.fr.cos.com.

POLICY ANALYSIS

Experts undertake policy analysis to determine the impact that a policy will have if enacted and the impact that an already enacted policy has had. In this section, the question "What impact will a proposed policy or policy amendment have?" is addressed. The question of the impact of an existing policy is taken up at the end of this chapter.

When a legislative body is deliberating a policy proposal, it wants to know what impact the policy will eventually have so that it can select a course of action. Analysis at this stage may make use of already existing data. For example, work programs for welfare recipients existed prior to the passage of TANF, and there were data that addressed questions about the availability of child care and how the lack of child care affected the ability of welfare recipients to work (see chapter 10). These data informed policy development in two ways: they made it clear that provisions for day care would have to be included in the policy and that the cost of providing day care had to be a part of the evaluation of program costs.

When a policy is proposed, you should be concerned with an analysis that will help you decide whether to support or oppose the proposal, in whole or in part. Professional organizations, such as the NASW, the Children's Defense Funds, the American Human Services Association (formerly, the American Public Welfare Association), and other research institutions prepare policy analyses, which may be available online. You may find that reviewing and comparing the analyses of "conservative" and "liberal" writers from the different groups will help you to (1) learn enough about the issues to adopt a stance in favor of or opposed to a proposal, (2) prepare testimony for a legislative committee or hearing, or (3) join a write-in campaign to express your point of view.

Several versions of a proposed policy may be presented before a legislative body settles on a final version. Each version may differ with respect to goals, methods of goal attainment, funding schemes, and other provisions. Each proposal will have a different "price tag" attached to it, with the costs arrived at by using statistical techniques and "modeling." Models are based on assumptions about the number of beneficiaries under different eligibility rules, costs associated with different benefits, and with whether the program will be federally financed or financed jointly by the federal government and the states. We know from the discussion in chapter 7 that changes to current legislation that would result in increases in mandatory spending or decreases in current revenue sources must be offset by spending cuts in other parts of the budget or by revenue increases. This "pay-as-you-go" provision is designed to prevent increases in the deficit as a result of new legislative enactments. Analysts generally begin their work with the first proposal and modify their conclusions as the process proceeds. By approaching analysis in an incremental manner, a complete review of the final proposal can be issued contemporaneous with legislative enactment of a policy.

Finally, you should be mindful of the fact that when policies are first enacted their precise impact on clients cannot always be ascertained, because some terms are vague and some provisions are not yet specified. Regulations that specify what is required of implementers will not be available for months and, in some cases, for a year or more (chapter 6). For example, final regulations for TANF were issued in April 1999, two and one-half years after the legislation was enacted.[11] The advocate who is preparing for testimony or lobbying will likely proceed without all of the information she or he would like to have.

As a policy practitioner you may conduct your own analysis, but answering the question "How will clients be affected?" is complex. For example, certain of the changes embodied in the PRWOA are immediately clear. Most parents would be disqualified from the TANF provisions in the PRWOA after sixty months in the program (chapter 10). This time limit makes it clear that the entitlement that had existed under AFDC had ended. The expectation that most parents would go to work is also clear. However, TANF provided that states may include a hardship exemption for 20 percent of the TANF caseload, but left it to the states to decide what groups to exempt. If you work with people with physical disabilities, you would have no way of knowing when TANF was passed how the work requirements would apply to your clients, and your advocacy efforts could focus on trying to ensure inclusion for those that you represent.

The information in the discussion on page 388 shows an approach to a very basic policy analysis using the Food Stamp Program for purposes of illustration. Information is usually reported by the listed categories. At a minimum, the information that must be considered includes (1) the purpose of the policy; (2) eligibility rules; (3) definitions, which in the provided example specify the benefit provided; and (4) funding sources.

Your ability to conduct a basis analysis of policy assumes that you have some expertise in the area of concern, for example, that you have knowledge of government food programs against which you can compare a new proposal and identify its strengths and weaknesses in relation to prior policies. With this in mind, consider the following:

The "Purpose" section of the policy states that its objective is to provide access to food and to improve nutrition. From your understanding of earlier food programs that distributed commodities, you may know that reduction of food surpluses depressing the farm economy and not meeting the nutritional needs of people was the driving force behind commodities-distribution programs (chapter 11). Thus, the new policy goal should better serve client need than the goal of the commodities distribution program.

All policies embrace an "intervention" that policymakers assume will facilitate goal attainment. Here, the intervention, which is synonymous with the benefit provided, is the provision of food stamps, which can be used in limited ways that are referred to under the "Definitions" section. This intervention assumes that the provision of stamps will enable households to acquire food that will provide a nutritionally balanced diet. There are two points to note. It is assumed that the chances of improving nutrition will be enhanced by defining food with reference to products for home consumption thus, precluding the use of stamps for nonfood items such as alcohol or tobacco and fast foods. The second point also contains an assumption, which is that recipients know how to select food items based on their nutritional value and that they will select food items with this in mind. As an advocate, you may need to anticipate and challenge these assumptions.

The section headed "Eligibility" contains several important points. First, the reference to national standards for eligibility tells you that the federal government will establish rules for eligibility and that unlike TANF, where each state may have different eligibility standards, a person who is eligible for food stamps in one state is eligible in any state. The eligibility section of the statute contains detailed rules for determining eligibility that are not reported in the illustration. Second, note that eligibility is based on low income and that there is a work requirement. The latter supports, but does not mandate, that recipients actually work. For example, an applicant could meet the work requirement by registering for work and by providing information to allow the agency to determine the employment status or the job availability of the individual. As stated in the eligibility section, "participation is limited to *households*" [emphasis added] meaning that the household, not the individual, is the beneficiary. Had Congress intended the individual to be the "unit" for eligibility it would have said so. You can never assume the meaning of words and phrases in policy. For this reason, all policies have a "Definition" section to which you must refer to learn the meaning of terms that are subject to differential interpretation. Whether eligibility for a policy is "linked" to other policies will be noted, as is the case in the last paragraph in the "Eligibility" section that states that households receiving benefits under either TANF or Supplemental Security Income are eligible for food stamps, precluding the necessity of a client applying separately for each program.

Finally, because the Food Stamps Program is an entitlement program, the "Funding" section states that necessary funds are to be appropriated, as in any entitlement program, in an amount sufficient to meet the needs of those eligible. When program funding is capped, the legislation will either specify a dollar amount or state that the costs are not to exceed those spent in an identified year. When programs are not entitlements, whether funds allocated are "sufficient" may be difficult to judge. In some cases, the goals to be realized by a policy will remain unchanged, but funding levels may decrease, as with the Title XX Social Services Block Grant. In such a situation, congressional intent not to sustain a commitment to the goals of the policy is easily inferred.

THE FOOD STAMP PROGRAM

§ *2011. Purpose.* [To] promote the general welfare, to safeguard the health and well-being of the Nation's population by raising levels of nutrition among low-income households. Congress finds that the limited food purchasing power of low-income households contributes to hunger and malnutrition among [household] members. . . . To alleviate . . . hunger and malnutrition, a food stamp program is . . . authorized [to] permit low-income households to obtain a more nutritious diet . . . by increasing food purchasing power for all eligible households who apply for participation.

§ *2014. Eligible households.* The[re] [shall be] uniform national standards of eligibility. Participation . . . [is] limited to . . . households whose income and other financial resources . . . are determined to be a substantial limiting factor in permitting them to obtain a more nutritious diet.

. . . [H]ouseholds in which each member receives benefits under the [Temporary Assistance to Needy Families Program] or supplemental security income benefits shall be eligible to participate in the food stamp program.

§ *2015. Eligibility Disqualifications.* No physically and mentally fit individual over the age of 15 and under the age of 60 [is] eligible to participate in the food stamp program if the individual refuses to register for employment, or refuses, without good cause (i) to participate in an employment and training program, (ii) to accept an offer of employment . . . (iii) to provide a State agency with . . . information to allow the . . . agency to determine the employment status or the job availability of the individual; (iv) voluntarily . . . quits a job; or reduces work effort [so that the individual] is working less than 30 hours per week. Each State . . . shall implement an employment and training program . . . [to] assist members of households . . . in gaining skills, training, work, or experience that will increase their ability to obtain regular employment.

§ *2012. Definitions.* [Benefit: Food Stamps may be used to acquire] "Food" [which refers to] (1) any food or food product for home consumption except alcoholic beverages, tobacco, and hot foods or hot food products ready for immediate consumption . . . and seeds and plants for use in gardens to produce food for the personal consumption of the eligible household.

[Beneficiary is the] "Household" which is defined as (1) an individual who lives alone or who, while living with others, customarily purchases food and prepares meals for home consumption separate and apart from the others, or (2) a group of individuals who live together and customarily purchase food and prepare meals together for home consumption.

§ *2027. Funding.* [Congress] authorize[s] to be appropriated such sums as are necessary for fiscal years 1996 through 2002.

Source: Compiled by the author from 7 U.S.C. § 2011 *et seq.*

TESTIFYING

The *Code of Ethics* of the NASW reminds us that testifying before legislative bodies is a professional obligation. Testimony may be written, oral, or both. If you have unique expertise in an area of interest to a legislative body, you may be invited to testify or you may attend a public hearing and sign up to give testimony. Written testimony may be read into the record if you are not present to speak, or written testimony may be distributed after oral testimony is provided.

Legislators are likely to be responsive to real-life stories and to testimony from clients who tell of their experiences in trying to obtain benefits. You may share stories about clients, assigning fictitious names to protect client confidentiality, that illustrate the difficulties that clients face in accessing benefits. You may also ask clients if they would tell their stories to legislative committees. Real-life stories capture the imagination of the public and of politicians in ways that statistics do not, and stories, when publicized, may elicit the public support that legislators need to justify their actions on behalf of marginalized groups, especially when the action requires large outlays of public funds. At times, however, a practitioner's best efforts to advance a client's agenda prove fruitless. Agency administrators may be indifferent to requests for change and legislative doors may be locked. Social workers, therefore, have sometimes collaborated with attorneys by providing them with information that they need to file suit against state agencies on behalf of clients. Their information or direct testimony is another way to influence agenda setting and policymaking by the courts.[12]

LOBBYING

Professional organizations and other special interest groups may employ lobbyists to advocate for the group's cause with members of legislative committees and with legislators. The NASW suggests that preparation for meetings is critical and that the informed advocate should establish an agenda and goals for a meeting. The advocate should identify in advance the subject to be addressed and limit the discussion to key points that can be addressed in depth rather than engaging in a broad overview of issues. In addition, you should prepare for a meeting by deciding what you would like to get out of it, for example, a commitment to introduce an issue, a commitment to support an already introduced issue, or simply the opportunity to gather or to provide information. If you visit as a member of a group, decide who will start the discussion and put your agenda on the table. If there are various topics to be addressed, assign one individual in your group to lead off each segment of the discussion. Sometimes, simply establishing contact is a good goal without getting commitments or specifics.

PUBLIC DEMONSTRATIONS

Media attention plays a role in advancing a policy issue (chapter 5), but individuals and small groups, unless they have high public visibility, have difficulty in gaining media attention. Public demonstrations are one way of attracting such attention. Consider the following. Before the availability of protease inhibitors promised to prolong the life of people who tested positive for Human Immunodeficiency Virus (HIV) and to restore physical well-being to individuals with Acquired Immune Deficiency Syndrome (AIDS), a diagnosis of AIDS was tantamount to a death sentence. The federal government and pharmaceutical companies undertook experiments to develop treatments for the HIV and AIDS. However, before a new drug can be tested, and before tested drugs become available to consumers, the United States Food and Drug Administration (FDA) must approve both the testing and subsequent marketing. The FDA's procedures have been criticized because their application means that years may pass between the time that a drug trial begins and the time that a drug becomes available. Critics have questioned why this process takes so long in the United States compared to Canada, Japan, Great Britain, and other European countries.[13]

In 1987, a group of AIDS activists calling themselves the AIDS Coalition to Unleash Power (ACT-UP) took it upon itself to change the drug-approval policies of the FDA. Group members argued that a person for whom early death was inevitable should be allowed to take experimental drugs as long as they held out any promise for improving health and were not demonstrably harmful. The group brought its message to public attention through a series of demonstrations, including protest marches, picketing outside of hospitals, demonstrations at federal court-houses and at the White House, blocking access to the FDA's headquarters, and demonstrating at public appearances where FDA officials made presentations. Co-alitions were formed with physicians, other health care professionals, and members of conservative think tanks, all of whom supported changing the FDA's approval process. It is probably the case that conservative groups were concerned less with the benefits of early approval for people with AIDS than with saving pharmaceutical companies the extraordinary expenses of extensive drug trials and the limits that this places on an early fiscal return for their investment.

In 1992, the FDA's policies were changed to permit accelerated or expedited approval of drugs, and the policy change was credited in large part to the pressure from ACT-UP and other advocacy groups.

POLICY IMPACT

Policy practice does not stop when policy is enacted but continues in order to determine whether an enacted policy is having the impact intended by policymak-ers. Impact studies are carried out directly by government agencies and by con-sulting firms, research organizations, and universities working under contract with a unit of government or supported by a foundation.

Investigators employ a variety of methods to ascertain whether programs are having their intended effect. For example, throughout this text I have referred to impact studies conducted by federal agencies, other research groups, and university-based researchers. Researchers use a variety of methods to learn about program impact, including (1) interviewing program officials and line staff; (2) reviewing agency records and abstracting data that describe the activities of agency staff in providing services; (3) employing statistical techniques to databases, for example, income data compiled by the Census Bureau to learn whether decreased rates of unemployment have had an impact on the number of individuals in poverty; (4) using single-subject designs to study the effects of interventions on individual clients; and (5) using experimental designs to study the impact of programs on groups, including longitudinal studies to determine the long-range impact of social welfare programs and services.

Despite the efforts of researchers, many questions about program impact go unanswered because professionals do not agree on what indicators to use to deter-mine whether a program has been successful. The likelihood of agreement on what indicators to use is greatest when outcome measures are purely quantitative. For example, it is not difficult to determine the number of clients whose income rose above the poverty level when cash benefits were adjusted to reflect increases in the cost of living, and all might agree that increased income will improve the quality of a person's life, but the latter is more easily inferred than empirically determined.

Consider another example. Provisions in the Adoption and Safe Families Act (ASFA) provide for incentive payments to states that increase the number of children adopted (chapter 15). The impact of the ASFA on adoptions is easy to determine as long as the program's success is judged solely on the basis of the number of children adopted. However, you might argue that this measure of impact, while meaningful, falls short because it fails to take into account child well-being subsequent to adoption. The difficult issue for the policy practitioner who studies program impact lies in getting agreement on the indicators of well-being, determining how to measure the agreed upon indicators, and obtaining the funds necessary to undertake a research program. The difficulty in obtaining agreement on proper indicators of well-being and determining how to measure them, probably explains, at least in part, why the Department of Health and Human Services has not identified outcomes for Head Start despite a congressional mandate that it do so (chapter 16).

A further difficulty in agreeing on indicators may lie in staff resistance to being evaluated. Evaluations are time consuming, often requiring staff to complete paperwork solely for the purpose of the evaluation. They are also intrusive, because someone is scrutinizing one's work. Most of us probably do not like the idea of having someone "look over our shoulder" for this purpose. Another concern is that an unfavorable evaluation could result in a loss of program funding. Dislike of evaluation probably increases if we know or have reason to believe that a program was not implemented in a manner likely to achieve the goals set by policymakers and if we are uncertain about the efficacy of the problem-solving methods that we employ.

Summary

The social worker as policy practitioner strives to improve the lives of clients by affecting the process by which policy is developed and implemented. Policy practice requires knowledge of the legislative process and expertise in the subject matter covered by the policy the practitioner seeks to affect. Whether the social worker works alone or with others, the tasks that define this area of social work practice include (1) advocacy; (2) agenda setting; (3) assessing the feasibility of change; (4) policy analysis; (5) testifying before policymakers; (6) lobbying policymakers; (7) engaging, at times, in public demonstrations to draw attention to an issue; and (8) evaluating the impact that policy has on the clients. The *Code of Ethics* of the NASW supports the tasks that define policy practice and the willingness of social workers to engage in policy practice reflects a professional commitment to improving client's lives.

Guide to On-Line Research

In this guide, I identify by Web address some Internet sites that contain material that may be useful to the policy researcher. Material is organized by the following categories: (1) research groups, (2) membership organizations, (3) advocacy groups, and (4) government sites. The categories are somewhat misleading because some groups, for example, the Children's Defense Fund, is listed as an advocacy group but also produces policy analyses.

The list is not inclusive. New sites are continually added to the Internet, some disappear, and some change their address. If you are looking for a site and the provided address does not get you there, try to locate a new site by using the search engine. Note that search engines use different search conventions, and you should read the instructions provided on-line. A number of sites provide list serves. Sites with list serves will note this, and they will provide instructions for having your E-mail address added to their list serve. If you subscribe (subscriptions are generally free), you will be notified each time new documents are added to the site.

Research Groups

www.jcpr.org   Joint Center for Poverty Research
www.mdrc.org   Manpower Demonstration Research Corporation
www.rand.org   Rand Corporation
www.brook.edu   The Brookings Institution
www.aei.org   The American Enterprise Institute
www.cnponline.org   Center for National Policy
www.epn.org   The Electronic Policy Network
www.urban.org   The Urban Institute
www.nyu.edu/socialwork/wwwrsw/   World Wide Web Resources for Social Workers

www.iwpr.org   The Institute for Women's Policy Research
www.kff.org   The Kaiser Family Foundation
www.cbpp.org   Center on Budget and Policy Priorities
www.tcf.org   The Century Foundation (formerly the 20th Century Foundation)
www-hoover.stanford.edu/pubaffairs/we/default.html   The Hoover Institution
www.claremont.org   The Claremont Institute
www.heritage.org   The Heritage Institute
www.cato.org   The CATO Institute
www.fordfound.org   The Ford Foundation
www.ilr.cornell.edu/library/e_archive   Catherwood Library at Cornell University
cpmcnet.columbia.edu./dept/nccp   National Center for Children in Poverty
www.adainfo.org   Americans with Disabilities Act Information Center

Membership Organizations

www.aarp.org   The American Association of Retired Persons
www.naswdc.org   The National Association of Social Workers
www.aphsa.org   American Public Human Services Association
www.geron.org   Gerontological Society of America
www.openadoption.org   American Association of Open Adoption Agencies

Advocacy Groups

www.childrensdefense.org   The Children's Defense Fund
www.aecf.org   The Annie E. Casey Foundation
www.hrc.org   The Human Rights Campaign Fund
www.now.org   The National Organization for Women
www.cwla.org   Child Welfare League of America
www.familiesusa.org   Families USA
www.opensecrets.org   Center for Responsive Politics
www.pfaw.org   People for the American Way
www.ngltf.org   National Gay and Lesbian Task Force
www.commoncause.org   Common Cause
www.minorityrights.org   Minority Rights International

Government Sites

www.aoa.dhhs.gov/   Administration on Aging
www.cdc.gov   Centers for Disease Control
www.acf.dhhs.gov/programs/cb/stats/afcars   Foster Care and Adoption Statistics
www.hcfa.gov   Health Care Financing Administration
www.gao.gov   The General Accounting Office

www.dhhs.gov   Department of Health and Human Services

www.access.gpo.gov/congress/wm001.html   House Committee on Ways and
Means (this committee has jurisdiction over social welfare)

www.medicare.gov   Medicare (Medicaid information is found through the
Health Care Financing Administration)

www.nimh.gov   National Institute of Mental Health

www.hud.gov   Department of Housing and Urban Development (extending
the address by adding, after "gov", /pih/pih/html brings you to a Web site
with information on public housing and Indian housing)

www.census.gov   United States Census Bureau

www.usda.gov   United States Department of Agriculture

www.ed.gov   United States Department of Education

www.access.gpo.gov   United States Government Printing Office

www.doj.gov   United States Department of Justice

www.samhsa.gov   Substance Abuse and Mental Health Services
Administration

www.senate.gov   United States Senate

www.house.gov   United States House of Representatives

www.whitehouse.gov   The White House

www.fedstats.gov   The FedStats Web page provides access to statistical
information from seventy federal agencies

www.ojp.usdoj.gov/vawo/   Violence Against Women Office

www.whitehouse.gov/omb/   Office of Management and Budget

www.financenet.gov/financenet/state/stbudget.htm   United States, state and
local budget information

www.acf.dhhs.gov/programs   Administration for Children and Families:
Programs and Services

Miscellaneous

www.FDNCenter.org   The Foundation Center (information concerning
projects funded by foundations)

www.stonewallrevisited.com   Lesbian and Gay issues

www-lib.usc.edu/~retter/main.html   Lesbian History Group

otes

CHAPTER ONE

1. Richard M. Titmus, *Social Policy: An Introduction* (London: George Allen and Unwin, 1977), Introduction.

2. The Civil Rights Act of 1964 precludes discrimination based on race, color, religion, sex, or national origin. 42 U.S.C.A. §2000e, *et seq.* When discussing civil rights policies, I refer to race- and gender-based discrimination because these are the most common forms of discrimination encountered by social workers. Sexual orientation is not included in the Civil Rights Act of 1964. Whatever civil rights protections are available to lesbians and gay men are found in discrete orders, such as President Clinton's Executive Order 13087 (May 1998) that precludes employment-based discrimination based on sexual orientation by federal agencies (63 FR 30097, 1998 WL 279809, May 1998) and in the laws of several states (see, for example, MA-ST-ANN, §151B §4 and WI-ST-ANN, §106.04). See, generally, Theodore J. Stein, *The Social Welfare of Women and Children with HIV and AIDS: Legal Protections, Policy, and Programs* (New York: Oxford University Press, 1998).

3. Diana M. DiNitto, *Social Welfare: Politics and Public Policy*, 4th ed. (Boston: Allyn and Bacon, 1995), 2; Thomas R. Dye, *Understanding Public Policy*, 9th ed. (New Jersey, Prentice-Hall, 1998), 2.

4. Bruce S. Jansson, *The Reluctant Welfare State: A History of American Social Welfare Policies*, 2nd ed. (Pacific Grove, Calif.: Brooks/Cole, 1993), 2.

5. Robert Morris, *Social Policy of the American Welfare State: An Introduction to Policy Analysis*, 2nd ed. (New York: Longman, 1985), 3, citing Thomas Humphrey Marshall, *Social Policy in the Twentieth Century*, 4th ed. (London, Hutchinson, 1975).

6. Titmus, *Social Policy*, 23.

7. 42 U.S.C. §601 *et seq.* (West 1999).

8. 42 U.S.C. §601(a)(1).

9. 42 U.S.C. §601(B).

10. 42 U.S.C. §601(a)(2) through (4).

11. 42 U.S.C.A. §670 (West 1997).

12. See 45 C.F.R. §400.118 and 45 C.F.R. Pt. 96. Appendix A (West 1999).

13. *Bragdon v. Abbott*, 118 S. Ct. 2196 (1998).

14. Richard D. Kahlenberg, *The Remedy: Class, Race, and Affirmative Action* (New York: Basic Books, 1996).

15. 26 FR 1977, 1961 WL 8178.

16. 42 U.S.C. §2000e-2 (West 1999). This provision in the Civil Rights Act applied only to tests. It had no bearing on the requirement for a high school diploma.

17. See, for example CA-ST-ANN, California Constitution, Art. II, §8 on the voter initiative and §9 on voter referenda (West 1997). The number of states with the initiative and referenda is reported in Nathaniel A. Persily, "The Peculiar Geography of Direct Democracy: Why the Initiative, Referendum and Recall Developed in the American West," *Michigan Law and Policy Review* 2 (1997): 11–41.

18. The court's criminal agenda is affected mainly by law enforcement officials who decide whether to pursue criminal charges against an alleged perpetrator.

19. Titmus, *Social Policy*, 31.

20. Nathan Glazer, *The Limits of Social Policy* (Cambridge, Mass.: Harvard University Press, 1990), 3.

21. *Sullivan v. Zebly*, 110 S. Ct. 885 (1990).

22. 20 C.F.R. 416.924(a)(1)(2).

23. A report by the U.S. General Accounting Office found no support for the suggestion that parents coached their children to fake mental impairments. See U.S. General Accounting Office, *Social Security—New Functional Assessments for Children Raise Eligibility Questions*, Report No. 95-66, 1995.

24. Senate Report 104-96, 104th Cong., 1st sess. (June 9, 1995).

25. U.S. General Accounting Office, *Teen Mothers—Selected Social-Demographic Characteristics and Risk Factors* (Washington, D.C.: U.S. Department of Health, Education, and Human Services Division B-280170, 1998), 13–14.

26. Richard Wertheimer and Kristin Moore, *Childbearing by Teens: Links to Welfare Reform* (Washington, D.C.: Urban Institute, 1998).

27. Nina Bernstein, "Illness, a New Baby, and Then a Struggle for Assistance," *New York Times*, August 17, 1998, p. B4.

28. Census Bureau, *Current Population Reports: Health Coverage 1997* (Washington, D.C.: U.S. Department of Commerce, 1998).

29. 140 *Cong. Rec.* Senate S12153-01 (Friday, August 19, 1994).

30. Jacob S. Hacker, *The Road to Nowhere: The Genesis of President Clinton's Plan for Health Security* (New Jersey: Princeton University Press, 1997); Paul Elwood, "Interview," *Hospitals* 67 (1993): 46.

31. Jack K. Kilcullen, "Groping for the Reins: ERISA, HMO Malpractice, and Enterprise Liability," *American Journal of Law and Medicine* 22 (1996): 7–50.

32. The figure of 36 million can be found in Commission on Behavioral and Social Sciences, National Research Council, *The Social Impact of AIDS in the United States* (Washington, D.C.: National Academy Press, 1993), 46. For the source of the 1997 figure, see note 28.

33. Peter T. Kilborn, "Voters' Anger at H.M.O.'s Plays as Hot Political Issue," *New York Times*, May 17, 1998, p. A1; Robert Pear, "Move Under Way to Try to Block Health Care Bills," *New York Times*, November 4, 1997, p. A1.

34. Kahlenberg, *The Remedy*, p. x, note 1.

35. Michael S. Greve, "Hopwood and Its Consequences," *Pace Law Review*, 17 (Winter 1996): 1–26; Richard H. Pildes, "Principled Limitations on Racial and Partisan Redistricting," *Yale Law Journal*, 106 (June 1997): 2505–2561.

36. Kahlenberg, *The Remedy*, 72.

37. Lawrence Harrison, "A Dream Not Really Deferred: America Is Quietly Getting Closer to Martin Luther King's Vision," *Washington Post*, January 17, 1993, p. C5.

38. Ellen Ladowsky, "That No White Male. . . . " *Wall Street Journal*, March 27, 1995, p. A20.

39. *Employment Non-Discrimination Act of 1994*, 140 *Cong. Rec.* S7561-02, (Thursday, June 23, 1994).

40. Editorial Desk, *New York Times*, October 28, 1995, p. A20 (President Clinton, advocating that the Congress hold hearings on ENDA, said "it would be an insult to the majority of Americans who oppose discrimination against homosexuals for the measure to be denied hearings); National Desk, *New York Times*, November 9, 1997, p. A30 (polling has shown broad support for the notion of equal protection for homosexuals under the law); Richard L. Berke, "The Nation: Chasing the Polls on Gay Rights," *New York Times*, August 2, 1998, Week in Review, p. 3 (discussing President Clinton's executive order barring federal agencies from discriminating against homosexuals, noting that the president's action "may have been shrewd . . . [because] the most pronounced shift in attitudes toward homosexuals in recent years has been a steady increase in support for equal rights in employment, housing and job protections. A survey by the President's pollsters . . . showed that 70 percent of Americans support Mr. Clinton's order").

41. Glazer, *Limits of Social Policy*, 3.

42. *Public Welfare Amendments of 1962*, Public Law 87-543, 87th Cong., 2nd sess. 1962 U.S.C.C.A.N. 1943, Senate Report No. 87-1589, June 14, 1962.

43. *Public Welfare Amendments of 1962*, Public Law 87-543, Section III, General Discussion. Improvement in Services to Reduce or Prevent Dependency.

44. Gilbert Y. Steiner, *Social Insecurity: The Politics of Welfare* (New York: Rand McNally, 1966), 181; Winifred Bell, *Aid to Dependent Children* (New York: Columbia University Press, 1965), 38.

45. Gilbert Y. Steiner, *The State of Welfare* (Washington, D.C.: Brookings Institution, 1971).

46. Steiner, *Social Insecurity*, 40.

47. *McCain v. Dinkins*, No. 58, 84 N.Y.2d 216 at 224 (New York 1994).

48. Shawn G. Kennedy, "Housing List in New York Hits Record," *New York Times*, December 27, 1992, p. C31.

49. Steiner, *Social Insecurity*, 146.

CHAPTER TWO

1. *Arneth v. Gross*, 699 F.Supp. 450 (S.D. N.Y. 1988).

2. *NASW Code of Ethics*, Standard 5: "Social Workers' Ethical Responsibilities to the Social Work Profession" (Washington, D.C.: National Association of Social Workers, 1998).

3. Robert H. Bremmer and others, *Children and Youth in America: A Documentary History: Volume I: 1600–1865* (Cambridge, Mass.: Harvard University Press, 1970), 398.

4. Richard Hofstadter, *Social Darwinism in American Thought* (Boston: Beacon Press, 1992), 41.

5. Walter I. Trattner, *From Poor Law to Welfare State: A History of Social Welfare in America*, 4th ed. (New York: Free Press, 1989), 54.

6. Ibid., 63.

7. Ibid., 64.

8. Bruce S. Jansson, *The Reluctant Welfare State: A History of American Social Welfare Policies*, 2nd ed. (Pacific Grove, Calif.: Brooks/Cole, 1993), 72.

9. Roy Lubove, *The Professional Altruist: The Emergence of Social Work as a Career 1880–1930* (Cambridge, Mass.: Harvard University Press, 1965), 1.

10. Ibid., 116.

11. Some settlements were religious missions whose workers saw little of value in the cultural differences of newly arrived immigrants who they sought to "Americanize." The workers in these settlements were less "aggressive[ly] moralistic" than charity organization society workers. Trattner, *From Poor Law to Welfare State*, 150–151.

12. Allen F. Davis, *Spearheads for Reform: The Social Settlements and the Progressive Movement 1890–1914* (New York: Oxford University Press, 1967), 266, note 21; Lela B. Costin, *Two Sisters for Social Justice: A Biography of Grace and Edith Abbott* (Chicago: University of Illinois Press, 1983), 45.

13. Davis, *Spearheads for Reform*, ch. 1 and 3.

14. Ibid., viii.

15. Trattner, *From Poor Law to Welfare State*, 160, note 6.

16. John Daniels, a settlement house worker in Boston, studied similar issues in that city, and Louise de Koven Brown and fellow settlement workers studied the lives of African Americans in Chicago. Davis, *Spearheads for Reform*, 96–98; Trattner, *From Poor Law to Welfare State*, 161.

17. Robert H. Bremmer and others, *Children and Youth in America: A Documentary History: Volume II: 1866–1932* (Cambridge, Mass.: Harvard University Press, 1970), 18.

18. Davis, *Spearheads for Reform*, 95, 96.

19. *Indian General Allotment Act of 1887* (The Dawes Act) 42 U.S.C.A. §3331 *et seq.*

20. Larry Kramer, "What's a Constitution for Anyway? Of History and Theory, Bruce Ackerman and the New Deal," *Case Western Reserve Law Review* 46 (1996): 924–925.

21. Edith Abbott, *Some American Pioneers in Social Welfare* (New York: Russell and Russell, 1963), 107–108.

22. Bremmer, *Children and Youth in America, Volume I*, 789.

23. *Hammer v. Dagenhart*, 247 U.S. 251.

24. *Bailey, Collector of Internal Revenue v. Drexel Furniture Company*, 259, U.S. Reports 20 (1922).

25. *United States v. Darby*, 312 U.S. 1 (1941).

26. *Tenement House Department of the City of New York v. Muenchen*, 72 N.E. 231 (1904).

27. Davis, *Spearheads for Reform*, 74–75.

28. Grace Abbott, *The Child and the State* (Chicago: University of Chicago Press, 1938), 229–231.

29. Costin, *Two Sisters*, 102.

30. *Lochner v. New York*, 198 U.S. 45 (1905).

31. 57 S. Ct. 578, 582 (1937).

32. Sybil Lipschultz, "Social Feminism and Legal Discourse: 1908–1923," *Yale Journal of Law and Feminism* 2 (1989): 131–160.

33. *Muller v. Oregon*, 52 L.Ed. 551 (1908).

34. David J. Rothman, *Discovery of the Asylum: Social Order and Disorder in the New Republic* (Boston: Little, Brown, 1971), 209.

35. Trattner, *From Poor Law to Welfare State*, 115.

36. James Leiby, *A History of Social Welfare and Social Work in the United States* (New York: Columbia University Press, 1978), 147.

37. Trattner, *From Poor Law to Welfare State*, 194.

38. Costin, *Two Sisters*, 130.

39. Davis, *Spearheads for Reform*, 219.

40. Ibid., 221.

41. Trattner, *From Poor Law to Welfare State*, ch. 11.

42. Ibid., 222–223.

43. Ibid., 231.

44. Lubove, *The Professional Altruist*, 48; Trattner, *From Poor Law to Welfare State*, 219.

45. Lubove, *The Professional Altruist*, 47; Trattner, *From Poor Law to Welfare State*, 219.
46. Trattner, *From Poor Law to Welfare State*, 234.
47. Ibid.

CHAPTER THREE

1. The data in this paragraph are derived from Margaret Gibelman and Philip H. Schervish, *Who We Are: A Second Look* (Washington, D.C.: National Association of Social Workers, 1997).
2. *McKinney's Consolidated Laws of New York State*, Executive Law, ch. 18, art. 21.
3. Carol J. DeVita, "Nonprofits and Devolution: What Do We Know?" in Elizabeth T. Boris and C. Eugene Steuerle, eds., *Nonprofits and Government: Collaboration and Conflict*, 219 (Washington, D.C.: Urban Institute, 1999).
4. See, for example, "President's Private Sector Survey on Cost Control," Executive Order 12369, 1982 (charged with studying how the federal government could reduce costs); President's Commission on Housing, Executive Order 12310, 1982 (governmental functions should be transferred to the private sector.); President's Commission on Indian Reservation Economies, Executive Order 12401, 1984 (charged with studying and providing advice to the president on ways to reduce the dependence of tribes on federal government and on how to strengthen private sector investments on the reservations); President's Commission on Privatization, Executive Order 12607, 1988 (review the current activities of the federal government and identify those functions that are not properly the responsibility of the federal government and should be divested or transferred to the private sector).
5. 42 U.S.C.A. §604a (1998).
6. Introduced as the Freedom from Government Competition Act. See 143 Cong. Rec. S7664-01, 7667.
7. 105th Congress, 1st sess., Public Law 105-270.
8. On privatization, see, generally, Keon S. Chi and Cindy Jasper, *Private Practices: A Review of Privatization in State Government* (Lexington, Ky.: Council of State Governments, 1998); Sara S. Bachman, "Why Do States Privatize Mental Health Services? Six State Experiences," *Journal of Health Politics, Policy and Law* 21 (Winter 1996): 807; U.S. General Accounting Office, *Privatization: Lessons Learned by State and Local Governments* (Washington, D.C.: Report No. GAO/GGD 97-48, 1997).
9. John O'Looney, "Beyond Privatization and Service Integration: Organizational Models for Service Delivery," *Social Service Review* 67, 4 (December 1993): 501–534; Richard Bartley, "Public-Private Relationships and Performance in Service Provision," *Urban Studies* 33, 4/5 (May 1996): 723–751.
10. U.S. General Accounting Office, *Private and Public Prisons: Studies Comparing Operational Costs and/or Quality Service*, Report. No. 96-158 (Washington, D.C., 1996).
11. Outsourcing is a generic term that refers to contracting for services, granting service franchises to private firms, and utilizing volunteers to deliver public services. When a service is outsourced, the government retains full responsibility for providing services and full control over management decisions while another entity operates the function or performs the service. See U.S. General Accounting Office, *Privatization*, 46.
12. U.S. General Accounting Office, *Privatization*, 27, 29, 31.
13. Chi and Jasper, *Private Practices*, 1, 12.
14. Ibid., appendices to report.
15. Ibid., 21–49
16. U.S. General Accounting Office, *Private and Public Prisons*, 1.
17. 117 S. Ct. 2100 (June 1997).
18. Chi and Jasper, *Private Practices*, 18.

19. David Cohen, "Democracy and the Intersection of Prisons, Racism and Capital: Review Essay," *National Black Law Journal* 15 (1997–98): 87–108.

20. Jeremy Lutsky, "Is Your Physician Becoming a Teamster? The Rising Trend of Physicians Joining Labor Unions in the Late 1990s," *DePaul Journal of Health Care Law* 2 (Fall 1997): 55–102.

21. Mark S. Kaduboski, "A Skirmish in the Battle for the Soul of Massachusetts State Government: Privatization of Government Services and the Constitutionality of Appropriation Restriction Measures," *Boston College Law Review* 38 (May 1997): 541–568.

22. Gibelman and Schervish, *Who We Are*, 19.

23. CO-ST-ANN §12-43-405 (West 1997); ALA-ST-ANN §34-30-3 (West 1998).

24. *Dunn v. Catholic Home Bureau*, 142 Misc.2d 316 (S. Ct. N.Y. 1989).

25. *Jaffee v. Redmond*, 116 S. Ct. 1923 (1996).

26. See, in general, Theodore J. Stein, *Child Welfare and the Law*, revised edition (Washington, D.C.: Child Welfare League of America, 1998).

27. National Association of Social Workers, *Code of Ethics*, Standard 1.07, Privacy and Confidentiality (Washington, D.C.: National Association of Social Workers).

28. The National Conference of Commissioners on Uniform State Laws (NCCUSL) is a group of attorneys, judges, law professors, and legislators who are appointed by state governors to propose uniform state laws. Adoption of uniform laws helps to overcome problems created by variations in state laws, for example, regarding control of and access to confidential information. The NCCUSL has no legislative authority and cannot impose its recommendations.

29. Ryan White Comprehensive AIDS Resources Emergency Act, 101st Cong., 1st sess., Public Law 101-381, 104 Stat 576, (August 18, 1990).

30. 42 U.S.C.S. §12112(d)(3)(B) (West 1999).

31. 42 C.F.R. §2.31 (West 1999).

32. 5 U.S.C.A. §552a(b) (West 1999).

33. 5 U.S.C.A. §552a (West 1999).

34. Paul M. Schwartz, "The Protection of Privacy in Health Care Reform," *Vanderbilt Law Review* 48 (1996): 295–347.

35. 5 U.S.C.A. §552 (West 1999).

36. See, for example, *Baldridge v. Shapiro*, 102 S. Ct. 1103 (1982); *United States v. Provenzano*, 105 S. Ct. 413 (1984); *Church of Scientology v. Internal Revenue Service*, 108 S. Ct. 271 (1987); *United States v. Julian*, 108 S. Ct. 1606 (1988).

37. 104th Cong., 2nd sess., Public Law 104-191, 110 Stat 1936 (August 21, 1996).

38. Committee on Maintaining Privacy and Security in Health Care Applications, *For the Record: Protecting Electronic Health Information* (Washington, D.C.: National Academy of Sciences Press, 1997).

39. Medical clearinghouses collect medical information regarding individuals and provide information to subscribers for a fee. Data are given to clearinghouses by insurance companies, and the clearinghouses compile data from third party treatment records and their own investigations of individuals. Their subscribers have virtually instantaneous access to this information. The system "operates in the shadows. Its integrity is untested and the accuracy or security of the accumulated data is seldom questioned and poses a risk to everyone who applies for health or life insurance, or who joins a Health Maintenance Organization. Individuals with grievances against clearinghouses may look to the federal Consumer Credit Protection Act that grants to individuals the right to inspect and challenge the data collected and to seek sanctions for abusive practices." Robert J. Conroy and Mark D. Brylski, "Access to Medical Records vs. Patient's Privacy Interests," *New Jersey Lawyer* 173 (December 1995): 25.

40. See note 37.

41. Committee on Maintaining Privacy, *For the Record*, 89.
42. Editorial, "Quest for Health Information Privacy Law Likely to be Long and Full of Pitfalls," *Health Legislation and Regulation* 23, 24 (1997): 1.
43. *Whalen v. Roe*, 97 S. Ct. 869 (1977).
44. *Tarasoff v. The Regents of the University of California*, 526 P.2d 553 (Cal. 1974).
45. *Tarasoff v. The Regents of the University of California*, 551 P.2d 334 (Cal. 1976).
46. 614 P.2d 728 (Cal. 1980).
47. Ibid., 752.
48. See, for example, DE-ST-ANN §5402 *et seq.* (West 1998); NJ-ST-ANN §2A:62A-16 (West 1998); LS-ST-ANN §9:2800.2 (West 1998).
49. See AZ-ST-ANN §S36-517.02 (West 1997); CO-ST-ANN §13-21-117 (West 1998); DE-ST-ANN §5402 (West 1997); ID-ST-ANN §9-1902 (West 1998); IND. CODE ANN. §§34-4-12.4-1 to -4 (West Supp. 1988); KY-ST-ANN §202A.400 (West 1998); LA-ST-ANN §9:2800.2 (West 1998); MI-ST-ANN §330.1946 (West 1998); MN-ST-ANN §148-975 (West 1998); MT-ST-ANN §§27-1-1101 to -1103; NB-ST-ANN §71-1,206.30 (West 1998); NH-ST- ANN §329:31 (West 1998); NJ-ST-ANN §2A:62A-16 (West 1998); UT-ST-ANN §S 78-14a-102 (West 1998); WA-ST-ANN §71.05.120 (West 1998).
50. *Kerrville State Hospital v. Clark*, 900 S.W.2d 425 (TX. Ct. App. 3rd Dist. 1995) *rev'd* for other reasons; *Schuster v. Altenberg*, 424 N.W.2d 159 (Wisc. 1988).
51. *Santa Cruz v. Northwest Dade Community Health Center*, 590 So.2d 444, review denied, 599 So.2d 238 (Fla. 1992); *Boulanger v. Pol*, 900 P.2d 823 (Kan. 1995); *Nasser v. Parker*, 455 S.E.2d 502 (Va. 1995); *Ellis v. Peter*, 211 A.D.2d 353 (Dept. 2nd 1995).
52. *Tenuto v. Lederle Laboratories and Bishop, N.Y.*, Slip Op. 08771 (Ct. App. 1997).
53. *Ellis v. Peter*, 211 A.D.2d 353 (Dept. 2nd 1995).
54. *Pike v. Honsinger*, 49 N.E. 760, 762 (1898).
55. *Oelsner v. New York*, 66 N.Y. 2d 636 (New York 1985).
56. *Schrempf v. New York*, 66 N.Y.2d 289 (New York 1985); *Topel v. Long Island Jewish Medical Center*, 55 N.Y. 2d 682 (New York 1981); *McDonnell v. County of Nassau*, N.Y. S. Ct., Nassau county. No. 11152/73, unreported (1986).
57. *Yula v. State*, 127 N.Y.S.2d 147 (A.D. 2nd Dept. 1954); *Centeno v. New York*, 40 N.Y.2d 932 (New York 1976); *Fiederlein v. New York Health and Hospitals Corp.*, 56 N.Y.2d 573 (New York 1982).
58. See *O'Shea v. United States*, 623 F. Supp. 380 (E.D.N.Y. 1985).
59. *Homere v. State*, 361 N.Y.S.2d 820 (Ct. of Claims 1974); *Bell v. New York City Health and Hospitals Corp.*, 456 N.Y.S.2d 787 (A.D. 2nd Dept. 1982); *Huntley v. New York*, 62 N.Y.2d 134 (New York 1984).
60. *Cohen v. New York*, 51 A.D.2d 494 (3rd Dept. 1976) affirmed (1977), 41 N.Y.2d 1086.
61. *Harlow v. Fitzgerald*, 102 S. Ct. 2727 (1982).
62. 12 F. Supp.2d 640 (E.D.MI. 1998).
63. *Sherman v. Four County Counseling Center*, 987 F.2d 397 (7th Cir. 1993); see also *Frazier v. Bailey*, 957 F.2d 920 (1st Cir. 1991) (social workers under contract to perform statutorily mandated governmental duties were entitled to raise qualified immunity as functionally governmental employees).

CHAPTER FOUR

1. Walter I. Trattner, *From Poor Law to Welfare State: A History of Social Welfare in America*, 4th ed. (New York: Free Press, 1989), 15.
2. During the reign of Henry VIII (1509–1547), and after the formation of the Church of England, a process of codifying the system of ecclesiastical poor relief that had existed under the Roman Catholic Church began. A number of miscellaneous civil

statutes were enacted in the sixteenth century, culminating in 1601 in the passage of the Poor Law, which unified into a single statue the previously enacted codes. See Larry Cata Backer, "Medieval Poor Law in Twentieth Century America: Looking Back Towards a General Theory of Modern American Poor Relief," *Case Western Reserve Law Review* 44 (Spring/Summer 1995): 871.

3. Statutes in the early colonies distinguished the workhouse from the almshouse. The workhouse was used to support settlement law provisions by threatening "rogues and vagabonds" with incarceration at hard labor if they moved into a new community and sought aid. In contrast, the almshouse (or poorhouse) was used to feed, lodge, and perhaps employ the needy people of a town. See David J. Rothman, *The Discovery of the Asylum: Social Order in the New Republic* (Boston: Little, Brown, 1971), 25–29.

4. William P. Quigley, "Rumblings of Reform: Northern Poor Relief Legislation in Antebellum America, 1820–1860," *Capital University Law Review* 26 1997): 739–774.

5. Jonathan A. Bush, "Free to Enslave: The Foundations of Colonial American Slave Law," *Yale Journal of Law and the Humanities* 5 (Summer 1993): 417–470. In contrast, Louisiana, whose laws derive from the Napoleonic Code, not the English Common Law, had its infamous Black Codes under which slaves were deemed to be the property of their masters, who were free to seize, sell, or mortgage them. The Black Codes prevented slaves from leaving plantations without written permission of their owners, unless they were accompanied by a white person.

6. Ibid., 421.

7. *Stewart v. Somerset*, 98 Eng. Rep. (1 Lofft) 499 [K.B.1772].

8. Fugitive Slave Clause, art. IV, §2. Fugitive Slave Act of 1793 (Act of Feb. 12, 1793, ch. 7, 1 Stat. 302); Fugitive Slave Law of September 18, 1850; ch. 60, 9 Stat. 462).

9. Paul Finkelman, "Symposium: Race Relations and the United States Constitution: From Fugitive Slaves to Affirmative Action: Sorting Out *Prigg v. Pennsylvania*," *Rutgers Law Journal* 24 (Spring 1993): 605–665.

10. The Fugitive Slave Act of 1850 was part of the Compromise of 1850 (Sept. 9 thru Sept. 20, 1850, chs. 49, 50, 51, 55, 63; 9 Stat. 446, 452, 453, 462; 467) under which California entered the Union as a non-slave state; New Mexico and Utah were designated territories that could join the Union as slave or non-slave states; and the District of Columbia was allowed to be a slave-holding state but was precluded from engaging in the slave trade. The compromise also settled boundary claims and debts that concerned the Republic of Texas.

11. *Commonwealth v. Aves*, 18 Pick. 193 (1836).

12. 41 U.S. 539 (January 1842).

13. Report of the Secretary of State, *Relief and Settlement of the Poor* (1824), reprinted in 1 New York State Bd. of Charities, Annual Report for the Year 1900, 949–953 (1901).

14. Other institutional arrangements included "asylums for the insane and blind, nurseries for poor and destitute children, [and] state reform schools." Quigley, "Rumblings of Reform." The work of Charles Loring Brace of the Children's Aid Society of New York provides an exception to the use of institutions. Based on his conviction that family life (although not necessarily the biological family of the immigrant children) provided the best setting for raising children, and that the children of immigrant families to whom he referred to as the "dangerous classes" posed a danger to life in New York City, Brace and his colleagues were responsible for sending more than 90,000 children out west, from the mid-1800s until the end of the century, where they provided free labor on farms.

15. Ely and Bodenheimer (1986) report that outdoor relief remained normative in the Southern states before the Civil War. European migration had little effect on the South, whose ongoing plantation economy allowed it to escape the problems associated with

industrialization in the Northern states. Slaves received whatever care was provided for them on the plantations where they lived, and the south did not enforce the Laws of Settlement. J. W. Ely, Jr. and D. J. Bodenheimer, "Regionalism and American Legal History: The Southern Experience," *Vanderbilt Law Review* 39 (April 1986): 539–567.

16. 60 U.S. 393 (1857).

17. *Emancipation Proclamation*, 12 Stat. 1268 (1863).

18. A. Leon Higginbotham Jr. and F. Michael Higginbotham, "Yearning to Breathe Free: Legal Barriers Against and Options in Favor of Liberty in Antebellum Virginia," *New York University Law Review* 68 (December 1993): 1213–1271.

19. Trattner, *From Poor Law to Welfare State*, 74.

20. Robert J. Kaczorowski, "Federal Enforcement of Civil Rights During the First Reconstruction," *Fordham Urban Journal* 23 (Fall 1995): 156–157.

21. Freedman's Bureau Bills (Mar. 3, 1865), ch. 90, 13 Stat. 507.

22. For newly freed slaves, the Fourteenth Amendment was "designed to insure to the colored race the enjoyment of all the rights that under the law are enjoyed by white persons, and to give to that race the protection of the general government in that enjoyment whenever it should be denied by the states." *Strauder v. West Virginia*, 100 U.S. 303 (1879); see also *Ex parte Virginia*, 100 U.S. 339 (1879).

23. *Barron v. City of Baltimore*, 32 U.S. 243 (1833).

24. Ch. 31, 14 Stat. 217 (1866).

25. Robert J. Kaczorowski, "Revolutionary Constitutionalism in the Era of the Civil War and Reconstruction," *New York University Law Review* 61 (November 1986): 863–940.

26. Ch. 114, 16 Stat. 140 (1870).

27. *Ku Klux Klan Act of 1871*, ch. 22, 17 Stat. 13.

28. Constitution of the United States, Amendment XV (1870).

29. 42 U.S.C.A. §1973 (West 1998).

30. 3 S. Ct. 18 (1883).

31. Ibid., 28.

32. 163 U.S. 537

33. Charles J. McClain, "The Chinese Struggle for Civil Rights in Nineteenth Century America: The First Phase, 1850–1870," *California Law Review* 72 (July 1984): 529–568.

34. Ibid., 529, 539–540. The Capitation Tax was deemed unconstitutional in 1857; see *People v. Downer*, 7 Cal. 169 (1857).

35. John Hayakawa Torok, "Reconstruction and Racial Nativism: Chinese Immigrants and the Debates on the Thirteenth, Fourteenth, and Fifteenth Amendments and Civil Rights Laws," *Asian Law Journal* 3 (May 1996): 55–103.

36. McClain, "The Chinese Struggle," 555.

37. *Yick Wo v. Hopkins*, 118 U.S. 356, 373 (1886).

38. *In re Ah Chong*, 2 F. 733 (C.C.D.C. 1880).

39. *In re Tiburcio Parrott*, 1 F. 481 (C.C.C. 1880).

40. Bruce Ackerman and David Golove, "Is NAFTA Constitutional," *Harvard Law Review* 108 (1995): 799–929.

41. Executive Order Number 9066, 7 Fed. Reg. 1407 (February 19, 1942); Act of March 21, 1942, 56 Stat. 173.

42. *Korematsu v. United States*, 65 S. Ct. 193 (1944).

43. "Restitution for World War II Internment of Japanese-Americans and Aleuts," 50 U.S.C.A. §1989 (West 1988).

44. Charles J. McClain, "Tortuous Path, Elusive Goal: The Asian Quest for American Citizenship," *Asian Law Journal* 2 (May 1995): 33–46.

45. *In re Ah Yup*, 1 F. Cas. 223 (C.C.D.C. April 29, 1878); *Ozawa v. United States*, 42 S. Ct. 65 (November 13, 1922). Citizenship was granted to Native Americans in a piecemeal

manner until 1924 when there was a blanket grant of citizenship to all Native Americans on whom citizenship was not previously conferred. Citizens of Mexico who were living in the territories ceded to the United States at the end of the Mexican-American War were offered citizenship if they remained in the United States. See *Treaty of Guadalupe-Hidalgo*, 9 Stat. 922 (February 1848) and Act of June 2, 1924, Ch. 233, 43 Stat. 253.

46. Torok, "Reconstruction and Racial Nativism."

47. 8 U.S.C.A. Ch. 7, Chinese Exclusion Acts, Temporary Act of May 6, 1882, 22 Stat. 58; Act of May 6, 1892, 27 Stat. 25; Act of April 27, 1904, 33 Stat. 428, amending Act of April 29, 1902, 32 Stat. 176).

48. Act of May 6, 1882, 22 Stat. at 59–61.

49. Titled also *An Act to Prohibit the Coming of Chinese Persons to the United States*. Act of May 6, 1892, 27 Stat. 25.

50. *Chae Chan Ping v. United States*, 9 S. Ct. 623 (May 13, 1989); *Fong Yue Ting v. United States*, 13 S. Ct. 1016 (May 15 1893).

51. Burlingame Treaty, 16 Stat. 739, (July 28, 1868).

52. 66 Stat. 163 (1952).

53. *Porterfield v. Webb*, 44 S. Ct. 21 (1923); *Cockrill v. California*, 268 U.S. 258 (1925); *Terrace v. Thompson*, 44 S. Ct. 15 (1923).

54. Feb. 2, 1848, 9 Stat. 922; 1848.

55. Richard Griswold del Castillo, "Symposium: Manifest Destiny: The Mexican-American War and the Treaty of Guadalupe Hidalgo," *Southwestern Journal of Law and Trade in the Americas*, 5 (Spring 1998): 31–43. In 1898, as part of the settlement that ended the Spanish-American War, Spain ceded Puerto Rico, Guam, the Philippine Islands, and Hawaii to the United States. In the early 1900s, the United States acquired part of Samoa in transactions with Samoan chiefs; in 1916, the United States purchased part of the Virgin Islands from Denmark, and after World War II the Northern Mariana Islands, which had been under control of the Japanese government, came under the control of the United States.

56. The Treaty of Guadalupe-Hidalgo and the protocol did not apply to Texas, which had been admitted to the Union before the treaty was signed. (*McKinney v. Saviego* 18 U.S. 235 [1856]). Texas law prevented a person who owned land in that state when it was a part of Mexico, who moved back to and remained in Mexico before Texas declared its independence, to lay claim to the earlier owned land.

57. *Northwestern Bands of Shoshone Indians v. U.S.*, 65 S. Ct. 690 (1945). The Protocol of Queretaro replaced Article X of the Treaty of Guadalupe-Hidalgo. Article X was rejected by Congress when the treaty was signed because it was interpreted as binding the United States to honor all grants whether or not the grants had been perfected under Mexican law. *Cessna v. United States*, 169 U.S. 165 (1898).

58. Guadalupe T. Luna, "En El Nombre De Dios Todo-Poderoso: The Treaty of Guadalupe Hidalgo and Narrativos Legales," *Southwestern Journal of Law and Trade in the Americas*, 5 (Spring 1998): 45–107.

59. Robert E. Lutz, "The Mexican War and the Treaty of Guadalupe Hidalgo: What's Best and Worst About Us?" *Southwestern Journal of Law and Trade in the Americas* 5 (Spring 1998): 27–30.

60. Land Act, Mar. 3, 1851, ch. 41, 9 Stat. 631. See also *Botiller v. Dominguez*, 9 S. Ct. 525 (1889).

61. del Castillo, "Symposium: Manifest Destiny."

62. Act of Feb. 5, 1917, ch. 29, § 3, 39 Stat. 874 (1917).

63. The agreements of 1942 and 1943 were informal. There was no specific act of Congress to create them. The 1943 agreement was financed through appropriations under Pub-

lic Law 45, approved April 29, 1943. Public Law 229 of 1944 continued these appropriations, and they were extended through December 1945 under Public Law 529.

64. Treaty making is governed by Article II, Section 2 of the United States Constitution that provides for the president to make treaties that must be approved by two-thirds of the Senate.

65. U.S.C.A. "Ordinance of 1787: The Northwest Territorial Government," Article III.

66. *Worcester v. Georgia* 31 US 515 (1832).

67. Arlene Hirschfelder and Martha K. de Montano, *The Native American Almanac: A Portrait of Native America Today* (New York: Macmillan, 1993), 53–58.

68. See, for example, Matthew Atkinson, "Red Tape: How American Laws Ensnare Native American Lands, Resources, and People," *Oklahoma City University Law Review* 23 (Spring-Summer 1998): 379–431; Raymond Cross, "Sovereign Bargains, Indian Takings, and the Preservation of Indian Country in the Twenty-First Century," *Arizona Law Review* 40 (Summer 1998): 425–509; Alexandra New Holy, "The Heart of Everything That Is: PAHA SAPA, Treaties, and Lakota Identity," *Oklahoma City University Law Review* 23 (Spring-Summer 1998): 317–352.

69. *Cherokee Nation v. Georgia*, 30 U.S. 1 (1831); *Worcester v. Georgia*, 31 U.S. 515 (1832).

70. Indian Removal Act of May 28, 1830, ch. 148, 4 Stat. 411.

71. Geoffrey C. Heisey, "Oliphant and Tribal Criminal Jurisdiction Over Non-Indians: Asserting Congress's Plenary Power to Restore Territorial Jurisdiction," *Indiana Law Journal* 73 (Summer 1998): 1051–1078.

72. Indian Appropriation Act of March 3, 1871 (Ch. 120, 16 Stat. 544).

73. *United States v. Kagama*, 118 U.S. 375 (1886); *Stephens v. Cherokee Nation*, 174 U.S. 445 (1899); *Lone Wolf v. Hitchcock*, 187 U.S. 553 (1903).

74. *Stephens v. Cherokee Nation*, 174 U.S. 445 (1899).

75. *Lone Wolf v. Hitchcock*, 187 U.S. 553 (1903); *Rosebud Sioux Tribe v. State*, 97 S. Ct. 1361 (1977).

76. Act of June 18, 1934, 48 Stat. 984 (June 18, 1934). Some of the provisions found in the 1934 act were later applied to natives of Alaska and native tribes in Oklahoma under separate statutes. See Act of June 26, 1936, 49 Stat. 1967 (Oklahoma Indian Welfare Act); Act of May 1, 1936, 49 Stat. 1250 (Alaska Native Reorganization Act).

77. *Talton v. Mayes*, 163 U.S. 376 (1896).

78. 25 U.S.C. §1301 *et seq.* (West 1997).

79. The Bureau of Indian Affairs was established in 1824. 25 U.S.C.A. §1a *et seq.* (West 1998).

80. Before 1978, federal recognition of Native tribes required an act of Congress or an executive order. In 1978, the Bureau of Indian Affairs created the Federal Acknowledgment Project for the purpose of evaluating tribal petitions for federal recognition. (See Bureau of Indian Affairs, "Procedures for Establishing That an American Indian Group Exists as an Indian Tribe" 25 C.F.R. Part 83 (Friday, February 25, 1994.) Criteria for recognition are set forth in federal regulations (see 25 C.F.R. §83.7) and include a long list of factors that may constitute evidence of group identity. For example, the following, alone or in combination, may constitute grounds for recognition: (1) identification by the federal government or relationships or dealing with state and local units of government; (2) identification as an Indian entity by anthropologists, historians, and/or other scholars; or (3) identification as an Indian entity in newspapers and books.

81. 25 U.S.C.A. §13 (1998).

82. The information concerning tribal governments is taken from Robert J. Lyttle, "Tribal Government," in Hirschfelder and de Montano, *The Native American Almanac*, 71–82.

83. 25 C.F.R. 11.100.

84. Melissa L. Koehn, "Civil Jurisdiction: The Boundaries Between Federal and Tribal Courts," *Arizona State Law Journal* 10 (Fall 1997): 705–768.

85. 18 U.S.C.A. §1153 (West 1998).

86. Indian Tribal Justice Act of 1993, 25 U.S.C.A. §3601 *et seq.* (West 1998).

87. *Shapiro v. Thompson*, 89 S. Ct. 1322.

CHAPTER FIVE

1. See Erwin Chemerinsky, "Evaluating Judicial Candidates," *Southern California Law Review* (1988) for a discussion of a "carefully orchestrated media campaign" to depict justices as soft on crime. Chemerinsky reports that "three justices were removed from the (California) bench because people perceived them as unwilling to execute a sufficient number of prisoners." The legacy of this might be that judges who are facing retention elections "will decide cases with an eye, perhaps subconsciously, on how their rulings will affect their chances at the polls."

2. Roger W. Cobb and Charles D. Elder, *Participation in American Politics: The Dynamics of Agenda-Building* (Boston: Allyn and Bacon, 1972): 161.

3. John W. Kingdon, *Agendas, Alternatives, and Public Policies*, 2nd ed. (New York: Addison-Wesley, 1995), 90.

4. Maxwell E. McCombs, "The Evolution of Agenda-Setting Research: Twenty-Five Years in the Marketplace of Ideas," *Journal of Communications* 43, 2 (Spring 1993): 62.

5. M. E. McCombs and D. L. Shaw, "The Agenda-Setting Function of Mass Media," *Public Opinion Quarterly* 36 (1972): 176–189.

6. Shanto Iyengar, Mark C. Peters, and Donald R. Kinder, "Experimental Demonstrations of the 'Not-So-Minimal' Consequences of Television News Programs," *American Political Science Review* 76 (1982): 848–858.

7. See McCombs, "The Evolution of Agenda-Setting Research," 63.

8. Kathryn L. Braun and Christopher R. Conybeare, "Health Scope: A Model for a Low Cost Health Education Program Using Commercial Television," *Public Health Reports* (Washington, D.C.: U.S. Department of Health and Human Services, July/August 1995), 483–491.

9. Robert E. Shephard Jr., "How the Media Misrepresents Juvenile Policies," *Criminal Justice* 12 (Winter 1998).

10. *United States v. Clary*, 846 F. Supp. 768 (E. Dist. MO., February 1994). Possession of 50 grams of crack cocaine carried a mandatory minimum sentence of 10 years, whereas one would have to be convicted of possession 5,000 grams of powder cocaine to receive the same sentence.

11. Barbara Nelson, *Making an Issue of Child Abuse: Political Agenda Setting for Social Problems* (Chicago: University of Chicago Press, 1984), 129.

12. Jacob S. Hacker, *The Road to Nowhere: The Genesis of President Clinton's Plan for Health Security* (New Jersey: Princeton University Press, 1997), 63.

13. Ibid., 139–140.

14. Peter A. Lauricella, "The Real 'Contract with America': The Original Intent of the Tenth Amendment and the Commerce Clause," *Albany Law Review* 60 (1997): 1377–1426.

15. Deborah Stone, *Policy Paradox: The Art of Political Decision Making* (New York: W. W. Norton, 1997), ch. 6.

16. For the position of the Democratic party, see "The Democratic Platform: Excerpts from the Platform: A 'New Covenant' With Americans," *New York Times,* July 15, 1992, sect. A, p. 10; col. 1; the conservative Republican opinion has been expressed by Heidi Stirrup, speaking on behalf of the Christian Coalition. See Heidi Stirrup, Testimony

before the Committee on Finance of the United States Senate, hearing on "The National Governors' Association Recent Resolutions Restructuring Welfare Reform," 1996. See also "Quayle Distorts Democratic Platform on Gays," *New York Times*, October 9, 1992, sect. A, col. 4, p. 32. Former Vice President Quayle claimed that the platform of the Democratic Party called for affirmative action to remedy discrimination against lesbians and gays.

17. Stone, *Policy Paradox*, 113.

18. Senate, Proceedings and Debates of the 101st Congress, 2nd sess., *Cong. Rec.* (Wednesday, October 3).

19. Clay Shaw, Testimony before the House of Representatives Ways and Means Committee Concerning Poverty and Out-of-Wedlock Births, March 12, 1996.

20. Caryl Rivers, "Ideas/Earth to Media: The Stable Family Is Alive," *New York Newsday*, June 2, 1996, p. A44.

21. R. W. Apple Jr., "Politics: The Issues—Interview with Newt Gingrich," *New York Times*, June 25, 1996, sect. A, p. 18, col. 1.

22. Stirrup, Testimony before the Committee on Finance.

23. Apple, "Politics: The Issues."

24. Arlene Skolnick, *Embattled Paradise: The American Family in the Age of Uncertainty* (New York: Basic Books, 1991).

25. From a speech given by President Clinton on July 31, 1996, entitled "The Welfare Bill," reprinted in *New York Times*, August 1, 1996, sect. A, col. 1, p. 24. See also Shaw, Testimony before the House.

26. Joseph I. Lieberman, "Welfare as We Know It," *New York Times*, July 25, 1996, sect. A, col. 1, p. 23.

27. Robert Rector, "Welfare Reforms Will Help Kids," reprinted from *New York Newsday* in the *Buffalo News*, *Viewpoints*, August 29, 1996, city ed., p. 3B. See also Stirrup, Testimony before the Committee on Finance.

28. Charles Murray, Testimony before the Subcommittee on Human Resources of the Committee on Ways and Means, House of Representatives, July 29, 1994.

29. Stirrup, Testimony before the Committee on Finance.

30. Murray, Testimony before the Subcommittee on Human Resources.

31. Clay Shaw, "Supporting True Welfare Reform," *Cong. Rec.* E857-01, 104th Cong., 2nd sess (May 21, 1996).

32. Senate, *The Work First and Personal Responsibility Act of 1996*, 104th Cong., 2nd sess., House Bill 3612, June 19, 1996.

33. See 104th Cong., 2nd sess., House Bill 4 (1995) (note 32).

34. Kingdon, *Agendas, Alternatives, and Public Policies*.

35. For a discussion of hate crime statutes, see George P. Choundas, "Neither Equal Nor Protected: The Invisible Law of Equal Protection, The Legal Invisibility of Its Gender-Based Victims," *Emory Law Journal* 44 (Summer 1995). The statutes of twenty-one states do not include gender in their protected categories.

36. The number of published articles was determined by searching the Lexis/Nexis newspaper database.

37. Scott Baldauf, "Do Homosexuals Need More Legal Protection?" *Christian Science Monitor*, October 14, 1998, p. 3. 28 U.S.C. §534 provides that the Attorney General shall acquire data each year about crimes where there is evidence of prejudice based on race, religion, disability, sexual orientation, or ethnicity. See Public Law 101-275 as amended 110 Stat. 1394 (July 1996).

38. James Brooke, "Gay Man Dies from Attack, Fanning Outrage and Debate," *New York Times*, October 12, 1998, sect. A, col. 1.

39. "Hate Crimes Legislation Is Defeated in Wyoming," *Houston Chronicle*, Thursday, Feb-

ruary 4, 1999; R. Geringer, "Awareness Rose, Despite Failure to Pass Bias Crimes Law," *Associated Press*, Sunday, February 7, 1999.

40. Anthony Downs, "Up and Down with Ecology: The Issue-Attention Cycle," *Public Interest* 28 (1972): 38–50.

41. Nelson, *Making an Issue of Child Abuse*, 129.

42. Randy Shilts, *And the Band Played On* (New York: St. Martin's, 1987), 201.

43. Throughout the country, newspaper coverage of AIDS peaked around 1987 at 626 articles in Southeastern newspapers and more than 1,000 articles published in West Coast newspapers. The number of newspaper articles was obtained by searching the Lexis/Nexis news database.

44. See Testimony of Dr. Donald Francis reported in Theodore J. Stein, *The Social Welfare of Women and Children with HIV and AIDS: Legal Protections, Policy, and Programs* (New York: Oxford University Press, 1998), p. 154, note 5. The federal government was not alone in turning away from the AIDS epidemic. Surveys of state legislative bodies and state governors indicated their desire to stay away from issues involving AIDS. Charles Backstrom and Leonard Robins, "State AIDS Policy Making: Perspective of Legislative Health Committee Chairs," *AIDS and Public Policy Journal* 10 (1995): 238–248.

45. Centers for Disease Control, *AIDS Surveillance in the Americas: Quarterly Report* (Washington, D.C.: United States Department of Health and Human Services, December 1995).

46. Stein, *Social Welfare of Women and Children*, p. 156, note 30; ch. 6.

47. Scott P. Hays and Henry R. Glick, "The Role of Agenda Setting in Policy Innovation," *American Politics Quarterly* 25, 4 (October 1997): 497–517.

48. Shilts, *And the Band Played On*, 143.

49. *Ryan White Comprehensive AIDS Resources Emergency Act of 1990*, Senate Report No. 273, 101st Cong., 2nd sess., 1990, 1990 U.S.C.C.A.N. 862, Public Law 101-381.

50. In 1992, the Supreme Court ruled that children could not bring suit against state government in which they alleged that the state had failed to provide benefits to which they were entitled under the Adoption Assistance and Child Welfare Act (*Suter v. Artist*, 112 S. Ct. 1360). In 1994, Congress overturned most of the High Court's decision, leaving intact that part of the Court's ruling that held that children could not sue for a state's failure to make reasonable efforts to prevent placement in foster care (42 U.S.C.A. §1320–2).

51. Senate, 104th Cong., 2nd sess., H. R. 3612.

52. Michael Kelly, "Outlaw Deeds, Not Thoughts," *New York Post*, October 14, 1998, Opinion, p. 29.

53. *Calendars of the United States House of Representatives and History of Legislation* (Washington, D.C.: U.S. Government Printing Office, 1997), unnumbered table, headed "Statistical Recapitulation and Comparison: 104th Congress; 103rd Congress; 102nd Congress; 100th Congress."

54. On National Dessert Day see House, *Cong. Rec.*, 103rd Cong., 1st sess., Wednesday, October 6, 1993, E2356; on National Grapefruit Month, see Eric J. Gouvin, "Truth in Savings and the Failure of Legislative Methodology," *Cincinnati Law Review* 62 (Spring 1994): 1281–1390.

55. H.R. 1946, 104th Cong., 1st sess. (1995); S. 984 104th Cong., 1st sess. (1995).

56. Summary of the testimony of Michael P. Farris on the Parental Rights and Responsibilities Act before the Subcommittee on Administrative Oversights and the Courts, Senate, December 5, 1995.

57. National Parent Teacher Association, Testimony before the Judiciary Committee of the House of Representatives, October 26, 1996, and Sammy Quintana, president of the National School Boards Association, Testimony before the Senate Judiciary Committee, December 5, 1995.

58. Testimony of Margaret F. Brinig, Professor of Law, before the Senate Judiciary Committee, December 5, 1995.

59. Some of the bills affected government agencies such as the Federal Aeronautics Administration; other legislation concerned matters such as memorial services for victims of airline crashes, conveyance of federal property to state or local control, the governance of the District of Columbia, absentee voting for citizens residing overseas, and relief of named individuals for special service, for example, providing back pay for individuals teaching overseas.

60. Cited in Paula D. McClain, *Minority Group Influence: Agenda Setting, Formulation and Public Policy* (Westport, Conn.: Greenwood Press, 1993), 3.

61. McClain, *Minority Group Influence*, 3.

62. 42 U.S.C. §1973 *et seq.* (West 1999).

63. Carl E. Meacham, "State of New York Minority Internship Program: Avenue to Gaining Access in the Public Policy Arena," in McClain, *Minority Group Influence*, ch. 9, 147–168.

64. Cheryl M. Miller, "Issue Selection by State Legislative Black Caucuses in the South," in McClain, *Minority Group Influence*, ch. 7, 112–125.

65. Benjamin Marquez, "The Industrial Areas Foundation and the Mexican-American Community in Texas: The Politics of Issue Mobilization," in McClain, *Minority Group Influence*, ch. 8, 128–146.

66. Thomas L. Friedman, "Gay Rights in the Military: Chiefs Back Clinton on Gay-Troop Plan; President Admits Revised Policy Isn't Perfect," *New York Times*, July 20, 1993, sect. A, col. 1.

67. See, for example, *San Francisco Chronicle*, July 24, 1993, p. A4; Senate, *Cong. Rec.*, Proceedings and Debates of the 103rd Cong., 1st sess. (May 28, 1993); House, *Cong. Rec.*, Proceedings and Debates of the 103rd Cong., 1st sess. (June 22, 1993); House, *Cong. Rec.*, Proceedings and Debates of the 103rd Cong., 1st sess. (June 24, 1993); House, *Cong. Rec.*, Proceedings and Debates of the 103rd Cong., 1st sess. (June 23, 1993); *Cong. Rec.*, Extension of Remarks Proceedings and Debates of the 103rd Cong., 1st sess. (June 24, 1993); House, *Cong. Rec.*, Proceedings and Debates of the 103rd Cong., 1st sess. (July 14, 1993); House, *Cong. Rec.*, Proceedings and Debates of the 103rd Cong., 1st sess. (July 14, 1993).

68. Dan Coats, Senate, *Cong. Rec.*, Proceedings and Debates of the 103rd Cong., 1st sess. (May 28, 1993).

69. House, *Cong. Rec.*, Proceedings and Debates of the 103rd Cong., 1st sess. (July 14, 1993).

70. 10 U.S.C. §654 (West 1998).

71. The phrase "don't pursue" is said to mean that no investigations or inquiries will be conducted solely to determine a service member's sexual orientation, but this phrase was admittedly ambivalent. Questioning the Joint Chiefs of Staff on this point, Senator Sam Nunn asked whether a commander would be able to commence an investigation on the basis of a single report that a service member was homosexual. Senator Les Aspin and General Colin Powell conceded that the decision was up to the discretion of any commander and that this aspect of the directive had to be "pinned down." Martin Kasindorf, "Joint Chiefs Back Policy on Gays," *New York Newsday*, July 21, 1993, p. 13.

72. Gabriel Rotello, "Democrats Give Gay Rights a Belated but Heartfelt Embrace," *New York Newsday*, July 14, 1992, p. 79.

73. 10 U.S.C.A. §654 (15).

74. Congress may thwart the president's efforts to appoint government officials when there are ideological differences between the president and the Congress. For example, despite the fact that there were sixty-six judicial vacancies in 1996, twenty-three of

which were classified as emergency vacancies because of the duration of the vacancy, the Senate was on the verge of breaking the record for the fewest number of judicial confirmations in any year in the preceding two decades. Editorial, *National Law Journal*, July 22, 1996, A14, col. 1.

75. Eric M. Freedman, "A Lot More Comes into Focus When You Remove the Lens Cap: Why Proliferating New Communications Techniques Make it Particularly Urgent for the Supreme Court to Abandon Its Inside-Out Approach to Freedom of Speech and Bring Obscenity, Fighting Words, and Group Libel Within the First Amendment," *Iowa Law Review*, 81 (1996): 883–936; Warren Weaver, *New York Times Abstracts*, June 24, 1973, sect. 4, col. 1, p. 3.

76. Kingdon, *Agendas, Alternatives, and Public Policies*, ch. 9.

77. *Hopwood v. Texas*, 78 F.3d 932 (5th Cir. 1996).

78. *Regents of the University of California v. Bakke*, 98 S. Ct. 2733 (June 28, 1978).

79. The number of published articles was determined by searching the Lexis/Nexis newspaper database for the state of California.

80. *Coalition for Economic Equity v. Wilson*, 122 F.3d 692 (9th Cir. 1997): 5–6.

81. Complainants generally file suit first with the Equal Employment Opportunity Commission (EEOC). The number of filed complaints makes the odds that the EEOC will pursue a lawsuit on behalf of an aggrieved individual slight. The complainant, after a statutorily imposed period time, may request a "right to sue" letter from the EEOC, which must be issued, allowing the individual to bring suit in federal court. 29 C.F.R. §1602.28 (West 1999). To bring suit, a party must establish that she or he (1) is a member of a class covered by the Civil Rights Act (e.g., based on race or gender, for example); (2) applied for and was qualified for the position sought; (3) was rejected despite being qualified for the position; that the position remained open after the applicant was rejected; and that the employer's search for applicants with the same qualifications as the party bringing suit continued. *McDonnell Douglas Corp. v. Green*, 93 S. Ct. 1817 (1973).

82. *The Consolidated Rescissions and Appropriations Act of 1996*, Public Law 104-134, Section 504, codified at 110 Stat. 1321.

83. W. H. Perry, *Deciding to Decide: Agenda Setting in the United States Supreme Court* (Cambridge, Mass.: Harvard University Press. 1991), 201. Unless otherwise noted, Perry's book was my information source for this section.

84. U.S. S. Ct. Rule 10, 28 U.S.C.A.

85. Gregory A. Caldeira and John R. Wright, "Organized Interests and Agenda Setting in the U.S. Supreme Court," *American Political Science Review* 82, 4 (December 1988), 1113–1123; Kevin T. McGuire and Gregory A. Caldeira, "Lawyers, Organized Interests, and the Law of Obscenity: Agenda Setting in the Supreme Court," *American Political Science Review* 87, 3 (September 1993), 717–726. But see John R. Hermann, "American Indian Interests and Supreme Court Agenda Setting," *American Politics Quarterly* 25, 2 (April 1997), 241–250 (amicus briefs are important only when filed by the solicitor general).

86. *Naim v. Naim*, 76 S. Ct. 472 (March 1956).

87. *Loving v. Virginia*, 87 S. Ct. 1817 (1967).

88. Perry, *Deciding to Decide*, 255.

89. *Barnes v. Moore*, 970 F.2d 12 (5th Cir. 1992) cert denied 113 S. Ct. 659 (1992).

90. Sanford Levinson, Review of *Strategy, Jurisprudence, and Certiorari. Deciding to Decide: Agenda Setting in the United States Supreme Court* by H. W. Perry Jr., *Virginia Law Review* 79 (1993): 717–739.

91. Perry, *Deciding to Decide*, 257.

CHAPTER SIX

1. For a discussion of state-by-state variations, see Virginia Gray, Russell L. Hanson, and Herbert Jacob, *Politics in the American States: A Comparative Analysis* (Washington, D.C.: Congressional Quarterly Press, 1999), ch. 5.

2. James E. Anderson, *Public Policymaking*, 3rd ed. (New York: Houghton Mifflin, 1997), 158.

3. Ibid., 137.

4. U.S. General Accounting Office, *Welfare to Work—State Programs Have Tested Some of the Proposed Reforms*, Report No. 95-26 (1995), 103. Services included education and training, help in preparing for the high school equivalency examination, assistance in acquiring proficiency in English, acquisition of job skills, and training for job readiness. For a discussion of how states handled child care, see Jan L. Hagen and Irene Lurie, "The Job Opportunities and Basic Skills Training Program and Child Care: Initial State Developments," *Social Service Review* 67 (1993): 198–216.

5. Robert Pear, "Budget Agency Says Welfare Bill Would Cut Rolls by Millions," *New York Times*, July 16, 1996, p. A 12.

6. Charles E. Lindblom, *The Policy Making Process* (Englewood Cliffs, N.J.: Prentice-Hall, 1968).

7. Federal law governing political action committees is found at 2 U.S.C.A. §431 *et seq.* and 11 C.F.R. §100.5 *et seq.* (West 1999).

8. 2 U.S.C.A., §441(a) (West 1999).

9. These data are found on the Federal Election Commission's Web site at www.fec.com.

10. The Federal Election Commission categorizes PACs as "separate segregated funds" (SSF), which are PACs established by membership organizations, corporations, labor or trade organizations, or cooperatives. Nonconnected PACs are not affiliated with a political party, an authorized candidate's committee, or an SSF. 2 U.S.C.A. §431 (West 1999).

11. Gray et al., *Politics in the American States*, 126.

12. The Heritage Foundation at www.heritage.org/mission/html.

13. The Center on Budget and Policy Priorities can be accessed through www.epn.org.

14. The American Association of Retired Persons is found at www.aarp.com.

15. *National Voter Turnout in Federal Elections: 1960–1996.* (Washington, D.C.: Federal Election Commission, 1999).

16. *Voter Registration and Turnout in Federal Elections by Age: 1972–1996* (Washington, D.C.: Federal Election Commission, 1999).

17. Charles Murray, *Losing Ground* (New York: Basic Books, 1984), ch. 1.

18. The Republican Congress tried also to change the Medicaid Program (see chapter 11) into a block grant but was not successful.

19. See, for example, Jason De Parle, "The Ellwoods: Mugged by Reality," *New York Times*, December 8, 1996, sect. 6, p. 64; Robert Pear, "Agreement Struck on Most Elements for Welfare Bill," *New York Times*, July 30, 1996, sect. A, p. 1; Bob Herbert, "In America; The Real Welfare Cheats," *New York Times*, April 26, 1996, sect. A, p. 31.

20. Alexi Bayer, "The Survival of the Most Efficient," *New York Times*, December 8, 1996, sect. 3, p. 14.

21. *Field v. Clark*, 12 S. Ct. 495 (1892).

22. *Buttfield v. Stranahan*, 48 L. Ed. 525 (1904).

23. *Yakus v. United States*, 64 S. Ct. 660 (1944).

24. Administrative law judges are appointed by agencies of the executive branch, for example, the Social Security Administration. (5 U.S.C.A. §3105). When individuals wish to appeal a denial of benefits, the first appeal is to an administrative law judge.

If the judge's ruling is not favorable, the individual may appeal to a federal district court.

25. H.R. Report No. 485(II), 101st Cong., 2nd sess. 1990; 1990 U.S.C.C.A.N. §303. Report 485, entitled "The Americans with Disabilities Act of 1990" was issued in four parts, numbered I through IV and reprinted at 1990 U.S.C.C.A.N. §§267 (Part I), 303 (Part II), 445 (Part III), and 512 (Part IV).

26. 29 C.F.R. §1630.2 (h)(1) & (2).

27. 5 U.S.C.A. §551 *et seq.* (West 1998).

28. 5 U.S.C.A. §552 (West 1999). Rules may be supplemented by the language in a statue; for example, environmental impact statements are required by the Natural Environmental Policy Act (42 U.S.C. 4332(2)(C). Executive orders may supplement agency rules. President Reagan and President Clinton issued executive orders requiring cost-benefits analysis when new regulations were issued. See Executive Order 12,291, 3 C.F.R. 128 (1981); Executive Order 12,866, 3 C.F.R. 638 (1993).

29. 5 U.S.C.A. §551(4) (West 1999).

30. An agency may avoid publication after a finding of good cause that notice is "impracticable, unnecessary, or contrary to the public interest" (5 U.S.C.A. 553(b)(B)(West 1998). When final rules are issued, a brief statement of the reasons for not publishing the rule is required.

31. 5 U.S.C.A. §553(c) (West 1999).

32. 5 U.S.C.A. §553(c) and §§556 and 557 (West 1999).

33. 5 U.S.C.A. §701 *et seq.* (West 1999).

34. 42 U.S.C.A. §300 *et seq.* (West 1999).

35. *Rust v. Sullivan,* 111 S. Ct. 1759 (1991).

36. In its 1974 report on the use of executive orders, a Senate committee concluded that it was not possible to distinguish situations where a directive was denominated an executive order or a proclamation, noting that President Eisenhower issued an executive order to facilitate integration of schools in the South while President Kennedy issued a proclamation to accomplish the same goal. Senate Committee on National Emergencies and Delegated Emergency Powers, *Executive Orders in Times of War and National Emergency,* 93rd Cong., 2nd sess., Report No. 93-1280 (October 1974), 4; hereafter referred to as the Executive Orders Report.

37. 44 U.S.C.A. §1505 (West 1998).

38. Executive Orders Report. In 1973, Congress passed the War Powers Resolution Act to impose restrictions on the President's powers to make war without Congressional acquiescence. See Peter E. Quint, "The Separation of Powers Under Nixon: Reflections on Constitutional Liberties and the Rule of Law," *Duke Law Journal* 1981, pp. 1–70.

39. The number of executive orders issued since the founding of the country cannot be determined because they were never systematically recorded until 1935, when the *Federal Register* was first published. Since that time, all such orders have been numbered consecutively and published in the *Register.* Senate Committee on the Judiciary, *Separation of Powers Annual Report,* 93rd Cong., 2nd sess., Report No. 93-1195 (September 1974); hereafter referred to as the Separation Report.

40. Executive Orders Report, 31.

41. Executive Orders Report, 2, Separation Report, 24.

42. *Youngstown Sheet and Tube v. Sawyer,* 72 S. Ct. 863 (1952).

43. The states are Alaska, Arizona, Arkansas, California, Colorado, Florida, Idaho, Illinois, Maine, Massachusetts, Michigan, Missouri, Montana, Nebraska, Nevada, North Dakota, Ohio, Oklahoma, Oregon, South Dakota, Utah, and Washington.

44. Constitution of the State of California, Article II, Voting, Initiative and Referendum, and Recall, §9(a).
45. Ibid., §8.
46. Constitution of the State of Colorado, Article 5, §1 General Assembly—Initiative and Referendum (West 1999).
47. *Buckley v. American Constitutional Law Foundation, Inc.*, 119 S. Ct. 636 (January 1999).
48. "Initiatives: Use and Abuse," *Los Angeles Times*, Sunday, April 19, 1998, Editorial, p. 4.
49. *Coalition for Economic Equity v. Wilson*, 946 F. Supp. 1480, 1499 (D.C.N.D. 1996), stay denied 1997 WL 70641, vacated 110 F.3d 1431, cert denied, 118 S. Ct. 397 (1997).
50. *Romer v. Evans*, 116 S. Ct. 1620 (1996). In *Equality Foundation of Greater Cincinnati v. City of Cincinnati*, 1998 WL 248349 (6th Cir. 1997), cert denied, 119 S. Ct. 365 (1998). The City Charter of the City of Cincinnati was amended to remove homosexuals, gays, lesbians, and bisexuals from any protection contained in municipal antidiscrimination ordinances. The amendment precluded restoring protected status. The 6th Circuit Court of Appeals found that the amendment did not violate the Constitution and distinguished *Cincinnati* from the *Romer* decision on two grounds: (1) the amendment did not disenfranchise any group or citizen from gaining special protection at all levels of state government, but affected only municipally enacted protections; and (2) the charter amendment eliminated only "special class status" and "preferential treatment for gays as gays," leaving untouched the application to gay citizens of any and all legal rights generally accorded by the municipal government to all persons as persons. In denying cert, Chief Justice Rehnquist took pains to note that a denial of cert was not a ruling on the merits of the case, thus quieting any suggestion that the Court had turned its back on its *Romer* decision.
51. *Buckley v. American Constitutional Law Foundation, Inc.*, 119 S. Ct. 636 (January 1999). In dissent, three justices found the financial disclosure and registered voter requirements constitutional.
52. Constitution of the United States, Article III, §2.
53. *Brown v. Board of Education*, 74 S. Ct. 686 (1954) [Brown I] *Brown v. Board of Education*, 75 S. Ct. 783 (1955) [Brown II].
54. *Swann v. Charlotte-Mecklenburg*, 402 U.S. 1, 1971.
55. *Juan F. v. Weicker*, 37 F.3d 874 (2nd Cir. 1994).
56. For consent decrees concerning child welfare agencies, see *Lynch v. King*, 550 F. Supp. 325 (D.C.Mass. 1982), *sub nom, Lynch v. Dukakis*, 719 F.2d 504 (1st Cir. 1983); *G. L. v. Zumwalt sub nom G. L. v. Stangler*, 873 F.Supp. 252 (W.D.MO. 1994); *Wilder v. Sugarman*, 385 F. Supp. 1013 (S.D.N.Y. 1974) *sub nom, Wilder v. Bernstein*, 499 F. Supp. 980 (S.D.N.Y. 1980); *L. J. v. Massinga*, 838 F.2d 118 (4th Cir. 1988), cert denied, 109 S. Ct. 816 (1989); *B. H. v. Johnson*, 715 F.Supp. 1387 (N.D.Ill 1989); *Juan F. v. O'Neil, sub nom Juan F. v. Weicker*, 37 F.3d 874 (2nd Cir. 1994); for examples concerning mental hospitals, see *Wyatt v. Stickney*, 325 F.Supp. 781 (M.D.Ala. 1971), 344 F.Supp. 387 (1972); *aff'd Wyatt v. Aderholt*, 503 F.2d 1305 (5th Cir. 1974) *New York State Association for Retarded Children v. Rockefeller*, 357 F.Supp. 752 (E.D.N.Y. 1975); *Halderman v. Pennhurst State School and Hospital*, 446 F.Supp. 1295 (E.D.Pa. 1977) *aff'd* in part, rev'd in part 612 F.2d 84 (3rd Cir. 1979), cert granted 102 S. Ct. 2956 (1982), motion for dismissal denied 463 S. Ct. 1251 (1983); for cases concerning prisons, see *Rhodes v. Chapman*, 452 U.S.337 (1981); *Harris v. Thigpen*, 727 F.Supp. 1564 (M.D.Ala. 1990) *aff'd* in part vacated in part 941 F.2d 1495 (11th Cir. 1991); *Doe v. Meachum*, 1990 WL 261348 (D.Conn. 1990); for an example concerning police, see *Rizzo v. Goode*, 423 U.S. 362 (1976).
57. *Horton v. Merrill Lynch, Pierce, Fenner & Smith, Inc.*, 855 F.Supp. (825 D.C.N.C. 1994).
58. Ellen Ash Peters, "Common Law Judging in a Statutory World," *University of Pittsburgh Law Review* 42 (Summer 1982): 995–1011.

59. Martha A. Field, "Sources of Law: The Scope of Federal Common Law," *Harvard Law Review* 99 (1986): 883–984.

60. Benjamin N. Cardozo, *The Nature of the Judicial Process* (New Haven: Yale University Press, 1921); Oliver W. Holmes, *The Common Law* (New York: Dover, 1881).

61. Judith S. Kaye, "Brennan Lecture: State Courts at the Dawn of a New Century: Common Law Courts Reading Statutes and Constitutions," *New York University Law Review* 70 (April 1995): 1–35.

62. Ibid. For a discussion of legislative avoidance and court intervention.

63. *Fosmire v. Nicoleau*, 551 N.E.2d 77 (N.Y. 1990).

64. *Fosmire v. Nicoleau*, 551 N.E.2d 77 (N.Y. 1990).

65. *Griswold v. Connecticut*, 85 S. Ct. 1678 (1965).

66. *Roe v. Wade*, 93 S. Ct. 705 (1965).

67. *Whalen v. Roe*, 97 S. Ct. 869 (1977).

68. *Pierce v. Society of Sisters*, 45 S. Ct. 571 (1925).

69. *Loving v. Virginia*, 87 S. Ct. 1817 (1967).

70. For the right to procreate, see *Skinner v. Oklahoma* 62 S. Ct. 1110 (1942); the right to obtain contraceptives, see *Griswold v. Connecticut*, 85 S. Ct. 1678 (1965); and the right to terminate a pregnancy, see *Roe v. Wade*, 93 S. Ct. 705 (1965).

71. For discussions of original intent, see Erwin Chemerinsky, "The Supreme Court, 1988 Term: Foreword: The Vanishing Constitution," *Harvard Law Review* 103 (1989): 43–104.

72. Ronald Dworkin, *A Matter of Principle* (Cambridge: Harvard University Press, 1985), ch. 1.

73. R. Randall Kelso and Charles D. Kelso, "How the Supreme Court Is Dealing with Precedents in Constitutional Cases," *Brooklyn Law Review* 62 (Fall 1996): 973–1038.

74. *Bowers v. Hardwick*, 106 S. Ct. 2841 (1986).

75. Kaye, Brennan Lecture.

76. *Planned Parenthood of Southeastern Pennsylvania v. Casey*, 112 S. Ct. 2791, 2808 (1992).

77. Oliver Wendell Holmes, "The Path of the Law," a speech delivered at a dedication ceremony at the Boston University School of Law, reprinted in the *Harvard Law Review* 110 (1997): 991–1009.

78. *Bowers v. Hardwick*, 106 S. Ct. 2841 (1986).

79. *Bowers v. Hardwick*, 106 S. Ct. 2841 (1986).

80. Kelso and Kelso, "Precedents in Constitutional Cases."

81. *Plessy v. Ferguson*, 163 U.S. 537.

82. *Brown v. Board of Education*, 74 S. Ct. 686 (1954) [Brown I] *Brown v. Board of Education*, 75 S. Ct. 783 (1955) [Brown II].

83. Brown I, 691.

84. *Planned Parenthood v. Casey*, 2813–2814. Another significant shift in Supreme Court jurisprudence occurred in 1905 when, in *Lochner v. New York*, 25 S. Ct. 539 (1905), the Court overturned a New York law that sought to regulate labor by limiting the number of hours that bakers could work because the regulations infringed on an individual's right to contract. In 1937 in *West Coast Hotel Co. v. Parrish*, 57 S. Ct. 578, the Court overturned *Lochner* due largely to the conditions that had been created by the Depression of 1929 and the "unparalleled demands for relief" (at 585) that the depression gave rise to.

85. *Maher v. Roe*, 97 S. Ct. 2376(1977); *Harris v. McRae*, 100 S. Ct. 2671 (1980).

86. *Webster v. Reproductive Health Services*, 109 S. Ct. 3040 (1986).

87. *Planned Parenthood of Central Missouri v. Danforth*, 96 S. Ct. 2831 (1976).

88. *Hodgson v. Minnesota*, 110 S. Ct. 2926 (1990).

89. *City of Akron v. Akron Center for Reproductive Health*, 103 S. Ct. 2481 (1983).

90. *Thornburgh v. American College of Obstetricians and Gynecologists,* 106 S. Ct. 2169 (1986).
91. *Planned Parenthood v. Casey,* 855–856.
92. *Cabell v. Markham,* 148 F.2d 737, 739 (2nd Cir. 1945).
93. The New York Court of Appeals is the state's highest court and the Supreme Court is the trial court.
94. Kaye, "Brennan Lecture," 26.
95. 42 U.S.C.A. §12201(a) (West 1999).
96. *Public Citizen v. United States,* 109 S. Ct. 2558, 2567 (1989).
97. *Blanchard v. Bergeron,* 109 S. Ct. 939, 947 (1989).
98. Kaye, "Brennan Lecture."
99. *Braschi v. Stahl,* 544 N.Y.S.2d 784 (1987).
100. *Braschi v. Stahl,* 788.

CHAPTER SEVEN

1. U.S. General Accounting Office, *A Glossary of Terms Used in the Federal Budget Process: Exposure Draft,* Revised January 1993, GAO/AFMD-2.1.1:87 (1995). Hereafter referred to as *Glossary.*
2. The U.S. General Accounting Office and the Office of Management and the Budget issue documents that provide detailed information regarding the federal budget process. See, for example, *Glossary* and the next publication in note 3.
3. Office of Management and Budget, *Budget of the United States Government: Fiscal Year 2000* (Washington, D.C., March 1999).
4. Ibid., ch. 2.
5. 42 U.S.C.A. §402 (West 1998). See chapter 10 on the Social Security Disability Insurance program compared to the Supplemental Security Income program.
6. Don Nickles, "Policy Essay: Retiring in America: Why the United States Needs a New Kind of Social Security for the New Millennium," *Harvard Journal on Legislation* 36 (Winter 1999): 77–114.
7. Public Law No. 92-603. Codified at 86 Stat. 1329.
8. House, Committee on Ways and Means, 104th Cong., 2nd sess., "Section 7, Aid to Families with Dependent Children and Temporary Assistance for Needy Families," *Green Book* (Washington, D.C., 1996), 405, 503–504.
9. Unfunded Mandates Reform Act of 1995, Public Law 104-4 codified at 109 Stat. 48. States may impose unfunded mandates on local units of government but the 1995 legislation affects only federal action.
10. Exempted are federal mandates "that enforce constitutional rights; prohibit discrimination on account of race, color, religion, sex, national origin, age, handicap or disability; or impose accounting and auditing requirements for federal funds." Also exempt are "mandates that are imposed as part of a disaster relief program requested by the state; that are 'necessary for the national security' or to implement treaties; that the President and Congress designate as emergency legislation; or that relate to the old age, survivors, and disability insurance program under Title II of the Social Security Act." Editorial Board, "Federalism: Intergovernmental Relations—Congress Requires a Separate, Recorded Vote for any Provision Establishing an Unfunded Mandate," *Harvard Law Review* 109 (April 1996): 1469–1474.
11. Information concerning the EEOC is taken from *U.S. Equal Employment Opportunity Commission: An Overview* (1999); *U.S. Equal Employment Opportunity Commission National Enforcement Plan* (1999); and *U.S. Equal Employment Opportunity Commission Filings Under all Statutes* (1999). Available at www.eeoc.gov/overview.html.
12. Patricia Wilson-Coker, Theodore J. Stein, and Robert C. Zampano, *First Implementation*

and Monitoring Report of the DCYS Monitoring Panel (New Haven, Conn.: December 9, 1991). On record at the federal district court in Hartford, Conn. Copy on file with the author.

13. *Wyatt v. Stickney,* 344 F.Supp. 373 (M.D. Ala. 1972).

14. Phillip J. Cooper, *Hard Judicial Choices: Federal District Court Judges and State and Local Officials* (New York: Oxford University Press, 1988).

15. *Glossary.*

16. Public Law No. 67-13, 42 Stat. 20 (codified as amended in various sections of 31 U.S.C.).

17. At any one time, federal agencies deal with three fiscal years. The current year whose budget they are executing, the new fiscal year that will begin on October 1 for which they are preparing their budget request, and the next fiscal year for which they must gather information.

18. Constitution of the United States, Article I, §8.

19. 42 U.S.C.A. §620 (West 1998).

20. 20 U.S.C.A. §1406 (West 1998).

21. 2 U.S.C.A. §641 (West 1998).

22. 2 U.S.C.A. §632 (West 1998).

23. 2 U.S.C.A. §632 (West 1999).

24. The seventeen categories that address national need are (1) national defense; (2) international affairs; (3) general science, space, and technology; (4) energy; (5) natural resources and environment; (6) agriculture; (7) commerce and housing credit; (8) transportation; (9) education, training, employment, and social services; (10) health; (11) Medicare; (12) income security; (13) social security; (14) veterans benefits and services; (15) administration of justice; (16) general government; and (17) community and regional development. U.S. General Accounting Office, *Budget Function Classifications: Origins, Trends, and Implications for Current Uses,* GAO/AFMD-98-67 (1998): 4.

25. Ibid.

26. James E. Anderson, *Public Policymaking: An Introduction* (Boston: Houghton Mifflin, 1997): 188.

27. *Glossary,* 100–101.

28. The data reported here were taken from House, *Green Book,* 104th Cong., 2nd sess., 1996, 104–114.

29. The AFDC program was eliminated in 1996 and replaced by the Temporary Assistance to Needy Families Program (see chapter 10).

30. The data reported here were taken from House, *Green Book,* 104th Cong., 2nd sess., 104–114.

31. For a history of efforts to amend the Constitution to achieve a balanced budget, see Senate, *The Balanced-Budget Constitutional Amendment,* Senate Report No. 3, 105th Cong., 1st sess. (1977).

32. 118 S. Ct. 2091.

33. Public Law No. 99-177, 99 Stat. 1037 (codified as amended in various sections of 2, 31, and 42 of the U.S.C.).

34. Donald B. Tobin, "Less Is More: A Move Toward Sanity in the Budget Process," *Saint Louis University Public Law Review* 26 (1996): 115–147.

35. 2 U.S.C.A. §900 *et seq.* The BEA was enacted as part of the Omnibus Budget Reconciliation Act of 1990. Public Law 101-508, 104 Stat. at 1388–573 (codified as amended throughout 2 U.S.C., 15 U.S.C. 1022, 31 U.S.C. 11055, 1341, 1342 (Supp. IV 1992). The BEA was extended in 1993 through the Omnibus Budget Reconciliation Act of that year (Public Law No. 103-66, §§14001–14004, 107 Stat. 312, 683–85 (codified as

amended in 2 U.S.C. §§665, 900–902, 904) and again in 1997 (extending the BEA through FY2002).

36. *Glossary*, 73–76.

37. Anita S. Krishnakumar, "Reconciliation and the Fiscal Constitution: The Anatomy of the 1995–96 Budget 'Train Wreck,'" *Harvard Journal on Legislation* 35 (1998): 589–622.

38. The government uses the Current Population Survey to obtain employment data (see chapter 8.) Each month Census Bureau employees interview individuals in the CPS household sample, which consists of approximately 50,000 households. Each person over the age of sixteen who lives in the household and is not on active duty in the armed forces is classified according to labor force activity during the "reference week," which is the week that includes the twelfth of the month. Labor force activity is defined to include jobholding activity, job-seeking activity, or non-labor force activity. The result is a threefold classification where (1) people with part- or full-time jobs, whether permanent or temporary, are employed, and employed individuals include individuals who do chores on a family farm or who help out in a family business for at least fifteen hours a week whether or not they are paid; (2) those without jobs, looking for work and who are available to work are unemployed; and (3) those who are neither employed nor unemployed are not in the labor force. U.S. Department of Labor, Bureau of Labor Statistics, *How the Government Measures Unemployment*, Report 864 (Washington, D.C., 1994).

CHAPTER EIGHT

1. U.S. Census Bureau, *Current Population Survey Reports, Measuring 50 Years of Economic Change Using the March Current Population Survey* (Washington, D.C., 1998). Hereafter referred to as *Measuring Economic Change*.

2. U.S. General Accounting Office, *Poverty Measurement: Issues in Revising and Updating the Official Definition*, GAO/AFMD-97-38 (1997), 4. Hereafter referred to as *Issues in Revising*.

3. Before implementation of the Orshansky model, poverty data were culled from social work literature, especially the writings of settlement house workers (see chapter 2); literature that was produced by labor unions; and miscellaneous state and federal reports.

4. Panel on Poverty and Family Assistance, Committee on National Statistics of the National Research Council, *Measuring Poverty: A New Approach* (Washington, D.C.: National Academy Press, 1996); *Issues in Revising*.

5. *Issues in Revising*.

6. Data from the Current Population Survey can be found in *Measuring Economic Change;* see also Joseph Dalaker and Mary Naifeh, *Poverty in the United States: 1997* (Washington D.C.: U.S. Department of Commerce, 1998).

7. See *Issues in Revising*. See also D. Vaughan, *Reflections on the Income Estimates from the Initial Panel of the Survey of Income and Program Participation*, Working Paper No. 83 (Washington, D.C.: U.S. Department of Commerce, n.d.).

8. The Survey of Income and Program Participation (SIPP) is an alternative approach to measuring poverty that was first used in 1983. The SIPP was developed by the CB to remedy deficiencies in the CPS. For example, SIPP interviewers ask about support that is received from federal, state, and local aid programs. Although the SIPP is operative, the data are not used as an alternative approach to determining the number of people in poverty. The SIPP compiles data describing (1) labor force activity; (2) assets and wealth; (3) pension coverage; (4) health insurance coverage; (5) disability and health status; (5) work history; (6) marital and family history; (7) educational costs and financing; (8) shelter costs and work expenses; (9) child care arrangements and

costs; and (10) interhousehold transfers of income and support services. The SIPP covers the United States civilian noninstitutionalized population and members of the armed forces living off post or with their families on post. The reporting unit is the household and respondents are household members aged fifteen years and up. See Vaughn, *Reflections,* and *Issues in Revising.*

9. *Issues in Revising.*

10. For discussions concerning the continued use of the Orshansky model, see *Issues in Revising;* U.S. General Accounting Office, *Poverty Measurement: Adjusting for Geographic Cost-of-Living Difference,* GAO/GGD-95-64 (1995); Panel on Poverty and Family Assistance, *Measuring Poverty.*

11. Panel on Poverty and Family Assistance, *Measuring Poverty.*

12. *Issues in Revising,* 9.

13. *Issues in Revising.*

14. Poverty data for Native American people, Eskimos, and Aleuts are not separately reported. U.S. Census Bureau, *Resident Population of the United States Estimates by Sex, Race and Hispanic Origin, with Median Age* (Washington, D.C., 1998).

15. U.S. Department of Housing and Urban Development, *Now Is the Time: Places Left Behind in the New Economy* (Washington, D.C., 1999), Table 11.

16. *Measuring Economic Change,* app. A, A-2.

17. Dalaker and Naifeh, *Poverty in the United States,* Table C-7.

18. U.S. Department of Labor, Bureau of Labor Statistics, *A Profile of the Working Poor* (Washington, D.C., 1996).

19. U.S. Department of Labor, Bureau of Labor Statistics, *Worker Displacement, 1995–1997* (Washington, D.C., 1998).

20. Edward C. Banfield, *The Unheavenly City* (Boston, Little, Brown, 1974); Oscar Lewis, "The Culture of Poverty," *Scientific American* 215 (October 1966): 19–25. See also Lewis's 1961 book, *The Children of Sanchez* (New York: Random House).

21. Mary Jo Bane and David T. Ellwood, *Welfare Realities: From Rhetoric to Reform* (Cambridge, Mass: Harvard University Press, 1994), 78–81; William Julius Wilson, *When Work Disappears: The World of the New Urban Poor* (New York: Alfred A. Knopf, 1997), 72.

22. Wilson, *When Work Disappears,* ch. 1 and 3.

23. See, for example, 142 *Cong. Rec.* Senate 9387-01; 144 *Cong. Rec.* Senate 7815-01. "Welfare reform is to end the culture of poverty. And yet the very rules that we now have reinforce the culture of poverty." "We all acknowledge that our current welfare system . . . has failed to move people from welfare to work, and has created a culture of poverty that has ensnared generations of our most vulnerable citizens in poverty and dependency." "By creating an underclass culture of poverty, dependency, and violence, we have been destroying the very people we have been claiming to help."

24. These data come from two reports of the U.S. General Accounting Office: *Textile Trade: Operations of the Committee for the Implementation of Textile Agreements,* Report No. 96-186 (1996), and *Caribbean Basin: Worker Rights Progress Made, but Enforcement Issues Remain,* Report No. 98-205 (1998).

25. These data come from two reports of the U.S. Department of Labor, Bureau of Labor Statistics: *The Employment Situation* (Washington, D.C., 1999). *Emerging Trends in the Information Technology Job Market: How Should the Public and Private Sectors Respond?* (Washington, D.C., 1999).

26. Robert I. Lerman, Testimony before the Subcommittee on Oversight and Investigations, Committee on Education and the Workforce, U.S. House of Representatives, 1998.

27. The new system will be used by the United States, Canada, and Mexico. See Eco-

nomic Classification Policy Committee, *New Data for a New Economy* (Washington, D.C.: U.S. Department of Labor, 1999).

28. Ibid.

29. Daily Labor Report (BNA) No. 131, at A4-A5 (July 9, 1997).

CHAPTER NINE

1. *Steward v. Davis,* 57 S. Ct. 883 (1937). The largest appropriation in American history, almost $5 billion, was dedicated to the Works Progress Administration (WPA). The WPA put millions of the unemployed to work on projects ranging from public works construction projects (libraries, municipal buildings) to ventures involving the fine arts. A portion of the funds went to the Resettlement Administration, which pursued a variety of rural relief programs, including the financing of a limited number of new communities for the rural poor. See Robert L. Rabin, "Federal Regulation in Historical Perspective," *Stanford Law Review* 38 (May 1986); 1243–1326.

2. On Senator Long's Plan, see Rabin, "Federal Regulation"; on the Townsend Plan, see Gilbert Steiner, *Social Insecurity: The Politics of Welfare* (New York: Rand McNally, 1966).

3. The Court's unwillingness to uphold New Deal legislation so frustrated President Roosevelt that in 1937 he proposed what came to be called his "court packing plan." Roosevelt argued that he be allowed to nominate a new justice for every sitting justice that was at least seventy years of age who refused to retire. At the time, the Court had six justices over the age of seventy. Thus, Roosevelt would have been allowed to appoint six new justices and increase the size of the Court to fifteen. The six new appointees would have given the president the majority that he needed to support his New Deal programs. The plan became unnecessary when two of the justices reversed their position, giving the president a 5 to 4 majority that upheld New Deal legislation.

4. Rabin, "Federal Regulation."

5. *Schechter Poultry v. U.S.,* 55 S. Ct. 837 (1935).

6. *United States v. Butler,* 56 S. Ct. 312 (1937).

7. Constitution of the United States, Amendment X.

8. Constitution of the United States, Article 1, section 8, clause 1.

9. 57 S. Ct. 883, May 24, 1937.

10. *Steward,* 890.

11. *Helvering v. Davis,* 57 S. Ct. 904 (1937): 909.

12. *Steward,* 891.

13. Michele L. Landis, "Let Me Next Time be 'Tried by Fire': Disaster Relief and the Origins of the American Welfare State 1789–1874," *Northwestern University Law Review* 73 (1998): 967–1034.

14. Martha Derthick, *Policymaking for Social Security* (Washington, D.C.: Brookings Institute, 1979), 199.

15. Ibid.

16. *Fleming v. Nestor,* 80 S. Ct. 1367 (1960).

17. The act is Public Law 74-271, 49 Stat. 620.

18. Derthick, *Policymaking for Social Security,* ch. 1.

19. House, Committee on Ways and Means, 105th Cong., 2nd sess., "Section 1: Social Security: The Old-Age, Survivors, and Disability Insurance (OASDI) Programs," *Green Book: Background Material and Data on Programs Within the Jurisdiction of the Committee on Ways and Means* (Washington, D.C., 1998).

20. Derthick, *Policymaking for Social Security,* 185.

21. *Green Book,* Section 1, 60. Federal employees are covered by the Federal Civil Service Retirement System, 5 U.S.C. §8331 *et seq.*

22. 42 U.S.C. §301 *et seq.* (West 1999).
23. 42 U.S.C. §401 *et seq.* (West 1999).
24. 23 U.S.C. §3301 *et seq.* (West 1999).
25. 42 U.S.C. §602 *et seq.* (West 1999).
26. 42 U.S.C. §701 *et seq.* (West 1999).
27. 42 U.S.C. §1202. (West 1999).
28. 42 U.S.C. §1382 *et seq.* (West 1999).
29. Of the $32 billion, $27.8 billion (87 percent) was for retirement benefits and $4.2 billion (13 percent) was for disability benefits.
30. Testimony of David Walker, Comptroller General of the United States, before the House Subcommittee on Social Security, Committee on Ways and Means, *Social Security: Criteria for Evaluating Social Security Reform Proposals* (U.S. General Accounting Office, GAO/T-HEHS-99-94, 1999), 3.
31. Dependent benefits are available to the eligible worker's spouse who is (1) sixty-two years of age or older or, if younger, the caretaker of the worker's entitled child; (2) a sixty-two-year-old never-remarried divorced spouse whose marriage to the eligible worker lasted for at least 10 years; (3) a sixty-year-old widow(er), or the fifty-year-old disabled widow(er); (4) a dependent, unmarried child, stepchild, or grandchild; or (5) a sixty-two-year-old parent who was dependent on the deceased worker at the time of death, who is not married and was receiving at least one-half of his or her support from the eligible worker. Dependent children are those (1) younger than eighteen years of age; (2) younger than 19 years of age attending elementary or secondary school full time; or (3) with a disability who are age eighteen or older if the disability began before age twenty-two. *Green Book*, Section 1, 28.
32. *Green Book*, Section 1, Table 1–10, "Monthly Benefit Amounts for Selected Beneficiary Families with First Eligibility in 1996, for Selected Wage Levels, December 1996."
33. *Green Book*, Section 1, 19.
34. *Senior Citizens Freedom to Work Act*, Public Law 106-182, 114 Stat. 198.
35. Omnibus Budget Reconciliation Act of 1993, Public Law 103-66.
36. *Green Book*, Section 1, 40.
37. The definition of disability for Title XVI is found at 42 U.S.C. §1382c(a)(3)(B) and for Title II at 42 U.S.C. §423(d)(1)(A)(B).
38. 20 C.F.R. §§404 & 416
39. 20 C.F.R. 404.1590 (West 1999).
40. 20 C.F.R. §404.1574 (West 1999). Medical benefits during the trial work period are found at 42 U.S.C.A. §426(b) as amended by Public Law 106-170, *Ticket to Work and Work Incentives Improvement Act of 1999*, 113 Stat. 1860 (1999).
41. See the *Green Book*, Section 1, 14, and 20 C.F.R. §404.1576 (West 1999).
42. *Green Book*, Section 1, 7
43. *Green Book*, Section 1, app. 1, Table 1.4, "Congressional Budget Office, Mandatory Outlay Projects for Selected Programs Within the Jurisdiction of the Committee on Ways and Means, Fiscal Years 1996–2002."
44. *Green Book*, Section 1, 66
45. See *Report of the 1994–1996 Advisory Council on Social Security*, vol. 1, app. 2 (Washington, D.C.: Advisory Council on Social Security, 1997). Other proposals, too numerous to go into in this text, have been made. See U.S. General Accounting Office, *Social Security: Different Approaches for Addressing Solvency Problems*, Report GAO/HEHS 98-33 (Washington, D.C., 1998), hereafter referred to as *Social Security*, testimony of David M. Walker, note 30.
46. At present, benefits are calculated by adding together the retiree's earnings for the "best" thirty-five years of taxable earnings and dividing the sum by 420, the number

of months in thirty-five years. One suggestion calls for increasing the number of years from thirty-five to forty. This should increase the number of years in which earnings were low, thus yielding a smaller benefit. This proposal would have negative effects for those who delay their entry into the workforce. For example, adults who delay entry into the workforce until their children are grown are not likely to have the currently required thirty-five years. Increasing the number of years with no earnings would reduce the received benefit.

47. Don Nickles, "Policy Essay: Retiring in America: Why the United States Needs a New Kind of Social Security for the New Millennium," *Harvard Journal on Legislation* 36 (Winter 1999): 97–98.

48. *Social Security*, 4.

49. Several states provided compensation to unemployed workers before passage of the act, but many were reluctant to exact an UI tax on their industries lest they place themselves at a competitive disadvantage with industries in states with no UI tax. *Steward v. Davis*, 891.

50. U.S. General Accounting Office, *Unemployment Insurance—Millions in Benefits Overpaid to Military Reservists*, GAO/HHS 96-101 (Washington, D.C., August 1996).

51. 26 U.S.C. §3301 *et seq*. A covered employer is one who (1) paid wages of at least $1,500 in any quarter in a year; (2) employed at least one worker for at least one day in each of twenty weeks in the current or prior year; (3) employed agricultural labor to whom cash wages of at least $20,000 were paid in any calendar quarter; (4) employed ten or more workers on at least one day in each of twenty different weeks in the current or prior year; and (5) employed domestic workers to whom cash wages of $1,000 or more are paid in any calendar quarter in the current or prior year. Nonprofit organizations and state and local governments need not pay federal unemployment taxes; instead, they may choose to reimburse the UI program for benefits paid to their laid-off employees. In general, none of the states provide unemployment coverage to (1) the self-employed, (2) agricultural and domestic workers except as noted above, (3) student interns, (4) alien farm workers, (5) seasonal camp workers, and (6) railroad workers who have their own unemployment program.

52. House, Committee on Ways and Means, 105th Cong., 2nd sess, "Section 4: Unemployment Compensation," *Green Book: Background Material and Data on Programs Within the Jurisdiction of the Committee on Ways and Means* (Washington, D.C., 1998), 331.

53. *Green Book*, Section 4, 334.

54. Of the 17.3 million claims that were filed in 1996, 23.8 percent were disqualified because the claimant (1) was not available for work (4.4 percent),(2) voluntarily left the job without good cause (6.3 percent), (3) was fired for work-related misconduct (4.1 percent), or (4) refused suitable work (0.3 percent) or was refused benefits for other unspecified disqualifying acts (8.7 percent). Disqualification rates ranged from a low of 7.5 percent in Tennessee to a high of 114.8 percent in Nebraska, with Colorado the next highest at 68.7 percent. Since a claimant may be disqualified more than once in any claim period, the number of denied claims may exceed the number of claimants.

55. 20 C.F.R. Part 615 (West 1999).

56. 20 C.F.R. Part 602. Appendix A (West 1999).

57. U.S. Department of Labor, *Consolidated Financial Statement Audit—Supplemental Report on Income Maintenance* (Washington, D.C., 1999).

58. *Green Book*, Section 4, 342.

59. Ibid.

60. See, for example, the Federal-State Extended Unemployment Compensation Act of 1970, Public Law No. 91-373, §524, 84 Stat. 695; Omnibus Budget Reconciliation Act

of 1981, Public Law No. 97-35, S 2401, 95 Stat. 357, 874–76 (amending Federal-State Extended Unemployment Compensation Act of 1970).

61. Stephen Bingham, "Replace Welfare for Contingent Workers with Unemployment Compensation," *Fordham Urban Law Journal* 22 (1995): 937–959.

62. Council of State Governments, *The Book of the States: Volume 32* (Lexington, Ky.: Council of State Governments, 1998), 413–414.

63. U.S. General Accounting Office, *Social Security Disability Programs Lag in Promoting Return to Work*, Report GAO/HEHS 97-46 (Washington, D.C., 1997).

64. See, for example, *Pitter v. Gussini Shoes*, 614 N.Y.S.2d 568 (A.D.2 Dept. 1994); *Kristiansen v. Morgan*, 708 A.D.2d 1173 (N.J.S. Ct. 1998).

65. Council of State Governments, *Book of the States*, Table 8.19.

66. Office of Worker's Compensation Programs, *Annual Report to Congress, FY 1996.* (Washington, D.C.: U.S. Department of Labor, 1997).

67. House, Committee on Ways and Means, 105th Cong., 2nd sess., "Section 13: Tax Provisions Related to Retirement, Health, Poverty, Employment, Disability and Other Social Issues," *Green Book: Background Material and Data on Programs Within the Jurisdiction of the Committee on Ways and Means* (Washington, D.C., 1998) 867.

68. The Personal Responsibility and Work Opportunity Act of 1996 is Public Law 104-193, 110 Stat. 2105, 2105–2355 (codified in scattered sections of the United States Code).

69. *Green Book*, Section 13, 869.

70. U.S. General Accounting Office, *Earned Income Credit—Targeting to the Working Poor* (Washington, D.C., 1995). A compliance study conducted by the IRS in 1994 produced a noncompliance rate of 29 percent during a two-week period of time in January 1994.

71. Nicholas Johnson and Ed Lazere, *Rising Number of States Offer Earned Income Tax Credits* (Washington, D.C.: Center on Budget and Policy Priorities, 1998).

72. *Green Book*, Section 13, 870.

CHAPTER TEN

1. See Winifred Bell, *Aid to Dependent Children* (New York: Columbia University Press, 1965), 6–7; and 141 *Cong. Rec.* Senate 10860-02 (July 28, 1995).

2. Martha Derthick, *Policymaking for Social Security* (Washington, D.C.: Brookings Institute, 1979), 25.

3. Frances Fox Piven and Richard A. Cloward, *Regulating the Poor: The Functions of Public Welfare* (New York: Pantheon Books, 1971), 175–176.

4. Bell, *Aid to Dependent Children*, 46.

5. Social Security Act of 1935, Title IV, §406(a).

6. Bell, *Aid to Dependent Children*, 35–36.

7. 42 U.S.C.A. §601. Amendments of August 1, 1956, 70 Stat. 848.

8. Public Law 87-543, Title I, §104(a)(4), (c)(2), 76 Stat. 185. July 25, 1962.

9. Piven and Cloward, *Regulating the Poor*, 183.

10. Public Law 90-248, §§204, 208(b). 81 Stat. 821, 884–90, 894 (amended 1971).

11. Public Law 100-485, 102 Stat. 2343 (1988). Codified in scattered sections of 42 U.S.C.A. §601.

12. Job development programs are under the authority of the Department of Health and Human Services (DHHS) or the Department of Labor (DOL). WIN and JOBS were DHHS programs. At the local level, WIN and JOBS programs are usually administered by a welfare agency and DOL programs are run by a state employment service. In 1998, Congress authorized the Workforce Investment Act (WIA) and vested program authority in the DOL. WIA, like the Job Partnership Training Program (JPTA) it replaced, serves economically disadvantaged adults, some of whom are welfare re-

cipients. Public Law 105-220, 112 Stat. 1059 (1998). An objective of WIA is to bring public employment programs together in a "one-stop" career center, but the law does not mandate that work services provided under TANF be included in one-stop centers. "Welfare-to-work" (WTW) grants, discussed in a later section, serve TANF clients and are administratively managed by DHHS and DOL. Successful implementation of WTW will require coordination between local labor and welfare systems. See John Trutko, Nancy Pindus, Burt S. Barnow, and Demetra Smith Nightingale, *Early Implementation of the Welfare-to-Work Program* (Washington, D.C.: Urban Institute, 1999), 3.

13. U.S. General Accounting Office, *Welfare to Work: Participants' Characteristics and Services Provided in JOBS,* GAO/HEHS-95-93 (Washington, DC., 1995); U.S. General Accounting Office, *Welfare Reform: Three States' Approaches Show Promise of Increasing Work Participation,* GAO/HEHS-97-80 (Washington, DC., 1997).

14. Senate Report No. 599, 89th Cong., 1st sess. 1965, 1965 U.S.C.C.A.N. 3501 concerning Public Law 89-253, the Economic Opportunity Amendment of 1965 (August 13, 1965).

15. War on Poverty programs included (1) Volunteers in Service to America (VISTA, a domestic peace corps); (2) Upward Bound (a program that encouraged poor children to go to college); (3) the Neighborhood Youth Corp (a program to help unemployed teens find work); (4) Head Start (preschool); (5) Community Action Programs (designed to mobilize community resources); (6) grant and loan programs for rural families and migrant workers; (7) legal services for poor people; (8) the Model Cities Program; (8) the Job Corps (a manpower program providing job training to disadvantaged youth aged sixteen to twenty-one); and (9) the Economic Development Act of 1965 that provided states with grants and loans for public works and technical assistance.

16. Piven and Cloward, *Regulating the Poor,* 250.

17. Ibid., 322.

18. For an excellent discussion of problems that plagued War on Poverty programs, see Eugene Bardach, *The Implementation Game: What Happens After a Bill Becomes Law* (Cambridge, Mass: MIT Press, 1977).

19. House, Committee on Ways and Means, 105th Cong., 2nd sess., "Section 7: Aid to Families with Dependent Children and Temporary Assistance for Needy Families (Title IV-A)," *Green Book: Background Material and Data on Programs Within the Jurisdiction of the Committee on Ways and Means* (Washington, D.C., 1998), 413.

20. Rebecca A. Maynard, ed., *Kids Having Kids: Economic Costs and Social Consequences of Teen Pregnancy* (Washington, D.C.: Urban Institute, 1997).

21. Ibid.

22. There are few sources of reliable data for researchers to determine time on welfare. The General Accounting Office concluded that the DHHS would not be able to monitor the sixty-month time limit for receipt of TANF benefits because state data, to the extent that they are available, are often incomplete or inconsistent. U.S. General Accounting Office, *Major Management Challenges and Program Risks: Department of Health and Human Services* (Washington, D.C., 1999). There are two databases that researchers use: (1) the Panel Study of Income Dynamics (PSID) that contains data compiled by the Institute for Social Research at the University of Michigan, and (2) data from the National longitudinal Survey of Youth (NLSY) compiled by the Bureau of Labor Statistics. These data sets are different, and the same questions asked of each will yield different answers. The PSID data cannot be used to observe monthly movement on and off of the welfare rolls. Thus, a "spell" on welfare, defined as the number of consecutive months on welfare, will be longer using PSID data than a spell that is measured using the NLSY database. For example, if in the space of twelve consecutive months the Brown family is on welfare in January and February, leaves the rolls in March or April, returns for May through August, leaves once again in September to

return in November for the remainder of the year, this family will have three spells, using NLSY data, and an average of 6.6 months on welfare. Using PSID data, this family would have a single spell of twelve months' duration. Spells on and off of welfare have implications for policy if they reflect cyclical workforce participation, for example, jobs obtained during tourist season and lost when the season ends. However, caution must be exercised in assuming that spells off of the rolls are the result of work. They may be due to administrative matters, such as a determination of noneligibility.

23. LaDonna Pavetti and Gregory Acs, *Moving Up, Moving Out or Going Nowhere? A Study of the Employment Patterns of Young Women* (Washington, D.C.: Urban Institute, 1997).

24. *Green Book*, Section 7, 531–532.

25. *Green Book*, Section 7, 398.

26. On March 24, 1995, the House of Representatives passed the Personal Responsibility Act, which in modified form passed the Senate as the Personal Responsibility and Work Opportunity Act of 1995. House, *Personal Responsibility and Work Opportunities Act of 1995*, H.R. Conf. Report 430, 104th Cong., 1st sess. (March 24, 1995). The legislation was vetoed by President Clinton on January 9, 1996. On May 22, the Personal Responsibility and Work Opportunity Act (PRWOA) of 1996 was introduced in the House and the Senate. This legislation passed both Houses in midsummer and was signed by President Clinton in August 1996. See Public Law 104-193, *Personal Responsibility and Work Opportunity Reconciliation Act of 1996*, H.R. 3734, Part A: Block Grants for States for Temporary Assistance for Needy Families, Sec. 402(B)(3), 104th Cong., 2d sess. 142, Slip Opinion (August 8, 1996).

27. The Emergency Assistance for Needy Families program, funded in equal amounts by the federal government and states, provided cash aid to families with children if funds were needed to prevent a child from becoming homeless and to prevent other forms of destitution of a child. Aid was limited to a period not to exceed thirty days in any twelve-month period.

28. *Green Book*, Section 7, 425.

29. Olivia A. Golden, *Statement Concerning Native American and Alaskan Tribal Affairs Presented to the Senate Indian Affairs Committee*, available at www.hhs.gov under the link Welfare Reform Implementation.

30. 42 U.S.C.A. §608(4)(A)(B); (5)(A)(i) (West 1999).

31. 42 U.S.C.A. §602(a)(1)(A) (West 1999).

32. House, Committee on Ways and Means, 105th Cong., 2nd sess, "Appendix L. Summary of Welfare Reforms Made by Public Law 104-193, The Personal Responsibility and Work Opportunity Reconciliation Act and Associated Legislation," *Green Book: Background Material and Data on Programs Within the Jurisdiction of the Committee on Ways and Means* (Washington, D.C., 1998), 1333.

33. U.S. General Accounting Office, *Welfare Reform: Early Fiscal Effects of the TANF Block Grant*, GAO/AIMD-98-137 (Washington, D.C., 1998), 10–11. States that draw funds from their treasury accounts must match withdrawn funds with funds from their maintenance of efforts accounts. This prevents states from building an excess of state reserves by drawing funds from the treasury alone.

34. Raymond Hernandez, "New York Gets Big Windfall from Welfare," *New York Times*, February 9, 1996.

35. 42 U.S.C.A. §§603(a)(3), 606, 606(b) (West 1999).

36. Jason DeParle, "As Welfare Benefits Expire, Second Thoughts," *New York Times*, October 10, 1999.

37. 45 CFR §260.31 (West 1999).

38. 42 U.S.C.A. §608(a)(7)(C)(i) (West 1999).

39. Judith M. Gueron, *Welfare Time Limits: An Interim Report Card* (Manpower Demonstra-

tion Research Corporation, 1999). All MDRC reports cited in this chapter were obtained at www.mdrc.org.

40. States choose to either supervise program operations, in which case local units of government pay a part of program costs and have the freedom to tailor programs to local needs within a framework set at the state level, or to administer programs in which case the state foots the entire bill and sets the rules.

41. 42 U.S.C.A. §§607 and 607(a)(2) (West 1999).

42. Robert Pear, "Most States Meet Work Requirement of Welfare Law," *New York Times*, December 30, 1998, sect. C, p. 6.

43. 42 U.S.C.A. §607 (West 1999).

44. *Green Book*, Section 7, 497.

45. S.C.A. §607(e)(1)(B)(2) (West 1999).

46. S.C.A. §608(b)(1) (West 1999).

47. *Green Book*, Section 7, Table 7.23.

48. *Green Book*, Section 7, Table 7.7.

49. 42 U.S.C.A. §602 (West 1999).

50. C.G.S.A. §17b-112. Temporary Family Assistance Program (West 1999).

51. Ibid. See also McKinney's Consolidated Laws of New York, Social Services Law, Assistance and Care §131a (West 1999).

52. U.S. General Accounting Office, *Welfare Reform: Many States Continue Some Federal or State Benefits for Immigrants*, GAO/HEHS-98-132 (Washington, D.C., 1998), 5.

53. U.S. General Accounting Office, *States Are Restructuring Programs to Reduce Welfare Dependency*, GAO/HEHS-98-109 (Washington, D.C., 1998), 65. Hereafter referred to as *Restructuring Programs*.

54. Ibid.

55. OR-ST-ANN §411.877 (West 1998).

56. Wisconsin Administrative Code, §1203 Definitions (West 1999).

57. Peter W. Slasich, "Low Income Housing Crisis Has Not Disappeared," *Journal of Affordable Housing and Community Development Law* 7 (Fall 1997), 8–10.

58. Amy Brown, *Work First: How to Implement an Employment-Focused Approach to Welfare Reform* (Manpower Demonstration Research Corporation, 1997), 4.

59. Ibid., 9–10.

60. *Restructuring Programs*, 85.

61. U.S. General Accounting Office, *States' Experience in Providing Employment Assistance to TANF Clients*, GAO/HEHS-99-22 (Washington, D.C., 1998), 13.

62. U.S. General Accounting Office, *Welfare Reform: Early Fiscal Effects*, 8.

63. *Restructuring Programs*, 39.

64. *Restructuring Programs*, 39.

65. As of October 1997, thirty-nine states had increased their countable asset limits, forty-eight states had increased their vehicle allowances, and forty-two states had changed their earnings disregard policies, as compared with what was allowed under AFDC.

66. Public Law 105-33, §5001, 111 Stat. 576 (August 5, 1997) codified in scattered sections of 42 U.S.C.A. §601 (West 1999).

67. 20 C.F.R. §645.212 (West 1999).

68. 42 U.S.C.A. §9908 (West 1999).

69. Trutko et al., *Early Implementation*, 7.

70. 42 U.S.C.A. §9858 (West 1999).

71. 42 U.S.C.A. §9858c. A child care certificate may be a check or some other disbursement provided directly to a parent by a state or local unit of government. The certificate is to be used only to pay for child care services that may be purchased from sectarian as well as nonsectarian child care services.

72. House, Committee on Ways and Means, 105th Cong., 2nd sess, "Section 9: "Child Care," *Green Book: Background Material and Data on Programs Within the Jurisdiction of the Committee on Ways and Means* (Washington, D.C., 1998), 686.

73. U.S. General Accounting Office, *Welfare Reform: States' Efforts to Expand Child Care Programs,* GAO/HEHS-98-27 (Washington, D.C., 1998).

74. U.S. General Accounting Office, *Education and Care: Early Childhood Programs and Services for Low-Income Families,* GAO/HEHS-00-11 (Washington, D.C., 1999).

75. "Citing Drop in Welfare Rolls, Clinton to Seek Further Cuts," *New York Times,* January 25, 1999, p. A14; "Clinton Says Welfare Rolls Have Fallen to 30-Year Low," *Wall Street Journal,* April 12, 1999, p. C16; "More Good News on Welfare Reform," *New York Post,* May 15, 1999, p. 16; Laura Meckler, "GOP Leaders Celebrate Welfare Success," *Associated Press,* May 27, 1999.

76. U.S. General Accounting Office, *Welfare Reform: State's Implementation Progress and Information on Former Recipients,*. GAO/HEHS-99-116 (Washington, D.C., 1999). Hereafter referred to as *Former Recipients.*

77. Robert I. Lerman, Pamela Loprest, and Caroline Ratcliffe, *How Well Can Urban Labor Markets Absorb Welfare Recipients?* Paper No. A-33 in the series New Federalism: Issues and Options for the States (Washington, D.C.: Urban Institute, 1999).

78. Public Welfare Amendments of 1962, Public Law 87-543, codified as amended at 42 U.S.C.S. §1315 (Law. Co-Op. 1996).

79. *Restructuring Programs,* app. II.

80. 42 U.S.C.A. §615 (West 1999).

81. Alberto Martini and Michael Wiseman, *Explaining the Recent Decline in Welfare Caseloads: Is the Council of Economic Advisors Right?* (Washington, D.C.: Urban Institute, 1997).

82. U.S. General Accounting Office, *Welfare Reform: Three States' Approaches Show Promise of Increasing Workforce Participation,* GAO/HEHS-97-80 (Washington, D.C., 1997).

83. *Restructuring Programs,* 98.

84. *Former Recipients;* Saran Brauner and Pamela Loprest, *Where Are They Now? What States' Studies of People Who Left Welfare Tell Us* (Washington, D.C.: Urban Institute, 1999). The GAO and Brauner and Loprest reviewed studies from Indiana, Wisconsin, Maryland, Iowa, Michigan, South Carolina, Tennessee, and Washington. In addition, the GAO reviewed reports from Idaho, Kentucky, Louisiana, Montana, New Jersey, New Mexico, Oklahoma, Pennsylvania, and Wyoming. Brauner and Loprest reviewed reports from Ohio and Texas.

85. These data can be found in Jo Anna Hunter-Manns and Dan Bloom, *Connecticut Post-Time Limit Tracking Study: Six-Month Survey Results* (Manpower Demonstration Research Corporation, 1999). On the subject of what happens to recipients after they leave the welfare rolls, see also Sharon Parrott, *Welfare Recipients Who Find Jobs: What Do We Know About Their Employment and Earnings?* (Washington, D.C.: Center on Budget and Policy Priorities, 1998); *Former Recipients,* 3.

86. Pamela Loprest, *Families Who Left Welfare: Who Are They and How Are They Doing?* (Washington, D.C.: Urban Institute, 1999). Loprest used data from the National Survey of American Families, a database compiled by the Urban Institute and consisting of a nationally representative survey of the noninstitutionalized, civilian population under the age of sixty-five and their families.

87. Judith M. Gueron, *Welfare Time Limits: An Interim Report Card* (Manpower Demonstration Research Corporation, 1999).

88. Gayle Hamilton, Thomas Brock, Mary Farrell, and others, *Evaluating Two Welfare-to-Work Program Approaches: Two-Year Findings on the Labor Force Attachment and Human Capital Development Programs in Three Sites* (New York: Manpower Demonstration Research Cor-

poration, 1997); Amy Brown, *Work First: How to Implement an Employment-Focused Approach to Welfare Reform* (New York: Manpower Demonstration Research Corporation, 1997).

89. Gordon L. Berlin, *Encouraging Work Reducing Poverty: The Impact of Work Incentive Programs* (New York: Manpower Demonstration Research Corporation, 2000), 36. Berlin reports that there is no evidence to suggest that the enhanced benefit increased the number of people applying for welfare.

90. Virginia Knox, Cynthia Miller, and Lisa A. Gennetian, *Reforming Welfare and Rewarding Work: A Summary of the Final Report on the Minnesota Family Investment Program* (New York: Manpower Demonstration Research Corporation, 2000), Table 3.

91. Ibid., 12.

92. Susan Scrivener, Gayle Hamilton, Mary Farrell, and others, *National Evaluation of Welfare-to-Work Strategies: Implementation, Participation Patterns, Costs, and Two-Year Impacts of the Portland (Oregon) Welfare-to-Work Program* (New York: Manpower Demonstration Research Corporation, 1998).

93. Sheila R. Zedlewski, *Work Activity and Obstacles to Work Among TANF Recipients* (Washington, D.C.: Urban Institute, 1999), 2.

94. *Restructuring Programs*, 111.

95. Dan Bloom, *The Cross-State Study of Time-Limited Welfare: An Interim Report Card* (Manpower Demonstration Research Corporation, 1999).

96. U.S. General Accounting Office, *Welfare Reform: Implementing DOT's Access to Jobs Program in Its First Year* (Washington, D.C., 1999), 1.

97. Public Law 105-178, 112 Stat. 107 (1998).

98. U.S. General Accounting Office, *Welfare to Work—State Programs Have Tested Some of the Proposed Reforms*, Report No. 95-26 (Washington, D.C., 1995).

99. U.S. General Accounting Office, *Welfare Reform: Implications of Increased Work Participation for Child Care*, GAO/HEHS-97-75 (Washington, D.C., 1998).

100. 42 U.S.C.A. §1381 *et seq.*, (West 1995).

101. The Old Age, Survivors, and Disability Insurance Program, TANF, Medicare, and Medicaid are available in the Territories. For a discussion of social welfare programs in the Territories, see House, Committee on Ways and Means, 105th Cong., 2nd sess, "Section 12, Social Welfare Programs and the Territories," *Green Book: Background Material and Data on Programs Within the Jurisdiction of the Committee on Ways and Means* (Washington, D.C., 1998). Discussing why residents of Puerto Rico are not eligible for SSI, the Supreme Court noted that residents of Puerto Rico do not pay income tax. Thus, they do not contribute to the public treasury whose funds provide the basic SSI grant. The Court acknowledges also the government's argument that the cost of including residents of Puerto Rico in the SSI program would be an estimated $300 million per year. *Califano v. Torres et al.*, 55 L.Ed.2d 65 (1978).

102. House, Committee on Ways and Means, 105th Cong., 2nd sess., "Section 3: Supplement Security Income (SSI)," *Green Book: Background Material and Data on Programs Within the Jurisdiction of the Committee on Ways and Means* (Washington, D.C., 1998), 403.

103. The definition of disability for Title XVI is found at 42 U.S.C.A. §1382c(a)(3)(B) (West 1999).

104. 42 U.S.C.A. §1382b(1) through (4) (West 1998).

105. *Green Book*, Section 3, 268.

106. 20 C.F.R. §§404 & 416 (West 1999).

107. See 20 C.F.R. 416.924(b). A listing of child impairments is found at 20 C.F.R. pt. 404, subpt. P, App. 1 (pt. B) (1993); adult impairments are found in pt. A. (West 1998).

108. *Contract with American Advancement Act of 1996*, Public Law 104-121, codified at 110 Stat. 847 (March 29,1996).

109. 20 C.F.R. §416.920(e)-(f); 20 C.F.R. §1520(e)-(f) (West 1998).

110. *Noncitizen Benefit Clarification and Other Technical Amendments Act of 1998*, Public Law 105-306, 105th Cong., 2nd sess. (September 1998).

111. In 1990, the Supreme Court, in *Sullivan v. Zebly* (110 S. Ct. 885) held that a child's rights were violated when her claim was denied based on a determination at step 3 without considering additional factors. The Court established the IFA that Congress overturned in 1996.

112. U.S. General Accounting Office, *Supplemental Security Income: Progress Made in Implementing Welfare Reform Changes: More Action Needed* Report No. 99-103 (Washington, D.C., 1999).

113. Regulations covering disability reviews, work incentives, participation in vocational rehabilitation programs, and earnings disregards are found at 20 C.F.R. §§416.213; 416.974; 416.990; 416.1112; 416.1118; 416.1220 and 416.2201 (West 1998).

114. *Employment Opportunities for Disabled Americans Act*, Public Law 99-643, 100 Stat. 3574.

115. *Ticket to Work and Work Incentives Improvement Act of 1999*, Public Law 106-170, 113 Stat. 1860 (1999).

116. Cori E. Uccello and L. Jerome Gallagher, *General Assistance Programs: The State-Based Part of the Safety Net* (Washington, D.C.: Urban Institute, 1997).

117. Ibid.

118. McKinney's Social Services Law, §§131, 159(2) Safety Net Assistance. California Welfare and Institutions Code, §§17200, 170006(f)(i) (West 1998).

119. C.G.S.A. 17b-118(a) (West 1999).

120. Smith-Hurd Illinois Compiled Statutes, §5/6–1.4. (West 1999).

121. The Refugee Assistance Act is found at 8 U.S.C.A. 1522 (West 1998) The definition of refugee is found 8 U.S.C.A. §1101 (West 1998).

122. 20 C.F.R. §416.268 (West 1999).

CHAPTER ELEVEN

1. Information concerning the National Center for Health Statistics is available at the Centers for Disease Control's web page at www.cdc.gov.

2. Jodie Levin-Epstein, ed., *A CLASP Report on Welfare Reform Developments* (Washington, D.C.: Center on Law and the Study of Social Policy, 1999).

3. *Agricultural Adjustment Act* (August 24, 1935) codified at 7 U.S.C.A. §612c (West 1999).

4. Karen Terhune, "Reformation of the Food Stamp Act: Abating Domestic Hunger Means Resisting 'Legislative Junk Food,'" *Catholic University Law Review* 41 (1992): 421–468.

5. Michael Lipsky and Marc A. Thibodeau, "Domestic Food Policy in the United States" *Journal of Health Politics, Policy and Law* 15 (1990): 321.

6. Special Committee on Aging of the U.S. Senate, 105th Cong., 1st sess, *Developments in Aging: 1996, Vol. I*. Senate Report 105-36(I) (1997). The first "stamp" program was a 1939 demonstration project.

7. 7 U.S.C.A. §2028 (West 1999); 7 C.F.R. §285.2 (West 1999).

8. 7 U.S.C.A. §2011 *et seq.* (West 1999).

9. U.S. General Accounting Office, *Food Stamp Program: Various Factors Have Led to Declining Participation*, GAO/RCED-99-185 (Washington, D.C., 1999), 1.

10. U.S. General Accounting Office, *Declining Participation*, 9.

11. 7 U.S.C.A. §2014 (West 1999).

12. Food and Nutrition Services, *Food Stamps: Income, Resources and Deductibles* (Washington, D.C.: U.S. Department of Agriculture, 1999).

13. U.S. General Accounting Office, *Declining Participation*, 3.

14. 7 U.S.C.A. §2015 (West 1999).

15. Included are people granted political asylum, immigrants from Cuba and Haiti, and

Amerasians and persons whose deportation has been withheld. People in these groups are eligible to receive food stamps for seven years.

16. 8 U.S.C.A. §1612 (West 1999).

17. *Balanced Budget Act of 1997,* Public Law 105-33, 111 Stat 291, 292; *Agricultural Research, Extension, and Education Reform Act of 1998,* Public Law 105-185, 112 Stat 523.

18. Kelly Carmody and Stacy Dean, *New Federal Food Stamp Restoration for Legal Immigrants: Implications and Implementation Issues* (Washington, D.C.: Center on Budget and Policy Priorities, 1998).

19. The states are California, Connecticut, Illinois, Maine, Maryland, Massachusetts, Nebraska, New Jersey, New York, Ohio, Rhode Island, Washington, and Wisconsin. Food and Nutrition Services, *State-Funded Food Programs for Legal Immigrants* (Washington, D.C.: U.S. Department of Agriculture, 1999).

20. U.S. General Accounting Office, *Food Stamp Program: How States Are Using Federal Waivers of the Work Requirement,* GAO/RCED-00-5 (Washington, D.C., 1999).

21. 7 C.F.R. §273.7(e) (West 1999).

22. U.S. General Accounting Office, *Food Stamp Program: Households Collect Benefits for Persons Disqualified for Intentional Program Violations,* GAO/RCED-99-180 (Washington, D.C., 1999); U.S. General Accounting Office, *Food Stamp Overpayments: Households in Different States Collect Benefits for the Same Individuals,* GAO/RCED-98-228 (Washington, D.C, 1999), 2; U.S. General Accounting Office, *Food Stamp Overpayments: Thousands of Deceased Individuals Are Being Counted as Household Members,* GAO/RCED-98-53 (Washington, D.C., 1998), 3.

23. U.S. General Accounting Office, *"Persons Disqualified for Intentional Program Violations."*

24. U.S. Department of Agriculture, *USDA Catches 331 Food Stamp Retailers in Fraud Sweep,* Release No. 0224.96 (Washington, D.C., September 1999).

25. Robert Pear, "Non-Profit Groups Accused of Bilking Lunch Programs," *New York Times,* October 3, 1999, p. C6.

26. 7 U.S.C.A. §7501–7516 (West 1999).

27. 7 C.F.R. §251.1 (West 1999).

28. See the Federal Food Programs, Emergency Food Assistance Program at www.frac.org.

29. 42 U.S.C.A. §1758 (West 1999).

30. 42 U.S.C.A. §1751 (West 1999).

31. CACFP also subsidizes meals served to chronically impaired adults in adult day care centers, but few participate. Total program costs are less than 2 percent of all CACFP funds. House, Committee on Ways and Means, "Section 9: Child Care," *Green Book* (Washington, D.C., 1998), 687.

32. Centers for Disease Control and Prevention, *Pregnancy Nutrition Surveillance Report* (Washington, D.C.: Department of Health and Human Services, 1996).

33. U.S. General Accounting Office, *Food Assistance: Working Women's Access to WIC Benefits,* GAO/RCED-98-19 (Washington, D.C., 1998), 2.

34. 42 U.S.C.A. §1786 (West 1999).

35. Children's Defense Fund, *Children Deserve a Fair Share of the Federal Budget Surplus* (Washington, D.C., 1999).

36. Food and Nutrition Services, *WIC Farmers' Market Nutrition Program* (Washington, D.C.: U.S. Department of Agriculture, 1999).

37. Senate, Committee on Labor and Human Resources, *Older Americans Act Amendments of 1996,* Senate Report No. 104-344 (Washington, D.C., 1996), 29.

38. 42 U.S.C.A. §3001 *et seq.* (West 1999).

39. 42 U.S.C.A. §3030a (West 1999).

40. There is authority under Title VI for nutrition programs directed toward elderly Na-

tive Americans and Native Hawaiians, who are also eligible under Title III. Eligibility is limited to tribal organizations with at least fifty members older than sixty years of age. In fiscal year 1996, more than 200 Native American Tribal organizations and one Native Hawaiian organization received Title IV funds. Senate, Special Committee on Aging of the 105th Cong., 1st sess., *Developments in Aging: 1996*, Vol. 1, Senate Report No. 105-36(I) (Washington, D.C., 1997).

41. 45 C.F.R. §1321.63 (West 1999).
42. Administration on Aging, *Elderly Nutrition Program* (Washington, D.C.: Department of Health and Human Services, 1999), 2.
43. Ibid.
44. Senate, *Older Americans Act Amendments of 1996*, 572.
45. 45 C.F.R. §1321.67 (West 1999).
46. Ibid.
47. Some programs for the homeless are administered by the Farmers Home Administration, the Department of Veteran's Affairs, Health and Human Services, Labor and Education.
48. 42 U.S.C.A. §1437 (West 1999).
49. 42 U.S.C.A. §12702 (West 1999).
50. Allison D. Christians, "Breaking the Subsidy Cycle: A Proposal for Affordable Housing," *Columbia Journal of Law and Social Problems* 32 (1999): 131–157.
51. Ibid., 131–157.
52. The percentages vary state by state. For example, in Montana, 13 percentage of families live in public housing and 27 percent receive rent subsidies, but in Arizona 6.5 percent live in public housing and 8.6 percent receive rent subsidies. House, Committee on Ways and Means, "Section 7: Aid to Families with Dependent Children and Temporary Assistance for Needy Families (Title IV-A)," *Green Book* (Washington, D.C., 1998), Table 7–26.
53. Press release issued by the HUD in 1998 entitled "President Clinton Signs Best HUD Budget in a Decade, Including Historic Measures to Transform Public Housing, Create New Housing Vouchers and Raise FHA Loan Limits." Available at www.hud.gov.
54. House, Committee on Ways and Means, "Section 15: Other Programs," *Green Book* (Washington, D.C., 1998), 992.
55. 42 U.S.C.A. §1434 (West 1999).
56. Sandra J. Newman and Joseph Harkness, "The Effects of Welfare Reform on Housing: A National Analysis" in Sandra J. Newman, ed., *The Home Front: Implications of Welfare Reform for Housing Policy*, ch. 2 (Washington, D.C.: Urban Institute, 1999).
57. Thomas G. Kingsely, *Federal Housing Assistance and Welfare Reform: Uncharted Territory* (Washington, D.C.: Urban Institute, 1999).
58. 42 U.S.C.A. §12705 (West 1999).
59. The preference for serving people with low incomes is found at 42 U.S.C.A. §12806 (West 1999); for helping people with disabilities, at 42 U.S.C.A. §8013 (West 1999); for rehabilitating structures, at 42 U.S.C.A. §12742 (West 1999); and for the Low Income Housing Tax Credit, at 26 U.S.C.A. §42 (West 1999).
60. *Housing and Community Development Act of 1992*, Public Law 102-550, 106 Stat. 3672, amending the National Affordable Housing Act of 1990.
61. Bruce C. Ramsey, James N. Broder, Anne J. Chiaviello, and others, "The Cranston-Gonzalez National Affordable Housing Act: An Overview," *Real Property, Probate and Trust Journal* 28 (1993): 177–256.
62. U.S. General Accounting Office, *Homelessness: Coordination and Evaluation of Programs Are Essential* (Washington, D.C., 1999), 86–88.
63. Christopher Walker, Sheila O. O'Leary, Patrick Boxall, and others, *Expanding the Na-*

tion's Supply of Affordable Housing: An Evaluation of the Home Investment Partnerships Program (Washington, D.C.: U.S. Department of Housing and Urban Development, 1998).

64. 42 U.S.C.A. §12891 (West 1999).

65. Abt Associates, Inc., *Evaluation of the HOPE 3 Program: Final Report* (Rockville, MD: U.S. Department of Housing and Urban Development, 1996).

66. Provisions of the National Affordable Housing Act provided for the sale of units in public housing projects under the HOPE I program and sale of publicly owned-multifamily properties under the HOPE II program. Due to tenant's financial problems and a lack of interest in low-valued property, no more than 25 percent of the units in public housing projects were sold. Robert Halpern, *Rebuilding the Inner City: A History of Neighborhood Initiatives to Address Poverty in the United States* (New York: Columbia University Press, 1995).

67. *The Quality Housing and Work Responsibility Act of 1998,* Public Law 105-276, 105th Cong., 2nd sess. (1998) §32. The Resident Home Ownership Program.

68. 42 U.S.C.A. §8011 (West 1999).

69. 42 U.S.C.A. §8013 (West 1999).

70. Statement of Henry Cisneros, Secretary of the U.S. Department of Housing and Urban Development, March 27, 1996, 1996 WL 139523.

71. Public Law 105-276, 112 Stat. 2461, §533, 105th Cong. 2nd sess. (October 1998).

72. 42 U.S.C.A. §14371 (West 1999) and 26 U.S.C.A. §42 (West 1999), the Low Income Housing Tax Credit (LIHTC).

73. U.S. General Accounting Office, *Public Housing: HUD Has Several Opportunities to Promote Private Management,* GAO/RCED-99-210 (Washington, D.C., 1999), 5.

74. 24 C.F.R. §982.203 (West 1999).

75. 24 C.F.R. §§96.204 through 96.207 (West 1999).

76. Memo from President Clinton to HUD Secretary on "One Strike and You're Out Guidelines," March 28, 1996, 1996 WL 139528. 42 U.S.C.A. §1437d (West 1999); 24 C.F.R. §966.4 (West 1999).

77. *Syracuse Housing Authority v. Boule,* 658 N.Y.S.2d 776 (City Ct. 1996); *City of South San Francisco v. Gillory,* 49 Cal.Rptr.2d 367 (CA: Super. 1995); *Housing Authority of New Orleans v. Green,* 657 So.2d 552 (La. App. 4 Cir. 1995) cert denied, 116 S. Ct. 1571 (1996).

78. 24 C.F.R. §982.1 Subpart A (West 1999).

79. Charles L. Edson and Richard M. Price, "Mark-to-Market: HUD Reengineers its Multi-Family Portfolio," *Probate and Property* 12 (1998): 17–20.

80. 24 C.F.R. §5.410 (West 1999) and 42 U.S.C.A. §1437d(o) (West 1999).

81. 24 C.F.R. §§960.204, 960.205. 960.209 (West 1999).

82. U.S. General Accounting Office, *Section 8 Project-Based Rental Assistance: HUD's Processes for Evaluating and Using Unexpended Balances Are Ineffective,* GAO/RCED-98-202 (Washington, D.C., 1998), 12.

83. Conference Report of the U.S. House of Representatives, Report No. 105-769, 105th Cong., 2nd sess. (1998).

84. Department of Housing and Urban Development, *Section 8 Rental Voucher Program and the Section 8 Rental Certificate Program* (Washington, D.C., 1999).

85. A single program is operated by the Federal Emergency Management Administration, eight by the Department of Health and Human Services, eleven by the Department of Housing and Urban Development, and three by the Veteran's Administration. U.S. General Accounting Office, *Homelessness: Coordination and Evaluation of Programs Is Essential,* GAO/RCED-99-49 (Washington, D.C., 1999), 8.

86. Public Law 100-77, 101 Stat. 482, codified as 42 U.S.C.A. §11381 *et seq.* (West 1999).

87. 42 U.S.C.A. §11301 (West 1999).

88. 42 U.S.C.A. §11431 (West 1999).

89. 42 U.S.C.A. §11381 (West 1999).

90. 42 U.S.C.A. §11403 (West 1999).

91. 42 USCS §12901 *et seq* (1999).

92. Office of HIV/AIDS Housing, U.S. Department of Housing and Urban Development, *HOPWA Formula Programs: 1994 Summary* (August 1995).

93. 25 U.S.C.A. §4101 *et seq.* (West 1999). With HUD approval, assistance may be provided to families who are not low income when the housing needs of such families cannot be met in other ways. Non-Indian families who are living on an Indian reservation may also receive assistance if the presence of the non-Indian family is "essential to the well-being of Indian families" and the non-Indian family's need for housing assistance cannot be met in other ways.

94. Ibid.

95. Information concerning CDCs and NCIDs comes from Christopher Walker and Mark Weinheimer, *Community Development in the 1990s* (Washington, D.C.: Urban Institute, 1998), 16.

96. 42 U.S.C.A. §5301 *et seq.* (West 1999).

97. Walker and Weinheimer, *Community Development in the 1990s.*

98. 42 U.S.C.A. §10418(a) (West 1999).

99. U.S. General Accounting Office, *Homelessness: State and Local Efforts to Integrate and Evaluate Homeless Assistance Programs*, Report No. GAO/RCED-99-178 (Washington, D.C., 1999).

100. Marybeth Shinn and Beth Weitzman, "Predictors of Homelessness Among Families in New York City: From Shelter Request to Housing," *American Journal of Public Health.* 88, 11 (1998): 1651–1658.

CHAPTER TWELVE

1. John K. Iglehart, "The American Health Care System—Expenditures," *New England Journal of Medicine* 340 (1999): 70–76.

2. U.S. Census Bureau, *Current Population Survey—Health Insurance Coverage: 1997* (Washington, D.C., 1997).

3. Len M. Nichols, Linda J. Blumberg, Gregory P. Acs, and others, *Small Employers: Their Diversity and Health Insurance* (Washington, D.C.: Urban Institute, 1997).

4. 42 U.S.C.A. §§1395 *et seq.* (West 1999).

5. Unless otherwise noted, my source for information concerning the Medicare Program is House, Committee on Ways and Means, "Section 2: Medicare," *Green Book* (Washington, D.C., 1998). For the Medicaid Program, my source is House, Committee on Ways and Means, "Section 15: Other Programs," *Green Book* (Washington, D.C., 1998).

6. 42 U.S.C.A. §§1395c & d (West 1999).

7. 42 U.S.C.A. §1395x (West 1999).

8. 42 U.S.C.A. §§1395d & e (West 1999).

9. *Social Security Amendments of 1983*, Public Law 98-21, 97 Stat. 65. Codified at 42 U.S.C.A. §1395ww (West 1999).

10. House, Committee on Ways and Means, "Appendix D: Medicare Reimbursement to Hospitals," *Green Book* (Washington, D.C., 1998).

11. 42 U.S.C.A. §1395y(a)(1)(A) (West 1999).

12. 42 U.S.C.A. §1395w-21 (West 1999).

13. Marilyn Moon, Barbara Gage, and Alison Evans, *An Examination of Key Medicare Provisions in the Balanced Budget Act of 1997* (Washington, D.C.: Urban Institute, 1997).

14. See the Tax Equity and Fiscal Responsibility Act (TEFRA) §114(a) (1982) 42 U.S.C.A. §1395mm. (West 1999).

15. U.S. General Accounting Office, *Medicare + Choice: Impact of 1997 Balanced Budget Act Payment Reforms on Beneficiaries and Plans*, GAO/T-HEHS-99-137 (Washington, D.C., 1999).

16. Diana Joseph Bearden and Bryan J. Maedgen, "Emerging Theories of Liability in the Managed Health Care Industry," *Baylor Law Review* 47 (1995): 285–340; Joe Baker, *Medicare HMOs and the Medicare + Choice Program*, Document No. FO-OOO1Z (New York: Practicing Law Institute, 1998).

17. *The Balanced Budget Amendment of 1997*, Public Law 105-33, §1855(d)(1).

18. Health Care Financing Administration, *Medicare: Medical Savings Accounts*, Publication No. HCFA 02-02137 (Washington, D.C.: Department of Health and Human Services, 1998).

19. When services are denied, the MCP must provide a written notice stating the reason for denial and the participant's right to appeal, including the right to an expedited appeal if a speedy decision is necessary to protect the beneficiary's health or life. If the beneficiary appeals, the plan must review its initial decision. If the result is not favorable to the plan participant, the appeal is to be sent automatically to the Center for Health Dispute Resolution, a private organization under contract to the Health Care Financing Administration. This group may support or overturn the plan's decision. Further appeal to an Administrative Law Judge (see chapter 6) is possible as is appeal to a federal district court. 62 FR 25844, 42 C.F.R. Parts 405, 417, 473 on general rules concerning appeals and 62 FR 23368, 42 C.F.R. Part 417 on expedited appeals.

20. Quality assurance programs are to (1) emphasize health outcomes and other quality-of-care indicators; (2) monitor and evaluate the effectiveness of services to patients at high risk; (3) evaluate the continuity and coordination of care that enrollees receive; (4) include measures of consumer satisfaction; (5) provide for evaluation by physicians and other health care providers of the processes that are followed in providing services; and (6) allow for the detection of underutilization and overutilization of services. Information that is compiled through quality assurance reviews must be available to beneficiaries so that they may compare health plan options. *Balanced Budget Act of 1997*, Public Law 105-33, 111 Stat 291, 292.

21. 42 U.S.C.A. §1395ss (West 1999).

22. *Omnibus Budget Reconciliation Act of 1990*, Public Law 101-508, 104 Stat 1388.

23. U.S. General Accounting Office, *Physician Shortage Areas: Medicare Incentive Payment Not an Effective Approach to Improve Access*, HEHS-99-36 (Washington, D.C., 1999). A number of programs seek to increase physician availability to the underserved, including (1) the Health Center Program, (2) National Health Service Corps., and (3) the Rural Health Clinic Program. U.S. General Accounting Office, *Physician Shortage Areas*.

24. 42 U.S.C.A. §1396 *et seq.* (West 1999).

25. *Green Book*, Section 2.

26. In 1997, Medicaid rolls declined nationwide by approximately 3 percent. The decline was attributed to the fact that TANF recipients were not automatically eligible for Medicaid as were AFDC recipients and to the failure of welfare workers to inform those diverted from TANF and those deemed not eligible for cash assistance that they might be eligible for Medicaid. Marilyn Ellwood, *The Medicaid Eligibility Maze: Coverage Expands, but Enrollment Problems Persist: Findings from a Five-State Study* (Washington, D.C.: Urban Institute, 1999).

27. A. Schneider, K. Fennell, and P. Long, *Medicaid Eligibility for Families and Children* (Washington, D.C.: Kaiser Family Foundation, 1998), part 4.

28. 142 *Cong. Rec.* H8829 (July 30, 1996).

29. Julie Darnell, Hye Sun Lee, Jonah Murdock, and others, *Medicaid and Welfare Reform:*

States' Use of the $500 Million Federal Fund (Menlo Park, Calif.: Kaiser Commission on Medicaid and the Uninsured, 1999).

30. *Green Book*, Section 2.

31. John Holahan, Suresh Rangarajan, and Matthew Schirmer, *Medicaid Managed Care Payment Methods and Capitation Rates: Results of a National Survey,* Occupational Paper No. 26 (Washington, D.C.: Urban Institute, 1999).

32. House, Subcommittee on Human Resources and Intergovernmental Relations, *AIDS Treatment and Care: Who Cares?* 101st Cong., 2nd sess., Report No. 674 (1994), note 150; Robert M. Williams, "The Costs of Visits to Emergency Departments," *New England Journal of Medicine* 334 (1996): 642–646.

33. 42 U.S.C.A. §1396(a)(1)(2)(3)(4B) and (5) (West 1999).

34. John Holahan, Teresa Coughlin, Korbin Liu, and others, *Cutting Medicaid Spending in Response to Budget Caps* (Washington, D.C.: Urban Institute, 1995), 8.

35. 42 U.S.C.A. §1396d(2)(B); 1396d(7)-(11) (West 1999).

36. 42 U.S.C.A. §1396n(b) (West 1999); 42 C.F.R §441.300; 42 C.F.R. §440.180(b)(1)-(8).

37. House, Committee on Ways and Means, "Appendix B: Health Status and Expenditures of the Elderly and Background Data on Long-Term Care," *Green Book* (Washington, D.C., 1998), 1059.

38. Ibid. The remaining 15 percent of long-term care costs are covered by private insurance and through miscellaneous federal and state programs.

39. 42 C.F.R. §435.1005 (West 1999).

40. 42 U.S.C.A. §1396r-5 (West 1999).

41. 42 U.S.C.A. §1382b (West 1999); 20 C.F.R. §416.1210 (West 1999).

42. Andy Schneider, Kristen Fennell, and Patricia Keenan, *Medicaid and the Uninsured* (Washington, D.C.: Kaiser Commission, 1999).

43. *Omnibus Budget Reconciliation Act of 1989,* Public Law 101-239 codified at 103 Stat. 2106 (1989); *Omnibus Budget Reconciliation Act of 1990,* Public Law 101-508, 104 Stat 1388 (November 5, 1990).

44. 42 U.S.C.A. §1396(a)(viii) (West 1999).

45. 42 C.F.R. §441.56 (West 1999).

46. 42 U.S.C.A. §701 (West 1999).

47. 42 U.S.C.A. §1397aa *et seq.* (West 1999). For data on the number of uninsured children, see "Health Insurance Coverage: 1997—Table 2," a document provided by the U.S. Census Bureau and available at www.census.gov.

48. Brian K. Bruen and Frank Ullman, *Children's Health Insurance Programs: Where States Are, Where They Are Headed* (Washington, D.C.: Urban Institute, 1998), 6–8.

49. Ibid.

50. U.S. General Accounting Office, *Children's Health Insurance Program: State Implementation Approaches Are Evolving* (Washington, D.C., 1999), 36–37.

51. See Alan Weil, *The New Children's Health Insurance Program: Should States Expand Medicaid?* (Washington, D.C.: Urban Institute, 1997); Frank Ullman, Brian Bruen, and John Holahan, *The State Children's Health Insurance Program: A Look at the Numbers* (Washington, D.C.: Urban Institute, 1998); U.S. General Accounting Office, *Children's Health Insurance.*

52. Vernon K. Smith, *Enrollment Increases in State CHIP Programs: December 1998 to June 1999* (Lansing, Mich.: Health Management Associates, 1999).

53. 42 U.S.C.A. §300gg-4 (West 1999).

54. 42 U.S.C.A. §300a *et seq.* (West 1999).

55. *Rust v. Sullivan,* 111 S. Ct. 1759 (1991).

56. 42 U.S.C.A. §1395dd (West 1999).

57. 42 U.S.C.A. §300ff-14(b)(A)(B) (West 1999).

58. 42 U.S.C.A. §300ff-51(b) & 52(a) (West 1999).

59. 42 U.S.C.A. §300ff-71 (West 1999).

60. 42 U.S.C.A. §300ff-91 (West 1999).

61. 42 U.S.C.A. §1601 *et seq.* (West 1999).

62. *Indian Health Care Improvement Act,* House Report 94-1026(I) 94th Cong., 2nd sess. (1976), Public Law 94-437, 1976, U.S.C.C.A.N. 2652.

63. *The Omnibus Budget Reconciliation Act of 1990,* Public Law 101-508, 104 Stat. 1388.

64. 29 U.S.C.A. §§1161–1168 (West 1998).

65. 29 U.S.C.A. §1162 (West 1999). The duration of coverage depends upon the "qualifying event" (29 U.S.C.A. §1163) that precipitated loss of employer-provided coverage. Qualifying events include (1) the death of the covered employee; (2) the termination (other than by reason of such employee's gross misconduct), or reduction of hours, of the covered employee's employment; (3) the divorce or legal separation of the covered employee from the employee's spouse; (4) the covered employee becoming entitled to benefits under title XVIII of the Social Security Act; (5) a dependent child ceasing to be a dependent child under the generally applicable requirements of the plan; (6) a proceeding in a case under Title 11, commencing on or after July 1, 1986, with respect to the employer from whose employment the covered employee retired at any time.

66. *Health Insurance Portability and Accountability Act of 1996,* Senate Report 104-156, 104th Cong., 1st sess. 1995 WL 624926.

67. 29 U.S.C.A. §1181 (West 1999).

68. U.S. General Accounting Office, *Private Health Insurance: Progress and Challenges in Implementing 1996 Federal Standards,* GAO/HEHS-99-100 (Washington, D.C., 1999).

69. 29 U.S.C.A. §1182 (West 1999).

70. 29 U.S.C.A. §1185a (West 1999).

71. "Collective Bargaining: AMA Officials Take First Steps to Create National Physicians' Bargaining Unit," *BNA Health Care Daily,* June 25, 1999, D8.

72. Julie Jacob, "Oxford Losses Raise Concerns for Industry's Staying Power," *American Medical News* 40 (1997): 43; "Omnicare Says That It Has Turned the Corner," *Mealey's Managed Care Liability Reporter* 21 (1998): 21; Monte Williams, "Medicare H.M.O. Cutbacks Strand Thousands of Clients," *New York Times,* November 14, 1998, C1.

73. U.S. General Accounting Office, *Medicare Managed Care Plans: Many Factors Contribute to Recent Withdrawals; Plan Interest Continues,* HEHS-99-91 (Washington, D.C., 1999); Ann Saphir and Chris Rauber, "Medicaid HMOs Exit Markets," *Modern Health Care* 29, 25 (1999): 46–48.

74. "Medicare: HCFA Report Warns HMOs Expected to Charge More Copayments for Drugs," *BNA Health Care Daily,* September 23, 1999; Robert Pear, "Medicare H.M.O.s to End Free Drugs, Report Says," *New York Times,* September 23, 1999.

75. Mary A. Laschober, Kathryn M. Langwell, Christopher Topoleski, and others, *How Medicare HMO Withdrawals Affect Beneficiary Benefits, Costs, and Continuity of Care* (Menlo Park, Calif.: Henry J. Kaiser Family Foundation, 1999), iii.

76. *Nursing Home Protection Amendments of 1999,* Public Law 106-4, 113 Stat 7, 106th Cong., 1st sess., March 25, 1999.

77. U.S. General Accounting Office, *Medicare Reform: Observations on the President's July 1999 Proposal* (Washington, D.C., 1999), Figure 1.

78. U.S. General Accounting Office, *Millions Can Be Saved by Screening Reports for Overused Services,* GAO/HEHS-96-49 (Washington, D.C., 1996); U.S. General Accounting Office, *Medicare: Program Safeguard Activities Expand, But Results Difficult to Measure,* GAO/HEHS-99-165 (Washington, D.C., 1999); U.S. General Accounting Office, *Medicare Fraud and Abuse: DOJ's Implementation of False Claims Act Guidance in National Initiatives Varies,* GAO/HEHS-99-170 (Washington, D.C., 1999).

79. Catherine Hoffman, *Uninsured in America* (Washington, D.C.: Henry J. Kaiser Family Foundation, 1998), 76–77.

80. Kenneth R. Wing, "The Impact of the Reagan-Era Politics on the Federal Medicaid Program," *Catholic University Law Review* 33 (1983): 1–93; Bruce J. Casino, "Federal Grants-in-Aid: Evolution, Crisis and Future," *Urban Lawyer* 20 (1988): 25–63.

81. Eileen R. Ellis and Vernon K. Smith, *Medicaid Enrollment in 21 States: June 1997 to June 1999* (Lansing, Mich.: Health Management Associates, 2000).

82. Jennifer A. Campbell, *Current Population Reports: Health Insurance Coverage 1998* (Washington, D.C.: U.S. Department of Commerce, U.S. Census Bureau, 1999). See Hoffman, *Uninsured in America*.

83. Nancy L. Johnson and Katherine Ryan Sullivan, "Long-Term Care Financing: Federal Policy Implications, Actions, and Options," *Quinnipiac Health Law Journal* 1 (1997).

84. Iglehart, "The American Health Care System."

85. "Comparison: Rising Costs an International Phenomenon," *Health Line* 1998, p. 2; "Health Costs: New Medical Technologies Drive Increases," *Health Line* 1999, p. 1.

86. *Medicare Program; Procedures for Making National Coverage Decisions*, 64 FR 22619, Tuesday, April 27, 1999.

87. U.S. General Accounting Office, *Prescription Drug Benefits: Implications for Beneficiaries of Medicare HMO Use of Formularies*, GAO/HEHS-99-166 (Washington, D.C., 1999).

88. U.S. General Accounting Office, *Medicare + Choice;* Constantine G. Papavizas and Norman F. Lent III, "Consumers and Providers Call for Regulation; The Managed Care Industry Would Disagree," *National Law Journal* 19 (1997): 32.

89. John D. Blum, "Symposium on Health Care Policy: What Lessons Have We Learned from the AIDS Pandemic: Safeguarding the Interests of People with AIDS in Managed Care Settings," *Albany Law Review* 61 (1998): 745–784.

90. Kaiser Family Foundation/Harvard University School of Public Health, *Survey of Physicians and Nurses* (Menlo Part, Calif.: Henry J. Kaiser Family Foundation, 1999).

91. Robert Pear, "Series of Rulings Eases Constraints on Suing H.M.O.s," *New York Times*, August 15, 1999, C6.

92. 140 *Cong. Rec.* Senate S12153-01 (Friday, August 19, 1994). Discussions of managed competition can be found in Jacob S. Hacker, *The Road to Nowhere: The Genesis of President Clinton's Plan for Health Security* (New Jersey: Princeton University Press, 1997); Paul Elwood, "Interview," *Hospitals* 67, 24 (1993): 46.

93. Iglehart, "The American Health Care System."

94. Arnold S. Relman, "Controlling Costs by 'Managed Competition'—Would It Work?" *New England Journal of Medicine* 328 (1993): 133–135.

95. Paul Wellstone and Ellen R. Shaffer, "The American Health Security Act—A Single-Payer Proposal," *New England Journal of Medicine* 328 (1993): 1489–1493.

96. Jeremy Lutsky, "Is Your Physician Becoming a Teamster? The Rising Trend of Physicians Joining Labor Unions in the Late 1990s," *DePaul Journal of Health Care Law* 2 (1997): 55–78.

97. Daniel Callahan, "Rationing Health Care: Social, Political and Legal Perspectives," *American Journal of Law and Medicine* 18 (1992): 1–4.

98. OR-ST-ANN, §414.025 et seq. (West 1998).

99. Lawrence Jacobs, Theodore Marmor, and Jonathan Oberlander, "The Oregon Health Plan and the Political Paradox of Rationing: What Advocates and Critics Have Claimed and What Oregon Did," *Journal of Health Politics, Policy and Law* 24 (1999): 161–179.

100. Thomas Bodenheimer, "The Oregon Health Plan: Lessons for the Nation," parts 1 and 2, *New England Journal of Medicine* 337 (1997): 651–655 and 337 (1997): 720–723.

101. Jacobs et al., "The Oregon Health Plan," 166–167.

CHAPTER THIRTEEN

1. *Gayle v. Browder,* 77 S. Ct. 145 (1956).
2. Estimates of the number of marchers varies within a narrow range. I obtained this figure from Paul Butler, Robert S. Chang, Charles J. Cooper, and others, "Race Law and Justice: The Rehnquist Court and the American Dilemma," *American University Law Review* (1996); 567–686.
3. Seeking to protect the voting rights of African Americans, Congress enacted civil rights statutes in 1957 and 1960. These acts, together with one section of the 1964 Civil Rights Act, provided legal remedies for discriminatory acts by the states. These statutes were not effective in removing state-erected barriers to voting. Passage, implementation and enforcement of the Voting Rights Act of 1965, which provides that "no voting qualification or prerequisite to voting, or standard, practice, or procedure shall be imposed or applied by any State or political subdivision to deny or abridge the right of any citizen of the United States to vote on account of race or color . . . " has accomplished much of what the earlier acts set out to do. (See chapter 5 on the Voting Rights Act of 1965.)
4. *Civil Rights Act of 1964,* Senate Report 88-872, 88th Cong., 2nd sess. (1964).
5. The Commerce Clause is found at Article I, §8, cl. 3; United States Constitution, Fourteenth Amendment, §5.
6. *Heart of Atlanta Motel, Inc. v. United States,* 85 S. Ct. 348 (1964).
7. Constitution of the United States, Article I, §8, cl. 3.
8. *Heart of Atlanta Motel Inc. v. United States.*
9. See *United States v. Lopez,* 115 S. Ct. 1624 (1995) (enactment of the Gun Free Zones Act of 1990 that prohibits the possession of a firearm in a school zone exceeded Congress' authority under the Commerce Clause); *Seminole Tribe of Florida v. Florida,* 116 S. Ct. 1114 (1996) (the Commerce Clause does not confer on Congress the authority to control state action concerning gaming regulations); *City of Boerne v. Flores,* 138 L.Ed.2d 624 (1997) (Congress exceeded its authority under Section 5 of the Fourteenth Amendment when it enacted the Religious Freedom Restoration Act that limits states in imposing regulations on religious organizations.)
10. 42 U.S.C.A §13981(b) (West 1999).
11. *Brzonkala v. Virginia Polytechnic Institute,* 169 F.3d 820 (4th Cir. 1999), aff'd 65 U.S.L.W. 4351 (2000).
12. *Civil Rights Act of 1964,* Public Law No. 88-352, 78 Stat. 241-67, codified at 42 U.S.C.A. §2000a *et seq.* (West 1999).
13. Title II does not include sex as a protected category. See *DeCrow v. Hotel Syracuse,* 288 F.Supp. 530 (N.D.N.Y. 1968).
14. 42 U.S.C.A. §1975a (West 1999).
15. The term "entities" is used to embrace the range of organizational arrangements that include large corporations, not-for-profit agencies, and private practitioners.
16. The Civil Rights Act of 1964 and the ADA define employer as one who employs fifteen or more people, whereas the ADEA defines an employer as one who employs twenty or more people.
17. 42 U.S.C.A. §2000e-2(a)(1) (West 1999).
18. Because Title VI applies only to recipients of federal funds, it does not contain the sweeping language prohibiting employment discrimination that is found in Title VII.
19. *Dothard v. Rawlinson,* 97 S. Ct. 2720 (1977).
20. *Harris v. Pan American World Airways, Inc.,* 649 F.2d 670 (9th Cir. 1980).
21. 42 U.S.C.A. §2000e(k) (West 1999).
22. Fawn H. Johnson, "Conference Report: OFCCP: New Review Process Gives Small

Agency Powerful Enforcement Tools Over Contractors," *BNA Labor Reporter,* Monday, August 16, 1999.

23. *Hopkins v. Price Waterhouse,* 618 F.Supp. 1109 (D.D.C. 1985); aff'd in part rev'd in part, 825 F.2d 458 (D.C. Cir. 1987), cert granted, 108 S. Ct. 1106, aff'd 920 F.2d 9676 (D.C. Cir. 1990).

24. Ibid., 1112.

25. Ibid., 1117, 1118.

26. Ibid.

27. Glass Ceiling Commission, *Good for Business: Making Full Use of the Nation's Human Capital* (Washington, D.C., 1995).

28. *Glass Ceiling Act of 1991,* Public Law 102-166, 105 Stat. 1081, §202. Findings.

29. Ibid., §210(a).

30. Glass Ceiling Commission, *A Solid Investment: Making Full Use of the Nation's Human Capital* (Washington, D.C., 1995).

31. Women's Bureau, "Women's Participation in the U.S. Workforce at All-Time High, Labor Department Reports," *BNA Employment Policy and Law Daily,* 1997 (3/28/97 EPLD d1).

32. President Johnson issued two executive orders requiring government contractors to take affirmative action. The first, issued on September 24, 1965, was Order No. 11246; the second, issued on October 13, 1967, was Order No. 11375. President Nixon's order is No. 11491. It was issued on October 29, 1969. Requirements for affirmative action in the VRA are found at 29 U.S.C.A. §701 (West 1999).

33. 42 U.S.C.A. §2000e-5(g)(1) (West 1999).

34. *Adarand v. Penna,* 115 S. Ct. 2097 (1995).

35. In 1997, a town in New Jersey decided to reduce the teaching staff in one of its departments and laid off a white teacher while retaining a black teacher. The teachers had been hired on the same day nine years earlier, they had equal seniority, and they were equally qualified. The decision to retain the African American teacher was based on the school board's desire to maintain diversity in its faculty. The Court of Appeals for the Third Circuit ruled that the diversity goal was an impermissible basis for the school's decision because the affirmative action plan was not remedial. The United States Supreme Court granted review of the case. Weeks before oral arguments were to take place, the case settled out of court. Legal scholars are in general agreement that the settlement was motivated, in part, by a fear that the High Court would use this case to make a sweeping and negative ruling on affirmative action. The decision to settle the case for the reasons noted is an excellent example of advocacy groups setting the agenda of the High Court. See *Taxman v. Board of Education,* 91 F.3d 1547 (3rd Cir. 1996); Philip T. K. Daniel and Kyle Edward Timken, "The Rumors of My Death Have Been Exaggerated: Hopwood's Error in "Discarding" Bakke," *Journal of Law and Education* (1999): 391–418; Constance Hawke, "Reframing the Rationale for Affirmative Action in Higher Education," *West's Education Law Reporter* (1999): 1–19; Lisa Estrada, "Buying the Status Quo on Affirmative Action: The Piscataway Settlement and Its Lessons About Interest Group Path Manipulation," *George Mason University Civil Rights Law Journal* 207–235.

36. *Civil Rights Act of 1964,* Senate Report 88-872, 88th Cong., 2nd sess. (1964).

37. Ibid.

38. Richard D. Kahlenberg, *The Remedy: Class, Race, and Affirmative Action* (Cambridge, Mass.: Harvard University Press, 1996), 40.

39. 98 S. Ct. 2733 (1978).

40. Ibid.

41. Ibid.

42. *Hopwood V. Texas.* 78 F.3d 932 (1996), cert denied 116 S. Ct. 2580 (1996).

43. Marina Angel, "Women in Legal Education: What It's Like to be Part of a Perpetual First Wave or the Case of the Disappearing Women," *Temple Law Review* 61 (1988): 799–841.

44. As an alternative to race-based admissions and in an effort to maintain student diversity, Texas will guarantee admission to a state institution of higher education to the top 10 percent of state high school graduates. Florida has voluntarily eliminated the use of affirmative action in college admissions and guarantees automatic admission to a state university or college for the top 20 percent of state high school graduates. California is implementing a plan to admit the top 5 percent. Jeffrey Selingo, "Texas Colleges Seek New Ways to Attract Minority Students," *Chronicle of Higher Education*, November 19, 1999, A35; Jeffrey Selingo, "Florida's University System Plans to End Affirmative Action in Admissions," *Chronicle of Higher Education*, November 19, 1999, A36.

45. *City of Richmond v. Croson,* 109 S. Ct. 706 (S. Ct. 1989).

46. *Hopwood v. Texas.* 78 F.3d 932 (1996), cert denied 116 S. Ct. 2580 (1996); *Eisenberg v. Montgomery County Public Schools,* 197 F.3d 123 (4th Cir. 1999), cert denied 120 S. Ct. 1420 (2000); *Wessmann v. Gittens,* 160 F.3d 790 (1st Cir. 1998).

47. *United Steelworkers v. Weber,* 99 S. Ct. 608 (1978). Weber involved an affirmative action plan in a collective bargaining agreement. The company's workforce was almost entirely white. Slots in a new training program were available to African American and white workers. Because African Americans had historically been excluded from craft unions, the bargaining agreement set aside 50 percent of the slots in the new training program for African Americans. This provision was to remain in effect until the percentage of African American workers in the plant was approximately equal to the percentage of African Americans in the local community.

48. If the job requires special skill or training, then the employer may compare the percentages of its minorities in those positions to the percentage of minorities in the general population who have those same special skills. *Johnson v. Transportation Agency,* 480 U.S. 616, 632 (1987).

49. 42 U.S.C.A. 2000e-5 g(1) (West 1999).

50. *United States v. Paradise,* 107 S. Ct. 1053 (1987).

51. Cited in Kahlenberg, *The Remedy.*

52. Stephen L. Carter, *Reflections of an Affirmative Action Baby* (New York: Basic Books, 1991), 72; William Julius Wilson, *When Work Disappears: The World of the New Urban Poor* (New York: Alfred A. Knopf, 1997), 197.

53. See *Employment Non-Discrimination Act,* Senate 2238, 103rd Cong. 2nd sess. (1994); *Employment Non-Discrimination Act,* H.R. 104-873, 104th Cong., 2nd sess. (1996); *Employment Non-Discrimination Act,* H.R. 1858, 105th Cong., 1st sess. (1997).

54. Statewide protection is found in California, Nevada, Minnesota, Wisconsin, Vermont, New Hampshire, Massachusetts, Rhode Island, Connecticut, New Jersey, and Hawaii. Executive orders protecting public employees are found in Washington, Colorado, New Mexico, New York, and Pennsylvania. The cities and counties that protect lesbians and gays against discrimination are too numerous to name. A map identifying states, cities, and counties can be found on the Internet at www.lambdalegal.org .

55. *Romer v. Evans,* 1116 S. Ct. 1620 (1996).

56. 29 C.F.R. §1604.11(a) (1999).

57. *Meritor Savings Bank v. Vinson,* 106 S. Ct. 2399 (1986); *Harris v. Forklift Systems,* 114 S. Ct. 367 (1993); *Faragher v. City of Boca Raton,* 118 S. Ct. 2275 (1998).

58. *Johnson v. Teamsters Local Union No. 559,* 102 F.3d 21 (1st Cir. 1996).

59. *Quinn v. Nassau County Police Department,* 53 F.Supp. 347 (E.D.N.Y. 1999); *Oncale v. Sundowner,* 118 S. Ct. 998 (1998).
60. *Oncale v. Sundowner,* 118 S. Ct. 998 (1998).
61. Equal Employment Opportunity Commission, *Enforcement Guidance: Vicarious Employer Liability for Unlawful Harassment by Supervisors* (Washington, D.C., 1999).
62. *Harris v. Forklift Systems,* 114 S. Ct. 367 (1993).
63. *Faragher v. City of Boca Raton,* 118 S. Ct. 2275 (1998).
64. *Harris v. Forklift Systems,* 114 S. Ct. 367 (1993).
65. *Burlington Industries, Inc. v. Ellerth,* 118 S. Ct. 2257 (1998), and *Faragher v. City of Boca Raton,* 118 S. Ct. 2275 (1998).
66. Equal Employment Opportunity Commission, *Enforcement Guidance.*
67. 20 U.S.C.A. §1681 (West 1999).
68. 42 U.S.C.A. §12111. (West 1999).
69. 29 U.S.C.A. §793(a) (West 1999); 41 C.F.R. 60.741.4.
70. The definition of disability in the ADA appears at 42 U.S.C.A. §12102(2)(A)-(C) (West 1999). For the VRA, see 29 U.S.C.A. §706(8)(b) (West 1999), and for the FHA, See, 42 U.S.C.A. §3602 (West 1999). Congress declined to create a definitive list of the conditions, diseases, or infections that might constitute physical or mental impairments. Guidance can be found in federal regulations that identify a variety of conditions, diseases, and disorders covered by the law. 29 C.F.R. §1630.2 (h)(1) & (2) defines physical or mental impairment as (1) any physiological disorder, or condition, cosmetic disfigurement, or anatomical loss affecting one or more of the following body systems: neurological, musculoskeletal, special sense organs, respiratory (including speech organs), cardiovascular, reproductive, digestive, genitourinary, hemic and lymphatic, skin, and endocrine; or (2) any mental or psychological disorder, such as mental retardation, organic brain syndrome, emotional or mental illness, and specific learning disabilities.
71. 45 C.F.R. §84.3(j)(2)(iii) (West, 1999).
72. 29 C.F.R. §1630.2(l)(1) thru (3) (1999).
73. 42 U.S.C.A. §3607(3)(B)(4) (West 1999).
74. 42 U.S.C.A. §12201(a) (West 1999).
75. 42 U.S.C.A. §12112(a) (West 1999).
76. 42 U.S.C.A. §12112(b)(1)-(7) (West 1999).
77. 42 U.S.C.A. §12111(8) (West 1999).
78. *Southeastern Community College v. Davis,* 99 S. Ct. 2361 (1979).
79. 42 U.S.C.A. §12111(9)(A)(B), (10) (West 1999); 29 C.F.R. §1630.2 (p)(1) & (p)(2)(i) through (iv).
80. 567 F. Supp. 369 (E.D. PA. 1983).
81. 29 U.S.C.A. §706 (8)(D) (West 1999).
82. *Bradley v. University of Texas A & M Medical Center,* 3 F.3d 922 at 924 (5th Cir. 1993); *Mauro v. Burgess Medical Center,* 886 F.Supp. 1349 at 1352–1353 (W.D.Mich. 1995).
83. 42 U.S.C.A. §12132 (West 1999).
84. 42 U.S.C.A. §12131(2) (West 1999).
85. 42 U.S.C.A. §12131(2) (West 1999).
86. 42 U.S.C.A. §12182(b)(2)(A)(iv) (West 1999).
87. 42 U.S.C.A. §12181(9) (West 1999).
88. 42 U.S.C.A. §12181(9)(A)-(D) (West 1999).
89. 49 U.S.C.A. §1374(c) (West 1999).
90. See 42 U.S.C.A. §12141(1); 12142 (a)-(c); §12143(c)(4) (West 1999).
91. Charles B. Craver, "The Application of the Age Discrimination in Employment Act to Persons Over Seventy," *George Washington Law Review* (1989): 58.

92. 29 U.S.C.A. §621 *et seq.* (West 1999). In January 2000, the U.S. Supreme Court ruled that the Eleventh Amendment prohibits suits against state government under the ADEA. The Eleventh Amendment proscribes lawsuits against states by citizens of "other" states, and the High Court extended this prohibition to citizen residents of the state being sued. *Kimel v. Florida Board of Regents,* 2000 WL 14165 (2000). The decision left intact the right to sue a private employer, and states can be sued under their own civil rights laws if they prohibit discrimination in employment based on age. See, for example, Code of Alabama, Industrial Relations, §Ch. 1, Art. 3 (West 2000); Code of Georgia, §34-1-2 (West 1999); Nevada Revised Statutes, §233.010 (West 1997); State of New Jersey, Law Against Discrimination, §10:5–12 (West 1999); McKinney's Executive Law of New York, §291 (West 1999); Oregon Revised Statutes, §659.030 (West 1998); Texas Labor Code, §21.051 (West 1999).

93. See *Hodgson v. Greyhound Lines, Inc.,* 499 F.2d 859 (7th Cir. 1974); *EEOC v. Trabucco,* 791 F.2d 1 (1st Cir. 1986).

94. The Equal Pay Act of 1963 was added to the Fair Labor Standards Act, enacted June 10, 1963, Public Law 88-38, 77 Stat 56, 29 U.S.C.A. §206(d) (West 1999). On the merit and seniority exceptions, see 29 U.S.C.A. §206(d)(1) (West 1999).

95. *County of Washington v. Gunther,* 68 L.Ed.2d 751 (1981).

96. 42 U.S.C.A. §3604(2)(A) through (C) (West 1999). On protection for foster parents, see *Gorski v. Troy,* 929 F.2d 1183 (7th Cir. 1991).

97. 42 U.S.C.A. §3602(b) & 3604(a)-(d) (West 1999).

98. 42 U.S.C.A. §3604 (West 1999).

99. 42 U.S.C.A. §3617 (West 1998).

100. 42 U.S.C.A. §3607 (West 1999) covers noncommercial buildings, private clubs, and elder housing. 42 U.S.C.A. §3603(b)(1) (West 1999) covers single-family housing sold or rented by an owner.

101. 42 U.S.C.A. §3604(f)(3)((C)(i)-(iii) (West 1999).

102. 42 U.S.C.A. §3604(f)(9) (West 1999).

CHAPTER FOURTEEN

1. Theodore J. Stein, *The Social Welfare of Women and Children With HIV and AIDS: Legal Protections, Policies and Programs* (New York: Oxford University Press, 1998), ch. 3.

2. *Social Security Amendments of 1956,* 84th Cong., 2nd sess. Public Law 84-80, 1956 U.S.C.C.A.N. 3877.

3. Elisa Vinson, *Governing-for-Results and Accountability: Performance Contracting in Six State Human Services Agencies* (Washington, D.C.: Urban Institute, 1999).

4. *National ADAP Monitoring Project: Annual Report,* Menlo Park, Calif.: Kaiser Family Foundation, 1999).

5. House, Committee on Ways and Means, "Section 10: Title XX Social Services Block Grant Program," *Green Book* (Washington, D.C., 1998), 723.

6. U.S. General Accounting Office, *Grant Programs—Design Features Shape Flexibility, Accountability, and Performance Evaluation* (Washington, D.C., 1998).

7. 42 U.S.C.A. §1397 *et seq.* (West 1999).

8. 42 U.S.C.A. §1397b(c) (West 1999).

9. 42 U.S.C.A. §1397 (West 1999).

10. U.S. General Accounting Office, *Community Development: Progress on Economic Development Activities Varies Among the Empowerment Zones* (Washington, D.C., 1998).

11. 42 U.S.C.A. §1397a (West 1999).

12. 42 U.S.C.A. §1397e (West 1999); 45 C.F.R. §96.74 (West 1999).

13. Children's Defense Fund, *Title XX on the Chopping Block Again!* (Washington, D.C., 1999).

14. Centers for Disease Control. *HIV/AIDS Surveillance Report: U.S. HIV and AIDS Cases Reported Through June 1999.* 1999 Mid-Year Edition. 11(1): 3, Table 1.

15. Scott Foster, Althea Gregory, Piet Niederhausen, and others, *Federal HIV/AIDS Spending: A Budget Chartbook* (Menlo Park, Calif.: Kaiser Family Foundation, 1998).

16. 42 U.S.C.A. §300ff-11 to -18 (West 1999).

17. 42 U.S.C.A. §300ff-12(b) (West 1999).

18. 42 U.S.C.A. §300ff-14(b)(A)(B) (West 1999).

19. 42 U.S.C.A. §300ff-21 to 30 (West 1999).

20. 42 U.S.C.A. §300ff-(25)-(26) (West 1999).

21. 42 U.S.C.A. §300ff-14 (West 1999); *Ryan White Care Reauthorization Act of 1996,* 104th Cong., 1st sess. S. 641 (1996) Part C-Early Intervention Services, codified at 42 U.S.C.A. §300ff-51(b) & 52(a) (West 1999). See also Conference Committee Report to accompany S. 641, 104th Cong., 2d sess. Report No. 545 (1996).

22. Ibid.

23. 42 U.S.C.A. §300ff-71 (West 1999).

24. 42 U.S.C.A. §300ff-91 (West 1999).

25. "Aids Funding" Testimony of the AIDS Action Council, before the House of Representatives, Subcommittee on Health and Environment of the Committee on Commerce (April 5, 1995); *Ryan White Care Act Amendments of 1995,* 104th Cong., 1st sess., House Report. No. 104-245 (September 14, 1995); U.S. General Accounting Office, Report to the Chairman, Committee on Labor and Human Resources, *Ryan White Care Act: Access to Services by Minorities, Women, and Substance Abusers* (Washington, D.C., 1995); American Indian Community House HIV/AIDS Project News, New York (1996): 21.

26. 42 U.S.C.A. §300x (West 1999).

27. 42 U.S.C.A. §290aa (West 1999).

28. Fernando J. Gutierrez, "Who Is Watching Big Brother When Big Brother Is Watching Mental Health Professionals: A Call for the Evolution of Mental Health Advocacy Programs," *Law and Psychology Review* 20 (1996): 57–96.

29. U.S. General Accounting Office. 1999. *Mental Health: Improper Restraint or Seclusion Use Places People at Risk GAO/HEHS-99-176.* Washington, D.C.:3.

30. Ibid.

31. Sara S. Bachman, "Why Do States Privatize Mental Health Services? Six State Experiences," *Journal of Health Politics, Policy and Law* 21 (1996): 807–846. In some states, priority populations are referred to as those with "serious" or "severe" mental illness, whereas other states provide for a state mental health department to establish priority populations. See CA-ST-ANN, §5600.2 (West 1998); MT-ST-ANN, §53–21–206 (West 1999); TN-ST-ANN §33–1–208 (West 1998), TX-ST-ANN §531.001 (West 1999).

32. David J. Rothman, *The Discovery of the Asylum: Social Order in the New Republic* (Boston: Little, Brown, 1971).

33. Patricia A. Streeter, "Incarceration of the Mentally Ill: Treatment or Warehousing?" *Michigan Bar Journal* 77 (1998): 166–169.

34. John Petrila, "Ethics, Money, and the Problem of Coercion in Managed Behavioral Health Care," *Saint Louis University Law Journal* 40 (1996), citing Gerald N. Grob, "Government and Mental Health Policy: A Structural Analysis," *Milbank Quarterly* 72 (1994): 491–492.

35. *Addington v. Texas,* 99 S. Ct. 1804 (1979).

36. *Jackson v. Indiana,* 92 S. Ct. 1845 (1972); *Lessard v. Schmidt,* 349 F. Supp. 1078, 1093 (E.D. Wis. 1972), vacated and remanded, 414 U.S. 473 (1974), on remand, 379 F. Supp. 1376 (E.D. Wis. 1974), vacated and remanded, 421 U.S. 957 (1975), reinstated, 413 F. Supp. 1318 (E.D. Wis. 1976).

37. In 1999, the U.S. Supreme Court issued a ruling in a case involving the voluntary incarceration in a psychiatric hospital of two mentally retarded women. The Court ruled that Title II of the Americans with Disabilities Act (ADA) (28 C.F.R. Section 35.130(d)) prohibits the exclusion of qualified individuals with disabilities from public programs. The law requires that states provide community-based treatment to people with mental health disabilities when professionals determine that community placement is appropriate and assuming that the patient does not oppose such placement. However, states may take into account available resources in determining whether patients have an entitlement to immediate community placement. Since states must strike a balance among competing groups of the mentally ill, the state will not be in violation of the ADA if it shows that is has a waiting list "that moves at a controlled pace, not controlled by the state's efforts to keep its institutions populated." *Olmstead v. Zimring* 119 S. Ct. 2176 (1999). Commenting on the Supreme Court decision, the Clinton administration took the position that the ruling applies to (1) people with physical as well as mental disabilities; (2) Medicaid recipients in private nursing homes; and (3) people living at home who are at risk of entering an institution. Letter to state Medicaid directors from U.S. Department of Health and Human Services, January 14, 2000.

38. *Halderman v. Pennhurst State School and Hospital,* 446 F. Supp. 1295 (ED Pa. 1977); *New York State Association for Retarded Children, Inc v. Rockefeller,* 357 F. Supp. 752 (EDNY 1973).

39. The act of 1963, codified at 42 U.S.C.A. §2689, has been repealed. The 1980 act was the Mental Health Systems Act, Public Law 96-398, 1980 U.S.C.C.A.N. 3372, 96th Cong., 2nd sess.

40. Joseph T. Carney, "American's Mentally Ill: Tormented Without Treatment," *George Mason University Civil Rights Law Journal* 3 (1992): 181–202.

41. Ibid.

42. Bachman, "Why Do States Privatize Mental Health Services?"

43. "The Police and Emotionally Disturbed People," *Time Magazine* 154, 11 (1999); Eric Fetmann, "The Problem Isn't Housing—It's Letting Madmen Roam Free," *New York Post,* January 10, 1999; Editorial, "Pataki's Mental Health Plan," *New York Post,* November 11, 1999.

44. Richard H. Lamb and Linda E. Weinberger, "Persons with Severe Mental Illness in Jails and Prisons: A Review," *Psychiatric Services* 49, 4 (1998): 483–492; Fuller E. Torrey, Joan Stieber, Jonathan Ezekiel, and others, *Criminalizing the Seriously Mentally Ill: The Abuse of Jails as Mental Hospitals* (Arlington, Va.: National Alliance for the Mentally Ill, 1992).

45. E. Fuller Torrey, "The Release of the Mentally Ill from Institutions: A Well-Intentioned Disaster," *Chronicle of Higher Education* 43, 40 (1997): B4.

46. See Torrey et al., *Criminalizing the Seriously Mentally Ill;* William G. Kearon, "Deinstitutionalization, Street Children, and the Coming AIDS Epidemic in the Adolescent Population," *Juvenile and Family Court Journal* 41, 1 (1990): 9–18.

47. On zoning issues and building permits, see Stein, *The Social Welfare of Women and Children With HIV and AIDS,* ch 2.; David Rothman and Sheila Rothman, *The Willowbrook Wars* (New York: Harper and Row, 1984).

48. *O'Connor v. Donaldson,* 95 S. Ct. 2486 (1975).

49. *Kendra's Law,* New York State Senate Bill No. 5762-A, Chapter 408 (1999).

50. *Mills v. Rogers,* 102 S. Ct. 2442 (1982); *Washington v. Gluchsbert,* 117 S. Ct. 2302 (1997).

51. 42 U.S.C.A. §300x-1 (West 1999).

52. 42 U.S.C.A. §290bb-32 (West 1999).

53. 42 U.S.C.A. §1396d(5) (West 1999).

54. 42 U.S.C.A. §290bb-31 (West 1999).

55. Congress noted that the accrediting activities undertaken by the private Joint Commission on Accreditation of Hospitals and the Health Care Financing Administration were not sufficient to protect patient rights because their visits to hospitals were scheduled in advance, and the focus of their visits was mainly on the institution's capacity to treat, not on the treatment provided on an individual basis.

56. Senate Report No. 99-109, 99th Cong., 1st sess. 1985, 1986 U.S.C.C.A.N. 1361, 42 U.S.C.A. §10801 *et seq.* (West 1999).

57. Beatrice A. Rouse, *Statistics Source Book 1998* (Washington, D.C.: Substance Abuse and Mental Health Administration, 1998), 20.

58. 42 U.S.C.A. §300x-21 *et seq.* (West 1999).

59. 45 C.F.R. §96.121 (West 1999).

60. 45 C.F.R. §96.135 (West 1999).

61. 45 C.F.R. §96.131 (West 1999).

62. Justice Research and Statistics Association, *Domestic and Sexual Violence Data Collection: A Report to Congress Under the Violence Against Women Act* (Washington, D.C.: National Institute of Justice, Bureau of Justice Statistics, 1996), 17, 61.

63. Violence Against Women, Hearing Before the Subcommittee on Crime and Criminal Justice Before the House of Representatives, 102d Cong., 2d sess. 70–82 (Feb 6, 1992) House Report. No. 103–395, at 27 (1993), cited in Darold W. Killmer and Mari Newman, "VAWA: A Civil Rights Tool for Victims of Gender-Motivated Violence," *Colorado Lawyer* 28 (1999): 77–81.

64. *State v. Daniel T.* 95 Misc.2d 639 (Criminal Court, King County 1978).

65. Catherine F. Klein and Leslye E. Orloff, "Providing Legal Protection for Battered Women: An Analysis of State Statutes and Case Law," *Hofstra Law Review* 21 (1993): 801–1189.

66. Gary Spencer, "Protection Order Abuse Elevated to Felony," *New York Law Journal* 216, 29 (1996): 1.

67. Justice Research and Statistics Association, *Domestic and Sexual Violence Data Collection,* 58.

68. The lower figure was reported by Carey Goldberg, citing Department of Justice statistics in "Spouse Abuse Crackdown, Surprisingly, Nets Many Women," *New York Times,* November 23, 1999. The figure of 4 million is found in Maurice Goldman, "The Violence Against Women Act: Meeting Its Goal in Protecting Battered Women," *Family and Conciliation Courts Review* 37 (1999).

69. Public Law 103-322, 103rd Cong., 2nd sess. 1994 U.S.C.C.A.N. 1839, codified in scattered sections of 42 U.S.C.

70. 42 U.S.C.A §13981(b) (West 1999).

71. Program descriptions are taken from the U.S. Department of Justice, Violence Against Women Office, *About Violence Against Women,* www.usdoj.gov.

72. 20 U.S.C.A. §1152 (West 1999).

73. Martha R. Burt, Adele V. Harrell, Lisa Jacobs Raymond, and others, *Evaluation of the STOP Formula Grants Under the Violence Against Women Act of 1994* (Washington, D.C.: Urban Institute, 1999).

74. Ibid.

75. Administration on Aging, *Profile of Older Americans: 1999.* Available at www.aoa.dhhs.gov/aoa/stats/profile/profile99.html. In 1998, people aged sixty-five to seventy-four represented approximately 18.4 million people or eight times the number of people that were in this age group in 1900, but the 12 million people aged seventy-five to eighty-four was sixteen times larger, and the 4 million people over the age of eighty-five was thirty-three times larger.

76. Marnie S. Saul, *Senior Community Service Employment—Program Reauthorization Issues that Affect Serving Disadvantaged Seniors*, 1999 WL 527511.

77. 105th Cong., 1st sess., *Development in Aging: 1996—Volume I*, Senate Report 36(I).

78. U.S. Department of Health and Human Services, *The Administration on Aging and the Older Americans Act* (Washington, D.C.: Administration on Aging, 1999. Available at www.aoa.dhhs.gov.

79. U.S. General Accounting Office, *Older Americans Act—Funding Formula Could Better Reflect State Needs*, GAO/HEHS-94-41 (Washington, D.C., 1994).

80. Henry Waxman, *National Family Caregiver Support Act*, Proceedings and Debates of the 106th Cong., 1st sess. 145 *Cong. Rec.* E745–03.

81. 42 U.S.C.A. §3001 (West 1999).

CHAPTER FIFTEEN

1. The final federal regulations that govern implementation of TANF provide that the funds may be used for family preservation, foster care, and adoption programs that are authorized under the Adoption Assistance and Child Welfare Act since the AACWA shares with TANF the purpose of "providing assistance to needy families so that children may be cared for in their own homes or in the homes of relatives." Elaine M. Ryan, *Financing Child Welfare Services Under TANF* (Washington, D.C.: American Public Human Services Association, 2000).

2. The studied states were Alabama, California, Colorado, Florida, Massachusetts, Michigan, Minnesota, Mississippi, New Jersey, New York, Texas, Washington, and Wisconsin. Kimura Flores and Toby Douglas, *The Children's Budget Report: A Detailed Analysis of Spending on Low-Income Children's Programs in 13 States* (Washington, D.C.: Urban Institute, 1998), 9.

3. For a review of the relationship between child welfare and the law, see Theodore J. Stein, *Child Welfare and the Law*, revised edition (Washington, D.C.: Child Welfare League of America, 1998).

4. 18 U.S.C.A. §5032 (West 1999).

5. 42 U.S.C.A. §5101 *et seq.* (West 1999).

6. The rate of substantiation has dropped steadily over time but remained at approximately 30 percent throughout the 1990s. Department of Health and Human Services, Administration for Children, Youth and Families, *The Scope and Problem of Child Maltreatment*. Available at www.acf.dhhs.gov/programs/cb/ncanprob.htm. See also Theodore J. Stein, "The Child Abuse Prevention and Treatment Act," *Social Service Review* 58, 2 (1984): 302–314; Theodore J. Stein, *Child Welfare and the Law*, ch. 4.

7. Rob Geen and Karen C. Tumlin, *State Efforts to Remake Child Welfare: Responses to New Challenges and Increased Scrutiny* (Washington, D.C.: Urban Institute, 1999).

8. 42 U.S.C.A. §5101 *et seq.* (West 1999).

9. 42 U.S.C.A. §5106a(b)(10) (West 1999).

10. 42 U.S.C.A. §5106a(b)(10) (West 1999).

11. Geen and Tumlin, *State Efforts to Remake Child Welfare*.

12. J. Doris, R. Mazur, and M. Thomas, "Training in Child Protective Services: A Commentary on the Amicus Brief of Bruck and Ceci," *Psychology, Public Policy and Law* 1 (1995): 479–491; D. J. Besharov, "Child Abuse: Arrest and Prosecution Decision Making," *American Criminal Law Review* 24 (1995): 315–327.

13. AR-ST-ANN §s9-16-106 (West, 1999); KY-ST-ANN §200.590 (West 1999); LA-ST-ANN §46:287.6 (West 1998); WA-ST-ANN §74.14C.005 (West 1999); FL-ST-ANN §415.515; Consolidated Laws of NY §409-a; CA WEL & INST §16500.5 (West 1999); IN-ST-ANN §12-14-25.5-2 (West 1999); IA-ST-ANN §232.102 (West 1998); NJ-ST-ANN

§30:4C-76 (West 1998); NC-ST-ANN §143B-150.6 (West 1999); TN-ST-ANN §37-3-602 (West 1999); PA-ST-ANN §62 (Purdon 1999); NM-ST-ANN §32A-17-3 (West 1998); UT-ST-ANN §62A-4a-103 (West 1999).

14. 42 U.S.C.A. §625 (West 1999).
15. 42 U.S.C.A. §670 (West 1999).
16. 42 U.S.C.A. §625(a)(1) (West 1999).
17. U.S. General Accounting Office, *Foster Care: HHS Could Better Facilitate the Interjurisdictional Adoption Process* (Washington, D.C., 1999), 1.
18. 42 U.S.C.A. §672 (West 1999).
19. 42 U.S.C.A. §671(a)(15) (West 1999).
20. West's Minnesota Statutes, 260 M.S.A. §260.012.
21. West's Florida Statutes, 39 F.S.A. §39.41(5)(b).
22. 45 C.F.R. §1356.21(d)(2) (West 1999).
23. 42 U.S.C.A. §675(5)(A) (West 1999).
24. 42 U.S.C.A. §675(5)(B) (West 1999).
25. *The Adoption and Safe Families Act of 1997*, Public Law 105-89 (November 19, 1997).
26. AACWA §675(5)(C) (West 1999).
27. 42 U.S.C.A. §673(c)(2) (West 1999).
28. U.S. General Accounting Office, *Foster Care: Implementation of the Multiethnic Placement Act Poses Difficult Challenges*, GAO/HEHS-98-204 (Washington, D.C., 1998), 1.
29. Public Law 108-382, 108 Stat. 4056 (1994).
30. Public Law 104-188, 110 Stat. 1903 (1996).
31. 42 U.S.C.A. §671(a)(19) (West 1999).
32. 42 U.S.C.A. §§671(a)(15)(F), 675(5)(C) (West 1999).
33. 42 U.S.C.A. §675(5)(E) (West 1999).
34. Using data supplied by the states, the secretary of the Department of Health and Human Services will establish a baseline of children adopted in each state for fiscal years 1995 through 2002. This baseline will be used to determine the number of children for whom the state is eligible for incentive payments (see the Adoption and Safe Families Act, section 201).
35. U. S. General Accounting Office, *Foster Care*.
36. Similar concerns arise around intercountry adoptions to which Americans have turned because of the paucity of infants available for adoption and previously existing rules limiting transracial adoptions. The Hague Convention on Protection of Children and Cooperation in Respect to Intercountry Adoptions 32 I.L.M. 1211 [1993]) is to intercountry adoptions what model laws are to intracountry adoptions. However, the United States is not a signatory to the convention and, although it may follow convention rules, it is free to adopt its own rules. 42 U.S.C.A. §673(a) (West 1999).
37. 42 U.S.C.A. §677 (West 1999).
38. Cynthia M. Fagnoni, *Foster Care: Challenges in Helping Youths Live Independently*, GAO/T-HEHS-99-121 (Washington, D.C. 1999); U.S. General Accounting Office, *Foster Care: Effectiveness of Independent Living Services Unknown*, GAO/HEHS-00-13 (Washington, D.C., 1999); *Foster Care Independence Act, Cong. Rec.* Senate 15227, December 3, 1999, 1999 WL 1091961.
39. U. S. General Accounting Office, *Foster Care: Effectiveness*. There has only been one national study completed since the 1985 initiative created the ILP.
40. House Report 106-199, 106th Cong., 1st sess., 1999 WL 422933.
41. 42 U.S.C.A. §1911 *et seq.* (West 1999).
42. 45 C.F.R. §1355.40 (West 1999).
43. U.S. Department of Health and Human Services, Administration for Children and Families, *Foster Care and Adoption: Current Statistics.* Available at www.acf.dhhs.gov/pro-

grams/cb/stats/afcars. Of forty-one states reporting foster care data, data from sixteen states was not used by DHHS. Reasons included issues concerning the quality of the data or because states asked that their data not be reported.

44. Transfer is not defined, but presumably it refers to the transfer of children to institutional care due to the need for assistance with physical or emotional impairments.

45. 42 U.S.C.A. §654 *et seq.* (West 1999). Unless otherwise noted, information concerning Child Support Enforcement Programs comes from House, Committee on Ways and Means, "Section 8: Child Support Enforcement Program," *Green Book*, (Washington, D.C., 1998).

46. 42 U.S.C.A. §602(a)(7)(A)(iii) (West 1999).

47. U.S. General Accounting Office, *Child Support Enforcement: Effects of Declining Welfare Caseloads are Beginning to Emerge*, Report No. GAO/HEHS-99-105 (Washington, D.C., 1999), 2.

48. 42 U.S.C.A. §653 (West 1999).

49. New York combines the income of both parents before calculating the support obligation, which is a percentage of income adjusted for the number of children. Child support orders are issued by state courts. To ensure that states enforce each other's support orders, TANF (42 U.S.C. §666) requires that all states adopt the Uniform Interstate Family Support Act. In addition, the Child Support Recovery Act (18 U.S.C. §228) provides that the federal government may jail a parent who, for more than one year, has deliberately avoided a support obligation and the amount owed exceeds $5,000.

50. See U.S. General Accounting Office, *Child Support Enforcement: Effects of Declining Welfare Caseloads are Beginning to Emerge*, Report No. GAO/HEHS-99-105 (Washington, D.C., 1999), 2; U.S. Department of Commerce, U.S. Census Bureau, *Child Support for Custodial Mothers and Fathers: 1995* (Washington, D.C., 1999); *Green Book*, Section 8, 608.

51. U.S. General Accounting Office, *Welfare Reform: Child Support an Uncertain Income Supplement for Families Leaving Welfare*, Report GAO/HEHS-98-168 (Washington, D.C., 1998), 2–3, 7–8.

52. Both states have sixty-month time limits, but both, having begun their welfare reform efforts in 1992 under Section 1115 waivers (see chapter 10), had families reaching their sixty-month limit in 1997.

CHAPTER SIXTEEN

1. 25 U.S.C.A. §450 *et seq.* (West 1999.), 20 U.S.C.A. §7801 *et seq.* (West 1999). Special provisions for Native Hawaiian children are found at 20 U.S.C.A. §7902 (West 1999) and for Native Alaskan children at 20 U.S.C.A. §7931 (West 1999).

2. The Family Educational Rights and Privacy Act of 1974 codified at 20 U.S.C.A. §1232g (West 1999).

3. U.S. General Accounting Office, *Federal Education Funding: Allocation to State and Local Agencies for 10 Programs*, GAO/HEHS-99-180 (Washington, D.C., 1999), 1.

4. 42 U.S.C.A. §9831 (West 1999).

5. House, Committee on Ways and Means, "Section 15: Other Programs," *Green Book* (Washington, D.C., 1998), 1009.

6. U.S. General Accounting Office, *Head Start Programs: Participant Characteristics, Services and Funding*, GAO/HEHS-98-65 (Washington, D.C., 1998), 5, 10.

7. U.S. General Accounting Office, *Head Start Programs*, 17–20.

8. The Department's Performance Plan is available at www.hhs.gov/progorg/fin/99perfpl.html.

9. U.S. General Accounting Office, *Head Start: Research Provides Little Information on Impact of Current Program* GAO/HEHS-97-59 (Washington, D.C., 1997).

10. U.S. General Accounting Office, *Head Start Programs*, 12.

11. Ruth McKey, *The Impact of Head Start on Children, Families, and Communities*, DHHS Publication No. (OHDS) 85-31193, 1, cited in U.S. General Accounting Office, *Head Start Programs*, 7.

12. Janet Currie and Thomas Duncan, "Does Head Start Make a Difference?" *American Economic Review* 85, 3 (1995): 341–364.

13. 20 U.S.C §6391 *et seq.* (West 1999).

14. Information on educational programs for the children of migrant farm workers was taken from U.S. General Accounting Office, *Migrant Children: Education and HHS Need to Improve Exchange of Participant Information* GAO/HEHS-00-4 (Washington, D.C., 1999).

15. 20 U.S.C.A. §6301 *et seq.* (West 1999). The name of the act was changed by amendment to the act in 1994. See Public Law 103-382, 108 Stat. 3518, 103rd Cong., 2nd sess. (1994).

16. Other programs seek to (1) increase literacy for adults and children (20 U.S.C. §6361), (2) improve teaching through professional development programs (20 U.S.C. §6601), (3) eliminate drug use and violence in schools (20 U.S.C. §7101), (4) support the development of innovative educational programs (20 U.S.C. §7301), and (5) support bilingual education (20 U.S.C.A §7401 [West 1999]).

17. *Goals 2000: Educate America Act*, Public Law 103-227, 108 Stat. 125, 103rd Cong., 2nd sess. (1994); codified at 20 U.S.C. §5801 *et seq.*

18. U.S. General Accounting Office, *Public Education: Title I Services Provided to Students with Limited English Proficiency* GAO/HEHS-00-25 (Washington, D.C., 1999), 5.

19. Jane Hannaway and Kristi Kimball, *Reports on Reform from the Field: District and State Survey Results* (Washington, D.C.: Urban Institute, 1997).

20. Alan L. Ginsburg, *Title I Education Funding*, testimony before the House Committee on Education and the Workforce. 1999 WL 16946013.

21. *Lau v. Nichols*, 94 S. Ct. 786 at 788 (1974).

22. 20 U.S.C.A. §1703(f) (West 1999).

23. U.S. General Accounting Office, *Title I Services*, 1.

24. See West Annotated California Education Code, Ch. 3 §306(d)

25. *Castaneda v. Pickard*, 648 F.2d 989 at 1009–1010 (5th Cir. 1981) (Castenada I), *Castaneda v. Pickard*, 781 F.2d 456 (5th Cir. 1986) (Castenada II), affirming Castenada I.

26. Leslie Slaughter, testimony before the House of Representatives, Education Subcommittee. 1998 WL 210930.

27. 42 U.S.C.A. §11431 *et seq.* (West 1999).

28. 42 U.S.C.A. §11432(g)(3)(A)(B) (West 1999).

29. See Theodore J. Stein, *Child Welfare and the Law*, revised edition (Washington, D.C.: Child Welfare League of America, 1998), ch. 4.

30. 20 U.S.C.A. §1400 (West 1999).

31. *Burlington v. Department of Education*, 736 F.2d. 773 (1st Cir. 1984), aff'd 105 S. Ct. 1996 (1985).

32. 20 U.S.C.A. §1400 *et seq.* (West 1999).

33. See Stein, *Child Welfare and the Law.*

34. 34 C.F.R. §§104.33; 104.35 and 104.36 (West 1999).

35. Requirement for outreach to "highly mobile" children is found at 34 C.F.R. §300.125(a)(2)(i) and for outreach to all private schools at 34 C.F.R. §300.451 (West 1999).

36. 34 C.F.R. §300.121 (West 1999).

37. *Board of Education v. Rowley*, 102 S. Ct. 3034 (1982).

38. Ibid.

39. *Rettig v. Kent City School District,* 720 F.2d 463 (6th Cir. 1983), cert denied, 104 S. Ct. 2379 (1984) later appeal 788 F.2d 328 (6th Cir. 1986) cert denied 106 S. Ct. 3297 (1986).
40. 34 C.F.R. §300.344(a)(1)-(3) (West 1999).
41. *Board of Education v. Dienelt,* 843 F.2d 813 (4th Cir. 1988).
42. *Seattle School District. v. B.S.,* 82 F.3d 1493 (1996).
43. *Jeremy H. v. Mount Lebanon School District,* 95 F.3d 272 (3rd Cir. 1996).
44. *Blazejewski v. Board of Education,* 560 F. Supp. 701 (W.D.N.Y. 1983), *Bonadonna v Cooperman,* 619 F. Supp. 401 (D.C.N.J. 1985).
45. 20 U.S.C.A. §1041(17) (West 1999)
46. *Agostini v. Felton,* 117 S. Ct.1997 (1997).
47. *Natchez-Adams School District v. Searing,* 918 F.Supp. 1028 (S.D.Miss. 1996).
48. 20 U.S.C.A. §1412(10)(A)(i)(II) (West 1999), 34 C.F.R. §300.403 (West 1999).
49. *K.R. v. Anderson Community School Corporation,* 81 F.3d 673 (7th Cir. 1996).
50. 34 C.F.R. §300.452 (West 1999).
51. *Burlington v. Department of Education.*
52. *Carter v. Florence County School District Four,* 950 F.2d 156 (4th Cir. 1991), *sub nom aff'd Florence County School District Four v. Carter,* 114 S. Ct. 361 (1993).
53. *Abrahamson v. Hershman,* 701 F.2d 223 (1st Cir. 1983); *Matthews v. Davis,* 742 F.2d 825 (4th Cir. 1984); *Drew P. v. Clarke County School District,* 877 F.2d 927 (11th Cir. 1989), cert denied 110 S. Ct. 1510 (1990).
54. *Vander Malle v. Ambach,* 667 F.Supp. 1015 (S.D.N.Y. 1987).
55. *McKenzie v. Smith* 1985; *King v. Pine Plains Central School District,* 771 F.2d 1527 (D.C.Cir. 1985).
56. *Ciresoli v. Maine School Administrative District,* 901 F.Supp. 378 (D.C.Me. 1995).
57. *Brown v. Wilson County School Board,* 747 F.Supp. 436 (M.D.Tenn. 1990).
58. 20 U.S.C.A. §1412(5)(B) (West 1999).
59. *Daniel R.R. v. State Board of Education,* 874 F.2d 1036 (5th Cir. 1989), *D.F. v. Western School Corporation,* 921 F.Supp. 559 (S.D. Ind. 1996), *Carter v. Florence County School District Four,* 950 F.2d 156 (4th Cir. 1991), *sub nom aff'd Florence County School District Four v. Carter,* 114 S. Ct. 361 (1993).
60. *Mavis v. Sobol,* 839 F.Supp 968 (N.D.N.Y. 1993).
61. *Daniel R.R. v. State Board of Education; Liscio v. Woodland Hills School District,* 734 F.Supp 689 (W.D.Pa. 1989), aff'd 902 F.2d 1561 (3rd Cir. 1990).
62. *Campbell v. Talladega County Board of Education,* 518 F.Supp. 47 (N.D.Ala. 1981).
63. *Roland M. v Concord School Committee,* 910 F.2d 983 (1st Cir. 1990), cert denied 111 S. Ct. 1122 (1991).
64. *Mavis v. Sobol.*
65. *Board of Education v. Illinois State Board of Education,* 41 F.3d 1162 (7th Cir. 1994).
66. *Capistrano Unified School District v. Wartenberg,* 59 F.3d 884 (9th Cir. 1995); *St. Louis Developmental Disabilities Treatment Center Parents Association v. Mallory,* 591 F.Supp. 1416 (W.D.Mo. 1984), aff'd 767 F.2d 518 (8th Cir. 1985).
67. *Learning Disabilities Association of Maryland, Inc. v. Board of Education of Baltimore County,* 837 F.Supp 717 (D.Md. 1993). *Farrell v. Carol Stream School District No. 25,* 1996 WL 364743, (N.D.Ill. 1996).
68. *Hall v. Shawnee Mission School District,* 856 F.Supp 1521 (D.C.Kan. 1994).
69. 34 CFR §300.519 (West 1999).
70. 34 CFR §300.520 (West 1999).
71. 20 U.S.C.A. §1415 (West 1999).
72. *Doe by & Through Doe v. Board of Education,* 15 A.D.D. 475 (N.D.Ill. 1996).
73. 20 U.S.C.A. §1415(a)-(d)(4) (West 1999).
74. Discretionary grant programs for infants and toddlers, from birth through age two,

are described at 20 U.S.C. §1471; for those aged three to five, including two-year-olds who will turn three during the school year, see 20 U.S.C §1419; and for children through age eight, at 20 U.S.C §1423.

75. 20 U.S.C.A. §1451 (West 1999).

CHAPTER SEVENTEEN

1. See David J. Rothman and Sheila M. Rothman, *The Willowbrook Wars* (New York: Harper and Row, 1984); Philip J. Cooper, *Hard Judicial Choices: Federal Court Orders and State and Local Officials* (New York: Oxford University Press, 1988); Michael A. Rebell and Arthur R. Block, *Educational Policy Making and the Courts: An Empirical Study of Judicial Activism* (Chicago: University of Chicago Press, 1982); Theodore J. Stein, "Issues in the Development, Implementation and Monitoring of Consent Decrees and Court Orders," *Public Law Review* 6 (1987): 141–160.

2. Theodore J. Stein, *Child Welfare and the Law* (Washington, D.C.: Child Welfare League of America, 1998), ch. 7.

3. Ibid.

4. *Wyatt v. Stickney,* 334 F. Supp. 1341 (M.D.Ala. 1971); 344 F. Supp. 373 (1972) aff'd in part, rev'd in part, *sub nom Wyatt v. Aderholt,* 503 F.2d 1305 (5th Cir. 1974).

5. Eugene Bardach, *The Implementation Game* (Cambridge, Mass.: MIT Press, 1977), 38–40.

6. 20 US.C.A. §8901 (West 1999).

7. Theodore J. Stein, *The Social Welfare of Women and Children with HIV and AIDS: Legal Protections, Policies and Programs* (New York: Oxford University Press, 1998), ch. 6.

8. Data describing teenage sexual behavior and condom use is compiled by the Center's for Disease Control's Youth Risk Behavior Survey. These data are available at http://www.cdc.gov/nccdphp/dash/yrbs/trend/htm.

9. For a review of this literature, see Theodore J. Stein, Eileen D. Gambrill, and Kermit Wiltse, *Children in Foster Care: Achieving Continuity-in-Care* (New York: Praeger, 1978).

10. 42 US.C.A. §675(1) (West 1999).

11. *Connecticut Department of Children and Youth Services v. Department of Health and Human Services,* 788 F. Supp. 573 (D.C.C. 1992), aff'd 9 F.3d 981 (1993).

12. U.S. General Accounting Office, *Medicaid and Special Education: Coordination of Services for Children with Disabilities Is Evolving,* GAO/HEHS-00-20 (Washington, D.C., 2000), 3.

13. Executive Order No. 156: codified at 9 NYCRR §4.156 (1999).

14. Susan J. Popkin and Mary K. Cunningham, *CHAC Section 8 Program: Barriers to Successful Leasing Up* (Washington, D.C.: Urban Institute, 1999).

15. Sylvia A. Law, "Symposium: The Legacy of *Goldberg v. Kelly:* A Twenty Year Perspective: Some Reflections on *Goldberg v. Kelly* at Twenty Years," *Brooklyn Law Review* 56 (1990): 805.

16. *Parrish v. Civil Service Commission,* 425 P.2d. 223 (1967).

17. *King v. Alabama,* 392 U.S. 309 (1968).

18. *Goldberg v. Kelly,* 25 L.Ed.2d 287 (1970).

19. *Beno v. Shalala,* 30 F.3d 1057 (1994).

20. New York State Constitution, Article 1, XVII, provides for the social welfare of the citizens of the state. New York administrative law (18 N.Y.C.R.R. §352.3) provides that "each social service district must provide a monthly allowance for rent . . . " and the regulations set maximums for each county. See *Jiggets v. Grinker,* 139 Misc.2d 476 (N.Y.Sup. 1988), rev'd, 543 N.Y.S.2d 414 (N.Y.A.D. 1989), rev'd 75 N.Y.2d 411 (N.Y. 1990), aff'd 689 N.Y.S.2d 482 (N.Y.A.D. 1999).

21. *Aliessa v. Whalen*, 694 N.Y.S.2d 308 (S.Ct.N.Y.Cty. 1999).

22. *City of Chicago v. Shalala*, 189 F.3d 598 (7th Cir. 1999).

23. *Saenz v. Roe*, 119 S. Ct. 1518 (1999).

24. Rob Geen and Karen C. Tumlin, *State Efforts to Remake Child Welfare: Responses to New Challenges and Increased Scrutiny* (Washington, D.C.: Urban Institute, 1999), 11.

25. Suits against state child welfare agencies generally allege that children are being denied services required by the AACWA and that denial of statutorily required services violates children's rights under the federal Constitution and federal and state statutes.

26. *Suter v. Artist*, 112 S. Ct. 1155 (1992).

27. Congress is free to overrule a ruling of the Supreme Court that rests on an interpretation of a congressional act. This freedom does not extend to interpretations of the federal Constitution. The congressional act overturning the Court is found at Public Law 103-432, codified at 108 Stat 4398, 103rd Cong., 2nd sess. (1994).

28. Robert T. Nakamura and Frank Smallwood, *The Politics of Policy Implementation* (New York: St. Martin's Press, 1980), 47.

29. Ibid.

30. Theodore J. Stein and Tina L. Rzepnicki, *Decision Making in Child Welfare Services: Intake and Planning* (Boston: Kluwer-Nijhoff Publishing, 1984).

31. Michelle Van Leeuwen, "The Politics of Adoptions Across Borders: Whose Interests Are Served?" *Pacific Rim Law and Policy Journal* 8 (1999): 218, note 45.

32. U.S. General Accounting Office, *Foster Care: Implementation of the Multiethnic Placement Act Poses Difficult Challenges*, GAO/HEHS-98-204 (Washington, D.C., 1998).

33. *Wilder v. Bernstein*, Opinion and Order, 78 Civ. 957(RJW). October 1986: 20.

34. Theodore J. Stein, *Wilder v. Bernstein: An Investigation into the Practices of New York City's Child Welfare Administration and Their Effect on the Implementation of the Wilder Settlement* (New York: American Civil Liberties Union Foundation, Children's Rights Project, 1990).

35. Robert A. Burt, "Pennhurst: A Parable," in R. H. Mnookin, ed., *In the Interest of Children: Advocacy, Law Reform and Public Policy,* 364 (New York: W. H. Freeman, 1985).

CHAPTER EIGHTEEN

1. Bruce S. Jansson, *Becoming an Effective Policy Advocate: From Policy Practice to Social Justice* (Pacific Grove, Calif.: Brooks/Cole, 1999), 10.

2. See, for example, Jansson, *Becoming an Effective Policy Advocate;* Edward Fitzgerald and John McNutt, "Electronic Advocacy in Policy Practice: A Framework for Teaching Technologically Based Practice," *Journal of Social Work Education* 35, 3(1999): 331–341; Cynthia J. Rocha and Alice K. Johnson, "Teaching Family Policy Through a Policy Practice Framework" *Journal of Social Work Education* 33, 3 (1997): 433–445; Demetrius S. Iatridis, "Policy Practice," in Richard L. Edwards, June G. Hopps, Diana M. DiNitto, and others, eds., *Encyclopedia of Social Work*, 19th ed., vol. 3, 1855–1866 (Washington, D.C.: National Association of Social Workers); Josefina Figueira-McDonough, "Policy Practice: The Neglected Side of Social Work Intervention," *Social Work* 38, 2 (1993): 179–188; Norman L. Wyers, "Policy Practice in Social Work: Models and Issues," *Journal of Social Work Education* 27, 3 (1991): 241–250.

3. www.statepolicy.org

4. National Association of Social Workers, *Code of Ethics,* "Standard 5: Social Workers' Ethical Responsibilities to the Social Work Profession," (Washington, D.C.: National Association of Social Workers, 1998).

5. Ibid.

6. In 1998, a federal district court considered whether a suit could be brought against the city under a Civil War Era statute that allows the federal government to sue a

"person" who files a false claim and receives triple damages if successful. The only question before the court was whether the city was a "person" for purposes of the suit. There was no direct testimony to prove or disprove the social worker's claims that she had tried to settle the matter within the agency. Thus, references to her behavior are phrased as "alleged" or "purported" actions. *United States v. City of New York*, 8 F.Supp.2d 343 (S.D.N.Y. 1998).

7. The social worker received 10 percent of the settlement ($4.9 million). See Nina Bernstein, "City and State to Pay $49 Million to Settle Foster-Care Fraud Suit," *New York Times*, Wednesday, November 11, 1998, B2; Pete Bowles, "Whistle-Blower Gets $4.9M," *Newsday*, Wednesday, November 11, 1998.

8. Federal law is found at 31 U.S.C.A. §3730(h) (West 1999); for examples of state laws, see McKinney's Civil Service Law of New York State, §75-b (West 1999); CA-ST-ANN, §8547 (West 1999–2000); AS-St-ANN, §39.90.100 (West 1999); Hawaii Revised Statutes, §378-61 (Matthew Bender & Co. 1999); IL-ST-ANN, §175/1 (West 1999); LA-ST-ANN, §440.3 (West 1999).

9. Whether the entire database contained in Westlaw or Lexis is available will vary according to the institutional subscription.

10. Elaine M. Ryan, *Financing Child Welfare Services Under TANF* (Washington, D.C.: American Public Human Services Association).

11. 64 *Federal Register* 17720 (April 12, 1999).

12. See Sylvia A. Law, "Symposium: The Legacy of *Goldberg v. Kelly*: A Twenty Year Perspective: Some Reflections on *Goldberg v. Kelly* at Twenty Years," *Brooklyn Law Review* 56 (1990): 805; Over the years, working on class action litigation against state child welfare agencies, I have met with social workers who provided information to further litigation against their employing agencies. In each case, the workers were reacting out of frustration with the unchanging nature of public bureaucracies and an unwillingness of administrators and others to listen to their pleas on behalf of clients.

13. Richard A. Merrill, "The Architecture of Government Regulation of Medical Products," *Virginia Law Review* 82 (1996): 1753–1866.

Bibliography

Abbott, Edith. 1963. *Some American Pioneers in Social Welfare.* New York: Russell and Russell.

Abbott, Grace. 1938. *The Child and the State.* Chicago: University of Chicago Press.

Abt Associates, Inc. 1996. *Evaluation of the HOPE 3 Program: Final Report.* Rockville, MD: U.S. Department of Housing and Urban Development.

Ackerman, Bruce and Golove, David. 1995. "Is NAFTA Constitutional?" *Harvard Law Review* 108.

Administration on Aging. 1999. *Elderly Nutrition Program.* Washington, D.C.: U.S. Department of Health and Human Services.

Advisory Council on Social Security. 1997. *Report of the 1994–1996 Advisory Council on Social Security,* vol. 1, app. 2. Washington, D.C.

Anderson, James E. 1997. *Public Policymaking.* 3rd ed. New York: Houghton Mifflin.

Angel, Marina. 1988. "Women in Legal Education: What It's Like to be Part of a Perpetual First Wave or the Case of the Disappearing Women." *Temple Law Review* 61.

Apple, R. W. Jr. 1996. "Politics: The Issues—Interview with Newt Gingrich." *New York Times,* June 25, sect. A, p. 18, col. 1.

Atkinson, Matthew. 1998. "Red Tape: How American Laws Ensnare Native American Lands, Resources, and People." *Oklahoma City University Law Review* 23.

Bachman, Sara S. 1996. "Why Do States Privatize Mental Health Services? Six State Experiences." *Journal of Health Politics, Policy and Law* 21.

Backer, Larry Cata. 1995. "Medieval Poor Law in Twentieth Century America: Looking Back Towards a General Theory of Modern American Poor Relief." *Case Western Reserve Law Review* 44.

Backstrom, Charles and Leonard Robins. 1995. "State AIDS Policy Making: Perspective of Legislative Health Committee Chairs." *AIDS and Public Policy Journal* 10.

Baker, Joe. 1998. *Medicare HMOs and the Medicare + Choice Program.* Document No. FO-OOO1Z. New York: Practicing Law Institute.

Baldauf, Scott. 1998. "Do Homosexuals Need More Legal Protection?" *Christian Science Monitor,* October 14, p. 3.

Bane, Mary Jo and David T. Ellwood. 1994. *Welfare Realities: From Rhetoric to Reform.* Cambridge, Mass: Harvard University Press.

Banfield, Edward C. 1974. *The Unheavenly City.* Boston: Little, Brown.

Bardach, Eugene. 1977. *The Implementation Game: What Happens After a Bill Becomes Law.* Cambridge, Mass: MIT Press.

Bartley, Richard. 1996. "Public-Private Relationships and Performance in Service Provision." *Urban Studies* 33 (4/5).

Bayer, Alexi. 1996. "The Survival of the Most Efficient." *New York Times,* December 8, sect. 3, p. 14.

Bearden, Diana Joseph and Bryan J. Maedgen. 1995. "Emerging Theories of Liability in the Managed Health Care Industry." *Baylor Law Review* 47.

Bell, Winifred. 1965. *Aid to Dependent Children.* New York: Columbia University Press.

Berke, Richard L. 1998. "The Nation: Chasing the Polls On Gay Rights." *New York Times,* August 2, Week in Review.

Berlin, Gordon L. 2000. *Encouraging Work Reducing Poverty: The Impact of Work Incentive Programs.* New York: Manpower Demonstration Research Corporation.

Bernstein, Nina. 1998. "Illness, a New Baby, and Then a Struggle for Assistance." *New York Times,* August 17, sect. B, p. 4.

Bernstein, Nina. 1998. "City and State to Pay $49 Million to Settle Foster-Care Fraud Suit." *New York Times,* November 11, sect. B, p. 2.

Besharov, D. J. 1986 "Child Abuse: Arrest and Prosecution Decision Making." *American Criminal Law Review* 24.

Bingham, Stephen. 1995. "Replace Welfare for Contingent Workers with Unemployment Compensation." *Fordham Urban Law Journal* 22.

Bloom, Dan. 1999. *The Cross-State Study of Time-Limited Welfare: An Interim Report Card.* New York: Manpower Demonstration Research Corporation.

Blum, John D. 1998. "Symposium on Health Care Policy: What Lessons Have We Learned from the AIDS Pandemic: Safeguarding the Interests of People with AIDS in Managed Care Settings." *Albany Law Review* 61.

Bodenheimer, Thomas. 1997. "The Oregon Health Plan: Lessons for the Nation." Parts 1 and 2. *New England Journal of Medicine* 337.

Boris, Elizabeth T. and C. Eugene Steuerle. 1999. *Nonprofits and Government: Collaboration and Conflict.* Washington, D.C.: Urban Institute.

Bowles, Pete. 1998. "Whistle-Blower Gets $4.9M." *Newsday,* November 11.

Braun, Kathryn L. and Christopher R. Conybeare. 1995. "Health Scope: A Model for a Low Cost Health Education Program Using Commercial Television." *Public Health Reports.* Washington, D.C.: U.S. Department of Health and Human Services.

Brauner, Saran and Pamela Loprest. 1999. *Where Are They Now? What States' Studies of People Who Left Welfare Tell Us.* Washington, D.C.: Urban Institute.

Bremmer, Robert H. and others. 1970. *Children and Youth in America: A Documentary History: Volume I: 1600–1865.* Cambridge, Mass.: Harvard University Press.

Bremmer, Robert H. and others. 1970. *Children and Youth in America: A Documentary History: Volume II: 1866–1932.* Cambridge, Mass.: Harvard University Press.

Brooke, James. 1998. "Gay Man Dies from Attack, Fanning Outrage and Debate." *New York Times,* October 12, sect. A., col. 1.

Brown, Amy. 1997. *Work First: How to Implement an Employment-Focused Approach to Welfare Reform.* New York: Manpower Demonstration Research Corporation.

Bruen, Brian K. and Frank Ullman. 1998. *Children's Health Insurance Programs: Where States Are, Where They Are Headed?* Washington, D.C.: Urban Institute.

Bureau of Indian Affairs. 1994. "Procedures for Establishing That an American Indian Group Exists as an Indian Tribe" 25 C.F.R. Part 83.

Burt, Martha R., Adele V. Harrell, Lisa Jacobs Raymond, and others. 1999. *Evaluation of the*

STOP Formula Grants Under the Violence Against Women Act of 1994. Washington, D.C.: Urban Institute.

Burt, Martha and Aron Laudan. 2000. *American's Homeless II: Populations and Services*. Washington, D.C.: Urban Institute.

Burt, Robert A. 1985. "Pennhurst: A Parable." In R. H. Mnookin, ed., *In the Interest of Children: Advocacy, Law Reform and Public Policy*, 265–364. New York: W. H. Freeman.

Bush, Jonathan, A. 1993. "Free to Enslave: The Foundations of Colonial American Slave Law." *Yale Journal of Law and the Humanities* 5.

Butler, Paul, Robert S. Chang, Charles J. Cooper, and others. 1996. "Race Law and Justice: The Rehnquist Court and the American Dilemma." *American University Law Review* 45.

Caldeira, Gregory A. and John R. Wright. 1998. "Organized Interests and Agenda Setting in the U.S. Supreme Court." *American Political Science Review* 82.

Callahan, Daniel. 1992. "Rationing Health Care: Social, Political and Legal Perspectives." *American Journal of Law and Medicine* 18.

Campbell, Jennifer A. 1999. *Current Population Reports: Health Insurance Coverage 1998*. Washington, D.C.: U.S. Department of Commerce, U.S. Census Bureau.

Cardozo, Benjamin N. 1921. *The Nature of the Judicial Process*. New Haven: Yale University Press.

Carney, Joseph T. 1992. "American's Mentally Ill: Tormented Without Treatment." *George Mason University Civil Rights Law Journal* 3.

Carmody, Kelly and Stacy Dean. 1998. *New Federal Food Stamp Restoration for Legal Immigrants: Implications and Implementation Issues*. Washington, D.C.: Center on Budget and Policy Priorities.

Carter, Stephen L. 1991. *Reflections of an Affirmative Action Baby*. New York: Basic Books.

Casino, Bruce, J. 1988. "Federal Grants-in-Aid: Evolution, Crisis and Future." *Urban Lawyer* 20.

Centers for Disease Control and Prevention. 1995. *AIDS Surveillance in the Americas: Quarterly Report*. Washington, D.C.: U.S. Department of Health and Human Services.

Centers for Disease Control and Prevention. 1996. *Pregnancy Nutrition Surveillance Report*. Washington, D.C.: U.S. Department of Health and Human Services.

Centers for Disease Control and Prevention. 1999. *HIV/AIDS Surveillance Report: U.S. HIV and AIDS Cases Reported Through June 1999*. Washington, D.C.: U.S. Department of Health and Human Services.

Chemerinsky, Erwin. 1989. "The Supreme Court, 1988 Term: Foreword: The Vanishing Constitution." *Harvard Law Review* 103.

Chemerinsky, Erwin. 1998. "Evaluating Judicial Candidates." *Southern California Law Review* 71.

Children's Defense Fund. 1999. *Children Deserve a Fair Share of the Federal Budget Surplus*. Washington, D.C.

Children's Defense Fund. 1999. *Title XX on the Chopping Block Again!* Washington, D.C.

Chi, Keon S. and Cindy Jasper. 1998. *Private Practices: A Review of Privatization in State Government*. Lexington, Ky.: Council of State Governments.

Choundas, George P. 1995. "Neither Equal Nor Protected: The Invisible Law of Equal Protection, The Legal Invisibility of Its Gender-Based Victims." *Emory Law Journal* 44.

Christians, Allison, D. 1999. "Breaking the Subsidy Cycle: A Proposal for Affordable Housing." *Columbia Journal of Law and Social Problems* 32.

Clinton, William Jefferson. 1996. "The Welfare Bill." Reprinted in *New York Times*, August 2, sect. A, col. 1, p. 24.

Clinton, William Jefferson. 1996. "One Strike and You're Out—Guidelines." March 28, 1996. 1996 WL 139528.

Coats, Daniel. 1993. *Congressional Record*, Senate, Proceedings and Debates of the 103rd Cong., 1st sess.

Cobb, Roger W. and Charles D. Elder. 1972. *Participation in American Politics: The Dynamics of Agenda-Building*. Boston: Allyn and Bacon.

Cohen, David. 1997–98. "Democracy and the Intersection of Prisons, Racism and Capital: Review Essay." *National Black Law Journal* 15.

"Collective Bargaining: AMA Officials Take First Steps to Create National Physicians' Bargaining Unit." 1999. *BNA Health Care Daily*, June 25, D8.

Commission on Behavioral and Social Sciences. National Research Council. 1993. *The Social Impact of AIDS in the United States*. Washington, D.C.: National Academy Press.

Committee on Maintaining Privacy and Security in Health Care Applications. 1997. *For the Record: Protecting Electronic Health Information*. Washington, D.C.: National Academy of Press.

Conroy, Robert J. and Mark D. Brylski. "Access to Medical Records vs. Patient's Privacy Interests." *New Jersey Lawyer* 173 (December 1995): 25.

Cooper, Phillip J. 1988. *Hard Judicial Choices: Federal District Court Judges and State and Local Officials*. New York: Oxford University Press.

Costin, Lela B. 1983. *Two Sisters for Social Justice: A Biography of Grace and Edith Abbott*. Chicago: University of Illinois Press.

Council of State Governments. 1998. *The Book of the States: Volume 32*. Lexington, Ky: Council of State Governments.

Craver, Charles B. 1989. "The Application of the Age Discrimination in Employment Act to Persons Over Seventy." *George Washington Law Review* 58.

Cross, Raymond. 1998. "Sovereign Bargains, Indian Takings, and the Preservation of Indian Country in the Twenty-First Century." *Arizona Law Review* 40.

Currie, Janet and Thomas Duncan. 1995. "Does Head Start Make a Difference?" *American Economic Review* 85.

Dalaker, Joseph and Mary Naifeh. 1998. *Poverty in the United States: 1997*. Washington D.C.: U.S. Department of Commerce.

Daniel, Philip T. K. and Kyle Edward Timken. 1999. "The Rumors of My Death Have Been Exaggerated: Hopwood's Error in "Discarding" Bakke." *Journal of Law and Education*.

Darnell, Julie, Hye Sun Lee, Jonah Murdock, and others. 1999. *Medicaid and Welfare Reform: States' Use of the $500 Million Federal Fund*. Menlo Park, Calif.: Kaiser Commission on Medicaid and the Uninsured.

Davis, Allen F. 1967. *Spearheads for Reform: The Social Settlements and the Progressive Movement 1890–1914*. New York: Oxford University Press.

"The Democratic Platform: Excerpts From the Platform: A 'New Covenant' With Americans." *New York Times*, July 15, 1992, sect. A, p. 10, col. 1.

De Parle, Jason. 1996. "The Ellwoods: Mugged by Reality." *New York Times*, December 8, sect. 6, p. 64.

Derthick, Martha. 1979. *Policymaking for Social Security*. Washington, D.C.: Brookings Institute.

DiNitto, Diana, M. 1995. *Social Welfare: Politics and Public Policy*. 4th ed. Boston: Allyn and Bacon.

Doris, J., R. Mazur, and M. Thomas. 1995. "Training in Child Protective Services: A Commentary on the Amicus Brief of Bruck and Ceci. *Psychology, Public Policy and Law* 1.

Downs, Anthony. 1972. "Up and Down with Ecology: The Issue-Attention Cycle." *Public Interest* 28.

Dworkin, Ronald. 1985. *A Matter of Principle*. Cambridge: Harvard University Press.

Dye, Thomas, R. 1998. *Understanding Public Policy*. 9th ed. New Jersey: Prentice-Hall.

Economic Classification Policy Committee. 1999. *New Data for a New Economy*. Washington, D.C.: U.S. Department of Labor.

Editorial Board. 1996. "Federalism: Intergovernmental Relations—Congress Requires a

Separate, Recorded Vote for any Provision Establishing an Unfunded Mandate." *Harvard Law Review* 109.

Edson, Charles L. and Richard M. Price. 1998. "Mark-to-Market: HUD Reengineers its Multi-Family Portfolio." *Probate and Property* 12.

Ellis, Eileen R. and Vernon K. Smith. 2000. *Medicaid Enrollment in 21 States: June 1997 to June 1999.* Lansing, Mich.: Health Management Associates.

Ellwood, Marilyn. 1999. *The Medicaid Eligibility Maze: Coverage Expands, but Enrollment Problems Persist: Findings from a Five-State Study.* Washington, D.C.: Urban Institute.

Elwood, Paul. 1993. "Interview." *Hospitals* 67.

Ely, James W. Jr. and David J. Bodenheimer. 1986. "Regionalism and American Legal History: The Southern Experience." *Vanderbilt Law Review* 39.

Equal Employment Opportunity Commission. 1999. *Enforcement Guidance: Vicarious Employer Liability for Unlawful Harassment by Supervisors.* Washington, D.C.

Estrada, Lisa. "Buying the Status Quo on Affirmative Action: The Piscataway Settlement and Its Lessons About Interest Group Path Manipulation." *George Mason University Civil Rights Law Journal.*

Fagnoni, Cynthia M. 1999. *Foster Care: Challenges in Helping Youths Live Independently.* GAO/T-HEHS-99-121. Washington, D.C.

Fetmann, Eric. 1999. "The Problem Isn't Housing—It's Letting Madmen Roam Free." *New York Post,* January 10, 1999.

Field, Martha A. 1986. "Sources of Law: The Scope of Federal Common Law." *Harvard Law Review* 99.

Finkelman, Paul. 1993. "Symposium: Race Relations and the United States Constitution: From Fugitive Slaves to Affirmative Action: Sorting Out *Prigg v. Pennsylvania.*" *Rutgers Law Journal* 24.

Flores, Kimura and Toby Douglas. 1998. *The Children's Budget Report: A Detailed Analysis of Spending on Low-Income Children's Programs in 13 States.* Washington, D.C.: Urban Institute.

Figueira-McDonough, Josefina. 1993. "Policy Practice: The Neglected Side of Social Work Intervention." *Social Work* 38.

Fitzgerald, Edward and John McNutt. 1999. "Electronic Advocacy in Policy Practice: A Framework for Teaching Technologically Based Practice." *Journal of Social Work Education* 35.

Food and Nutrition Services. 1999. *Food Stamps: Income, Resources and Deductibles.* Washington, D.C.: U.S. Department of Agriculture.

Food and Nutrition Services. 1999. *State-Funded Food Programs for Legal Immigrants.* Washington, D.C.: U.S. Department of Agriculture.

Food and Nutrition Services. 1999. *WIC Farmers' Market Nutrition Program.* Washington, D.C.: U.S. Department of Agriculture.

Foster, Scott, Althea Gregory, Piet Niederhausen, and others. 1998. *Federal HIV/AIDS Spending: A Budget Chartbook.* Menlo Park, Calif.: Kaiser Family Foundation.

Freedman, Eric M. 1996. "A Lot More Comes Into Focus When You Remove the Lens Cap: Why Proliferating New Communications Techniques Make it Particularly Urgent for the Supreme Court to Abandon its Inside-Out Approach to Freedom of Speech and Bring Obscenity, Fighting Words, and Group Libel within the First Amendment." *Iowa Law Review* 81.

Friedman, Thomas L. 1993. "Gay Rights in the Military: Chiefs Back Clinton on Gay-Troop Plan; President Admits Revised Policy Isn't Perfect." *New York Times,* July 20, sect. A, col. 1.

Geen, Rob and Karen C. Tumlin. 1999. *State Efforts to Remake Child Welfare: Responses to New Challenges and Increased Scrutiny.* Washington, D.C.: Urban Institute.

Geringer, R. 1999. "Awareness Rose, Despite Failure to Pass Bias Crimes Law." *Associated Press,* Sunday, February 7.

Glass Ceiling Commission. 1995. *A Solid Investment: Making Full Use of the Nation's Human Capital.* Washington, D.C.

Glass Ceiling Commission. 1995. *Good for Business: Making Full Use of the Nation's Human Capital.* Washington, D.C.

Goldman, Maurice. 1999. "The Violence Against Women Act: Meeting Its Goal in Protecting Battered Women." *Family and Conciliation Courts Review* 37.

Gibelman, Margaret and Philip H. Schervish. 1997. *Who We Are: A Second Look.* Washington, D.C.: National Association of Social Workers.

Ginsburg, Alan L. 1999. *Title I Education Funding.* Testimony before the House Committee on Education and the Workforce. 1999 WL 16946013.

Glazer, Nathan. 1990. *The Limits of Social Policy.* Cambridge, Mass.: Harvard University Press.

Gouvin, Eric J. 1994. "Truth in Savings and the Failure of Legislative Methodology." *Cincinnati Law Review* 62.

Gray, Virginia, Russell L. Hanson, and Herbert Jacob. 1999. *Politics in the American States: A Comparative Analysis.* Washington, D.C.: Congressional Quarterly Press.

Greve, Michael S. 1996. "Hopwood and Its Consequences." *Pace Law Review* 17.

Griswold del Castillo, Richard. 1998. "Symposium: Manifest Destiny: The Mexican-American War and the Treaty of Guadalupe Hidalgo." *Southwestern Journal of Law and Trade in the Americas* 5.

Grob, Gerald N. 1994. "Government and Mental Health Policy. A Structural Analysis." *Milbank Quarterly* 72.

Gueron, Judith M. 1999. *Welfare Time Limits: An Interim Report Card.* New York: Manpower Demonstration Research Corporation.

Gutierrez, Fernando J. 1996. "Who Is Watching Big Brother When Big Brother Is Watching Mental Health Professionals: A Call for the Evolution of Mental Health Advocacy Programs." *Law and Psychology Review* 20.

Hacker, Jacob S. 1997. *The Road to Nowhere: The Genesis of President Clinton's Plan for Health Security.* New Jersey: Princeton University Press.

Hagen, Jan L., and Irene Lurie. 1993. "The Job Opportunities and Basic Skills Training Program and Child Care: Initial State Developments." *Social Service Review* 67.

Halpern, Robert. 1995. *Rebuilding the Inner City: A History of Neighborhood Initiatives to Address Poverty in the United States.* New York: Columbia University Press.

Hamilton, Gayle, Thomas Brock, Mary Farrell, and others. 1997. *Evaluating Two Welfare-to-Work Program Approaches: Two-Year Findings on the Labor Force Attachment and Human Capital Development Programs in Three Sites.* New York: Manpower Demonstration Research Corporation.

Hannaway, Jane and Kristi Kimball. 1997. *Reports on Reform from the Field: District and State Survey Results.* Washington, D.C.: Urban Institute.

Harrison, Lawrence. 1993. "A Dream Not Really Deferred: America Is Quietly Getting Closer to Martin Luther King's Vision." *Washington Post,* January 17, sect. C, p. 5.

"Hate Crimes Legislation Is Defeated in Wyoming." 1999. Houston Chronicle, Thursday, February 4.

Hate Crimes Statistics Act. Public Law 101-275 as amended 110 Stat. 1394 (July 1996).

Hawke, Constance. 1999. "Reframing the Rationale for Affirmative Action in Higher Education." *West's Education Law Reporter.*

Hays, Scott P. and Henry R. Glick. 1997. "The Role of Agenda Setting in Policy Innovation." *American Politics Quarterly* 25.

Health Care Financing Administration. 1998. *Medicare: Medical Savings Accounts.* Publication

No. HCFA 02-02137. Washington, D.C.: U.S. Department of Health and Human Services.

Heisey, Geoffrey C. 1998. "Oliphant and Tribal Criminal Jurisdiction Over Non-Indians: Asserting Congress's Plenary Power to Restore Territorial Jurisdiction." *Indiana Law Journal* 73.

Herbert, Bob. 1996. "In America; The Real Welfare Cheats." *New York Times*, April 26, sect. A, p. 31.

Hermann, John R. 1997. "American Indian Interests and Supreme Court Agenda Setting." *American Politics Quarterly* 25.

Hernandez, Raymond. 1996. "New York Gets Big Windfall from Welfare." *New York Times*, February 9.

Higginbotham, A. Leon Jr. and F. Michael Higginbotham. 1993. "Yearning to Breathe Free: Legal Barriers Against and Options in Favor of Liberty in Antebellum Virginia." *New York University Law Review* 68.

Hirschfelder, Arlene and Martha K. de Montano. 1993. *The Native American Almanac: A Portrait of Native America Today*. New York: Macmillan.

Hoffman, Catherine. 1998. *Uninsured in America*. Washington, D.C.: Henry J. Kaiser Family Foundation.

Hofstadter, Richard. 1992. *Social Darwinism in American Thought*. Boston: Beacon Press.

Holahan, John, Teresa Coughlin, Korbin Liu, and others. 1995. *Cutting Medicaid Spending in Response to Budget Caps*. Washington, D.C.: Urban Institute.

Holahan, John, Suresh Rangarajan, and Matthew Schirmer. 1999. *Medicaid Managed Care Payment Methods and Capitation Rates: Results of a National Survey*. Occupational Paper No. 26. Washington, D.C.: Urban Institute.

Holmes, Oliver W. 1881. *The Common Law*. New York: Dover.

Holmes, Oliver W. 1881. "The Path of the Law." *Harvard Law Review*.

Holy, Alexandra New. 1998. "The Heart of Everything That Is: PAHA SAPA, Treaties, and Lakota Identity." *Oklahoma City University Law Review* 23.

Hunter-Manns, Jo Anna and Dan Bloom. 1999. *Connecticut Post-Time Limit Tracking Study: Six-Month Survey Results*. New York: Manpower Demonstration Research Corporation.

Iatridis, Demetrius S. 1995. "Policy Practice." In Richard L. Edwards, June G. Hopps, Diana M. DiNitto and others, eds., *Encyclopedia of Social Work*. 19th ed., vol. 3. Washington, D.C.: National Association of Social Workers.

Iglehart, John K. 1999. "The American Health Care System—Expenditures." *New England Journal of Medicine* 340.

Iyengar, Shanto, Mark C. Peters, and Donald R. Kinder. 1982. "Experimental Demonstrations of the 'Not-So-Minimal' Consequences of Television News Programs." *American Political Science Review* 76.

Jacob, Julie. 1997. "Oxford Losses Raise Concerns for Industry's Staying Power." *American Medical News* 40.

Jacobs, Lawrence, Theodore Marmor, and Jonathan Oberlander. 1999. "The Oregon Health Plan and the Political Paradox of Rationing: What Advocates and Critics Have Claimed and What Oregon Did." *Journal of Health Politics, Policy and Law* 24.

Jansson, Bruce S. 1993. *The Reluctant Welfare State: A History of American Social Welfare Policies*. 2nd ed. Pacific Grove, Calif.: Brooks/Cole.

Jansson, Bruce S. 1999. *Becoming an Effective Policy Advocate: From Policy Practice to Social Justice*. Pacific Grove, Calif.: Brooks/Cole.

Johnson, Fawn H. 1999. "Conference Report: OFCCP: New Review Process Gives Small Agency Powerful Enforcement Tools Over Contractors." *BNA Labor Reporter* 157 (August 16).

Johnson, Nancy L. and Katherine Ryan Sullivan. 1997. "Long-Term Care Financing: Federal Policy Implications, Actions, and Options." *Quinnipiac Health Law Journal* 1.

Johnson, Nicholas and Ed Lazere. 1998. *Rising Number of States Offer Earned Income Tax Credits.* Washington, D.C.: Center on Budget and Policy Priorities.

Justice Research and Statistics Association. 1996. *Domestic and Sexual Violence Data Collection: A Report to Congress Under the Violence Against Women Act.* Washington, D.C.: National Institute of Justice, Bureau of Justice Statistics.

Kaczorowski, Robert J. 1986. "Revolutionary Constitutionalism in the Era of the Civil War and Reconstruction." *New York University Law Review* 61.

Kaczorowski, Robert J. 1995. "Federal Enforcement of Civil Rights During the First Reconstruction." *Fordham Urban Journal* 23.

Kaduboski, Mark S. 1997. "A Skirmish in the Battle for the Soul of Massachusetts State Government: Privatization of Government Services and the Constitutionality of Appropriation Restriction Measures." *Boston College Law Review* 38.

Kahlenberg, Richard D. 1996. *The Remedy: Class, Race, and Affirmative Action.* Cambridge, Mass.: Harvard University Press.

Kaiser Family Foundation/Harvard University School of Public Health. 1999. *Survey of Physicians and Nurses.* Menlo Part, Calif.: Henry J. Kaiser Family Foundation.

Kelly, Michael. 1998. "Outlaw Deeds, Not Thoughts." *New York Post,* October 14, Opinion, p. 29.

Kaye, Judith S. 1995. "Brennan Lecture: State Courts at the Dawn of a New Century: Common Law Courts Reading Statutes and Constitutions." *New York University Law Review* 70.

Kearon, William G. 1990. "Deinstitutionalization, Street Children, and the Coming AIDS Epidemic in the Adolescent Population." *Juvenile and Family Court Journal* 41.

Kelso, R. Randall and Charles D. Kelso. 1996. "How the Supreme Court Is Dealing with Precedents in Constitutional Cases." *Brooklyn Law Review* 62.

Kennedy, Shawn G. 1992. "Housing List in New York Hits Record." *New York Times,* December 27, sect. C, p. 31.

Kilborn, Peter T. 1998. "Voters' Anger at H.M.O.'s Plays as Hot Political Issue." *New York Times,* May 17, sect. A, p. 1.

Kilcullen, Jack, K. 1996. "Groping for the Reins: ERISA, HMO Malpractice, and Enterprise Liability." *American Journal of Law and Medicine* 22.

Killmer, Darold W. and Mari Newman. 1999. "VAWA: A Civil Rights Tool for Victims of Gender-Motivated Violence." *Colorado Lawyer* 28.

Kingdon, John W. 1995. *Agendas, Alternatives, and Public Policies.* 2nd. ed. New York: Addison-Wesley.

Kingsely, Thomas G. 1999. *Federal Housing Assistance and Welfare Reform: Uncharted Territory.* Washington, D.C.: Urban Institute.

Klein, Catherine F. and Leslye E. Orloff. 1993. "Providing Legal Protection for Battered Women: An Analysis of State Statutes and Case Law." *Hofstra Law Review* 21.

Knox, Virginia, Cynthia Miller, and Lisa A. Gennetian. 2000. *Reforming Welfare and Rewarding Work: A Summary of the Final Report on the Minnesota Family Investment Program.* New York: Manpower Demonstration Research Corporation.

Koehn, Melissa L. 1997. "Civil Jurisdiction: The Boundaries Between Federal and Tribal Courts." *Arizona State Law Journal* 10.

Kramer, Larry. 1996. "What's a Constitution for Anyway? Of History and Theory, Bruce Ackerman and the New Deal." *Case Western Reserve Law Review* 46.

Krishnakumar, Anita S. 1998. "Reconciliation and the Fiscal Constitution: The Anatomy of the 1995–96 Budget 'Train Wreck.'" *Harvard Journal on Legislation* 35.

Ladowsky, Ellen. 1995. "That No White Male. . . . " *Wall Street Journal,* March 27, sect. A, p. 20.

Lamb, Richard H. and Linda E. Weinberger. 1998. "Persons with Severe Mental Illness in Jails and Prisons: A Review." *Psychiatric Services* 49.

Landis, Michele L. 1998. "Let Me Next Time be 'Tried by Fire': Disaster Relief and the Origins of the American Welfare State 1789–1874." *Northwestern University Law Review* 73.

Laschober, Mary A., Kathryn M. Langwell, Christopher Topoleski, and others. 1999. *How Medicare HMO Withdrawals Affect Beneficiary Benefits, Costs, and Continuity of Care.* Menlo Park, Calif.: Henry J. Kaiser Family Foundation.

Lauricella, Peter A. 1997. "The Real 'Contract with America': The Original Intent of the Tenth Amendment and the Commerce Clause." *Albany Law Review* 60.

Law, Sylvia A. 1990. "Symposium: The Legacy of *Goldberg v. Kelly:* A Twenty Year Perspective: Some Reflections on *Goldberg v. Kelly* at Twenty Years." *Brooklyn Law Review* 56.

Leiby, James. 1978. *A History of Social Welfare and Social Work in the United States.* New York: Columbia University Press.

Lerman, Robert I. 1998. Testimony before the Subcommittee on Oversight and Investigations. Committee on Education and the Workforce. U.S. House of Representatives.

Lerman, Robert I., Pamela Loprest, and Caroline Ratcliffe. 1999. *How Well Can Urban Labor Markets Absorb Welfare Recipients?* Paper No. A-33 in the series New Federalism: Issues and Options for the States. Washington, D.C.: Urban Institute.

Levin-Epstein, Jodie, ed. 1999. *A CLASP Report on Welfare Reform Developments.* Washington, D.C.: Center on Law and the Study of Social Policy.

Levinson, Sanford. 1993. Review of *Strategy, Jurisprudence, and Certiorari. Deciding to Decide: Agenda Setting in the United States Supreme Court,* by H. W. Perry Jr. *Virginia Law Review* 79.

Lewis, Oscar. 1961. *The Children of Sanchez.* New York: Random House.

Lewis, Oscar. 1966. "The Culture of Poverty." *Scientific American* 215.

Lieberman, Joseph. 1996. "Welfare as We Know It." *New York Times,* July 25, sect. A, col. 1, p. 23.

Lindblom, Charles E. 1968. *The Policy Making Process.* Englewood Cliffs, N.J.: Prentice-Hall.

Lipschultz, Sybil. 1989. "Social Feminism and Legal Discourse: 1908–1923." *Yale Journal of Law and Feminism* 2.

Lipsky, Michael and Marc A. Thibodeau. 1990. "Domestic Food Policy in the United States." *Journal of Health Politics, Policy and Law* 15.

Loprest, Pamela. 1999. *Families Who Left Welfare: Who Are They and How Are They Doing?* Washington, D.C.: Urban Institute.

Lubove, Roy. 1965. *The Professional Altruist: The Emergence of Social Work as a Career 1880–1930.* Cambridge, Mass.: Harvard University Press.

Luna, Guadalupe T. 1998. "En El Nombre De Dios Todo-Poderoso: The Treaty of Guadalupe Hidalgo and Narrativos Legales." *Southwestern Journal of Law and Trade in the Americas* 5.

Lutsky, Jeremy. 1997. "Is Your Physician Becoming a Teamster? The Rising Trend of Physicians Joining Labor Unions in the Late 1990s." *DePaul Journal of Health Care Law* 2.

Lutz, Robert E. 1998. "The Mexican War and the Treaty of Guadalupe Hidalgo: What's Best and Worst About Us?" *Southwestern Journal of Law and Trade in the Americas* 5.

Lyttle, Robert J. 1993. "Tribal Government." In Arlene Hirschfelder and Martha K. de Montano, eds., *The Native American Almanac: A Portrait of Native America Today.* New York: Macmillan.

Marshall, Thomas Humphrey. 1975. *Social Policy in the Twentieth Century.* 4th ed. London: Hutchinson.

Martini, Alberto and Michael Wiseman. 1997. *Explaining the Recent Decline in Welfare Caseloads: Is the Council of Economic Advisors Right?* Washington, D.C.: Urban Institute.

Maynard, Rebecca A., ed. 1997. *Kids Having Kids: Economic Costs and Social Consequences of Teen Pregnancy.* Washington, D.C.: Urban Institute.

McClain, Charles J. 1984. "The Chinese Struggle for Civil Rights in Nineteenth Century America: The First Phase, 1850–1870." *California Law Review* 72.

McClain, Charles J. 1995. "Tortuous Path, Elusive Goal: The Asian Quest for American Citizenship." *Asian Law Journal* 2.

McClain, Paula D. 1993. *Minority Group Influence: Agenda Setting, Formulation and Public Policy.* Westport, Conn.: Greenwood Press.

McCombs, M. E. and D. L. Shaw. 1972. "The Agenda-Setting Function of Mass Media." *Public Opinion Quarterly* 36.

McCombs, Maxwell E. 1993. "The Evolution of Agenda-Setting Research: Twenty-Five Years in the Marketplace of Ideas." *Journal of Communications* 43.

McGuire, Kevin T. and Gregory A. Caldeira. 1993. "Lawyers, Organized Interests, and the Law of Obscenity: Agenda Setting in the Supreme Court." *American Political Science Review* 87.

McKey, Ruth. 1985. *The Impact of Head Start on Children, Families, and Communities.* DHHS Publication No. (OHDS) 85-31193.

Meckler, Laura. 1999. "GOP Leaders Celebrate Welfare Success." *Associated Press,* May 27.

"Medicare: HCFA Report Warns HMOs Expected to Charge More Copayments for Drugs." 1999. *BNA Health Care Daily,* September 23.

Merrill, Richard A. 1996. "The Architecture of Government Regulation of Medical Products." *Virginia Law Review* 82.

Moon, Marilyn, Barbara Gage, and Alison Evans. 1997. *An Examination of Key Medicare Provisions in the Balanced Budget Act of 1997.* Washington, D.C.: Urban Institute.

Morris, Robert. 1985. *Social Policy of the American Welfare State: An Introduction to Policy Analysis.* 2nd ed. New York: Longman.

Murray, Charles. 1984. *Losing Ground.* New York: Basic Books.

Murray, Charles. 1994. Testimony before the Subcommittee on Human Resources of the Committee on Ways and Means, U. S. House of Representatives, July 29.

Nakamura, Robert T. and Frank Smallwood. 1980. *The Politics of Policy Implementation.* New York: St. Martin's Press.

National ADAP Monitoring Project: Annual Report. 1999. Menlo Park, Calif.: Kaiser Family Foundation.

National Association of Social Workers. 1998. *Code of Ethics.* Washington, D.C.: National Association of Social Workers.

National Voter Turnout in Federal Elections: 1960–1996. 1999. Washington, D.C.: Federal Election Commission.

Nelson, Barbara. 1984. *Making an Issue of Child Abuse: Political Agenda Setting for Social Problems.* Chicago: University of Chicago Press.

Newman, Sandra J. and Joseph Harkness. 1999. "The Effects of Welfare Reform on Housing: A National Analysis." In Sandra J. Newman, ed., *The Home Front: Implications of Welfare Reform for Housing Policy.* Washington, D.C.: Urban Institute.

Nickles, Don. 1999. "Policy Essay: Retiring in America: Why the United States Needs a New Kind of Social Security for the New Millennium." *Harvard Journal on Legislation* 36.

Nichols, Len M., Linda J. Blumberg, Gregory P. Acs, and others. 1997. *Small Employers: Their Diversity and Health Insurance.* Washington, D.C.: Urban Institute.

O'Looney, John. 1993. "Beyond Privatization and Service Integration: Organizational Models for Service Delivery." *Social Service Review* 67.

Office of Management and Budget. 1999. *Budget of the United States Government: Fiscal Year 2000.* Washington, D.C., March.

Office of Worker's Compensation Programs. 1997. *Annual Report to Congress, FY 1996.* Washington, D.C.: U.S. Department of Labor.

Panel on Poverty and Family Assistance. 1996. Committee on National Statistics of the National Research Council. *Measuring Poverty: A New Approach.* Washington, D.C.: National Academy Press.

Papavizas, Constantine G. and Norman F. Lent III. 1997. "Consumers and Providers Call for Regulation; The Managed Care Industry Would Disagree." *National Law Journal* 19.

Parrott, Sharon. 1998. *Welfare Recipients Who Find Jobs: What Do We Know About Their Employment and Earnings?* Washington, D.C.: Center on Budget and Policy Priorities.

Pavetti, LaDonna and Gregory Acs. 1997. *Moving Up, Moving Out or Going Nowhere? A Study of the Employment Patterns of Young Women.* Washington, D.C.: Urban Institute.

Pear, Robert. 1996. "Budget Agency Says Welfare Bill Would Cut Rolls by Millions." *New York Times,* July 16, sect. A, p. 12.

Pear, Robert. 1996. "Agreement Struck on Most Elements for Welfare Bill." *New York Times,* July 30, sect. A, p. 1.

Pear, Robert. 1997. "Move Under Way to Try to Block Health Care Bills." *New York Times,* November 4, sect. A, p. 1.

Pear, Robert. 1998. "Most States Meet Work Requirement of Welfare Law." *New York Times,* December 30, sect. C, p. 6.

Pear, Robert. 1999. "Non-Profit Groups Accused of Bilking Lunch Programs." *New York Times,* October 3, sect. C, p. 6.

Pear, Robert. 1999. "Series of Rulings Eases Constraints on Suing H.M.O.s." *New York Times,* August 15, sect. C, p. 6.

Perry, W. H. 1991. *Deciding to Decide: Agenda Setting in the United States Supreme Court.* Cambridge, Mass.: Harvard University Press.

Persily, Nathaniel, A. 1997. "The Peculiar Geography of Direct Democracy: Why the Initiative, Referendum and Recall Developed in the American West." *Michigan Law and Policy Review* 2.

Peters, Ellen Ash. 1982. "Common Law Judging in a Statutory World." *University of Pittsburgh Law Review* 42.

Petrila, John. 1996. "Ethics, Money, and the Problem of Coercion in Managed Behavioral Health Care." *Saint Louis University Law Journal* 40.

Piven, Frances Fox and Richard A. Cloward. 1971. *Regulating the Poor: The Functions of Public Welfare.* New York: Pantheon Books.

"The Police and Emotionally Disturbed People." 1999. *Time Magazine* 154.

Popkin, Susan J. and Mary K. Cunningham. 1999. *CHAC Section 8 Program: Barriers to Successful Leasing Up.* Washington, D.C.: Urban Institute.

Pildes, Richard, H. 1997. "Principled Limitations on Racial and Partisan Redistricting." *Yale Law Journal* 106.

"Quayle Distorts Democratic Platform on Gays." 1992. *New York Times,* October 9, sect. A, col. 4, p. 32.

Quigley, William P. 1997. "Rumblings of Reform: Northern Poor Relief Legislation in Antebellum America, 1820–1860." *Capital University Law Review* 26.

Quint, Peter E. 1981. "The Separation of Powers Under Nixon: Reflections on Constitutional Liberties and the Rule of Law." *Duke Law Journal.*

Rabin, Robert L. 1986. "Federal Regulation in Historical Perspective." *Stanford Law Review* 38.

Ramsey, Bruce C., James N. Broder, Anne J. Chiaviello, and others. 1993. "The Cranston-Gonzalez National Affordable Housing Act: An Overview." *Real Property, Probate and Trust Journal* 28.

Rebell, Michael A. and Arthur R. Block. 1982. *Educational Policy Making and the Courts: An Empirical Study of Judicial Activism.* Chicago: University of Chicago Press.

Rector, Robert. "Welfare Reforms Will Help Kids." *New York Newsday.* Reprinted in *Buffalo News, Viewpoints,* August 29, 1996, city ed., p. 3B.

Relman, Arnold S. 1993. "Controlling Costs by 'Managed Competition'—Would It Work?" *New England Journal of Medicine* 328.

Report of the Secretary of State. 1824. *Relief and Settlement of the Poor.* Reprinted in New York State Board of Charities, Annual Report for the Year 1900, vol. 1, 949–953, 1901.

Rivers, Caryl. 1996. "Ideas/Earth to Media: The Stable Family Is Alive." *New York Newsday,* June 2, sect. A, p. 44.

Rocha, Cynthia J. and Alice K. Johnson. 1997. "Teaching Family Policy Through a Policy Practice Framework." *Journal of Social Work Education* 33.

Rotello, Gabriel. 1992. "Democrats Give Gay Rights a Belated but Heartfelt Embrace." *New York Newsday,* July 14, p. 79.

Rothman, David J. 1971. *The Discovery of the Asylum: Social Order and Disorder in the New Republic.* Boston: Little, Brown.

Rothman, David J. and Sheila M. Rothman. 1984. *The Willowbrook Wars.* New York: Harper and Row.

Rouse, Beatrice A. *Statistics Source Book 1998.* Washington, D.C.: Substance Abuse and Mental Health Administration.

Ryan, Elaine M. 2000. *Financing Child Welfare Services Under TANF.* Washington, D.C.: American Public Human Services Association.

Ryan White Comprehensive AIDS Resources Emergency Act of 1990. Senate Report No. 273, 101st Cong., 2nd sess., 1990, 1990 U.S.C.C.A.N. 862, Public Law 101-381.

Saphir, Ann and Chris Rauber. 1999. "Medicaid HMOs Exit Markets." *Modern Health Care* 29.

Saul, Marnie S. 1999. *Senior Community Service Employment—Program Reauthorization Issues that Affect Serving Disadvantaged Seniors.* 1999 WL 527511. GAO/HEHS-99-126. Washington, D.C.

Schneider, Andy, Kristen Fennell, and P. Long. 1998. *Medicaid Eligibility for Families and Children,* part 4. Washington, D.C.: Kaiser Family Foundation.

Schneider, Andy, Kristen Fennell, and Patricia Keenan. 1999. *Medicaid and the Uninsured.* Washington, D.C.: Kaiser Commission.

Schwartz, Paul M. 1996. "The Protection of Privacy in Health Care Reform." *Vanderbilt Review* 48.

Scrivener, Susan, Gayle Hamilton, Mary Farrell, and others. 1998. *National Evaluation of Welfare-to-Work Strategies: Implementation, Participation Patterns, Costs, and Two-Year Impacts of the Portland (Oregon) Welfare-to-Work Program.* New York: Manpower Demonstration Research Corporation.

Shaw, Clay. 1996. "Supporting True Welfare Reform." *Cong. Rec.* 142 CR E857-01142. 104th Cong., 2nd sess.

Shaw, Clay. 1996. "Testimony before the House of Representatives Ways and Means Committee Concerning Poverty and Out-Of-Wedlock Births." 1996 WL 108745.

Shephard, Robert E. Jr. 1998. "How the Media Misrepresents Juvenile Policies." *Criminal Justice* 12.

Shilts, Randy. 1987. *And the Band Played On.* New York: St. Martin's.

Shinn, Marybeth and Beth Weitzman. 1998. "Predictors of Homelessness Among Families in New York City: From Shelter Request to Housing." *American Journal of Public Health* 88.

Skolnick, Arlene. 1991. *Embattled Paradise: The American Family in the Age of Uncertainty.* New York: Basic Books.

Slasich, Peter W. 1997. "Low Income Housing Crisis Has Not Disappeared." *Journal of Afford-able Housing and Community Development Law* 7.

Slaughter, Leslie. 1998. Testimony before the House of Representatives, Education Subcommittee. 1998 WL 210930.

Smith, Vernon K. *Enrollment Increases in State CHIP Programs: December 1998 to June 1999*. Lansing, Mich.: Health Management Associates, 1999.

Spencer, Gary. 1996. "Protection Order Abuse Elevated to Felony." *New York Law Journal* 216.

Stein, Theodore J. 1984. "The Child Abuse Prevention and Treatment Act." *Social Service Review* 58.

Stein, Theodore J. 1987. "Issues in the Development, Implementation and Monitoring of Consent Decrees and Court Orders." *Public Law Review* 6.

Stein, Theodore J. 1990. *Wilder v. Bernstein: An Investigation into the Practices of New York City's Child Welfare Administration and Their Effect on the Implementation of the Wilder Settlement*. New York: American Civil Liberties Union Foundation, Children's Rights Project.

Stein, Theodore J. 1998. *The Social Welfare of Women and Children with HIV and AIDS: Legal Protections, Policy, and Programs*. New York: Oxford University Press.

Stein, Theodore J. 1998. *Child Welfare and the Law*. Revised Edition. Washington, D.C.: Child Welfare League of America.

Stein, Theodore J., Eileen D. Gambrill, and Kermit Wiltse. 1978. *Children in Foster Care: Achieving Continuity-in-Care*. New York: Praeger.

Stein, Theodore J. and Tina L. Rzepnicki. 1984. *Decision Making in Child Welfare Services: Intake and Planning*. Boston: Kluwer-Nijhoff.

Steiner, Gilbert. 1966. *Social Insecurity: The Politics of Welfare*. Chicago: Rand McNally.

Steiner, Gilbert Y. 1971. *The State of Welfare*. Washington, D.C.: Brookings Institution.

Stirrup, Heidi. 1996. Testimony before the Committee on Finance of the United States Senate. "The National Governors' Association Recent Resolutions Restructuring Welfare Reform." 1996 WL 90840.

Stone, Deborah. 1997. *Policy Paradox: The Art of Political Decision Making*. New York: W. W. Norton.

Streeter, Patricia A. 1998. "Incarceration of the Mentally Ill: Treatment of Warehousing?" *Michigan Bar Journal* 77.

Terhune, Karen. 1992. "Reformation of the Food Stamp Act: Abating Domestic Hunger Means Resisting 'Legislative Junk Food.'" *Catholic University Law Review* 41.

Titmus, Richard, M. 1977. *Social Policy: An Introduction*. London: George Allen and Unwin.

Tobin, Donald B. 1996. "Less Is More: A Move Toward Sanity in the Budget Process." *Saint Louis University Public Law Review* 26.

Torok, John Hayakawa. 1996. "Reconstruction and Racial Nativism: Chinese Immigrants and the Debates on the Thirteenth, Fourteenth, and Fifteenth Amendments and Civil Rights Laws." *Asian Law Journal* 3.

Torrey, E. Fuller. 1997. "The Release of the Mentally Ill from Institutions: A Well-Intentioned Disaster." *Chronicle of Higher Education* 43, 40: B4.

Torrey, E. Fuller, Joan Stieber, Jonathan Ezekiel, and others. 1992. *Criminalizing the Seriously Mentally Ill: The Abuse of Jails as Mental Hospitals*. Arlington, Va.: National Alliance for the Mentally Ill.

Trattner, Walter I. 1989. *From Poor Law to Welfare State: A History of Social Welfare in America*. 4th ed. New York: Free Press.

Trutko, John, Nancy Pindus, Burt S. Barnow, and Demetra Smith Nightingale. 1999. *Early Implementation of the Welfare-to-Work Program*. Washington, D.C.: Urban Institute.

Uccello, Cori E. and L. Jerome Gallagher. 1997. *General Assistance Programs: The State-Based Part of the Safety Net*. Washington, D.C.: Urban Institute.

Ullman, Frank, Brian Bruen, and John Holahan. 1998. *The State Children's Health Insurance Program: A Look at the Numbers.* Washington, D.C.: Urban Institute.

U.S. Census Bureau. 1997. *Current Population Reports. Health Insurance Coverage: 1997.* Washington, D.C.

U.S. Census Bureau. 1998. *Current Population Reports. Measuring 50 Years of Economic Change Using the March Current Population Survey.* Washington, D.C.

U.S. Census Bureau. 1998. *Current Population Reports. Health Coverage 1997.* Washington, D.C.: U.S. Department of Commerce.

U.S. Census Bureau. 1998. *Current Population Reports. Poverty in the United States: 1997.* Washington, D.C.: U.S. Department of Commerce.

U.S. Census Bureau. 1998. *Resident Population of the United States Estimates by Sex, Race and Hispanic Origin, with Median Age.* Washington, D.C.

U.S. Census Bureau. 1999. *Money Income in the United States.* Washington, D.C.: U.S. Department of Commerce.

U.S. Census Bureau. 1999. *Poverty in the United States.* Washington, D.C.: U.S. Department of Commerce.

U.S. Department of Agriculture. 1999. *USDA Catches 331 Food Stamp Retailers in Fraud Sweep.* Release No. 0224.96. Washington, D.C.

U.S. Department of Health and Human Services. 1999. *The Administration on Aging and the Older Americans Act.* Washington, D.C.

U.S. Department of Housing and Urban Development. 1995. Office of HIV/AIDS Housing. *HOPWA Formula Programs: 1994 Summary.* Washington, D.C.

U.S. Department of Housing and Urban Development. 1999. *Now Is the Time: Places Left Behind in the New Economy.* Washington, D.C.

U.S. Department of Housing and Urban Development. 1999. *Section 8 Rental Voucher Program and the Section 8 Rental Certificate Program.* Washington, D.C.

U.S. Department of Labor. 1994. Bureau of Labor Statistics. *How the Government Measures Unemployment.* Report 864. Washington, D.C.

U.S. Department of Labor. 1996. Bureau of Labor Statistics. *A Profile of the Working Poor.* Washington, D.C.

U.S. Department of Labor 1998. Bureau of Labor Statistics. *Worker Displacement, 1995–1997.* Washington, D.C.

U.S. Department of Labor 1999. Bureau of Labor Statistics. *The Employment Situation.* Washington, D.C.

U.S. Department of Labor. 1999. *Consolidated Financial Statement Audit—Supplemental Report on Income Maintenance.* Washington, D.C.

U.S. Department of Labor. 1999. *Emerging Trends in the Information Technology Job Market: How Should the Public and Private Sectors Respond?* Washington, D.C.

U.S. Federal Election Commission. 1999. *Voter Registration and Turnout in Federal Elections by Age: 1972–1996.* Washington, D.C.

U.S. General Accounting Office. 1994. *Older Americans Act—Funding Formula Could Better Reflect State Needs.* GAO/HEHS-94-41. Washington, D.C.

U.S. General Accounting Office. 1995. *Earned Income Credit—Targeting to the Working Poor.* GAO/GGD 95-122BR. Washington, D.C.

U.S. General Accounting Office. 1995. *A Glossary of Terms Used in the Federal Budget Process: Exposure Draft.* GAO/AFMD-2.1.1:87. Revised January 1993. Washington, D.C.

U.S. General Accounting Office. 1995. *Poverty Measurement: Adjusting for Geographic Cost-of-Living Difference.* GAO/GGD-95-64. Washington, D.C.

U.S. General Accounting Office. 1995. Report to the Chairman, Committee on Labor and Human Resources. *Ryan White Care Act: Access to Services by Minorities, Women, and Substance Abusers.* Washington, D.C.

U.S. General Accounting Office. 1995. *Social Security—New Functional Assessments for Children Raise Eligibility Questions.* Report No. 95-66.

U.S. General Accounting Office. 1995. *Welfare to Work: Participants' Characteristics and Services Provided in JOBS.* GAO/HEHS-95-93. Washington, D.C.

U.S. General Accounting Office. 1995. *Welfare to Work—State Programs Have Tested Some of the Proposed Reforms.* Report No. 95-26. Washington, D.C.

U.S. General Accounting Office. 1996. *Millions Can Be Saved by Screening Reports for Overused Services.* GAO/HEHS-96-49. Washington, D.C.

U.S. General Accounting Office. 1996. *Private and Public Prisons: Studies Comparing Operational Costs and/or Quality Service.* Report No. 96-158. Washington, D.C.

U.S. General Accounting Office. 1996. *Textile Trade: Operations of the Committee for the Implementation of Textile Agreements.* Report No. 96-186. Washington, D.C.

U.S. General Accounting Office. 1996. *Unemployment Insurance—Millions in Benefits Overpaid to Military Reservists.* GAO/HHS-96-101. Washington, D.C.

U.S. General Accounting Office. 1997. *Head Start: Research Provides Little Information on Impact of Current Program.* GAO/HEHS-97-59. Washington, D.C.

U.S. General Accounting Office. 1997. *Poverty Measurement: Issues in Revising and Updating the Official Definition.* GAO/AFMD-97-38. Washington, D.C.

U.S. General Accounting Office. 1997. *Privatization: Lessons Learned by State and Local Governments.* GAO/GGD-97-48. Washington, D.C.

U.S. General Accounting Office. 1997. *Social Security Disability Programs Lag in Promoting Return to Work.* GAO/HEHS-97-46. Washington, D.C.

U.S. General Accounting Office. 1997. *Welfare Reform: Three States' Approaches Show Promise of Increasing Workforce Participation.* GAO/HEHS-97-80. Washington, D.C.

U.S. General Accounting Office. 1998. *Budget Function Classifications: Origins, Trends, and Implications for Current Uses.* GAO/AFMD-98-67. Washington, D.C.

U.S. General Accounting Office. 1998. *Caribbean Basin: Worker Rights Progress Made, but Enforcement Issues Remain.* Report No. 98-205. Washington, D.C.

U.S. General Accounting Office. 1998. *Community Development: Progress on Economic Development Activities Varies Among the Empowerment Zones.* Washington, D.C.

U.S. General Accounting Office. 1998. *Food Assistance: Working Women's Access to WIC Benefits.* GAO/RCED-98-19. Washington, D.C.

U.S. General Accounting Office 1998. *Food Stamp Overpayments: Thousands of Deceased Individuals Are Being Counted as Household Members.* GAO/RCED-98-53. Washington, D.C.

U.S. General Accounting Office. 1998. *Foster Care: Implementation of the Multiethnic Placement Act Poses Difficult Challenges.* GAO/HEHS-98-204. Washington, D.C.

U.S. General Accounting Office. 1998. *Grant Programs—Design Features Shape Flexibility, Accountability, and Performance Evaluation.* GAO/GGD 98-137. Washington, D.C.

U.S. General Accounting Office. 1998. *Head Start Programs: Participant Characteristics, Services and Funding.* GAO/HEHS-98-65. Washington, D.C.

U.S. General Accounting Office. 1998. *Section 8 Project-Based Rental Assistance: HUD's Processes for Evaluating and Using Unexpended Balances Are Ineffective.* GAO/RCED-98-202. Washington, D.C.

U.S. General Accounting Office. 1998. *Social Security: Different Approaches for Addressing Solvency Problems.* GAO/HEHS-98-33. Washington, D.C.

U.S. General Accounting Office. 1998. *States Are Restructuring Programs to Reduce Welfare Dependency.* GAO/HEHS-98-109. Washington, D.C.

U.S. General Accounting Office. 1998. *States' Experience in Providing Employment Assistance to TANF Clients.* GAO/HEHS-99-22. Washington, D.C.

U.S. General Accounting Office. 1998. *Teen Mothers—Selected Social-Demographic Characteristics and Risk Factors.* GAO/HEHS 98-141.Washington, D.C.

U.S. General Accounting Office. 1998. *Welfare Reform: Child Support an Uncertain Income Supplement for Families Leaving Welfare.* GAO/HEHS-98-168. Washington, D.C.

U.S. General Accounting Office. 1998. *Welfare Reform: Early Fiscal Effects of the TANF Block Grant.* GAO/AIMD-98-137. Washington, D.C.

U.S. General Accounting Office. 1998. *Welfare Reform: Implications of Increased Work Participation for Child Care.* GAO/HEHS-97-75. Washington, D.C.

U.S. General Accounting Office. 1998. *Welfare Reform: Many States Continue Some Federal or State Benefits for Immigrants.* GAO/HEHS-98-132. Washington, D.C.

U.S. General Accounting Office. 1998. *Welfare Reform: States' Efforts to Expand Child Care Programs.* GAO/HEHS-98-27. Washington, D.C.

U.S. General Accounting Office. 1999. *Child Support Enforcement: Effects of Declining Welfare Caseloads are Beginning to Emerge.* GAO/HEHS-99-105. Washington, D.C.

U.S. General Accounting Office. 1999. *Children's Health Insurance Program: State Implementation Approaches Are Evolving.* GAO/HEHS 99-65. Washington, D.C.

U.S. General Accounting Office. 1999. *Education and Care: Early Childhood Programs and Services for Low-Income Families.* GAO/HEHS-00-11. Washington, D.C.

U.S. General Accounting Office. 1999. *Federal Education Funding: Allocation to State and Local Agencies for 10 Programs.* GAO/HEHS-99-180. Washington, D.C.

U.S. General Accounting Office. 1999. *Food Stamp Overpayments: Households in Different States Collect Benefits for the Same Individuals.* GAO/RCED-98-228. Washington, D.C.

U.S. General Accounting Office. 1999. *Food Stamp Program: Households Collect Benefits for Persons Disqualified for Intentional Program Violations.* GAO/RCED-99-180. Washington, D.C.

U.S. General Accounting Office. 1999. *Food Stamp Program: How States Are Using Federal Waivers of the Work Requirement.* GAO/RCED-00-5. Washington, D.C.

U.S. General Accounting Office. 1999. *Food Stamp Program: Various Factors Have Led to Declining Participation.* GAO/RCED-99-185. Washington, D.C.

U.S. General Accounting Office. 1999. *Foster Care: Effectiveness of Independent Living Services Unknown.* GAO/HEHS-00-13. Washington, D.C.

U.S. General Accounting Office. 1999. *Foster Care: HHS Could Better Facilitate the Interjurisdictional Adoption Process.* GAO-HEHS 00-12. Washington, D.C.

U.S. General Accounting Office. 1999. *Homelessness: Coordination and Evaluation of Programs Are Essential.* GAO/RCED-99-49. Washington, D.C.

U.S. General Accounting Office. 1999. *Homelessness: State and Local Efforts to Integrate and Evaluate Homeless Assistance Programs.* GAO/RCED-99-178. Washington, D.C.

U.S. General Accounting Office. 1999. *Medicare + Choice: Impact of 1997 Balanced Budget Act Payment Reforms on Beneficiaries and Plans.* GAO/T-HEHS-99-137. Washington, D.C.

U.S. General Accounting Offices. 1999. *Major Management Challenges and Program Risks: Department of Health and Human Services.* GAO/OCG 99-7. Washington, D.C.

U.S. General Accounting Office. 1999. *Medicare Fraud and Abuse: DOJ's Implementation of False Claims Act Guidance in National Initiatives Varies.* GAO/HEHS-99-170. Washington, D.C.

U.S. General Accounting Office. 1999. *Medicare Managed Care Plans: Many Factors Contribute to Recent Withdrawals; Plan Interest Continues.* HEHS-99-91. Washington, D.C.

U.S. General Accounting Office. 1999. *Medicare: Program Safeguard Activities Expand, But Results Difficult to Measure.* GAO/HEHS-99-165. Washington, D.C.

U.S. General Accounting Office. 1999. *Medicare Reform: Observations on the President's July 1999 Proposal,* Figure 1. Washington, D.C.

U.S. General Accounting Office. 1999. *Mental Health: Improper Restraint or Seclusion Use Places People at Risk,* 3. GAO/HEHS-99-176. Washington, D.C.

U.S. General Accounting Office. 1999. *Migrant Children: Education and HHS Need to Improve Exchange of Participant Information.* GAO/HEHS-00-4. Washington, D.C.

U.S. General Accounting Office. 1999. *Physician Shortage Areas: Medicare Incentive Payments Not an Effective Approach to Improve Access.* GAO/HEHS-99-36. Washington, D.C.

U.S. General Accounting Office. 1999. *Prescription Drug Benefits: Implications for Beneficiaries of Medicare HMO Use of Formularies.* GAO/HEHS-99-166. Washington, D.C.

U.S. General Accounting Office. 1999. *Private Health Insurance: Progress and Challenges in Implementing 1996 Federal Standards.* GAO/HEHS-99-100. Washington, D.C.

U.S. General Accounting Office. 1999. *Public Education: Title I Services Provided to Students with Limited English Proficiency.* GAO/HEHS-00-25. Washington, D.C.

U.S. General Accounting Office. 1999. *Public Housing: HUD Has Several Opportunities to Promote Private Management.* GAO/RCED-99-210. Washington, D.C.

U.S. General Accounting Office. 1999. *Supplemental Security Income: Progress Made in Implementing Welfare Reform Changes: More Action Needed.* Report No. 99-103. Washington, D.C.

U.S. General Accounting Office. 1999. *Welfare Reform: Implementing DOT's Access to Jobs Program in Its First Year.* GAO/RCED 00-14. Washington, D.C.

U.S. General Accounting Office. 1999. *Welfare Reform: State's Implementation Progress and Information on Former Recipients.* GAO/HEHS-99-116. Washington, D.C.

U.S. General Accounting Office. 2000. *Medicaid and Special Education: Coordination of Services for Children with Disabilities Is Evolving.* GAO/HEHS-00-20. Washington, D.C.

U.S. House of Representatives. 1990. *Americans with Disabilities Act.* Report No. 485(II), 101st Cong., 2nd sess. 1990.

U.S. House of Representatives. 1994. Subcommittee on Human Resources and Intergovernmental Relations. *AIDS Treatment and Care: Who Cares?* Report No. 674. 101st Cong., 2nd sess.

U.S. House of Representatives. 1995. *Aids Funding.* Testimony of the AIDS Action Council before the Subcommittee on Health and Environment of the Committee on Commerce. 1995 WL 146461.

U.S. House of Representatives. 1995. *Personal Responsibility and Work Opportunities Act of 1995.* Conference Report 430, 104th Cong., 1st sess.

U.S. House of Representatives. 1996. Committee on Ways and Means. *Green Book.* 104th Cong., 2nd sess.

U.S. House of Representatives. 1998. Committee on Ways and Means. *Green Book.* Washington, D.C.

U.S. Senate. 1974. Committee on the Judiciary. *Separation of Powers Annual Report.* 93rd Cong., 2nd sess., Report No. 93-1195.

U.S. Senate. 1974. Committee on National Emergencies and Delegated Emergency Powers. *Executive Orders in Times of War and National Emergency,* 93rd Cong., 2nd sess., Report No. 93-1280.

U.S. Senate. 1990. *Cong. Rec.* Proceedings and Debates of the 101st Congress. 2nd sess. Wednesday, October 3.

U.S. Senate. 1994. *Employment Non-Discrimination Act of 1994.* 140 *Cong. Rec.* S7561-02. Thursday, June 23.

U.S. Senate. 1996. *The Work First and Personal Responsibility Act of 1996.* 104th Cong., 2nd sess., House Bill 3612. June 19.

U.S. Senate. 1996. *Older Americans Act Amendments of 1996.* Committee on Labor and Human Resources. Senate Report No. 104-344.

U.S. Senate. 1997. *The Balanced-Budget Constitutional Amendment.* Senate Report No. 3, 105th Cong., 1st sess.

U.S. Senate. 1997. *Developments in Aging: 1996.* Vol. 1. Report No.105-36(I). Special Committee on Aging of the 105th Cong., 1st sess.

Van Leeuwen, Michelle. 1999. "The Politics of Adoptions Across Borders: Whose Interests Are Served?" *Pacific Rim Law and Policy Journal* 8.

Vaughan, D. n.d. *Reflections on the Income Estimates from the Initial Panel of the Survey of Income and Program Participation.* Working Paper No. 83. Washington, D.C.: U.S. Department of Commerce.

Vinson, Elisa. 1999. *Governing-for-Results and Accountability: Performance Contracting in Six State Human Services Agencies.* Washington, D.C.: Urban Institute.

Walker, Christopher, Sheila O. O'Leary, Patrick Boxall, and others. 1998. *Expanding the Nation's Supply of Affordable Housing: An Evaluation of the Home Investment Partnerships Program.* Washington, D.C.: U.S. Department of Housing and Urban Development.

Walker, Christopher and Mark Weinheimer. 1998. *Community Development in the 1990s.* Washington, D.C.: Urban Institute.

Walker, David. 1999. Testimony before the Subcommittee on Social Security, Committee on Ways and Means, House of Representatives. *Social Security: Criteria for Evaluating Social Security Reform Proposals.* Washington, D.C.: U.S. General Accounting Office, GAO/T-HEHS-99-94, p. 3.

Waxman, Henry. *National Family Caregiver Support Act.* Proceedings and Debates of the 106th Cong., 1st sess. 145 *Cong. Rec.* E745-03.

Weaver, Warren. 1973. *New York Times Abstracts,* June 24, sect. 4, col. 1, p. 3.

Weil, Alan. 1997. *The New Children's Health Insurance Program: Should States Expand Medicaid?* Washington, D.C.: Urban Institute.

Wellstone, Paul and Ellen R. Shaffer. 1993. "The American Health Security Act—A Single-Payer Proposal." *New England Journal of Medicine* 328.

Wertheimer, Richard and Kristin Moore. 1998. *Childbearing by Teens: Links to Welfare Reform.* Washington, D.C.: Urban Institute.

Williams, Monte. 1998. "Medicare H.M.O. Cutbacks Strand Thousands of Clients." *New York Times,* November 16, sect. C, p. 1.

Williams, Robert M. 1996. "The Costs of Visits to Emergency Departments." *New England Journal of Medicine* 334.

Wilson-Coker, Patricia, Theodore J. Stein, and Robert C. Zampano. 1991. *First Implementation and Monitoring Report of the DCYS Monitoring Panel.* New Haven, Conn., December 9. On record at the federal district court in Hartford, Conn.

Wilson, William Julius. 1997. *When Work Disappears: The World of the New Urban Poor.* New York: Alfred A. Knopf.

Wing, Kenneth R. 1983. "The Impact of the Reagan-Era Politics on the Federal Medicaid Program." *Catholic University Law Review* 33.

Women's Bureau. 1997. "Women's Participation in the U.S. Workforce at All-Time High, Labor Department Reports." *BNA Employment Policy and Law Daily,* 3/28/97 EPLD d1.

Wyers, Norman L. 1991. "Policy Practice in Social Work: Models and Issues." *Journal of Social Work Education* 27.

Zedlewski, Sheila R. 1999. *Work Activity and Obstacles to Work Among TANF Recipients.* Washington, D.C.: Urban Institute.

Index